Skills for Managerial Success

Theory, Experience, and Practice

Laird W. Mealiea
Dalhousie University

Gary P. Latham
University of Toronto

Chicago • Bogotá • Boston • Buenos Aires • Caracas
London • Madrid • Mexico City • Sydney • Toronto

Times Mirror
Higher Education Group

Irwin Book Team
Executive editor: Kurt L. Strand
Marketing manager: Michael Campbell
Project editor: Waivah Clement
Production supervisor: Lara Feinberg
Assistant manager, desktop services: Jon Christopher
Designer: Heidi J. Baughman
Compositor: Douglas & Gayle Limited
Typeface: 10/12 Times Roman
Printer: R. R. Donnelley & Sons Company

Library of Congress Cataloging-In-Publication Data

Mealiea, Laird.
    Skills For Managerial Success: Theory, Experience, and
Practice / Laird W. Mealiea, Gary P. Latham.
        p.   cm.
    Includes index.
    ISBN 0-256-12454-X
    1. Management.   I. Latham, Gary P.   II. Title
HD31.M3878   1996
658—dc20   95–12121

Printed in the United States of America

1 2 3 4 5 6 7 8 9 0 DO 2 1 0 9 8 7 6 5

To my daughter Jennifer Rose and son David, who continually give me joy and hope for the future.

Laird W. Mealiea

To my sons, Bryan and Brandon, who taught me the art as well as the science of management.

Gary Latham

PREFACE

AN UNDERLYING RATIONALE

This book reflects our experience wearing two professional hats. As professors, we interact with students who want to develop skills that will enable them to become effective managers; as consultants, we educate people who want to improve their managerial skills. In both instances, the feedback on the usefulness of the topics covered in this text has been overwhelmingly positive. In the case of students, the most telling responses come after they have had the opportunity to manage others. The following statement represents a typical comment from these individuals: "When it comes to managing and making my job easier, your course was among the most practical and useful."

For functioning managers, the relevance of the material is more immediate. These experiences contribute to their ability to accurately assess the appropriateness of transferring what is being learned in the classroom, or workshop, to organizational situations. The flavor of their comments is captured by the following statements taken from several program evaluations: "I wish I had had this when I first became a manager. If I had had this information earlier, it would have made my job a lot easier." "I found the topics covered relevant to my work. I will be putting them to good use. Oh, by the way, can I send my boss to the next session?" It is feedback such as this, the desire to use this material when teaching our own students, and the urging from both colleagues and friends to write a text on management skill development, that has motivated us to put our ideas into print.

Before you begin reading the chapters that follow, it would be helpful to consider the underlying rationale for topic selection and the book's format. Such decisions reflect our belief that the key ingredient to any increase in productivity is the employees who are asked to perform effectively within organizations.

It is employees who use their on-the-job experience to figure out how to better use the technology and other materials with which they must work. In other words, employees are the driving force behind productivity and quality improvements; they make the productivity ratio larger.[1] To be a successful manager, to obtain increased levels of output resulting from subordinate effort and ability, one must learn to work effectively with people. Thus, the primary focus of this text is on manager-subordinate interactions, especially the managerial behaviors needed to develop and maintain positive and productive relationships with subordinates, peers, superiors, and individuals external to the organization.

Topic selection, including the design of case studies, role plays, and experiential exercises, reflects our belief that the ability to manage effectively is a function of the degree to which you possess the *attitudes, knowledge,* and *skills* necessary to perform well within a particular organizational setting. What is your attitude toward ethics in management, employee participation in decision making, assertiveness and followership? Chapter 3 addresses the question of what constitutes appropriate attitudes for managers in the 1990s.

Knowledge is critical to managerial success because it establishes the base upon which decisions are made and the behaviors that are appropriate in a given situation. As a result, each chapter carefully integrates content knowledge with a discussion of appropriate behaviors needed to demonstrate the skill or activity being considered. Chapter 2 (knowledge about the self) and Chapter 15 (knowledge about the organization and its environment) describe the knowledge that must be acquired about one's self, one's organization, and the organization's environment.

The sequencing of chapters is designed to logically move through a building process based on content and prerequisite knowledge, skills or activities. Chapter 1 explains the manager's role and the environmental trends managers are likely to face throughout the 1990s and into the 21st century. Chapter 2 encourages students to evaluate their personal goals, needs, self-efficacy, and interpersonal style, and to assess how their personal profile will affect their ability to manage. Chapter 3 articulates key attitudes managers need to function effectively. Chapters 4 through 7 (stress/time management, communications, and negotiations) focus on support skills that allow the manager to effectively carry out other activities such as performance appraisal, counseling, coaching, progressive discipline, and so on. Chapter 8 considers what a manager should do when required to select the most qualified employees. Chapter 9 describes the goal-setting process and how it can be used to motivate people to perform at, or near, their peak capabilities.

---

[1] W. B. Werther, Jr., W. A. Ruch, and L. McClure, *Productivity Through People,* West Publishing Company, St. Paul, 1986: 4.

Goal attainment is facilitated when there is an effective team climate in which subordinates are willing to innovate rather than resist change, and where the negative effects of conflict are minimized. In an attempt to improve understanding of the skills necessary to perform effectively in each of these areas, team building will be covered in Chapter 10, innovation in Chapter 11, and managing conflict and anger in Chapter 12. Chapter 13 considers the topic of performance evaluation and how the manager can use performance reviews for employee coaching and development. Along with conducting performance appraisal for administrative and developmental purposes, managers are increasingly required to engage in counseling activities. To help managers carry out employee counseling, Chapter 14 develops a counseling model designed specifically for managers who want to help their employees. We end the book at the macro level (Chapter 15). This last chapter was included to emphasize that managers function within an organizational system. If they are to perform effectively, they must understand system components.

In an attempt to facilitate the transfer of identified knowledge, attitudes, and skills to the real world, students are provided with opportunities to practice key concepts. Exercises are designed to provide hands-on experience by requiring students to simulate real work behavior. The exercises vary from chapter to chapter because of the wide range of topics covered and the inherent differences in content. Most exercises are designed to be carried out in a classroom setting; some will require preclassroom work to be performed well.

SKILLS VERSUS ACTIVITIES

It is often difficult to separate the skills required for success from the activities that these skills are designed to support. For each activity or functional area there are certain skills that must be carried out if the manager is to be successful. For example, to be successful, managers must be competent in such areas as goal setting, performance evaluation, or counseling. However, to be effective in these areas, managers also need to be skilled in the science of negotiation, conflict management, and change management. To negotiate or counsel effectively, managers should be skilled in the areas of probing, reflecting, listening, giving feedback, nonverbal communications, and so on. Therefore, some chapters deal with activities such as counseling or performance evaluations, while others deal with supporting skills such as communications. After reading this book, students will be able to successfully implement important managerial activities by drawing on the appropriate support skills.

Laird W. Mealiea
Gary P. Latham

CONTENTS IN BRIEF

CONTENTS

**15   Understanding the Organization
and Its Environment: A Macro
Perspective   639**

THE ROLE OF MANAGEMENT

1

Objectives:

- Explain the role of management in organizations that are moving into the 21st century.
- Articulate important environmental trends that will affect the manager's ability to perform appropriately.
- Define the underlying themes upon which subsequent chapters are based.

Understanding the Role of Management

Managers organize the enterprise's physical and technical resources; they manage the organization's financial resources; they develop and maintain market share; they deal with external constituencies, such as government and suppliers; and most importantly, they manage others or their work. Management is the process of getting others to perform activities necessary to achieve organizational and personal goals.[1] Therefore, we are not surprised when Tom Monahan, founder and president of Domino's Pizza—one of the wonder firms of the 1980s—stated, "You cannot have a successful business with just good management at the top . . . It [good management] has to go right down to the lowest levels of the organization."

Given the key role that human resources play in determining organizational productivity[2] this book focuses on the interactions between managers and their subordinates, and managers and relevant others. Relevant others include individuals with whom managers must interact in order to obtain desired levels of output and quality. By focusing on these areas, it is possible to provide the required depth of study necessary to facilitate understanding and the transfer of newly acquired skills to the job.

The ability of 1990s managers to successfully fulfill their responsibilities in these two areas has come into serious question. A key reason we experience difficulty competing with such countries as Japan, Germany, and Korea is our lack of good managers. Tom Peters emphasized this problem in his book, *Thriving on Chaos:*

> Consider this statement from Nucor Corporation's president, Ken Iverson: "I've heard people say that Nucor is proof that unions per se have a negative impact on worker productivity. That's nonsense! That conveniently ignores vital questions like: What's the quality of direction being given the workers? What are the resources the workers need to get the job done? Where's the opportunity for workers to contribute ideas about how to do the job better? The real impediment to producing a higher-quality product more efficiently isn't the workers, union or nonunion, it's management." W. Edwards Deming is a little kinder, insisting that management is merely 90 percent of the problem.[3]

The New York Times[4] argued that American managers hold the view "that there is no need to invent, build or develop anything yourself—given the capital and good financial management, anything of value can be bought and any problem can be sold. A sense of commitment—to one's workers, customers, suppliers, even one's fellow managers—is an impediment." Similarly, Mintzberg, in Canada, concluded that management has become so ineffective that it prevents economic growth.[5] Organizations, in Mintzberg's view, put people last, foster the growth of political warfare, undermine loyalty, and prevent creative leadership. Excellence in North American organizations may become a thing of the past.

Without productive employees there are no productive organizations. As Tom Peters stated, "despite the accelerating technology/automation revolution, our organizations must become more dependent on people (line workers). To be sure, fewer people will work on the line in a given factory or operations center, but those who do will be more important to and responsible for the company's success than ever before."[6] What we must realize is that technology is introduced not for the primary purpose of replacing human labor, but rather to make the human resource more productive. This only occurs if the human resource is managed effectively and thereby accepts the new technology.

The need for new management skills and behaviors not only applies to senior managers but to front-line supervisors as well. "Experts agree that the first line supervisor's role will change dramatically...They aren't going to control people anymore. They have to coach them, help to do the planning, approve organizational direction, and make sure the directions are clear. It will be an enabling function rather than a control function."[7] The era in which managers function as heroes and "carry" their group is rapidly drawing to a close. Instead, the adaptive manager must recognize the changes in the environment and take the time to continually improve existing skills and acquire new ones.

An Environmental Imperative

As managers attempt to develop and grow, create an environment that empowers employees, and at the same time remain competitive, they will encounter fundamental changes in their environment. If managers refuse to adapt to these changes, it is unlikely that they will be able to create an organizational climate in which their subordinates can perform at, or near, their peak capabilities. To fully appreciate the changes that managers face, it is necessary to articulate a number of trends shaping their environment in the 1990s (see Figure 1.1). It is within this changing environment that managers must learn to apply the material presented in the chapters that follow.

When considering these trends, it is important to keep these points in mind: First, the impact of many trends has already been felt by managers and their organizations. However, their ultimate impact has not yet fully worked its way through the North American enterprise system. Second, the trends are often interdependent. For example, the fact that employees are demanding a greater role in organizational decision making is a function of their increased education, better training, an increased awareness of personal rights, an increased reliance on self-control and self-help, and other related factors.

Increased Desire on the Part of Employees to Participate

Employees in Canada and the United States want to function within a work environment that provides some level of participation in decision making.[8] The pressure for greater participation is likely to increase as employees continue to increase their education, and as organizations attempt to restructure themselves in an effort to become competitive. Clemmer and McNeil pointed out that we now have "gold-collar" employees, resulting from our information

FIGURE 1.1

Environmental trends of the 1990s: What the manager faces now and in the future

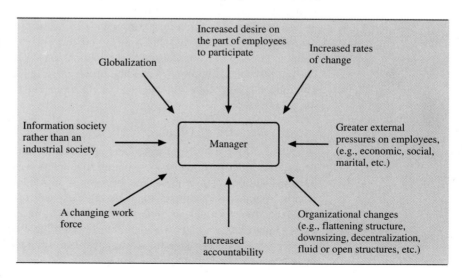

age and more knowledgeable individuals, who "offer their employers imagination and original thought but at a price: they are not nearly as docile as the workers they replaced. Often knowing more than the managers who supervise them, they place a high value on getting along with their co-workers and are difficult, if not impossible, to manipulate. Their respect for authority is conditional—based on proven expertise or actual results, rather than a job title or size of office. They offer loyalty, but expect recognition and opportunities for participation in return."[9] If this is the type of employee that managers will now supervise, then managers must act to create opportunities for employee participation and self-management. However, managerial success will require more than simply increasing levels of employee participation. Managers will have to learn to negotiate, manage conflicts, effectively probe and listen to employees, manage change, and do this with the utmost integrity. If not, employee loyalty, motivation, and service will be lost.

Before moving on to the next trend, it is necessary to offer a word of caution. Managers should not assume that all employees have the same desire to participate in decision making, or need the same level of information about their work environment.[10] A desire to participate occurs if the employee is interested in the issues under consideration and if he or she has the self-confidence to believe that such efforts would be successful. Employees are likely to ask, "Do I have the knowledge, skills, and ideas that would make my contribution valuable?" A "no" response to this question is likely to dampen desire to participate. Individual differences in terms of career stage, personality, desire to fulfill higher order needs (growth, achievement, recognition, etc.) are also likely to affect an employee's desire for participation in decision making. An employee who *(a)* has reached a career plateau and no longer seeks advancement, *(b)* is close to retirement, *(c)* is an isolate (desires to be left alone), or *(d)* is more interested in job security than an enriched job environment, may avoid such opportunities.

Managers can stimulate participation by informing subordinates of their desire to have them participate, sharing all relevant information with subordinates, educating subordinates on how and when to participate, providing opportunities in which subordinates can participate, creating a trusting and supporting environment, and providing positive consequences for participative efforts when they do occur.

Increased Rates of Change

A second major trend that must be addressed by tomorrow's managers is a change rate that is increasing exponentially, and a series of steady states (i.e., periods without change) that are becoming shorter and shorter.[11] Rosabeth Kanter stated that managers must become masters of change if they want to be effective.[12] Kanter argued in her recent book, *When Giants Learn to Dance,* that the rate of change and competition have accelerated to such high levels that, to survive, organizations must become innovative and flexible. If not, they will become extinct.[13]

To achieve this reality, managers will have to develop a new mind set.[14] They must be willing to break with the past and articulate strategic visions that motivate and challenge their employees. Part of this mind set must include an emphasis on urgency. For example, to effectively compete in the auto industry, North American firms must strive to shorten the time needed to bring new products to the market. As Ulrich and Wiersema pointed out, the norm for North American firms is 48 months as compared to 18 for the Japanese.[15] Shortened product cycles and increased environmental turbulence will require North American managers to alter their mega change "home run" philosophy to one supporting smaller and more frequent incremental changes. Such an approach minimizes the risks associated with incorrect decisions.

Table 1.1 presents a sampling of the changes that have been taking place and that are likely to continue throughout the 1990s and beyond. Therefore managers must accept their role as change agents. They must plan for change, and seek out opportunities in which to innovate, while at the same time find ways to overcome the resistance of employees who seek to hold on to a familiar past.

Greater External Pressures on Employees

Given the increased turbulence of our environment, employees now face levels of personal stress significantly greater than a decade ago. Existing stress factors reflect the social problems affecting North America, such as a decline in the disposable income of the middle class, dual-career families, high divorce rates, drugs, alcoholism, changes in family size and structure, crime, AIDS, etc. These issues threaten the psychological and emotional stability of all organizational participants. Yesterday's managers would have argued that this is not their problem so long as the employees do their job. Managers of the 1990s must recognize that the employee who walks through the organization's front door does

---

TABLE 1.1   Evidence of a Turbulent Environment

• Fluctuations in exchange rates	• Political upheavals (China/Eastern Europe/Gulf War)
• Fluctuations in interest rates	
• Fluctuations in energy prices	• Increased availability of new venture capital
• Unstable Third World	
• Technological revolution	• Reduced jobs in large-scale mfg. and increases in small-scale mfg.—demassification
• Increased international competition	
• International interdependence (e.g., globalization)	• Increased rate of product change and new-product introduction (e.g., computer industry)
• Shifts in work force demographics	
• Fluctuations in stock markets	• Significant shifts in the family structure (i.e., dual-career families, single parents, independent living)
• Fluctuations in the rate of inflation	

not leave unwanted psychological and emotional problems behind.[16] Managers must realize that they are functioning in a period in which employee stress is one of the fastest growing occupational diseases.[17] Such stress, or conflict, debilitates the employee, saps required energy, obstructs critical thinking, and prevents employees from fulfilling their potential.[18] The result is marginal employees producing at unacceptable levels. Under such conditions, managers themselves run the risk of being classified as marginal.

The negative effects of stress may not be immediately observed.[19] Instead, individuals may first attempt to adapt in some way to stressful situations and they may be able to maintain existing performance levels. Such adaptive strategies, however, do take their toll by depleting physical or psychic energy reserves. As a result, individuals eventually become irritable, less tolerant of future stress, and eventually experience burnout.

Again, the pressure is on managers to change and adapt their behavior to better manage the level of stress within the system. This can only be accomplished if they develop skills useful both for identifying employees in need, and for helping to reduce or offset unwanted pressures.

Organizational Changes

Pressures that threaten the psychological and emotional balance of employees are not limited to those in their personal lives. Environmental turbulence also exists within the organization. As we approach the 21st century, the structure and internal dynamics of North American organizations will also change. As indicated above, changes in the external environment will force internal changes within the organization. External pressures include new consumer demands that require the development of new products; greater external controls and audits that result in expanded legal departments, better quality control, and changes in existing products (e.g., safety features on North American automobiles); and the rapid advances in technology that force firms to introduce new technologies in order to be competitive.[20] However, the area likely to experience the most dramatic change in the 1990s is the organization's internal structure. The pyramidal, boxed, structure so often used to describe organizations will likely give way to more open and fluid designs as described by Tom Peters and shown in Figure 1.2. Similarly, Naisbitt and Aburdene argued that the top-down pyramid-type structure will be replaced by a network-type structure where employees interact with each other by crossing formalized departmental boundaries.[21]

The traditional system, which is predominantly rule-determined, inflexible, and highly structured, is giving way to a structure that is flexible, open, adaptive, unstructured, and often ambiguous. Although such changes are necessary to remain competitive in a turbulent environment, employees are likely to experience uncertainty and stress during the changeover. Managers in the 1990s must ensure that subordinates remain productive by facilitating their ability to adapt to new organizational designs.

FIGURE 1.2

Organizational structure then and now

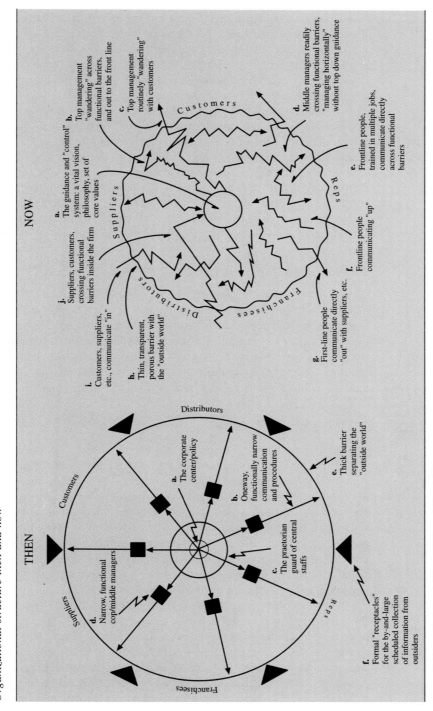

Source: T. Peters, *Thriving on Chaos*, 1987, pp. 657 and 661.

To become increasingly efficient and improve their competitive edge, North American organizations are taking steps to downsize their operations.[22] Once viewed as an effective means to lessen financial pressures, organizations now see downsizing as a management prerogative during both good and bad times. Even as the American economy moves out of the recession of the early 1990s, corporate goliaths continue their downsizing mania.[23] At the same time, demographics predict a significant increase in the number of individuals available to move into middle management.[24] The result of these two trends is a reduction of promotional opportunities for middle managers at a time when competition for such promotions is increasing because of numbers.

Downsizing also affects individuals who remain with the organization. Remaining employees become concerned about their own security and continued relevance of their personal skills. This is especially true when downsizing occurs in small frequent steps or when the organization fails to provide sufficient information to reduce employee uncertainty.[25]

Increased Accountability

Along with increases in freedom, greater personal opportunity, interdependence, and access to information, come increases in accountability. The activities of managers are under increasing scrutiny of other managers, unions, government agencies, and external activist groups. Managers are embracing managerial integrity as desirable in its own right. Where a relationship between managers and their subordinates is built upon integrity and trust, managers can eliminate the controlling or policing behaviors used in the past.

A Changing Work Force

The makeup of the North American labor force is changing. The phrase "browning of America" refers to the fact that Americans of European descent may become a minority group in the 21st century.[26] Whereas in the 1930s to 1950s a large percentage of immigrants were from European countries, an increasing number of today's immigrants are coming from Third World countries, notably in Central and South America, as well as in Asia. For example, the number of Hispanic workers will be up 74 percent by the year 2000 and will represent 10 percent of the United States work force. Similarly, Asian and other racial groups will grow at an annual rate of 3.9 percent and will account for approximately 11 percent of all new workers by 2000.[27]

These employees are coming from cultures that may not readily accept the current cultural values in North America. Some immigrant groups will not have the educational background to facilitate amalgamation into a highly industrialized society. For example, script literacy requirement for effective job performance continues to increase and currently starts at grade 12 equivalency for the average job.[28] Similarly, "smart machines" and improved technologies used by organizations to remain competitive require employees to demonstrate strong cognitive skills.[29] Employees will increasingly be called upon to analyze and diagnose their work environments and subsequently make independent judgments or decisions as to appropriate courses of action. Furthermore, employees will likely be asked to use such cognitive skills under conditions of increased time pressure.

Also affecting the racial mix of the U.S. work force is the estimate that between now and the year 2000 a third of the individuals entering the work force will be minority group members.[30] Unfortunately, over half of these individuals are currently living in poverty and receiving substandard training and education.[31] Further complicating the mix of minorities in the work force is the prediction that by the year 2000 employed black women will outnumber employed black males.[32]

The increasing role of women within organizations represents another major change in the North American work force. In the United States the percentage of women in the active work force increased from 33 percent in 1960 to over 45 percent in 1991.[33] This particular trend takes on greater significance, given that women are also beginning their working careers early. Similarly, women are now returning to work in record numbers immediately after having children. The trends in Canada are similar (see Table 1.2).

Women are expected to account for approximately 60 percent of new entrants into the U.S. work force between 1985 and the year 2000, resulting in a "feminization" of the work force.[34] Women are becoming more educated, more aware of their own rights, and they are moving in greater numbers into nontraditional female occupations, such as management, medicine, law, and engineering.[35] For example, while women currently account for 30 percent of internal auditing and accounting professionals, it is estimated that by the year 2000 they will account for at least 50 percent of the professionals performing in these two areas.[36] Because women are becoming better educated, and prove themselves to be highly qualified graduates, organizations that fail to tap into this pool of potential applicants run the risk of losing superior employees to those organizations who actively recruit females. Not hiring or promoting individuals because they are women will not only be grounds for discrimination but will also be bad for business.[37] Organizations that fail to actively recruit females also run the risk that they will have to dig more deeply into traditional sources of applicants to find qualified individuals. When this occurs, the result is likely to be new hires who are less qualified to do the job.

The effect of an increased number of women in the work force also impacts the type of service that organizations will be required to provide for their employees. Females classified as "mothers with infants" is one of the fastest growing groups in the U.S. labor force. It is reported that in 1987 approximately 53 percent of mothers with children under one year of age were active in the labor market. This figure is more than twice the number recorded by the U.S. Bureau of Labor Statistics in 1970.[38] As a result, there has been a 300 percent increase during the 1980s in the number of firms that provide childcare services.[39]

TABLE 1.2   **Labor Force Participation Rate for Canadian Women**
(by age group)

Age	1961	1975	1985	1995
15–24	39.3%	56.8%	64.7%	72.0%
25–44	29.2	52.3	70.3	76.2
45–64	28.5	39.4	46.9	50.1
65+	5.9	4.9	4.8	7.2
Average	28.7	44.4	54.2	57.0

Source: *Canadian Personnel/Human Resource Management,* G. Milkovich, W. Glueck, R. Barth, and S. McShane, Irwin, Burr Ridge, Ill., 1988, 47.

A third demographic trend which will have a significant effect on managers is the dominant role that will be played by baby boomers. For example, in 1975 there were approximately 39 million employees in the 25–44 age bracket in the United States. During the 1990s this number should swell to over 60 million. It will account for over 50 percent of the total work force.[40] Between 1986 and the year 2000, the number of individuals in the 35 to 47 age bracket will grow by 38 percent, and individuals in the 48 to 57 age bracket will grow by 67 percent.[41]

Similar statistics are available for Canada.[42] In 1976, the 35 to 49 age group accounted for approximately 16 percent of the Canadian work force. It is predicted that in 1996 this percentage will increase to approximately 24 percent. What is important is that these individuals are more likely to be competing for promotions, recognition, and increased responsibility. Such increased pressures will be coming at a time when the number of middle management positions will be decreasing as organizations restructure and flatten. Such an imbalance will place great demands on management to create an environment for their subordinates that will both motivate and provide opportunities for development.

At the same time that the baby boomers are aging, there are fewer young people entering the work force.[43] Such a double-barreled effect increases the number and variety of problems facing organizations attempting to deal with an aging work force. A work force characterized by seniority is likely to have the effect of increasing organizational payrolls. In addition, as employees age and their advancement slows, organizational resources will have to be directed toward retraining, motivation, retirement counseling, etc. On the input side, the search for young employees will become increasingly competitive, and nontraditional sources of new recruits will have to be tapped, especially women, minorities, and immigrants.

In summary, the consequences of these factors are likely to challenge the creativity and resources of existing recruiting, selecting, training, and development functions within many organizations. At the same time, such changes in the work force will also challenge managers' ability to motivate and lead their subordinates as the range of individual differences increases.

Information Society Rather than an Industrial Society

In the 1990s one descriptive label that frequently appears in business literature and the popular media is the term *age of information* (or *the information economy*).[44] Managers at all levels now have more access than ever before to a broad range of information data about themselves, the organization, the organization's environment, and external constituencies, that are relevant and appropriate for a particular managerial need. This benefit to managers has occurred on three levels.[45] Managers have access to a large volume of information when making decisions or assessing their own performance. Online information was a $6 to $7 billion industry in 1990 and is predicted to grow at an annual rate of 20 percent. There are currently over 4,500 databases available in the world.[46] Next, the speed of information transfer has greatly increased with the use of modern information technologies. Information technology has also allowed managers to simultaneously transfer large volumes of data to geographically dispersed end points. These three trends facilitate managers acting together to solve existing or potential problems.

The availability of such information can be of significant benefit to future managers. First, because of the dynamics and complexity of the manager's environment, as well as the interdependence of our markets, industries, and organizations, an access to a wide range of information is a necessary condition for success. On the macro level, managers must have ongoing information about the organization's environment, mission, structure, norms, and politics. Without this information, managers cannot expect to navigate a successful course through all the potential pitfalls that await them. Second, this information will allow them to be proactive by scanning and identifying opportunities for improvement and developing strategic plans necessary to survive in a turbulent world.

On a personal level, managers must have accurate information about their own needs, values, objectives, strengths, and weaknesses. If managers do not understand themselves, they increase the probability of creating a work environment in conflict with their own personalities. The probable consequences of such a conflict are increased dissatisfaction, absenteeism, turnover, and decreased personal effort. Furthermore, if managers fail to behave in a manner consistent with their personalities, the impact on subordinates is typically negative; that is, such behavior is likely to communicate conflicting messages about personal goals, expectations, and preferred behaviors from subordinates. When this occurs, subordinates become suspicious or distrustful. This in turn will produce barriers to effective interactions between manager and subordinate.

Similarly, information about the manager's departmental team is critical to success. The more information a manager has about subordinates' needs, values, beliefs, strengths, and weaknesses, the more likely he or she is to make accurate decisions on how to manage subordinates in such areas as training needs, assignments, delegation, coaching, and counseling. However, to make use of this information, managers will have to scan the environment to determine what information is available. To do this effectively, managers must actively network by freely interacting with customers, subordinates, peers, and superiors. They must increase the level of subordinate participation and interaction.

A word of caution, however, must be expressed. The benefits just described can only be recognized when manager-leaders of the future learn to manage available data and transform it into usable information. Managers will need to develop skills in data collection, integration, analysis, problem solving, and distribution to take full advantage of available information. They will by necessity have to develop skills with the same degree of sophistication as the new technologies that are driving the move toward an information age.[47]

Globalization

One of the most significant challenges facing managers in the 1990s is the pressures resulting from globalization. Although no universally accepted definition of *globalization* exists,[48] the term can be understood if we consider the concepts of *market*[49] and *structure*.[50] In terms of market, globalization implies that an organization's product distribution traverses national boundaries. Defined in this way, organizations can vary by the degree of globalization. Those organizations that only traverse some national boundaries are experiencing limited globalization. If an organization's markets traverse all national boundaries, then it is completely global. Structurally, an organization is considered global when it is able to balance centralized control of assets, resources, responsibilities, and corporate strategy, yet at the same time take advantage of market differences and linkages. For example, Johansson of Electrolux was able to implement a strategy of coordinating the goals of newly acquired firms in different countries, but at the same time allowing for local market differentiation in terms of how products were sold, promotion in local media, and the use of local brand names.[51]

A number of factors account for the trend toward globalization. The increased ease by which information, resources, and products pass from country to country continues to stimulate organizational interest in world markets. We have also seen the establishment of the European Free Trade Association and the Free Trade deal between the United States and Canada. The potential also exists for a linking of Russia with its breakaway republics and for Eastern European countries to form a trading bloc in the area of 800 million people. Similarly, Pacific Rim countries are likely to form a Far Eastern trading bloc. The United States, Mexico, and Canada have joined to form the second largest trading bloc in the world.[52] The appearance of large trading blocs adds to the pressure for organizations to compete globally. Even smaller organizations are likely to become global as they develop alliances through joint ventures and minority participation.

In addition to a movement toward a borderless world,[53] globalization also reflects changes in the expectations and buying habits of consumers.[54] Consumers are wealthier, more diverse in their needs and expectations, and at the same time demonstrate a greater awareness of the availability of products in the marketplace. They have become more concerned about a product's status appeal, quality, comfort, and time-saving qualities, than its national origin. These trends are reflected in the competitive threat to U.S. firms in areas they once dominated (see Table 1.3).

In an effort to compete and survive, organizations themselves have also fueled the movement toward globalization. Organizations often seek to move into less developed countries not only to find cheaper labor but to find new markets. Emerging nations also provide the greatest opportunity for developing markets with the potential for rapid growth. At the same time, location of manufacturing facilities in less developed countries offers organizations the opportunity to build new facilities with the latest technologies. Such facilities allow the organization to either achieve or maintain a competitive edge.

TABLE 1.3   Changing Pattern of Industrial Leadership

Industry	Leaders 1950–1975	Challengers 1980...
Automotive	GM Ford	Toyota Nissan Honda
Semiconductors	TI Motorola	Toshiba Fujitsu Hitachi
Tires	Goodyear Firestone	Michelin Bridgestone
Medical systems	GE Philips Siemens	Hitachi Toshiba
Consumer electronics	GE RCA Philips	Matsushita Sony
Photographic	Kodak	Fuji
Xerography	Xerox	Fuji
Earth moving equipment	Caterpillar	Komatsu

Source: C. K. Prahalad, "Globalization: The intellectual and managerial challenges," *Human Resource*, Vol. 29, No. 1, Spring 1990, pp. 27–37.

The impact of globalization on organizations is likely to be profound and will add to the pressure for managers to develop a new set of competencies for the 1990s and the 21st century. Successful managers in the global arena will have to become strategic opportunists, architects of organizational structure, and coordinators of people. They will have to be able to manage highly decentralized organizations under conditions of increased competition and uncertainty. In addition, managers in the global arena must become increasingly sensitive to product and human diversity. Finally, global managers must be willing to develop and fine-tune analytical skills as they attempt to identify and adjust to global trends.

In summary, a manager's success in the 1990s will depend upon *(a)* recognizing the trends likely to affect the ability to manage, and *(b)* developing and applying the appropriate behaviors necessary to adapt to a changing world.

An Underlying Philosophy

To perform effectively in a changing environment, it is necessary for managers to clarify a number of assumptions. The following list attempts to articulate these assumptions and describe how they can be acted upon to help ensure managerial success (see Figure 1.3). Such a discussion will also clarify the authors' personal philosophies of management and facilitate the student's understanding of the material presented in subsequent chapters.

FIGURE 1.3

*Underlying philosophy:
Some key dimensions*

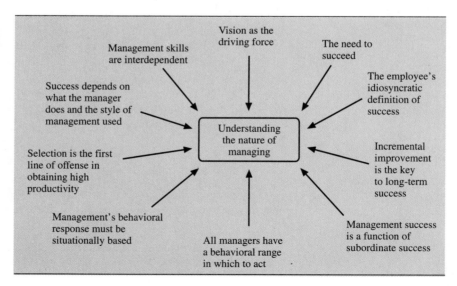

Vision as the Driving Force

To be successful, managers must bring into focus a vision that acts to energize organizational participants.[55] It is this vision that clarifies expectations on the part of subordinates, gives hope for a better tomorrow, and clarifies in the minds of others what will be the organization's (or unit's) preferred future state. What goals should be achieved and where the department or organization should be in, say, six months or a year are visualized when considering such variables as size, production, or quality or what type of climate should be created within the department and the organization at large. A vision that is accepted by subordinates motivates them to *(a)* perform effectively, even under adverse conditions, *(b)* experiment and create in order to reach goals that only yesterday appeared unreachable, *(c)* strive to develop new skills that will facilitate success in the future, and *(d)* remain on course when attempting to achieve stated objectives.

To be able to bring their vision into focus, managers must know their organization; understand its external environment; know their own needs, values, and preferred future state; and be able to translate personal ideas and goals into understandable messages. Two additional conditions must be met if managerial visions are to have their desired impact. First, managers must demonstrate an emotional commitment to the vision. More specifically, the vision must be perceived by others as a driving force within the manager. Only when managers are emotionally committed can they hope to "sell" their vision to others. Second, managers' vision of the future must have substance. Without substance you cannot have understanding, and without understanding you cannot create a clear picture in the minds of others. Therefore, before a manager can sell a vision to others he or she must have clearly thought out its content. It is this clear picture that produces the desired future state that others will want to move on to.

For managers to develop a clear vision that is in harmony with organizational goals, they must link their goals to the organization's overall strategic planning process. Such linking helps minimize conflict and gives credibility to a manager's departmental vision. To gain acceptance by subordinates, a manager must effectively communicate the ideas to others and negotiate where differences exist. In so doing, managers are attempting to jointly develop goals with their subordinates and thereby obtain their support.

The Need to Succeed

Next, management must assume that individuals seeking a long-term relationship with an organization have an underlying desire to be successful within that environment. This should be true regardless of organizational level. An individual will be successful to the degree that he or she achieves sought-after incentives or goals.[56] The value of such incentives or goals reflects the degree to which they can satisfy internal needs, thereby balancing internal tensions.[57]

Such an assumption is critical if management is to be successful in motivating employees to perform at, or near, their peak capabilities.

It is important to realize that only if employees have the need to succeed will it be meaningful for management to attempt to create an environment that facilitates employee success, that is, goal achievement. Managers can facilitate goal achievement and provide the necessary outcomes to maintain the desired intensity and direction of employee behavior.[58] If these conditions do not exist within the organization, then subordinates will become marginal employees, or withdraw physically or psychologically from their environment. If the latter conditions prevail, then management itself will be, by default, marginal. (As will be discussed later, individuals who do not have this underlying drive will voluntarily leave the organization after limited tenure, or if they do not leave voluntarily should be selectively removed through the organization's own evaluation process.)

The Importance of Individual Differences

As indicated above, success for each employee will be defined by the degree to which outcomes, both intrinsic and extrinsic, satisfy his or her unique internal needs or drives. Such internal needs and drives will reflect the individual's unique personality. Individual differences are also likely to affect the type of work environment preferred by employees and the level of satisfaction experienced.

Holland argued in his personality-job fit theory that employees' felt satisfaction with their work environment and the propensity to leave their current job reflects the degree of match between the employee's personality and the occupational setting.[59] For example, individuals who prefer social rather than physical or intellectual activities would be more satisfied with, and less likely to leave, jobs that emphasized interpersonal interactions (e.g., foreign service, hotel management, clinical psychology).

Five personality attributes frequently discussed in the "organizational behavior" literature also appear to have predictive utility in understanding employee differences.[60] They are locus of control orientation, achievement orientation, Machiavellianism, propensity for risk taking, and authoritarianism.

Locus of control orientation relates to individual differences in perceived source of reinforcement. Internals believe that outcomes received are a result of their own behavior, whereas externals believe that personal outcomes are a result of events beyond their control, that is, fate or chance.[61] Internals, when compared to externals, demonstrate a stronger preference for work environments that allow for participation and self-control.

Individuals who demonstrate a high need for *achievement* prefer tasks of moderate difficulty with immediate and reliable feedback.[62] At the same time, high achievers will avoid tasks that are so difficult that there is no chance of success.

Machiavellian personalities are not easily distracted, are oriented toward self-defined goals and task success, and believe that the ends justify the means. As employees, they function best in situations that allow for face-to-face interactions, have a minimum of rules or regulations, and where means to the ends are not clearly defined.[63]

High-risk-takers have a greater willingness to make quick decisions under conditions of uncertainty.[64] Such individuals are likely to perform well in environments that are unstructured and experiencing rapid change.

The interest in authoritarianism reflects the important role that authority, participation, and followership play in determining managerial success.[65] The authoritarian personality represents a set of beliefs and attitudes that can affect individuals' behavior on the job.[66] Its most prominent characteristics are (1) a rigid and moralistic adherence to middle class values, (2) a high sensitivity to authority relationships, that is, power and dominance, (3) submission to directives from above and exploitation of those below, (4) dogmatic thinking, (5) distrust, and (6) resistance to change.[67] Although few organizational members would be classified as extremely high-authoritarian, research suggests that they would have difficulty dealing with the feelings of others, that they would feel more comfortable with structured and directive leaders, that they would evaluate their leaders in terms of status and power, and be less likely than low-authoritarian employees to respond negatively toward managers in high status positions.[68]

Effective management must not only take individual differences into account, but create a climate that can, within acceptable limits, accommodate them. How managers accomplish this is covered in the goal-setting chapter but would also require that they use skills covered throughout the text.

Incremental Improvement is the Key to Long-Term Success

The concept of managerial success must recognize that as the environment changes, some subordinates may not be able, or willing, to perform at satisfactory levels. When this occurs, managers must *(a)* recognize the existence of such problem subordinates, and *(b)* take the necessary action to turn the marginal, or unsatisfactory, employee around. It is unlikely that such turnarounds will result from a single feedback, coaching, training, or disciplinary session. It may be necessary for the manager to work through a sequence of incremental improvement steps in order to achieve desired performance from subordinates.[69]

A corollary to this is that management performance should be evaluated on improvement over time rather than by fixed absolutes derived from unilaterally determined goals and objectives. It should also be realized that because situations are continually changing it may be impossible to maximize individual or group productivity. Consequently, "satisficing" may become the appropriate measure of success. Satisficing occurs when an individual establishes a level of acceptability that is below some maximum or ideal level. As the individual screens or experiences alternatives, he or she selects the first one that exceeds the stated level of acceptability. This may occur in spite of the fact that better alternatives still exist within the environment.

Management Success is a Function of Subordinate Success

To be truly successful, managers should free themselves from the burden of attempting to carry subordinates. Again, managers who can accomplish this will be highly valued by their organizations. Managers who select good employees; train and develop subordinates; negotiate and set demanding, but achievable, goals; monitor both results and behavior; and effectively coach, counsel, and provide meaningful feedback do increase the probability that their subordinates will provide the performance required. When this occurs, subordinates are carrying the manager and increasing the probability of managerial success.

All Managers Have a Behavioral Range in Which to Act

Societal norms, unions, activist groups, top management, one's immediate boss and subordinates define the extreme limits of a manager's behavior within any organizational setting (see Figure 1.4). The actual width of each manager's range varies, depending on the particular situation, the degree of managerial experience, and one's past track record. This range allows managers to modify the material presented within this book so as to satisfy individual personalities. At the same time, it offers managers an opportunity to experiment with delivery style so as to maximize the fit with their unique situation. Therefore, although significant increases in productivity will be achieved if the recommended behaviors described in this book are implemented, there always exists a flexibility range capable of accommodating individual behavioral differences.

FIGURE 1.4

Management's discretionary range of behavior

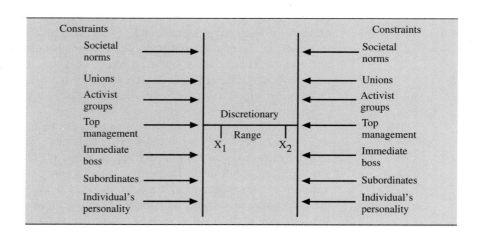

The existence of an available behavioral range also facilitates managers' ability to differentially reward staff within their departments. Assume, if you will, that point X_2 on the right-hand side of Figure 1.4 represents positive behaviors a manager can direct toward subordinates (i.e., recognition, social support, positive feedback, autonomy, rewards under his or her control), while point X_1 on the left-hand side of the range represents the withholdings of these positive behaviors. If subordinates support and carry out the jointly set departmental (organizational) goals, then managers can reinforce that behavior with selected positive consequences under their control. On the other hand, if subordinates do not support and carry out the jointly set goals, then similar positive reinforcements will be withheld. In extreme cases, disruptive employees will be punished in a more punitive manner, that is, fired, transferred, or suspended. In other words, the existence of a behavior range allows managers to create an effective motivational climate, one in which reinforcement and punishment are directly linked to performance.

Management's Behavioral Response Must Be Situationally Based

Related to the last point is need for a situational, or contingent, approach to management. Such an approach requires that managers diagnose their environments and then scan their environments to collect relevant information. To diagnose effectively, managers first articulate the issues or problems being considered. Once sufficient information is collected, a manager selects what he or she believes to be the most appropriate course of action to follow—by linking relevant facts, personal goals, and appropriate theories. For example, if a manager is attempting to assess what leadership style is appropriate in a given situation, he or she will have to collect information about subordinates' ability, willingness to perform, consequences of failure, employee expectations, etc. The manager then selects what he or she considers the most appropriate leadership style.

Therefore, whether managers use an autocratic or participative style of leadership, one-way or two-way communication, delegate or make unilateral decisions, have a wide or narrow span of control, etc., depends on the situation. Managers must ultimately develop a style that is both flexible and consistent: flexible in that it changes the behaviors used as a situation changes, but consistent in that it employs the same behaviors in the same situations. In this way, a manager can be perceived as both fair and predictable.

Selection Is the First Line of Offense in Obtaining High Productivity

To take full advantage of the skills described in this book, the manager must have subordinates who have the aptitude and willingness to learn new behaviors. This implies that the "first line of offense" in attempting to achieve high levels of productivity is selection. Unfortunately, this is not always possible where the manager does not control selection decisions. For example, the manager may be newly promoted and as a result have inherited individuals who are unable to perform at desired levels. Also, political realities may force a manager to select an individual who is not able to perform at desired levels. The more frequently poor selection occurs, the lower the probability of managerial success. A detailed discussion of selection issues is presented in Chapter 8.

Success Depends on What the Manager Does and the Interpersonal Style Used

Managerial success is a function of the manager's technical competencies and the interpersonal style he or she uses. Technical competencies relate to the skills presented in this text and the functional area the manager is responsible for. Interpersonal style refers to the way the manager relates to others from day to day. Important elements of interpersonal style are the level of interpersonal sensitivity,[70] the level of self-disclosure or openness,[71] and the degree of trust expressed toward others.[72]

Interpersonal sensitivity means that individuals consider how relationships are working and the interpersonal impact individuals are having on one another. Self-disclosure reflects an individual's willingness to share personal information, feeling, and perceptions. Trust implies that individuals are willing to take personal risks by either putting their goals in the hands of others or by offering services to others without any guarantee of acceptance or personal benefit. As will be discussed in Chapter 2, subordinates are more likely to support and accept managers who are interpersonally sensitive, open, and trusting. Managers who reject this point of view, because it is philosophically alien to their present management style or personality, will likely find others increasingly resistant to their actions.

Management Skills are Interdependent

The topics presented in this book are highly interdependent. For example, you cannot have good performance appraisal unless you have engaged in successful goal setting, nor can you have successful goal setting unless you know and understand the environment in which you function, and are able to negotiate effectively. Students must realize that as they proceed through this text sequentially, there will be a cumulative positive impact on their ability to manage others. Consequently, maximum benefit for the reader can only be obtained after the material covered in each chapter has been mastered.

Having been introduced to the text's scope, environmental trends in the 1990s, and the authors' underlying approach to management, you are now ready to begin mastering the skills necessary for successful management. However, remember that what you read is relevant only if you attempt to apply the material in organizational settings and then assess its consequences. If the consequences are the ones you desire, then repeat those behaviors when similar situations occur. If the consequences are negative, or leave room for improvement, then analyze the cause and effect links that exist within the environment and attempt to make changes in your future behaviors so as to bring about improved performance for yourself and those around you.

Opportunity with Constraint

The 1980s will become known as the decade of excess. It was a period of record economic growth, organizational takeovers, junk bonds, appearance of new business, deregulation, personal computers, fax machines, etc. In the United States, President Reagan proclaimed it was "morning in America," and it appeared that it was, as Americans rushed out to spend their newly enacted tax cuts and at the same time borrow on their futures. However, as North America progresses through the 1990s and beyond, all is not well. There are increasing signs that the decade of prosperity has come to an end, that resources are not endless, that mergers and takeovers do not ensure an effective production system or more and better products, and that foreign trading blocs threaten North America's economic future. At the same time, however, there are increasing opportunities resulting from globalization, from the opening up of new markets in Eastern Europe, Russia, and China, and from the North American Free Trade Agreement (NAFTA) among the United States, Canada, and Mexico.

Organizations in North America are now facing a period of both opportunity and constraint. Unfortunately, many organizations have not responded to the challenge, nor to the need to improve their management to meet the competition head on. It is this failure that concerns Kanter when she says that giants (North America's large organizations) must learn to dance. In Kanter's view, the ultimate corporate balancing act will take place when organizations attempt to do more with less, and learn to grow while cutting back.[73] Fewer employees will be present within organizations because of downsizing, as technologies allow organizations to trim their work force without reducing the level of output. If fewer employees are able to maintain the same level of output, it logically follows that the negative impact of poor performers is likely to have a proportionately greater impact on an organization's success, that is, their effect relative to the number of total employees will grow. To help overcome this dilemma, management must be able to fine-tune its managerial skills and thereby increase its ability to get more out of its subordinates. This truly is the challenge for management throughout the 1990s and beyond.

Summary

As individuals attempt to manage in the 1990s and beyond, they will increasingly be forced to adjust their behaviors to fit environmental realities. Environmental imperatives such as the employee's desire to participate, globalization, increased rates of internal and external change, forced accountability, a changing work force, and greater access to information, will dramatically affect the way individuals manage. The key to success is whether managers recognize these imperatives and adjust their behaviors accordingly. This chapter also presented a number of underlying assumptions made by the authors that will facilitate the reader's understanding of material presented in subsequent chapters. Finally, it was argued that although managers face environmental constraints and uncertainty, they have an opportunity to manage more effectively.

EXERCISES

1.1 Clarifying Student Responsibilities: A Psychological Contract*

The purpose of this exercise is to consider course expectations for both the professor and the students. You are to assume that the instructor has already considered what is expected from the students and how course material is to be presented to the class. Please take 45 minutes to carry out Steps 1 and 2 to facilitate a meaningful discussion about expectations and responsibilities.

Step 1.   The class will form small groups of five to six students each. During Step 1, each group will select one member to present output. Each group will be provided with transparencies and felt-tip markers to prepare for the presentation.

Step 2.   Each small group will take 40 minutes to develop a response to the questions below. When developing the group's position, use the open group discussion process; that is, group members state their personal views openly to the rest of the group. At the same time, they must be willing to listen to the views of other group members.

Questions to consider:

- Given your knowledge of the present course and its professor, what do you want to accomplish by the end of the term? What do you believe are the instructor's goals and the students' expectations? If the goals and expectations are not the same, explain why. You also should consider whether it is desirable for the instructor's goals and student expectations to be the same.
- When considering classroom activities, and responsibilities, what do you believe to be desirable behaviors on the part of instructor and students?
- What behaviors of instructor and students are likely to have a negative impact on student performance during the course?
- What can the instructor and students do to ensure that negative behaviors do not occur or that their impact can be neutralized if they do occur?

---

*A psychological contract between professors and students implicitly defines the performance and behavioral expectations these individuals have of each other. Such expectations are likely to reflect personal standards, experiences, and the educational institution attended.

Step 3. The class will assemble, and selected group representatives will make their presentations. Students will be allowed to ask questions for clarification purposes but will not be allowed to add to the presenting group's response. Time permitting, each group will have a chance to make its presentation.

Step 4. The professor will lead the class in an open discussion of group presentations. Student perceptions will be compared with the instructor's expectations.

Step 5. Each student will prepare a written statement listing what he or she can do to make the class a positive learning experience. (Step 5 is optional)

Please proceed

1.2. What Needs to Be Done During the First Six Months on the Job

Very often, the most difficult transition for a new manager occurs during the first six months on the job. If the new employee does not perform well, take the initiative, or demonstrate value to the organization, management may question the wisdom of hiring the individual. Although the pressure is on the new employee to perform, he or she will most often ask, "What should I do first?" This exercise is designed to give you an opportunity to think through what your answer should be to this question and how best to approach the first six months on the job. Please follow the steps outlined below.

Step 1. Students will form small groups of five to six individuals. They should select one member of the group to act as group spokesperson.

Step 2. Read individually the background material presented below.

Step 3. Through group discussion, develop a list of 12 to 15 recommendations to guide newly hired managers. These guidelines should act as a road map for what the new manager should or should not do when taking over a department. Try to be as imaginative and specific as possible. To breathe life into your discussion, feel free to make additional assumptions about the new job and organization for which you will be working. The only constraint is that the assumptions must be realistic and consistent with the jobs for which graduate business students are typically hired.

Step 4. At the end of 40 minutes, one or more groups will present their lists. Each group will be provided with overhead transparencies and felt-tip overhead markers. After group lists have been discussed, they will be compared to the experts' list.

You have 40 minutes to develop your list and prepare for the forthcoming presentation.

Background

Assume that you are L. Timmons. You have a degree from a well-known business school and have just been hired by a rapidly growing organization located in the Northeast. You will have 12 subordinates reporting to you. Your department's primary task is to do research to update a database that your company sells to both government and private industry. The position you are filling is not a new one, and your staff have been with the organization an average of five years. You soon discover that you would like to change some activities and procedures in your department. Top management has also hinted that your predecessor was transferred in part because he could not manage effectively or get things done. You can assume that no specific problems need to be solved immediately; there are no crises.

1.3. Understanding the Manager's Role

Success of managers very often depends on understanding what is expected of them by the organization, other managers, and subordinates. This understanding is also critical when attempting to define personal expectations, organizational needs, and potential areas of development. Since many students will become managers, take the time to articulate what you believe to be appropriate managerial roles. Please follow the steps outlined below.

Step 1.   The class will form small groups of five to six individuals each.

Step 2.   Through group discussion, develop a list of behaviors and responsibilities that clearly define the manager's job. When developing your list of behaviors and responsibilities, consider the manager's short-term and long-term horizon. If individuals in your group are currently managers, ask what they are doing now and what they would like to do in the future. If you are not a manager, but currently employed, consider what your employer might need or expect from your immediate superior. Do not list specific types of tasks performed by managers (e.g., completing personnel reports). Instead, list the general types of behaviors or responsibilities that describe a manager's role. (Step 2 should take approximately 30 minutes.)

Step 3.   From its list of behaviors and responsibilities, each group will determine the five that it believes are most important. Your reduced list should be ranked 1 through 5 with 1 indicating the most critical, 2 the next most important, to 5 the least critical. (Step 3 should take approximately 30 minutes.)

Step 4.   The class will assemble and discuss group results.

End Notes

1. R. L. Daft, *Management,* Dryden Press, New York, 1988: 5; J. L. Gibson, J.M. Ivancevich, and J. H. Donnelly, Jr., *Organizations,* 8th ed., Irwin, Burr Ridge, Ill., 1994: 743.

2. R. E. Kopelman, *Managing Productivity in Organizations,* McGraw-Hill, New York, 1986; W. B. Werther, Jr., W. A. Ruch and L. McClure, *Productivity through People,* West Publishing, St. Paul, Minn., 1986; and A. Szilagyi, *Management and Performance,* 3rd ed., Scott, Foresman, Glenview, Ill., 1988.

3. T. Peters, *Thriving on Chaos,* Harper & Row, New York, 1988: 345.

4. R. H. Hayes and W. Abernathy, "Management Minus Invention," *The New York Times,* August 20, 1980: D2.

5. Henry Mintzberg, *Mintzberg on Management,* Free Press, London, 1989.

6. Peters, 1988: 344.

7. "Special Report," *Business Week,* April 25, 1983: 74.

8. V. Vroom, *Some personality determinants of the effects of participations,* Prentice Hall, Englewood Cliffs, N.J., 1960; H. A. Tosi, "A reexamination of personality as a determinant of the effect of participation," *Personnel Psychology,* Vol. 23, 1970: 91–99; J. M. Ivancevich, "An analysis of participation in decision making among project engineers," *Academy of Management Journal,* Vol. 22, 1979: 253–269; E. A. Locke, P. M. Schweiger, and G. P. Latham, "Participation in decision making—When should it be used?" *Organizational Dynamics,* Spring 1986: 65–79; M. Shaskin, "Participative management is an ethical imperative," *Organizational Dynamics,* Summer 1986: 86–75.

9. Jim Clemmer and Art McNeil, *The VIP Strategy: Leadership Skills for Exceptional Performance,* Key Porter Books, Toronto, 1988: 9.

10. R. W. Clement, "Happy employees are not all alike," *Across the Board,* Vol. 30, January–February 1993: 51–52

11. Rosabeth M. Kanter, *When Giants Learn to Dance,* Simon & Schuster, New York, 1989; J. Naisbitt, *Megatrends: Ten New Directions Transforming Our Lives,* Warner Books, New York, 1985; J. Naisbitt and P. Aburdene, *Megatrends 2000,* Morrow, New York, 1990; J. Naisbitt and P. Aburdene, *Re-inventing the Corporation: Transforming Your Job and Your Organization for the New Information Age,* Warner Books, New York, 1985.

12. Rosabeth M. Kanter, *The Change Masters,* Simon & Schuster, New York, 1983.

13. Kanter, 1989.

14. D. Ulrich and M. F. Wiersema, "Gaining strategic and organizational capability in a turbulent business environment," *The Academy of Management Executive,* Vol. 3, No. 2, 1989: 115–122.

15. Ulrich and Wiersema, 1989.

16. D. L. Nelson and C. Sutton, "Chronic work stress and coping: A longitudinal study and suggested new directions," *Academy of Management Journal,* Vol. 33, No. 4, 1990: 859–869.

17. R. J. Hendrickson, "Proactive approach to minimize stress on the job," *Professional Safety,* Vol. 34, No. 11, November 1989: 29–32.

18. J. E. McGrath, "Stress and behavior in organizations," *Handbook of Industrial and Organizational Psychology,* ed. M. D. Dunnette, Rand McNally, Chicago, 1976; T. Cox, *Stress,* University Park Press, Baltimore, 1978; H. Benson and R. L. Allen, "How much stress is too much?" *Harvard Business Review,* September–October, 1980: 86–92; J. M. Ivancevich and M. T Matteson, *Stress and Behavior in Organizations,* Scott, Foresman, Glenview, Ill., 1981; R. D. Allen, M. A. Hitt, and C. R. Greer, "Occupational stress and perceived organizational effectiveness in formal groups: An examination of stress level and stress type," *Personnel Psychology,* Summer 1982: 359–370; W. Gmelch, *Beyond Stress to Effective Management,* John Wiley & Sons, New York, 1982; Hendrickson, 1989; D. C. M. Anderson, "A departmental stress management plan," *Health Care Supervisor,* Vol. 8, No. 4, July 1990: 1–8.

19. D. C. Glass and J. E. Singer, *Urban Stress,* Academic Press, New York, 1972; S. Cohen, "Aftereffects of stress on human performance and social behavior: A review of research and theory," *Psychological Bulletin,* Vol. 88, 1980: 82–108.

20. R. H. Hayes and W. J. Abernathy, "Managing our way to economic decline," W. B. Werther, Jr., W. A. Ruch, and L. McClure, 1986: 9–23; E. Block, "Technology policy and U.S. competitiveness," *Chemical Engineering News,* Vol. 69, May 27, 1991: 32–36; J. Morkes, "U.S. losing ground in critical technologies," *Research and Development,* Vol. 33, June 1991: 18; H. Kleiman, "Lessons from yesterday: How we can recapture the technological lead," *Industry Week,* Vol. 244, February 17, 1992: 54 + .

21. Naisbitt and Aburdene, 1985.

22. L. R. Offermann and K. K. Gowing, "Organizations of the future," *American Psychologist,* Vol. 45, No. 2, February 1990: 95–108.

23. G. Church, "Job in an age of insecurity," *Time,* November 22, 1993: 22–28.

24. Offermann and Gowing, 1990.

25. Church, 1993: 22–28.

26. S. Liss, "America's immigration challenge," *Time,* Special Issue, Fall 1993 Vol. 142, No. 21, 1993: 3–7.

27. George T. Milkovich and William F. McShane, *Canadian Personnel/Human Resource Management,* Business Publications, Plano, Tex., 1988.

28. L. Mikulecky, "Basic skill impediments to communication between management and hourly employees," *Management Communication Quarterly,* Vol. 3, No. 4, May 1990: 452–473.

29. I. L. Goldstein and P. Gilliam, "Training issues in the year 2000," *American Psychologist,* Vol. 45, No. 2, February 1990: 134–143.

30. W. B. Johnston and A. H. Packer, *Workforce 2000: Work and Workers for the Twenty-First Century,* Hudson Institute, Indianapolis, Ind., 1987.

31. F. D. Horowitz and M. O'Brien, "In the interest of the nation: A reflective essay on the state of our knowledge and the challenges before us," *American Psychologist,* Vol. 44, 1989: 441–445.

32. Johnston and Packer, 1987.

33. U.S. Bureau of the Census, Statistical Abstract of the United States 1991, 11th ed., U.S. Government Printing Office, Washington, D.C., 1991: 388.

34. Johnston and Packer, 1987.

35. "Women in the Work Force: Innovation in Canada," Research Report prepared for the Economic Council of Canada, Ministry of Supply and Services, Ottawa: Canada, 1987, Cat. No. EC22–141/1987E, chap. 9.

36. J. Kusel and T. H. Oxner, "Women in internal auditing," *Internal Auditor,* Vol. 9, No. 2, 1990: 9–12.

37. S. J. Patel and B. H. Kleiner, " The price corporations must pay for women executives," *Equal Opportunities International,* Vol. 9, No. 2, 1990: 9–12; F. J. Segal and G. G. Marcial, "Corporate women," *Business Week,* June 8, 1992: 74–83.

38. Offermann and Gowing, 1990.

39. B. Leibson, "Corporate child care: 'Junior execs' on the job," *Facilities Design and Management,* Vol. 9, No. 7, July 1990: 32–37.

40. George T. Milkovich and William F. Glueck, *Personnel/Human Resource Management,* Business Publications, Plano, Tex., 1985: 36.

41. Johnston and Packer, 1987.

42. G. T. Milkovich, W. Glueck, R. Barth, and F. S. McShane, *Canadian Personnel/Human Resource Management,* Irwin, Burr Ridge, Ill. 1988: 47.

43. Offermann and Gowing, 1990.

44. D. Bell, *The Coming of Post Industrial Society,* Basic Books, New York, 1973; A. Toffler, *The Third Wave,* Bantam, New York, 1980; J. Naisbitt, *Megatrends,* Warner Books, New York, 1984; Interview with W. David Penniman, "Defining the information age," *Bulletin of the American Society for Information Science,* December/January 1989: 18–20; S. Alter, *Information Systems: A Management Perspective,* Addison-Wesley Publishing, Reading, Mass., 1992.

45. J. E. Bredehoft and B. Kleiner, "Communications revolution and its impact on managing," *Industrial Management & Data Systems,* Vol. 91, No. 7, 1991: 15–19.

46. A. Prozes, "The electronic information age," *Business Quarterly,* Vol. 55, No. 1, Summer 1990: 80–84.

47. H. E. Dolenga, "Management paradigms and practices in the information age," SAM *Advanced Management Journal,* Vol. 57, No. 1, Winter 1992: 25–29.

48. W. A. Spivey and D. T. Lawrason, "Global management: Concepts, themes, problems, and research," *Human Resource Management,* Vol. 29, No. 1, Spring 1990: 85–97.

49. P. Danos and R. L. Measelle, "Globalization of the business environment: Implications for the accounting profession and business education," *Human Resource Management,* Vol. 29, No. 1, Spring 1990: 77–84.

50. C. A. Bartlett and S. Ghoshal, "What is a global manager?" *Harvard Business Review,* September–October, 1992: 124–132; Spivey and Lawrason, Spring 1990: 85–97.

51. Bartlett and Ghoshal, 1992.

52. D. N. Thompson, "The triad, reciprocity and alliances: New realities for trade," *Business Quarterly,* Vol. 55, No. 1, Summer 1990: 25–29.

53. K. Ohmae, *The Borderless World: Power and Strategy in the Interlinked Economy,* Harper Collins College Publications, New York, 1991.

54. S. Koh, "Corporate globalization: A new trend," *Academy of Management Executive,* Vol. 6, No. 1, February 1992: 89–96.

55. Kanter, 1983; Clemmer and McNeil, 1988; R. H. Rosen, *The Healthy Company: Eight Strategies to Develop People, Productivity, and Profits,* Jeremy P. Tarcher, Inc., Los Angeles, 1991; J. A. Belasco, *Teaching the Elephant to Dance,* Penguin Group, New York, 1991.

56. R. M. Steers and L. W. Porter, *Motivation and Work Behavior,* 4th ed., McGraw-Hill, New York, 1987.

57. M. D. Dunnette and W. K. Kirchner, *Psychology Applied to Industry,* Appleton-Century-Crofts, New York, 1965.

58. Steers and Porter, 1987.
59. J. L. Holland, *Making Vocational Choices: A Theory of Vocational Personalities and Work Environments,* Prentice Hall, Englewood Cliffs, N.J., 1985; A. R. Spokane, "A review of research on person-environment congruence in Holland's theory of careers," *Journal of Vocational Behavior,* June 1985: 306–43; D. Brown, "The status of Holland's theory of career choice," *Career Development Journal,* September 1987: 13–23.
60. F. Luthans, *Organizational Behavior,* 5th ed., McGraw-Hill, New York, 1989; S. P. Robbins and M. C. Butler, *Organizational Behavior: Concepts, Controversies, and Applications,* Prentice Hall, Englewood Cliffs, N.J., 1991; J. L. Gibson, J. M. Ivancevich, and J. H. Donnelly, Jr., *Organizations: Behavior, Structure, Process,* Irwin, Burr Ridge, Ill., 1994.
61. J. B. Rotter, "Generalized expectancies for internal versus external control of reinforcement," *Psychological Monographs: General and Applied,* Vol. 80, No. 1, 1966: 5 + ; T. R. Mitchell, C. M. Smyser and S. E.Weed, "Locus of control: Supervision and work satisfaction," *Academy of Management Journal,* September 1975: 623–631; P. E. Spector, "Behavior in organizations as a function of employee's locus of control," *Psychological Bulletin,* May 1982: 482–497; G. J. Blau, "Locus of control as a potential moderator of the turnover process," *Journal of Occupational Psychology,* Fall 1987: 21–29.
62. D. C. McClelland, "Business drive and national achievement," *Harvard Business Review,* July–August 1962: 99–112; D. C. McClelland, "Toward a theory of motive acquisition," *American Psychologist,* May 1965: 321–333; D. C. McClelland and D. Burnham, "Power is the great motivator," *Harvard Business Review,* March–April 1976: 100–111; Gibson, Ivancevich, and Donnelly, Jr., 8th ed. 1994: 157–160.
63. R. Christie and F. L. Geis, *Studies in Machiavellianism,* Academic Press, Hinsdale, Ill., 1970.
64. I. L. Janis and L. Mann, *Decision Making: A Psychological Analysis of Conflict, Choice, and Commitment,* The Free Press, New York, 1977; B. M. Bass, *Organizational Decision Making,* Irwin, Burr Ridge, Ill., 1983.
65. R. M. Stogdill, *Handbook of Leadership: A Survey of Theory and Research,* The Free Press, New York, 1974.
66. H. Gough, "Personality and personality assessment," in M. D. Dunnette (ed.), *Handbook of Industrial and Organizational Psychology,* Chicago, Rand McNally, 1976, 579; R. M. Stogdill, 1974.
67. T. W. Adorno, E. Frenkel-Brunswik, D. J. Levinson, and R. N. Sanford, *The Authoritarian Personality,* New York, Harper & Row, 1950; H. Gleitman, *Psychology,* New York, W. W. Norton & Company, 1981.
68. Gough, 1976; Stogdill, 1974.
69. L. W. Mealiea, "Learned behavior: The key to understanding and preventing employee resistance to change," *Group & Organizational Studies,* Vol. 3, No. 2, June 1978: 211–223; Peters, 1988; D. Nadler, "Managing transitions to uncertain future states," *Organizational Dynamics,* Vol. II, 1982: 37–45.
70. A. G. Athos and J. J. Gabarro, *Interpersonal Behavior: Communicating and Understanding Relationships,* Prentice Hall, New Jersey, 1978; R. L. Weaver II, *Understanding Interpersonal Communications,* Harper Collins College Publishers, New York, 1993; L. P. Porter and L. E. McKibbin, *Management Education and Development: Drift or Thrust in the 21st Century?* McGraw-Hill, New York, 1988; "Chicago's B-School Goes Touchy-Feely," *Newsweek,* November 27, 1989: 140.
71. Weaver II, 1993; J. Hall, "Communication revisited," *California Management Review,* Fall 1973: 56–67; P. W. Cozby, "Self-disclosure: A literature review," *Psychological Bulletin,* Vol. 79, 1973: 73–91.
72. Weaver II, 1993; Athos and Gabarro, 1978.
73. Kanter, 1989: 31.

UNDERSTANDING WHO YOU ARE

Objectives:

- Learn behavioral concepts that facilitate self-understanding.
- Clarify the impact of personality and self-concept* on personal behavior within an organizational setting.
- Describe conceptual models that will guide decision making when dealing with the personality/environmental interface.
- Articulate the consequences of a match between the individual and the environmental setting.

The Importance of Understanding the Self

As discussed in Chapter 1, managers have a range in which they can perform without experiencing conflict. A manager's personality is an important variable in determining the upper and lower boundaries of this range. Personality is *a relatively stable set of characteristics, tendencies, and temperaments that have been significantly formed by inheritance and by social, cultural, and environmental factors. This set of variables determines the commonalities and differences in the behavior of the individual.*[1] Associated with an individual's unique personality is a set of preferred behaviors.[2] The free expression of such behaviors represents a goal for employees as they interact within their environment. When free self-expression is blocked, employees experience internal tension or frustration.[3]

---

*Self-concept defines how individuals view themselves based upon knowledge about personal goals, motives, attitudes, behaviors, etc. A person's self-concept is also influenced by relevant others with whom he or she interacts, such as parents, siblings, spouse, co-workers, and boss.[4]

The consequences of internal tension or frustration can be negative or positive. On the negative side, internal tension can be exhibited through expressed job dissatisfaction, reduced effort, work sabotage, and psychological or physical flight.[5] Psychological flight occurs when employees daydream, or give minimum attention to tasks being performed. Physical flight occurs when individuals take inappropriate sick days and extended lunch hours or coffee breaks. In extreme cases of physical flight, employees may voluntarily quit and seek employment elsewhere in an attempt to achieve a match between their personalities and job characteristics. On the positive side, managers may be motivated by internal tension or frustration to take steps to increase their understanding of the environment, initiate changes where possible, or accept situations that cannot be changed.

To deal effectively with this internal tension, managers must understand their own personalities. By knowing themselves, managers increase their ability to find those organizational environments that are likely to produce a match with their personalities, develop change strategies designed to produce a desired match, or leave environments that are unacceptable to them. Personal knowledge of self also facilitates interpersonal sensitivity by allowing managers to better understand their own behavior and its effect on others.

This chapter focuses on four areas that are important when attempting to assess the match between individuals and their environments. They are: personal career management and goal setting, self-efficacy, interpersonal needs, and interpersonal style (see Figure 2.1). Individuals who take the time to know

FIGURE 2.1

Personality factors

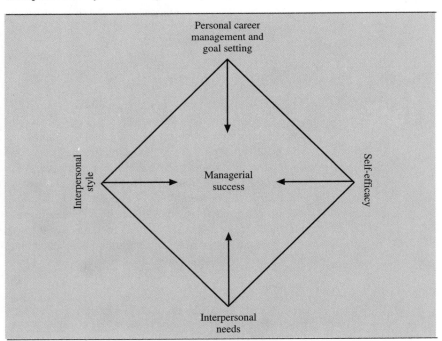

themselves have a greater likelihood of developing change strategies that will facilitate growth and personal health.[6]

Personal Career Management and Goal Setting

Personal career management is a process "by which individuals can guide, direct, and influence the course of their careers."[7] The term *career* refers to the full range of work experiences that an individual engages in during his or her lifetime and the individual's subjective interpretation of these events— that is, the individual's aspirations, needs, feelings, etc. Defined in this way, the concept of career is not limited to a particular profession, sequence of advancements, or occupations within a particular organization.[8] Figure 2.2 describes such a career management process and the variables that help explain

FIGURE 2.2

A model of career management

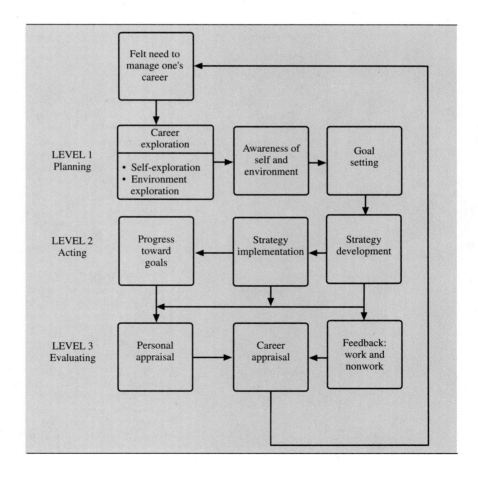

how the process works.[9] Of particular relevance to this chapter is the activity of personal goal setting and the key role it plays in decision making and strategy development.[10]

Successful career management and personal goal setting are often associated with the concept of career stages and the setting and implementation of appropriate goals at each stage.[11] While currently cited models differ in the number of stages described, and the labels used, it is sufficient for our purposes to consider the five stages listed in Table 2.1[12] and the major issues confronted at each stage. Issue differences between stages require individuals to seek information, establish goals, and develop strategies that are unique to the career stage at which they are currently functioning.

For example, individuals at the entry into the work force stage are more likely to establish goals that deal with making a realistic and valid job choice, doing well in selection interviews, or identifying organizations that satisfy personal needs or wants. At the early career stage, individuals are likely to set

TABLE 2.1   Career Stages and Related Issues

Career Stage	Issues
• Prework period	Defining the self; obtaining appropriate education or training; developing basic life skills; developing understanding of available occupational choices and personal preferences.
• Entry into the work force	Identifying potential employers; landing a first job; negotiating terms of employment; managing the transition from being unemployed to employed; adjusting to daily work activity or routines.
• Early career	Developing one's skills and knowledge base, gaining acceptance and credibility, balancing personal independence and dependence on others; assessing the match between the initial job and personal needs, interests, and talents; selection of a specialty; deciding whether to stay on initial job or seek a better job elsewhere; developing one's long-term career plans.
• Middle career	Continued relevance of job skills when remaining with area of specialization; appropriateness of becoming a generalist; reappraising one's career before it is too late to make changes; gaining full understanding of the total organization and its strategic plans, customer needs, new product possibilities, etc.
• Late career	Maintain value to the organization by becoming a mentor, that is, imparting organizational wisdom and insight to fledglings; using organizational wisdom and insight to cope with reduced power or influence; recognizing that a promotion to senior management may not be an option; and planning for retirement.

goals that center on getting established on the job, achieving initial successes, gaining credibility through specialization, learning to get along with the first boss, and finding out about the organization in which they function. Individuals at the middle career stage are more likely to establish goals associated with career reappraisal, overcoming obsolescence due to technological changes, moving away from technical or specialized areas and becoming more of a generalist. Individuals at the late career stage are more likely to be concerned with finding new sources of enjoyment outside the work environment, preparing for retirement, and retaining a personal identity that is not job related.[13]

Movement from one career stage to another will require individuals to update self and environmental awareness information and to appropriately change goals when required. Unfortunately, the danger exists that individuals will continue to seek goals when they are no longer appropriate to their current situation.[14] Complicating the process are within-stage differences that occur due to individual differences. Such differences reflect the unique set of needs, wants, interests, and talents possessed by each individual.[15]

Self-Exploration and Awareness

Exploration and awareness of the self and one's environment are necessary conditions to establish personal career goals. Self-exploration allows individuals to achieve self-awareness, and environmental exploration facilitates environmental awareness.[16] While it is recognized that environmental exploration and awareness are necessary for successful goal setting, a detailed discussion of these topics will be postponed until Chapter 15. This chapter emphasizes the process of self-exploration and awareness. Individuals who are proactive and collect relevant information about personal needs, values, interests, talents, and lifestyle preferences are likely to *(a)* be more satisfied and productive when searching for acceptable job opportunities, *(b)* develop clearer career plans and expectations, and *(c)* be more productive on the job.[17]

When collecting or processing information about the self, individuals have four primary alternative modes for self-exploration. There are the individuals themselves; others with whom they interact, such as co-workers, supervisors, friends, and family members; counseling and testing services provided by the organization; and counseling and testing services provided by third-party professionals.[18] Of primary interest to the present discussion is the individual's own self exploration. By placing emphasis on the individual's own efforts, it is assumed "that with some guidance and understanding of the process, any careful and thoughtful person can generate personal information, assess its usefulness, and draw conclusions from it that will be helpful, even extremely helpful, in making career-related decisions."[19] However, self-assessment alone will not capture all the needed information necessary to make career decisions. Whenever possible, self-generated information should be supplemented with information and interpretive support from the other sources to help ensure relevance and accuracy of personal conclusions.[20]

At the personal level, it is possible for individuals to engage in a number of self-evaluation techniques that will facilitate data collection and self-analysis. The levels of probing of such techniques range from the simple to the complex probing. The type selected by the individual will reflect his or her ability and commitment and the level of support provided within the environment.[21] Whichever technique is used, the goal is to answer the question, "Who am I?" Table 2.2 lists a number of often-cited techniques designed to collect and organize information about the self, and gain greater self awareness.[22] Whichever technique is used, the output should define or articulate aspects of the individual's life in concrete or behaviorally specific terms. The individual then analyzes and reflects on available information to identify common themes or inferences about the self.

TABLE 2.2   Individual Control Self-Assessment Techniques

- Self-written interviews, life story, autobiographical story—this technique requires an individual to write an autobiography that describes his or her life. It is a written narrative of personal history. Specific content statements would describe life events, education, hobbies, major changes that have occurred in the past, consequences of the described events, and the individual's feelings about these events. Also included is a description of turning points in one's life and the pros and cons of past career decisions.

- Daily or weekly logs—As individuals pass through a particular time period they write down events and decisions made, and the time devoted to these activities. When constructing such a diary, it is desirable to include both work and nonwork days.

- Written daydreams—The individual first stimulates a fantasy or vision about the future or a currently preferred surrounding. Individuals then record what they have visualized for future analysis.

- Written future obituaries or retirement speeches—Individuals write personal obituaries or retirement speeches that might be given at the time of their death or retirement. The individual describes what he or she would be remembered for and the comments made by co-workers and acquaintances.

- Ranking of significant work values—The individual lists what he or she believes are important or relevant values and then ranks them in terms of appropriateness or desirability. Listed values may relate to the following general categories: money, financial security, material gain; helping people, social contribution; power over self, self-improvement; security, stability, predictability; mental challenge and mental stimulation.

- Assets and liabilities balance sheet—The individual makes two lists. The first list articulates assets or strengths, the second articulates liabilities or weaknesses. When using this technique, it is desirable to have individuals describe specific situations and behaviors to help ensure accurate and complete assessment of personal assets and liabilities.

- Lifestyle representation—Individuals describe their current lifestyle in either written or pictorial form. When using this technique, individuals are encouraged to be as behaviorally specific as possible.

The following example provided by an individual who completed an autobiographical narrative demonstrates how these techniques can facilitate self-exploration and analysis. Let us call him Bob. Bob's narrative included a number of statements that described activities at his university and while working during the summer.

> Each time I would get an accounting or operations research assignment, I would just about die. Working through these assignments always appeared to take longer than they actually did. Even though I typically got good grades (well above the average, I might add) it didn't do anything for me.
>
> During the summer I would work in my neighbor's nursery (trees and plants). What I liked about the job was being outdoors and interacting with the customers. I really got off on working with customers to solve their particular yard problems and then designing a landscaping package that fitted their needs.

After receiving his MBA, Bob went to work for a Chartered Accounting firm. He lasted about three years and then left to open a tree and plant nursery with his brother. After 15 years, Bob and his brother continue to own and manage their nursery. Although only a single incident, it demonstrates the importance of self-awareness and the need to translate it into career goals that fit the individual's self concept, personality, interests, and talents.

Goal Setting

As indicated in Figure 2.2, career goals link awareness to the design and implementation of career strategies. Career goals give direction to what individuals want to accomplish.[23] At the same time, career goals provide individuals with a structure that helps answer the questions "Why am I here?" and "Why am I doing this?" Greenhaus lists five reasons why goal setting can have a significant effect on behavior and performance. Goals can stimulate high effort, give focus of direction, elevate persistence levels, facilitate strategy formation, and provide the basis upon which to gain meaningful and timely feedback.[24] When translating personal and environmental awareness into personal goals, it is helpful to follow some basic rules. The following **"SMART"** acronym is a useful technique designed to help you remember the characteristics of well-thought-out career goals. Its component parts are:

S   Goals should be specific
M   Goals should be measurable
A   Goals should be attainable but challenging
R   Goals should be relevant and recorded
T   Goals should have a time frame

Goals Should Be Specific

Career goals vary in terms of their time frame and degree of specificity.[25] Conceptual, long-term, career goals describe the general experiences an individual seeks to achieve in the long run. In our nursery example above, Bob, before graduation, could have established the long-term conceptual goal that he wanted a career that would allow him to interact with people, combined planning and organizing skills with the ability to help others, be his own boss, and work in an area linked in some way to the out-of-doors. Goal specificity, however, is also needed to achieve the benefits of goal setting.[26] Therefore, even when dealing with long-term goals it is desirable to be specific. This can be accomplished by turning long-term conceptual goals into long-term operational goals.[27] By articulating long-term operational goals, the individual outlines long-term specific goals he or she would like to achieve. In Bob's case, he may specify that in five years after graduating with his MBA, he will own his own plant and tree nursery. Greater specificity can be added if Bob also includes his desire that the business be a joint venture with his brother, and that the nursery should be within commuting distance of his mother's home, should it be necessary to provide care in her senior years.

Movement toward long-term conceptual or operational goals is made up of a sequence of compatible action plans or short-term subgoals.[28] The individual identifies a sequence of short-term operational career subgoals that move him or her incrementally closer to long-term goals. Goal specificity is increased by breaking a large goal into smaller manageable units, and by bringing an action-oriented goal into the short-run. Bob can increase goal specificity by setting short-term goals: take a job with one of the large nurseries in the area immediately after graduation, take a horticulture course each term at the local junior college, and save a minimum of 20 percent of his monthly salary.

Goals Should Be Measurable

To determine if career goals have been achieved, it is necessary to build measurement characteristics into one's stated goals.[29] This requires that individuals articulate criteria of success and identify the techniques necessary to evaluate performance. Typically, performance is measured in physical units, such as courses taken, promotions received, jobs worked; deadlines; and money earned, saved or expenses incurred.[30] Such objective measures allow the individual to build numerical criteria into the goals.

It is also possible to apply subjective criteria when measuring goals.[31] Career goals can fulfill the individual's desire to satisfy intrinsic and instrumental needs.[32] In the case of intrinsic needs, goal-related experiences can satisfy the individual's need to engage in work activities that are enjoyable, use relevant skills, and enhance lifestyle preferences. Instrumental needs refer to the degree to which completed goals facilitate the achievement of future goals. In Bob's case, the ability to find a job with, and successfully work for, a local nursery facilitated the movement toward owning his own nursery in the future. It gave him the needed experience and added credibility to future attempts to obtain a small business loan. When using subjective measures it is important to attempt to identify indicators that lend themselves to measurement and evaluation.[33] For example, the degree to which intrinsic needs have been fulfilled may be indicated by the level of expressed satisfaction, the number of voluntary or unpaid hours worked, unscheduled sick days, or job attendance.

Goals Should Be Attainable and Challenging

Next, goals, and the behaviors required, should be attainable. Research suggests a linear relationship between goal difficulty and task performance.[34] Goals set too low are not challenging, typically do not use relevant skills, and often fail to maximize the effort–reward relationship. Consequently, low levels of goal difficulty result in low levels of performance. However, if the individual has the ability, or is likely to be rewarded for partial success, setting goals that are challenging has a greater likelihood of leading to high performance. If goals are set too high, or require behaviors that are beyond the individual's ability level, they are unlikely to be carried out. In other words, because effort is insufficient for success, commitment to the goal will be low.

Goals Should Be Relevant and Recorded

Individuals differ in terms of personal interests, values, lifestyle preferences, and talents.[35] Goal relevancy occurs when the career-planning process, either at the organizational or individual level, considers these differences.[36] Increased goal relevancy is likely to have a positive impact on the individual's motivation to achieve stated goals and ultimately on the level of satisfaction and productivity experienced during one's career.[37] Historically, career-planning programs were primarily designed to achieve organizational staffing needs rather than to satisfy the needs of the employees.[38] Today, the effort is being made to consider employee relevance within organizational career-planning programs. This shift has occurred in response to changes in employee values; employee demands for jobs that are challenging, self-fulfilling, and provide for growth; employee demands for self-control; the desire to achieve a balance between work and family life; and increased social pressure on organizations to be more responsible.[39] Consequently, the 1990s have seen a significant number of organizations building employee relevancy into their career-development programs by involving employees in self-assessment activities.

Research indicates that individuals who record their goal statement outperform their counterparts who do not.[40] Lee Iacocca stated in his autobiography that the best thing he learned at Ford was to write down his goals and objectives, as this forced him to think them through and at the same time keep them visible.[41] This is necessary because writing goal statements forces you to think through what you are proposing in terms of possible, consistent, and properly sequenced steps. Written statements help keep you focused on what has to be done to attain your goals.

Goals Should Have Time Schedules

The element of time is critical to the process of goal setting. It ensures that the individual involved does not postpone engaging in those behaviors or activities that will facilitate goal achievement. Without a specific statement about time, a feeling of urgency is rarely associated with goal statements. The absence of self-urgency will permit the individual to push off until tomorrow what should have been done today. It is the interaction between importance and urgency that affects the individual's priorities. Therefore, when the individual states, "In three years I want to be promoted to general manager," he or she is more likely to act by planning and implementing a course of action.

How to operationalize the **SMART** goal setting process just described is demonstrated by the experience of a successful account executive working for a national brokerage firm. During a consulting project with the firm, we had the opportunity to discuss with one of the firm's top account executives how he had gone about setting personal goals. He had an undergraduate degree in finance and had been a successful book salesperson before joining the brokerage firm. This individual, upon joining the brokerage firm and going through the firm's orientation program, had written down a five-year plan of how much money he would earn. Based upon personal history, and suggestions from the firm, the new account executive set his first year's earnings 40 percent over the stated average for first-year account executives. Similarly, based upon the track record of two big-hitters in the company (larger-volume account executives), the new account executive also set the goal of 30 percent increases over each of the first three years. Finally, the individual set the goal that at the end of three years he would be the highest-volume individual in his office, and the highest-volume account executive in the Eastern region in five years. The successful account executive also added that he had taken steps to ensure that these goals and resulting behavior did not interfere with other personal goals. As a result, he found time to swim in the mornings, spend time with his family, and take several vacation trips each year.

This account executive also took specific steps to ensure that he moved toward his goals. For example, time is a critical commodity for account executives. If they are not scanning for new accounts, actively trading, etc., they are not making money. As a result, good time-management skills are necessary if success is to be achieved. To develop these skills, this account executive hired a local consultant to spend several days shadowing him and giving recommendations that would help him make optimal use of his time. The account executive believed that such goal-setting behavior played an important role in allowing him to achieve success.

The Effect of Self-Efficacy on Personal Well-Being

Research has demonstrated that it is self-efficacy that determines the type of goals selected, level of goal commitment, and task performance.[42] Perceived self-efficacy relates to how individuals assess their ability "to mobilize the motivational, cognitive resources, and courses of action needed to exercise control over events in their lives."[43] Defined in this way, perceived self-efficacy does not refer to specific skills but rather the ability to combine multiple skills in a flexible manner to cope with a changing environment to attain one's goals. Individuals may have the motor skills to drive a car but personally believe that they cannot successfully maneuver it in downtown traffic. Such self-doubt can be strong enough to cause the individual to refuse to drive in city traffic or become so nervous that an accident occurs. It is this element of forethought, or personal self-assessment, that plays an important role in determining future behavior or activity, thought patterns, or personal responses to one's environment. It is only when our perceptions about our capabilities are accurate, that we make correct decisions about how to act in different situations, how we can improve, should personal deficiencies exist, and what type of support we might need from others to facilitate performance. It is our self-efficacy, rather than our actual ability, that gives us the courage to "take the hill."

Perceived Self-Efficacy and Its Effect on Personal Well-Being

The importance of perceived self-efficacy is best understood by considering its effect on how individuals behave. Perceived self-efficacy affects what activities individuals choose to engage in, and the environmental settings they will enter.[44] Individuals will avoid situations in which self-efficacy is perceived to be low and seek out situations where self-efficacy is perceived to be high. Such action will also affect the range of choices open to the individual. Those individuals having high self-efficacy will, by definition, enter a larger number of situations and therefore have a wide range of choices open to them. Exposure to a larger number of relevant experiences also results in a greater opportunity for growth and development. The reverse will be true for low-self-efficacy individuals. They are less willing to expose themselves to varied situations and therefore less likely to experience growth and development opportunities.

Motivation, or the level of perceived effort, is also affected by the individual's perceived self-efficacy.[45] When individuals with high perceived self-efficacy encounter difficult or challenging tasks, they exert higher levels of effort than individuals with low perceived self-efficacy. Individuals with high self-efficiency are willing to persist and put out greater effort to overcome challenges or threats existing within their environments. Increased levels of personal effort, resulting from high perceived self-efficacy, often result in increases in the level of performance.[46] When compared to past performance, self-efficacy appears to be a better predictor of future performance.[47]

The emotional response of individuals also correlates with perceived self-efficacy.[48] Individuals with high perceived self-efficacy demonstrate less distress before performing an activity. They are also less likely to dwell on personal deficiencies that may cause them to fail. They are more likely to approach an up-coming task in a positive frame of mind. Individuals with low levels of perceived self-efficacy, while exhibiting a preoccupation with self-deficiencies, are more likely to approach an upcoming task with heightened anxiety. Additionally, individuals experiencing low self-efficacy will devalue their self-worth, and experience personal depression. This last effect, personal depression, often causes the low self-efficacy person to dwell on what benefits they will likely miss, given poor performance.

An individual's goal-setting process is also affected by perceived self-efficacy.[49] Individuals' willingness to set goals for themselves and others is a function of their perceived ability to carry out the complex set of cognitive and motor tasks required for performance. Before committing time, energy, or resources to an activity, most people answer the question, "Do I have the capability to perform in the manner required?" The more positive the response to this question (i.e., the higher the perceived self-efficacy) the higher will be the set goals and the greater will be the individual's personal commitment to attain them. High self-efficacy individuals also demonstrate an increased ability to visualize ways to solve problems and construct cognitive scenarios likely to lead to successful performance.[50] Such ability further increases the likelihood of setting higher goals.

Lastly, self-efficacy affects the individual's ability and willingness to change.[51] As indicated above, individuals with high self-efficacy demonstrate the following characteristics:

1. Expose themselves to a wider choice of options.
2. Set high goals.
3. Are more willing to try new alternatives.
4. Are able to visualize corrective alternatives when needed.
5. Are more likely to persevere when faced with challenges and threats.
6. Do not shield themselves from personal weaknesses or negative self-conceptions.

Such characteristics facilitate the ability of individuals to identify, plan for, and carry out corrective changes designed to improve personal success. For example, if individuals deny that they have deficiencies or avoid situations that challenge their personal capabilities, there will be no incentive to change. Similarly, if they have a low self-image or believe that they cannot overcome obstacles to effective learning or change, then they will quickly give up when confronted with obstacles to goals.

Linking Expectations about Outcomes, Perceived Self-Efficacy, and Behavior

It is the interaction between perceived self-efficacy and expectations about outcomes that energizes the individual to behave, that is, either to act or to withdraw from situations (see Figure 2.3). Individuals with high perceived self-efficacy and positive expectations about the link between outcomes and performance are highly motivated. When the link between performance and

Interactive effects of self-efficacy and anticipated outcomes

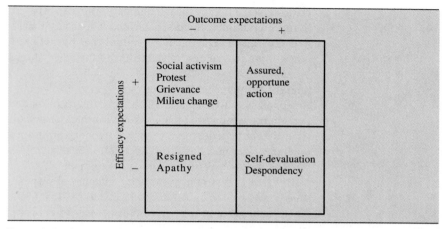

Source: A. Bandura, "Self-efficacy mechanism in human agency," *American Psychologist*, Vol. 37, February 1982, p. 140. Copyright 1982 by the American Psychological Association. Reprinted by permission.

outcomes is perceived to be negative, or outcomes are not as expected, high self-efficacy individuals will intensify their personal efforts. If increased efforts do not produce results, they will protest, or otherwise attempt to change the situation. If change is not truly possible, they will leave the situation and seek out situations that better fit their skills.

Where individuals have a low perceived self-efficacy, and a negative expectancy about receiving outcomes, they will likely withdraw. Simply put, low-efficacious individuals will readily give up. Where low-efficacious individuals see a positive link between performance and outcomes, they are most likely to self-devaluate or become emotionally despondent or depressed. Under these conditions the low self-efficacy people assume that they will fail and they realize that desired rewards will therefore not be forthcoming.

Clearly, it is individuals who have high self-efficacy who will likely be the most effective within the organizational context.

Sources of Perceived Self-Efficacy

There are four primary mechanisms that can increase an individual's perceived self-efficacy.[52] They are mastery experiences, social comparisons and modeling, social persuasion, and personal assessment of one's emotional or physical state (physiological).

Mastery Experiences

Of the four building blocks, mastery experiences are likely to have the greatest impact on individuals. Each time individuals attempt performance, they will assess the degree of success or failure achieved. This will occur either through personal assessment or as a result of feedback received from others. If individuals have a broad range of performance experiences, and these experiences have been repeatedly successful, it is likely that they will develop positive self-efficacy in those areas. Alternatively, if their experiences result in repeated failure, there is a greater probability that they will develop a negative self-image. Thus, it is important that trainers sequence tasks in an order that all but guarantees mastery during the early stages of learning.

Social Comparison and Modeling

A second way to increase self-efficacy is to imitate others who are currently performing well within the work environment. For example, if a co-worker has recently graduated from the same university program as the observer, is about the same age, and has about the same level of real-world experience, he or she can act as a valid source of comparison. If the comparison person does well, there is a strong probability that the observer will attempt to do well. Assessments such as these are likely to lead to higher self-efficacy. Similar others who are performing well are likely to exhibit behaviors necessary for successful performance. By observing these behaviors it is likely that the observer will gain insight into what is required to be successful. The ability to imitate such behavior increases feelings of self-confidence. Thus, trainers and mentors should identify people whom an employee admires and with whom the employee can identify! Such people serve as models who, in turn, increase the self-efficacy of the observer.

Persuasion: Supporting and Encouraging Statements

Rarely do people perform their jobs without interacting with others (i.e., the boss, peers, subordinates, and even family members and friends). It is during these interactions that relevant others can play an important role in helping people to develop a positive self-image by overcoming self-doubts. If relevant others offer support and encouraging statements to individuals (e.g., "You can do it," "Try it again, you've done it before," "Just a little more and you'll have it!") it is possible to remove or dampen self-doubts and increase their perceived self-efficacy. When attempting to use this mechanism to motivate the self-doubter to develop and grow, it should be made clear that the evaluation is based on the individual's past performance and not the performance of others.

It is important that supporting and encouraging statements are realistic. Statements that motivate individuals to perform in areas above their present skill levels will likely lead to failure. Encouraging or supporting statements that lead to failure will have a double negative impact. The doubting individual will not only develop low self-efficacy, but will also learn to distrust those who initially attempted to help.

Self-statements are especially persuasive. We do what we say we can do. This is illustrated well in the children's story about the little individual engine who mastered an extremely difficult task while repeatedly uttering the statement, "I think I can, I think I can." By helping a person see the relationship between past successes and present challenges, and by helping them to utter positive self-statements, self-efficacy increases. There are few sources of persuasion more persuasive than one's self.

Physiological Arousal

When assessing their capability to perform, individuals will also consider physiological and emotional factors relevant to the task at hand. Excessive fatigue, stress, anxiety, anger, poor conditioning, etc., are all likely to affect the individual's perceived self-efficacy. For example, wise skiers will assess their physical condition at day's end before attempting that last ski trail. If their legs feel rubbery it would be an unwise decision to attempt the challenge—even if they successfully skied it in the morning.

It is possible for individuals to manage many of the physical and emotional threats to positive self-efficacy. They begin by understanding their dominant responses, either physical or emotional, to a broad range of situations. To facilitate the process, individuals can ask such questions as: "Do I easily become tired?" "Can I control my emotions even when tired or attacked by others?" "How much stress can I handle before losing control?" "Do I easily become tense or anxious when confronted with the unknown or changing situations?"

The next step is for the individual to assess upcoming tasks and task environments, and determine the likelihood that they may trigger emotional and physical responses capable of reducing perceived self-efficacy. In those situations where the likelihood is high, the individual should take preventive or buffering action to remove or offset emotional or physical problems likely to arise. This type of preventing or buffering behavior occurs when the opera singer physically works out to keep in shape, the football star gets a good night's sleep before the big game, or the manager controls environmental stressors so as not to be stressed out during an upcoming negotiation or project.

Interpersonal Needs

To help ensure that goal relevancy exists, individuals must take steps to identify important personal needs and develop goals that are compatible. A need that is common to popular motivational content models is the individual's need to interact or establish interpersonal relationships with others.[53] The intensity or strength of this need reflects a variety of conditions that motivate an individual to seek interaction with others. Individuals will seek out others (1) for practical reasons, (2) to reduce anxiety, and (3) to help define the self.

A Practical Need

The most obvious reason for seeking others is that the individual is a single entity and therefore cannot independently accomplish all those things he or she would like to achieve. Consequently, the individual must seek out others to obtain the support or unity of action that will allow goal achievement. We can refer to this as the practical side of the individual. In other words, managers are being pragmatic when they seek to join others because they rely on subordinates and relevant others (peers, senior management, staff personnel, suppliers, etc.) to achieve desired levels of output.

If subordinates are marginal, it is likely that the manager's performance will suffer. To help ensure that subordinates are productive, managers engage in directing, controlling, evaluating, coordinating, coaching, counseling, training, and developing activities. Although such a list is not exhaustive, it does suggest the high level of interaction required to maintain desired levels of output. In the case of relevant others, interactions will be required to obtain desired information, support, and resources. Interactions with relevant others may also result from a practical need to explain one's position or protect staff from outside pressure. In the latter situation, managers can act to buffer and protect subordinates by requiring that stressful communications be given to them rather than to their subordinates.

A Need to Reduce Anxiety

When faced with anxiety-producing situations, individuals will often seek similar and familiar others. Such people are likely to listen, share information, or support and comfort individuals experiencing the stressful situations. Such behavior by others helps reduce the level of anxiety being experienced. It does not take individuals long to learn that others can be helpful in buffering them from an uncertain, turbulent environment or can offer the emotional support necessary to maintain one's internal balance. Therefore, even before the stress or anxiety is experienced, the effective manager is building a network of similar and familiar others who can be called upon if the need arises.[54]

A Need to Define One's Self

A third reason given for the drive to interact with others is the desire of individuals to define who and what they are. Behavioral scientists have found that individuals seek to interact with others because of a need for social comparison.[55] In the simplest of terms, other individuals are used as a means of personal comparison. This is important because when considering the life space of an individual, there are two types of realities that they face: physical and social. In terms of physical or objective reality, individuals can determine whether an object is hard, soft, or heavy by merely touching it, lifting it, or hitting it with a hammer. Testing procedures such as these do not require that individuals interact with others and therefore produce no motivation for them to seek out others.

It is the second type of reality, social or subjective reality, which motivates individuals to seek out others. Social reality involves areas that are ambiguous and which require social comparisons for clarification. For example, individuals may ask themselves, "Am I a good manager?" "Am I a good skier?" "Am I intelligent?" The answer to these and similar questions can only be obtained through interaction with others or, more specifically, through a comparison with others. Consequently, to know and understand themselves, individuals seek out and interact with others.

A Basic Model

An alternative approach to understanding why individuals seek out others is explained in a classic model developed by W. Schutz (see Figure 2.4).[56] The model integrates three internal needs in an attempt to explain a person's behavior in an interpersonal situation. These three needs are (1) need for inclusion, (2) need for control, and (3) need for affection. As we will see shortly, it is

FIGURE 2.4

Model of social interaction

Need for	Satisfying relationship	Relevant feeling	Self-concept	Level of emphasis
Inclusion	Initiate/originate interactions with relevant others on a range from all others to no others Allow relevant others to initiate interactions on a range from all others to no others	Level of perceived interest expressed between individuals	Degree of perceived self-significance and worth	Formation of relationships
Control	Controlling all the behaviors of relevant others on a range from all behaviors to no behaviors Allow relevant others to control personal behaviors on a range from all behaviors to no behaviors	Level of perceived respect for the competence and responsibleness of others	Degree of perceived self-capability, assertiveness, and inner direction	Ongoing power relationships
Affection	Initiate close relationships with relevant others on a range from all others to no others Allow relevant others to initiate close personal relationships on a range from all others to no others	Level of perceived mutual affection between individuals	Degree to which the self is perceived to be likable, lovable, and trusting	Emotional closeness

also possible to talk about each of the three needs at a "feeling" and "self-concept" level. What we are interested in here is what feelings and self-concepts exist that activate, help support, or maintain each need level.

Need for Inclusion

The interpersonal need for inclusion is defined as the individual's desire to establish and maintain a satisfactory level of interaction with others. In other words, there is a desire to belong when placed within a social environment. The key here is what level of inclusion or interaction with others is psychologically comfortable for the individual. The actual range of inclusion or interaction will vary from "all others" to "no others" and all possible points in between.

We can, however, look at individuals' need for inclusion on two different levels. First, what levels of inclusion will individuals themselves seek out when others are present within the environment? If individuals have a high need for inclusion, then the actual number of attempts to personally initiate interactions will likely be quite high. Conversely, if the need is relatively low, few, if any, personal attempts to initiate interactions will occur. The second level deals with the number of initiations the individual will tolerate when those are initiated by others in the environment. In other words, does the individual feel psychologically comfortable when interactions are initiated by others? If the individual does not feel comfortable with such attempts, then he or she will not become involved or will quickly withdraw from such exchanges.

The feeling associated with the felt need for inclusion is that of mutual interest. Again, the presence of relevant feelings works in both directions. In the case of individuals who initiate interaction, it is a comfortable, or satisfying feeling to take an interest in other individuals. With such feelings in place, it is easy to understand why individuals will seek others who function within their life space. Conversely, when the drive for inclusion is initiated from others, it is the feeling on the part of individuals that it is satisfactory, or comfortable, for others to have an interest, which allows them to respond positively to such initiatives. For the drive for inclusion to be activated and maintained in either direction, individuals must have a positive concept of self. In this case, individuals will perceive themselves as having significance and worth.

Need for Control

The interpersonal need for control is defined as the desire on the part of individuals to establish and maintain a satisfactory power relationship with others within the environment. The use of power in personal interactions defines the impact one individual has on another.[57] The individual might seek control to satisfy his or her need for dominance or a personal need to minimize threats or felt stress. The actual need for control will likely manifest itself through behaviors linked to leadership, competitive or aggressive behavior, accomplishment, attempted intellectual superiority, and preferred action situations.[58] The key here is what level of control is psychologically comfortable for the individual.

The potential range of control available will vary from control over all the behavior of others to controlling none of the behavior of others, and all possible points in between. Again, the direction of discussion can be from the individual to others or from others to the individual and what level of control is appropriate to the situation. Therefore, the question becomes how much control do individuals desire over the behavior of others, and how much control of their own behavior are individuals willing to give up to others? When considering this question, managers should differentiate between appropriate and inappropriate control. Control that is used to coerce or manipulate others when they have the skill to function effectively without being controlled should be considered inappropriate. (It is assumed here that effective implies that the individual's performance would be consistent with the would-be controller's personal needs.) Appropriate control occurs when it provides structure and guidance to those who cannot yet function on their own. However, as the individual develops, established controls are relaxed to increase the individual's freedom.

The feelings that are most critical to the question of control and attempted use of power deal with the issues of perceived competence and sense of responsibility of both the self and relevant others. If individuals perceive themselves as more competent and responsible than a particular relevant other, then they are likely to attempt to extend personal control and power over that other individual. Similarly, if such a perception exists, it is unlikely that individuals will allow the relevant other to obtain a position of control or power. This would only be perceived as a condition likely to reduce individuals' expectations of future success. Conversely, if individuals perceive a relevant other as more competent and responsible then they are, then there will be an increased likelihood of those individuals giving up personal control and power to the relevant other. It is also implied that one's willingness to control, or be controlled, will likely vary from one situation to another, or from one relevant other to another as the ratio of perceived competence and responsibility changes.

Finally, the degree to which individuals strive for personal control and power, or are willing to be controlled by others, will be greatly affected by their concept of self. If individuals perceive themselves as capable, assertive, and inner-directed, then the tendency will be to control and not to be controlled by others. Conversely, if individuals perceive themselves as inexperienced, passive, and outer-directed, then the tendency will be to abdicate or withdraw from opportunities to control others and instead take on a follower role.

Need for Affection

The interpersonal need for affection is defined as the individual's desire to establish and maintain a satisfactory level of affection with relevant others within the environment.[59] The actual need for affection will likely manifest itself through behaviors linked to openness, overall liking and responsiveness, and an interpersonal sharing of innermost anxieties, wishes, and feelings. The key here is what level of closeness is psychologically comfortable for the individual. As was the case for the previous two needs, the need for affection can also be expressed in two directions. In the first case, the individual will establish close personal relations along some dimension anchored by all relevant others at one end and no relevant others at the opposite end. Alternatively, the individual will allow close relationships initiated by relevant others along some dimension again anchored by all relevant others at one end and no relevant others at the opposite end. Here again, where on the two dimensions individuals will seek to function depends upon what they perceive as psychologically comfortable.

At the feeling level, the need for affection is expressed through a mutual affection with relevant others. Typically, such feelings are associated with dyadic relationships, that is, mentor relationships, friendships, dating, marriage, etc., and reflect strong emotional ties between the individuals involved. Such relationships also reflect a strong positive self-concept.

Within the organizational context, it is important that individuals recognize their personal profile with respect to these three drives. Because the role of manager requires individuals to interact with and direct others, it is critical to understand how comfortable they feel about the issue of inclusion, power, and affection or closeness. This knowledge will also help managers understand and predict their own behavior. At the same time, managers are able to determine whether their preferred position fits environmental requirements of the situation or the expectations of others with whom they interact. Finally, knowing the demands of a given situation, and the degree of match between preferred and required interpersonal styles, managers will be able to identify personal weaknesses and thereby engage in self-adjustment or development.

Interpersonal Style and Strategy

Interpersonal style is the manner in which individuals relate to one another. When two individuals interact, it is possible to discuss the level of interpersonal sensitivity being exhibited by each individual as an individual's interpersonal style. The following discussion focuses on two areas that are important for maintaining positive and productive interpersonal relations. The first deals with self-disclosure and feedback-seeking behaviors, and the second deals with how one responds to others.

Self-Disclosure and Feedback-Seeking Behavior

Self-disclosure occurs when managers are willing to communicate those feelings, perceptions, needs, and expectations that relate to on-the-job performance and the development of a positive interpersonal relationship with others. By engaging in self-disclosure, managers force themselves to assess who and what they are, allow others to better predict their behavior, and facilitate trust by demonstrating a willingness to share.[60] Feedback-seeking behaviors reflect an effort by managers to motivate others to provide them with needed information about what has been happening. The monitoring and truthful evaluation of feedback facilitates behavior changes necessary to improve interpersonal relations and job performance.[61]

A Basic Model of Interpersonal Style

By combining these two dimensions (see Figure 2.5), it is possible to identify four interpersonal styles used by managers when interacting with others.[62] The specific style used by managers affects the interpersonal relationship that develops between them and relevant others and can act as a model for others within their departments. The two larger arrows in Figure 2.5 indicate that the decision to disclose or ask for feedback is not a "yes" or "no" proposition. Instead, the level of disclosure or amount of feedback requested varies along a continuum ranging from no disclosure or feedback requests to full disclosure or frequent feedback requests. This variance can be referred to as style intensity. The mix selected by a manager will reflect his or her personality, assessment of relevant others, and the climate in which the individual is deciding. The four smaller arrows indicate a directional relationship between style and consequence. For example, in the upper left-hand quadrant, the manager is using a balance style represented by high self-disclosure and frequent requests for feedback. The consequence of such a style is an open relationship in which participants understand one another.[63] A detailed description of the four cells is given below:[64]

FIGURE 2.5*

Interpersonal style based upon level of self-disclosure and feedback sought

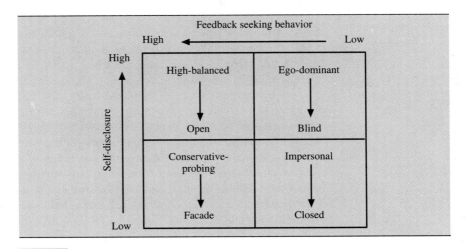

*This model reflects the authors' interpretation of material presented in J. Hall, "Communication revisited," *California Management Review,* Vol. 15, No. 3, Spring 1973: 56–67; J. Luft, *Group Processes: An Introduction to Group Dynamics,* National Press Books, Palo Alto, Calif., 1984; R. L. Weaver, Il, 1993.

- **High-Balanced/Open**—Managers using this style actively seek feedback from others and at the same time are willing to self-disclose. Managers using this style know and understand themselves and are secure enough to share this information with others. They also have confidence in others and respect their input. In addition, they are secure enough to accept timely and accurate feedback and make appropriate changes. The result is a full sharing of information, mutual understanding, and mutual trust; in other words, an open and positive relationship. An open environment also increases the comfort level of others and thereby increases the likelihood that they will maintain open channels of communication once established.

- **Ego-Dominant/Blind**—Managers using this style over-use self-disclosure and fail to balance disclosure with feedback-seeking behaviors. These managers rate their own skills highly and are likely to become egoistically involved in the correctness or importance of their actions. Furthermore, they tend to dominate and seek compliance from relevant others without seeking their feelings or perceptions. Consequently, ego-dominant managers fail to be aware of their impact on others and at the same time miss opportunities to allow others to participate in the decision-making process. The result of this style is a blind spot in which managers are unaware of the perceptions and feelings of others. When relevant others believe that managers are not interested in their feelings and perceptions, they are likely to feel disenfranchised and withdraw their support for the relationship.

- **Conservative-Probing/Facade**—Managers using this style have an aversion to self-disclosure, but still seek to maintain open channels of communication with others by seeking feedback. A failure to self-disclose may reflect a manager's own insecurity or a mistrust of others. Whatever the reason, conservative-probing managers are likely to create personal facades designed to mislead relevant others. Unfortunately, once such behavior is recognized, relevant others are likely to withdraw their willingness to provide meaningful and candid feedback about the situation or themselves. The result may ultimately be isolation and mistrust on the part of relevant others.

- **Impersonal/Closed**—Managers using this last style minimize the use of both self-disclosure and feedback-seeking behaviors. Such relationships tend to be impersonal with relevant others unaware of how these managers feel, and what information they (relevant others) might have to contribute to the situation. While such managers minimize their risks during interpersonal exchanges, they create an environment characterized by withdrawal, detachment, and a reliance on rules as the basis for control. The result of such a style is an environment characterized by closed impersonal relationships and a minimum level of interaction and creativity within the system. Relevant others are also likely to experience frustrations as they begin to perceive the manager's behavior as an obstacle to their own need for achievement.

In an ideal environment, a "high-balanced" interpersonal style would produce the maximum benefits for the manager. In such an environment, the manager would be fully understood by others, and he or she would fully understand others. Decisions would be based upon complete information. Unfortunately, the world is not a perfect place and the ideal is rarely, if ever, achieved. What is an appropriate style would be a function of differences in situational characteristics as well as differences in the participants themselves. It would be in the manager's best interest to develop a strategy for determining the appropriate level of self-disclosure and feedback-seeking behavior when interacting with others.

Guidelines for Self-Disclosure

Self-disclosure provides others with information about one's self that would not otherwise be available. Such information not only can increase the recipient's understanding of the sender but can also increase the recipient's power and influence within the relationship. However, information and power in the hands of a relevant other who does not reciprocate, or who cannot be trusted, places the sender at risk. To minimize this risk, managers should develop a strategy for determining the appropriate level of self-disclosure in each situation. The following four steps can be used as a guide in determining the appropriate level of self-disclosure.[65]

Step 1. Managers should begin the process of self-disclosure by *(a)* determining their own strengths and weaknesses in areas that relate to on-the-job performance, *(b)* identifying areas that they would like to see others disclose so as to develop positive interpersonal relationships, that is, areas such as hobbies, sports, educational background, current events, and *(c)* assessing group norms that might set limits on the level of disclosure that is considered appropriate. Also important at this stage is the manager's ability to identify individual differences that might exist within the group of relevant others being considered. Not all individuals approve of disclosing behaviors, especially while on the job.

Step 2. During initial encounters, especially when dealing with unfamiliar others, self-disclosure should deal with topics that limit personal risk. It is often desirable to assess personal risk before exposing oneself emotionally or psychologically. For example, when attempting to negotiate with an unfamiliar counterpart, a manager would be ill advised to indicate his or her best offer before obtaining some understanding of the other person. During early encounters it is also considered inappropriate to disclose negative information about oneself. Such disclosures are considered too personal to be offered too soon in a developing relationship.

Step 3. Gradually move to more personal or intimate areas of personal disclosure. The speed with which this occurs should be dictated by the response of relevant others. The manager might ask the following questions. "Does the relevant other reciprocate by engaging in self-disclosing behaviors?" "Has the relationship grown in terms of interpersonal liking and trust?" "What has been the recipient's response to disclosed information, especially in terms of reciprocated disclosures?" "Do I or does the relevant other have the personal self-esteem to handle more intimate disclosures?" If the answers to these questions have been positive, then it may be desirable to move to a higher level of self-disclosure. If a manager is dealing with a well-known subordinate who shares a common vision with the manager, and who has dealt well with negative and positive information in the past, then full disclosure of personally held information would likely be appropriate.

Step 4. Limit the disclosure of intimate or very personal information to ongoing, long-term, relationships. Such relationships are often necessary to ensure a required level of trust has been achieved. If not, the sender may be incurring too great a personal risk. Time-proven relationships also minimize the potential of a contrast effect from the recipient. A contrast effect occurs when the recipient becomes embarrassed or resentful by the disclosure and attempts to withdraw from the relationship in some way.

Guidelines for Feedback-Seeking Behaviors

To be successful within one's environment it is important that managers know and understand that environment. In those areas where conflict exists between behaviors and existing demands within the environment, managers will be required to adjust their behaviors or change the environment. Where environmental demands cannot be changed, managers will increase their emphasis on personal adjustments. Feedback-seeking behaviors are an important initial step in collecting the required information needed *(a)* to identify areas in which conflict exists, and *(b)* in situations where environmental demands cannot be changed.

In an effort to use feedback-seeking behaviors to assess the correctness and adequacy of effort designed to achieve desired goals, managers can use two strategies for collecting feedback information.[66] Managers can obtain meaningful feedback by actively monitoring their environment by observing the behavior of others. In this case, there is no attempt on the manager's part to directly interact with relevant others. Information is obtained by vicariously observing how others respond to their behavior, and how others are responded to or are reinforced. Alternatively, managers can play a more direct role by specifically asking relevant others how they feel about or would evaluate their behavior. The relevant question is not should managers seek feedback, but rather how should they go about obtaining needed feedback? The following seven steps are designed to help answer this question.

Step 1. Managers should first identify those areas in which feedback would be of value. Perceived value is determined by the importance of additional information to goal achievement or the reduction of environmental uncertainty. In the latter case, would additional information improve the manager's decision-making capabilities? Also worth considering is the success of recent feedback-seeking behaviors. If the manager is familiar with the situation because of past monitoring or inquiry behaviors, then it is unlikely that new feedback efforts will be worth the time and effort. The value of feedback is greater in new environments. As managers gain experience and tenure, the incremental benefit of feedback-seeking behaviors decline.

Step 2. Managers should attempt to assess the relative value of monitoring versus inquiring behaviors. Monitoring behaviors are less visible than inquiring behaviors, and as a result minimize the potential loss of credibility by not making it appear that managers lack knowledge or understanding of their environment. Unfortunately, monitoring behavior takes longer as managers wait for desired behaviors or activities to take place. Monitoring also requires the manager to rely on his or her inferential and cognitive skills to interpret each situation. Inquiring behaviors allow the manager to take direct control of the situation and ask specific questions of specific individuals. Although managers can increase personal control, there is an accompanying cost, namely, time and effort to track down relevant others, finding free time to discuss target areas, and having to explain why the information is needed.

At this point, the steps taken will vary depending on whether the manager chooses the monitoring or inquiring alternative. Due to space considerations, and a bias toward direct managerial interventions, the following steps will focus on inquiring activities.

Step 3. Managers should inform relevant others of the specific areas in which they desire feedback. They should attempt to be specific and provide as much guidance and information to the target individual(s) as possible. Managers should also take the time to educate relevant others about the characteristics of effective feedback. This can be accomplished by descriptive dialogue or through example, that is, the manager acts as a model when giving feedback to others. For a discussion of these characteristics refer to Chapter 13.

Managers should ask for feedback only in areas where they want or need feedback. Individuals who take the time to provide feedback are likely to be turned off if they see their efforts discarded because the information provided relates to an area of little interest to the manager.

Step 4. To facilitate the feedback process, managers should make themselves accessible to relevant others. This can be accomplished by setting aside time for feedback encounters, walking through one's department, allowing sufficient time at the end of planned meetings for receiving feedback, or engaging in probing behaviors designed to open channels of communication (See Chapter 4).

Step 5. Managers should monitor their own behavior to ensure that verbal and nonverbal behaviors are not in conflict. It is easy to shut down a feedback exchange by giving nonverbal cues that indicate indifference, impatience, or even anger. Managers who ask for feedback and arrange to meet with a subordinate are facilitating the feedback process. However, if during the feedback session managers continue to look at their watches or shake their heads back and forth in disapproval of comments made, it is likely that subordinates will limit the amount of feedback given as well as its content.

Step 6. During the feedback exchange, managers should ensure that they have understood the sender's message. Techniques such as probing, summarizing, reflecting, and active listening will be reviewed in detail in Chapter 4.

Step 7. Where possible, managers should attempt to provide positive consequence for feedback provided by others. This can be accomplished during the feedback exchange by good eye contact, smiling when good points are made, up and down motions of the head, etc. It would also be desirable to thank the individual giving the feedback for his or her efforts. The manager should never attack or personally criticize the feedback given. If the feedback is inappropriate, attempt to explain why. Similarly, if nothing can be done in response to the feedback received, also explain why this is the case.

After the feedback has been received and accepted, the best type of reinforcement for the manager is to make appropriate changes or to maintain behaviors where feedback is positive. Where necessary, the manager may want to point out changed or maintained behaviors to the individual who provided the feedback.

How We Respond to Others

How managers respond to others is an important factor in determining the success of interpersonal relations and it reflects their unique personalities. The actual range of behavioral responses that are linked with personality is quite large and is reflected in the broad range of existing personality tests and theories currently available. However, not all response behaviors are equally relevant to managerial performance or the manager–subordinate and management–other interface. Therefore, because of both relevancy and space considerations our discussion will be limited to the behavioral dimensions listed in Figure 2.8.[67]

The seven dimensions listed in Figure 2.8 can be used to describe any manager relating to others. The set of ratings given to the individual represents a dominant response profile for that person. A dominant response profile is the set of behaviors that an individual feels comfortable in using and which reflects his or her personality. In listing the seven dimensions there has been no attempt to anchor the end points with either positive or negative values. This is because the effectiveness of any particular profile will be a function of the specific situation in which the individual functions. However, as organizations move into the 21st century, and increasingly face the trends described in Chapter 1, a manager whose profile is to the right on this continuum will, in the view of the authors, have a greater likelihood of succeeding.

Acting in the Here and Now versus Planning for the Future
Individuals falling on the left of this dimension tend to be decisive and consequently prefer to take immediate action and receive immediate gratification.

FIGURE 2.8

Behavioral dimensions relevant to the manager–subordinate interface

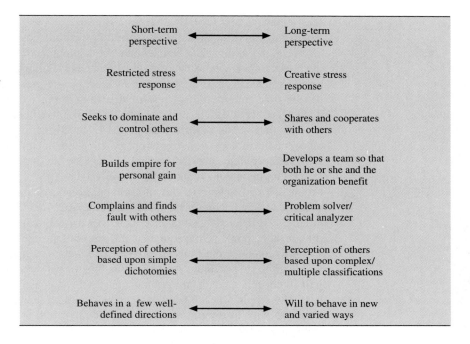

When immediate action and gratification are not possible, these individuals tend to lose interest in the current problem or situation. Diminished interest will likely cause them to look elsewhere for reinforcement.

For the now-oriented individuals, decisions are frequently made on the basis of sequential rather than parallel searches. During sequential searches, the individual selects the first alternative that satisfies his or her needs. In the case of parallel searches, the individual collects data on a number of choices before selecting the ones that best satisfy his or her needs. Unfortunately, such a now-orientation frequently prevents people from adequately scanning their environments for alternatives. At the very minimum it will short-circuit the creative process designed to identify viable alternatives. Here-and-now managers also devote less time to activities associated with follow-through once the decisions have been made. Instead, here-and-now managers are more likely to move to new problems, and to look for fires to put out. The behavioral characteristics just described closely parallel those associated with a Type A impulsive personality (see Chapter 5 for information on Type A personalities).

Individuals functioning toward the right side of this continuum exhibit behaviors opposite to those just described. Future-oriented individuals demonstrate a greater willingness to wait, engage in parallel searches when attempting to assess decision alternatives, bring decisions into the future, and place greater emphasis on the need to plan for the future. Such an individual demonstrates tolerance for ambiguity and uncertainty as well as a willingness to allow others to participate.

Restricted versus Creative Stress Response

When faced with a stressful situation, the response options open to individuals are many and varied. Some behavioral scientists have attempted to define the stress response in terms of three alternatives (i.e., fight, flight, and freeze).[68] Such direct action alternatives, however, ignore cognitive alternatives that can be used to cope with stressful situations.[69] For example, individuals may deny the threat exists or treat the stressor in an analytical and detached manner that is something to be studied. The fight, flight, and freeze model also does not fully develop problem-focused options that are designed to solve the problem or problems being faced by the individual.[70]

Individuals who function on the left side of the continuum tend to apply the stress response without thought, analysis, or consideration of consequence. In other words, it tends to be automatic. In addition, individuals classified as "restricted" also tend to have hair triggers when it comes to initiating the stress response. Consequently, it does not take much of an environmental stimulus to cause the individual to initiate a stress response.

For those individuals classified as "restricted," the actual stress response will likely reflect their unique personality. In the case of "restricted" individuals who emphasize the fight or aggressive mode, there appears to be a strong desire to win. Furthermore, those individuals by their very nature tend to be fighters or aggressors. Such individuals are often overly sensitive to people or things that might potentially be perceived as a threat. Therefore, if anything or anyone stands between them and a personal goal, they are ready to fight first and ask questions later (if at all). "Restricted" individuals who choose the flight response are typically taking the easy way out. Such individuals have a passive nature and are likely to experience a greater level of self-doubt or insecurity. Consequently, these individuals are more likely to withdraw (psychologically or physically) from the situation to remove themselves from the threat zone and thereby reduce the probability of confrontation. Unfortunately, such behavior does not solve the underlying problem, but allows it to fester and grow. Last, "restricted" individuals who freeze when under stress appear to be the most vulnerable because they do not defend themselves or get out of harm's way. Consequently, unless these individuals face a minimum threat, they will run the risk of experiencing the greatest personal damage.

On the other end of the continuum, "creative" individuals have less of a hair-trigger reaction and are more likely to allow the rational adult, rather than the emotional self, to take charge. In this way, they are likely to analyze the consequences of personal behavior. For example, "creative" individuals are likely to ask questions such as "What do I really gain from fighting back, taking flight, or doing nothing?" "Is it really worth the battle?" "What will happen if I just leave or ignore the problem?" "How can I change my behavior to change the situation and thereby reduce the stress I feel?" By analyzing the situation and asking these questions, these individuals are more likely to maintain self-control, assert themselves without being aggressive, or let the other side win if and when such action is in their own long-term best interest. At this side of the continuum, these individuals will make a decision and see it through to its conclusion. But even here "creative" individuals monitor and adjust to a changing environment. Personal energy may even be directed to some type of problem-solving behavior designed to overcome the conflict without activating the normal stress response. More is said about effective conflict management techniques in Chapter 12.

Dominating versus Sharing with Others

Where individuals are placed on this dimension appears to be closely related to their need for power and its use.[71] Individuals who function toward the left side of the continuum seek to dominate and control others and as a result perceive their world in terms of power and influence. These individuals view their organizational life as a sequence of struggles to come out on top. Individuals on the left side of the continuum view such struggles as zero-sum exchanges (i.e., if you don't win, you lose). Their interactions with the outside world are predicated on the assumption that if you act in a powerful manner toward others you will be recognized, rewarded, and ultimately promoted. Unfortunately, dominating behavior builds in a predisposition for interpersonal conflict within the organization. Such individuals can best be described as "personal power managers" who use power for personal gain.[72] "Personal power managers" appear to be less effective than "institutional managers" who use their power to achieve organizational goals.[73]

Individuals on the sharing end of the continuum differ on the basic assumptions that drive their behavior. Although they recognize and accept power and influence as an organizational reality, they do not see it as their only option. Therefore, it is not necessary to wear oneself down through constant struggle and competition. Instead, it is possible to cooperate, share, and jointly problem solve your way to a workable solution. This also reflects the belief that the organizational pie is not fixed but in fact can be expanded. Consequently, each party is not in a struggle to win at the expense of the other.

Empire Building versus Team Development

Closely related to the last dimension is the issue of personal empire building at the expense of being a team player. Individuals who seek to build their personal empires appear to be egoistically tied to organizational territory. Because of this egoistic involvement, organizational expansion is linked with the extension of the self. For such individuals bigger would be better, not only in terms of space but also in terms of organizational budgets, information, and activities performed. The need here is to expand for the sake of expanding, not to expand based on well thought-out need. Furthermore, individuals functioning to the left on this continuum find it difficult to give anything up or even to delegate. Frequently, the net result is fragmentation of the organization and increased organizational conflict.

Individuals functioning on the opposite end of the continuum recognize the importance of territorial rights but do so by clearly defining its limits and basing it on need and ultimately on organizational success. They are less concerned with departmental or functional boundaries and more concerned with developing interdepartmental or functional links. It is this willingness to transcend boundaries and functions that allows the individual to develop a team orientation rather than a we–them orientation. A final difference between individuals functioning at the two end-points is that team-oriented managers look at their job as "a job" while empire builders look at their job as "my" job. As a result, team players are less likely to be egoistically involved, ritualistic, or territorial when making decisions that relate to their department or functional area.

Complaining versus Problem Solving

A major issue that affects where individuals will fall on this dimension is one of attribution. As events take place within their environment, there is a natural drive to locate cause. In the broadest sense cause can be located in the people themselves or in the surrounding environment. The first can be classified as internal causation and the latter as external causation. Those individuals who function to the left of this continuum tend to place causation in the external environment and as a result never see themselves as the problem. Besides placing cause in the external environment, the complainer does not suffer in silence. Instead, individuals will complain to anyone who will listen their beliefs as to the cause of existing problems or events.

Complainers often believe that they have all the information needed to make good decisions.[74] As a result they will fail to seek out additional information, analyze the cause-and-effect relationships that exist within the environment, or in any way become a critical thinker. The difficulty here is that when a problem occurs, or a decision turns out to be a poor one, complainers tend to focus on people (not including themselves) rather than the process or content of the problem. These behaviors are likely to have a negative impact on the productivity and internal satisfaction of any department. If the manager is a complainer and openly places blame on others, then there is a high probability that relevant others will withdraw either physically or psychologically. More specifically, they will be less willing to take the initiative, experiment, or take any chance that will produce the typical negative response from their boss. Similarly, the manager's negative behavior may cause subordinates to take on an "I'm OK, You're (the boss) Not OK" attitude. If this happens, subordinates will be less likely to share with, trust, or support that manager.

The other end of this continuum reflects behaviors that are opposite to those just described. At the problem-solver end, the individual is willing to accept either internal or external causes to problems or environmental events. Furthermore, the individual accepts that there may be relevant information within the environment that must be uncovered and analyzed before blame can be placed. Once sufficient information is obtained and cause and effect relationships are understood as best as possible, then instead of confronting others, the problem solver attempts to work with others to find an acceptable solution. Behaviors such as these are more likely to result in a learning and adaptive style on the part of the manager. Similarly, these behaviors are less likely to result in subordinates withdrawing or taking on the "I'm OK, You're Not OK" position.

Simple Dichotomies versus Complex Multiple Classifications

Individuals differ in terms of the ways in which they perceive and classify their environment. Some individuals use only a few lenses or a small number of concepts to define their world, while others use a rich and varied set of concepts to define and understand what is taking place around them. Individuals who use few concepts or constructs to define their perception of others are said to be cognitively simple, and individuals who use a rich and varied range of concepts and constructs to define their perception of others are said to be cognitively complex. Although there is some controversy as to one's ability to generalize research findings across situations, the concept of cognitive simplicity–complexity can help us better understand how individuals relate to their environment and other people.

An individual who is cognitively simple tends to emphasize similarities between themselves and relevant others, while cognitively complex individuals tend to be sensitive to differences between individuals. At first glance this might appear to be an advantage for the cognitively simple. But what very often happens is that because the cognitively complex individual is able to use multiple and varied concepts and constructs to evaluate differences, differences tend to be tolerated. The implication here is that cognitively simple people may be less able to tolerate difference because they do not have the frame of reference needed to classify these differences. One possibility is that the cognitively simple person may respond in the following manner, "Like me and you are OK. Not like me and you are not OK, or at least suspect."

Another difference between cognitively simple and cognitively complex individuals is their ability to adjust to, or cope with, environmental variety. When the environment of individuals is complicated and ambiguous, it is important that they are able to make sense of the multiple and varied stimuli being received. In other words, they want to identify usable patterns and relationships that exist in the environment. It is the knowledge of usable patterns and relationships that facilitates future prediction and control over one's environment. It would appear that the cognitively complex individual is able to understand and organize the stimuli received from a complicated and ambiguous environment.

Behaving in Few versus Many Ways

There is sufficient evidence to indicate that individuals vary in the range of behaviors in which they are willing to engage. Actual variance among individuals is primarily a function of personality and experience. In terms of personality, people's willingness to attempt new and different behaviors will be a function of the degree to which they are sensation seekers and risk takers. Put another way, what is the individual's perceived level of self-confidence when attempting new behaviors? Personality will play a significant role in determining whether new and varied behaviors will be attempted by different individuals; it is not a guarantee that they will become part of their behavioral repertoire.

The likelihood of new behaviors becoming a permanent part of one's behavioral repertoire will be a function of the individual's experience when such behaviors were attempted. This is especially true for initial attempts with new behaviors. Specifically, how successful were the individuals when they attempted the new behaviors, and what were their consequences? Clearly, early successes when attempting new behaviors increase the individual's expectancy that future attempts will be equally successful. This will increase the probability that those behaviors will be repeated in the future. Furthermore, if the behavior produced positive consequences for the individual, then there would be an even higher probability of the attempted behavior becoming a permanent part of the individual's behavioral repertoire.

Therefore, if we accept a wide range of personality differences within any given group, as well as the likelihood of individuals having different experience, it is not surprising to find individuals functioning at different points along this continuum. What is important is that the manager recognizes these differences and understands the cause and effect relationships that brought them about.

Relevance to Managers

Managers need to understand their dominant profile. This knowledge is important for assessing the match between their profile and the situation—either prior to entering the situation or when attempting to function within a particular situation. Concomitantly, knowledge of one's dominant behavior response profile helps the individual to better assess existing strengths and weaknesses and thereby helps develop strategies for self-development if and when needed.

As with interpersonal style, the key for managers is to introduce a process by which they can collect accurate and timely information about their profile. Again, self-evaluation and feedback from others will play a critical role in satisfying the managers' need to know.

Summary

The ability of managers to perform effectively is a function of how well individuals know themselves. This chapter described four key areas relating to the "self" that are critical in determining the manager's personal success within the organization. When individuals understand their basic values or beliefs about management, their interpersonal style, interpersonal needs, dominant behavioral responses, personal goal structure, and perceived self-efficacy, there is a greater likelihood of making appropriate decisions about *(a)* the type of organization, or organizational environment, that will best match their perceived self, *(b)* how to adjust to organizational changes when they occur, and *(c)* what type of self-development activities will best prepare them for the future.

EXERCISES

2.1 Self-Assessment: Identifying Career and Life Values

Self-exploration is an important activity if individuals are going to identify what is important to them. Understanding personal needs, values, interests, talents, and lifestyle preferences helps individuals select a career path that is satisfying. The activity that follows is a simple exercise that can help individuals identify what is important to them. Please follow the steps outlined below.

Step 1. Before the next class, individually write out an autobiography that describes your life. An autobiography is a written narrative of your personal history. It includes items such as life events, education, hobbies, and major changes that occurred in the past. Narrative material should also include feelings or emotions associated with these events. Your autobiography should also include a description of turning points in your life and the pros and cons of past career choices. If you have not already started a career, point out and discuss the pros and cons of major decisions you have made in your life thus far, such as choosing friends, and summer jobs, selecting a university to attend, your university major, and courses taken.

Step 2. During next class, you will break up into groups of two individuals each. Then members of the group will exchange narratives.

Step 3. Each participant will take 30 minutes to review his or her partner's narrative. As you read through this material, you will be picking out major events, activities, or behaviors. You should also be linking events, activities, or behaviors with expressed feelings and personal responses. As you read on, you will begin to identify feelings, emotions, or inferences about your partner that recur. Similarly, you will begin to identify common threads that run through several events, activities, or behaviors. Based upon this analysis, identify or infer your partner's needs, values, talents, lifestyle preferences, etc. Write down these conclusions and support them with specific statements that were made in your partner's narrative.

Step 4. Group members should take turns sharing their observations and conclusions with their partners. Discussions should be two-way exchanges that allow the listener to respond to what is being presented. The person listening can ask questions, offer additional information, or even disagree with what is being stated by the speaker. Students find it helpful if they deal with one value, need, lifestyle preference, or talent at a time. While discussing each conclusion, presenters should support their views with support statements from the other member's autobiography. It is important that you do not rush Step 4. (While carrying out Step 4, remember that individuals are complex and that self-exploration can be demanding and emotional. Also remember that any detailed self-analysis takes time and that this is just a beginning. Step 4 should take approximately 30 minutes.)

Step 5. After each participant's presentation/discussion, group members should jointly discuss the implication of identified values, needs, talents, and lifestyle preferences on that person's future career choices and job satisfaction. (10 minutes)

2.2 Writing Out Your Retirement Speech[75]

A simple exercise designed to bring one's personal career goals into clearer focus is to write out one's own retirement speech. In other words, if you were retiring today, what would you like to have accomplished in your life and what would you like other people to be saying about you? This exercise is designed to bring these issues into better focus. Please follow the steps outlined below.

Step 1. The class will break up into groups of two individuals each.

Step 2. Individually take 10 minutes to fill in the blank retirement speech provided below. You should assume that you are now 55 years old and taking early retirement. For each of the eight items you listed, write out a statement explaining why they were listed.

Step 3. Upon completion of steps 1 and 2, each group member should take a turn reading his or her retirement speech and explanation statements to the other person. The listener is free to ask questions to ensure understanding. Step 3 should result in a list of values, needs, and lifestyle preferences that are important to the person writing his or her own retirement speech. (30 minutes)

Step 4. After each participant's presentation/discussion, group members should jointly discuss the implication of identified values, needs, talents and lifestyle preferences on that person's future career choices and job satisfaction. (10 minutes)

MY RETIREMENT

WE ARE HERE TODAY TO HONOR SOMEONE WHO AFTER BEING WITH OUR

COMPANY FOR OVER _____ YEARS, AND ACHIEVING THE POSITION OF

_____ , HAS DECIDED TO RETIRE.

AS _____ RETIRES WE SHOULD NOT FORGET

THE NUMEROUS CONTRIBUTIONS (HE/SHE) HAS MADE TO OUR ORGANIZATION.

AT THE VERY LEAST (HE/SHE) SHOULD BE REMEMBERED FOR—

    1.

    2.

    3.

    4.

HOWEVER, HAVING WORKED WITH _____ FOR THESE
MANY YEARS, I BELIEVE THE MOST FITTING TRIBUTE WE COULD GIVE
WOULD BE TO READ A FEW OF THE MANY COMMENTS MADE ABOUT
_____ BY (HIS/HER) CO-WORKERS HERE AT
_____ .

    5.

    6.

    7.

    8.

AS I CLOSE, AND WE GIVE _____ THE KEYS TO A PART-
ING GIFT, LET US ALL STAND AND SAY "BON VOYAGE!"

2.3. Interpersonal Perception Exercise

Important to the process of interpersonal perception are the manner in which we perceive ourselves, the way others perceive us, and the level of agreement that exists between the two. To understand the process and the degree of interpersonal agreement, please follow the steps outlined below.

Step 1. Students will form groups of two. Where possible, each group should consist of individuals who know each other well enough to assess their interpersonal style and dominant response behaviors. Once your group is formed, the individuals should rate themselves in column A on the 36 dimensions listed on the Personal Profile Form. Rate each item on a five-point scale. Use 1 to indicate a low occurrence of the described behavior and 5 to indicate a high occurrence. Use NA (not applicable) for behaviors that are perceived as inappropriate in describing the focus person. To identify your form, place your initials in the upper right-hand corner. When you are finished with step 1, fold the left-hand side of the form vertically so that only columns B and C are visible.

Step 2. Pass your Personal Profile Form to the other group member. Each individual will now assess his or her partner in Column B. Use the same five-point rating scale and NA (where appropriate) that you used for Column A. Place your initials to the right of the B at the top of the column so that the focus person can identify the assessor for later discussion. When all students have completed Step 2, pass the completed Personal Profile Form back to the focus person. (If you belong to a three-person group, have the third group member repeat Step 2 in Column C.)

Step 3. Group members should unfold their own forms and review the various ratings. Items that received the same rating, or are within one scale point of each other, fall into the Quadrant 1 category of the Johari window, that is, the open area of interpersonal perceptions (A description of the four quadrants of the Johari window is presented below.) This means that the behavior and its frequency are recognized and agreed upon by both individuals. Items that the focus person indicates occur frequently but which are assigned NA or are perceived as occurring infrequently by the other group member fall into the Quadrant 3 category of the Johari window, the hidden self. Items that are assigned NA or are rated as occurring infrequently by the focus person, but which are perceived as occurring frequently by the other group member, fall into Quadrant 2 of the Johari window, the blind self. In this case, the behavior is recognized by others but not by the focus person.

- The Open quadrant represents a situation where information about personal characteristics is known to the self and others.

- The Hidden quadrant represents a situation where information about personal characteristics is known to the self but not to others.

- The Blind quadrant represents a situation where information about personal characteristics is not known to the self but known to others.

- The Unknown quadrant represents a situation where information about personal characteristics is not known to either the self or others.

Step 4. Each group should discuss the results. The discussion will be more lively if each individual selects at least three items on which the group members have significant disagreement. Each individual may choose to discuss hidden or blind areas of interpersonal perception. For example, the focus person may want to verify the perceptions of others—that is, what situations have produced the other's response; the focus person may want to explain self-perceptions to give others a better understanding. (30 minutes)

Other questions to ask may include: Why was there agreement or disagreement? How comfortable did you feel discussing areas of agreement or disagreement? Would the results have been different had the exercise been carried out with a casual acquaintance or a stranger? How could you go about increasing the accuracy of interpersonal perceptions?

Note. Because this exercise deals with potentially sensitive material, students who are uncomfortable discussing their responses should feel free to omit Step 4. However, if any items are of particular concern, a student might wish to discuss them with the partner or with the instructor.

Initials _____

PERSONAL PROFILE FORM

A	B	C	Are you someone who tends to:
__	__	__	1. Interrupt others while they are talking?
__	__	__	2. Always agree with others? As a result, other people can never really tell how you feel.
__	__	__	3. Dominate other people or situations?
__	__	__	4. Engage in irritating personal habits, such as tapping a pencil, jingling keys, fussing with your hair, overuse a particular word?
__	__	__	5. Talk in an aloof or condescending manner?

—— —— —— 6. Help others?

—— —— —— 7. Not listen to the points of view of others?

—— —— —— 8. Support, and sympathize with, others?

—— —— —— 9. Not follow through on a commitment?

—— —— —— 10. Be friendly toward others?

—— —— —— 11. Be critical of others?

—— —— —— 12. Be agreeable and cooperative?

—— —— —— 13. Depend on others?

—— —— —— 14. Trust others?

—— —— —— 15. Give up easily or not stand up for your rights?

—— —— —— 16. Give positive reinforcement when it is deserved?

—— —— —— 17. Make snap decisions without checking the facts?

—— —— —— 18. Overreact to minor problems?

—— —— —— 19. Self-condemnation?

—— —— —— 20. Be too personal, especially in inappropriate situations?

—— —— —— 21. Be suspicious and distrustful of others?

—— —— —— 22. Not allow others to forget their mistakes?

—— —— —— 23. Be insecure when faced with a new situation or unfamiliar people?

—— —— —— 24. Find it difficult to be sociable or relaxed?

—— —— —— 25. Be moody or exhibit sudden or unexplained mood swings?

—— —— —— 26. Interfere in matters that do not concern you?

—— —— —— 27. Be assertive and firm when dealing with others?

—— —— —— 28. Have a short-term perspective?

—— —— —— 29. Have a long-term perspective?

—— —— —— 30. Not help others even when you have the time or resources?

—— —— —— 31. Hold back information from others until it is too late?

—— —— —— 32. Complain about everything that is said?

—— —— —— 33. Overdo reinforcement behaviors, such as smiling, nodding your head in agreement, or saying uh-huh?

—— —— —— 34. See things in black and white with no middle ground?

—— —— —— 35. Be unwilling to change or try new behaviors?

—— —— —— 36. Value friendship above personal gain?

2.4. Goal Setting/Time Scheduling

It is important for managers to develop and use techniques that help them organize and schedule their time. This exercise is designed to provide students with practice using several common organizing and scheduling techniques. Your task in this exercise is to complete the three Goal Setting/Time Organizing forms. Please follow the steps outlined below:

Step 1. The class will be asked to break up into groups of two members each. Each group should work jointly through the goal setting/scheduling process for one member.

Step 2. Decide which member of the group this exercise will focus on. Try to select the individual whose university program provides the richest source of information and who evidently wishes to get control over his or her life.

Step 3. If the second group member is not familiar with the other person's program, it is necessary for the focus person to briefly summarize the present course load, (courses in which the focus person is enrolled), and related activities and projects. It may also be desirable for the focus person to articulate long-term career objectives.

Step 4. You are now ready to complete the *Goals–Objectives Analysis Sheet.* This form is intended to reflect those major tasks, objectives, and projects that the focus person seeks to accomplish in the next two to three months or the quarter or semester.

First, list all the tasks, objectives, and projects you want to accomplish during this period. Your goals are likely to be generated either by you or an external third party (e.g., professor, friends, spouse). The items listed do not need to relate only to university activities. Any goal, objective, or project that takes time to complete, and which you value, is fair game.

Second, determine the due dates for each item and the approximate amount of time needed to complete each. An awareness of due dates and time needed to complete each task, objective, and project, facilitates the identification of future starting times, appropriate sequencing, and the establishment of priorities. Because you are still at the "general" level, you may only be dealing with "guestimates." Consequently, as you continue through the total planning process, you will likely fine-tune your estimates.

Third, list your goals in order of priority. Use an ABC priority system; that is, write a capital A to the left of those items that have the most value or have the greatest potential payoff; a B for those items with a medium value; and C for those items with a low value. As you do this, you will realize that to some extent you're guessing. You're not sure you'll be right on target in terms of value. By comparing the items with one another you will be able to come up with the ABC priority for every entry on the Goals–Objectives Analysis Sheet. Relative value will also help the focus person determine how much time and energy to devote to each project.

Finally, under the column titled "Other" you may want to indicate the people you are likely to be working with on each project, what their strengths and weaknesses are, and the type of review schedule needed. It may also be helpful to indicate the level of difficulty likely to be encountered in each project. The level of anticipated difficulty will help you determine the amount of time you should devote to each project.

During this step, the other person in the group is responsible for asking relevant questions to ensure that correct and complete information is listed on the goals–objectives form. Why was a particular goal, objective, or project listed? Should a particular goal, objective or project take that long? Should it take more or less time to complete? Are the assigned priorities correct? Are goals, objectives or projects consistent with the stated career goals or program goals stated by the student?

Step 5. This step requires that you fill out the *Subgoal—Action Plan Analysis Sheet*. Here you take one or two of your major goals–objectives and break them down into action plans. Action plans represent subgoals of the larger, more general goals and projects. In other words, what subgoals of each project must be accomplished for you to achieve success in the longer term? (Make sure that the goal–objective you select is of sufficient complexity or size that it has to be broken down into more manageable parts.) At this point, you are not concerned with behaviors but with the next level of specificity needed to fine-tune and give direction to your future activities. Direction provides motivation and forces you to think through your projects.

Next, indicate the appropriate sequence position for each subgoal. Then determine how much time will be required to perform each activity and the starting dates. As with the Goals–Objectives—Analysis Sheet, you should indicate in the "Other" column who is responsible for the successful completion of each action plan, the individual's strengths and weaknesses, and so on.

Again, the nonfocus person has the responsibility of asking relevant questions to ensure that both correct and complete information is recorded. This is a joint effort. The following are some questions that should be considered: Are the due dates and sequencing logical and consistent? Are any additional steps or action plans to be included? Do I have sufficient detail to begin considering specific behaviors necessary to achieve the action plan? Is the allocation of work between group members appropriate? In a real world situation, it may be necessary to develop multiple levels of action plans as you move from general, conceptual, goals and objectives to specific behaviors.

Step 6. Once you have broken down your goals, objectives, and projects into sufficient detail, you are ready to begin looking at specific behaviors or attainment steps necessary to achieve each action plan. Continue by filling out the Attainment Steps/Behaviors Analysis Sheet. Again, consider appropriate sequencing, time needed, due dates, and who should be acting out these behaviors. Because of limited class time, consider only *one* action plan or subgoal. However, select one of sufficient complexity that requires multiple behaviors or activities to accomplish.

With this degree of detail you can easily schedule *(a)* when these behaviors should be carried out and *(b)* who will act them out. Finally, the nonfocus person will again ensure that all relevant questions have been asked. For example: Did the focus person leave out any behaviors? Are the persons selected able and willing to perform the required behaviors? Does the focus person have the time, energy, and resources to carry out listed behaviors?

Participants should add questions they believe will help the focus person ensure that all relevant issues have been considered.

GOALS–OBJECTIVES ANALYSIS SHEET

G/O NO.	GOAL/OBJECTIVE DESCRIPTION	PRI-ORITY	DUE DATE	TIME NEEDED	OTHER

SUBGOAL—ACTION PLAN ANALYSIS SHEET

SUBGOAL—A/P DESCRIPTION	SEQUENCE	DUE DATE	TIME NEEDED	OTHER

ATTAINMENT STEPS/BEHAVIORS ANALYSIS SHEET

ATTAINMENT STEPS/BEHAVIORS	SEQUENCE	DUE DATE	TIME NEEDED	OTHER

End Notes

1. J. L. Gibson, J. M. Ivancevich and J. H. Donnelly, Jr., *Organizations: Behavior, Structure, Process,* Irwin, Burr Ridge, Ill., 1994: 78.

2. C. S. Hall and G. Lindzey, *Theories of Personality,* John Wiley & Sons, New York, 1957; A. J. DuBrin, *Effective Business Psychology,* 2nd ed., Reston Publishing, Reston, Va, 1985; S. R. Maddi, *Personality Theories: A Comparative Analysis,* Dorsey Press, Burr Ridge, Ill, 1989.

3. Hall and Lindzey, 1957; Maddi, 1989.

4. R. L. Weaver II, *Understanding Interpersonal Communications,* Harper Collins College Publishers, New York, 1993; A. G. Athos and J. J. Gararro, *Interpersonal Behavior,* Prentice Hall, Englewood Cliffs, N. J. 1978; G. A. Kimble and N. Garmezy, *Principles of General Psychology,* 3rd ed., The Ronald Press Company, New York, 1968.

5. T. W. Costello and S. S. Zalkind, *Psychology in Administration: A Research Orientation,* Prentice Hall, Englewood Cliffs, N. J., 1963; A. C. Parham, *Basic Psychology for the Work Life,* South-Western Publishing, Cincinnati, Oh, 1983; J. L. Holland, *Making Vocational Choices: A Theory of Vocational Personalities and Work Environments,* Prentice Hall, Englewood Cliffs, N. J., 1985; A. R. Spokane, "A review of research on person–environment congruence in Holland's theory of careers," *Journal of Vocational Behavior,* June 1985: 306–43; D. Brown, "The status of Holland's theory of career choice," *Career Development Journal,* September 1987: 13–23.

6. C. R. Rogers, *On Becoming a Person,* Houghton Mifflin, Boston, Mass., 1961; P. J. Brouwer, "The power to see ourselves," *Harvard Business Review,* Vol. 42, 1964: 156–165; DuBrin, 1985; J. H. Greenhaus, *Career Management,* The Dryden Press, Chicago, 1987; C. B. Smith, "Designing and facilitating a self-assessment experience," in *Career Growth and Human Resource Strategies,* ed. M. London, and E. M. Mone, Quorum Books, New York, 1988: 157–171; M. Csikszentmihalyi, *The Evolving Self: A Psychology for the Third Millennium,* Harper Collins Publishers, New York, 1993; R. Ornstein, *The Roots of the Self: Unraveling the Mystery of Who You Are,* Harper Collins Publishers, New York, 1993.

7. Greenhaus, 1987.

8. J. H. Greenhaus, 1987; H. Gunz, "The meaning of managerial careers: Organizational and individuals' levels of analysis," *Journal of Management Studies,* Vol. 26, No. 3, May 1989: 225–250; D. T. Hall, *Careers in Organizations,* Goodyear Publishing, Pacific Palisades, Calif., 1976.

9. The model described in Figure 2.1 is based upon the career management model found in J. H. Greenhaus, *Career Management,* the Dryden Press, Chicago, Ill., 1987: 18.

10. G. P. Latham and G. A. Yukl, "A review of research on the application of goal setting in organizations," *Academy of Management Journal,* Vol. 18. 1975: 824–845; E. A. Locke, K. N. Shaw, L. M. Saari, and G. P. Latham, "Goal setting and task performance: 1969–1980," *Psychological Bulletin,* Vol. 90, 1981: 125–152; Greenhaus, 1987; S. A. McIntire and E. L. Levine, "Combining personality variables and goals to predict performance," *Journal of Vocational Behavior,* Vol. 38, 1991: 288–301.

11. D. T. Hall, 1976; E. H. Schein, *Career Dynamics: Matching Individual and Organizational Needs,* Addison-Wesley Publishing, Reading, Mass., 1978; D. E. Super, "A life-span, life-space approach to career development," *Journal of Vocational Behavior,* Vol. 16, 1980: 859–865; J. H. Greenhaus, 1987; J. E. A. Russell, "Career development interventions in organizations," *Journal of Vocational Behavior,* Vol. 38, 1991: 237–287; K. Labich, "Taking control of your career," *Fortune,* Vol. 124, part 2, November 18, 1991: 87+.

12. The stages and issues presented in Table 2.1 are based upon material presented in D. C. Miller and W. H. Form, *Industrial Sociology,* Harper & Row, New York, 1951; D. T. Hall, 1976; Schein, 1978; Super, 1980; Greenhaus, 1987; Russell, 1991: 237–287; Labich, 1991: 87+.

13. Hall, 1976; M. London and S. A. Stumph, *Managing Careers,* Addison-Wesley Publishing, Reading, Mass., 1982; Greenhaus, 1987; Russell, 1991; Labich, 1991.

14. B. M. Staw, "The escalation of commitment to a course of action," *Academy of Management Review,* Vol. 6, 1981: 577–587.

15. S. H. Osipow, *Theories of Career Development,* Appleton-Century-Crofts, New York, 1968; Greenhaus, 1987; Gunz, 1989.

16. London and Stumph, 1982; Greenhaus, 1987; J. G. Clawson, J. P. Kotter, V. A. Faux and C. C. McArthur, *Self-Assessment and Career Development,* Prentice Hall, Englewood Cliffs, N. J., 1985; Smith, 1988, 157–171.

17. J. H. Greenhaus, B. L. Hawkins, and O. C. Brenner, "The impact of career exploration on the career decision-making process," *Journal of College Student Personnel,* Vol. 24, 1983: 495–502; S. Gould, "Characteristics of career planners in upwardly mobile occupations," *Academy of Management Journal,* Vol. 22, 1979: 539–550; Greenhaus, 1987; S. A. Stumpf and K. Hartman, "Individual exploration to occupational commitment or withdrawal," *Academy of Management Journal,* Vol. 27, 1984: 308–329; J. H. Greenhaus and H. K, Springgob, "Managerial perceptions of career planning information," *Journal of Management,* Vol. 6, No. 1, 1980: 79–88.

18. London and Stumph, 1982; W. B. Walsh and S. H. Osipow, *Handbook Of Vocational Psychology, Vol. 2,* Lawrence Erlbaum Associates, Publishers, Hillside, N. J., 1983; Clawson, Kotter, Faux and McArthur, 1985; Greenhaus, 1987; Smith, 1988; Cohen, "Applying the data base," *Training and Development Journal,* September 1989: 65–69; R. J. Sahl, "Probing how people think," *Personnel Journal,* December 1990: 48–56.

19. Clawson, Kotter, Faux and McArthur, 1985: 5.

20. For a discussion of alternate sources such as self-assessment workshops, interest and work value inventories, aptitudes, see Walsh and Osipow, 1983; Clawson, Kotter, Faux, and McArthur, 1985; London and Stumph, 1982; Smith, 1988.

21. Smith, 1988; Clawson, Kotter, Faux and McAruthur, 1985; Greenhaus, 1987.

22. London and Stumph, 1982; Clawson, Kotter, Faux and McArthur, 1985; Smith, 1988; Greenhaus, 1987.

23. G. P. Latham, and G. A. Yukl, "A review of research on the application of goal setting in organizations," *Academy of Management Journal,* Vol. 18, 1975: 824–845; E. A. Locke, K. N. Shaw, L. M. Saari, and G. P. Latham, "Goal setting and task performance: 1969–1980," *Psychological Bulletin,* Vol. 90, 1981: 125–152; E. A. Locke, E. Frederick, C. Lee, and P. Bobko, "Effects of self-efficacy, goals, and task strategies on task performance," *Journal of Applied Psychology,* Vol. 69, 1984: 241–251; K. L. Johnson, "How to turn goals into reality," *Broker World,* Vol. 10, No. 1, January 1990: 108–110; L. G. Ecroyd, "Planning to live forever?" *Association Management,* Vol. 44, No. 9, September 1992: 52–55; R. Dobbins and B. O. Pettman, "The psychology of success," *Equal Opportunities International,* Vol. 11, No. 1, 1992: 12–16.

24. Greenhaus, 1987.

25. Greenhaus, 1987.

26. Locke, Shaw. Saari, and Latham, 1981; A. J. Mento, R. P. Steel, and R. J. Karren, "A meta-analytic study of effects of goal setting on task performance," *Organizational Behavior and Human Decision Making,* Vol. 39, 1987: 52–83.

27. Greenhaus, 1987.

28. G. A. Steiner, *Strategic Planning: What Every Manager Must Know,* The Free Press, 1979.

29. A. D. Szilagyi, Jr., *Management and Performance,* 3rd ed., Scott, Foresman, Glenview, Ill., 1988.

30. E. A. Locke and G. P. Latham, *Goal Setting: A Motivational Technique that Works,* Prentice Hall, Englewood Cliffs, N. J., 1984.

31. Szilagyi, Jr., 1988.

32. Greenhaus, 1987.

33. R. F. Mager, Goal Analysis, Belmont, California, Fearon Publisher 1972; R. F. Mager, *Preparing Instructional Objectives* (2nd ed.), Belmont, California, Fearon, 1975.

34. Locke and Latham, 1990; Locke, Shaw, Saari, and Latham, 1981; Mento, Steel, and Karren, 1987.

35. D. E. Super, *Work Values Inventory,* Houghton Mifflin, New York, 1970; J. L. Holland, *Making Vocational Choices: A Theory of Careers,* Prentice Hall, Englewood Cliffs, N. J., 1973; Hall, 1976; Walsh Osipow, 1983; Greenhaus, 1987; Gunz, 1989.

36. Greenhaus, 1987.

37. Greenhaus, 1987.

38. Russell, 1991.

39. Russell, 1991.

40. Johnson, 1990: 108–110.

41. L. Iacocca, with W. Novak, *Iacocca: An Autobiography,* Bantam Books, 1984.

42. Locke, Frederick, Lee and Bobko, 1984; Latham and E. A. Locke, "Self-regulation through goal setting," *Organizational Behavior and Human Decision Processes,* Vol. 50, 1990: 212–247.

43. R. Wood and A. Bandura, "Social cognitive theory of organizational management," *Academy of Management Review,* Vol. 14, No. 3, 1989; 361–384.

44. A. Bandura, "Reflections on self-efficacy," *Advances in Behavior Research and Therapy*, Vol. 1, 1978, 237–269; A. Bandura, "Self-efficacy mechanism in human agency," *American Psychologist*, Vol. 37, No. 2, 1982; 122–147; N. E. Betz and G. Hackett, "Applications of self-efficacy theory to understanding career choice behavior," *Journal of Social and Clinical Psychology*, Vol. 4, 1986, 279–289; R. W. Lent and G. Hackett, "Career self-efficacy: empirical status and future directions, *Journal of Vocational Behavior*, 1987: 347–382; J. K. Ford, M. A. Quinones, D. J. Sego, and J. S. Sorra, "Factors affecting the opportunity to perform trained tasks on the job," *Personnel Psychology,* Vol. 45, No. 3, Autumn 1992: 511–527.

45. I. Brown, Jr., and D. K. Inouye, "Learned helplessness through modeling: The role of perceived similarity in competence, *Journal of Personality and Social Psychology*, Vol. 36, 1978: 900–908; D. H. Schunk, "Modeling and attributional effects on children's achievement: A self-efficacy analysis," *Journal of Educational Psychology,* Vol. 73, 1981: 93–105; A. Bandura and N. E. Cervone, "Differential engagement of self-reactive influences in cognitive motivation," *Organizational Behavior and Human Decision Processes*, Vol. 38, 1986: 92–113; D. Cervone and P. K. Peake, "Anchoring, efficacy, and action: The influence of judgment heuristics on self-efficacy," *Journal of Personality and Social Psychology*, Vol. 50, 1986: 492–501; A. Bandura, "Self-regulation of motivation and action through goal systems," in *Cognitive Perspectives on Emotion Motivation*, ed. V. Hamilton, G. H. Bower, and N. H. Frijda, Kluwer Academic Publishers, Dordrecht, Netherlands, 1988: 37–61; M. E. Gist, and T. R. Mitchell, "Self-efficacy: A theoretical analysis of its determinants and malleability," *Academy of Management Review,* Vol. 17, No. 2, April 1992: 183-211.

46. A. Bandura, L. Reese and N. Adams, "Attitudes and social cognition," *Journal of Personality and Social Psychology*, Vol. 43. No. 1, 1982: 5–21.

47. Bandura, "Recycling misconceptions of perceived self-efficacy," *Cognitive Theory and Research*, Vol. 8, No. 3, 1984: 231–255.

48. Bandura, Reese, and Adams, 1982; F. H. Kanfer and A. M. Zeiss, "Depression, interpersonal standard setting, and judgments of self-efficacy," *Journal of Abnormal Psychology* Vol. 92, 1983: 319–329; R. S. Lazarus and S. Folkman, *Stress, Appraisal, and Coping*, Springer, New York, 1984; A. Bandura, "Self-efficacy conception of anxiety," *Anxiety Research*, Vol. 1, 1988: 77–98; R. F. Mager, "No self-efficacy, no performance," *Training,* Vol. 29, No. 4, April 1992: 32–36.

49. Locke, Frederick, Lee, and Bobko, 1984; P. C. Earley, and T. R. Lituchy, ""Defining goal and efficacy effects: A test of three models," *Journal of Applied Psychology,* Vol. 76, No. 1, February 1991: 81–98.

50. G. P. Latham, D. C. Winters, and E. A. Locke, "Cognitive and motivational effects of participation: A mediator study," *Journal of Organizational Behavior,* 1994.

51. A. Bandura and N. E. Adams, "Analysis of self-efficacy theory of behavior change," *Cognitive Therapy and Research*, Vol. 1, 1977: 287–308; Bandura, 1978.

52. Wood and Bandura, 1989: 361–384.

53. J. L. Gibson, J. M. Ivancevich, and J. H. Donnelly, Jr., *Organizations, Behavior, Structure, Process,* Irwin, Burr Ridge, Ill., 1994.

54. K. E. Kram and D. T. Hall, "Mentoring as an antidote to stress during corporate trauma," *Human Resource Management,* Winter 1989, Vol. 28, No. 4: 493–510.

55. L. A. Festinger, "A theory of social comparison," *Human Relations,* Vol. 7, 1954: 117–140; B. Latane, "Studies in social comparison," *Journal of Experimental Social Psychology,* 1966, Supplement 1; L. Wheeler, "Social comparison and selective affiliation," in T. L. Huston, (ed.) *Foundations of Interpersonal Attraction,* Academic Press, New York, 1974; Athos, Gararro, 1978; A. Bandura, *Social Learning Theory,* Prentice Hall, Englewood Cliffs, N. J., 1977; R. Kreitner and F. Luthans, "A social learning approach to behavioral management: Radical behavioralists'mellowing out,'" *Organizational Dynamics,* Autumn 1984: 47–65; D. A. Gioia and C. C. Manz, "Linking cognition and behavior: A script processing interpretation of vicarious learning," *Academy of Management Review,* July 1985: 527–539; Wood and Bandura, 1989.

56. Figure 2.4 is based upon material presented in W. Schutz, *FIRO: A Three Dimensional Theory of*

Interpersonal Behavior, Holt, Rinehart & Winston, New York, 1958; L. R. Ryan, *Clinical Interpretation of the FIRO-B,* Counsulting Psychologists Press, Palo Alto, Calif., 1970; R. E. Hill, "Interpersonal needs and functional areas of management," *Journal of Vocational Behavior,* Vol. 4, 1974: 15–24.

57. D. C. McClelland, *Power: The Inner Experience,* Irvington, New York, 1975.

58. Schutz, 1958; McClelland, 1975.

59. Schutz, 1958.

60. Weaver II, 1993: 149; V. J. Callan, "Subordinate-manager communication in different sex dyads: Consequences for job satisfaction," *Journal of Occupational & Organizational Psychology,* Vol. 66, No. 1, March 1993: 13–27; W. J. A. Marshall, "The importance of being earnest: A primer for leaders," *Management Quarterly,* Vol. 27, No. 2, Summer 1986: 7–12; R. Hossack, "Male executives: Challenged by a gender bind," *CMA Magazine,* Vol. 67, No. 5, June 1993: 5; S. M. Jourard, *The Transparent Self,* Van Nostrand, New York, 1971; J. Powell, *Why Am I Afraid to Tell You Who I Am?* Argus Communications, Chicago, 1969.

61. S. Ashford, "Feedback-seeking in individual adaptation: A resource perspective," *Academy of Management Journal,* September 1986: 465–487; G. B. Northcraft and S. J. Ashford, "The preservation of self in everyday life: The effects of performance expectations and feedback context on feedback inquiry," *Organizational Behavior & Human Decision Processes,* Vol. 47, No. 1, October 1990: 42–64; P. L. McLeod, J. K. Liker, and S. A., Lobel, "Process feedback in task groups: An application of goal setting," *Journal of Applied Behavioral Science,* Vol. 28, No. 1, March 1992: 15–41; H. J. Leavitt and R.A.H., Mueller, "Some effects of feedback on communication," in *Interpersonal Communications: Survey and Studies,* Dean Barnlund, ed., Houghton Mifflin, Boston, Mass., 1968: 251–259.

62. The interpersonal model discussed by the authors is based upon the following sources: R. L. Weaver II, 1993: 149–164; Gibson, Ivancevich, and Donnelly, Jr., 1991: 549–551; Hall, 1973; Luft, 1984.

63. Weaver II, 1993; Gibson, Ivancevich, and Donnelly, Jr., 1994: 584–587; Hall, 1973; Luft, 1984.

64. Our description of cell content reflects the material presented in Weaver II, 1993; Gibson, Ivancevich, and Donnelly, Jr., 1994: 584–587; Hall, 1973; Luft, 1984; Ashford, 1986.

65. Weaver II, 1993; R. F. Verderber and K.S. Verderber, *Inter-Act: Using Interpersonal Communication Skills,* 5th ed., Wadsworth, Belmont, Calif., 1989; J. J. Gilbert, "Empirical and theoretical extensions of self-disclosure," in *Explorations in Interpersonal Communication,* G. R. Miller, ed., Sage Publications, Beverly Hills, Calif., 1976: 200+; P. W. Cozy, "Self-disclosure: A literature review," *Psychological Bulletin,* Vol. 79, 1973: 73–91.

66. Ashford and Cummings, "Feedback as an individual resource: Personal strategies of creating information," *Organizational Behavior and Human Performance,* Vol. 32, 1983: 370–398.

67. The following discussion is based, in part, of the material presented in A. J. Bernstein and S. Rozen, *Dinosaur Brains: Dealing with All Those Impossible People at Work,* Ballantine Books, New York, 1989.

68. T. Cox, *Stress,* University Park Press, Baltimore, 1978.

69. R. S. Lazarus, *Psychological Stress and Coping Process,* McGraw-Hill, New York, 1966; R.S. Lazarus, *Patterns of Adjustment,* McGraw-Hill, New York, 1976.

70. S. Folkman, "Personal control and stress coping processes: A theoretical analysis," *Journal of Personality and Social Psychology,* Vol. 64, No. 4, 1984: 839–852; P. J. Dewe, "Examining the nature of work stress: Individual evaluations of stressful experiences and coping," *Human Relations,* Vol. 42, No. 1, 1989: 993–1013; P. J. Dewe, "Applying the concept of appraisal to work stressors: Some exploratory analysis," *Human Relations,* Vol. 45, No. 2, 1992: 143–165.

71. McClelland, 1975; Bernstein and Rozen, 1989.

72. McClelland and D. H. Burnham, "Power is the great motivator," *Harvard Business Review,* March–April, 1976: 100–110.

73. McClelland and Burnham, 1976.

74. Bernstein and Rozen, 1989.

75. This exercise is based upon material presented in J. W. Lee, with M. Pierce, *Hour Power,* Dow Jones-Irwin, Burr Ridge, Ill., 1980.

ATTITUDES AND VALUE SYSTEMS NECESSARY FOR SUCCESS

Objectives:

- Discuss environmental factors that affect the link between management attitudes, values, and behavior.
- Articulate those values and beliefs most likely to shape managerial attitudes and values in the next decade.
- Highlight important management attitudes that directly impact on the success of the manager–subordinate interface.
- Give you an opportunity to examine your attitudes and value systems relative to organizational issues.

The Role of Feelings, Beliefs, Attitudes and Values in Shaping Management Behavior

Managerial behavior, in response to organizational events, reflects a complicated mixture of what we often refer to as factual beliefs, attitudes, value systems, and environmental realities.[1] To fully appreciate the importance of these variables, we must consider how they relate to one another, and how managerial behavior in the present affects managerial attitudes and values in the future. These relationships are described in Figure 3.1.

Attitudes consist of feelings, beliefs, and predispositions to behave in certain ways. The integration of attitudes forms an individual's personal value system.[2] As is the case with attitudes, an individual's value system also produces behavioral intentions. However, because an individual's personality is acted out within an environment, an internal predisposition is not always manifested.[3] For example, an individual may have a negative attitude toward another person but refuse to express it or act it out because it would be socially inappropriate

FIGURE 3.1

*Attitude components
and relationships*

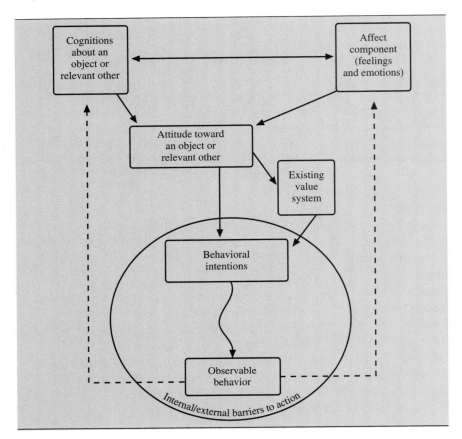

to do so. As Rokeach[4] pointed out, how individuals express their attitudes about objects is likely to be affected by the situations in which they are encountered and the individual's attitudes about the situation. The reason can be found in the building blocks of the model shown in Figure 3.1.

The Cognitive Component

Information about one's environment facilitates personal decision making and increases the likelihood of success (see Chapter 15). Therefore, people try to internally define and understand their external environment. In doing so, managers create a cognitive map of the world around them. This cognitive map consists of "factual beliefs," that is, characteristics of environmental objects and the perceived relationships that exist among these objects.[5]

Cognitions (beliefs, memories) represent a perceptual interpretation of the external environment that may be true or false. Regardless of the level of accuracy, the individual believes that they are true and acts accordingly.

The Affect Component

Affect is the emotional or feeling component of attitudes. It determines the individual's response to environmental objects, that is, a positive or negative evaluation of the general value or appropriateness of an object, or a symbol of that object.[6] Individuals who place a positive value on an object, or its symbol, tend to seek out, or approach, that object. Conversely, individuals who place a negative value on an object, or its symbol, tend to avoid, attack, or reject that object.[7] The affect component of attitudes is due in part to subtle classical conditioning over time.[8]

As individuals interact with their environment, conditioned emotional responses are developed. Positive feelings usually occur in situations where an individual satisfies personal needs such as completing a challenging task, receiving reinforcement through praise from significant others, receiving an award, etc. These feelings are usually linked to other objects or individuals present during the positive experience. Furthermore, feelings can even generalize to objects and individuals not present during the initial event but which have common, or similar, characteristics to those that were present. For example, an individual may have a positive response to an individual who reminds him or her of a warm or affectionate parent.

The affect component of attitudes also reflects the social input that individuals receive from others.[9] Therefore, the attitudes that employees develop about their work will often reflect information received from co-workers. Similarly, the individual's personality affects the feelings that help shape job attitudes. Staw and Ross found that individuals who have a predisposition to experience negative emotional states (i.e., feel nervous, anxious, distressed) are more likely to develop negative attitudes toward themselves, their work, and others, than are individuals who demonstrate a positive predisposition.[10]

The intensity of feelings and emotions can vary significantly among individuals, and can change dramatically from one time to another. Intensity plays a direct role in determining attitude strength, behavioral intent, and the willingness to carry out intentions.

If people believe an issue is central to their self-concept, the affective response is likely to be strong. For example, two managers may hold the belief that an employee's gender is unrelated to on-the-job performance, but only one of the managers may have strong feelings on the subject. If both managers were to observe an act of employee discrimination that was based upon gender differences alone, the behavioral intentions for each individual would likely differ. For the manager with strong feelings, open support of the employee would likely occur. But taking strong supporting action is not likely to be contemplated by the manager who does not possess strong feelings on this issue. Furthermore, the manager with intense feelings would likely be able to withstand social and organizational pressures to ignore what had taken place.

The Central Role of Attitudes

Although attitudes do not always predict specific behaviors, knowledge of underlying attitudes does allow the manager to predict general behavior patterns over the long run. Through an understanding of underlying personal attitudes of employees, managers are able to match long-term general behaviors to situational requirements and personal needs. Understanding attitudes is also important because they affect a number of psychological processes likely to determine a manager's success. Specifically, attitudes help shape and maintain four personality functions, namely, adjustment, ego defense, value expression, and knowledge.[11]

1. **The adjustment function** is the process by which individuals develop favorable or unfavorable attitudes about objects. It guides future interactions with the same or similar objects, it maximizes need satisfaction through goal achievement.

2. **The ego-defensive function** is the process by which individuals develop attitudes that protect the ego from threatening external forces, as well as one's own personal behaviors and internal feelings. Such attitudes enable individuals to rationalize, project, or displace internal conflicts and thereby again achieve balance.

3. **The value-expressive function** enables individuals to obtain satisfaction from expressing attitudes which reflect their personal values and self-concept.

4. **The knowledge function** permits individuals to use attitudes to give structure and meaning to their environment. This is accomplished by seeking information about the characteristics of objects and the relationships among them.

By understanding the adjustment function, managers should open themselves up to new experiences and objectively assess the consequences of behaving in new ways. Attitudes formed in this manner can act to ensure that managers are current and that their attitude structure matches the requirements of changing situations. If a manager finds it necessary to empower subordinates by giving them increased responsibility for self-direction and assessment, even though he or she has resisted such action in the past, and finds the experiencing satisfying, it is likely that the manager's attitudes toward empowerment will change in a positive direction. The manager's changed attitude toward empowerment increases the probability that he or she will use the technique in the future.

By recognizing the dangers of ego protection—rationalization (finding good reason for one's undesirable behavior), projection (finding one's own traits in others, usually negative traits), and displacement (an expression of any behavioral tendency that is directed toward some object or person other than the one causing the behavior)—managers can assess their inner motives when interacting with others.[12] Such inner honesty increases the likelihood of positive interpersonal relationships and at the same time reduces the probability of self-fulfilling prophecies. By recognizing the benefits of the value-expressive function in establishing one's personal self-identity, managers can open up to relevant others. Managers who develop open, honest, and self-expressing relationships will increase the probability of mutual understanding between themselves and others. Last, by recognizing the knowledge function, managers actively seek information about the characteristics of, and relationships among, important objects within their environment. Knowledge and understanding about one's environment increase the likelihood that managers will become better decision makers.

The Link Between Attitudes and Values

As we have stated above, an individual's attitude set can be organized into a meaningful hierarchical structure that effectively establishes his or her internal value system. Value systems, once formed, are enduring and act to provide guidance to the individual when considering modes of conduct and desired end states. However, individuals often do not exhibit behavior that is consistent with their value systems. They may not even be consciously aware of the specific values they hold.[13]

External–Internal Barriers to Action

The wavy line between behavioral intentions and observable behaviors in Figure 3.1 indicates that individuals do not always act out their intentions. Behavioral intentions can be short-circuited because of internal and external barriers.[14] Internally, the individual's attitude set, or value system, is made up of a number of specific attitudes. At any given moment, certain attitudes or values will be active while others will be passive in terms of their relative impact on behavior. In the case of passive attitudes, little observable evidence of their presence will exist until some external event brings them to the active level.

Because the individual is likely to have multiple attitudes and values, the potential for conflict with behavior intentions also exists. As we will see in Chapter 12, internal conflict can result in individuals suppressing one or both of the conflicting behavioral intentions as they seek internal balance. Personality also plays a role in determining whether an individual acts out behavioral intentions. For example, individuals who have high self-esteem are more likely than low self-esteem individuals to take risks, choose unconventional jobs, resist external influences to conform, and take unpopular stands.[15] Similarly, the external environment makes it difficult to predict which of the conflicting attitudes and values will cause the individual to behave in a certain way.[16] For example, employees who value the protection of the environment may nevertheless be willing to damage it by dispensing toxic chemicals to prevent an explosion from spilled gasoline at the work site. Similarly, students may have a negative attitude toward a particular course but not express their view because the professor is present.

Externally, the individual is faced with a broad range of potential barriers that can block behavioral intentions. As discussed earlier, the upcoming decade is likely to reflect a period of reduced resources. Under conditions of increased scarcity, it may be difficult to effectively carry out one's behavioral intentions. For example, you may have a very negative attitude toward a particular professor but nevertheless enroll in the class. The conflict occurs because the course in question is a required course and this particular professor, because of reductions in faculty, is the only one who teaches it. Lack of support or social acceptance is often cited as another barrier to the free expression of one's attitudes. Consequently, if the individual is a "minority of one," he or she often suppresses poorly supported behavioral intentions. This may occur because the individual is a new member of the group and therefore feels inferior to the remaining members. As a result, the individual conforms.[17] Similarly, if the group's position relates to a pivotal, or important, norm[18] there is pressure for the individual to conform as a prerequisite for remaining a group member. Individuals may also hold attitudes that supersede the one in conflict, and thereby conform to support the higher order attitude.[19] Other environmental factors, such as organizational tradition, organizational structure, distribution of power and influence, organizational rules and regulations, can also dampen the desire to act out behavioral intentions if the cost of doing so outweighs the benefits.

The Role of One's Moral Code

When decisions have to be made about moral issues, it is the individual's moral code that determines whether a particular act or behavior is right or wrong. Here again, however, a direct link does not exist between an individual's moral code and observed behavior. As you will recall, confounding factors in the environment may prevent the full expression of a person's behavior. Consequently, managers may believe it is incorrect to fix prices, offer a bribe, give a gift to win a contract, or discriminate because of race. Nevertheless, pressures within the environment may cause them to do just that. If managers are given the choice to lose their job, or fix prices, or falsify a report as requested by senior management, they may ignore their moral code and comply with an immoral request.[20]

Impact of Behaviors on Beliefs and Feelings

The two dashed arrows in Figure 3.1 indicate that behavior can alter either the cognitive or affective components of an attitude.[21] The underlying logic supporting this position is that individuals seek both an internal and external balance.[22] Balance is a state in which important variables fit together harmoniously.[23] If a balanced state between held attitudes and behavior is disrupted, the individual seeks to correct the situation. For example, consider a manager who holds a negative attitude toward subordinate participation. The manager's negative attitude may reflect a belief that subordinates are inherently selfish, and will make decisions that are to their benefit. This attitude may also be based on being severely reprimanded for project failures resulting from previous subordinate mistakes. If senior executives force this manager to share decision making with subordinates, the individual will experience an imbalance.

Managers attempt to regain balance by changing something under their control. One alternative open to managers is to refuse to delegate decision-making authority to subordinates. Such a course of action, however, is likely to produce a negative response from both senior management and subordinates. A second alternative is for managers to rationalize their behaviors by arguing that a participative management style is being forced upon them by top management, and therefore they have been given no other choice. However, if the process works well, managers can alter their beliefs, or given the altered beliefs and the good feeling resulting from the positive participative encounter, change their feelings toward involving subordinates in decision making.[24]

In summary, to understand behavior it is necessary to consider the cognitive and affective components of attitudes, the full set of attitudes held by the individual that are relevant to a particular situation, the individual's value and moral systems, and the environment in which the behavior occurs. At the same time, expressed behavior can alter specific attitudes by influencing their cognitive or affective components. It is the complexity and dynamics of the model described in Figure 3.1 that equip managers to adjust to the complexity and dynamics of their own behavior.

It is now possible to turn our attention to a discussion of important areas in which management attitudes and values can have a significant impact on individual and organizational success. The areas selected reflect the authors' assessment of what values and attitudes must be understood to allow managers to deal effectively with the trends described in Chapter 1. The first such area is that of business ethics.

The Issue of Ethics

The 1980s were characterized as a decade of excess and self-indulgence. In this decade, the issue of business ethics has become a topic of considerable concern. With media headlines depicting brokerage house fraud, overruns in defense contracts, improper advertising, insider trading, judges indicted on tax evasion, and the conscious destruction of the environment for financial gain, the ethical conduct of leaders is being questioned. Faced with mounting concerns about the appropriateness of behavior, managers face the issue of determining just what should be their attitude toward ethical conduct by their organization.

The individual's ethical system is made up of a set of interrelated attitudes and values relating to preferable modes of behavior. In other words, an ethical system represents a set of ground rules that are followed when making decisions about correct behavior. Ethics is concerned with answering the question "What should I do so that I am good and not bad, right and not wrong, just and not unjust?" Business ethics asks the same questions in the context of organizational behavior. The answer to this question is a function of the ethical system followed by managers when faced with choices among alternative courses of action. The response to these questions plays a significant role in the long-term success of any business.[25]

Ethical dilemmas occur in a broad range of situations that arise in the context of doing one's job. For example:[26]

- In the 1970s a number of companies manufacturing children's pajamas discovered that the pajamas they were selling were made with a flame-retardant chemical found to cause kidney cancer in children. Because of the toxic chemical, the garments could not be thrown away or sold in the United States. However, the financial loss to the companies manufacturing the garments would be significant. Unable to get financial compensations from government or the manufacturer of the toxic chemical, some companies sold their flame-retardant garments to exporters at 10 to 30 percent of wholesale. Clearly the intention of these companies was to dump the product in foreign markets and thereby reduce the companies' financial loss.

- To sell custom-made brake assemblies to be used in Air Force military planes, a major manufacturer offered to deliver a new four-disk brake system at a ridiculously low price. The offer was too good to refuse, and the company got the contract. Unfortunately, a four-disk brake system was insufficient to withstand the high internal heat generated when the aircraft landed. They continually failed preshipment tests. Nevertheless, company officials continued to communicate positive results to the purchaser of the brakes. In response to the test failures, senior company officials pressured those responsible for preshipment tests to prepare results that would qualify the brakes for shipment. The brakes eventually failed during flight tests, and the participating engineers informed the FBI of what had happened. In response to the controversy, the company recalled the qualifying report and shipped five-disk brakes that worked.

- In the late 1960s, a North American automobile company was faced with gas tank problems on one of its cars. Yet they wanted to be able to compete with foreign imports by selling a car that weighed under 2,000 pounds and was priced under $2,000. The decision facing the company was whether to go with the existing design that incorporated a gas tank system that failed the National Highway Traffic Safety Administration's proposed safety standards. Of the 11 cars tested, the only 3 that passed were equipped with fuel tank modifications. Since the estimated costs of modifications were greater than the estimated social benefits, the company proceeded with the original design.

- A manager of a department store struggled with a decision to put hidden microphones in restrooms, lounge areas, and stockrooms, and a hidden camera in the checkout section of the jewelry department. The motivation behind such a move was to stem the high level of theft being experienced in the jewelry department. After trying other alternatives without success, the manager finally agreed to install hidden cameras and microphones. In 10 days the hidden camera had identified the thief. Although the hidden microphones were not helpful in catching the thief, they provided information about employees selling drugs, individuals planning to quit, employees fraudulently receiving food stamps, and a buyer who wanted to discredit the store. The manager was now faced with the issue of what to do with the obtained information.

Four Ethical Systems

At best, four ethical systems explain the ethical behavior of individuals (see Figure 3.2). *End-result ethics* (commonly known as utilitarianism) defines rightness in terms of the degree to which a decision's consequences promote happiness (pleasure) rather than unhappiness (pain). However, the happiness or unhappiness described is not at the individual level, but rather for all the concerned parties. *Rule ethics* is based upon the assumption that there exists a set of universal rules that can be used to guide ethical decisions (that is,

FIGURE 3.2

Principal ethical systems

Ethical System	Proponent	Definition
End-Result Ethics	John Stuart Mill (1806–1873)	The moral rightness of an action is determined by considering its consequences.
Rule Ethics	Immanuel Kant (1724–1804)	The moral rightness of an action is determined by laws and standards.
Social Contract Ethics	Jean Jacques Rousseau (1712–1778)	The moral rightness of an action is determined by the customs and norms of a particular community.
Personalistic Ethics	Martin Buber (1878–1965)	The moral rightness of an action is determined by one's conscience.

Source: Taken from William D. Hitt, *Ethics and Leadership: Putting Theory into Practice,* Battelle Press, Columbus, Ohio, 1990.

"do unto others as you would have them do unto you," as quoted in Webster, "treat others as an end in themselves, never merely as a means.") In this case, the good life is not a function of end results but of whether individuals fit their behavior to the moral code. An ethical system based upon *social contracts*

TABLE 3.1   Ethical Systems and the Questions They Raise

End-Result Ethics

- How does one define happiness, pleasure, and utility?
- How does one go about measuring happiness, pleasure, and utility?
- How does one predict the outcome of a particular action?
- How does one choose between short-term happiness and long-term happiness?
- If 90 percent of the people were free and 10 percent were slaves, would this satisfy the greatest happiness principle?
- If you could sit in a pleasure-inducing booth for the rest of your life, would you choose to do it?

Rule Ethics

- By what authority do we accept particular rules and the goodness of these rules?
- What rule do we follow in choosing between conflicting rules?
- How do we adapt general rules to fit specific situations or circumstances?
- Why should we follow a given rule if the consequences are likely to be bad?
- Is there such a thing as a rule with absolutely no exceptions?

Social Contract Ethics

- How do we determine the general (community) will?
- What is meant by the common good?
- What is to be done about independent thinkers of outspoken opinion?
- According to social contract ethics, would Hitler's Nazi Germany be considered a moral society?
- Is the general community the "measure of all things"?

Personalistic Ethics

- How could we justify our actions except by saying, "Well, it felt like the right thing for me to do"?
- How could we resolve conflicting views of two different persons?
- What would be the common bond in a team that fostered personalistic ethics?
- How could an organization assure uniformity in ethics if it promoted personalistic ethics?

Source: William D. Hitt, *Ethics and Leadership: Putting Theory into Practice*, Battelle Press, 1990, pp. 97–129.

assumes that when individuals join a group, community, or organization to gain support and protection from the larger group, they sacrifice some personal freedoms and autonomy. Once formed, the large group establishes a set of laws that are designed to guide its members when making ethical decisions. Under this system, members should participate in the making of laws, but once decided upon by the majority, are bound by them even though they may not have supported their creation. In the case of *personalistic ethics*, the focal point of truth is within the individual rather than in the consequences, higher principles (e.g., all persons are created equal), or community laws. According to personalistic ethics, it is peoples' consciences that guide them through the daily maze of ethical issues.

No one system can be relied upon to cover all situations (see Table 3.1). To overcome this problem, each ethical system should be considered as part of a total ethical map designed to guide the decision maker. Rational processes allow people to draw from each system the perspective that is needed to make the right ethical decision.

Blanchard and Peale's "ethics check questions" represent a similar approach for assessing the appropriateness of ethical decisions (see Table 3.2). The manager who uses these questions is incorporating key aspects of the ethical systems discussed above.

Three Levels of Ethics

When discussing business ethics, there are three distinct but related levels of analyses.[27] First, business ethics can be considered an internal process or activity by which individuals reflect and decide what they should do (an internal cognitive process). Second, the term can refer to principles that guide the individual when making a decision about appropriate behavior (internally held or externally stated). Last, it can refer to the actual behaviors exhibited

---

TABLE 3.2   The Ethics Check Questions

> 1. Is it legal?
>   Will I be violating either a civil law or company policy?
> 2. Is it balanced?
>   Is it fair to all concerned in the short term as well as in the long term?
>   Does it promote win–win relationships?
> 3. How will it make me feel about myself?
>   Would it make me proud?
>   Would I feel good if my decision was published in the newspaper?
>   Would I feel good if my family knew about it?

Source: Kenneth Blanchard and Norman Vincent Peale, *The Power of Ethical Management*, William Morrow, 1988, p. 27.

by the individual (acted out and observed). Each level plays a critical role in determining the effectiveness of the manager's behavior within the existing system.

The Need for a Socratic Approach to Ethical Decision Making

Given that no one system can answer all the manager's ethical questions, there exists a need for a Socratic approach to ethical decision making. Specifically, as managers reflect and choose what should be done, rational and analytical abilities must be used to collect and process all available information. Managers should examine their own values, the conflicting and competing attitudes, the beliefs that exist within the system, and the arguments offered to support such conflicting views. They should then relate these insights to known ethical systems. Such an examination of the organization's environment, consequences, and internal value systems will help ensure that they do not automatically accept the moral–ethical codes espoused by others. Once managers have identified the set of principles that will guide their behavior, it is desirable to openly state these principles. Verbalization of ethical principles allows others to know where a manager stands, creates the opportunity for others to make constructive comments, and increases the likelihood that a manager will act upon principles. Behavior is important, as it represents the acting out of the manager's ethical principles. In this way, managers are able to test the first two levels of business ethics and assess the degree to which they fit reality. If they do fit well, a manager's attitudes and values will be reinforced. If they do not, then a manager is likely to alter the attitudes and values. By acting out all three levels, a manager increases the probability that the ethical system followed will produce "good," "right," and "just" behavior.

Ethical Encounters with Subordinates

The following discussion highlights five prescriptive issues concerning the manager–subordinate interface.

Issue 1: Sharing Information.   Because of the structure and nature of most organizations, managers traditionally have greater access to information than do subordinates. This information often gives a manager power and influence over others. When this information is relevant to subordinates' performance and interests, it is desirable to share such information with them.[28] This action empowers employees by making them important components in the information-sharing process.

Issue 2: Rewards for Performance.   The concept of differential reward implies that individuals should be rewarded in proportion to their overall contribution or rate of improvement. If two individuals contribute or improve at the same rate, they should receive rewards of like value. Therefore, such things as gender, race, social familiarity, relationship to others, etc., should not be considerations in the manager's decision.

Issue 3: Sharing Recognition.   Closely related to Issue 2 is that of sharing one's success with those who have contributed to it. Given the complexity, dynamics, and interrelated nature of most organizations, it is unlikely that a manager will achieve success without the help of others. It is therefore important for managers to give credit where credit is due, by ensuring that top management and relevant others within the organization know the contribution others have made to the success.

Issue 4: Subordinate Development.   Managers should do whatever they can to ensure that employees fulfill their potential. This will enable the manager and the organization to reach their goals.[29]

Issue 5: Mixed Signals.   The move toward ethical behavior on the part of managers, and organizational members in general, is often short-circuited because of the mixed signals received from top management—especially the immediate boss. Statements such as "It doesn't matter to me how you do it, just do it!" "If you could sell $250,000 last quarter you should be able to do $350,000 next quarter!" "Either John is let go, or you go!" fail to communicate to the receiver appropriate or ethical behavior. Because of the ambiguity of these statements, employees are free to interpret them as implying that any tactics are acceptable when attempting to achieve results.[30] This is especially true when rewards are tied primarily to results and not behavior.[31] To overcome this problem, managers should articulate ethical codes that are specific in terms of behavior, and well enforced.

Conversely, when managers are given a directive by their immediate boss, it is equally important to assess the degree to which such communications incorporate these characteristics. If they do not, ethical managers will ask for clarification. This detailed information can then be processed by them to determine whether such a directive is consistent with the "ethics check questions" outlined above.

While these five issues demonstrate appropriate ethical behavior over the next decade, they also point to a number of additional topic areas where managers' attitudes, values, and, ultimately, behavior will prove critical in determining their success. The specific areas that come to mind are *managerial sensitivity toward others, employee involvement, assertiveness,* and *followership.* Let us consider each of these topic areas and what should be the appropriate attitudes, values, and behaviors for the present decade.

Managerial Sensitivity

Although the emphasis of the present text is the manager–employee interface, it is important to realize that a manager interacts with a wide range of individuals in carrying out job-related responsibilities (see Figure 3.3). At each interaction point, it is important that the manager develop an interpersonal style that will produce a long-term positive relationship among the parties

FIGURE 3.3

*Interpersonal
Exchanges*

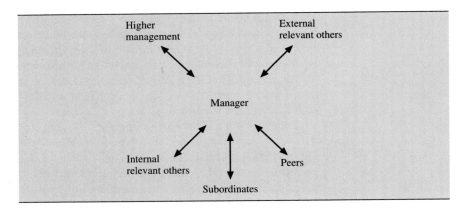

involved. Critical to the development of such a relationship is the manager's ability to interact with others in an interpersonally sensitive manner. For our purposes, interpersonal sensitivity occurs on two levels simultaneously. Managers are interpersonally sensitive when they consider the psychological and physical needs of others in planning for, or engaging in, an interpersonal exchange. Similarly, sensitive managers also consider the impact that their behavior is likely to have on others. Unfortunately, instead of being interpersonally sensitive, many managers make two critical errors when interacting with others. First, they often assume that others behave and think the way they do and therefore only have to know themselves, and second, that if relevant others are different, they will have to accept what managers do as the normal or correct way of behaving. Both premises are likely to increase the probability of interpersonal failure.

The question that must be clarified in each manager's mind is, "Why does interpersonal competence play such a critical role in managerial success?" To answer this question it is necessary to consider the factual beliefs and feelings that relate to this issue.

Required Interactions

By definition, managers must interact with others both internal and external to the organization. However, for interactions to be maintained at levels necessary to accomplish the manager's goals, they must satisfy certain conditions. One such condition is that the individuals with whom the manager interacts must believe that they are receiving something of value from the exchange.[32] Given the trends cited in Chapter 1, it is unlikely that economic benefits alone will be sufficient to balance the exchange equation between the manager and "relevant others." Organizational outcomes in the form of recognition, personal acceptance, shared information, and participation in the organization's decision-making process have become equally important in satisfying employee needs.

Interpersonal exchanges also have value because they can be helpful in answering key questions about the "self" and the interpersonal climate in which the exchanges occur. Individuals want to know if they will be accepted, whether they are important and have value, and the degree to which they belong. Individuals will also use interpersonal exchanges to assess the degree of personal warmth likely to be exhibited by others. In this way, individuals measure the degree to which they can develop a close, intimate relationship, and whether they can feel free to express affection. In short, an interpersonally sensitive manager can make others feel comfortable and relaxed—a reward often overlooked in our busy world.

Interpersonal sensitivity is also an important building block for mutual trust. Managers who willingly consider and accept individual differences are more likely to be trusted by others. The logic here is that a manager who is interpersonally sensitive is more likely to listen to and accept the needs, opinions, attitudes, and values of other individuals. Individuals who develop a trusting relationship with others are more likely to share information with the other person.

Individual Differences

To fully appreciate the range of individual differences faced by North American managers in the 1990s, it is again important to reflect back on the demographic changes taking place. Globalization and the "browning" of North America will significantly increase the range of individual differences experienced by the typical manager. By the year 2000, 80 percent of the North American work force will be made up of minorities, women, and immigrants.[33] Therefore, proactive companies must develop strategies on how to use this resource effectively. In addition, managers must develop behavioral styles that will take into account the wide range of differences that are likely to exist among employees. To do so they must:[34]

1. Consider what it might feel like to be different. An easy way of doing this is to reflect back on those situations in which you were the different person. To get maximum impact out of the exercise, write down what you felt. When we have done this with our students, they often use such words as frustrated, angry, upset, afraid, and uncomfortable. However, once these feelings are recognized, it is best to look upon individuals with differences as unique, special, gifted, innovative, etc. In other words, they provide opportunities for us rather than threats.

2. Reflect back on previous situations that are similar to the one you are now experiencing. In other words, learn from your own past behavior. If you did something before and it worked, do it again. If it didn't work, try to analyze the situation and your behaviors to determine why failure occurred. If you find something that appears to be correctable, change the behavior and give it another try.

3. Discuss the differences you are experiencing in your interactions with others who have had similar experiences. There is no need to reinvent the wheel. Managers can learn vicariously from other people's successes and failures.

4. In those areas in which you are dealing with groups who are different, use community resources or agencies who have a working knowledge of the group in question.

5. Talk directly to the individual involved. Managers should not be embarrassed by acknowledging their lack of experience. Hanamura gives the example of a manager who has never worked with a physically challenged employee.[35] He suggested approaching the person and stating "I want to help all new employees perform well on the job. Having never worked with someone with your particular challenge I would appreciate if you would let me know of any problems or needs you might have when carrying out your assignments."

6. Stay in touch with the popular media and formal research that deal directly with individual differences. By so doing, managers can take advantage of the material being written about non-whites, women, physically disabled, and immigrants regarding their unique needs.

7. Place yourself in nonthreatening situations, or other than work-related situations, where you can simulate the interactions likely to occur within your department. This could come in the form of asking organizational peers (friends) to act out stressful job-related interactions. Alternatively, new behaviors could be attempted during noncritical or critical job assignments to reduce the impact of failure. Such situations allow managers to concentrate on the interaction rather than the task.

8. Consider the interactions you have with people who are different from you as a learning process that works for both parties. You can learn from others who are different from you. At the same time, you can be educating others about yourself, how you function, and what you seek to achieve through the exchange.

Employee Involvement

Employee involvement takes place in four general categories involving important areas of an organization's work environment: work processes, communication, compensation, and personnel actions (see Table 3.3).[36] Reasons for the ongoing interest in employee involvement reflect a number of changes within the business environment, and a realization that employee empowerment can produce positive benefits for the organization. Many of these changes reflect what Bell[37] refers to as a "post-industrial society." As discussed in

TABLE 3.3   Categories of Employee Involvement

Work Processing

- Self-pacing
- Autonomous work teams
- Problem-solving committees
- Quality circles
- Flex-time
- Job rotation

Communication

- Consultation meetings
- Management by objectives
- Counselors or ombudsmen
- Attitude surveys
- Representation on policy-making bodies

Compensation

- Stock distribution plans
- Incentive systems
- Profit sharing

Personnel Actions

- Selection of new co-workers
- Wages, promotions, merit, etc.
- Selection of supervisor

Chapter 1, today's organizations face task environments that are growing exceedingly complex; an explosion of information and information technology; rapid, if not turbulent, external environments, and more sophisticated employees who desire increased levels of self-control. The following examples indicate the positive impact of employee involvement:[38]

> In 1988 IBM paid out $107 million to employees for their suggestions and saved $98 million in the first year alone.

> The Lockheed Corporation spent $700,000 to introduce quality circles and in a four-year period has saved over $5 million.

> The National Association of Suggestion Systems (NASS) indicates that in 1988 its members saved on average about $7,663 for every employee suggestion implemented.

> NASS indicates that in 1988 there was a total bottom-line saving of $2.2 billion resulting from employee participation programs.

Extensive review of the research literature on participative management techniques, however, indicates that the impact of participation is likely to vary depending upon the situational factors found in each setting.[39] By recognizing the complexity and dynamics of the process and determining the situational conditions that support employee involvement, it is possible to reap its benefits.

Necessary Conditions for Employee Involvement

Because employee involvement techniques will not work in all situations, it is managers' responsibility to assess their environment and determine when this management tool should be used. The following represent the six *key dimensions* that impact the viability of employee participation.

Employee Interest

A key element in any attempt to introduce participative management is the degree to which employees want to support the process. Individual differences resulting from personality, age, experience, interest, demographics, and cultural differences have been shown to affect the degree to which employees seek to participate or otherwise enrich their jobs.[40] If employees demonstrate no interest in participating, then it is unlikely that an extensive employee involvement program will work. Any one of these differences can be translated into an unwillingness to take on added responsibility. For example, when Honda attempted to introduce participative management techniques in their new plant in Marysville, Ohio, they were told by many employees that whatever the company wanted was just fine. However, because employees are not interested does not mean that they should not be kept informed, have an open invitation to participate in decision making, or be gradually educated to make their ideas known to management.

Competency

Participative endeavors should reflect a balance between employee competencies and participative requirements. Participation in decision making is effective only if individuals involved in the process have the necessary skills and knowledge.[41] Prerequisite skills and knowledge include content (knowledge about the problem being considered) and process dimensions (problem solving, communication skills, etc.). However, it may be desirable to set task requirements just beyond the present abilities of employees to provide opportunities for them to develop their skills. Employees so challenged show increased motivation and growth.

When considering the issue of competency it is important to ensure that steps have been taken to educate and train participants. Margulies and Black[42] point out that a "fatal flaw" often causing participative decision–making programs to fail is the inadequate training provided to the participants. In many instances, it is necessary to take time to train participants in even the most basic skills of communication, interpersonal dynamics, and problem solving to make participation a viable option.[43]

Time Available

Time must be available to plan and organize the training of individuals who will take part in the decision-making process.[44] To understand why time is such an important resource in the design and implementation of a participative system, we can look at the five process stages Fisher[45] argued managers must work through to make such a system work (see Table 3.4). In those instances where participation is not introduced on a systemwide basis, each of these steps will still have to be considered in some modified form by the implementing manager.

If subordinates possess the relevant information and skills to perform effectively, managers will save time by allowing them to act at their own discretion. This is why the benefits of employee participation are situationally specific.

Managerial Support

For participative management programs to survive and prosper, the manager in charge must be supportive of the process, and must behave in a manner to help ensure its success.[46] As many as 80 percent of North American managers exhibit aspects of a Type A personality.[47] As a group, Type A managers

---

TABLE 3.4   Five Stages of Participative Management Systems Development

1. *Conception:* The point at which a small group of managers conceives the idea of (a) developing a new start-up participative management work system or (b) changing an existing nonparticipative system to a participative management work system. These managers are typically charismatic leaders who will champion the participative philosophy through the early stages of participative management system development.

2. *Incubation:* During this stage, the managers' original ideas are translated into an action plan capable of transforming the organization into a participative management work system. It is during this stage that managers generate and demonstrate organizational support for the participated management system being developed.

3. *Implementation:* At this stage, managers bring on line the structural, process, and ethical/value changes needed to support the new participative management system. Specific changes are likely to occur in existing rules, policies, procedures, job designs, reward and appraisal systems, and training and orientation programs.

4. *Transition:* This stage signifies the end of implementation efforts and the adjustment of organizational members to the new participative management system. It is also the period during which organizational members develop the required competencies to function within and maintain the new management system, and senior management begins to transfer authority and autonomy to lower levels within the organization.

5. *Maturity:* In the mature system, the participative system is in place and fully functional. However, the system continues to evolve as the environment in which the organization functions continue to change.

exhibit behavioral patterns of impatience, irritation, anger, and aggression. These behavioral traits are often in conflict with an employee involvement philosophy. Even if managers verbally support the introduction of employee participation, their dominant behavior short-circuits such support. If the manager is unwilling to transfer power and control to subordinates, and subordinates are not willing to take on new responsibility, there is a tacit "conspiracy of dependence."[48] In other words, subordinates remain dependent upon the decisions of higher management and consequently resist any attempts to introduce participative programs.

Managers who seek to introduce participative programs in their departments must make a conscious effort to understand their own personal motives and control personal impatience or the desire to dominate employees. Without this effort participative programs cannot work.

Cooperative Goals

Cooperative goals lead to perceived goal interdependence for the parties engaged in joint activities. When this occurs, the success of the two parties is linked. Both perceive the likelihood of their success enhanced if the other party succeeds. Consequently, each party attempts to help the other be successful. The net result is that cooperative endeavors result in greater joint performance, especially for complex tasks.[49] The implication for the manager attempting to join forces with subordinates for a cooperative effort is to take steps to ensure that there is perceived goal congruence. This can be accomplished by clearly communicating objectives, negotiating payoff distributions, and openly sharing resources (including information).

Interpersonal Dynamics

It is unlikely that two or more individuals coming from two different organizational levels, groups, or functional areas will agree 100 percent of the time. They are likely to have different views, preferences, information, reference points, and structural orientations. Therefore, the success of any participative effort will be a function of the manner in which the participating individuals interact to solve problems and conflicts when they occur. Because managers are attempting to develop a long-term working relationship with their subordinates, it is important that controversy on important issues is allowed to surface rather than remain hidden and fester.

This is because expressed controversy sensitizes the participants that all is not well. It ensures that questionable views, or courses of action, will not go unchallenged. Such critical challenges represent an important check-and-balance component in the decision-making process. It is the ability of group members to be openly critical of their own actions that helps to ensure high-quality decisions. A classic example of what can happen when controversy is not allowed to surface is the Bay of Pigs fiasco in 1961.[50] In this instance, the late President Kennedy's advisers failed to express their concerns. As a result, poor quality decisions were made. Controversy, when properly handled, also increases the probability that participants buy into and commit to participative efforts. Here again, the manager can play a critical role in helping to ensure success.

First, managers must develop an interpersonal style that does not continually dominate or challenge group members. Next, they must ensure that each participant in the participative effort recognizes the importance of controversy. This can be directly accomplished by *(a)* getting each member to accept the role of a critical evaluator of all group decisions and *(b)* linking free and open communications with the accomplishment of cooperative goals. At the same time, managers must take steps to ensure that they have the necessary skills to handle interpersonal conflicts, encourage team development, facilitate principled negotiations, build rapport and ensure active listening among the group's members. (These topics will be taken up in subsequent chapters.)

Task Complexity

Latham, Winters, and Locke[51] found that when tasks are complex for individuals, participation in decision making is more effective in solving them than if individuals work alone. This only occurs if the participation leads to the discovery of effective task strategies and an increase in the person's self-confidence so that the strategies can be implemented. Strategies and self-confidence have a reciprocal effect on each other. If through participation self-confidence is increased, people persist at a task until they discover effective strategies.

Assertiveness

As environments become more turbulent and complex, organizations are asked to do more with less, structures flatten, and the ranks of middle management dwindle, it is increasingly important that managers value assertive behavior. It is assertive behavior that helps ensure that the manager's needs, values, and expectations are considered by others within, and outside, the organization. In short, it represents an alternative to the manager being powerless, manipulated, and passed by as his or her environment changes. "Assertive behaviors promote equality in human relationships, enabling us to act in our own best interests, to stand up for ourselves without undue anxiety, to express honest feelings comfortably, to exercise personal rights without denying the rights of others."[52]

This definition implies four of the core elements critical to the understanding of assertiveness. First, assertive people are comfortable in communicating and behaving in a manner capable of transmitting their needs, values, beliefs, expectations, and self-image. Next, assertive behaviors involve individuals standing up for their rights and doing so in an interpersonally sensitive manner. Third, although assertive people act to express (protect) their rights, they also consider the rights of others. Last, when attempting to assert themselves within a changing, social environment, individuals must accept personal risk. Personal risk occurs because there is no way of predicting how others will react to assertive behavior.

The Importance of Individual Rights

Personal rights are central to any assertive behavior model. It is only when individuals accept that they have rights that assertive behaviors are likely to be displayed during interpersonal exchanges. Rights are the building blocks upon which we build long-term interpersonal relationships. The question that is often asked, however, is "Where do these rights come from?" In the simplest of terms, these rights come from the recognition that we are human beings and that regardless of roles, position, organizational setting, or country, all individuals have rights. The existence of such rights was expressed in the "Universal Declaration of Human Rights" passed by the United Nations General Assembly in 1948, and is clearly reflected in the recent events in Eastern Europe and the former Soviet Union. The list presented in Table 3.5 represents those rights most often mentioned as the basis of an assertive style. When you approach all interpersonal relationships with the realization that all parties have the same rights (one person's rights cannot automatically negate the rights of others) your approach to management will begin to change.

Mini exercise—To help you appreciate the importance of personal rights, try the following exercise. Begin by selecting one of the rights listed in Table 3.5 to act as the basis for an imaginary daydream. To obtain the most from your daydream, you should select a right which, although important to you, you would have the most difficulty accepting. Once you have made your selection and satisfied yourself that you understand what that right implies, please complete the following steps:

Step 1. Place yourself in a comfortable position, take a few deep breaths and relax.

TABLE 3.5   Personal Rights

• The right to have rights	• The right to be independent
• The right to be successful	• The right not to assert one's self
• The right to be listened to	• The right to refuse requests without feeling guilty
• The right to be left alone	
• The right to ask for what you want	• The right to make mistakes
• The right to take full responsibility for one's self	• The right not to explain
	• The right to change one's mind
• The right to say "I don't know."	• The right to not be liked
• The right to say "I don't understand."	• The right to appear illogical to others
	• The right to say "I don't care."

Step 2. Close your eyes and imagine that you have the right that you have selected. Imagine how your life would change (e.g., your interaction with others; how you would feel about yourself and other people; and if the outcomes from the interpersonal exchange would change in any way). To breathe life into your fantasy, you might want to think about a particular situation either at work or at home. Take about two to three minutes to complete Step 2. (Relax for a few minutes before going on to Step 3.)

Step 3. Close your eyes for a second time and imagine that the right you were given in Step 2 has been suddenly taken away. Again think about how your life would change and how you would behave without that right. Do you feel worse off for having lost the right so recently gained? How do you feel about yourself and others? Would you like to have that right back? Allow this second fantasy to continue for a minute or two.

Step 4. (optional) After completing Steps 1 through 3 you may want to discuss your experience with a close friend. At this point, you may want to consider the following questions: What right did you select and why? What did you learn about rights and assertiveness by doing this mini exercise? Did you find that you felt either better about yourself or freer when the right was yours to use?

The Passive–Aggressive Continuum

When discussing the concept of assertiveness, it is useful to do so in terms of the passive–aggressive continuum (see Figure 3.4). Where managers fall on this continuum reflects how they would respond to questions about winning and losing, staff competencies, life positions, individual rights, personal responsibilities, etc. It is the authors' belief that the appropriate position for managers in the upcoming decade is to behave in the assertive zone.

The term *zone* is used to imply that appropriate assertive behavior is not the midpoint between passive and aggressive behavior. Instead, assertive behavior is made up of both initiating and responding components. Depending upon the situation, manager's assertive behavior may move toward the aggressive or passive sides of the continuum. However, assertive managers never disregard the underlying attitudes and beliefs that support an assertive stance, nor do they ever behave in an interpersonally insensitive manner. As we will see in Chapter 12, managers may correctly ignore an existing conflict within their department because long-term objectives would be better served by doing so, or the feelings and rights of others would be better served by such action. On the surface, the managers' behavior appears passive in nature but instead reflects their right not to assert themselves. When dealing with a crisis, however, it may be more appropriate for managers to assert themselves or even to behave

FIGURE 3.4

The passive–aggressive continuum

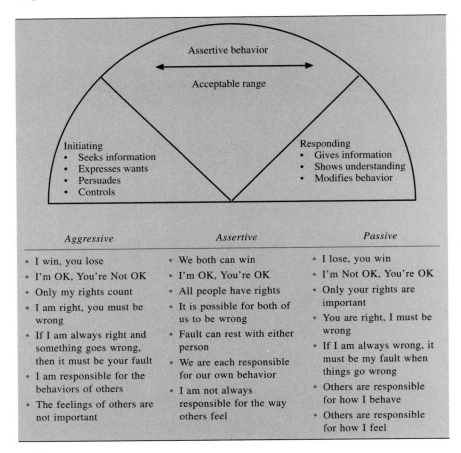

Aggressive	Assertive	Passive
• I win, you lose	• We both can win	• I lose, you win
• I'm OK, You're Not OK	• I'm OK, You're OK	• I'm Not OK, You're OK
• Only my rights count	• All people have rights	• Only your rights are important
• I am right, you must be wrong	• It is possible for both of us to be wrong	• You are right, I must be wrong
• If I am always right and something goes wrong, then it must be your fault	• Fault can rest with either person	• If I am always wrong, it must be my fault when things go wrong
• I am responsible for the behaviors of others	• We are each responsible for our own behavior	• Others are responsible for how I behave
• The feelings of others are not important	• I am not always responsible for the way others feel	• Others are responsible for how I feel

in an aggressive manner. A shift to the left on the aggressive–passive continuum might be necessary to achieve long-term goals, better serve the rights of others, or because there is insufficient time to wait and see what happens next.

Behavioral and Emotional Consequences of Assertiveness

One direct benefit of assertive behavior is that managers increase the probability that they will achieve personal goals and objectives. Furthermore, assertive managers are more likely to develop feelings of self-confidence and self-esteem by achieving more, and by developing positive and open relationships with others. Others are also more likely to respect and value managers who are upfront, honest, and interpersonally sensitive. Table 3.6 presents five techniques generally associated with assertive behavior.

TABLE 3.6 Assertive Techniques for the Manager

Be persistent	Repeat your request over and over again. Repeated communications will be interpersonally sensitive, well timed and present positions in new and different ways—possibly with additional support material.
Conduct principled negotiations	Offer to negotiate with the other party to arrive at a solution that will satisfy both individuals and at the same time allow both to maintain their dignity (the concept of principled negotiation will be covered in Chapters 6 and 7).
Share information	Be willing to share all information that is relevant to the issue at hand. This will include information about one's self—feelings, needs, expectations, values, etc.
Take risks	Be willing to be converted, listen to the views of the other individual. If necessary, agree in principle or go with the odds.
Seek out negative feedback	Demonstrate a willingness to accept constructive criticism by seeking out and responding to feedback which addresses personal weaknesses and errors.

Followership and Managing One's Boss

"Organizations stand and fall partly on the basis of how well their leaders lead, but partly also on the basis of how well their followers follow."[53] Some behavioral scientists argue that activities associated with the follower role dominate most of the manager's time and energy, and account for most of an organization's success.[54] It is time that we change our attitudes toward followership and begin to understand what we must do to become effective followers as well as effective leaders.

Characteristics of Effective Followers

There are two behavioral dimensions that are critical in predicting the overall success of a follower: independent critical thinking and active assertive behavior.[55] These two dimensions can be used to describe a number of follower types—only one of which is likely to be effective (see Figure 3.5).

Among ineffective followers those who are classified as *sheep* are passive and dependent. They need constant supervision and direction and will only perform tasks that are assigned to them. They are poor followers because they take up the leader's time, do not cope well with change, and contribute little to the innovation and creativity of an organization.

Alienated followers—critical thinkers who function independently—are passive in their response to what takes place within the organization. This passivity may reflect their personality, the organizational culture, or the fact that this particular employee has been "turned off" by a boss. In the latter

FIGURE 3.5

Follower types

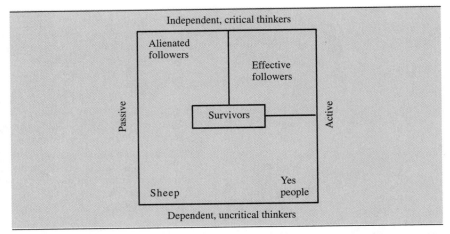

Source: "In Praise of Followers," by Robert Kelly, *Harvard Business Review,* November–December, 1988, p. 142.

case, alienated followers may develop a negative perception of the organization as a whole. Such individuals may become withdrawn critics and, by so doing, threaten the morale of other employees.

Yes people are active but derive all their direction from the boss. They are individuals who try to focus on what they believe will make the boss happy. They spend more time analyzing their boss rather than the relevant characteristics of the situation. Such individuals work well with bosses who are dogmatic, autocratic, or who do not like confrontation. The net impact can be a stagnant, unresponsive department that is unable to adjust to changing environmental demands.

The fourth category of less-than-effective followers is the *survivor*. They engage in just enough initiative and critical thinking to get by, but no more. Consequently, survivors give their bosses a false sense of security but never really contribute to their potential.

Effective followers are critical thinkers who can act independently of the boss, and at the same time be proactive rather than reactive when interacting with their environment. They provide the boss with the resources necessary to achieve excellence. As for specific attributes, effective followers have the following qualities:

1. Self-management.   In essence, effective followers manage themselves. They are able to develop a relationship with the boss that can be best described as a team of two—more like equals than superior and subordinate. Perceived in this manner, effective followers are individuals who readily accept the process of delegation and employee participation. In keeping with the proactive stance of effective followers, they will seek out opportunities to take on unsupervised responsibilities. The process of self-management, when tied to empowerment, lightens the supervisory responsibilities of the boss and thereby allows a wider span of control.

2. Flexible commitment.   Effective followers buy into the goals and objectives of the organization. Linked with item 1, these individuals see themselves working jointly with their boss to achieve organizational objectives.

3. Scanning.   Closely related is the need for followers to continually scan their environment for potential problems and opportunities. It is the subordinate who is closest to the action who is the richest source of information. Effective followers gladly take on the role of scanner as a shared responsibility with their boss.

4. Competence.   Effective followers actively seek *(a)* those skills necessary for personal success, and *(b)* training and development opportunities in those attitude, skill, and knowledge areas identified as deficient. The ongoing drive for growth and improvement on the part of followers ensures that they are not only able to perform core tasks but will also be ready to undertake new and challenging tasks not previously encountered.

5. Courage.   Ultimately, effective followers have the courage to act on their own, to stand for what they believe to be right, and to interact freely and openly with the boss. Where effective followership is not rewarded, managers must also have the courage to leave the company if necessary.

> For example, Kelly describes the action of an employee at Beech-Nut who demonstrated such courage.[56] The employee suspected that the apple juice being purchased at below market cost was adulterated. On the basis of this suspicion, the employee suggested to his boss that the company no longer use the new supplier. The employee's suggestion was turned down and he was told to back up these suspicions with proof. After collecting what he believed was strong evidence, the employee again approached management to recommend a change in suppliers. When no action was taken, the employee went higher up the scalar chain of authority but instead of getting action was threatened with dismissal for not being a team player. Finally, the employee approached the company's president but the results were the same—no action. For his efforts, the employee received a performance appraisal that indicated that although he was competent and loyal, he was naive and allowed impractical ideals to color his judgment. Ultimately, the employee resigned. Several years later, Beech-Nut and two members of management were indicted for conspiracy to commit fraud. In the end, the company pleaded guilty. The episode resulted in a $2 million fine and an estimated 20 percent loss in market share.

In this example, followership was operational but leadership was not.

Managing Your Boss

A discussion of followership would be incomplete if we did not consider the manner in which subordinates interact with their bosses. Managers predominately direct their influence downward in the direction of subordinates, as opposed to upward in the direction of their boss. It is the authors' belief that managerial success, and value to the organization, can be enhanced if managers learn to manage the boss. This can be accomplished by using the appropriate attitudes, skills, and knowledge (ASKs) covered in this text when interacting with the boss.

An important first step in managing your boss is to identify the strengths and weaknesses, work style, expectations, and needs that you both bring to the relationship. With this information you are better able to recognize areas of potential conflict and attempt to work in the direction of overcoming, or preventing, these conflicts from interfering with future interactions. This can be accomplished by informing the boss of those areas representing potential differences and suggesting a time and place to discuss these differences in an open and constructive manner. Here too, interpersonal sensitivity plays an important role in producing constructive discussions rather than a negative response from your boss.

The following statements can be helpful when attempting to initiate such an exchange: "This may only represent a misunderstanding on my part but _____," "Let me see if I understand this correctly _____," and "I am not sure if this is important but could we discuss _____." When attempting to address these issues the manager should consider the timing and the number of issues considered.

Closely related is the issue of goal setting. It is important that managers tune into the goals of their boss to correctly establish priorities and allocate resources. If the boss's goals are not apparent, steps should be taken to clarify what they are. Again, this can be accomplished by requesting a meeting devoted to an open discussion of the boss's goals and how they fit with your expectations and departmental needs. It is important that when entering into such a discussion with your boss you are prepared and willing to share all relevant information.

A third aspect of managing your boss is the ability to identify and reward desired behavior. Not only do managers have to identify which subordinate behaviors are important to making them more successful, but the same holds true when subordinates interact with the boss. Just what is it that you want from the boss? Once this decision has been made and examples of this behavior are exhibited by the boss, reward it. A simple sincere "thank you" is often sufficient. If this is insufficient, then a more detailed feedback exchange is required. The key is to keep in mind that positive reinforcement increases desired behaviors. If desired behaviors are not forthcoming, then it is suggested that you revert to the previous example and attempt to communicate to the boss those behaviors that would make your job easier.

Because your boss is an individual, you must accept that he or she has the same feelings and emotions as do other employees. To put this statement in perspective, remember that you are likely to be someone else's boss and we could be talking about you. Once managers accept this fact about their boss, it becomes easier to consider the boss's feelings and emotions. For example, you can assume that your boss does not want to be embarrassed. An embarrassing exchange is likely to attack the boss's self-concept and cause him or her to become defensive or go on the offensive. Therefore, a basic rule in effectively managing bosses is that you should never surprise them. If there is a problem to be discussed always attempt to alert them to any planned exchange. This allows bosses to think the issue through and thereby reduce the likelihood of a defensive response.

All bosses should want to improve the performance of their subordinates. This can often be done through the right type of training and development program specifically designed for the subordinate. Unfortunately, not all organizations have an effective Human Resource Department, or managers with the time to identify training needs and design such a program. Therefore, based upon the characteristics of the effective follower, the subordinate can facilitate the process by identifying his or her own training needs and communicate these needs to the boss. What is important is that you do the leg work and come prepared to explain exactly what you need, why you believe you need the training, and some of the options available with the associated costs. Often the money is there for training, it is just that the manager does not have the time to figure out who needs what, and why.

An ideal way to manage your boss is to free sufficient personal time to be able to offer to take on some of his or her responsibilities. Some managers ask "where do they get this extra time?" The secret is to do all the ASKs covered in this text. If you do, we are confident that you will significantly increase the time available to practice this type of boss management. Next, identify those activities your boss is likely to delegate and at the same time will act as a developmental assignment for you. Carry out this process several times and you significantly increase your value and influence within the department. (This type of boss management assumes that your boss is reasonable and fair, and that he or she will not take advantage of your offer.)

Summary

To be successful in the upcoming decade, managers will have to bring into focus the attitudes and values they bring to organizations. This chapter has attempted to highlight five areas in which management attitude and values will play an important role in determining organizational fit and, ultimately, managerial success. First, managers must deal with their subordinates in an ethical manner. Second, managers must deal with others in an interpersonally sensitive manner, or otherwise long-term relationships will suffer. Third, it was argued that, given the changes in employee characteristics and values, the successful manager in the forthcoming decade will likely increase the role of employee involvement. With employees who are better educated, more in control, more mobile, and better informed, participation in decision making is likely to be a primary technique used to gain subordinates' understanding of and commitment to attaining the organization's goals. Next, given the rates of change facing organizations, the flattening of structures, and the need to do more with less, it is the assertive manager who will survive. Finally, managers of the future must recognize their dual role—that of leader and follower. Effective followership is often overlooked as an ingredient necessary to energize the organization and fuse it into a functional whole.

EXERCISE

3.1. Appropriate Values and Attitudes: EverBright Electrical In-Basket

The EverBright Electrical in-basket case is designed to give each student the opportunity to play the role of Larry Benton, a senior executive in a local utility. The actions Larry takes in response to items in his in-basket reflect his attitudes and values. To obtain the most from this exercise, please follow the steps outlined below.

Step 1. Before the next class meeting, read through the in-basket items for EverBright Electrical presented on the following pages. Do not attempt to respond to any memos, or write any comments on the in-basket. You will have plenty of time to do this during Step 2. Step 1 is your opportunity to read through the entire in-basket without the pressure to act. In this way, you will get a feel for the kind of memos that pass across Larry's desk, the organization for which he works, and the type of people he works with.

Step 2. (Step 2 will also be performed before the next class.) Complete the EverBright in-basket as though you were Larry Benton. Take as long as you want to respond to the memos in the in-basket. To facilitate the organization of your thoughts, write your responses on the bottom or back of each memo. Note that not all memos require action. Some memos provide information only and, once understood, should be filed.

Step 3. (Steps 3 and 4 will be carried out during the next class meeting.) During Step 3, you will meet in small groups of five to six individuals. Each group will review the actions taken by the group's members for each memo and reach a group consensus on what the correct response to each memo should be. In reaching consensus, you should consider *(a)* why each group member responded as he or she did, *(b)* the impact of such action on others, and *(c)* how such action is attuned to the organizational environment likely to exist in the 1990s.

Step 4. The class will assemble and compare group results with the instructor's master list.

Student Instructions for the EverBright Electrical In-Basket

You are asked to assume the role of Larry Benton, Vice President of Human Resource Management for EverBright Electrical. You officially return from a month's vacation on Monday, September 23rd. While you were away, a number of important events occurred. Mary, your executive secretary, had to leave unexpectedly because of personal problems. Her replacement, Ethel, has been acting executive secretary for two and one-half weeks. In addition, a major move was planned for that period and the personnel offices, including training, were moved from downtown to the new uptown utility center during your absence. The offices in the new facility are still being renovated.

Prior to coming to EverBright, you worked in another state for a small utility where you were in charge of the payroll department. You have a total working experience of about 15 years in the utility industry and have been with EverBright for one year. Two years ago, when Bob Headman took over as president of the corporation, he made it clear that he would fill key organizational positions with individuals whose management philosophy was similar to his. To help clarify what makes up an appropriate management philosophy, Bob Headman hired a local consulting group to provide values training for all senior managers at EverBright Electrical. Currently, only 40 percent of EverBright's senior managers have taken the values training.

You return from your vacation Friday, September 20, and are surprised to receive an urgent call from Bob Headman. Circumstances beyond the president's control forced him to ask you to leave immediately for a two-week fact-finding trip to Capital City. While there, you are to assess the political implications of constructing a nuclear power plant at the edge of the country's largest national park. The president asks you to catch a plane to Capital City on Sunday evening, September 22, so that you are ready for an early start on Monday morning.

You couldn't make it to your office on Saturday because of a previous family commitment, your nephew's wedding. You were so rushed in getting ready for your trip to Capital City that you decided to stop at your new office on the way to the airport and complete whatever business was in your in-basket. You believe that to let this sit for another two weeks after your month's vacation is asking for trouble. Although you have not talked to any of your staff since your return, you have had several conversations with Mr. Headman. You call Ethel to introduce yourself and alert her of your plans, but find that she is away for the weekend. You ask her house-sitter to tell Ethel that you plan to stop at the office Sunday to review your in-basket. As a final point, you tell the sitter that you plan to leave instructions for Ethel as part of your review.

You arrive at the office at 4:00 P.M. and find it deserted, as you expected. Although there is little reason for your staff to come in on weekends, you realize that this may produce a problem because all the main office files are locked and there will be no support staff. Your personal files are in transit from the downtown office and will be delivered to the new office facility on Monday. Further complicating your task is the fact that the telephone system is not functioning. Consequently, the only way you can communicate with others on a Sunday is to leave written messages.

The memos and other correspondence that appear on the following pages represent what you find in your in-basket. You have also been provided with a two-month calendar and an organization chart for your personal use.

September						
Sunday	*Monday*	*Tuesday*	*Wednesday*	*Thursday*	*Friday*	*Saturday*
1	2	3	4	5	6	7
8	9	10	11	12	13	14
15	16	17	18	19	20	21
22	23	24	25	26	27	28
29	30					

October						
Sunday	*Monday*	*Tuesday*	*Wednesday*	*Thursday*	*Friday*	*Saturday*
		1	2	3	4	5
6	7	8	9	10	11	12
13	14	15	16	17	18	19
20	21	22	23	24	25	26
27	28	29	30	31		

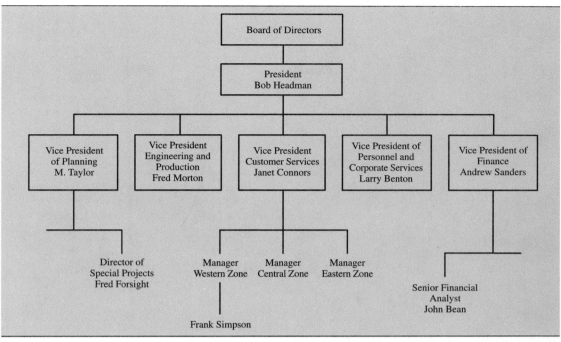

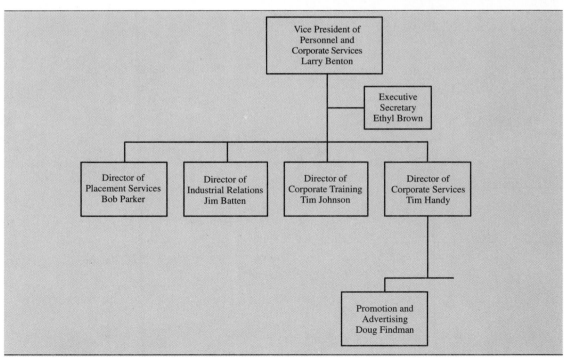

Item 1

To: Larry Benton, Vice President, Human Resource Management
From: Ethel Brown
Date: September 16, 1994

Dear Mr. Benton:

This is my first day on the job and I wanted to thank you in writing for agreeing to give me the chance to act as your executive secretary. I know that Mr. Headman has been in touch with you several times while you were on vacation to discuss this matter. I have also had the opportunity to meet with Mary before she left and have been following her instructions on how you like the office managed.

I am sure that upon your return, we will have ample time to discuss such matters in greater detail and develop the same type of positive relationship you and Mary had.

I look forward to your return.

Item 2

To: Larry Benton, Vice President Human Resource Management
From: Bob Parker, Placement Services
Date: September 18, 1994

CONFIDENTIAL

As I mentioned before you left on vacation, I followed up on the applicants for the new position in customer services. As you recall, my special interest in one candidate stemmed from his working for the government agency directly responsible for environment and environmental impact studies. As it turns out, I think we can get this person if we give him what he wants. To do so we have to bend a few of the rules and give him a salary about 10 percent above the salary range for that position.

I think we should do it because he indicated he would bring with him three confidential data disks from the agency that would save us thousands of hours to research and duplicate. If we had that data now we would blow the government's case out of the water and have a clear shot at locating the new power plant at the edge of the national park.

All I need is your approval and it's a go.

Item 3

First Federal Bank

September 10, 1994

Mr. Larry Benton, Vice President,
Human Resource Management
EverBright Electrical
Box 1641
Seashore, Maine
01256

Dear Mr. Benton:

I am writing to ask for assistance in a matter of some importance. We have always appreciated the relationship between First Federal and EverBright and look forward to providing your organization with these services in the future.

Allow me, however, to get directly to the reason I am writing. One of your company's employees, David P. Preston, has asked for a rather large loan at our bank. Because of the nature of the loan, the short length of time Mr. Preston has lived in Seashore, Maine, and the fact that EverBright has been his sole employer since his arrival, I hope that you will give us some much needed information. Specifically, please consider the following questions and jot down your opinions as they relate to Mr. Preston.

- Is he a dependable employee?

- Have you had disciplinary problems with Mr. Preston? If so, what kinds of problems?

- Does the employee have any problems with substance abuse?

- How does this employee get along with other employees?

- Has the employee been part of any employee assistance program?

I would greatly appreciate whatever assistance you could give in this matter, and I look forward to our continued cooperation. If you have any questions, please feel free to give me a call.

Sincerely,

John Needsit
V.P. Consumer Loans

Item 4

To: Larry Benton, Vice President, Human Resource Management
From: Jim Batten, Director, Industrial Relations
Date: September 19, 1994

Re: Forthcoming Negotiations with CUTD Local 234

We have to get together as soon as you get back from vacation to discuss our negotiation strategy with the CUTD. I think that this is a year that we can really put it to the union and take advantage of the unexpected surge in revenues. I would appreciate if you would consider the following points before we meet.

- The national union has recently fought several large strikes and its war chest is greatly depleted.
- The economy in our region is at an all-time low resulting in a minimum of employee mobility.
- Internal politics in the union make it unlikely they will reach a consensus soon.
- The union's chief negotiator has minimal experience and lacks aggressiveness. How he got in is beyond me.

See you when you return.

Item 5

To: Larry Benton, Vice President, Human Resource Management
From: Bob Headman
Date: August 23, 1994

Just a quick note on what we discussed this morning. (I realize you will be on vacation when this reaches your desk, but it will act as a reminder when you return.) We clarified some key points but I want to make sure there is total agreement. Allow me to express my perceptions of what we decided.

- That 1995 would be a year of expansion for EverBright and that your department would undertake the needed human resources studies to ensure the needed supply of competent staff. These reports will be on my desk by December 1st.

(Item 5 continued)

(Item 5 concluded)

- Some effort should be made to have a better representation of minorities within our work force. This will not be done through a quota system but by working with local organizations to ensure that qualified applicants are found and that they apply.
- Given the difficulty we have had with pay equity problems in the past six months, begin an analysis of how to cut down on such problems in the future.
- Have your department make recommendations as to whether or not the personnel function at EverBright should be further decentralized so as to better reflect the geographical dispersion of our company.
- Because you are heading up the special task force on nuclear power generation, and will frequently be called out of town unexpectedly, we agreed that you would make no new external commitments that would lock you into specific dates for at least the next six months.

Item 6

Larry Benton, Vice President, Human Resource Management
EverBright Electric
Box 1641
Seashore, Maine   02156
August 15, 1994

Dear Mr. Benton:

It is once again time to plan for the 1995 Business Conference sponsored by the MBAs at Northern University. The topic this year is "The Personnel Function in the 1990s." We again plan to welcome over 150 business people and approximately 400 of our students. The date of this year's conference is February 4th and 5th. A closing dinner will be held on the second evening.

The members of the organizing committee were so impressed with your workshop on information systems in the human resource management function that they decided to invite you to be our keynote speaker at this year's conference. I recall that you were interested in taking on such a task. As we discussed last year, all expenses will be paid and you will receive a small stipend as keynote speaker.

I have also enclosed the tentative program for the two-day conference and the proposed topics for each of the planning and working sessions. Our group looks forward to your participation. Please write or call to confirm your continued interest.

Respectfully,

Thomas Johns
Program Coordinator

Item 7

To: Larry Benton, Vice President, Human Resource Management
From: Ray Harden, Office Manager—Camden, Western Zone
Date: September 4, 1994

I am writing to you as a person of last resort. I have a cashier clerk under my supervision, Helen Weldon, who has been nothing but trouble since I hired her. My recommendation to Frank Simpson, my immediate supervisor was that she should not be hired. He ignored my recommendation and put forth her name alone to personnel and payroll as the person to be hired. Helen does not carry her share of the work, is absent far more than anyone else, and continually comes in late. She is also disrespectful toward customers. When I bring these matters to Mr. Simpson's attention, he tells me that part of my job is to train and develop my staff and that it's up to me to solve employee problems.

I am not one to gossip, but I do know that Mr. Simpson is a married man and I have now observed both him and Ms. Weldon in somewhat compromising situations—once at a local theater and once at a neighborhood lounge.

I don't know where else to turn and felt that you would be the person to contact. Please help me out of this situation.

Item 8

September 10, 1994

Larry Benton, Vice President, Human Resource Management
EverBright Electrical
Box 1641
Seashore, Maine
01256

Dear Mr. Benton:

Allow me to introduce myself. My name is Frank Spears and I am the Human Resource Manager for Central Michigan Electric. I attended a conference this past week in New Orleans and had a conversation with Bob Headman, your CEO, at one of the sessions. He mentioned that you were in the early stages of setting up an assessment center for the analysis of selection and training needs. It so happens that we just brought such a center on-line. It took us about two years to get the bugs worked out. As president of the Michigan Association for the Advancement of Assessment Center Technology, Headman suggested that I forward our package to you. You will find the following materials enclosed:

(Item 8 continued)

(Item 8 concluded)

- Overview of structure and schedule for setting up a three and one-half day assessment center.
- Six samples of our simulations that act as core material to our program.
- Training package for assessors.
- Instruction manual for running team meetings to achieve a consensus on rating assessment center participants.
- Support forms and analysis sheets.

Should you have any questions on the enclosed material, feel free to give me a call. I would be more than happy to discuss some of our ups and downs. The only thing that I ask in return is that you send me a copy of your final AC package when it is completed and that you share your results with local industry.

Respectfully,

Frank Spears
Human Resource Manager

Item 9

To: Larry Benton, Vice President, Human Resource Management
From: Bob Headman
Date: September 10, 1994

While you were away, I ran across the following article. I thought it might be helpful in both designing and establishing some normative data for our planned organizational study.

**ARTICLE TITLE: North American Workers Need Respect:
                              Survey Finds Managers Lack Interest**

(Assume article's text and survey results appear here.)

Areas surveyed: job content, benefits, how work is organized, pay, quality of products and customer services, management effectiveness, relevance of job performance and review process, relevance of career development and training.

Item 10

To: Larry Benton, Vice President, Human Resource Management
From: Tim Johnson, Director of Corporate Training
Date: September 1, 1994

Here are the data you asked me to collect for you. I have found two programs that fit your needs. I believe that if you go to either one you will significantly improve the contribution you make to the long-term planning of this organization. In fact, they are programs from which several of our senior people might gain.

Program A	*Program B*
• Dalton University, Senior Management Program for Strategic Planning, Boston	• Center for Strategic Studies, Residence Program, Toronto
• Program offers option for university MBA credit if participant takes written exam at the end of the program and writes a term paper.	• No university credit available, but participant does receive a certificate of completion.
• Three-week program in one-week modules, spread over six months.	• Combination residence and correspondence. Residence made up of two one-week sessions over a six-month period; correspondence involves 20 written units plus textbook analysis and assignments.

Program A		*Program B*	
• Tuition—$2,900 U.S.		• Tuition—$3,100 U.S.	
• Additional expenses (U.S.)		• Additional expenses (U.S.)	
• Meals	$1,050	• Meals	$1,050
• Accommodations	525	• Accommodations	1,400
• Airfare	750	• Airfare	900
	$2,325		$3,350

Program A	*Program B*
• Tuition payable prior to start of program.	• Tuition payable prior to start of program.
• Initial in-residence week scheduled for November 15, 1994. Next program July 1995.	• Initial in-residence week scheduled for November 1, 1994. Next program unscheduled.
• General industry acceptance: medium to high based on sample of 36 past attendees.	• General industry acceptance: high based on sample of 27 past attendees.

If you need further information or the raw data supporting these figures, you should feel free to give me a call.

Item 11

To: All Vice Presidents, Directors, and Department Heads
From: Bob Headman
Date: September 1, 1994
Subject: Budget Overruns

As you all know, the Public Utilities Board has put aside our application for an increase in rates. Given the makeup of the Board and the present economic climate, it is unlikely that we will see a significant increase in the near future. Therefore, we have to take steps to ensure that we stay within our projected budgets. To facilitate this move to control expenditures, I am requesting that any overrun in budget be first approved through this office. This must be done account by account; in other words, intradepartmental transfers between accounts cannot be used to bypass this request.

Item 12

To: Larry Benton, Vice President, Human Resource Management
From: John Bean, Senior Financial Analyst
Date: September 20, 1994

Attached, you will find the third quarter, cumulative budget for the Human Resource Management Department. Data collection techniques are consistent with those used for Quarters 1 and 2. Should you have questions, please give me a call.

Projected and Cumulative Budget
Human Resource Management Department
Third Quarter—August 31, 1994
Year-end—December 31, 1994

Account	Projected Budget (in dollars)	Cumulated Actual Expenditures (August 31, 1991)
Travel	$ 7,500	$ 4,320
Training and Development	45,000	44,000
Salary	600,000	450,000
Advertising	15,000	10,750
Office Supplies	5,000	4,200
Office Equipment	22,500	11,047
Telephone and Long Distance Charges	2,500	1,000
Planning Retreat	5,000	0

Item 13

August 6, 1994

Larry Benton, Vice President, Human Resource Management
EverBright Electrical
Box 1641
Seashore, Maine 01245

Dear Mr. Benton:

As the local president of the Affirmative Action Association of America (AAAA), I am writing to ask for your assistance in collecting information about the affirmative action programs implemented by local organizations. For our group to be effective in redressing past injustices, it is important for us to better understand the role of local industry. Therefore, we are asking directors, vice presidents, and managers of the human resource function to complete a brief questionnaire and return it to us in the return envelope provided.

If you have any questions, please feel free to contact me at 952-5763 or my administrative assistant, Brenda Whitton, at 952-5762.

Thank you for your assistance.

Respectfully,

Alfred P. Boltson
President

Item 14

September 5, 1994

Larry Benton, Vice President, Human Resource Management
EverBright Electrical
Box 1641
Seashore, Maine 01245

Dear Mr. Benton:

Several weeks ago we sent you a questionnaire and asked you to complete it at your convenience. We at Affirmative Action Association of America (AAAA) are attempting to improve the employment opportunities for minority groups in this area. To date, we have not received a response from your organization. Realizing that you are all busy, I would nonetheless appreciate it if you could complete and mail your questionnaire as soon as possible. In the event that you have lost or misplaced your original, I have enclosed a second copy with a self-addressed envelope.

Again, thank you for your time.

Respectfully,

Alfred P. Boltson
President

Item 15

To: ___Larry Benton___

Date: ___Sept 18th___   Time ___9:30 a.m.___

Message

Mr. Ms. ___Alfred P. Boltson___

Of ___AAAA___

Telephone___( )___   ___952-5763___
Area Code   Number   Extension

Telephoned		Wants to see you	
Will call back		Returned your call	
Please call		Urgent	

Indicated that he would like you to call him back and indicate whether we are going to participate in his survey—I attempted to explain that you were out of town but this didn't seem to make any difference

Received by _____

Item 16

To: Larry Benton, Vice President, Human Resource Management
From: Tim Banks, Plant Manager
        Nuclear Plant 1
Date: September 14, 1994

Larry:

I would like to thank you for offering to help with some of my problems here at the plant. Making some of these administrative decisions has been difficult, because I am new on the job, and have spent most of my career on the technical side. As requested, I have outlined two cases that I hope you will comment on. In other words, how can I increase the effectiveness of my staff? Your speedy response would be greatly appreciated because I have to take action on two of these cases next week.

Thanks again,

CASE 1

As you know, we occasionally have to buy new vehicles for our transmission and distribution people. My predecessor always made the decision for the men, to ensure that the poorest truck was replaced and to make sure that the men wouldn't fight over who received new equipment. Unfortunately, no one ever seemed happy with the plant manager's decision except the individual who received the new truck. Rarely was the poorest truck driven by the most senior, best, or safest driver. Consequently, it took weeks before the morale of our drivers got back to normal.

I have always found our drivers to be reasonable individuals and believe there must be a better way to allocate new vehicles. We are scheduled to bring in two new trucks next week.

CASE 2

Looking at the safety record for this plant, I have noticed that we have more than our share of breakdowns in the reactor's cooling system. This is partly due to the age of the plant and the equipment, which represents first-generation nuclear technology. The problem represents the number of instances where the potential for radioactive release may have occurred or may be about to occur. The practice followed by the maintenance supervisor has been to allow crew members to determine who goes into contaminated areas. Again, the results obtained by the maintenance supervisor are less than desired. When the decision was left to them, the crew members traditionally selected the most junior and inexperienced individuals to go into the contaminated areas and make repairs. Unfortunately, not all crew members are equally experienced. Even when they are, it is unlikely they will complete repairs in the same length of time. I like the idea of getting employee involvement in management decisions, but the results in this instance don't appear to satisfy our needs.

Item 17

To: Larry Benton, Vice President, Human Resource Management
From: Fred Forsight, Director of Special Projects
Date: September 12, 1994

I am happy to inform you that the new capital budget from Headman's office has been approved. Included in the budget was a go-ahead for the planning phase of the new training facilities at head office. As it stands now, it looks as though approximately $150,000 will be available for the new space. Obviously, you are a hit with Headman. The training facilities should fit in well with the new renovations that are taking place.

The only thing required is that you come up with some preliminary plans as to what you need in the new training center. We do have some time, but I hope you can get back to me by the end of October.

Item 18

To: Larry Benton, Vice President, Human Resource Management
From: Bob Parker, Placement Services
Date: September 2, 1994

CONFIDENTIAL

Larry:

Pursuant to our conversation about Headman rejecting your proposal on affirmative action programs, I want to make the following suggestions. I have been around here a lot longer than most, and I have come to understand the old man better than anyone. The best that I can figure is that your proposals were acceptable, but weren't packaged correctly. Headman has always been impressed with fancy presentations filled with charts, tables, and detailed print-outs. Your presentation just didn't fill this need. Therefore, forget that he told you to start from scratch and that the report and supporting data were not worthy of a vice president in his organization.

I have your report. Just give me the go-ahead and I will use a new piece of software I have to rework your data, put it in a form that will knock the old man's socks off, and get you off the hook. It's amazing what this new software can do to old data. To start from scratch would just be a waste of your time. It could take you months to do what he wants. I'll modify the data just enough so that he'll think it's all new.

The only thing I ask in return is that if the affirmative programs are brought on-line, I am allowed to coordinate them and present our results to the next Human Resource Management conference scheduled for next spring in California.

Thanks,

Item 19

To: Larry Benton, Vice President, Human Resource Management
From: Doug Findman, Promotion & Advertising
Date: September 18, 1994

Here we go again — the people down at *The Gazette* blew another one of our ads. It was the full-page ad you and I wrote to counter the union's charge that we were involved in brainwashing training techniques and engaged in union-busting practices.

(Item 19 continued)

(Item 19 concluded)

As is standing practice, my department provided a rough sketch for them to use in designing a layout. Not only did they do a terrible job on the layout (the worst job I've seen yet), but they put it in the paper on the wrong day and got some key phrases mixed up. It sounded as though we were agreeing with what the union said. Nevertheless, they still want us to pay—$2,500. I talked to the editor, but she said the only person she wants to hear from is you —and what she wants to hear is the sound of money. I guess I'm just not senior enough.

The editor's name and address are:

Betty Sandford, Managing Editor
Daily Gazette
P.O. Box 1118
Seashore, Maine
01256

I'm sure you'll know what to do.

Thanks,

cc: Tim Handy
Director of Corporate Services

Item 20

To: Larry Benton
From: Bob Parker, Placement
Date: September 16, 1994

In keeping with our affirmative action guidelines, we have recently hired a qualified employee from a minority (Native American). He will begin work as a lineman in the Western zone on October 18. Do you want to do anything to facilitate his entry into the work group and thus reduce any problems associated with differences in culture or crew expectations?

We have several weeks to plan for this but I think it is important enough that we take the necessary steps to ensure that no problems occur.

Item 21

September 16, 1994

Larry Benton, Vice President, Human Resource Management
EverBright Electrical
Box 1641
Seashore, Maine 01256

Dear Mr. Benton:

I am writing to bring to your attention a matter that I believe represents a problem in EverBright's promotion policy. I have been with the company for 22 years and have always been considered a good employee. I believe that my personnel file and performance reviews speak for themselves. In addition, I have been a collections and customer records supervisor for the past six and one-half years. During that time I have filled in on three occasions for Bill Fillmore, the credit and collections manager during his illnesses and rehabilitation. My tenure as acting manager ranged from three to six months. In each instance, I was told that I had discharged my duties above expectations. Because of this experience and my expressed interest, I thought that if the position of credit and collections manager ever went on the board for open competition I would have an excellent chance to get it. Therefore, when it was announced that Bill Fillmore would go on permanent long-term disability, I truly believed that I had a shot for the position. I now know that I was wrong!!!!!

To begin with, the job was never even posted on the board and was filled with an internal candidate from another department. This particular individual has only been with the company for 10 years and, in my opinion, has little or no experience in collections. Although I try to be positive and upbeat at all times, this entire affair has been a personal blow to me.

I hope that you will look into this matter. I trust that in the future this type of backroom decision making will be discontinued.

Respectfully,

Jeff Backmen

Item 22

To: Larry Benton, Vice President, Human Resource Management
From: Tim Johnson
Date: September 20, 1994

I realize that you will be out of town, but I wanted to bring the following item to your attention. As you requested in August, the department's planning retreat was postponed for three months until the weekend of November 9. In the past, the location, agenda, problem areas, process, and who should attend was determined by Jim Harden, your predecessor. I would like to know if you are going to follow this procedure and, if so, when we might get together to discuss the matter.

Item 23

To: Larry Benton, Vice President, Human Resource Management
From: Tim Johnson
Date: September 4, 1994

Here are the evaluation data on the outside trainers we have used in the past 12 months. On the basis of the objective criteria we established, I have ordered by rank the individuals or companies used. This information should prove helpful when selecting external resource people in the future.

Firm Individuals Rank High (1) to Low (6)	Random Participant Evaluations, 1 to 10 Scale (10 High)	Performance Test, 1 to 10 Scale (10 High)	Average Cost per Diem
1. Jim Hilton Hilton Associates	10	10	$ 950
2. Betty Steadmen PMJ, Inc.	9	8	950
3. Protrain, Inc.	10	7	1,500
4. Bob Kidmore	7	7	1,000
5. Janet Sullivan	7	5	1,000
6. Lester Small, Excellence, Inc.	5	5	1,750

Not only does Jim Hilton head the list but he has indicated a willingness to reserve a large block of his time over the next nine months.

Item 24

To: Larry Benton, Vice President, Human Resource Management
From: Bob Headman
Date: September 19, 1994

While you were away, I had a meeting with Lester Small from Excellence, Inc. As you know, Excellence, Inc., has done considerable performance improvement training and has done some training for us in the past. Les made a presentation on what he and his group would do if they received the contract for the senior and midmanagement training we have scheduled beginning in January. I don't want to impinge on your area, but I was considerably impressed with what he had to say and suggest that we use his program.

I think we should move quickly on this so we don't lose the opportunity to get Les's commitment for the 60 days of training we need.

Item 25

To: All Vice Presidents, Directors, and Department Heads
From: Andrew Sanders, V.P. Finance
Date: September 20, 1994

Re: Financial Constraint

As you all know, EverBright is in the process of expansion and is proposing construction of a new nuclear plant at Point Hope. Because of the uncertainty of the project and the need to direct our funds to key expansion projects, all managers are advised to plan for a 10 percent across-the-board budget cut for the 1995 fiscal year. The board, Robert Headman, and I know that we can count on all managers to support this effort. You all realize that in the long run we will be better for it.

Item 26

To: Larry Benton, Vice President, Human Resource Management
From: Jim Batten
Date: August 22, 1994

Attached you will find the report you wanted on the five-year forecast for labor supply and demand likely to be faced by EverBright. It took considerable effort to bring together, and I know I would not have been able to do the subject justice had it not been for my staff. Should you have any questions on its contents, appendixes, data, and conclusions, please feel free to give me a call.

Item 27

To: Larry Benton, Vice President, Human Resource Management
From: Bob Headman
Date: September 19, 1994

I will not get a chance to talk to you personally before you leave on your trip— so I want to mention that I presented to the board of directors your report on the five-year forecast for the supply and demand of labor in this region. The board was greatly appreciative of your efforts. Most directors said it was one of the finest reports received in a long time. Keep up the good work.

End Notes

1. D. Katz, "The functional approach to the study of attitudes," *Public Opinion Quarterly,* Vol. 24, 1960: 163–176; J. J. Rosenberg, "A structural theory of attitudes," *Public Opinion Quarterly,* Summer 1960: 319–40; M. Fishbein and I. Ajzen, *Belief, Attitude, Intention, and Behavior: An Introduction to Theory and Research,* Addison-Wesley Publishing, Reading, Mass, 1975; D. W. Organ and T. Bateman, *Organizational Behavior: An Applied Psychological Approach,* 3rd ed., Business Publications, Plano, Tex, 1986: 191–222; T. Tourangeau and K. A. Rasinski, "Cognitive processes underlying context effects in attitude measurement," *Psychological Bulletin,* Vol. 103, 1988: 299–314.

2. Katz, 1960.

3. M. Rokeach, "Attitude change and opinion change," *Public Opinion Quarterly,* Vol. 30, 1966: 529–548; L. Mann, *Social Psychology,* John Wiley & Sons, New York, 1969; A. W. Wicker, "Attitudes versus actions: The relationship of verbal and overt behavioral responses to attitude objects," *Journal of Social Issues,* Vol. 25, 1969: 41–78; M. Fishbein and I. Ajzen, 1975; Organ and Bateman, 1986; Tourangeau and Rasinski, 1988.

4. Rokeach, 1966.

5. E. E. Jones and H. B. Gerard, *Foundations of Social Psychology,* John Wiley & Sons, New York, 1967; Organ and Bateman, 1986.

6. H. W. Dickson and E. McGinnies, "Affectivity and arousal of attitudes as measured by galvanic skin responses," *American Journal of Psychology,* October 1966: 584–589; Jones and Gerard, 1967; A. J. DuBrin, *Effective Business Psychology,* Reston Publishing, Reston, Va., 1985; J. L. Gibson, J. M. Ivancevich, and J. H. Donnelly, Jr., *Organizations: Behavior, Structure, Process,* Irwin, Burr Ridge, Ill., 1994.

7. Jones and Gerard, 1967.

8. Jones and Gerard, 1967; Organ and Bateman, 1986.

9. G. Salanick and J. Pfeffer, "A social information-processing approach to job attitudes and task design," *Administrative Science Quarterly,* June 1978: 224–253; Dubrin, 1985.

10. B. M. Staw and J. Ross, "Stability in the midst of change: A dispositional approach to job attitudes," *Journal of Applied Psychology,* Vol. 70, 1985: 469–480.

11. Katz, 1960; R. B. McAfee and P. J. Champagne, *Organizational Behavior: A Manager's View,* West Publishing, St. Paul, Minn., 1987: 38–39.

12. Katz, 1960.

13. L. Cochran, "Implicit versus explicit importance of career values in making career decisions," *Journal of Counseling Psychology,* Vol. 30, No. 2, 1983: 189–193; R. B. Cialdini, R. E. Petty, and J. T. Cacioppo, "Attitude and attitude change," *Annual Review of Psychology,* Vol. 32, 1981: 357–404; R. Brannon, "Attitudes and the prediction of behavior," in *Social Psychology: An Introduction,* ed. B. Seidenberg and A. Snadowsky, The Free Press, New York, 1976: 145–198: C. A. Kiesler and P. A. Mirson, "Attitudes and opinions," in *Annual Review of Psychology,* Vol. 26, ed. M. R. Rosenzweig and L. W. Porter, Annual Reviews, Inc., Palo Alto, Calif.; M. Fishbein, "The relationships between beliefs, attitudes, and behavior," in *Cognitive Consistency,* ed. S. Feldman, Academic Press, New York, 1966; 1975: 415–456; D. Wrench, *Psychology: A Social Approach,* McGraw-Hill, New York, 1969.

14. A. W. Wicker, "Attitudes versus actions: The relationship of verbal and overt behavioral responses to attitude objects," *Journal of Social Issues,* Vol. 25, 1969: 41–78; M. Fishbein and I. Ajzen, 1975.

15. J. Brockner, *Self-Esteem at Work,* Lexington Books, Lexington, Mass., 1988.

16. Mann, 1969.

17. B. Berelson and G. A. Steiner, *Human Behavior: An Inventory of Scientific Findings,* Harcourt, Brace & World, New York, 1964.

18. E. Schein, "The individual, the organization, and the career: A perceptual scheme," *Journal of Applied Behavioral Science,* Vol. 7, 1971: 401-426.

19. Rokeach, 1966.

20. W. H. Shaw, *Business Ethics,* Wadsworth, Belmont, Calif., 1991.

21. D. J. Bem and A. Allan, "On predicting some of the people some of the time: The search for cross-situational consistencies in behavior," *Psychological Review,* Vol. 81, 1974: 506–520; R. G. Brannon, G. Cyphers, S. Hesse, S. Hesselbart, R. Keane, H. Scheiman, T. Vicarro, and D. Wright, "Attitude and action: A field experiment joined to a general population survey," *American*

Sociological Review, Vol. 38, 1973: 625–636; J. W. Brehm, *Responses to Loss of Freedom: A Theory of Psychological Reactance,* General Learning Press, Morristown, N. J., 1972.

22. M. Rokeach and G. Rothman, "The principle of belief congruence and the congruity principle as models of cognitive interaction," *Psychological Review,* Vol. 72, 1965:128-172; C. Osgood and P. Tannenbaum, "The principle of congruity in the prediction of attitude change," *Psychological Review,* Vol. 62, 1955: 42–55; F. Heider, "Attitudes and cognitive organization," *Journal of Psychology*, Vol. 21, 1946: 107–112; F. Heider, *The Psychology of Interpersonal Relations,* John Wiley and Sons, New York, 1958; M. Rosenberg and R. Albelson, "An analysis of cognitive balancing," in *Attitude Organization and Change,* ed. C. Hovland and M. Rosenberg, Yale University Press, New Haven, 1960; L. Festinger, *A Theory of Cognitive Dissonance,* Stanford University Press, Stanford, 1957; B. M. Staw, "Attitudinal and behavioral consequences of changing a major organizational reward: A natural field experiment," *Journal of Personality and Social Psychology,* Vol. 9, 1974; 742–751.

23. Heider, 1946: 107–112; Heider, 1958.

24. E. Aronson, "The rationalizing animal," *Psychology Today,* May 1973: 46–52; B. M. Staw, "Knee-deep in the big muddy: A study of escalating commitment to a chosen course of action," *Organizational Behavior and Human Performance,* Vol. 16, 1976: 27–44.

25. J. A. Timmons, L. E. Smollen, and A. Dingee, Jr., *New Venture Creation,* 2d ed., Irwin, Burr Ridge, Ill., 1985.

26. The following examples are taken from Shaw, *Business Ethics,* Wadsworth Publishing Co., Belmont, Calif., 1991.

27. Eric H. Beverslvis, "Is there no such thing as business ethics?" *Journal of Business Ethics*, Vol. 3, 1987: 81–88.

28. Rosabeth M. Kanter, *The Change Masters*, Simon & Schuster, New York, 1983.

29. G. P. Latham, "Human Resource training and development," *Annual Review of Psychology,* Vol. 39, 1988: 545–582.

30. P. E. Murphy, "Implementing business ethics," *Journal of Business Ethics,* Vol. 7, 1988: 907–915.

31. G. P. Latham, and K. N. Wexley, *Increasing Productivity Through Performance Appraisal,* 2d ed., Addison-Wesley Publishing Company, 1994.

32. J. W. Thibaut and H. H. Kelly, *The Social Psychology of Groups,* John Wiley and Sons, New York, 1959; G. Homans, *Social Behaviors: The Elementary Forms,* Harcourt Brace Jovanovich, New York, 1961; J. S. Adams, "Inequity in social exchange," in *Advances in Experimental Social Psychology*, ed. L. Berkowitz, Academic Press, New York, 1965.

33. S. J. Patel and B. H. Kleiner, "The price corporations must pay for women executives," *Equal Opportunities International,* Vol. 9, No. 2, 1990: 9–12.

34. Steve Hanamura, "Working with people who are different," *Training and Development Journal*, June 1989: 110–114.

35. Hanamura, 1989.

36. W. E. Halal and B. S. Brown, "Participative management: Myth and reality," *California Management Review,* Vol. 23, No. 4, Summer 1981: 20–32.

37. Daniel Bell, *The Coming Post-industrial Society*, Basic Books, New York, 1973.

38. D. Nichols, "Bottom-up strategies: Asking the employees for advice," *Management Review,* December, 1989: 44–49.

39. Edwin A. Locke and David M. Schweiger, "Participation in decision making: One more look," in *Research in Organization Behavior*, ed. Barry M. Staw and H. Greenwich, JAI Press, Greenwich, Conn., 1979: 205–339; E. A. Locke, P. M. Schweiger, and G. P. Latham, "Participation in decision making—When should it be used?" *Organizational Dynamics,* Spring 1986: 65–79; V. Govindarajan, "Impact of participation in the budgetary process on managerial attitudes and performance: Universalistic and contingency perspectives," *Decision Sciences,* Vol. 17, Fall 1986: 496–516; D. Tjosvold, "Participation: A close look at its dynamics," *Journal of Management,* Vol. 13, No. 4, 1987: 739–750; N. Margulies and S. Black, "Perspectives on the implementation of participative approaches," *Human Resource Management,* Vol. 26, No. 3, Fall 1987: 385–412; W. A. Pasmore and M. R. Fagans, "Participation, individual development, and organizational change: A review and synthesis," *Journal of Management,* Vol. 18, No. 2, 1992: 375–397.

40. V. Vroom, *Some Personality Determinants of the Effects of Participation,* Prentice Hall, Englewood Cliffs, N.J., 1960; K. E. Runyon, "Some interactions between personality variables and management styles," *Journal of Applied Psychology,* Vol. 57, 1973: 288–294; J. M. Ivancevich, "An analysis of participation in decision making among project engineers," *Academy of Management Journal,* Vol. 22, 1979: 253–269; Tjosvold, 1987; Margulies and Black, Fall 1987.

41. Locke and Schweiger, 1979; Margulies and Black, Fall 1987.

42. Margulies and Black, Fall 1987.

43. M. A. Verespej, "No empowerment without education: And often workers will need even the most basic skills," *Industry Week,* Vol. 240, April 1, 1991: 28–29.

44. Locke and Schweiger, 1979; K. K. Fisher, "Management role in the implementation of participative management systems," *Human Resource Management,* Vol. 25 No. 3, Fall 1986: 459-479; Margulies and Black, Fall 1987.

45. Fisher, Fall 1986.

46. Locke, Schweiger and Latham, 1986; Fisher, Fall 1986; Margulies and Black, Fall 1987.

47. L. A. Pace and W. W. Suajanen, "Addictive Type A behavior undermines employee involvement," *Personnel Journal,* June 1988: 36.

48. W. E. Halal and B. S. Brown, Summer 1981; William Winpisinger, "Job enrichment: A union view," *Monthly Labor Review,* Vol. 96, April 1973: 56.

49. D. W. Johnson, G. Maruyama, R. T. Johnson, D. Nelson, and S. Skon, "Effects of cooperative, competitive, and individualistic goal structures on achievement: A meta-analysis," *Psychological Bulletin,* Vol. 89, 1981: 47–62.

50. I. Janis, *Victims of Groupthink: A Psychological Study of Foreign Policy Decisions and Fiascos,* Houghton Mifflin, Boston, 1973.

51. G. P. Latham, D. C. Winters, and E. D. Locke, "Cognitive and motivation effects of participation: A mediator study," *Journal of Organizational Behavior,* Vol. 15, January, 1994: 49–63.

52. R. E. Alberti and M. L. Emmons, *Your Perfect Right,* Impact Publishers, Calif., 1986.

53. R. E. Kelly, "In praise of followers," *Harvard Business Review,* November–December 1988: 142.

54. J. Pfeffer, "The ambiguity of leadership," *Academy of Management Review,* Vol. 2, 1977: 104–112; J. R. Meindl, S. B. Ehrlich and J. M. Dukerich, "The romance of leadership," *Administrative Science Quarterly*, Vol. 30, 1985: 78–102; J. Kiechel III, "The case against leaders," *Fortune,* November 21, 1988: 217–220; Kelly, 1988; R.E. Kelly, *The Power of Followership,* Doubleday, New York, 1992.

55. Kelly, 1988: 142–147.

56. Kelly, 1988.

EFFECTIVE COMMUNICATION FOR THE 1990s

Objectives:

- To familiarize students with communication concepts critical to building positive relationships between the manager and others internal and external to the organization.
- To sensitize students to the importance of cross-cultural differences when attempting to communicate within the global community.
- To provide students with the opportunity to practice appropriate behavior in the areas of listening, rapport building, and nonverbal communications.

Communication—Helping to Achieve Managerial Excellence

"...The difference between the right word and the almost right word is the difference between lightning and lightning bug."

Mark Twain

Much of the conflict, confrontation, discord, and general misunderstanding that occurs between managers and others within an organization could be avoided if the basic components of the communication process were understood and used in interpersonal relationships. The recognition of communication as an important variable in obtaining managerial success is not new. In 1938, Chester Barnard argued that the development and maintenance of an effective communication process were key responsibilities of the executive.[1]

The relative importance of effective communications continues to become more central and pervasive as *(a)* the environment in which managers function becomes increasingly turbulent and uncertain, and *(b)* their subordinates

127

demand a greater role in the organization's decision-making process. In the latter case, subordinates demand more because of changing values, increased education, and a greater awareness of personal rights.

Furthermore, given the uncertainty and increased pressure experienced by subordinates and other organizational members, the manager must be able to understand and support those individuals in a position of stress. This supportive role, the desire to develop greater rapport with others, and an increased need for information, will result in a greater level of interaction and communication among organizational members. Therefore, as organizations move into the "information age," managers must learn to master communication processes that are dynamic and complex.

In this chapter, our emphasis is on those skills that facilitate rapport between the manager and other individuals. Specifically, this chapter focuses on the areas of effective listening, rapport building, and nonverbal assessment. If managers can master these three skills they will have gone a long way in better integrating the subordinate as a valuable resource and partner.

Understanding the Basics

The following definitions provide a good starting point for our discussion of communication.

- Communication is a generally predictable, continuous, and always-present process of the sharing of meaning through symbol interaction.[2]
- Communication is the transmission of information and understanding through the use of common symbols, verbal and/or nonverbal.[3]

The critical elements in these two definitions are the words *information*, *understanding*, *continuous*, *symbols*, and *process*. Participants involved in the communication process do not transmit meaning but rather only bits of information in the form of encoded messages using verbal and nonverbal symbols. Meaning exists only within the minds of each of the communicators. Participants achieve mutual understanding when there is a match between the sender's encoded message and the receiver's decoded message. This, then, is the ultimate goal of communications.

For example, let us consider what is happening between us as you read these words. As one of us sits in front of a word processor, we are attempting to encode, or translate, meaning that exists in our minds into a written message. If someone were to ask us if we know what meaning we wanted to transfer to the student, our answer would be "Yes!" Unfortunately, words by themselves do not transmit meaning. Whether there is mutual understanding will be a function of communication and how well we have encoded our thoughts on the pages of this text and how well you decode this written message, that is, give meaning to these words. Therefore, we can only hope that as you read these words you will understand what behavioral scientists have identified as effective management. If there is a one-to-one mapping of what is in our minds and what ends up in your mind as you read these pages, then there will be understanding. In this way we will have created meaning.

The Process of Communicating

There are numerous models[4] that depict the complex phenomenon called communications. A representative model is reproduced in Figure 4.1. A sender or communicator, in response to a perceived purpose, translates or encodes information into a message for transmission to a receiver. The receiver has to be aware of the incoming message to the extent of being able to interpret it or decode it. As the process is initiated and carried out, both the sender and the receiver are influenced by a wide range of factors called "filters" that can prevent, distort, change, or enhance the transmission of a message. Filters may exist either internally or externally to the individuals involved. Internal filters are in the form of needs, attitudes, experiences, and assumptions

FIGURE 4.1

The Tubbs communications model

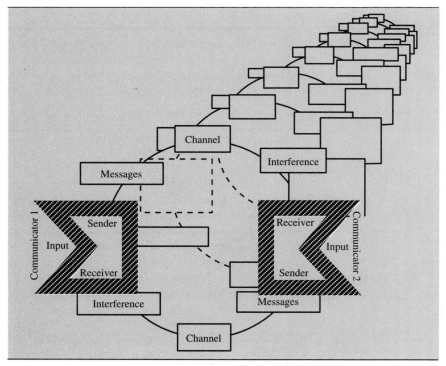

Source: Stewart Tubbs and Sylvia Moss, *Human Communications,* 1987, p. 7.

about reality, while external filters occur in the form of the environmental climate, context, and volume. Ultimately, as the two communicators interact, a feedback loop will be built into the system. This feedback loop allows the two communicators to assess the impact of their attempted communication on each other. It is the feedback loop and the information it carries that keeps the communication process open and free flowing. It is the feedback loop, verbal or nonverbal in content, which changes the role of the receiver into that of a communicator, and the original communicator into a receiver. This flip-flopping of roles will continue to spiral into the future until the objectives of at least one, if not both, of the communicators have been satisfied.

Therefore, communication is an ongoing process that can remain open indefinitely as long as *(a)* the participants believe that there is a joint benefit in continuing, *(b)* each communicator is willing to actively listen to the other, *(c)* there is an effort by one or both parties to maintain rapport, and *(d)* both communicators effectively respond to nonverbal cues.

Effective Listening

Four language-related behaviors include reading, writing, speaking, and listening. Of the four, listening takes the most time in an individual's average day. One early study put the figure at 53 percent.[5] Furthermore, effective listening is an essential ingredient in the mix of skills supporting managerial success. It is because organizational interactions rely so heavily on face-to-face encounters that effective listening is a necessity if managers are to understand the people around them. If we analyze the type of messages being sent, the manager may be dealing with directions from above, information describing future events, feedback, requests for help, explanations, etc. In each case, if one fails to understand correctly, failure of some kind will likely follow.

For example, a busy President relied upon his Vice President of Human Resource Management to explain the next item for the company's monthly executive meeting. The President failed to listen and from what was heard expected a consultant's proposal for identifying senior management competencies and a pay-for-performance system that incorporated these competencies. Unfortunately, the report he heard dealt with a companywide management training program that was designed around a recent needs analysis. Not hearing what was expected, the President became critical of the consultant's report and the Vice President's handling of the matter. Considerable time was lost attempting to get the meeting back on track.

Such listening failures are not limited to senior managers. During a recent training session, a participant provided the following example. He had a subordinate who complained about everything. The subordinate would complain about his health, the company, co-workers, or whatever else was on his mind.

Because the complaints were always unfounded and the employee's behavior could not be changed, the supervisor decided to ignore them. Unfortunately, one morning the employee complained about his wrist hurting and that he wanted to go home. The supervisor indicated that he should stay and stop complaining. As it turned out, the employee had fallen coming into work and had broken his wrist.

Equally important from the point of view of the manager–subordinate interface, effective listening is one of the most critical components in demonstrating personal empathy and understanding toward subordinates. Without empathy and understanding, the manager cannot develop the required interpersonal and leadership relationships necessary to survive in the 1990s and beyond.

Unfortunately, the amount of time we spend listening does not appear to support the old adage of "practice makes perfect." Evidence overwhelmingly indicates that most individuals are poor listeners. Research indicates that listeners remember about 50 percent of messages immediately after hearing them, and only remember 25 percent of the message two months later.[6] What are the underlying reasons for such poor listening performance by individuals? To begin with, many individuals fail to differentiate correctly between hearing and listening. Hearing is simply a neuro-physiological process by which people collect and register sound waves that exist externally to their bodies. In other words, sound waves are physically collected by the human ear, and vibrate the eardrum. It is at this point that listening begins. Once the pattern of vibrations is recognized, the individual can choose to interpret or ignore the patterns. If people decide to interpret, they will register the impulses, identify the stimuli by classifying and integrating the new input into an existing cognitive structure, and then evaluate what has been recorded. In this last step, individuals assess the significance, value, or appropriateness of the information that has been received. In other words, we hear with our ears and we listen with our brains.[7]

Therefore, although many individuals consider listening easy to do, the reality of the situation is that it is a difficult process to master, and a physically demanding activity to engage in. As a student, think back to one of those important lectures where you knew you had to pay attention. Now answer the question: How easy was it? When students are asked this question, most report it is difficult to do. Many experience headaches, back pain; one student even talked about breaking into a sweat. Put simply, listening can be hard work.

Next, of the four communicating behaviors, listening does not fare well in terms of personal preference. Research evidence[8] indicates that in terms of arousal, listening ranks third out of the four behaviors. Results indicated that individuals are most aroused when they are speaking, next when they are writing, and least when they are reading. The finding that individuals prefer to talk rather than listen was supported by Bostrom.[9] In this case, those individuals who talked most during a small group discussion were found to be the most satisfied. The converse, those individuals who talked least, were least satisfied.

Furthermore, listening is often ineffective because of the multiple factors that can prevent any message from being understood. The following two-person model clearly indicates the complexity of the process and why it often fails.

The Two-Person Model

This model developed by Hunt (Figure 4.2) describes a number of factors that impinge on the ultimate success of any attempt to listen. Because of individual variances, there will be a wide range of differences in the ability of individuals to concentrate, hear a message, or respond to visual cues. Weaknesses in any of these areas will reduce the individual's effectiveness as a listener. Similarly, if the sender is a poor communicator, then it is unlikely that the receiver will attempt to understand the intended message.

The two-person model also indicates that each participant will often have a history with the other person. Experiences may act to distort or block any incoming message. What is listened to will also be affected by the perceived utility of the message for either sender or receiver. Clearly, the more useful a message's content, the harder the receiver will work to understand it, or the sender to get it understood. Next, each exchange represents a different environmental situation and as such may differ in the number of constraints that can block the free flow of information. Last, the level of message difficulty, newness, and complexity often has an impact on the receiver's willingness to

FIGURE 4.2

Model of two-person speaker-listener relationship

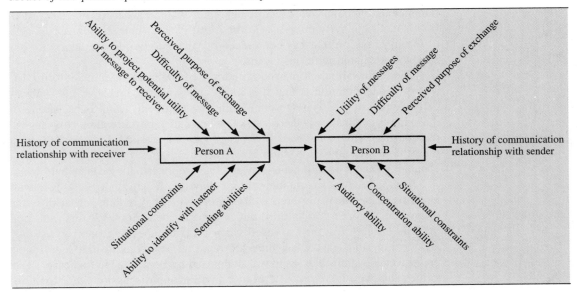

Source: Gary T. Hunt, *Communication Skills in the Organization,* 1989, p. 81. Copyright 1989 by Allyn and Bacon, Reprinted by permission.

make the effort to listen and understand. Therefore, if the message is perceived as too difficult or complex, and thus beyond the individual's comprehension level, the individual will begin to tune out what is being sent.

The Listening Encounter

As we try to understand what makes a good listener, significant improvement in listening style can be achieved if managers prepare for listening encounters, actively listen, and evaluate their performance.[10] Figure 4.3 briefly outlines the listening process and how these three variables fit together. Proactive managers continually monitor their environments for listening opportunities. However, because managers have limited time and energy, they must then rank each potential encounter in terms of importance. The actual level of perceived importance will be a function of encounter relevance to personal goal achievement and urgency.

Once listening opportunities are ranked, then managers can map out and assess the communication styles, skills, and backgrounds of the individuals involved. The more that is known about senders, the more likely you will understand their points of reference. Concomitantly, the more you understand the

FIGURE 4.3

Preparing for effective listening

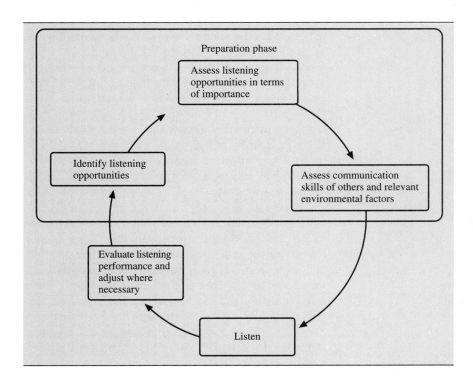

individuals involved, the greater the probability you will understand their messages as they would like you to. To further increase effectiveness, proactive listeners will also consider such issues as potential environmental distractions, emotional distractions, physical conditions of the communicators, and the content of the message.[11] Without this initial step there is no planning or preparation process.

The next step is to engage in the communication exchange and listen to what is being transmitted. However, given the potential for error and poor listening performance by many listeners, it is necessary to evaluate performance.[12] Listening performance can be evaluated on two levels.[13] The first level of evaluation reflects the assumption that individuals listen to achieve some purpose. For example, individuals listen for appreciation, discrimination, therapeutic value, comprehension, and critical analysis.[14]

When an individual listens for appreciation, the objective is pleasure and enjoyment. Individuals may go to a lecture series less for the content and more to hear a particular speaker because of his or her wit or humor. Nevertheless, a by-product of this type of listening may be intellectual or professional benefit. In the case of discriminative listening, the listener infers understanding about issues not mentioned (i.e., the sender's feelings, emotions, beliefs, and opinions). Discriminative listening requires that individuals listen to the speaker's words and observe his or her nonverbal behaviors. Therapeutic listening is designed to help the sender talk through a problem or engage in a process of personal catharsis. The listener is acting as a sounding board for the sender and in so doing, allows the individual to work through personal feelings. Listening for comprehension takes place when the listener is attempting to gain understanding, that is, the individual wants to accurately understand the information, ideas, and processes being described by the sender. Finally, critical listening allows the listener to interpret the message being received and assess its strengths and weaknesses. Critical listening ultimately allows the individual to assign value to the received message. During any listening encounter, it is possible for the individual to be listening for more than one purpose. A manager listening to a troubled subordinate may be listening for therapeutic, comprehension, and critical assessment reasons.

Listening is successful if it achieves the listener's goals. O'Hair and Friedrich[15] stated that an individual can objectively assess listening performance by asking questions relevant to personal goal achievement. The listener might ask, "Did I achieve my listening goal?" "In situations where I had more than one goal, how many of them did I achieve?" "Were the goals that I set for this listening situation realistic?" Answers to these questions, however, only address half of the performance question, that is, results or outcomes.[16] Alternatively, listeners can evaluate their performance in terms of personal behaviors that facilitate or hinder effective listening. The **SWOT** acronym identifies four areas in which listener behaviors can affect performance.[17]

1. Strengths refer to those behaviors the listener engages in that facilitate effective listening. For example, if an individual does not fully understand what is being transmitted, a good listener asks questions or provides clear feedback to the sender that he or she does not understand what has been said. Such behaviors should be continued by the listener.

2. Weaknesses refer to behaviors that reduce the effectiveness of the listening process. An individual is considered a poor listener if he or she pays more attention to personal characteristics than to the message's content. Similarly, poor listeners fail to take advantage of the differential between speech speed (125 to 150 wpm) and thought speed (400 to 500 wpm),[18] that is, to cognitively assess what is being heard or prepare for a response to the sender's message. Once weaknesses have been identified, it is possible for the individual to adjust his or her behavior to prevent or buffer their negative consequences.

3. Opportunities are unexpected chances within the listening encounter that, if taken advantage of, increase listening effectiveness. Such an opportunity may be when a student is too embarrassed to ask questions about a lecture that he or she does not understand. If a fellow student asks a relevant question the student should take advantage of the situation to improve his or her understanding. Once a question and answer sequence has been initiated by someone else, it may also be less stressful for the less assertive student to ask the second question.

4. Threats are factors that have the potential to disrupt the listening process. They can result from the listener's own behavior, the behavior of others, and events within the listening environment. A common threat to successful listening is the listener's own personality. For example, if he or she easily becomes emotional, such emotions can act as a disruptive filter. Others can interfere or disrupt the listening process by interrupting or in some way distracting the listener. Finally, environmental noise can directly block the message from being received and thereby cause the listener not to achieve his or her goals. The proactive listener scans his or her environment to identify potential threats and then takes action to prevent threats from occurring or to buffer their impact.

Using Attending and Responding Skills to Build Positive Relationships

Attending Behaviors

Attending behaviors are designed to allow the manager to tune into the subordinate's feelings, values, beliefs, and attitudes of others. Such skills primarily fall in the area of empathic listening, observation of nonverbal behaviors, and physically organizing the environment to facilitate interactions.[19] At this time we will limit our discussion to empathic listening and leave the discussion of nonverbal communications to a later point in this chapter. We will cover physical attending when discussing the concept of counseling in Chapter 14.

Empathy is the ability to "get inside" another person's mind and view the world through that individual's eyes.[20] Empathic (active) listening is the process by which the listener integrates "physical, emotional, and intellectual inputs in a search for meaning and understanding."[21] Empathic listening also implies that the listener is not attempting to judge or evaluate the sender. Defined in this way, the empathic listener is attempting to understand the total person, and not merely collecting information to recall it later or analyzing it to draw conclusions or critically assess content.[22] To be effective, empathic (active) listening must reflect the listener's attitudes toward others. Rogers and Farson[23] expressed such a view when they stated:

> To be effective, active listening must be firmly grounded in the basic attitudes of the user. We cannot employ it as a technique if our fundamental attitudes are in conflict with its basic concepts. If we try, our behavior will be empty and sterile, and our associates will be quick to recognize this. Until we can demonstrate a spirit which genuinely respects the potential worth of the individual, which considers his rights and trusts his capacity for self-direction, we cannot begin to be effective listeners.

Empathic listening also motivates the sender to respond with a similar listening style, thereby increasing the probability of mutual understanding or producing a correspondence of mood between the sender and the receiver.[24] Such a climate facilitates open communication and the development of mutual trust. The long-term consequences are positive interpersonal relationships and reduced employee complaints.[25]

Athos and Gabarro[26] articulated a set of guidelines that help a listener develop an empathic (active) listening style.

- A greater emphasis on listening than talking.

- Responding to that which is personal rather than abstract.

- Following others in their exploration rather than leading them into areas we think they should be exploring.

- Clarifying what others have said about their own thoughts and feelings rather than asking questions or telling them what we believe they should be thinking, seeing, or feeling.

- Responding to the feelings implicit in what others have said rather than the assumptions or "content" that they have talked about.

- Trying to get into the other's inner frame of reference rather than listening and responding from our own frame of reference.

- Responding with empathic understanding and acceptance rather than unconcern, distanced objectivity, or over-identification (i.e., internalizing the problem so that it also becomes our own).

- Refraining from making early evaluations of what the speaker is saying. (This last point has been added by the authors.)

The following exchange between a manager and her subordinate is an example of poor empathic (active) listening.

Manager: "John, have you had a chance to try out that new desktop publishing package?"
Subordinate: "Well, Mary, this desktop publishing business is pretty complicated stuff."
Manager: "It is difficult, but it's the best package out there and our competitors use it."
Subordinate: "Maybe I'm too old to learn about computers. The old way seemed OK to me."
Manager: "Were you unable to work the DTP self-help disk designed to get you started?"
Subordinate: "Does it matter? Does this company ever ask its employees how they feel about new things and new computers? It just appeared on my desk."
Manager: "Of course it matters. I'll send down someone from systems to show you how the self-help disk works."
Subordinate: "Well, I just don't want to look dumb."
Manager: "You know, all people need support with new computer software—our people in systems have had a lot of experience in training. I'm sure you'll be on top of the situation in a week."
Subordinate: "Well, maybe someone goofed by expecting me to figure it out by myself. If I get the self-help disk working maybe I'll be OK. But I still think I've been treated badly, and in a week you're going to ask my advice on whether to return this program or buy it."
Manager: "I'm glad we had a chance to talk and straighten out your problem—see you in a week. If you have any problems let me know."

As we look at this exchange, each time the manager responds to the subordinate it is obvious she fails to effectively listen to his feelings and attitudes. In the early part of the exchange, the manager has failed to realize that the subordinate is frightened by the new software package. Later, the manager fails to respond to the subordinate's anxiety over changing from an old system that he already knew how to operate effectively. Finally, the manager fails to tune in to the subordinate's belief that management does not consider the needs, feelings, or ideas of subordinates. It is unlikely that after several of these exchanges John will again try to communicate with Mary. She doesn't listen to him.

Let us now turn our attention to the issue of responding behaviors designed to keep the channels of communication open and to develop manager–subordinate rapport.

Responding Behaviors

Responding behaviors are designed to keep the channels of communication open and the interpersonal exchange running smoothly.[27] To keep communication channels open and process available information, the manager must learn

TABLE 4.1   **The Gibb Categories of Defensive and Supportive Response Behaviors**

Defensive Behavior	*Supportive Behavior*
1. Evaluation	1. Description
2. Control	2. Problem orientation
3. Strategy	3. Spontaneity
4. Neutrality	4. Empathy
5. Superiority	5. Equality
6. Certainty	6. Provisionalism

and apply responding behaviors. The actual success of any interaction will reflect the degree to which the manager applies behaviors designed to build interpersonal rapport. The clarification of appropriate behaviors is the topic of this section.

In any exchange between the manager and a subordinate, it is typically the subordinate who will decide whether the encounter is threatening. Gibb[28] isolated six defense-causing verbal behaviors. If you use one or more of these verbal behaviors, you run the risk of threatening the other person's self-esteem. If such situations do develop, it is unlikely that managers will be able to build the desired level of rapport with their subordinates. Gibb juxtaposed these six defensive-inducing behaviors with six types of verbal behaviors likely to produce a positive relationship. The two varieties of behaviors are listed in Table 4.1.

Evaluation versus Description

The position of managers easily allows for evaluative statements because part of their function is to set goals and engage in performance appraisal and review. Consider the following statement made by a manager to a subordinate: "Larry, you should have known better than to let Peter handle the delivery on his own—he's just not ready for that kind of responsibility. Now look at the mess we are in!" You probably can sense Larry's stress from being criticized by his boss. A subordinate who is faced with this situation is likely to feel uncomfortable and defensive. We use evaluative statements so easily because we have been exposed to them thousands of times from parents, teachers, friends, and spouses. This is sometimes referred to as "you" language because most evaluative response statements begin with the word "you" and are of an accusing nature: "You should have known better—," "You idiot, don't—," or "You'll be sorry if—."[29]

In contrast, descriptive statements tend to arouse significantly less tension or threat. A descriptive statement presents feelings, information, events, or perceptions that do not put receivers on the spot or require them to defend their personal decisions or actions. Unfortunately, the overexposure we have all had to evaluative statements requires that managers attempt to shift from them to descriptive statements. Descriptive statements are "I" language.[30] They are less judgmental. In the above case, the manager may have had a more positive effect on Larry if he or she had said: "Larry, I reviewed Peter's report on the P-26 delivery. I see that it was three days behind schedule. I know Peter is relatively new here and I am a bit concerned—let me know if there is anything I should be aware of or any additional support I can give you." A descriptive statement such as this is more likely to lead to an open discussion of the issue.

Control versus Problem Orientation

Response behaviors or messages that imply control over ideas, attitudes, or behavior often make the receiver defensive. The implication is that the manager knows what is best; therefore, the receiver feels slighted, put down, manipulated, or taken advantage of. A major complaint subordinates make about their bosses is that they make decisions without fully considering subordinates' views. This is not to imply that control type messages cannot be used, but rather that they are frequently misinterpreted by subordinates as implying lack of concern, sincerity, or interest on the part of managers. Consequently, subordinates can easily rationalize their lack of cooperation with managers because the subordinates were not responsible for the decision.

A problem-oriented message, on the other hand, implies that managers are interested in exploring with subordinates the parameters involved in a particular issue or problem. In this case, managers are interested in the cooperation and input of subordinates. Consequently, managers are open to subordinates being active participants in those issues or problems which *(a)* are likely to be of interest to the subordinates, *(b)* the subordinates are likely to have relevant input on, or *(c)* are potentially developmental for the subordinates. By allowing the subordinates to feel that they have had a major role in deciding future directions or actions, you enhance their feelings of adequacy and competency and make it easier for them to cooperate. In other words, managers are increasing the level of positive rapport between themselves and the subordinates.

Strategy versus Spontaneity

Tom Sawyer manipulated his friends into whitewashing the fence through the use of strategy: "Boy, I'm really lucky to be doing this—and I'm really sad that you can't have fun like me." Had his friends been fully aware of the ploy, Tom would have spent a very hot afternoon whitewashing the fence by himself. Strategies are used by all of us to manipulate others; however, if receivers realize or believe that they are being manipulated, they will react negatively. Think back to some of the strategies your parents or teachers used to get you to do something. You probably did not like what happened, especially if the demands on you were not in full agreement with your own needs.

If your behavior is viewed as spontaneous and genuine, you are more likely to put those with whom you are interacting at ease. Such individuals will be more responsive to any message you may be sending their way.

Neutrality versus Empathy

Neutral statements imply an indifference to the other individual participating in the exchange. Managers who take on such a detached (aloof) role run the risk of alienating their subordinates. Subordinates need to feel worthwhile and that their needs and concerns are perceived as legitimate, and so the right alternative is to demonstrate empathy toward one's subordinates. Recognizing subordinates as individuals, feeling for their concerns, and trying to understand their points of view will help to develop a positive relationship between subordinate and manager. The manager in our active listening example above remained neutral to the subordinate's feelings and emotions. Recall the following exchange:

Manager: "Were you unable to work the DTP self-help disk designed to get you started?"
Subordinate: "Does it matter? Does this company ever ask its employees how they feel about new things and new computers? It just appeared on my desk."
Manager: "Of course it matters. I'll send down someone from systems to show you how the self-help disk works."
Subordinate: "Well, I just don't want to look dumb."
Manager: "You know, all people need support with new computer software—our people in systems have had a lot of experience in training. I'm sure you'll be on top of the situation in a week."

Both of the manager's responses failed to address the subordinate's fears and concerns. Consequently, the subordinate is likely to feel that the manager is indifferent or uncaring.

Superiority versus Equality

By the nature of the organization, managers are put in a hierarchical position higher than subordinates. However, this does not imply that managers must continually behave as if they are better than their subordinates. Managers should convey a sense of competency based upon their expertise and their ability to satisfy subordinates' needs. A manager can communicate a willingness to involve subordinates in departmental matters by treating them as equal partners when addressing certain issues or problems. Clearly, a team philosophy will be appropriate only in those areas where the subordinate has the interest, skill, knowledge, and time to address the issue being considered. Similarly, the issue being considered must be one that the manager can appropriately share with the subordinate. Therefore, equality does not mean equal in terms of authority or responsibility, but rather in terms of individuals coming together and sharing an experience, with the mutual goal of jointly solving a problem or addressing an important issue.

Certainty versus Provisionalism

There are times when it is important for managers to express themselves in firm and definite terms. However, a constant dogmatic style of "knowing it all" can keep them from effectively developing positive relations with others. Subordinates may feel that there is no way to communicate or share with such managers, particularly from their perspective. Provisionalism allows managers to show subordinates that they are interested in their opinions and feelings and that they are open and flexible to reinterpretation of their own position. However, as was the case with a dogmatic style, a constant provisional style will also have its negative effects. Managers who can never make decisions, continually shift their positions to fit those of subordinates, will gain the reputation of being indecisive, and will run the risk of damaging their credibility.

Useful Statements for the Manager

To fully understand how best to keep channels open and interactions running smoothly, we have found it helpful to list a set of statements the manager can use when attempting to understand or collect information from subordinates. The following list represents statements the manager can make. Each statement is classified as to whether it will have a positive or negative impact on manager–subordinate rapport.[31] The first five, which have a positive impact, are described further below.

- Stem questions (positive).
- Probing statements (positive).
- Reflective/understanding statements (positive).
- Supportive statements (positive).
- Summarizing statements (positive).
- Irrelevant statements (negative).
- Evaluative statements (negative).
- Interpretive statements (negative).

Stem Questions

A stem question is an opening statement designed to initiate a desired exchange. When stem questions are embedded in an ongoing exchange, they are typically designed to redirect the conversation in a new direction. In the exchange described earlier between Mary and John, the manager's opening statement "John, have you had the time to try out that new desk top publishing package?" is an example of a stem question. Stem questions may be the result of the internal drive of the individual to find out information, or the result of verbal or nonverbal cues received from relevant others. In the above example, the question therefore could have been asked because Mary was personally interested in knowing how John was getting on with the new software, or because of a confused look on John's face.

Probing Statements

Probing statements are questions designed to clarify or draw out additional information from the sender of a particular message. The need for probing is predicated on the assumption that individuals often fail to give a clear or accurate assessment of their feelings, values, beliefs, or attitudes. Lack of clarity may occur because of inexperience, perceived time constraints, perceived needs of the listener, or a felt insecurity by the sender. Consequently, it is the listener's responsibility to probe, in order to ensure as clear and accurate an understanding as possible of what has been said by the other individual. When attempting to clarify or dig further, the listener will likely zero in on the who? what? where? when? components of the sender's initial statement. The listener can further clarify messages by asking for additional detail, examples of critical incidents, or a further explanation of points just made. All such probing questions are designed to ensure that the listener has an accurate mental picture of what the sender has in mind.

Reflecting or Understanding Statements

The reflecting or understanding statement is designed to inform senders how you think they feel. This is done with a minimum of words but yet with sufficient interpretation to demonstrate that the manager does care about what the subordinate is saying. When using a reflecting or understanding statement, the intensity of emotions should be consistent with those expressed by the sender. Extreme differences in expressed emotion are likely to have a negative affect on the ongoing relationship between the sender and the listener. Also, do not be concerned that your interpretation is inaccurate. It is trying to understand how the other person is feeling that is important.

Managers may initially find it difficult to use reflecting or understanding statements. The typical remarks made by such managers are that they feel awkward or that their statements come across as hollow or insincere. This often happens because the managers are merely repeating the statements made by the sender.

Subordinate: "I'm afraid that I am too old to learn new procedures."
Manager: "You feel afraid."

The manager has accurately reflected the subordinate's feeling, but gives the impression of not really caring. It would have been much more productive to say, "You are concerned that you'll have difficulty understanding the new package" or "You are afraid that your old skills will no longer apply." After practicing these statements and reviewing personal experiences, managers are typically able to master this skill.

Supportive Statements

Supportive statements are based upon active listening and are designed to communicate to senders that it is OK to feel the way they do. It is also logical to link supportive statements with reflecting or understanding statements. Once the listener has concluded that he or she understands fully the feelings, values, beliefs, and attitudes of the sender, and they are acceptable or appropriate, it is desirable to communicate this fact to the other person. Therefore, the supportive listener would likely state, "It is OK to feel that way," or "If I were in your shoes I would have reacted the same way." The point should also be made that because supportive statements are designed to reassure the sender, they often represent end points of an avenue of consideration. As a result, supportive statements tend to conclude the current avenue of exploration, but at the same time can set the stage for a new direction to be pursued by the listener.

Summarizing Statements

These statements are periodically used to summarize large blocks of information that have been exchanged between two individuals. Such statements tend to represent a standard communication technique designed to ensure that the listener has heard and understood what the sender has been saying. By summarizing what the listener believes has been said, the responsibility of ensuring understanding is placed back on the shoulders of the sender. In other words, if the sender does not believe the listener has understood (this will be reflected in the listener's summary) then the sender must point out this inconsistency and restate his or her position. It is hoped the restated position will improve the level of understanding between sender and listener.

Nonverbal Behavior

One of the major differences between verbal and nonverbal communication is that verbal communication only has two channels (verbal and written, i.e., dealing with the words themselves), while nonverbal communication has many. Nevertheless, a message and its received meaning will always be based upon two components: (*a*) verbal behavior and (*b*) nonverbal behavior. In addition, both components interact with one another, and this interaction can serve to either facilitate or hinder the transmission of understanding. For example, the verbal statement "We will not tolerate any acts of sexual harassment in this organization," in combination with a wink, wave of the hand, or a laugh, creates confusion in the employee's mind as to the communicator's true feeling.

Similarly, the verbal statement "I respect your decision" can have different meanings depending upon the accompanying nonverbal behaviors. The statement "I respect your decision" delivered in an even but firm tone, backed up with a gentle pat on the arm, an up-down nod of the head, and physical closeness, would likely signal a genuine acceptance of the individual's stated position. The same words being delivered as the sender withdraws from the receiver, and where emphasis is placed on the word "I" followed by a pause, and then the words "respect your decision" spoken in a questioning and lower tone, with emphasis on the word "your," is likely to communicate a negative or doubting response.

Nevertheless, to effectively attend to others, it is important for the manager to be able to respond to the nonverbal cues that exist within any given situation. It is in the area of feelings and emotions (i.e., overall interpersonal responsiveness, level of liking, and felt dominance or submission) that nonverbal behaviors appear to be most important. In the area of face-to-face communication, which is often open to the greatest perceptual distortion, researchers estimate that from 65 percent[32] to 93 percent[33] of social meaning is based upon nonverbal behavior.

Unfortunately, there are very few universals in the area of nonverbal communication. The typical exceptions are nonverbal cues associated with interest, joy, surprise, fear, sadness, anger, and disgust. However, even here there can be cross-cultural differences in the level of intensity associated with different cues. Consequently, much of the information we can obtain from nonverbal communication remains situational (individual) specific. In other words, our ability to understand the nonverbal behaviors of others is directly correlated with the development and frequency of interpersonal relationships. To understand nonverbal communication, you must know and understand those around you. This statement points out a critical reason why some individuals are not effective when dealing with nonverbal communication. Put simply, some individuals refuse to get close enough to their subordinates, or observe them frequently enough, to make sense of the multiple nonverbal messages being received.

The following anecdote demonstrates the relevance of nonverbal communication. A vice president of finance explained why he was able to interact well with his subordinates. He always made it a practice to take walks through the office to observe his people under as many conditions as possible. He went on to say that with 90 percent of his staff he was eventually able to read their feelings and emotions. When pressed, the VP agreed that he was talking about nonverbal behaviors. The VP said he could tell when someone was having a good day and therefore could be pushed a little harder. Conversely, he could tell when someone was stressed and therefore needed to be left alone. Also, the VP indicated that when probing subordinates he could tell when individuals were holding back, or had nothing more to offer. The conclusion, he argued, was that his success with people was a result of an ability to tune in on subordinates' moods even when nothing was mentioned verbally.

Channels of Nonverbal Behavior

To take advantage of nonverbal messages, managers must familiarize themselves with the alternative channels through which nonverbal communications can flow. Once these channels are understood, it is the responsibility of managers to observe relevant others frequently enough, and over a broad range of circumstances, to understand the unique nonverbal behaviors of each subordinate. Let us consider the seven most common channels of nonverbal behavior (see Figure 4.4).[34]

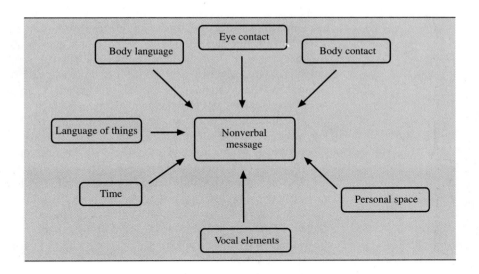

Body Language

Body language deals with the nonverbal messages transmitted through body movements. It is important to develop an appreciation of the role body movement plays in transmitting information, because not only are there cultural differences, but also gender differences within each culture. Misunderstanding of such messages is likely to lead to conflict and thereby reduce the level of rapport between managers and their subordinates. According to Ekman and Friesen[35] there are five major purposes served directly through the use of these five body languages (i.e., emblems, illustrators, affect displays, regulators, and adaptors). Let us consider each briefly.

Emblems are nonverbal cues that can be directly translated into words. If people are moving toward you and you would like them to stop, you can raise your hand, palm facing them, and they will likely understand that you want them to stop. Another example would be when you touch your thumb and forefinger together to form an O, extend the remaining three fingers, hold your palm facing the receiver, and make short jerky movements—this is likely to be interpreted as meaning "OK" in North America. The point, however, must be made that the meaning of emblems is often culturally based.

Illustrators are used by communicators to supplement, clarify, or reinforce what is being said by the sender. Therefore, if you want to tell someone you just caught a big fish, you do more than just say you caught a big fish. To make your point you use both hands and arms to indicate the size. The use of illustrators tends to increase when the topic is more important to the sender or the sender is excited. However, because the use of illustrators varies greatly between individuals, it is important to know the people around you and what behaviors are considered normal. In this way, the observer can better assess the importance being placed on both the illustrator and the message being sent. In the case above, if the fisherman sending the message rarely used illustrators to emphasize his or her verbal messages, their use now would indicate extra excitement about catching the fish, and that it was really big.

Affect displays relate to body movements and facial expressions that express the emotional state of the sender. For example, in the VP story above, one of the ways in which he assessed subordinates' moods was to observe their walk or posture. If subordinates were slumped in posture and walked more slowly than usual, they were in a down mood.

It is because many individuals do not consciously attempt to control their nonverbal behavior that the greatest potential for unintended leakage occurs. Therefore, to reduce the number of mixed messages, the manager must learn to pay attention to his own "affect display," but at the same time tune in to those of subordinates as a mechanism for assessing verbally unexpressed inner states.

But here again, the relevance of body positioning must be interpreted based upon the manager's knowledge of the sender. The significance of the receiver leaning toward the sender, legs or arms crossed, or leaning away from the sender, must be interpreted in terms of one's knowledge about that individual. A brief example will demonstrate this point. Several years ago a well-known national political figure was discussant on a university panel. After the session a colleague spoke with the gentleman for several minutes. Later, our colleague indicated that he did not like the political figure because he was cold and aloof. When asked why he felt that way, our colleague described the political figure's erect and stiff body positioning. Our response to this statement was that perhaps such an erect and stiff stance was the result of the accident he had been in several months before. Without more knowledge of the political figure and more personal experience with him, this question could not be answered.

Regulators are designed to help control or regulate the flow of verbal messages occurring between individuals. For example, a nod of the receiver's head will indicate understanding of the message being transmitted, and at the same time tell the sender to continue. Conversely, the lack of regulators is often taken as a signal that the receiver is uninterested in what the sender is saying. The use of regulators also tends to increase as the verbal messages become more complex.

Adaptors are often the most difficult to give meaning to, or understand. Adaptors tend to reflect the unique personality of the sender and therefore can only be understood in terms of one's experiences with the sender. Pencil chewing, leg shaking, nail biting, or head scratching may have little or no meaning when transmitted by some individuals, but significant meaning when used by others. It is the manager's responsibility to know which extreme is an accurate interpretation of a particular situation.

Eye Contact

Eye contact and movement have long been recognized as a key source of information about the feelings and emotions of others. Such emphasis is clearly indicated by the many everyday expressions dealing with eye contact and movement (e.g., "if looks could kill" or "his icy stare"). Researchers[36] indicate that eye movement and eye contact can be useful in indicating (*a*) thought, (*b*) understanding, (*c*) willingness of the receiver to respond, and (*d*) emotional response of the receiver.

It is generally argued that people who make good eye contact are indicating that they are cognitively receptive, while those who look away are not. Alternatively, if someone is making good eye contact, that individual likely understands what the speaker is saying. However, if the receiver looks away during a conversation this might imply that the individual is either thinking over what has been said and that the sender should slow down or pause while the receiver is thinking it over, or may, in fact be uninterested and therefore not paying attention. Researchers have further indicated that the receivers' eyes, including eyebrows, eyelids, and surrounding area, can be one of the richest sources of information about their emotional response to the sender's message, that is, anger, disgust, happiness, or embarrassment.

However, as implied in each of the above statements, there is no guarantee that the receivers of the nonverbal cue are correct in their interpretation. The words "generally," "might," or "can be" are designed to impart a degree of uncertainty in any interpretation and thereby warn the receivers to cross-check their inferences. Because we are dealing with inferences, there will always be a probability of error. To reduce this probability, the manager must continually update his or her cognitive database of subordinate behaviors.

Body Contact

Heslim[37] has classified touching behaviors into five categories: (1) functional/ professional, (2) social/polite, (3) friendship/warmth, (4) love/intimacy, and (5) sexual/arousal. These five categories appear to represent increasing levels of closeness, familiarity, support, or intimacy between two individuals. If one allows another person to shake one's hand, it implies a certain level of closeness, but not as much closeness as two individuals who hug. However, Heslim's categories fail to recognize the possibility of negative messages sent by touch. Clearly, if someone slaps another, a strong message of anger or dislike is communicated. Touch, and who initiates the touching, may also imply perceived dominance. Henley[38] argued that individuals who perceive themselves as having power or dominance over others are more likely to touch.

The potential for conflict occurs when the two individuals involved in an exchange do not agree as to appropriate levels of tactile response, or if one participant in an interpersonal exchange is perceived as going beyond an acceptable level of familiarity or intimacy. For example, in the mid 1980s, the Queen, while visiting Canada and mingling with the crowds, was held on the arm by a Lieutenant Governor. While most of us would find this to be a common courtesy, the English press were horrified that anyone would become that familiar with the Queen, even if he was a well-known political figure. When dealing with tactile behavior, managers must realize that what is perceived as appropriate will be a function of the individual, the situation, and the individual's cultural background.

Personal Space

The distance allowed between individuals can be used to communicate the degree of liking between two individuals. One of the most detailed scales for social distance was developed by Hall[39] and described the relationship between distance, level of intimacy, vocal characteristics, and message content (see Table 4.2). Clearly, this social distance model tells us that the degree to which we allow others to invade our social space can communicate the degree of liking and overall responsiveness toward another individual. However, the actual distancing allowed by a particular individual will be a function of his or her culture, personality, and gender. Consequently, when managers attempt to interpret feelings and emotions, they must base their decision not only on a social distance scale developed by a behavioral scientist, but also upon their personal experience and insight into each significant other.

TABLE 4.2 Social Distance Zones

Distance	Description of Distance	Vocal Characteristics	Message Content
0–6 inches	Intimate (close phase)	Soft whisper	Top secret
6–18 inches	Intimate (far phase)	Audible whispers	Very confidential
1.5–2.5 feet	Personal (close phase)	Soft voice	Personal subject matter
2.5–4 feet	Personal (far phase)	Slightly lowered voice	Personal subject matter
4.0–7 feet	Social (close phase)	Full voice	Nonpersonal information
7–12 feet	Social (far phase)	Full voice, slight overloudness	Public information for others to hear
12–25 feet	Public (close phase)	Loud voice talking to a group	Public information for others to hear
25 feet or more	Public (far phase)	Loudest voice	Hailing, departures

Source: Stewart L. Tubbs and Sylvia Moss, *Human Communication*. Used by permission of Random House, Inc., p. 146, © 1987.

Vocal Elements

Vocal components of speech involve word stress, inflection, vocal rate, loudness, enunciation, and other vocalizations such as laughing, crying, sighing, yawning, etc. Mehrabian looks at paralanguage in an interesting way when he concludes that vocal information is "what is lost when speech is written down." The importance of vocal information is further brought into perspective when we consider Mehrabian's conclusions that approximately 38 percent of social meaning is a result of paralanguage.[40] The importance of vocal communication is that its use can change the meaning of the words being spoken. The following example will demonstrate this point. During the Nixon years in the White House, Robert MacCloskey, working out of the State Department, used a phrase that took on several meanings depending upon the paralanguage used. It was not long before the press corps understood the different meanings MacCloskey was trying to get across when answering their questions. The specific phrase used was "I would not speculate." From this one sentence he was able to transmit three different messages to those asking him questions. If the statement was made without any accent on any of the four words, MacCloskey was saying that he really didn't know the answer to the question. Alternatively, if the accent was on the "I" followed by a brief pause before completing the sentence, the intended message was "I would not speculate but you can if you want to." Finally, if the accent was on the word "speculate" preceded by a pause, the premise of the question was probably wrong and it was not worth pursuing.

We see, therefore, that the same words stated three different ways resulted in three different meanings that were clearly understood by the press corps. The question is, how do these different meanings become generally accepted by others. The key is observation, tuning in to vocal differences, and linking the information with the situation and specific consequences. The longer this process is continued, the more accurate the receiver's interpretation of the intended meaning will be.

Time

Time is a variable that appears to be critical to most North Americans and a nonverbal cue used to give meaning to messages received. Culture and individual differences also play a role in how people relate to time. However, the two dimensions that appear to be most critical are the promptness dimension (early versus late) and the degree of specificity.[41] North Americans tend to place a high value on time and therefore promptness. Similarly, North Americans, on average, tend to place a greater value on specificity than do other cultures. When they are part of the interpersonal relationship, differences in the application of time can communicate differences in feeling and emotion. For example, if you ask a friend a favor (assume that the issue is important to you), and the friend agrees to do it for you within a specified period of time but fails to deliver as promised, a number of conclusions will be drawn. First, the friend may not be as dependable as you thought, may not be as good a friend as you thought, or may have placed a significantly lower value on the request than you did. Similarly, if your boss makes a request and states that you should have it done in "a week or so," you are likely to interpret it as having low priority. However, if the boss had been specific and stated he wanted it by 3:00 P.M. on Friday, you are likely to give it a higher priority.

Language of Things

Language of things typically deals with the physical artifacts over which individuals have control. These may include the manager's automobile, dress, office furnishings, or items on the desk. Whether consciously or unconsciously, individuals communicate messages through objects used. Therefore, for managers to interact effectively and understand those around them, or for that matter control their own behavior, an effort should be made to tune in to this channel of nonverbal behavior. Let us consider two examples.

One of the more commonly talked-about areas of object language is that of personal dress. The students of the authors often joke that they can tell when we are out making money—we have our three-piece suits on. The underlying assumption is that to be perceived as a business professional in the real world (when an academic works as a consultant), one must dress the part. If one does not dress the part, or live up to the expectations of others, then conflict will occur in the mind of the receiver. Therefore, we find researchers who argue that if you want to be influential and have power over others you must dress accordingly.

Similar advice has been directed specifically toward women. The following quote from Tubbs and Moss[42] is a case in point:

> According to some fashion consultants and consumer research groups, a problem has developed over the last few years: suits have become so popular—even among secretaries—that female executives can no longer distinguish themselves from other working women on the basis of what they wear. Thus one clothing consultant advised that a woman executive should also add "powerful" dresses to her wardrobe—that is, dresses that have shoulder pads. Another consultant, noting that dress codes for women have relaxed somewhat, counseled that a female executive does not have to wear a suit "if she is willing to wear something equally dark, conservative, and asexual."

Another potential message that may be communicated by dress is individualism, dominance, and/or power. Individuals who dress differently from those around them, or in a nontraditional manner, are frequently perceived as aggressive and independent.

The physical environment that managers create and function within may also communicate the type of individuals they are.[43] Two examples will demonstrate the relevance of physical surroundings.

In one organization, in the accounts payable department, an incident occurred which demonstrates how individuals draw inferences based merely on physical surroundings. Specifically, a new manager was offered the position of vice president of the division. A set of offices was organized and furnished before he arrived, so that all would be ready on his first day. Prior to the official day, the new VP made a surprise visit to his suite of offices. Once there he informed the powers that be that the offices were not suitable. In response, the organization gave the new VP authority to redecorate his offices. The following invoices were received by the accounts payable people: antique wall clock, antique desk and chair, antique couch, antique globe, antique wastepaper basket, antique rug, etc. Based on this information about object language, the people in the accounts payable department began to joke about the new VP and how he might behave. He was soon being described as stuffy, old, straight-laced, and rigid. This, in spite of the fact that they had never met the individual.

A second example involves a manager who was in the process of making a selection decision. One of the individuals who had applied for the position in question already worked in the manager's department as an administrative assistant. This particular individual, however, was often criticized for keeping a sloppy desk and work area. During a conversation with the manager, the issue of the pending selection decision and the administrative assistant's application came up. The manager indicated that although eligible for the promotion, that employee appeared unorganized and undependable. When pressed for a reason, the manager made several references about the employee's sloppy desk and office and stated that it would be hard to promote such a disorganized person. Although the condition of the employee's desk and office were not valid predictors of success in the new position, the manager was clearly being affected by the employee's physical surroundings.

Cross-Cultural Communications

As discussed earlier, managers increasingly find themselves functioning within a global environment. This trend toward a borderless world complicates the communication process and thereby threatens the manager's success when attempting to build rapport, probe for information, and interpret nonverbal behaviors.[44] We begin this discussion by explaining the role culture plays in the communication process, and by pointing out key factors that increase the likelihood of mutual understanding.

Culture and Its Impact on Interpersonal Communications

Culture can be defined as "the collective programming of the mind which distinguishes the members of one human group from another, ... the interactive aggregate of common characteristics that influence a human group's response to its environment."[45] At the same time, it represents the social legacy that is passed down from generation to generation and reflects what a particular group or society has found to work best within their environment. However, most cultural assumptions and perceptions that direct our behavior exist on a subconscious level.[46]

Culture affects the communication process by influencing an individual's values, attitudes, language, thought processes and nonverbal communicative behavior.[47] The likelihood of successful communication taking place will therefore be a function of the compatibility of two cultures or the degree to which each communicator is willing and able to adjust to cultural differences. In other words, culture can be considered noise that interferes with the effective exchange of information (see Figure 4.5). As communicators attempt to cut across cultural boundaries, the sender must encode thoughts using one cultural framework, while the receiver must decode it in another. As environmental noise, culture acts to distort the message that is being sent and thereby produces a mismatch between the sender's meaning and the receiver's interpretation of that meaning. Such filtering produces a situation of perceived conflict rather than actual conflict. Miller and Steinberg[48] referred to such filtering as pseudoconflict because the misunderstanding does not exist in reality but rather results from a misunderstanding of each other's culture. Unfortunately, if pse o- conflicts are allowed to exist because of a lack of sensitivity to cultural d ences, the consequences are indeed real.

It is, however, possible for managers to reduce the frequency of doconflict. The first step is for managers to accept the existence of c difference and the role it plays in the communication process. The step is for managers to engage in formal or informal training desi provide insight into the culture and the behaviors necessary to facilit personal exchanges.

Unfortunately many managers fail to accept that a problem exists and therefore do not adequately adjust to cross-cultural differences. To understand why, consider how normative behavior is developed. In each culture, individuals behave as they do because such behavior has worked for them in the past. The consequence is that individuals from a particular culture perceive their behavior as logical and appropriate and the behavior of individuals in other cultures as inferior or illogical.[49] Further complicating cross-cultural communication is the process by which individuals attribute meaning to what they hear or see.[50] Whatever meaning a manager gives to what is seen or heard often reflects his or her experiences. The greater the difference between communicator experiences, the greater the likelihood their attributions will be different. Such an ethnocentric view not only causes managers to reject the values, meanings, and nonverbal behavior of others, but also increases the probability that they will antagonize others involved in the interpersonal exchange. Ultimately, interpersonal communications and relationships break down.

Cross-Cultural Factors Affecting Communication

The following factors demonstrate some of the difficulties managers can experience when dealing with other cultures. Our list of factors, however, is not intended to represent the full range of possibilities managers might encounter.

FIGURE 4.5

Communication and Cultural Noise

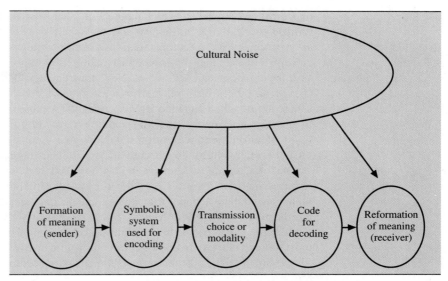

Source: S. Ronen, *Comparative and Multinational Management,* John Wiley & Sons, New York, 1986, p. 95. Copyright © 1986 by S. Ronen. Reprinted by permission of John Wiley & Sons.

Instead, it is designed to sensitize the reader to the importance of taking cultural differences into account and subsequently developing the appropriate skills and knowledge to reduce the likelihood that communication breakdown will occur. During real world encounters, potential breakdowns reflect the unique characteristics of each culture and the subcultures to which the manager is exposed. The examples given below involve three important factors affecting cross-cultural communications. Specifically, they deal with thought processing, language, and nonverbal behaviors.

Thought Processing

The way people interpret their environment is by thought processing.[51] Important to the present discussion are cross-cultural differences in the way in which individuals define authority relationships, environmental context, and social and family relationships. Three differences in these areas can directly affect how individuals communicate and how they respond to what is seen and heard.

1. We have argued that to be successful, North American managers must learn to empower subordinates. Empowered employees will have greater control over their own activities and participate in a broader range of management decisions. In Chapter 10, "Building an Effective Team," it is argued that managers should take steps to build teams in which subordinates share leadership responsibilities, engage in civilized disagreement, and interact on an informal as well as formal level. Similarly, in Chapter 11, "Creativity and the Problem

of Employee Resistance to Change," it is argued that employees must be willing to challenge authority and the traditional way in which activities are performed. Such recommendations are compatible with our North American culture, but can they be universally applied to other cultures? The answer to this question appears to be "No." Laurent asked managers in 12 countries if they believed that the main purpose of the organization's hierarchy was to define who had authority over whom.[52] Among countries, the percentage of managers agreeing with the statement varied considerably. The lowest level of agreement was obtained from managers in the United States— 18 percent, whereas 86 percent of Indonesian managers agreed with the statement. Cultural differences in how authority or power is distributed within cultures was also demonstrated by Hofstede.[53] Hofstede evaluated the degree to which society accepts that power and influence are concentrated in the hands of a few, rather than being more equally distributed within the population. Countries with the highest acceptance of power distance between individuals (highest first) were the Philippines, Mexico, Venezuela, India, Singapore, Brazil, Hong Kong, France, and Columbia. The countries with the lowest acceptance of power distance (lowest first) were Austria, Israel, Denmark, New Zealand, Ireland, Sweden, Norway, Finland, and Switzerland. The United States demonstrated moderate acceptance to power distance between individuals.

These results indicate that in certain cultures, authority is accepted often without question and even to the point that subordinates prefer a "bossy boss."[54] If a North American is managing in the Philippines and asks a subordinate to participate in a production decision, it is likely that the individual will refuse. The Philippine employee would prefer to be told what to do and would not question management decisions. Such a hesitancy may be perceived by the manager as the employee does not want to take on any responsibility, whereas the employee questions the manager's competency. If the manager continues to probe and question (i.e., press the employee to participate), the employee will increasingly see the manager in a negative light and may even refuse to work for the foreign manager. If such a scenario were to occur, empowerment and probing behaviors would have a negative effect on communications and the existing relationship between the manager and his or her subordinate.

2. Communicators rely heavily upon the words themselves and the context or environment in which the message is sent. For the moment, let us turn our attention to the degree to which cultures rely on context as a source of meaning. Hall[55] indicated that the environment or context encompasses five categories of events that can be taken into account by communicators. They are the subject or activity being considered, the situation, one's social status, experience, and culture.

Cultures differ in the degree to which they consciously or unconsciously draw upon the context to achieve understanding. High-context situations occur when most of the message's meaning is drawn from the environment, or internalized in the sender and receiver, Conversely, low-context situations occur when most of the message's meaning is drawn from the words being used. There are a number of differences between high- and low-context cultures.[56]

Individuals immersed in low-context cultures de-emphasize the context and often fail to learn how to effectively draw on the environment for meaning. The net result is that low-context individuals rely much more heavily on verbalization to achieve understanding. Low-context messages are therefore highly specific, elaborate, and clearly communicated. In contrast, individuals immersed in high-context cultures are more effective in reading nonverbal behaviors and expect others to be as adept in reading their environments. As a result, there is significantly less reliance on verbalization to achieve understanding. Supporting this view are data from a cross-cultural survey by Ishii and Kloph.[57] They found that the average individual in the United States spends about double the amount of time in conversations each day as do contemporaries in Japan: 6 hours, 43 minutes, versus 3 hours, 31 minutes.

Difficulties occur when individuals from low-context cultures attempt to communicate with individuals from high-context cultures. (See Figure 4.6 for a brief listing of high-and low-context countries.) Individuals from each culture behave in a way consistent with their ethnocentric view of how best to communicate. Many Americans therefore complain that the Japanese never get to the point or are too ambiguous. Conversely, many Japanese complain that Americans are too talkative, belabor the point, and are continually stating the obvious. The situation can further escalate as the American probes, mirrors, and

FIGURE 4.6

High- and low-context cultures

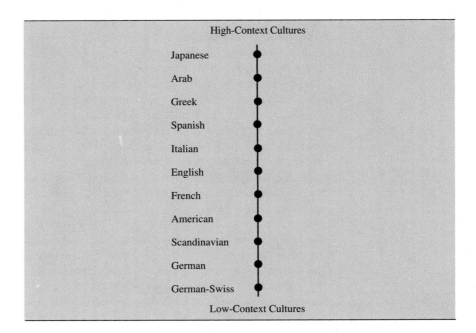

reflects more to achieve understanding. Unfortunately, the communicator from Japan may find the American too aggressive and incompetent, while the American finds the Japanese communicator uncooperative and elusive. Such negative views can cause participants to become hostile toward each other and ultimately cause participants to withdraw emotionally or physically from the communication exchange.

3. The role family and friends play within social encounters varies among cultures.[58] In many countries, especially in the Middle East, Africa, and Asia, family relationships are close and place great demands on individual family members. These cultures also place high value on friendship as a social support mechanism to help individuals satisfy personal needs. Close friendships are developed slowly over time and are perceived as prerequisites for social and business success. Therefore, when functioning within these countries, North Americans should not be surprised when business schedules are disrupted or delayed by friends or relatives of a foreign national. North Americans should also not be surprised if foreign nationals question or respond negatively to a decision to hire a qualified stranger over an organizational member's friend or relative. Responding negatively to such behavior communicates an intolerance for what is considered normal behavior within the host country. Such ethnocentric behavior demonstrates a lack of empathy and can have a negative impact on future communications.

Verbal Language

Language "is an organized, generally agreed upon, learned system used to represent human experiences within a geographic or cultural community."[59] What individuals see, hear, and feel is given labels arbitrarily that make sense within their particular culture. More specifically, language is designed to allow individuals to communicate those things, ideas, or symbols that are considered important in a particular society. As a result, language is at best an inexact system of labels representing reality. It is possible that the frameworks upon which two cultures have built their languages are not compatible, or that one culture has selected words that specifically satisfy social or interpersonal needs that are irrelevant in other cultures. Thus, it is easy to understand how and why managers of different cultures often misunderstand one another. A number of examples should sensitize you to the importance of understanding the host country's language and the reference base upon which it is built.

Translating and Interpretive Errors.   Direct errors that occur when translating one's message into another language can cause problems for organizations. Borisoff and Victor[60] described a number of incidents of gross errors that have occurred when translating a simple message into the language of another culture. For example, a United States deodorant company made an obvious error when translating their slogan, "If you use our deodorant, you won't be embarrassed" into Spanish for use in the Mexican market. To shorten the process, they used a translation used in Spain. The Spanish slogan used the word "embarazada" that translates into embarrassed, but in Mexican, embarazada means "pregnant." Clearly, the message sent was not the one intended. Similarly, when General Motors translated "Body by Fisher" for use in their Belgium market the message became "Corpse by Fisher." General Motors also ran into difficulty when they attempted to sell the Chevrolet Nova in Puerto Rico. The direct translation of Nova means star, but the verbal pronunciation of Nova (i.e., no va) means "it does not go."[61]

The Ford Motor Company has also made comparable translation errors when attempting to sell their product in foreign countries.[62] When Ford marketed a low-cost truck in Third World countries under the name "Fiera," they found that the word translated in Spanish into "ugly old woman." In the case of the Comet, which Ford marketed in Mexico under the name "Caliente," sales were less than expected until they realized that Caliente is a slang term meaning "streetwalker." Finally, Ford stopped using the name Pinto in Brazil when they discovered that the slang interpretation was "a small male appendage." Even though such errors are usually avoided, they cause people outside North America to question our ability and sensitivity.

Breakdowns Resulting from Subtle Differences in Accents, Style, and Linguistic Codes. Linguistic difficulties during cross-cultural exchanges are not limited to translation or interpretive errors. Subtle differences in accents, especially in how one enunciates or pronounces a word, as well as style and linguistic codes that go unnoticed, can also cause communications to fail. For example, in China there are four dominant tones used in the spoken language. As the people change the tone used, they also change the meaning of the spoken word.[63] Eastern cultures have also been heavily affected by Confucianism. Central to such a philosophy is the importance of developing and maintaining positive personal relationships. As a result, East Asians frequently engage in small talk before any effort to get down to business.[64] Similarly, Arabs prefer to have a "run-in period" for work-related encounters. During this time they prefer to engage in informal conversations. Asian linguistic codes also appear to differ significantly from those found in North America. For example, Americans can quickly change from using last names during an interpersonal exchange to using first names. Such shifts can occur within minutes. In contrast, to shift from the formal to the informal address elsewhere may require a long acquaintance and may not occur at all.[65]

Cultures also differ in terms of the value they place on interpersonal relationships. Eastern cultures place high value on one's ability to develop and maintain proper human relationships. This sensitivity toward others and their feelings often results in a level of politeness that the average North American would find confusing if not unacceptable. The Japanese will go to great lengths to ensure that others can "save face" during interpersonal exchanges.[66] North Americans believe in direct and forceful communications; the Japanese prefer indirect and vague communications.[67] If an American wants a door shut because he or she feels cold, that person is likely to specifically ask someone to shut the door. A Japanese person experiencing the same situation may simply state that it is a rather cold day. In this way, the Japanese communicator does not put someone else on the spot, but nevertheless hopes his or her message will be received and that the door will be shut.

Similarly, a Japanese businessperson will avoid using the word "no" so as not to cause others to lose face. Instead, the Japanese may say yes to a request and then go on to give a detailed explanation. If the receiver is paying attention to the long and detailed explanation, it will soon become evident that the Japanese manager has just said no even though the spoken word was yes.[68]

Nonverbal Behavior

As indicated above, nonverbal communications can play a significant role in what is communicated between parties. This is especially true during cross-cultural exchanges. Both senders and receivers must be sensitive to how representatives from different cultures are likely to express themselves nonverbally and to the potential consequences of how each views the other's behavior. Given the complexity of nonverbal behavior, and the enormous variations among cultures, we must again limit our discussion to specific examples dealing with time, space, and gaze or eye contact.

Time.   Hall[69] distinguishes between cultures that perceive time as linear (Monochronic or M-time), and those that view time as being less well defined and fluid (Polychronic or P-time). Individuals who view time as linear prefer to do one thing at a time. Time is viewed as a mechanism for communicating information or demonstrating power.[70] M-time individuals therefore place greater weight on the scheduling of time than on developing relationships. Conversely, individuals who view time as flexible and fluid believe that it is both desirable and possible to be involved in several things at the same time. As a result, schedules become less important than developing and maintaining relationships. Therefore, it is not uncommon for a P-time manager to fail to complete a business meeting because of interruptions or because of a desire to learn more about the person he or she is dealing with.

Interpersonal difficulties occur when M-time and P-time managers interact but fail to consider the other person's time orientation. The following example depicts a typical exchange between a Mexican manager and the North American counterpart. Assume that the American manager while in Mexico has been asked to meet with a Mexican manager at a set time. The American manager arrives several minutes before the scheduled meeting time, but the Mexican manager is unavailable and does not arrive for several hours. When the meeting does begin, the Mexican manager prefers to talk about the

American's personal background and the background of the project without discussing issues relevant to the meeting. The Mexican manager also allows others to interrupt the meeting, thereby preventing meaningful progress towards a successful completion of the stated agenda. As a result, another meeting has to be scheduled to complete the business planned for the first meeting.

In such a situation, the American would likely feel that he or she has been treated poorly, because the Mexican has wasted precious time and has behaved unprofessionally. Given the American's need for closure, this person is likely to press for action, attempt to get the meeting back on track, and be hesitant to discuss personal matters or the project's background. As a result, the Mexican finds the American manager cold, aloof, and too aggressive as an individual. Ultimately, the Mexican manager may question doing business with the American. In both cases, impressions are being communicated that do not fit the motives or actual behavior of either individual. Instead, the pseudo-conflict exists because both managers have failed to respond effectively to cultural differences.

Interpersonal Space.   There is significance in the physical distance between individuals, their physical orientation (i.e., how one sits, stands, or positions one's self when dealing with others), and the use of one's space. Here again, cultures differ in terms of how they deal with the issue.[71] Individuals from Arab and Latin cultures tend to interact at closer distances than do North Americans.[72] In cultures that expect encounters based upon physical closeness and touch, American managers who distance themselves or refuse to engage in physical contact are likely to communicate a wrong message. They may appear cold and aloof and thereby have a negative effect on the interpersonal relationship that the parties involved are trying to develop.

Cross-cultural differences also occur when considering a manager's physical surroundings. German managers prefer surroundings that emphasize privacy and reinforce social distance. Their offices are often constructed with soundproofing materials, heavy drapes, and impressive doors, thereby physically separating them from others within the organization.[73] Alternatively, a Japanese manager's office is likely to be open, physically shared with subordinates. There is usually little in the way of physical artifacts to distinguish one individual's office from another.[74] Such a physical layout is designed to stimulate open communication and a team environment. Nevertheless, there still exists a strict status ranking based on physical location within the room and in which room one is located. Individuals in the open office are not equal. The high status individual is usually seated farthest from the door and closest to the window.

Sensitivity to preferred, or appropriate body positioning, is important when dealing with other cultures. North Americans usually prefer to sit facing one another, whereas the Chinese prefer to sit side by side.[75] In Japan, one communicates the level of interpersonal deference to another person by bowing.

Gaze or Eye Contact. North Americans can also run into difficulty in determining what is considered proper eye contact.[76] North Americans have been educated that eye contact is desirable to demonstrate listening and sensitivity to what the other person is saying. If failure to maintain eye contact is interpreted as an indication of suspicious or dishonest behavior, such behavior may also be considered disrespectful or threatening to the speaker. But not all cultures place value on eye contact. Arabs, Latins and some African countries (e.g., Nigeria) exhibit the greatest levels of eye contact, and Northern Europeans and Indians exhibit the lowest.[77] An Arab businessperson may gaze with such intensity that he or she can embarrass the American manager, who typically expects moderate eye contact.

In Japan, children are educated not to maintain eye contact. In adult life, Japanese demonstrate respect by lowering their gaze when communicating with someone of high social or organizational status. Therefore, if a North American businessperson interacts with a high status Japanese manager and maintains extended eye contact, it may be misinterpreted as a sign of disrespect. Alternatively, if the North American manager is interacting with a Japanese manager of lower status and that manager fails to maintain good eye contact, the North American manager may become suspicious of the person's motives.

Given these examples of cross-cultural communication, the reader should recognize that the ability to demonstrate empathy, engage in rapport-building behavior, and accurately respond to nonverbal cues is usually more difficult when interacting with foreign nationals. A key to overcoming these difficulties is a willingness to inform oneself of cross-cultural differences, and be willing to alter one's style to accommodate the culturally specific needs of each situation.

Summary

Communication skills presented in this chapter are designed to facilitate rapport building and information processing among managers and other individuals. This can be accomplished through active listening; probing, reflecting, summarizing, and making supportive statements; and developing one's ability to control and observe nonverbal behavior. Such rapport building, attending, and responding behaviors also increase the probability that managers will be able to both recognize and respond to individual differences that are likely to exist in members of their staff and others with whom they must interact. A final discussion focused on the effect of cross-cultural differences on the communication process and the need for managers to *(a)* be sensitive to such global differences and *(b)* adjust their style to facilitate open communications, rapport building, and data collection within an expanding global community.

EXERCISES

4.1 Empathic Listening

An empathic or active listening style is important when you are trying to *(a)* develop rapport with others and *(b)* demonstrate a supportive interpersonal style. Active listeners attempt to go beyond the spoken words and get at the feelings and emotions expressed by others. Active listeners put themselves into other people's inner frames of reference rather than being aware of only their own frame of reference. This exercise is designed to give you an opportunity to better understand the concept of active listening and to practice your active listening skills. Please follow the steps outlined below.

Step 1. The class will break up into groups of two.

Step 2. Following Step 3 you will find nine messages that have been sent from one person to another. In each case, the group will assume that the sender of the message is waiting for an empathic (active listening) response. Develop a short script of what you believe is an empathic (active) response for each message. When developing your script, consider the likely context in which the message was made, the general conversation that led up to the message, and so forth. Your script should include not only the appropriate empathic response but also several lines of conversation that lead up to the sender's message, and several lines of appropriate conversation following the empathic response.

Groups also are encouraged to make realistic assumptions about the environment in which the message is sent. The only constraint is that the assumptions should be consistent with the types of jobs and situations in which graduating MBAs might find themselves.

Groups should also select a member to play the roles of sender and receiver. A recommended approach is to alternate the role for each message. Depending on the efficiency of your group, allow time to practice each of the message–response scenarios. Because different people may interpret the messages differently, the entire class will be asked to make comments or suggestions in response to each role play.

When developing your mini scripts, keep in mind the following characteristics of active listening:

- The active listener puts a greater emphasis on listening than talking.
- The active listener responds to both the feelings and emotions of the sender and the content of the message.
- The active listener explores areas that the other person wants to go to rather than leading that person into them.
- The active listener seeks to clarify what the other person has said rather than giving his or her own interpretation.
- The active listener demonstrates sincere concern.
- The active listener avoids evaluating the sender's feelings or emotions.
  (30 minutes)

Step 3. Groups will be selected at random to role-play the exchange between the sender and the receiver.

Role-Play Messages

1. I can do the job as well as Linda. I don't understand why she was given the project.

2. I've been using the manual system for 10 years now, and it never produced this many errors. I don't see why we had to change to the new system.

3. Does it matter what I think? Does this company ever ask its employees how they feel about new things and new computers? It just appeared on my desk.

4. I turned in that major report and all Frank said was "thanks." I never heard about it again. Heck, I must have spent four months getting it completed.

5. If you want me to do it that way, I guess it can be done.

6. All I know is that I have budgets to complete, people to train, and time sheets to fill out. Now you ask me if I have any free time.

7. I came up with that idea, and my name wasn't even mentioned at the meeting.

8. If it weren't for him, I wouldn't be in this mess now.

9. I don't know why I wasn't invited to the party. I know that John was there, and he isn't even from our department.

4.2 Probing, Reflecting, Summarizing, and Empathizing: Digging for Complete Information

This exercise gives students an opportunity to better understand the mechanics and the importance of stem questions, probes, reflecting statements, summarizing statements, and supportive statements. Each of these statements is defined below.

Stem question. An opening question designed to initiate a desired exchange.

Probe. A question that seeks to clarify or draw out additional information.

Understanding or **reflecting statement.** A statement designed to mirror what someone else has said. Paraphrasing the original statement helps ensure understanding.

Summarizing statement. A statement used periodically to summarize large blocks of information that have been exchanged between two individuals.

Supportive statement. A statement based on active listening and designed to communicate that it is OK to feel a certain way.

This exercise allows you to practice your skills in using rapport-building questions and statements in collecting and processing information. It also gives you an opportunity to practice your interpersonal skills when interacting with others. Please follow the steps outlined below.

Step 1. The class will break up into groups of two.

Step 2. First read through the material presented in Scenario 1. After reading the interpersonal exchange, indicate what type of rapport-building question or statement each of the manager's 10 statements represents. You also should explain why each classification was made and the rationale behind it that is, what was the manager trying to accomplish?

Step 3. The class will assemble and discuss group findings.

(Steps 2 and 3 can be eliminated if the instructor reviews Scenario 1 with the entire class.)

Step 4. Select one of the five work situations frequently faced by managers and in which the desired objective is the interpersonally sensitive collection and processing of relevant information. If you are not satisfied with the work situations provided at the end of Scenario 1, use a situation with which you are personally familiar and develop a scenario that effectively uses rapport-building questions and statements and at the same time collects and processes the desired information. Please use Scenario 1 as a guide. (30 minutes)

Step 5. The class will assemble and volunteers will be asked to act out their scenarios. After each student scenario is presented, the class will assess the degree to which (*a*) appropriate statements were used, (*b*) needed information was collected, (*c*) rapport was developed, and (*d*) channels of communication remained open.

Scenario 1

John, a regional manager for a local manufacturing firm, observes that an employee who reports to one of his subordinates, Frank, is acting depressed and withdrawn. To understand why, John initiates the following exchange.

John	Other
1. Bob, what seems to be the problem?	— I just can't seem to make Frank happy. I guess it's time I look for a new job!
2. What exactly has been happening—?	— You know—no matter what you do, Frank doesn't think it's acceptable.
3. Did something specific happen this morning to make you feel that way?	— Not that I can tell—one day appears to be like any other with Frank.
4. Well, could you give me a specific example of something that you did that Frank didn't appreciate?	— Well I'm not sure if I could give you a specific example—he just doesn't seem to appreciate anything you do.

John	*Other*
5. What about the last project you did for Frank? When it reached my desk it looked pretty good—what did he think about it?	— As I said, it's hard to know what Frank's opinion is—I turned in the report and he just took it and laid it on his desk. What made it even worse is that I put a lot of work into that report and I think it was really good.
6. In other words, you spent a lot of time on the project and you feel that Frank should have recognized your efforts.	— You got that right!
7. Does he treat all of his people the same way?	— Yeah—&^%$ *&^—the boys in Frank's department would die if he ever said thanks, let alone tell you what would happen next. Ask any of the guys—they would tell you the same thing.
8. Let me get this straight, no matter what anyone does, Frank doesn't reward them in any way.	— That's right—the only time you get any feedback from Frank is when he wants to bawl you out, or tell you what a dumb ass you are.
9. If I am hearing you right, then, what is really getting your back up is the fact that Frank gives you only negative feedback, and that when you do a good job he basically just ignores your efforts.	— I guess you could put it that way—as I said, nothing is acceptable to Frank and if I'm not going to be appreciated around here I'm going to quit. Hell, I didn't go to school all those years and work my butt off getting experience just to be treated like *&^^%$.
10. Gee, Bob, I can see why you're upset—everyone wants to know when they're doing a good job. Why don't you let me look into the situation before you take any drastic action—especially since Frank has only been here for several months.	— I appreciate what you're saying, John. Managers like you understand—but I doubt if Frank ever will. However, if you want to look into it, that's OK with me—as for quitting, I'm not going to leave until I find something worth leaving for.

Work Situations

1. You are about to interview a job applicant who will be reporting to you. You want to assess the individual's knowledge of one of the work procedures used in your department.

2. You want to find out what one of your employees does on the job. You plan to use collected information to develop a training module for new employees.

3. You want to determine an employee's detailed opinion about a new piece of equipment and whether this particular piece of equipment makes the job easier or more difficult. The equipment is on loan, and you will soon have to make a purchasing decision for the entire organization.

4. You are attempting to obtain the facts behind an incident that has made an employee angry (or depressed). Assume that the employee has calmed down enough to talk rationally about the situation.

5. One of your subordinates is not performing at his or her normally high level. You want to find out what is causing the slowdown.

If you are unable to write a scenario based on any of the above situations, feel free to select a work-related situation with which you are familiar.

4.3 Nonverbal Communications Exercise

The purpose of this exercise is to measure your ability to control and accurately assess nonverbal communications. Each group will play the role of Bob, Vice President of Production, who is meeting with a department head, a subordinate who is about to enter his office. During the role-play exchange, Bob will communicate the following information to the department head.

   (Name) , I've called you in because I have to talk to everyone, including you. As you know, we have a policy that all computer hardware and software must remain on company grounds. Unfortunately, it has come to my attention that some people are not only taking hardware and software home, but are making personal copies of copyrighted material. I'm not accusing anyone, because I don't have any hard evidence yet. If the offending parties are identified, I will take disciplinary action. To prevent future problems, you will be assigned a specific piece of hardware. Do you have any questions, ___(Name)_ ?

Step 1. The class will break up into groups of five to six individuals.

Step 2. Each group will select one of their group members to play the role of Bob, Vice President of Production. The instructor will play the role of the departmental head, a subordinate.

Step 3. Each group will be assigned an interpersonal stance about the department head—for example, the degree of liking, responsiveness, and perceived dominance.

Step 4. When developing Bob's role, build in as many nonverbal cues as possible to indicate clearly how you feel about the department head. Remember that you will give the same verbal message to all department heads, but you want to give a different nonverbal message to each individual.

You should give specific attention to the following:

- Initial greetings as the department head enters your office.

- Physical positioning; that is, do you stand or sit? How close do you stand or sit?

- Your general posture, tone, volume, and spacing of message sent.
- Eye contact/facial expression.
- Physical contact; for example, shaking hands.
- What you do as the department head leaves your office. (Approximately 10 to 15 minutes)

Step 5. Practice another encounter. Have a second group member play the role of the department head who will be coming to Bob's office.
(Approximately 10 to 15 minutes)

Step 6. The class assembles again. The instructor will select at random one student to play the role of Bob. The selected student will communicate the written message before class to a student to play the department head.

Step 7. After each role play, the class will indicate what nonverbal messages were getting through to the department head. Specific attention will be paid to nonverbal cues used by Bob.

Nonverbal Exercise: Role 1

Assume that you (*a*) distrust the employee, (*b*) dislike the employee, (*c*) consider yourself far superior to the employee, (*d*) believe that the employee is probably one of the main reasons why the boss asks you to change the current policy, and (*e*) wonder why the employee is allowed to remain in this position by the president.

Nonverbal Exercise: Role 2

Assume that you (*a*) trust the employee 100 percent, (*b*) like the employee a lot— you started with the company at the same time, 15 years ago, and frequently get together to talk about company politics, (*c*) consider the employee your equal even though you are the employee's boss, (*d*) believe that this employee is not responsible for the supervisor asking you to change the existing policy, and (*e*) you will promote this employee first the next time an opening occurs at your level.

4.4 Adjusting to Cultural Differences in a Global Economy

Given the wide range of cultures, values, attitudes, and acceptable behaviors that currently exist among countries, it is not hard to imagine nationals from the parent company engaging in behavior abroad that might offend or otherwise confuse individuals from the host country. A first step in minimizing the occurrence of problems is for all employees to take the host country's culture into consideration when working in a foreign country. This exercise is designed to help students bring this need into better focus. Please follow the steps outlined below.

Step 1. The class will break up into small groups of five to six individuals each.

Step 2. Read independently the first scenario presented below. After all group members have read Scenario 1, each small group will discuss how the employee should act. (10–15 minutes)

Step 3. The class will assemble and discuss group recommendations. (10–15 minutes)

Step 4. Repeat Steps 2 and 3 for the remaining scenarios.

Scenario 1

Bob Frederick, an American, has recently received his MBA degree. He also has an undergraduate degree in chemical engineering. After taking a job with Eastern Oil, Bob was assigned to manage an oil distribution center in a Middle Eastern country. He had never been to the Middle East before his final meeting with the owners of the company. Bob does, however, have five years' experience working in the oil industry in the southeastern United States.

Because of the location of the oil distribution center, the host company had a difficult time hiring a manager from North America. However, it did want someone in the position who was from the West and could interact easily with European and North American representatives. Four technical assistants and one support person are reporting to Bob. All five are nationals of the host country and all speak fluent English. Bob has been on the job for about three months.

To increase the efficiency of all departments, the decision was made to computerize the process of distribution and customer billing for the center. Through informal discussions, Bob learns that the two younger technical support people (ages 26 and 24), already are computer literate. Two older technical support people (ages 57 and 61) are not; both have been with the host company for 20 years and are comfortable with the manual system. Bob is concerned that these two individuals cannot adapt easily to the new technology. Despite his concerns, Bob introduces the new system.

One of the older employees readily accepts the change and has no difficulty learning to use the new computers and the accompanying software. The second, the older of the two, refuses to use the new system and makes every effort to point out why it won't work or why it is inappropriate for the type of work being done. Bob has tried several times with very little impact to talk things over with the employee. The situation worsens each time Bob talks to the resistant employee. It also appears that the employee's behavior is having a negative impact on the entire staff.

1. How would you view this situation as a North American manager dealing with North American workers?

2. How do you think the answer to Question 1 would differ if you were a North American manager in the Middle East?

3. How should Bob respond to the older employee who is resisting the change?

Scenario 2

Water purification, or water sweetening, is an issue of major concern in many Middle Eastern countries. Governments in the area are continually looking for more effective and cheaper ways to purify saltwater and make it suitable for human consumption. A North American firm has recently introduced a new process that most people consider a major improvement. There has been increased demand for the process. One reason that the firm's process has become so popular is that it can easily be integrated with existing technologies. As a result, the company may receive contracts either to build a whole new facility or to integrate the new technology into an existing technology.

Increased demand for the process has also stretched the company's resources to the point that management is unable to send experienced representatives to manage new projects. In addition, management is unable to give its employees the depth of cultural training typically needed to ensure a working knowledge of the host country's culture, including behavioral do's and don'ts when interacting with the local population.

A new order was placed recently with the company and a seasoned company representative was assigned to lead the project. Unfortunately, he was stricken suddenly with a heart attack and had to return to North America. No manager equally experienced was available, so the company was forced to send a junior person, Tim Upton, who has little on-site experience in the host country. Nevertheless, Tim is put in charge of plant layout and design, and is responsible for ensuring that all the pieces fit together. The parent company believes that this is acceptable because Tim will be surrounded with knowledgeable assistants from the host country. Tim personally considers the new assignment as a major test of his ability. If he does well, future opportunities will come quickly.

Tim is comfortable with all the technical issues of the new water purification process. However, his level of confidence does not carry over into interaction with the government of the host country, dealing with construction tradespeople, local safety laws and regulations, local suppliers and contractual requirements, and so on. He expresses some relief when reviewing the credentials of the people who will be reporting to him. As it turns out, at least one individual appears to be knowledgeable in each of the problem areas.

1. How should Tim go about ensuring that he will get the best cooperation from the individuals who report to him?

Scenario 3

Several months ago, while looking through the trade journals, you read a want ad for a fish plant manager. The company placing the advertisement is located in the Middle East, and the facility is on the Persian Gulf. The placement information indicates that the successful candidate should be familiar with the fishing industry and have a minimum of 10 years of management experience.

You have over 20 years of experience as captain on several large fishing vessels with responsibility for a crew as large as 64. However, as you have grown older, you no longer enjoy long periods of isolation at sea. At the same time, you believe that you are too young to retire. You never married so you have only yourself to consider. You apply for the position. You believe that your experience satisfies the listed job requirements. To your surprise, the processing company is interested and you get the job.

Soon after your arrival, the owner of the company formally invites you to his home for dinner. Although you know that the owner was educated in Europe and has a very attractive wife and three daughters, the invitation was vague and you are uncertain whether his family will be at the dinner or any of your associates. You had been out of the office most of the day and did not see the invitation until you returned. The staff had left for the day, and you did not feel like asking anyone else about how you should respond.

1. Before receiving additional information about the situation, what should the plant manager do to make dinner with the owner go well?

2. Should the plant manager bring anything for the owner or the wife?

3. How should the plant manager dress?

4. Should the plant manager bring a guest?

5. Should the plant manager come early, on time, or fashionably late?

6. Should the plant manager compliment the owner for his (*a*) achievements, (*b*) beautiful home, (*c*) hospitality, (*d*) generosity, (*e*) charming wife and family, (*f*) wisdom, (*g*) expensive collection of antique cars, (*h*) popularity among employees?

Scenario 4

Bruce Judge has just been transferred to Mexico City by a large American bank to manage a new data center. He has been with the bank for five years and considers the opportunity to manage the Mexican center a promotion. While Bruce has never been to Mexico, he looks forward to working in a different culture. Bruce received his MBA in information systems from a local university he attended as a part-time student. Bruce believes his strong background in information systems and several undergraduate Spanish courses that he had taken played an important role in his selection. Although Bruce can read some Spanish, he has difficulty speaking the language, and making matters worse, the undergraduate courses provided him with little insight into the Mexican people.

The establishment of a data center in Mexico reflects the bank's global orientation, and a desire to take advantage of the wage differential that currently exists between the Mexican labor market and what is normally paid to similar employees in the United States. The bank's management believes that the new information age allows for effective transfer of banking information between major financial centers, both in North America and Europe. As the center's manager, Bruce is responsible for 200 employees.

Bruce has five individuals reporting to him, a Director of Operations, Director of Systems Support, Director of Corporate and Human Services, Director of Customer Services, and an Administrative Assistant. All of Bruce's subordinates are Mexican. Unfortunately, since Bruce's arrival three weeks ago, he has been having a number of problems with his immediate subordinates. Although they are all technically competent, he is having a difficult time managing them. Bruce decides to mentally review a number of recent interactions he has had with his Administrative Assistant, Juan. It is Bruce's opinion that because he interacts more with Juan than with his other subordinates, it might be best to start with him. The following are several incidents that Bruce recalls.

- I gave Juan the opportunity to work on his own when handling two important reports. When the due dates for the reports passed and I asked Juan to explain, he merely indicated that he had been waiting for additional information or was waiting for me to act.

- The last two times I assigned work to Juan and asked for his estimate of how long it would take, he refused to set a deadline. Then, when I made a suggestion, he agreed. In the end, it took him twice as long to complete the assigned work.

- I asked Juan to give his opinion on a meeting I had with him and the directors. I felt that the meeting had gone poorly and asked Juan for his opinion. Juan responded by stating that he felt I had managed the meeting well and the other directors had supported my views. Subsequent events demonstrated that Juan's statements were not true.

- On three occasions, when I was meeting with Juan, he took telephone calls, worked on his daily planner, and left the room to talk to one of the support staff.

- Juan continues to ask me questions about my wife, parents, and siblings. It makes me feel a bit uncomfortable, since I don't know him very well and the questions he asks are so personal. On at least two occasions such questions interfered with the business we were dealing with at the time, and we had to schedule another meeting to complete our discussion.

- When dealing with support staff, Juan uses his position to make threats. As a result he appears to be pressuring others to work rather than motivating them.

1. Does Bruce have a problem? How should he respond to Juan?

Scenario 5

Econ, a rapidly growing electronics retailer located in the Southwest, is currently attempting to negotiate a number of agreements with manufacturers located in Japan and elsewhere in the Far East. Econ has a reputation for selling the newest products at discounted prices and, at the same time, having the largest inventory possible. Its slogan is, "Never be undersold or out of stock." To demonstrate their desire to develop close ties with the new suppliers, management has decided to send Peter Nelson, one of the firm's top purchasing agents, to the Far East. He has been given the responsibility to negotiate a set of contracts that will improve Econ's market share in the Southwest and, at the same time, enhance its reputation as an up-and-coming electronics firm. Accompanying Peter is Reid MacLeod, a technical expert in computer hardware and software.

One organization of particular interest to Econ is Nagaoka, Inc., a Japanese firm that has established itself as a leader in external hard disk drives and fax modems. Before leaving for Japan, Peter set up a number of meetings with Mr. Washsami, Nagaoka's Vice President of Sales. These meetings represent the first-time encounter with a Japanese firm for both Peter and Reid. Peter and Reid arrive at the Nagaoka plant as scheduled and are escorted to a well-appointed meeting room. Besides Mr. Washsami, there are three other individuals present. They are Mr. Asakawa, Director of Production, Mr. Matsuata, Mr. Asakawa's assistant, and Mr. Konatshima, the company's interpreter (Mr. Konatshima was asked to attend because only Mr. Washsami speaks English). After several minutes of formal introductions, the two sides sit down to begin discussions. To break the ice, Peter indicates to the interpreter that, since the group will be working together for several days, it would be desirable to use first names. He then repeats his and his colleague's first name. The Japanese nod their heads but continue to use last names. Peter tries a second time but the response is the same. He decides not to push the issue further, but wonders why the Japanese are being so formal.

Peter again takes charge by explaining what he and Reid hope to accomplish and Econ's business philosophy. Peter directs his comments to Mr. Washsami because he is the most senior person on the Japanese team. The interpreter repeats his comments for the benefit of the others. They respond by nodding followed by long periods of silence. Feeling uncomfortable with the silence, Peter begins to explain the specific needs that Econ has to Mr. Washsami. Of particular importance to Econ are discounts for large volumes and a multi-year contract. In response to Peter's comments, Mr. Washsami indicates that it would be difficult to make decisions so soon. He receives accepting glances from his colleagues. Not accepting Mr. Washsami's statements, Reid presses the issue of price. However, the more Peter and Reid press, the more adamant and withdrawn Mr. Washsami becomes and the longer the periods of silence. Finally, Peter and Reid accept Mr. Washsami's unwillingness to discuss price at this time.

Peter turns his attention to important technical specifications for the hard disk drives Nagaoka manufactures. In this case, Peter directs his comments to Mr. Asakawa, Director of Production. Peter assumes that because Mr. Asakawa is the Director, he is the person with the technical understanding to answer questions. In response to the questioning, Mr. Asakawa hesitates and, before responding, talks to his assistant. It soon becomes clear to Peter that the person with all the answers is not Mr. Asakawa, but his assistant. Peter, however, is confused because he does not want to offend the Director or place Mr. Matsuata in an awkward position with his boss. Peter attempts to overcome his dilemma by directing his comments to the interpreter without specific reference to either Mr. Asakawa or Mr. Matsuata. Unfortunately, such a strategy only confuses the interpreter and makes the situation worse.

The group has been meeting now for two hours and Peter is becoming anxious about the amount of progress being made. As far as he can see, there has been very little progress. Even worse, the Japanese negotiators' casual and relaxed style, coupled with their reluctance to talk, has given Peter the impression that they are not very interested in doing business with Econ. In a final attempt to salvage something from the meeting, Peter turns his attention to the issues of delivery dates and how long it would take to receive an order once it had been placed. Here again, the Japanese are reluctant to make a commitment on quantities and delivery times. However, sensing some movement by Mr. Washsami, Peter presses on. After about 30 minutes of interpreter-assisted conversation, Mr. Washsami finally says yes to the specific delivery date requested by Reid. Mr. Washsami's yes, however, is followed by a long explanation about why such a date would be difficult to meet and how it would put considerable strain on Nagaoka's production facility.

Believing that he has finally obtained a commitment from Mr. Washsami, Peter decides that this would be a great opportunity to begin writing down points of agreement. Peter continues by suggesting that, since there is agreement on a delivery date, they can begin to write up a tentative agreement between Econ and Nagaoka. At first the interpreter is reluctant to repeat Peter's comments, but finally translates the message. To Peter's surprise, the Japanese look shocked and indicate that there is still not agreement on a delivery date. Peter is totally confused and suggests that they take a luncheon break to reconsider their position. The two sides agree to meet at 2:00 P.M. and leave for lunch together.

1. What do you believe went wrong with the negotiations between Econ and Nagaoka?

2. Who is at fault?

3. What would you have done differently?

End Notes

1. C. I. Barnard, *The Functions of the Executive*, Harvard University Press, Cambridge, Mass., 1938.

2. G. E. Myers and M. T. Myers, *The Dynamics of Human Communication,* 3rd ed., McGraw-Hill, New York, 1980: 11.

3. J. L. Gibson, J. M. Ivancevich, and J. H. Donnelly, Jr., *Organizations: Behavior, Structure, Process,* 8th ed., Irwin, Burr Ridge, Ill., 1994: 770.

4. W. Schramm, ed., *The Process and Effects of Communication*, University of Illinois Press, Urbana, Ill., 1954; C. Shannon and W. Weaver, *The Mathematical Theory of Communication,* University of Illinois Press, Urbana, Ill., 1949; A. Sanford, G. Hunt and H. Bracey, *Communication Behavior in Organizations,* Charles Merrill, Columbus, Ohio, 1976; S. L. Tubbs and S. Moss, *Human Communication*, Random House, New York, 1987; D. O'Hair and G. W. Friedrich, *Strategic Communication in Business and the Professions,* Houghton Mifflin Company, Boston, Mass., 1992.

5. L. Barker, R. Edwards, C. Gaines, K. Gladney, and F. Holley, "An investigation of proportional time spent in various communication activities by college students," *Journal of Applied Communication Research*, Vol. 8, 1981: 101–109.

6. L. R. Barker, *Listening Behavior*, Prentice Hall, Englewood Cliffs, N. J., 1971.

7. B. E. Gronbeck, D. Ehninger, A. H. Monroe, and K. German, *Principles of Speech Communication,* Scott, Foresman, Glenview, Ill., 1988.

8. L. Crane, R. Dieker and C. Brown, "The physiological response to the communication modes: Reading, listening, writing, speaking and evaluating," *Journal of Communication*, Vol. 20, 1970: 231–240.

9. R. Bostrom, "Patterns of communication interaction in small groups," *Speech Monographs*, Vol. 37, 1970: 257–263.

10. J. VanLare, *The Professional Listener,* Training By Design, Inc., New York, 1983; Tubbs and Moss, 1987; O'Hair and Friedrich, 1992; R. L. Weaver,

Understanding Interpersonal Communication, Harper Collins College Publishers, New York, 1993.

11. O'Hair and Friedrich, 1992.
12. Barker, 1971.
13. O'Hair and Friedrich, 1992.
14. A. D. Wolvin and C. G. Coakley, *Listening,* Wm. C. Brown, Dubuque, Iowa, 1982; Gronbeck, Ehninger, Monroe, and German, 1988.
15. O'Hair and Friedrich, 1992.
16. E. A. Locke and G. P. Latham, *Goal Setting: A Motivational Technique that Works!* Prentice Hall, Englewood Cliffs, N. J., 1984; O'Hair, and Friedrich, 1992.
17. O'Hair and Friedrich, 1992.
18. B. Goss, *Processing Information,* Wadsworth, Belmont, Calif., 1982; Wolvin, and Coakley, 1982.
19. R. R. Carkhuff and B. G. Berenson, *Beyond Counseling and Therapy,* 2nd ed., Holt, Rinehart & Winston, New York, 1976.
20. G. Egan, *You and Me: The Skills of Communicating and Relating to Others,* Wadsworth, Belmont, Calif. 1977.
21. Weaver, 1993: 171.
22. Weaver, 1993.
23. As quoted in G. T. Hunt, *Communication Skills in the Organization*, Prentice Hall, Englewood Cliffs, N. J., p. 89.
24. Weaver, 1993.
25. L. Dryer, "Bringing human resources into the strategy formulation process," *Human Resource Management,* Vol. 22, No. 3, 1983: 257–271; A. D. Frank and J. L. Brownell, *Organizational Communication and Behavior: Communicating to Improve Performance,* Holt, Rinehart & Winston, New York, 1989.
26. A. G. Athos and J. J. Gabarro, *Interpersonal Behavior: Communication and Understanding in Relationships*, Prentice Hall, Englewood Cliffs, N.J., 1978: 417.
27. R. R. Carkhuff, "The development of systematic human resource development models," *Counselling Psychologist,* Vol. 3, 1972: 4–11; R. R. Carkhuff, "New training for helping professionals: Toward a technology for human and community resource development," *Counselling Psychologist,* Vol. 3, 1972: 12–30; Carkhuff and Berenson, 1976.
28. J. Gibb, "Defensive communications," *Journal of Communications,* Vol. 11, 1961: 141–148.
29. T. Gordon, *P.E.T.: Parent Effectiveness Training,* New American Library, New York, 1975.
30. Gordon, 1975.
31. The following discussion is based in part on material presented in E. Jackson, "Establishing rapport I: Verbal interaction," *Journal of Oral Medicine,* Vol. 30, No. 4, October/December, 1975.
32. R. L. Birdwhistell, *Kinesics and Context: Essay on Body Motion Communication*, University of Pennsylvania Press, Philadelphia, 1970.
33. A. Mehrabian, *Nonverbal Communication*, Aldine-Atherton, Chicago, 1972.
34. D. Borisoff and D. A. Victor, *Conflict Management: A Communication Skills Approach,* Prentice Hall, Englewood Cliffs, N. J., 1989.
35. P. Ekman and W. V. Friesen, "The repertoire of nonverbal behavior: Categories, origins, usage, and coding," *Semiotica,* Vol. 1, 1969: 49–98; P. Ekman and W. V. Friesen, "Nonverbal behavior in psychotherapy," in *The Psychology of Depression: Contemporary Theory and Research*, ed. R. J. Friedman and M. M. Katz, Winston & Sons, Washington D. C., 1974; P. Ekman and W. V. Friesen, *Unmasking the Face*, Prentice Hall, Englewood Cliffs, N. J., 1975.
36. M. Argyle, R. Inghan, F. Alkema, and M. McCallin, "The different functions of gaze," *Semiotica,* Vol. 7, 1973: 19–32; A. Kendon, "Some functions of gaze direction in social interaction," *Acta Psychologica,* Vol. 26, 1967: 22–63.
37. R. Heslim, "Steps toward a taxonomy of touching," paper presented at the Midwestern Psychological Association, Chicago, May 1974. Referenced in M. L. Knapp, *Essentials of Nonverbal Behavior*, Holt Rinehart & Winston, New York, 1980.
38. N. M. Henley, *Body Politics: Power, Sex and Nonverbal Communicatons*, Prentice Hall, Englewood Cliffs, N. J., 1977.
39. E. T. Hall, *The Silent Language,* Doubleday & Company, Garden City, New York, 1973.
40. A. Mehrabian, *Silent Messages: Implicit Communication of Emotions and Attitudes,* 2d ed., Wadsworth Publishing Company, Belmont, Calif., 1981.
41. E.T. Hall, 1973; E. T. Hall, *Beyond Culture,* Anchor Press, Doubleday & Company, Garden City, New York, 1976; S. Ronen, *Comparative and Multicultural Management,* John Wiley &

Sons, New York, 1986; Borisoff and Victor, 1989: J. Condon, "…So near the United States: Notes on communication between Mexican and North Americans," in L. A. Samovar, and R. E. Porter, *Intercultural Communications,* Wadsworth, Belmont, Calif., 1991.

42. Tubbs and Moss, 1987: 164.
43. R. Sommer, *Personal Space,* Prentice Hall, Englewood Cliffs, N. J., 1969; C. J. Drew, "Research on the psychological-behavioral effects of the physical environment," *Review of Educational Research,* Vol. 23, No. 2, 1972: 447–465.
44. L. A. Samovar and R. E. Porter, *Intercultural Communications,* Wadsworth, Belmont, Calif., 1991: 1.
45. G. Hofstede, *Culture's Consequences: International Differences in Work-Related Values,* Sage Publications, Beverly Hills, Calif., 1980: 25.
46. Borisoff and Victor, 1989.
47. N. Adler, *International Dimensions of Organizational Behavior,* Kent Publishing Company, Boston, Mass., 1986.
48. G. R. Miller and M. Steinberg, *Between People: A New Analysis of Interpersonal Communication,* Science Research Associates, Chicago, Ill., 1975.
49. A. Almaney, "Intercultural communication and the MNC executive," *Columbia Journal of World Business,* Vol. 9, No. 4, 1974; S. Ruhly, *Orientations to Intercultural Communication,* Science Research Associates, Palo Alto, Calif., 1976; S. Ronen, *Comparative and Multinational Management,* John Wiley & Sons, New York, 1986; Borisoff and Victor, 1989.
50. Ronen, 1986; Samovar and Porter, 1991.
51. Borisoff and Victor, 1989.
52. A. Laurent, "The cultural diversity of western conceptions of management," *International Studies of Management and Organization,* Vol. 13, No. 1-2: 75–96.
53. G. Hofstede, *Cultural Consequences* (abridged ed.), Sage Publications, Beverly Hills, Calif., 1982.
54. Ronen, 1986: 101.
55. *Communications,* Wadsworth, Belmont, Calif., 1991: 46–55.; L. Coopland and L. Griggs, *Going International: How to Deal Effectively in the Global Marketplace,* Random House, New York, 1985.
56. Samovar and Porter, 1991: 5–22.

57. S. Ishii and D. W. Kloph, "A comparison of communication activities of Japanese and American adults," *Eigo Tempo (ELEC Bulletin),* Vol. 53, 1976: 22–26.
58. M. Argyle, "Intercultural communication,"in Samovar and Porter, *Intercultural Communications,* Wadsworth, Belmont, Calif., 1991: 43; Borisoff and Victor, 1989; E. T. Hall, "The silent language in overseas business," *Harvard Business Review,* May–June, 1960: 87–96; E. T. Hall, *Beyond Culture,* Doubleday, New York, 1976.
59. R. E. Porter and L. A. Samovar, "Basic principles of intercultural communication," in L. A. Samovar and R. E. Porter, *Intercultural Communications,* Wadsworth, Belmont, Calif., 1991: 5–22.
60. Borisoff and Victor, 1989: 129.
61. S. Ronen, 1986; D. A. Ricks, *Big Business Blunders,* Irwin Professional Publishing, Burr Ridge, Ill., 1983.
62. Ronen, 1986; Ricks, 1983.
63. Hall, 1991: 46–55.
64. Yum, "The impact of Confucianism on interpersonal relationships and communication patterns in east Asia," in L.A. Samovar and R. E. Porter, *Intercultural Communications,* Wadsworth, Belmont, Calif., 1991: 66–96.
65. Yum, 1991: 66–96.
66. T. S. Lebra, *Japanese Patterns of Behavior,* The University Press of Hawaii, Honolulu, 1976.
67. R. Pascale and A. Athos, *The Art of Japanese Management; Application for American Executives,* Warner Communications, New York, 1981; R. Hirokawa, "Communication within the Japanese business organizations," in D. L. Kincaid, *Communication Theory: Eastern and Western Perspectives,* Academic Press, New York, 1987.
68. M. Imai, *Sixteen Ways to Avoid Saying No,* Nihon Keizai Shimbun, Tokyo, 1981.
69. E. T. Hall, *The Dance of Life: The Other Dimension of Time,* Doubleday and Company, New York, 1983; E. T. Hall, "Monochronic and polychronic time," in L. A. Samovar and R. E. Porter, *Intercultural Communications,* Wadsworth, Belmont, Calif., 1991: 332–339.
70. D. Borisoff and L. Merrill, *The Power to Communicate: Gender Differences as Barriers,* Waveland Press, Prospect Heights, Ill., 1985.
71. Hall, 1959; S. L. Tubbs and S. Tubbs, 1987.

72. R. E. Porter and L. A. Samovar, "Basic principles of intercultural communication," in Samovar and Porter, 1991: 5–22; C. Z. Dolphin, "Variables in the use of personal space in intercultural transactions," in Samovar and Porter, 1991: 320–331; E. T. Hall, *Beyond Culture,* 1976; E. T. Hall, *The Silent Language,* 1973; O. M. Watson, *Proxemic Behavior; A Cross-Cultural Study,* Mouton, The Hague, 1970.

73. Borisoff and Victor, 1989; J. S. Condon, *An Introduction to Intercultural Communication,* Macmillan, New York, 1985.

74. Borisoff and Victor, 1989; G. Fields, *From Bonsai to Levis, When West Meets East: An Insider's Surprising Account of How the Japanese Live,* New American Library, New York, 1983.

75. Samovar and Porter, 1991: 5–22.

76. P. R. Harris and R. T. Morgan, *Managing Cultural Differences, 2nd ed.,* Gulf Publishing Company, Houston, Tex., 1987; Borisoff and Victor, 1989; M. Argyle, "Intercultural communication," in Samovar and Porter, 1991: 33–45.

77. O. M. Watson, *Proxemic Behavior; A Cross-Cultural Study,* M. Argyle, 1991.

STRESS AND TIME MANAGEMENT: SURVIVAL SKILLS FOR THE 1990S

Objectives:

- To sensitize students to the effect of personal and subordinate stress on managerial performance.
- Identify those factors likely to have an impact on appraisal and coping behaviors.
- Identify a set of appropriate responses designed to prevent or offset the negative consequences of stress.
- Define the concept of time management and point out common time-wasters that reduce managerial efficiency and ultimately increase the manager's stress level.
- Give students practice in analyzing their own stress levels and developing techniques for minimizing the impact of stress.

The Importance of Managing Stress

It has already been stated that the next decade is likely to be a turbulent period during which managers must learn to deal with organizational change and uncertainty, increased competition, reduced demand for middle managers, pressures for on-the-job changes, and organizational environments that will require the manager to do more with fewer resources. Conditions such as these are likely to make job stress an epidemic in the forthcoming decade.[1] In addition, off the job, managers must cope with such factors as dual-career families, economic and social change, financial pressure, and changing demographics. Managers are therefore increasingly being exposed to environments that are likely to trigger a stress response. To function effectively in such environments, managers must develop coping strategies for stress. The need to manage stress is evident when we consider some of the statistics that indicate the magnitude of the problem facing North American firms.

Stress costs United States industry billions of dollars in absenteeism, turnover, decreased productivity, and health related problems.[2] Metropolitan Life Insurance Company estimates that a million individuals are absent daily because of stress, and that such absences cost United States firms $150 billion annually. Such estimates are not difficult to accept when we consider the following data. A recent survey of 1,000 businesspeople found that approximately 50 percent of the respondents experienced stress daily, and 80 percent felt stress at least once a week.[3] Similarly, a study conducted by Northwestern National Life of 600 full-time employees found that 46 percent of the respondents believed that they were highly stressed, and that 25 percent believed that they were experiencing stress-related illnesses.[4] In terms of medical treatment, costs, and time lost, it is estimated that stress cases can cost organizations approximately $15,000 each. This is about twice the cost associated with other workplace injuries.[5]

The following quote from *Fortune* magazine provides graphic detail.

> Sirota and Alpher Associates, a New York firm that surveys employee attitudes for corporations, has monitored more than one million workers at 171 big corporations over the past 18 years. The firm finds that the number of managers who say that they have too much to do has jumped from 34 percent to 46 percent in the past five years. In addition, 39 percent of nonmanagers say they have too much work versus 30 percent previously. Last year a Gallop survey of personnel and medical directors of 201 big and small corporations, showed that, on average, 25 percent of their companies' employees suffer from anxiety or stress-related disorders. Typically, the emotionally exhausted or depressed employee lost 16 days of work a year. According to the Research Triangle Institute, a North Carolina research firm, these disorders (and the frequent companion, substance abuse) cost $183 billion annually in lost productivity, job errors, and doctor's bills.[6]

Assigning Responsibility for Stress-Management Interventions

Traditionally managers have not considered it their responsibility to intervene on behalf of subordinates to prevent the occurrence of stress or to manage it when it is present.[7] Instead, efforts designed to manage stress have traditionally come from three sources, namely, the organizational level, the individual level, or from an outside third party.[8] Given the distribution of power that exists within organizations, a change in emphasis will not take place unless management alters its beliefs as to who is truly responsible for the control of stress. If managers accept their changing role (i.e., from controller or administrator to mentor, coach, helper, and team builder), they are more likely to accept the responsibility of creating a climate in which subordinates are less likely to fall victim to the negative consequences of stress.

If possible, it would be desirable and cost effective for managers to remove the underlying causes of stress. It is unlikely, however, that such an ideal state could ever be reached. Therefore, it will be necessary to supplement management interventions with stress management training, wellness programs, and employee counseling. However, because we are primarily interested in the interface between managers and their subordinates, our focus will be on the manager's role in managing organizational stress.

Managers function on two levels simultaneously when attempting to manage stress. On a personal level, managers must take the necessary steps to ensure that they have the requisite skills and knowledge necessary to either offset the potential effects of a stressful environment or create a new personal environment with more manageable stress levels. This can be done by working through one's immediate boss, existing company systems (Stress Management Training [SMT], wellness programs, etc.), or by unilaterally taking steps to build coping behaviors into one's management style. Such actions, when taken, are consistent with the authors' view of good followership and assertive management techniques.

On the subordinate level, the manager must act to create a work environment in which an optimal level of stress is achieved for each subordinate. This will require the manager to draw on the full range of behaviors being described in this text. In other words, the effective manager will actively intervene in the subordinate's environment to ensure that job design, levels of participative management, reward systems, stated goals, etc., reduce the probability that stress will have a negative impact on employee attitudes, productivity, and well-being.

An Optimum Level of Stress

We assume that there is an optimum level of stress that varies from individual to individual.[9] Therefore, the important question for managers to answer is "How much stress is the right amount?" Implied in this question is the generally accepted view that stress can have both positive and negative consequences. The potential for positive and negative consequences of stress is reflected in the performance curve shown in Figure 5.1. To be effective, managers must attempt to create an environment, both for themselves and subordinates, where the level of stress falls within the optimum stimulation zone. To create such an environment, managers must learn to manage stress and its causes. Given the shape of the curve, this means that in the under-stimulation zone managers must increase stimulation so that effort, creativity, change, and growth take place. In the over-stimulation zone, the manager must take steps to remove or offset those factors that are producing excessive levels of stress.

FIGURE 5.1

*Stress and
performance*

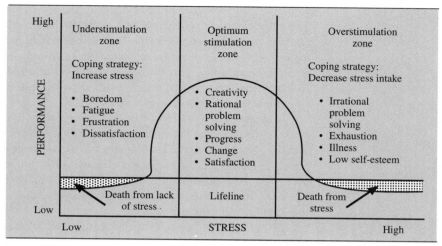

Source: Walter Gmelch, *Beyond Stress to Effective Management,* John Wiley & Sons, New York, 1982, p. 29.

Although the overstimulation zone appears to be the area of greatest concern to researchers and practitioners, the understimulation zone cannot be ignored. Low levels of stress can fail to motivate individuals to perform effectively. Without internal or external pressures, individuals may fail to use available, but untapped, abilities and resources, or fail to develop new skills and resources. Low levels of stress often result in boredom, fatigue, frustration, and dissatisfaction. Consequently, actual performance levels are likely to fall below potential performance levels. For example, Puffer and Brakefield[10] found that individuals performing simple tasks used less "behavior avoidant coping" (engaging in behaviors or activities that are unrelated to the task in question) when stress levels were high. The need for some level of stress to keep individuals on task can be partially explained by Sutton and Kahn's[11] detachment hypothesis. It suggests that busy people block out external pressures to maintain their focus on the present task. As a result, unless external pressure exceeds some threshold level, these individuals are not likely to alter their behavior or perform in desired directions. Alternatively, stress can heighten an individual's awareness of environmental cues and thereby cause the individual to act.[12] If an appropriate level of stress does not exist, the individual is unlikely to respond to external pressures.

Figure 5.1 also includes a lifeline superimposed on the bell-shaped stress–performance curve. The overlap produces a death zone when stress levels are very low or very high. Death, in the broad meaning of the term, does not necessarily mean physical death. In the present context, it can indicate professional death as well. The use of the terms *"RIPEs"* and *"Senators"* by two clients of our authors can be used to clarify what is meant by being professionally dead because of understimulation. The first term stands for "retired in place employees," namely, individuals who perform at marginal levels. The term *"Senator"* (taken from the political arena in Canada where members of the federal Senate are appointed for life) was also used to refer to individuals who act as if they have a lifetime appointment and as a result did not have to perform to keep their position.

Why are these individuals allowed to remain within the organization? The answer reflects environmental characteristics and the lack of pressure needed to cause change. Maintenance of such a system was possible because the two organizations in question held a near monopoly position in a growing market. There was little need for managers to concern themselves with employee productivity because increases in operational costs could quickly be passed on to customers by increasing the price of services offered to allow the organizations to maintain a healthy profit margin. Further, reinforcing the low pressure on employees to produce was a cultural system that valued individual freedom, minimum levels of interpersonal assessment, and a willingness to carry poor performers. When asked why such a system was maintained, employees responded by stating that it really didn't matter since company rewards were significantly above the industry averages.

Overstimulation can also threaten an individual's performance. For example, work overload (i.e., having too much to do, or doing work that is beyond one's current skill level), role conflict, or ambiguity can produce excessive strain for the job incumbent. Job strain can result in poor problem solving because of tunnel vision, inability of the problem solver to distinguish between the trivial and the important, failure to recognize or identify alternatives, exhaustion or burnout, illness, and low self-esteem. Long-term exposure to job strain may lead to physical or psychological harm (drug abuse) and terminal illnesses.[13]

Understanding the Stress Response

Figure 5.2[14] describes stress as an interactive or bidirectional process. In one direction, individuals are affected by environmental stressors that place excessive demands on the individual's emotional and physical resources. At the same time, what an individual defines as a stressor is likely to be shaped by past successes and failures in attempting to cope with felt stress, individual differences, perceptions, and coping strategies used.[15] The model shows how the various components interact and at the same time identifies a number of key areas in which the manager can intervene to manage the stress response for self or for subordinates.

Such a model demonstrates the complexity of the stress response. This complexity should not be viewed as a handicap but rather as multiple opportunities for the manager to have a positive impact on personal and subordinate stress. The key is to identify those areas that are relevant to one's own situation and respond in a manner that maximizes personal and subordinate performance and satisfaction. As described in Figure 5.2, there are four major sets of variables likely to interact with existing stressors to produce a stress

FIGURE 5.2

Understanding stress

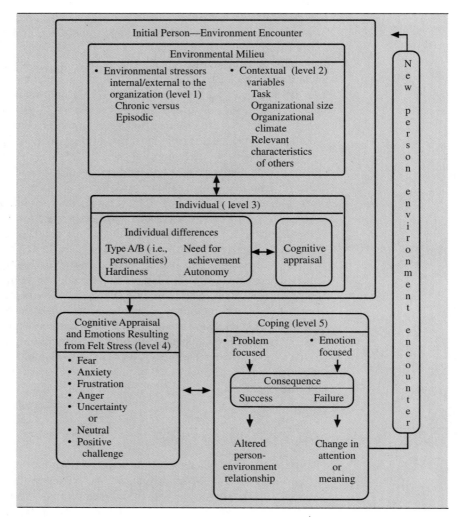

FIGURE 5.2

Understanding stress

response. Differences in environmental, individual, cognitive, and coping variables will play a significant role in determining the ultimate effect of stress.[16] Knowledge of these differences will facilitate efforts to minimize the negative effects of stress.

Let us consider each of the levels and assess the potential for managerial action.

Environmental Stressors

Early attempts to identify environmental stressors relied heavily on *a priori* lists to define the types of stressors most likely to have negative consequences for an individual.[17] These stressors included such items as:

1. Job demands and task characteristics (i.e., weekly work schedule, over- and underutilization, work pace, responsibility for work or things, travel, etc.).
2. Role demands and expectations (i.e., role overload, role conflict, role ambiguity, etc.).
3. Organizational characteristics (i.e., company size, job security, hours of work, sociotechnical changes, management style, organization climate, policies and procedures, etc.).
4. Demands and conditions external to the organization (i.e., route to and from work, number and nature of customers and clients, government laws and regulations, technological and scientific developments, suppliers, etc.).

Recent empirical research has demonstrated that interpersonal relationships, work overload and individual concerns also act as environmental stressors.[18] Interpersonal stressors included conflicts with aggressive or incompetent others, inconsiderate or inconsistent styles of management, and difficulties resulting from unreasonable, inconsistent, and insensitive colleagues. Workload stressors dealt with workload build-up; fluctuations in volume, pace, or complexity; and difficulties in meeting deadlines due to interruptions, extra unnecessary tasks, task complexity, and task importance. Last, stressors associated with individual concerns included such issues as career progress and development, competency, and health or well-being problems stemming from working conditions.

There is a relationship between stressors and job satisfaction, anxiety, and tension.[19] This is especially true when considering the effects of role conflict and ambiguity. Evidence has also been provided to support a moderate relationship between environmental stressors and behavioral consequences (i.e., absenteeism and job performance).[20]

Individuals do not enter the organization and leave their emotions and external experiences behind. Off-the-job pressures often play a significant role in determining the levels of distress symptoms reported or observed on the job. In a study of 97 newcomers to three organizations, Nelson and Sutton found that of the total explained variance in reported symptoms of distress (41 percent), 32 percent was explained by prior distress symptoms, and only 8 percent by existing work demands.[21]

There are chronic as well as episodic stressors. Chronic stressors relate to situational characteristics that are either ongoing or inherent to the environment. Chronic stressors can relate to the environment itself (e.g., heat and noise), the task (e.g., importance of decisions for air traffic controllers), or the level of activity (e.g., volume or pace). The impact associated with chronic stressors tends to be cumulative and therefore affects the individual over the long term. Therefore, chronic stressors appear to be better predictors of health-related disorders than are episodic stressors. Episodic stressors, on the other hand, relate to nonrecurring life events, incidents, or episodes. As such, they are short-term in nature.

Desired Managerial Response

Recognizing the presence of on-the-job stressors, the proactive manager must take steps to inventory chronic and episodic stressors likely to occur within the department and the total organization. The logic behind inventorying stressors is that the manager cannot change what he or she is not aware of. Once potential stressors are identified, it is necessary for managers to attempt to determine the probability of positive or negative consequences, not only for themselves, but for each of their subordinates. This step is necessary because it recognizes that each subordinate is likely to respond differently to potential stressors found within the work environment. To accomplish this, a manager will need to observe and record relevant information. This can be accomplished through observation, direct questioning, and assessment of available hard data (e.g., performance reviews, output data, grievances, etc.). If mechanisms designed to retrieve these data are not in place, the manager must take the necessary steps to implement them.

It is not necessary to go into great detail in each of these areas, as that is the intent of the various chapters found within this text. For example, if there are insufficient performance data, the manager may find it necessary to address the problem by implementing a performance-review mechanism. If the manager is not observing and recording relevant information, then he or she should regularly take walks through the department, or engage in counseling and coaching sessions with subordinates. Similarly, if the manager is finding it difficult to draw out the information even when questioning subordinates, then he or she should fine-tune probing, reflecting, supporting, and active listening skills. If, after review, a prime stressor is insufficient time, then the manager is well advised to identify and eliminate personal and subordinate time wasters. The argument being made here is that good management practices can go a long way in reducing not only the stress level experienced by the manager but also by his or her subordinates.

Last, inventorying will afford the opportunity to categorize relevant stressors as either chronic or episodic. The mix found within any department is likely to affect the type of intervention strategies that can be implemented by the manager. In the case of episodic stressors, the development of action–oriented and problem-solving skills would be appropriate. However, if the stressors are of a chronic nature, then the manager is more likely to deal with interventions that are emotion-focused or are capable of buffering the long-term impact of stress. It is in this area that wellness programs, counseling, and SMT programs are the most beneficial.

Contextual Moderators

An analysis limited to the identification of stressors and their relationship to affective and behavioral responses fails to adequately reflect the complexity of the stress process. As indicated by the model, an individual's response to stress will be affected by contextual or situational factors, individual differences, and how the individual appraises the situation.[22] We will first consider the effects of contextual or situational factors that can act as moderators. Moderators are environmental conditions separate from the stress encounter that nevertheless affect the level of felt stress.

1. Tasks performed. When considering the tasks performed, two variables have been shown to affect employee behavior. They are the technical and nontechnical characteristics of the task, and the level of task complexity. When the task involves technical problems as opposed to interpersonal problems, individuals are more likely to take action to solve the problem.[23] The implication here is that when the task or problem is tangible, and not people oriented, there is a higher probability of acting in the short run to solve the problem. If managers face a nontechnical task or problem, they are more likely to withdraw or hesitate when considering whether to take action.

A task is considered complex if it requires a large number of acts, significant information input, frequent coordination efforts, and involves frequent changes.[24] The level of task complexity will affect the individual's response to existing or potential stress. In the case of simple tasks, performance is dampened when the level of stress is low.[25] At the same time, individuals who perform simple tasks are less likely to engage in avoiding behavior when faced with a stressful situation. This may partly result from the fact that when stress does occur, there is a heightened awareness that action must be taken to solve the problem. It is also possible that employees who experience stress while performing a simple task have a greater expectation of succeeding if they try to remove the source of the stress. The greater the individual's expectancy of success, the greater his or her motivation to take action. Conversely, individuals experience greater stress from performing complex tasks. As a result, they engage in fewer active coping behaviors.

2. Organization size. One coping strategy for handling stress is to talk with others within the organization. Talking to peers is among the top five coping strategies in terms of frequency of use and effectiveness.[26] Individuals in large organizations have a greater likelihood of using the strategy of talking to immediate supervisors, other senior managers, and colleagues at the same level than their counterparts in smaller organizations.[27] The same study, however, found that individuals performing in large organizations were less likely to take action unilaterally to solve an existing problem. Therefore, individuals in larger organizations appear more likely to pursue social-support strategies than action-oriented strategies to cope with stress.

A number of explanations can be given to help clarify the role that organization size plays in the selection of coping strategies. In large organizations, individuals who experience stress may simply be responding to the increased number of others who are available as contact persons. In other words, the greater the availability of a given resource (potential helpers), the greater the likelihood that individuals will make use of that resource. In the area of taking direct action to solve an existing problem, it is possible that individuals who perform in small organizations are afforded greater control or influence in the decision-making process. Conversely, individuals who perform in large organizations may be less able to affect organization events, or the type of action taken to solve problems. The dilemma is faced often by students with two job offers, one from a large organization and the other from a small organization. Does the student want to become a "big fish" in a little pond or a "little fish" in a big pond? The implication, at least in the short run, is that the individual in the small pond (organization) will likely have greater influence over what happens within the organization than the individual who becomes a minor player in a large organization.

3. Organizational climate. The climate in which the individual functions will also affect the coping strategies used to handle existing stress.[28] Individuals when performing in warm, supportive, and open organizations, where managers are willing to tolerate mistakes and use them as a learning experience, are less likely to withdraw but will instead initiate action designed to solve the problem or discuss the problem with others, either to collect information or alert others to the existence of such a problem. Employees' work climate will also affect the level of participation afforded them by others in the organization. In situations where individuals are allowed to participate actively, their work-related stress will be reduced.[29]

4. Relevant characteristics of others. The characteristics of others affect the type of interpersonal support an individual believes is likely to be available within his or her work environment and the range of possible action alternatives when attempting to remove stressors from the work environment. It is commonly argued that social support is an important buffer in protecting individuals from the negative consequences of stress.[30] Social support occurs when individuals receive direct assistance form others. Affecting the individual's perception of available support is the sheer number of people that can be called upon to assist him or her in times of need. Clearly, the greater the perceived resource, the greater the individual's belief that social support exists. In addition, social support occurs when the stressed individual receives admiration and reinforcement of his or her own beliefs and behaviors from others. Individuals also experience increased feelings of support through networking and the establishing of relationships with others whose response can be described as exhibiting a high degree of liking.

The ability of others to give direct support is also affected by their personal characteristics. Support is more likely to be forthcoming if others (1) are aware that the individual is experiencing stress; (2) have the time and energy to intervene; and (3) have either information or skills that are likely to be relevant in dealing with the individual's stress. For example, an effective way for managers to deal with stress resulting from work overload is to delegate much of their routine activities to subordinates. Delegation to subordinates, however, will only work as a stress reliever if subordinates are willing to accept the new work assignment, have excess time or energy, or have relevant information or skills capable of being applied to the new assignment. If these conditions are not present, a manager's attempts to delegate may increase stress rather than reduce it. Increased stress for the manager can occur if the employee fails, becomes confrontational and complains, procrastinates, or requires significant coaching and counseling to perform the task.

Desired Managerial Application

By altering contextual moderators, managers can reduce the likelihood that stress will result in negative consequences for themselves or their subordinates. After a task has been constructed or designed, the manager should clearly communicate the steps necessary to complete the task successfully and to indicate the areas in which subordinates have control or authority to act unilaterally. Such clarification is especially important for nontechnical tasks likely to require a significant number of interpersonal exchanges, or where the sequences of task steps, or the consequences of the action taken, are ambiguous or uncertain.

For simple tasks the manager must ensure that the level of stress is sufficient to keep the subordinate focused on the task and not become complacent. This is sometimes necessary to ensure that the subordinate recognizes that the task is worth doing. This can sometimes be accomplished by clearly linking desired rewards with successful task completion.

In those situations where the task is complex and likely to produce excessive stress, the manager must take steps to simplify the task. This can be accomplished by breaking the task down into more digestible parts, thereby reducing the perceived complexity of the task or of the task sequence being performed. Managers can reduce the stress associated with complex tasks by increasing the subordinate's perceived self-efficacy. As indicated in Chapter 2, high self-efficacy individuals work harder and longer, and are more confident that if they try they will succeed on a given task. The self-efficacy of subordinates can be increased by allowing them to experience small successes before attempting big successes, providing them with relevant training and development opportunities, making available required tools and resources, and giving them relevant and timely feedback to ensure an accurate self-perception.

To overcome the difficulties associated with organization size differences, managers can build in the frequency of interpersonal contacts and networking opportunities for their subordinates. The development of an effective team can also help overcome the deleterious effect of organization size. In small organizations, networking ensures that the individual will interact with a sufficient number of others both inside and outside a given department. Teams also increase the probability that individuals will have the social support capable of motivating them to act. At the same time, teams increase the likelihood that group members will share similar values and develop positive relationships capable of sustaining individual performance during stressful periods. Last, team members are more likely to share relevant information and have complementary skills that can facilitate group performance. (See Chapter 10 for a detailed discussion of teams and their effect on individual performance.)

Activities such as performance evaluation, training and development, feedback, coaching, and counseling are options designed to increase the skill and confidence level of subordinates. With an increase in subordinate productivity and self-confidence, the manager increases the subordinate's expectancy that he or she will succeed if the effort to perform is made. Similarly, the confident, skillful, time-efficient subordinate is more likely to develop a positive perception of the manager and to respond favorably when given an opportunity to lighten the manager's workload by accepting a delegated task.

Managers must also realize that when it comes to the department's climate, they must act as a model for subordinates. Wherever possible, the manager must share available information with interested parties, respond to others in a positive and trusting manner, support subordinate efforts, empower subordinates by allowing them to participate in decision making and self-control, and allow subordinates to learn from their mistakes. By modeling these behaviors for subordinates, the manager increases the probability that subordinates will behave in a similar fashion.[31]

Individual Differences

The way in which employees appraise and cope with potential stressors is often a function of their personal characteristics. By failing to take into account their individual differences, a manager may fall victim to one of the most common and damaging errors that can be made when dealing with others, that is, assume that they think, behave, and respond the way he or she does. To sensitize managers to this problem, we will discuss three personality types that affect how individuals perceive and respond to stress, and additional factors that can influence how individuals respond to stress.

Key Personality Types

Personality types have attracted considerable attention in the stress literature. These are *Type A* and *Type B* personalities, *internal* and *external* personality types, and *hardiness* as a constellation of personality characteristics. Individuals having a Type A personality are characterized as being achievement oriented, hard driving, persistent, impatient, hasty, and having a feeling of being under pressure of time. The Type B personality would exhibit the opposite characteristics.[32] Type A personalities also demonstrate a strong desire to have control and mastery over their environments. Type A individuals may be hard driving and achievement oriented, not as a means to solve problems, but rather as a means of offsetting anxiety resulting from lack of control or mastery.[33]

When Type A personalities feel that they are out of control, or find that their skills are not applicable to the situation, their responses tend to be dysfunctional. Type A individuals under stress respond by demonstrating helplessness, frustration, anger, and resentment.[34] In addition, they are also more likely to delay working on complex tasks when placed under pressure or stress.

Internals and *externals* refer to personality types who believe they control fate or that fate controls them.[35] Internals believe that what happens to them is contingent largely upon their choice of behaviors. Consequently, positive or aversive consequences are received as a function of their own behavior. Externals, on the other hand, view consequences or outcomes as largely independent of what they do. The outcomes are perceived as largely a function of chance, fate, or powerful others. The outcomes are unpredictable. Therefore, the perceived focus of control is external to themselves.

Generalized beliefs about control have their greatest effect when the environment in which employees function is ambiguous, that is, when cause-and-effect relationships governing the environment are unclear, or when cues that help predict outcomes or levels of personal control are at a minimum. Under such conditions, internals are more likely to perceive that they have control, while externals are more likely to perceive that they are at the mercy of the environment.

Theory and research associated with the study of internals and externals indicate that each personality type has a preferred dominant response toward its environment.[36] Internals attempt to control and manipulate their environment. Externals appear less interested in controlling what happens within their work environments. Internals are more satisfied with their work environments, tend not to burn out, and enjoy opportunities to participate in decision making. Lack of control opportunities for internals may lead to feelings of low self-esteem and feelings of helplessness.[37]

Hardiness refers to a personality type characterized by commitment, control, and challenge.[38] Hardiness helps individuals buffer or offset the potential negative effects of stressful situations. The net effect of commitment is a predisposition to approach rather than avoid activities or others in their environment. These individuals tend to become fully involved in the activities they are engaged in. They are also more likely to find meaning in, or identify with, activities and others found in their environments.

Control fosters hardiness by causing individuals to believe that they can influence what happens around them. The basis for the perception of control is the individual's belief that he or she is imaginative, knowledgeable, skillful, and can make choices within the environment. Such individuals are less likely to feel overwhelmed by events in their environment because they can deal effectively with it. Individuals who believe they have control also tend to develop a broad repertoire of responses that they can draw upon to deal with environmental changes. This response repertoire also allows the individual to change the environment to make it less stressful.

Individuals who perceive challenge in their world see it as a place where change is a way of life. Such a predisposition allows individuals to view their environment as a sequence of stimulating opportunities for growth. Growth in turn implies that individuals can transform themselves and their environment into something better. The net impact of all three dispositions, namely commitment, control, and challenge, is to produce behaviors that can be characterized as open, flexible, and integrative.

Although not classified as personality types, there are a number of additional personality characteristics that affect the manner in which an individual responds to stressful situations. One factor of particular relevance to the present discussion is the differences that exist among individual *need profiles*. Unsatisfied needs are the "whys" of behavior; they directly affect how individuals respond to their environment. For example, an individual's long-term career need is likely to affect how he or she handles stress associated with career opportunities in the work environment.[39] Individuals who have a low need for advancement or who believe that they have reached their limits are less likely to become stressed if few career advancement opportunities exist within their environment. Individuals with a high need for autonomy are likely to become anxious if they are not given a wide range of discretionary control. However, research suggests that when faced with a stressful situation, individuals high in the need for autonomy prefer to take preparatory action (i.e., engage in problem appraisal activities, collect information, and seek alternative methods or solutions.)[40]

Additional Variables

Three additional variables, understanding, prediction, and control, also affect the way in which individuals perceive their world.[41] *Understanding* refers to the degree to which individuals are able to perceive how their environments work and why events take place. *Prediction* allows individuals to forecast the frequency, time, and duration of important events that are likely to have an impact on their success. Last, *control* implies that individuals can alter or influence events or relevant others within the environment. These three conditions, when achieved by individuals, can act as antidotes against the negative consequences of stress.

In a study of physicians, nurses, and dentists, it was found that understanding, prediction, and control had a significant moderating affect on perceived role stress.[42] However, only control had a direct positive impact on satisfaction. None of the three variables had a direct relationship to the subjects' well-being. Irrespective of the lack of a direct moderating relationship between understanding, prediction, and control and the subject's well-being, all three exhibited an indirect impact on psychological well-being due to a direct effect on the assessment of role stress.

Desired Managerial Application

Being aware of moderator variables, and their effect on the employee's assessment of potential stressors, managers are better able to manage their own work environment and the work environment of their subordinates. In the case of Type A individuals, managers would be best advised to break down complex tasks into digestible sub-parts, with each having its own assessment and feedback loop. This allows the Type A person to gain closure and a feeling of accomplishment. Subdividing tasks performed by Type A individuals into digestible units, supplemented with appropriate training, also satisfies their need for mastery and felt competence, and helps guarantee that they do not become impatient or bored. Should these efforts prove insufficient and subordinates demonstrate frustration and helplessness, managers must be prepared to engage in effective performance evaluation, feedback, coaching, and counseling (see Chapters 12 and 13).

When assigning work, or designing jobs, managers can consider the internal or external orientation of their subordinates. Since internals appear to prefer to control more, internalize cause and effect, and want to participate actively, it would be desirable to structure the internals' work environment to satisfy their job preferences. To minimize the impact of internal–external orientations, managers can also provide greater information and feedback to all subordinates. This will minimize the level of existing ambiguity and increase the relevance of environmental cues.

Given the research results on the effect of employee hardiness (commitment, control, and challenge), it is desirable for managers to create a climate capable of eliciting hardiness characteristics. In the area of commitment, the manager can increase subordinate participation (Chapter 3), work to build a departmental team (Chapter 10), and attempt to build into the job design those characteristics likely to match the employee's personal needs through effective goal setting and motivation (Chapter 9). To achieve a feeling of control, managers must learn to let go. This will require that managers allow subordinates to experience shared leadership and, at the same time, match the levels of responsibility that subordinates have with comparable levels of authority.

To help minimize the occurrence of negative stress, it is important for managers to recognize the differences that exist among subordinates. When considering subordinate needs, it is important to recognize that they will vary on such dimensions as need for autonomy, control, achievement, tolerance of ambiguity, inclusion, and power or dominance. It is therefore recommended that managers make every effort to collect relevant information about their subordinates. Given the available time and energy, successful managers will develop an implicit needs profile for each of their subordinates. Once collected, this information will facilitate such administrative decisions as delegation, work assignments, job design, group membership, and career pathing. Clearly, each time an administrative decision is made, managers should update their implicit needs profiles to reflect the newly acquired information.

As discussed above, understanding and prediction moderate how individuals respond to stress. Not only does the information allow employees to understand their work environment better, but it also allows them to increase the accuracy of their predictions about the future. Managers should therefore learn to keep the channels of information open in an attempt to ensure that all subordinates have access to needed information. Open channels can be initiated, and maintained, by developing positive rapport with others, responding in full to specific information requests when received, reinforcing offered information that is both relevant and timely, and by making available avenues of appeal.

Cognitive Appraisal

Cognitive appraisal refers to the process by which individuals give meaning to an encounter with their environment.[43] In other words, how do individuals perceive a situation. On the rational level, individuals objectively compare environmental demands with their ability to respond. Ultimately, individuals will assess the stressor's impact on personal well-being. Newton[44] has pointed out a number of relevant questions that individuals might ask when assessing a situation. These are: To what extent is X a problem for me? How much difficulty will I have coping with X? Why is X a problem for me? and Why do I have difficulty coping with X? The answers to these questions directly determine the level of felt stress or emotion that individuals attribute to their environment.

Behavioral scientists have also identified four issues that are likely to affect an individual's assessment of a given situation.[45] Specifically, when individuals attempt to assess whether an environmental encounter is irrelevant, benign, positive, or stressful, they consider how the encounter made them feel, how they would appear to others, the level of support from others, and the degree of personal control. Table 5.2 presents a listing of these four issues

TABLE 5.2   Factors Affecting Primary Appraisal

How will the individual be made to feel?
- Will I be made to feel uncomfortable?
- Will I be made to feel embarrassed?
- Will I be made to feel silly?
- Will I be made to feel responsible?
- Will I be made to feel concerned that personal expectations are not being met, or that I may not achieve an important goal?
- Will I lose the respect of someone important?
- Will I appear incompetent to relevant others?
- Will I be personally threatened?

How will the individual be viewed by others?
- Will I be viewed as nonsupportive?
- Will I be viewed as difficult to get along with?
- Will I be viewed as wrong?

What type of support will the individual receive from others?
- Are relevant others competent or incompetent?
- Will relevant others likely be hostile or difficult?
- What is the general level of support available?

What type of control does the individual have?
- Do I have control over events?
- Do I have control over the timing of tasks and duties?

and the supporting questions that can be used to define them. Individuals who believe that potentially stressful encounters will make them feel embarrassed or silly, who may be perceived as nonsupportive by relevant others, who must interact with others who are hostile or difficult, and who are made to act without control over events are likely to experience higher levels of stress than individuals facing opposite conditions.

For example, assume that a professor unexpectedly assigns a term paper to the class. Furthermore, assume that it will be a long and complex paper requiring more hours to complete than students can afford. As a result, students are likely going to experience increased anxiety. However, a particular student may reassess his or her environment and reduce felt stress by redefining the importance of the term paper. The student may conclude that he or she already has sufficient points to get a B+ in the course (a grade well within pre-class expectations), and because a full-time job after graduation has already been secured, a poor grade on the paper will have little effect on his or her life. Therefore, the student will experience minimum stress. A second student, however, who needs a good grade to pass the course and has no way of expanding personal time to cope with this assignment will likely experience a high level of stress.

The process component of appraisal indicates that individuals are involved in a dynamic exchange with their environment, and that the direction of influence is bidirectional, from the environment to the individual and vice versa. In this way, individuals assess their coping potential. At the process level, individuals are likely to ask, "What can I do to prevent the situation from occurring or continuing?" and "How can I minimize the effect of environmental events on me personally?" When answering these questions, they are likely to direct their attention to such issues as the physical, social, psychological, and material resources that can be brought to bear on the situation to effectively manage stressors or buffer their effects.

In the case of physical resources, individuals assess their general health, energy levels, and ability to maintain acceptable levels of energy output over extended periods of time. Social resources relate to the support systems that individuals can draw upon to help solve environmental problems or buffer their effects. Individuals who are members of organizational networks or effective teams are more likely to have access to needed information, social encouragement, or meaningful assistance from relevant others. In the area of psychological resources, individuals differ in the level of self-esteem, self-efficacy, or strong beliefs needed to sustain psychological balance during periods of stress. For example, individuals who have a proven track record of solving difficult personal or organizational problems are less likely to feel overwhelmed when confronted with a new problem. Last, individuals are likely to assess their access to material resources when evaluating what they might do to control stressors or buffer their negative effects. Individuals who have access to additional financial resources, tools, and equipment will assess their chance of success as higher than will others who do not have access to such resources.

Organizationally, individuals would likely assess *(a)* the presence of organizational or bureaucratic constraints, *(b)* the degree to which stressors have to be accepted, *(c)* the need to collect more information before any action can be taken, *(d)* the degree to which individuals have to hold themselves back, and *(e)* the degree to which individuals believe that they can change or do something about the situation.[46] If employees assess their environment as unencumbered by rules and regulations, feel comfortable with their information base, do not have to hold themselves back because of potentially adverse consequences, and believe that they can have an impact on their environments, they will view work situations as less stressful.

When individuals assess their coping potential they are not asking "How successful am I?" but rather "How successful might I be?" In other words, they are dealing with internal expectancies of what will happen. If they have high expectancies that they will be successful if they try, then felt stress will likely be low. Internal expectancies, however, are no guarantee that individuals will be successful once a selected coping strategy has been applied. They do, however, affect the degree of threat individuals are likely to perceive in their environments.

Desired Managerial Application to Appraisal

Managerial behavior has a direct impact on how employees appraise their environment. To ensure that employees' appraisals of potentially stressful encounters are accurate and positive, managers must take proactive measures to provide them with the appropriate levels of information, control, and skills. Clearly, managers cannot expend the same amount of time and energy with every employee or situation to ensure an effective subordinate stress response. Therefore, the degree to which they engage in such proactive measures should be defined by the importance and likelihood of a negative and disruptive stress response. Similarly, the experience, the ability to learn from and adjust to changing environments, and the track record of the employee will play an important role in determining how the manager should respond to the subordinate. The following are a number of managerial actions that can facilitate the appraisal process and help to minimize negative consequences.

By clearly articulating steps required to perform a newly assigned task, the consequences of successful and unsuccessful performance, and by highlighting potentially adverse situations that may interfere with a subordinate's success, managers can provide the necessary information to allow subordinates to answer key questions at the appraisal level. Many of these activities can be built into an ongoing goal-setting relationship between managers and their subordinates.

By facilitating open channels of communication, employee networking, and relevant and timely feedback, managers can also increase the probability that employees are able to determine the degree to which an environmental encounter will tax personal resources, that is, will the encounter be irrelevant, benign or positive, or stressful. Here again, other topics covered in this text will detail how to carry out these activities. For example, feedback can be used either independently of any other managerial activity or as part of a performance appraisal system, counseling encounter, or coaching session. Similarly, open communication can be facilitated by effective team building and rapport building by the manager and others within the organization.

Subordinates can be given greater control of their environment through a program of employee empowerment, participation, and task delegation. Such activities tend to reduce the use of rules for direction and control, and maximize the level of employee discretion when carrying out job-related responsibilities. By pushing control down to the subordinates' level, managers can demonstrate acceptance and recognition of subordinates' abilities. These strategies will also allow managers to lighten their own workload (e.g., by delegating activities of lesser value at their own level to subordinates who may find these activities challenging and developmental). However, before empowerment, participation, and delegation can have the desired effect, managers must first guarantee that subordinates are properly trained.

Training and development activities are crucial to any attempt to minimize the negative consequences of potentially stressful encounters. Subordinates who are properly trained and have been developed incrementally are more likely to develop high self-esteem, high self-efficacy, and personal confidence in their ability to overcome environmental stress. Such individuals, when assessing personal coping skills, are less likely to respond in an emotional or dysfunctional manner to environmental stressors.

Emotions Resulting from Felt Stress

It is the interaction among environmental stressors, contextual variables, individual differences, and cognitive appraisal that determines the level and type of emotional responses exhibited. In turn, it is the employee's emotional response that initiates a variety of coping strategies used to maximize personal payoffs or minimize personal pain. The desired response sought by managers is to have subordinates accept existing environmental conditions as normal and within their coping repertoire. When this occurs, then employee response to potentially stressful encounters is neutral, benign, or perceived as an opportunity for growth and development.

Negative emotions such as fear, anxiety, frustration, anger, and uncertainty increase the probability of dysfunctional behaviors being exhibited by subordinates. Negative emotions often interfere with performance in a number of ways. At one level, negative tension about an environmental encounter can cause individuals to redirect energies from current tasks to those encounters likely to be classified as emergencies because of the individuals' emotional response.[47] Unfortunately, there is no guarantee that such a reallocation of time and energy will maximize personal payoffs. Second, negative emotion can block effective problem solving.[48] This may occur because of cognitive breakdowns and irrelevant thought processes. Alternatively, negative emotions may disrupt interpersonal relationships needed to solve environmental problems.

Both positive and negative emotions can be a consequence of stressful encounters. Stressful encounters often trigger both negative and positive emotions from affected individuals. For example, the employee who is offered a new promotion feels excitement because of the recognition received, and the opportunity to have a greater impact on the organization. At the same time, the employee may feel fear because of the newness of the assignment and the possibility that he or she might fail.

Coping

"Coping refers to cognitive and behavioral efforts to master, reduce, or tolerate the internal and/or external demands that are created by the stressful transactions."[49] Defined in this way, coping does not refer to the level of success or failure of the coping effort. Instead it merely indicates that affected individuals have taken some type of action to manage their environments more effectively. Coping tactics used by individuals vary considerably and reflect their personalities, the resources available, and how they assess their environments. Table 5.3[50] gives some indication of the range of possibilities by describing six major coping strategies and representative support behaviors.

TABLE 5.3   Coping Strategies and Support Behaviors

1. Task-oriented coping behaviors
   - Setting priorities.
   - Taking some immediate action based on the present understanding of the situation.
   - Finding out more about the situation.
2. Emotional relief
   - Lose one's temper.
   - Express irritability to one's self.
   - Express feelings to co-workers or take feelings out on the staff.
3. Utilization of home resources
   - Talk things over with spouse when you get home at night.
   - Face the situation, knowing that your family and spouse give you help and a sense of proportion to the problem.
   - Take some of the work home and work on it there.
4. Preparation prior to action
   - Ignore the problem until you feel ready to handle it.
   - Take a break and come back to the problem later.
   - Tackle routine work so that you can cool down and get your composure back.
5. Distraction techniques
   - Go and have a few beers.
   - Become involved in nonwork activities.
   - Leave the office, go home early, or take a day off.
6. Passive attempts to tolerate the situation
   - Let the feeling wear off.
   - Give up and accept what's happening.
   - Try not to worry or think about it.

Coping Style versus Coping Behavior

To fully understand the coping process, it is necessary to discuss three additional issues. They are, the difference between a coping behavior and coping style, whether the coping style is emotion-focused or problem-focused and the effect of coping behavior on emotions and the environment. Coping style can be defined as follows:

> any pattern of coping which an individual exhibits over the longer-term, resulting either from the way the individual tends to appraise events, or from semi-habitual behavior which he or she employs. While such long-term coping patterns might exist relatively independently of the environment (i.e., as personality/behavioral traits), they might also be conditioned or be products of particular environmental contexts.[51]

Individuals have a dominant coping style that reflects organizational conditioning or socialization. Employees performing in an environment where individuals predominantly avoid problems or deny that problems exist will, over time, learn that avoiding or denying behaviors are appropriate and desirable. If a style proves unacceptable to an individual, if it is in conflict with his or her core beliefs or personality, then that individual will experience internal conflict. In attempting to produce internal balance, such individuals can attempt to change the system, engage in deviant behaviors, leave the organization, or conform to organizational standards.

In contrast to a coping style, there are coping behaviors. These are the actual behaviors that the individual applies to the stressful encounter. The consequence of such a distinction is that although an individual or organization may have a dominant style, it may be desirable to alter that style should the conditions of a specific situation require it. Therefore, it is likely that the most effective coping strategy would be to diagnose the situation (an analysis of situational, individual differences, and appraisal data) to determine what is the best coping response to be used. In other words, individuals must be willing to move away from their dominant style if that is the only way to remain effective or free of stress within a particular situation.

Emotion/Problem-Focused Coping

Coping serves two functions for the individual.[52] On the one hand, coping is designed to manage the emotions generated by the stressful encounter. Alternatively, problem-focused coping is designed to solve the problem or alter the cause and effect sequences that are producing the problem. In terms of the coping strategies listed in Table 5.3, Strategy 1 would best be described as a direct action, problem-focused alternative. Strategies 2 to 6 would, on the other hand, reflect emotion-focused alternatives. Although individuals are likely to engage in both problem- and emotion-focused strategies, the choice tends to be situational specific or will reflect the results of personal appraisals by affected individuals.

In those cases where the situation is assessed as being changeable, that is, implying some degree of personal control, individuals are more likely to use problem-focused strategies.[53] Problem-focused strategies are also more likely (holding other factors constant) in the short run or in response to episodic encounters.[54] Conversely, where change does not appear to be possible, individuals increase their use of emotion-focused strategies. When stress is chronic, and no acceptable alternatives exist, individuals increase the use of emotion-focused strategies.

Individuals are more likely to use emotional release and distraction strategies the more stressful the encounter, or when the stressor effect is negative (i.e., negative impact on performance, feelings or emotions) rather than positive (i.e., positive sense of involvement, or stimulating in terms of effort).[55] Similarly, individuals are more likely to use distraction strategies when the appraisal is that the job is meaningless, boring, or irrelevant. A later study found that individuals who appraise situations as providing little support are more likely to cope with stressful encounters by "trying not to let it get to them."[56] In addition, individuals were more likely to use family support systems when their concerns revolved around feelings rather than loss of control.

Although individuals use both emotion- and problem-focused coping behaviors, one style may dominate an individual's response to a stressful encounter. As indicated above, which style dominates will be a function of the stressors, individual differences, timing, and primary or secondary appraisals. A potential difficulty occurs when the initial and dominant response style is emotional in nature. If individuals deny, avoid, vent emotion, or attack others, they may never notice the underlying problem or the cause-and-effect relationships that caused the problem in the first place. Therefore, before individuals can effectively solve environmental problems, they must get their emotions under control.

Coping as a Mediating Variable

Coping behaviors designed to prevent, or buffer, the negative consequences of a stressful encounter can also affect emotions. If individuals cope with their environment by engaging in cognitive restructuring or reappraisal, that is, they mentally redefine reality, they can alter their own emotional states. For example, a student may respond to a poor grade by concluding that the poor grade resulted from lack of studying, and that by studying in the future, it will be possible to receive a good grade. Such a cognitive reappraisal will reduce the negative emotions in response to the poor grade and will reduce the level of felt stress when faced with future tests. In other words, because the environment is perceived to be under the control of the individual, he or she can prevent negative consequences from occurring. Similarly, if individuals reappraise a stressor to be unavoidable or something that must be accepted, they may feel less responsible for what is occurring, and they may stop worrying about it. Last, individuals engaged in planned problem solving often demonstrate an increase in positive emotions. A partial explanation of this finding is that individuals simply feel better when they begin to work on a problem that is giving them stress.[57]

Folkman and Lazarus found that when individuals use a confrontational coping style, they feel worse and experience increased fear and anger.[58] Such findings would indicate that the strategy of "getting it off your chest" does not necessarily work. "Getting it off your chest" can backfire when the communication is demeaning or abusive to the receiver or if it fails to address underlying issues. When this occurs, the person–environment relationship will suffer if conflict escalates. Coping behaviors in the form of reappraisal and distancing were found to have the effect of worsening the individual's emotional state. This occurs where the problem does not go away, and the individual realizes that the negative consequences of the problem will likely increase in the future. Similarly, stress worsens when distancing cannot be maintained. Individuals may argue to themselves that performance evaluations are unimportant, but are reminded of the value of good performance appraisals when others are promoted because they receive a high rating.

In those situations where individuals take direct action to remove potential stressors and their efforts have been successful, change will occur in the environment and within the individual. For example, if an individual, who is having conflict with a co-worker takes direct action to solve the conflict, he or she is likely to change the environment and his or her own self-image.

Assume the individual uses meaningful and timely feedback to solve the problem, and the feedback is understood, accepted, and results in a desired behavior change by the co-worker. The result of such an intervention is that the stressor has been removed, and the employee experiencing the stress is no longer angry, frustrated, or anxious. Furthermore, the individual is likely to feel more confident in his or her own interpersonal skills, and will likely assess similar conflicts in the future as less threatening. In other words, the individual has improved the person–environment relationship that is likely to exist in the future.

Desired Managerial Application

Although coping responsibilities primarily rest with those individuals who experience stress, managers play an important role in supporting, training, and modeling appropriate behaviors for subordinates. The following are a number of techniques managers can find useful when attempting to maximize the effectiveness of the subordinates' coping response.

Managers can model the willingness to demonstrate flexibility in the coping style used, and demonstrate that the application of coping styles should be situationally based. As Newton[59] pointed out, to cope effectively, managers must diagnose their environments and select the appropriate strategy to fit the situation. This will require that managers continually monitor their environments to obtain accurate and current information. Chapter 12 presents a detailed discussion of coping strategies for handling conflict, and of their situational nature.

Managers can also model the way they handle disruptive emotions such as anger, fear, and disliking people, things, or activities. The key is not to allow disruptive emotions to interfere with cognitive or rational thought processes, or interpersonal relations. This is not to say that managers should ignore their emotions, but rather that they should balance emotions with the need to analyze and solve problems, and to recognize when they themselves become dysfunctional. The discussion in Chapter 12 on how to handle the angry employee will provide a specific example of appropriate modeling behaviors.

Later in this chapter a discussion of how to overcome time wasters is presented. Effective management of time wasters is an effective mechanism for dealing with work overload. When managers exhibit these behaviors, they increase the probability that subordinates will behave in a similar manner.

In those areas where modeling is not an effective mechanism to change the subordinate's coping style, the manager can directly intervene through feedback, coaching, or counseling (FCC), or directing subordinates toward stress management training (SMT). In the case of FCC, managers are attempting to directly intercede and alter the manner in which subordinates cope. As will be discussed in Chapter 14, one of the goals of counseling is to ensure skill in decision making. If this can be accomplished, subordinates should increase their effectiveness and productivity. At the very minimum, they will demand less of their manager's time. Alternatively, managers can arrange for training designed to improve a subordinate's coping abilities. SMT provides subordinates an opportunity to develop coping techniques designed to help inoculate them against stress (i.e., self-diagnoses, improved life skills, balancing work–family perspective, relaxation techniques).

Managers can also facilitate subordinate coping by building "time out" periods within a normal work period. Time-outs can be used by subordinates to recharge their batteries through meditation, relaxation, or imagery, or they can use the time to plan creatively for upcoming events. For this technique to be effective, it may be necessary to incorporate free periods into the subordinate's work schedule and, where possible, to provide for quiet spaces in which these activities can be carried out. Time-out periods are especially effective in high-stress jobs or where employees must deal with emotional others.

To address the issue of chronic stressors, managers should periodically undertake departmental, or job design, audits to determine areas in which chronic stressors have been allowed to build up. Once these are identified, managers should take steps to remove or buffer subordinates from the long-term negative effects of chronic stress. Managers must also keep in mind that subordinates are typically the richest source of job-related information and are likely to be the individuals responsible for, or at least affected by, proposed job changes designed to remove chronic job stressors. Consequently, to achieve audit accuracy and subordinate buy-in, it is also recommended that managers involve subordinates at both the identification and problem solving levels.

Time Management

For managers to implement the recommendations presented in this and other chapters, it is important that they have the time to diagnose, implement, and monitor the required management interventions. Unfortunately, by failing to weed out time-wasters that creep into their everyday management style, managers reduce the time available to undertake productive behaviors. As a result, they become reactive rather than proactive managers. In addition, individuals who do not effectively manage their time-wasters will likely increase the level of their own personal stress as they are asked to do more with less.

Most managers have been exposed to some type of time management workshop and have read popular paperbacks or articles on how to manage time effectively. Managers are often told that time is money, or that if they manage their time effectively, they manage their organizational lives effectively. Unfortunately, these statements are not literally true. Individuals cannot do anything about time per se. This is because you do not manage time; rather, you manage yourself. That is, you manage the activities that you use to structure or fill up your time.

Activity alone is not an indication of value or the quality of an individual's output. It is the results that are produced by activities that are of value, and that will ultimately differentiate between successful and unsuccessful managers. To be effective, managers must engage in activities that provide maximum personal benefit. Consequences or payoffs will only have benefits to individuals if they satisfy personal goals or predetermined objectives. Time-wasters can therefore be defined as any behavior or activity that produces a payoff of less value than could have otherwise been obtained by performing an alternative activity or behavior. The way to become effective, therefore, is to replace activities of low personal value with activities that provide payoffs. Put another way, managers must continually ask themselves, "What is the best use of my time?"

To guide managers in how to handle effectively the problem of time-wasters, the remainder of this chapter is devoted to ways of eliminating destructive time-wasters. There are at least six techniques that can be used to reduce the occurrence of time-wasters. (Exercise material associated with this chapter will expand on the number of strategies.)

1. Planning and Organizing

The most frequently recommended technique for overcoming time-wasters is the use of an effective planning and organization process. Central to this process is the manager's ability to articulate personal goals for both the short and long term. As discussed earlier, a manager's long-term goals include both personal career goals and organization long-term goals. Long-term goals are often general or conceptual in nature. Short-term goals typically reflect an analysis of a relevant planning horizon unique to the individual or the organization. An individual's planning horizon may be as short as a single day, or as is the case for most managers, range somewhere between 3 to 12 months. A short-term planning horizon will also vary with the dynamics of the environment and organizational level at which the person functions. Managers who function within dynamic environments usually must shorten their planning horizon. At the same time, the higher up in the organization the manager functions, the longer the planning horizon is likely to be.[60] A machine repairman may have a planning horizon of a single day, whereas a senior manager's short-term planning horizon may be 12 months or more.

Long-term goals will vary among individuals and for the same individuals as they move through different life stages. Furthermore, long-term career goals tend to reflect a greater emphasis on results than on behavior. What is important is that individuals take the time to understand what they desire, given their present stage of development. Therefore, it is not surprising to find students just graduating from university to have one set of long-term objectives, individuals who are at a stable or maintenance stage of their career to have a different set, and employees close to retirement to have still another.[61]

Managers will eventually be required to consider their short-term planning horizon. When this occurs, managers must increase the level of detail and specificity of their planning. Managers will identify appropriate sub-goals, action plans, and behaviors that must be set and implemented to help ensure success. Individuals with busy schedules, or activity overload, are best advised to write down required behaviors and allot appropriate amounts of time to their completion. "To do lists" and "schedules" serve as guides for managers as they move into the future. Crises may disrupt or invalidate existing schedules. As a result, managers must be prepared to move away from predetermined plans as conditions change. Similarly, it is impractical for busy managers to schedule or plan their entire day. Effective managers, in dynamic environments, keep a portion of their time free so that they can respond effectively to interruptions or unscheduled conversations.[62]

Given limited time, energy, and resources, it is unlikely that managers will be able to carry out all identified behaviors and activities. As a result, effective managers establish priorities for themselves and others. If necessary, managers will verify established priorities with others (i.e., bosses, peers, and subordinates) to ensure accuracy and appropriateness. When setting priorities, it is important that managers consider the issues of importance and urgency. Importance should reflect a perceptual integration of the manager's own goals (both short- and long-term), and the goals of relevant others. Effective managers will have consciously made an effort to integrate their goal-setting process with the goal-setting process of others (see Chapter 9).

Urgency is a function of the actual date by which an activity or behavior has to be completed and the amount of time required to carry out the behavior or activity. Both variables must be considered to assess urgency accurately. For example, merely knowing that something is required in five weeks does little to establish urgency. However, if the manager knows that there is only limited time in which to successfully complete the required tasks, then the goals and required support activities take on an air of urgency. To assess how long it will take to complete a given activity, managers must have information about task complexity, task difficulty, coordination efforts required, and the possibility of disruptions due to adverse occurrences.

When the two dimensions are combined (see Figure 5.3), it is possible for managers to set their priorities accurately. Clearly, those activities or behaviors that are both important and urgent should be classified as the manager's highest priorities (call these your A's). Activities or behaviors that are important but not urgent are ranked lower in terms of the manager's priorities (call them your B's). In those instances where the activity or behavior is unimportant, yet urgent, it is advisable for the manager to classify these items as C's in terms of priority. If there are activities that are both unimportant and nonurgent, it is best to ignore these unless importance or urgency assessments change. Problems arise when managers waste time on their C's or irrelevant activities and thereby perform tasks of lesser value than could have otherwise been performed. In the authors' experience, most managers can find the time to do their A's and most if not all of their B's.

2. Delegation

Closely following planning and organizing in popularity as a technique for eliminating time-wasters, is delegation. Delegation is the process by which managers give things to other people to complete.[63] Of primary interest to our present discussion is downward delegation to subordinates. The use of delegation is useful for a number of reasons. First, managers can expand their performance capabilities from what they can do to what they can control. If managers, through selection, training, development, and motivation, can develop an effective work team with extra capacity, then they can use this excess to increase delegation. If a manager has 12 subordinates, and he or she can delegate one hour of work to each subordinate, his or her workday is expanded by 12 hours. Instead of 8 hours of productivity, the manager now has 20 hours in

FIGURE 5.3

Setting priorities

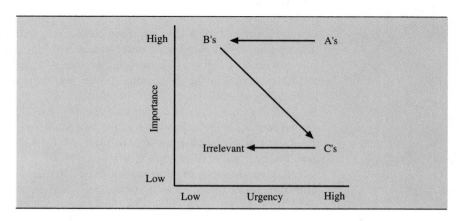

which to produce. Newly released time can be used for more creative activities, especially if the activities given up are routine for the manager. Managers with excess capacity can even ask their own boss how they might lighten the boss's routine to make him or her more productive. In either case, the managers increase their value to the organization.

Delegation also increases the probability of subordinate development. Even if the delegated tasks are routine for the manager, they may not be routine for subordinates. In this way, delegated tasks can be used as training vehicles designed to improve the long-term performance and potential for promotion of subordinates. Delegation of managerial responsibility also removes some of the misunderstanding, or information gaps, which sometimes exist between managers and their subordinates. By performing delegated tasks, subordinates gain a clearer understanding of what the boss does and why it is done.

Last, delegation helps maintain the appropriate level of activity or decision making. In our earlier discussion of participative management, it was noted that frequently the richest source of information or expertise is at the subordinate level and not at the boss's level. When this is the case, quality of performance or decision making can be enhanced by delegating task and/or decision-making responsibilities to subordinates. A spin-off benefit is that increased responsibility and autonomy can act as an important source of motivation to those individuals who are seeking growth opportunities on the job. Therefore, the question is not, should a manager delegate, but rather, what steps should be followed to make delegation work effectively. Below are *eight* steps managers can follow when attempting to delegate work to others.[64]

Select the Activities or Tasks to Be Delegated

Managers attending our workshops often express the concern that if they give away too much of their job they will lose control or reduce their value to the organization. Such concerns have validity only if managers do nothing with their extra time, or if there is so much slack in the system that there is nothing else that they can do. Managers can make effective use of their time by directing energies toward activities of greater value than those being given away. If managers give away routine, low-value activities, they should replace them with ones that are more challenging and of higher value. If the manager has a superior who is interested in developing subordinates, one way this can be accomplished is for the manager to approach the senior person, indicate the reason for the available time, and then express a willingness to help the boss perform some relevant task that would make his or her job easier. As for the second concern, it appears to be less relevant, as organizations move further into the 1990s and managers are asked to do more with less. Under such conditions, managers may be able to survive only if they improve subordinate performance and delegate effectively.

To carry out this step, managers should list all the things that they do as part of their job. Once these activities are listed, the manager can go through the list, and with each item as a focal point, ask the following questions:

Could any one of my subordinates do this activity instead of me? Could any one of my subordinates do this activity better, faster, or more cheaply than I can? Could such an activity act as a training vehicle so that I could save time in the future? Although this activity has become routine for me, would it be challenging to one of my subordinates? Is this an activity that would likely be interesting to one of my subordinates? Can the needed information to perform this task be made accessible to subordinates? Can I control or monitor the task or activity once it is given away? If the answer to one or more of these questions is yes, then the activity may be a candidate for delegation.

Analyze the Activities or Tasks to Be Delegated

A delegated task or activity is likely to be new to the subordinate being asked to perform the task. As a result the manager may be required to explain even the simplest or smallest step to ensure that the subordinate does not fail. Unfortunately, individuals who perform a task repeatedly begin to give only surface attention to the tasks being performed or leave out steps because of their familiarity with equipment or procedures. When this occurs, these gaps are likely to be unintentionally overlooked. To be able to explain adequately what is required of a subordinate when performing a delegated task, it may be necessary for the manager to analyze the task in great detail to ensure that nothing is left out.

The logic behind this step may become clear after you read the following story. A friend lived next to a well-known pianist who was known for his rendition of a particular piece. The neighbor would hear the pianist play the song many times and enjoyed hearing it each time. One night, however, the neighbor heard what appeared to be a novice playing the song. The individual played the notes very slowly and frequently repeated key bars. The next day when the neighbor met the pianist in the hall he asked if he had taken up teaching, and explained what he had heard the night before. The pianist said no, it was he who had been playing, and then explained that it was necessary to go through a familiar piece in that fashion so as not to forget the detail.

The manager, like the pianist, must occasionally reanalyze tasks performed so as to not forget the details, especially when preparing to explain them to someone else. Detailed analysis is also necessary to identify potential problems the subordinate may encounter, or critical points at which the subordinate should be observed.

Select the Subordinate to Whom the Work Will Be Delegated

This step rests on the assumption that the manager knows his or her subordinates well enough to answer the following questions. (Note: If the manager cannot answer these questions, then there is a need to collect more information before making any decision about delegating work.) The questions the manager should ask are: Which of my subordinates would enjoy doing this task? Which of my subordinates has the time, knowledge, and skill to do the work? Should the task be done brilliantly or quickly? If it should be done brilliantly, which of my subordinates can do it brilliantly? If it has to be done quickly, which of my subordinates can do it quickly? Would any of my subordinates have their motivation reduced by this task because their skills were far above what was required to perform well? Which of my subordinates would find this task demeaning or punishing? In each case, if managers fail to answer these questions correctly, they increase the probability that delegation will fail.

Create an Exact Plan for Delegating the Work

At this point, the manager is able to develop a detailed plan of when and how to delegate the work. Although the plan will vary from situation to situation there are a number of recommendations that appear to work well in most instances. Clearly, if conditions warrant deviation from the following recommendations, managers are well advised to make the changes.

Timing is a crucial variable in establishing a delegation plan. In deference to subordinates, they should be given as much lead time as possible before being asked to start a newly delegated task. Lead time allows subordinates to preplan and reorganize their schedule and thereby minimize disruptions. If a sufficient lead time cannot be given, the manager should, at the least, delegate the task the day before the individual is to begin the new assignment. This allows the individual the evening to prepare for the next day. The most disruptive alternative is to hit the subordinate with the newly delegated task first thing in the morning. By then the employee already has his or her day planned and will likely find major scheduling changes disrupting.

The manager's detailed plan should also include the decision to use face-to-face, two-way communication. Face-to-face communication allows managers to respond to nonverbal cues that might otherwise go unobserved. For example, the subordinate may verbally say yes to doing the task, but nonverbally communicate a desire not to get involved. If the delegation was done by telephone, or even worse by memo, the nonverbal message may be missed. Two-way communication ensures that the subordinate is allowed to ask questions and seek clarification of information or directions not clearly understood when first sent.

The manager's detailed delegation plan should also answer a number of key questions. One of the first is, "What results do I want the subordinate to achieve?" When managers answer this question, they are in effect establishing a standard against which the subordinate will be assessed. If delegation is being used as a developmental tool, the manager will likely want subordinates to try their best and, regardless of results, be willing to allow them to learn from their experience. Therefore, the criterion for success will be improvement. If managers seek high-quality results, they could possibly be looking for error-free performance. Alternatively, if managers desire a subordinate to be finished by a particular date, they in effect are establishing time as a standard of success. It is also possible that more than one standard will be applied to a particular situation, such as quality and speed of completion.

Next, the manager might ask, "What resources and information should I make available to the subordinate, and how much freedom should the person be given?" The answer to this question determines what the manager will bring to the delegation meeting and the degree of managerial supervision used while the subordinate performs the delegated task. The answer to this question may also be affected by the experience of the subordinate and the results the manager wants to achieve. For example, if the subordinate is inexperienced, and the manager wants to use the delegation process to develop the individual, he or she may bring considerable support information to the delegation meeting to spoon-feed the individual. At the same time, the manager may decide to allow minimum subordinate discretion and maximum supervision.

Delegate the Work

The act of delegating should occur during a face-to-face meeting between managers and subordinates. From a purely content point of view, the delegation meeting provides managers with an opportunity to communicate the details of their delegation plan. When subordinates leave this exchange, they should understand the steps to be followed, how they will be monitored and evaluated, deadlines if they exist, likely problems that may be encountered, and who might be of assistance should the subordinates need help. During the exchange, subordinates are also informed of what benefits both they and managers are likely to receive as a result of successful performance.

The delegation meeting also gives managers an opportunity to clarify concerns frequently expressed by subordinates who receive delegated tasks or activities. Subordinates often want to know why they are being asked to perform the assigned task. Common reasons for delegating work to subordinates are because they (*a*) have shown an interest in the task, (*b*) have free time, (*c*) need training or development in the task or activity, or (*d*) are next in line to do the work. Knowing the specific reason allows the subordinate to discuss the manager's assumptions.

Managers can greatly facilitate the delegation process if they show trust in their subordinates. Managers will exhibit high levels of trust in subordinates who (*a*) share their goals, (*b*) make every effort to do well, (*c*) are dependable, and (*d*) will likely succeed if they try. The manager who communicates these feelings and beliefs to subordinates will increase their self-efficacy, and hence their willingness to accept the delegated responsibilities now and in the future.

It is also desirable to give subordinates a say in the delegation decision, or allow them to alter the directions guiding their behavior. In the first instance, the subordinate may not be able to perform the would-be assignment, or may have no interest in performing the task in question. Therefore, if the manager miscalculated the subordinate's available time, skill, or interest, it may be necessary to withdraw the request. By allowing subordinates input in how the task will be performed, the manager reduces the likelihood of resistance later, and increases the feeling of subordinate ownership of the task. Both conditions significantly increase the probability of subordinate success.

Monitor the Subordinate's Progress

The ideal situation for managers is to be able to delegate and not have to monitor or assess the individual's performance. Then, if a manager does not hear from the individual again, he or she can assume that the job has been successfully completed. Unfortunately, this ideal is rarely reached. When it is not likely, managers must monitor the progress of the employee. The actual level of monitoring or supervision required may be different for each employee/task/environment combination.

Factors that the manager needs to consider when deciding upon the appropriate level of monitoring are the subordinate's experience level, the consequences of both success and failure, the dynamics of the environment, the complexity of the task, and the perceived level of trust existing among the individuals involved. Clearly, if the subordinate has little experience, and is performing an important but complex task, it is likely that close and frequent monitoring is required. The opposite conditions would allow managers to reduce monitoring activities to a minimum. Whatever the choice, managers should inform subordinates as to the level of monitoring or supervision that they will use. Simply put, the purpose is to minimize the occurrence of negative results.

Discuss Progress or Results with the Subordinate

Coaching or feedback exchanges with subordinates ensure that they understand how well they performed and how they might improve performance. Although such sessions can occur at any time, it is desirable, in most cases, to have a follow-up meeting with the subordinate. The purpose of the meeting is to answer both manager and subordinate questions. (There are delegated tasks that require no follow-up activity. This may occur when delegation is to occur only once, quality is unimportant, employee development is not an objective, when there is insufficient time, and when the goal is to allow subordinates to experience complete freedom on the job.)

Subordinates want answers to the following types of questions: How well have I done? Would I have improved performance by doing something differently? Am I likely to be asked to do this again, and if so how will it affect my job description or classification? Now that I have completed the assignment, what benefits do I receive? Now that I am done, is it business as usual? Positive answers to such questions help to ensure that the subordinate will *(a)* have a positive feeling toward the experience, and *(b)* show a positive response to future delegation.

Managers, on the other hand, would like answers to such questions as: Did the subordinate learn anything from the experience? If so, what? Did the subordinate enjoy doing the delegated task? If so, why? If not, why? Given the opportunity, would the subordinate like to perform the task again? Would the subordinate have done anything different if he or she had greater control or discretion? Was there a specific element of the task or activity that was particularly difficult to perform? Answers to these questions improve the manager's knowledge about subordinates and improve the decisions made during Steps 2 and 3 of the delegation process.

Reinforce or Reward Appropriate Behavior

Although many managers would argue that this step has already been carried out if the previous steps have been completed successfully, unfortunately this may not be the case in the eyes of the subordinate. Therefore, it is important to ensure that reinforcement or reward follows successful completion of the delegated task. To be effective, rewards offered subordinates must fit their needs and expectations. For example, if the subordinate expects an increase in responsibility, job variety, and autonomy after successfully completing the delegated task, it is in the manager's best interest to enrich the subordinate's job. Conversely, if the subordinate accepts the delegated task only because such acceptance will get him or her off the hook in the future, then the manager must ensure that the individual is temporarily taken out of the delegation loop.

Having studied these eight steps, you should realize by now that delegation is a process that transcends the act itself. To be effective, the delegation process must integrate analysis, planning, acting, and follow-up activities. Only then can the manager save time, reduce the level of felt stress, and satisfy the development needs of subordinates.

3. Overcoming Procrastination

There are many reasons why managers procrastinate, or can never get started on urgent projects. The reasons cited most frequently include being intimidated by large projects, inertia resulting from current activities, too many interruptions, classifying a task as a low priority item or simple enough to be done later, finding the task absolutely unbearable, difficulty making decisions, or having unclear instructions and therefore fear doing the wrong thing.[65] Unfortunately, procrastination increases the individual's stress level as deadlines draw nearer and third parties, or situational cues, remind the manager of the need for completion.

Although controlling procrastination is considered part of the study of time management, the solution to the problem rests within the individual. Individuals must be able to control these feelings and perceptions to ensure that important and value-producing activities are not deferred. The control of procrastination begins when managers establish clear priorities. By setting priorities, managers determine what activities or tasks produce the greatest return, and the date when these activities should be completed. The setting of priorities also forces managers into making decisions. Individuals have difficulty denying the importance of a task after they have devoted the time to planning and organizing activities, and have come up with a ranking of tasks based upon personal or organizational payoffs.

Procrastination can also be reduced by taking larger projects and breaking them down into manageable sub-tasks or goals. Once tasks have been divided into manageable parts, it is easier to place these parts into available time slots. For example, a manager who has nothing to do before leaving for lunch may not want to start on a large project because it is likely to take all afternoon. Instead of doing something with the free 15 minutes, the manager leaves early for lunch. If the project had been analyzed and broken down into manageable sub-parts, it is likely that the manager could have fit some of the required sub-activities into the 15 minute block of time (e.g., locating a file, ordering supplies, collecting information, or making several short telephone calls).

In those instances where procrastination is likely to result from fear of failure due to unclear instructions, the manager must take action to clarify what is expected from others. As noted in Chapter 3, managers can take assertive and proactive action by seeking to clarify role responsibilities with their boss. Such action is consistent with being an effective follower. Chapter 9 will also indicate that clarifying role responsibility is a legitimate goal-setting activity for managers. If a manager's boss fails to articulate role responsibilities, it is the manager's responsibility to seek clarification. If fear of failure results from low self-efficacy or inadequate skills, then the manager must initiate action to develop the skill necessary to perform the job effectively. This is especially crucial when the task being deferred is one that is likely to occur frequently.

In situations where frequent interruptions prevent managers from acting, it is desirable to set aside specific blocks of time (i.e., quiet time, that can be set aside to work on particular tasks). If such quiet time cannot easily be built into a manager's daily routine because others in the organization do not respect his or her time, then it may be necessary to use creative techniques to protect personal quiet time. One such technique is to schedule a meeting with yourself, either in your own office or elsewhere. Then when others request time, you simply state that you already have a meeting scheduled for that time slot. People rarely ask you to break a prearranged meeting. Furthermore, if the request deals with an activity of higher value than what was planned, it is a simple matter to break your meeting with yourself. This will also likely win you some points with the relevant other.

Before leaving the subject of procrastination, it is important to realize that there are times when deferring or delaying activity is appropriate.[66] Crises, or priorities, can produce situations during which activities or tasks of lesser value must be deferred. Such action allows managers to redirect their energies to more pressing, high-value, items. The net impact for managers who use creative procrastination is better utilization of available time.

4. Learning to Say NO!

Many managers fall into the trap of agreeing to do tasks that result in minimum payoff for the individual or the organization. When managers fail to say no, they are likely to increase their workload. There are many reasons why this occurs, ranging from lack of assertiveness to not wanting to offend others. The following example demonstrates how failing to say "no" can cost the manager hours of wasted time.

A friend of ours had just taken over as city manager of a large municipality. We will call him Bob. Bob considered himself a good manager and believed that subordinates should be able to function independently of their boss. He was a strong supporter of the principles espoused by Blanchard in his book, *Leadership and the One Minute Manager.*[67] Unfortunately, the previous city manager could never say no to his staff and, when asked, would solve their problems. It is worth noting, that the former city manager was described by city staff as a passive individual who disliked confrontation, and who, at the same time, had a strong need to be accepted and liked by his staff.

Soon after Bob became city manager, he noticed that subordinates were always in his office asking for assistance. It appeared that whenever his staff ran into a problem, they would come to him for advice. In addition, subordinates refused to make important decisions unless they got his approval first. To confirm his suspicion, Bob kept a time log for several weeks. At the end of two weeks, Bob estimated that subordinate requests on his time were consuming four to five hours a day. In other words, instead of the subordinates carrying Bob, he was carrying his subordinates. To correct the problem, Bob took the following action. At a scheduled meeting, Bob informed his staff that he wanted them to begin handling their own problems. He would start saying no to their requests for help in those areas where subordinates had enough experience or skill to act unilaterally. Bob also indicated that he would gradually wean them from the practice of using him as a crutch. Bob also indicated that in six months they would be functioning on their own. To dramatize his point, he put a sign on his door that read, "If I have to solve all your problems, then I don't really need you!" At the end of six months, Bob reassessed the amount of time he was spending on subordinate problems. He found that the four to five hours had dropped to less then one hour. His ability to say no to subordinates, supplemented with six months of coaching, counseling, and feedback, was saving him almost 20 hours a week.

Of particular relevance to the present discussion is the role that *time* and *detail* play in setting the trap into which many individuals fall when questioned. The *avoidance curve* depicted in Figure 5.4 demonstrates that the more detail the individual receives, or the closer he or she gets to the point of time at which action is required, the more likely he or she will attempt to avoid the activity. Individuals find it easier to agree to general statements. Therefore, if the boss asks a subordinate if he or she would like to help to make the organization more profitable, few would say no. However, if the boss was to specify the required behavior necessary to fulfill the employee's contractual agreement, the response may be totally different. For example, if the boss was to indicate later that the subordinate would have to take a 20 percent cut in pay, be transferred to a different plant, or even be laid off, the subordinate would likely resist. In other words, the subordinate would attempt to avoid honoring the agreement.

FIGURE 5.4

Impact of time and detail on our ability to say "No"

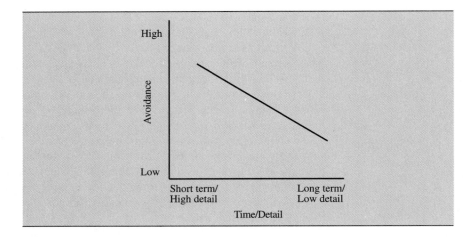

Time also plays a role in determining whether individuals respond yes or no to requests from others. When there is likely to be a significant time lapse between an initial request and the point at which the action is to be carried out, people are more likely to say yes. "Now" issues are more likely to be scrutinized by the individual because their impact is immediate. Similarly, *now* issues are frequently more certain and detailed than those that will happen in the future. The further off into the future the action is required, the individual feels less pressure and is less certain about consequences associated with success or failure. A yes answer also minimizes the probability of confrontation with the relevant other, or hurting the other's feelings. However, as time passes, the clearer and more certain the consequences and the sooner individuals will have to act, the greater the probability that they will seek to avoid their commitments.

The classic example of the impact of time on one's ability to say no (even when you know the impact is negative in the long run) is represented by the story of Faust, who sold his soul to the Devil. When Faust was young and unhappy he was quite willing to sell his soul to the Devil for money and health. However, as he grew older and the consequences of his action became clear, he tried by every means to get out of his contract with the Devil.

The key to learning to say no is a careful analysis of both short- and long-term consequences and then comparing these consequences to personal goals or priorities. A useful technique to help individuals recognize when to say no is the practice of visualization.[68] Visualization allows individuals to picture in their minds what life would be like as a result of a yes or no answer. For visualization to work, individuals have to have knowledge of likely events in the future (either through experiences or data collection) and must be honest with themselves as to how this information is interpreted. A second technique that individuals find useful in determining when to say "no" is the process of self-talk.[69] This technique forces the individual to walk through the problem, its component parts, and likely consequences of both yes and no responses. A by-product of engaging in self-talk is improved problem solving and decision making by managers. In other words, individuals talk through all relevant information and identify possible consequences. Predicted consequences are then compared with actual results. As individuals become experienced in visualization and self-talk, they are able to assess the appropriateness of a yes or no response to requests made by others.

5. *Handling the Drop-In Visitor*

Assume that you are in your room studying, a head is poked into the room and a voice asks, "Do you have a minute?" The possible motives behind such a request are many. The individual may want to socialize, put off doing work, ask for help, or help you with a problem you brought up earlier in the day. What is important about the request is that rarely does the individual only want a minute of your time. It addition, the possibility exists that the visitor's motivations are not compatible with your own personal goals. If you are studying for an exam and your visitor wants to waste time, escape, solve a problem of little relevance to your studies, then the longer he or she stays in your room the greater will be the amount of time wasted.

To handle drop-in visitors, managers must develop intervention tactics that limit or prevent drop-ins without damaging interpersonal relations. The first step in controlling drop-ins is to know one's own goals. Personal goals can then be compared to visitor motives. Such comparison allows you to assess the consequences of letting the would-be visitor into your room or office. Knowing one's own goals and the likely motives of the would-be visitor also allows you to be more assertive as a person. The assertive persons, if busy, will explain their situation and request that the individual return later. Alternatively, assertive persons are more likely to close their doors to create "quiet time" at least until personal goals have been satisfied.

If, however, you determine that it is in your best interest to allow the individual into your room or office, actions can still be taken to minimize the probability that the visitors will exceed their welcome. If you are concerned about the drop-in staying too long, you can simply set a time limit to the visitor's stay. When setting a time limit, it is desirable to obtain verification from the would-be visitors to ensure that they understand that a time limit exists. Alternatively, you can suggest that both you and the visitor move to a different location. The rationale behind such a tactic is that it is easier to leave if the exchange exceeds the preset limit than it is to ask visitors to leave once they have made themselves comfortable in your room or office.

If you cannot prevent the would-be visitor from entering your space, and it is not practical to move to an alternate location or set a viable time limit, you can still minimize the impact of drop-in visitors by altering the physical environment of your office. For example, if you must leave your door open, you can locate your desk so that it is not in view from the door. One of the authors initially had an office that could not allow such a physical change. As a result, every time someone passed the door there would be greetings and conversation. After several months and many interruptions and wasted time the author moved to a new office. The new office is L shaped, with the door at the end of the short leg and the desk at the end of the long leg. Consequently, even with the door fully open, passersby do not know someone is in the room. The result is few drop-in visitors.

There appears to be a direct relationship between the comfort level of an individual's work space and the number of drop-in visitors. Therefore, you can reduce the number of unwanted drop-ins by decreasing the comfort level of your room or office.[70] An example of a former colleague will help dramatize this point. The professor in question would frequently complain that he did not accomplish all that he wanted when in his office. The physical surroundings of his office helped explain why—it was more comfortable than the faculty lounge. The office was larger than average and there was the professor's chair plus three easy chairs. The professor rationalized the comfortable chairs because he met frequently with students to discuss classroom projects. In addition, our colleague enjoyed his coffee and had a rather large coffeemaker in his office. He always kept it full and loved to share it with other faculty members. Finally, his wife was a great baker and as a result frequently sent in samples of her efforts to be tasted by anyone who happened to stop by. To say the least, the comfort level of this professor's office was high. Therefore, it is not surprising that more times than not when you passed this professor's room there were always one or two other faculty members present.

If all else has failed, several options designed to control the drop-in still remain. You can begin by making concluding-type comments designed to communicate a desire to end the discussion. Verbal cues can be supplemented with nonverbal cues. You can increase the pauses between relevant responses, you can glance several times at your watch, or you can stand up and walk toward the door. Any one of these tactics is usually sufficient to remove an unwanted visitor.

6. Judicious Use of Meetings

Ask managers their opinion about meetings and they will invariably give a negative answer. They say that meetings take too long, occur too frequently, and their output is not worth the time and energy expended.[71] Managers are likely to spend at least 20 to 30 percent of their time attending meetings. As is the case with all potential time-wasters, managers must develop strategies and tactics that ensure time spent in meetings is productive. A critical first step in this process is to understand why a meeting is being held. If we know the reason, then it is possible to compare the benefits derived and the goals we want to achieve.

There are valid reasons why meetings should be held (see Table 5.5). In situations where information is dispersed throughout the organization, meetings are an effective vehicle through which managers can collect the needed

TABLE 5.5   **Why Have Meetings? Seven Legitimate Reasons**

- Information gathering.
- Decision making and problem solving.
- Information dispersal.
- Gaining commitment.
- Coordination.
- Team building.
- Human relations spin-offs.

information to make quality decisions. If the individuals involved have goals that are compatible with those of the manager, and are able to deal effectively with one another without engaging in dysfunctional conflicts, the manager can save significant personal time by delegating decision-making and problem-solving responsibilities to the group at meetings. Group decision making and problem solving by interested and qualified individuals also increase the likelihood that relevant others will buy into the decision reached and remain committed to action plans during their implementation.

Where individual differences, multiple demands on staff time, and numerous means–ends combinations exist, managers can effectively use meetings to coordinate activities of interested parties. Managers who rely on one-on-one interactions to coordinate activities of several subordinates or peers are likely to spend most of their time relaying messages between individuals. As is discussed in Chapter 10, managers increase the probability of personal success if they create a climate in which an effective team can develop. One way to accomplish this is for the manager to create meaningful group experiences. For example, if the meeting experience is successful, that is, participants achieve their goals, openly share information, and achieve consensus through managed disagreements, participants are more likely to perceive themselves as a team. Last, individuals want to belong, participate, and have control over what happens in their environment. Meetings offer the mechanism through which these needs can be satisfied.

Therefore, for meetings to be worthwhile, these seven potential benefits given in Table 5.5 must be compatible with your goals and produce a higher payoff than alternative activities that are currently available. Unfortunately, the benefits described above are not automatic and require significant effort and skill by the manager and meeting participants. Let us briefly look at some of the things that you can do to make meetings effective.

1. Schedule meetings only when there is a sufficient reason to have them. Managers who schedule a weekly meeting only for "show and tell" fail to recognize that you should have meetings only when they increase the effectiveness of the team. If there is no valid purpose, managers should call off the meeting.

2. If a meeting is necessary, ensure that participants know why, and that they have relevant support material before the meeting. Managers dealing with regularly occurring meetings should follow "the rules of halves and three quarters."[72] The rule of halves states that an item should not be put on the agenda unless it is received halfway between regular meetings. The logic supporting such a rule is that it takes time to organize, set priorities, and collect relevant support material. If sufficient time is not made available for these activities prior to the meeting, it is likely to lose effectiveness. The rule of three quarters indicates that three-quarters of the way through the normal period between scheduled meetings, an agenda and support material are sent out to participating members. When this is done, individuals have sufficient time to prepare for the upcoming meeting. Prepared individuals make relevant contributions; ill-informed participants are unlikely to do so.

3. Managers should ensure that meetings start and end on time. If starting times are loosely enforced, participants often respond to this flexibility by coming to meetings late. Once latecomers appear, and the behavior has been rewarded by a late start to the meeting, those present soon learn that it is better to come late than to sit there and wait for others. Such ragged beginnings waste significant corporate time and poison the atmosphere in which the participants are to function.

Similar problems occur if fixed ending times are not enforced. If participants are taught to believe that meetings can go on as long as there is work to be done, participants have little need to be efficient. As a result they are likely to expand their discussions, consider peripheral or secondary issues, engage in irrelevant side conversations, etc. When this occurs, managers are allowing meetings to expand in terms of duration and again run the risk of wasting valuable corporate time. A telling example happened within a hospital. The executive director decided to establish an executive committee to help create hospital policy and facilitate staff participation in important decisions. The executive committee was set to meet on alternate Wednesdays from 8:30 A.M. to 10:30 A.M., and was initially made up of the executive director, five directors, and three managers from staff departments. Within six months the guidelines just described were no longer in place. The meetings were being held every Wednesday, allowed to continue until 2:30 P.M., and involved no fewer than 23 hospital staff. The expanded meeting time had become accepted and the executive director was forced to supply coffee break treats and lunch. Clearly, the meetings had gotten out of hand.

4. How the leader, or chairperson, opens the meeting can play an important role in determining meeting efficiency. Openings are designed to direct and motivate participants so that as little time as possible is wasted in getting individuals to understand the meeting's purpose, and the appropriate role for both the chairperson and committee members. Poor openings are likely to result in participant disinterest and lack of contribution, confusion as to role responsibilities, and increased levels of intragroup conflict. Such negative consequences are likely to undermine group faith in the group meeting process.

To be effective, openings should include three elements. First, a good opening indicates the objectives of the meeting. Unfortunately, just because participants have an agenda, and have agreed to attend, there is no guarantee that participants agree on the meeting's purpose. Therefore, the leader, or chairperson, should articulate what is to be accomplished by meeting's end. Next, the leader, or chairperson, should summarize relevant background information to ensure that all participants have equal access to information. Such action helps ensure that all participants are functioning with approximately the same level of information. Last, the leader, or chairperson, should use the opening to explain and reinforce what members are expected to contribute, what their role will be, how the meeting will be run, and what the group can expect from the chair.

5. Meeting effectiveness can break down if agenda integrity is not maintained. Agenda integrity implies that an agenda has been set, that—time permitting—agenda items will be discussed, and that issues not listed on the agenda will not be discussed before the existing agenda items. Agenda integrity ensures that participants can predict what is going to be discussed, and therefore guides members on how to prepare for the meeting, and even whether the meeting is worth attending. If the chair frequently suspends the agenda in favor of an item not previously listed, participants are less likely to prepare for upcoming meetings. Lack of participant preparation will lead directly to wasted effort and poor group performance.

Summary

This chapter explained the concepts of stress and time management, their importance, and how managers can reduce negative effects where they may occur. A stress model was presented to demonstrate the complexity of the stress response and classify behaviors that can help individuals control their own stress and that of relevant others. Specific attention was directed at stressors, situational factors, individual differences, appraisal, and coping, in determining how to control the negative effects of stress. Stress was also described as an interactive process in which the environment affects the individual and the individual affects the environment.

This discussion should help you to understand and accept the importance of time-management concepts. The mini cases at the end of the chapter provide an opportunity to identify and discuss the full range of techniques you can use to reduce time-wasters. When effectively handling personal time-wasters, managers act as models for subordinates who, through vicarious learning, coaching, or feedback, can develop their own skills in managing time.

EXERCISES

5.1 Coping with Stress

Stressors are events or situations that place demands on the individual which have the potential of exceeding his or her capabilities. Individuals frequently differ in the way they appraise stressors and ultimately how they cope with stressful encounters. This exercise is designed to allow students to identify potential stressors in their environments, to rate them in terms of felt stress, and identify their personal coping strategies. Understanding, accepting, and discussing personal strategies for coping with stress can be an effective way of improving future performance. This is especially true when individuals have an opportunity to compare personal coping styles with the styles used by others. Please follow the steps outlined below. Steps 2, 3, and 4 can be completed at home to minimize classroom time needed for this exercise.

Step 1. The class will break up into groups of two.

Step 2. Students will list on a plain sheet of paper the potential stressors they believe occur in their environments. Remember, you are asked to list potential stressors, not those stressful events that presently exceed your physical or emotional ability to overcome. (10 minutes)

Step 3. Rate the degree to which each potential stressor has produced an emotional response—fear, frustration, anger, tension, or joy—some time in your recent past. Use a 1-to-10 scale to rate each potential stressor, with 1 indicating low fear, or other emotion and 10 indicating high fear, or other emotion. (10 minutes)

Step 4. Select the four items to which you gave the highest rating and list the behaviors you used to cope with each stressful encounter. Identify the specific coping behaviors in which you engaged and whether each response was problem-focused or emotion-focused. Item 1 in the following Coping Strategies and Support Behaviors table provides examples of problem-solving strategies, while Items 2 through 6 provide examples of emotion-coping strategies. Students are encouraged to be as creative as possible and not limit themselves to the examples provided in the table. You also should rate each encounter in terms of the degree that you believe you (*a*) were successful and (*b*) were satisfied with your performance. (10 minutes)

Coping Strategies and Support Behaviors

1. Task-oriented coping behaviors.
   _____ Set priorities.
   _____ Take immediate action based on your present understanding of the situation.
   _____ Find out more about the situation.

2. Emotional relief.
   _____ Lose your temper.

_____ Express anger or irritability with yourself.

_____ Express feelings to co-workers or take feelings out on staff.

3. Utilization of home resources.

_____ Talk things over with spouse at home.

_____ Face the situation knowing that your family and spouse support you and add a sense of proportion to the problem.

_____ Take some of your work home and work on it there.

4. Preparation prior to action.

_____ Ignore the problem until you feel ready to handle it.

_____ Take a break and come back to the problem later.

_____ Tackle routine work so that you can cool down and regain your composure.

5. Distraction techniques.

_____ Go and have a few beers.

_____ Become involved in nonwork activities.

_____ Leave the office, go home early, or take a day off.

6. Passive attempts to tolerate the situation.

_____ Let the feeling wear off.

_____ Give up and accept what's happening.

_____ Try not to worry or think about it.

Step 5. In their groups, individuals will take turns describing a single stressful encounter, explain why it was stressful, rate their success in coping with it, and measure their satisfaction with their coping behavior and the results. Once an encounter has been described, individuals will jointly consider the following questions:

- Why did the encounter produce stress?
- Were any environmental factors present that affected the level of stress experienced, that is, presence of other individuals, type of support offered, appraisal of consequences and their importance to the individual, past coping experiences, felt control or power, and so on?
- Could the individual have done anything differently to minimize the effects of existing stressors?

When carrying out Step 5, students often find it more effective to consider each stressful encounter in alternate turns. The first student describes an encounter which is then discussed by both students. Then the second student presents an encounter. This process continues until all encounters have been considered or time runs out. (Approximately 45 minutes)

Step 6. The class will assemble and discuss student experiences.

5.2 Delegation: Giving Work to Others

Delegation is an activity necessary for effective management. Unfortunately, managers often fail to delegate to promising or qualified subordinates. You will be asked to apply the learning points on how to delegate work responsibilities to a promising subordinate. (The instructor will distribute a printed copy of the appropriate learning behaviors.) You will prepare for role play with Laura Harding. Please carry out the steps below.

Step 1. The class will break up into small groups of five to six individuals each. Each group will select one of its members to play the role of John Fillmore, Vice President of the Human Resource Department at EverBright Electrical. (The role of Laura will be played by the instructor.)

Step 2. Read individually the background information that describes the situation in which John Fillmore finds himself and why he has decided to delegate the task of attending the first organizational strategic planning meeting to Laura Harding. (5 minutes)

Step 3. Each group will develop a script about John Fillmore's delegating the task to Laura Harding. You are allowed to make additional assumptions about EverBright and the people involved. The only constraint is that your assumptions must be consistent with conditions likely to exist in a utility employing 5,000 workers. (25 minutes)

Step 4. Each group should practice role-playing the encounter between John Fillmore and his subordinate. One of the group's members will play the role of Laura. The remaining group members will act as observers. (15 minutes)

Step 5. The class will assemble and one or more individuals will be selected to play the role of John Fillmore.

Background
Preparation and Role Play: Giving Work to Others

John Fillmore is the Vice President of the Human Resource Department at EverBright Electrical. He was asked by the president of the utility, Bob Headman, to attend a strategic planning session scheduled March 15. Unfortunately, John has already committed himself to represent EverBright at a national conference on the same day and will be out of town for at least one week. John will return on March 18, three days after the scheduled meeting. Consequently, John has found it necessary to select one of his staff to attend the strategic planning meeting in his place. Today is March 4.

Although the president had asked all vice presidents to participate in the new strategic planning process, he had also indicated that, in keeping with the corporation's new values, each vice president had the option of sending a qualified representative instead. If an alternate was selected, vice presidents also could allow that person to continue as the functional area's representative throughout the strategic planning process.

The driving force behind the introduction of a strategic planning process is Ever-Bright's decision to privatize after being a public utility for 22 years. The president intends to develop a set of appropriate strategies to facilitate the transition. He believes that the best way to plan this change is to involve a large number of individuals in a dynamic and ongoing planning process. Simply put, when the time to implement the strategies arrives, he wants everyone to be on board and supportive.

John has selected Laura Harding to take his place. She has been one of John's strongest supporters in the past and has been highly motivated whenever asked to handle special projects. Laura has worked for EverBright for 22 years. At one time, she left EverBright for three years to work for another utility, but decided to return when her present position was advertised. She has served five years in her current position as special assistant to the Vice President of Human Resource Management.

A number of recent tasks performed by Laura provide some idea of her experience and interests. Laura was the chief negotiator for EverBright during the last round of contract negotiations with the union. Through Laura's efforts, EverBright obtained not only one of the best collective agreements it has ever had with the militant union, but also a new positive relationship with union representatives. Laura also has been active in mapping out long-term personnel forecasts for EverBright. Finally, during the past year Laura redesigned the organization's performance appraisal system and created the training package designed to give line personnel the skills to implement the new system.

Other Relevant Facts

- To the best of John's knowledge, the president is serious about privatization and the drive to be the most efficient and profitable utility on the East Coast.

- In recent discussions with the president, John has the distinct impression that Bob Headman wants to see a more centralized human resource function. He wants to ensure greater consistency in decisions made within the corporation, and a centralized function will give the department greater credibility.

- At the present time, John believes he is the only vice president to send a representative to the first strategic planning meeting.

- Five vice presidents will be attending the first session: Andrew Sanders, Finance; Janet Connors, Customer Services; Fred Morton, Transmission and Distribution; Howard Bennett, Engineering; and Martin Taylor, Planning.

- During the past several months John has noticed that Fred Morton has become increasingly critical of Janet Connors. Fred surprised John and others in a recent meeting by criticizing Janet for turning the customer services function into a "pink ghetto." John had not previously considered Fred to be sexist.

- John has a strong personal preference to delegate more substantive activities and responsibility to his staff. He identifies individuals who want and can handle increased responsibility.

- John believes that individuals who perform well should be rewarded with more responsibility, training, good performance appraisals, advancement, and so forth.

- Although John has not yet established a complete agenda for the human resource function after the company's privatization, he has the following six points in mind:
  1. Corporate/human resource planning should be formalized. There should be a close relationship between corporate planning and human resource planning.
  2. Because EverBright's human resource characteristics are slow to change, there should be a long-term planning horizon at the management level for both the corporation and the human resource function. However, given the dynamics of the local environment, EverBright also should attempt to build in short-term monitoring and flexibility.

3. Given the organization's recent attempt to change its corporate culture, a greater effort should be made to socialize new corporate members. This will likely require an effort to develop an appropriate orientation package, training of staff in delivery, and so on.

4. Given the move to privatization, it is important to make explicit the logical career paths that exist at EverBright. This also will require that a strategic decision be made on how explicit the criteria for promotion should be. If the criteria are explicit and detailed, EverBright reduces its flexibility in promotion decisions but gives better direction to those employees who want to get ahead.

5. Given the company's need to improve its performance and to offset criticisms of ineffectiveness, it should look at the performance appraisal system and determine how best to make it work for the entire organization. Issues to consider are: (*a*) level of employee participation, (*b*) short- and long-term criteria and how to develop them, (*c*) purpose of the data, and (*d*) ratio of behavioral criteria to results-oriented criteria. Given the move to privatization, compensation issues must be assessed. To maximize employee acceptance and motivation, EverBright's system of compensation should have the following characteristics: externally competitive base salaries, internal pay equity, flexible packages to accommodate internal differences, long-term incentives, and short-term merit tied to standards in the industry. A final issue is whether EverBright should consider offering high-employment security to a core percentage of its work force.

6. Given the move to privatization, greater emphasis should be placed on both technical and nontechnical training. The best current estimates show that a 300 percent increase in training and development is necessary to bring the company in line with other private utilities.

• Recently, John has been made aware of a rumor that two of the strongest vice presidents—Fred Morton, of Transmission and Distribution, and Howard Bennett, of Engineering—have formed a coalition to fight the president on the introduction of further cultural changes into the system. Once EverBright moves out from under the watchful eyes of the government, there may be a move to oust Bob Headman.

5.3 Group Case: Managing Time-Wasters

Effective managers take the time during their busy days to assess how well they are doing. The process of mentally walking through one's experiences provides the insights necessary to improve future performance. If you have a bad day, try to identify what you did and others did that made it a bad day. Once you have identified these behaviors, you can plan changes in them that will make their occurrence less likely in the future. Similarly, if you have a good day, you should identify what you and others did that made it a good day. Again, once you have identified these behaviors, you can take steps to ensure that they occur in the future. This exercise is designed to give you experience in using this internal assessment process. If you can do it now, you will be able to do it when it really matters—in life. Please follow the steps outlined below.

Step 1. The class will break up into small groups of five to six individuals to consider the case of Will Wasteit.

Step 2. Quickly read the case individually. During Step 2, do not make any attempt to write down or in any way assess the various time wasters in which Will engages. A time-waster is defined as any stimulus or behavior that causes an individual to devote time to low-value activities, that is, those activities that are likely to result in lower potential payoffs for the individual. (5 minutes)

Step 3. Through group discussion, list the time-wasters in which Will engages. Once you have identified your list of time-wasters, construct a second list of steps, or behaviors, designed to prevent time-wasters from occurring. (45 minutes)

Step 4. The class will assemble to discuss group results and prepare a single list of behaviors to overcome the problem of time-wasters. The class's master list will then be compared with the professor's list of behaviors designed to help you overcome the problem of time-wasters.

Managing Time
The Case Of Will Wasteit

Will Wasteit is the manager of training for EverBright Electrical. EverBright is a medium-sized utility located in the eastern United States. His department is primarily concerned with the development and delivery of training curricula within the utility, but it is also involved in other human resource management issues. Will has been with the organization for about six months. He joined EverBright directly after completing his business degree at a local university. Unfortunately, Will's first six-months' performance review was below average. The following describes a typical day for Will.

Will got up about 6:00 A.M. to pack into his briefcase the work spread across the dining-room table. He had not finished reviewing the new design created by Tim (one of his staff) for a training program in effective goal setting that he had brought home the night before. He had forgotten that he had promised to attend his daughter's parent–student fall dance. The dance ended about 10:30 P.M. and Will had little time to spend on the report. When Will went to pack the report, he got quite a shock. During the night, his cat had jumped onto the table and played with Tim's report; the pages were spread all over the dining-room floor and several had bite and scratch marks on them.

Will was confident that he could finish Tim's report when he got to work. Will checked the day-planner he kept at home and it showed that nothing was scheduled for the day. Unfortunately, when Will arrived 20 minutes late at the public underground parking lot where he usually parked, he found that it was closed for the next three months. He had meant to write that fact down in his planner but had forgotten. He recalled that the day the memo had appeared on his electronic mail he had left his home day-planner in his other suit. (Will would later discover that he had written down this information on the day-planner on his office desk.) Will searched the local area for another parking lot that wasn't full or, if he was lucky, a space on the street. He finally found a lot and parked his car. Will got to his office 45 minutes late.

Will's routine each morning is to go through his mail. He believes that this is the best way to keep on top of things within the organization. He goes through his mail piece by piece, even though he has not yet checked the daily planner on the desk. He decides mentally that there is no need to check it because his home planner was blank. As he sorts through the mail, there is a knock on the door. John Crutch, a subordinate who does training for EverBright, pops into the office and asks Will if he has a minute. John comes into Will's office at least five times a day with some problem that he cannot solve. John is having a problem with a training program he was planning and just wants to ask a quick question. Will invites him in, but the "quick question" turns into a 30-minute discussion of how to design a session exercise. The training session isn't scheduled for four weeks. To get John out of his office, Will suggests that John leave the material so that he can look at it that evening. John Crutch leaves with a glow on his face and gives Will a warm "Thank you!"

It is now 10:30 A.M. Instead of finishing with his mail, Will goes to the cafeteria to get a cup of coffee. On the way there, however, Will's support person, Linda says that she is doing an important rush copying job and the copier is out of toner. Will says that there should be plenty of toner in the supply cabinet and asks the support person to follow him to check. Unfortunately, the cabinet is empty of toner. Will snaps, "You might know this would happen; it's Wednesday morning!" They return to Will's desk, where he locates the company's service department number under three layers of work. He personally calls to see how soon some more new toner can be sent over. Having placed the order, Will goes downstairs to borrow some toner from the payroll department because it has the same type of copier. When Will returns, he gives the toner to Linda and at last leaves for the cafeteria.

Will returns to his desk at 11:30 A.M. from his coffee break which he extended by 15 minutes because he ran into an old school friend and wanted to catch up on gossip. His phone rings, and it is the president of the company requesting that Will meet with him the next morning to discuss the new personnel forecasts for 1995. As soon as Will hangs up the telephone, he rushes to the file room to track down the appropriate files with the most recent personnel figures used in his department. Ten minutes pass and he does not find the material he wants. Fortunately for Will, Linda enters the filing room and finds the needed figures in about 10 seconds.

Since it is almost noon (11:47 A.M.), Will decides to leave for lunch. He usually takes his hour lunch between noon and 1:00 P.M. It is a warm fall day and Will takes a walk on the campus of the local university. The downtown campus reminds Will of his undergraduate school. As he is about to head back to the office, Will remembers that he wants to look up some material on quality circles and, if he has the time, pick up some additional material on John Crutch's project. At the university library, Will spots the new computerized ABI (Abstracted Business Index) and decides to give it a try. Will likes the system with its several rotating racks containing more than 400 CDs that house entire copies of 90 percent of the articles on the ABI. Although Will does not collect any of the information for which he came to the library, he feels good about learning how to use the new ABI system. It is almost 2:00 P.M. when Will arrives back at the office.

Upon arriving at the office, he finds that his 1:30 appointment is waiting for him: Betty Simms from a local software development group. Her firm is marketing a computerized performance appraisal and review system. According to the group's write-ups, the system is user-friendly and fully integrated, and it allows for direct data analysis. The president of EverBright is interested in the system and has asked Will to assess its potential. Will doesn't remember setting up the meeting or seeing it on his day planner. He apologizes to Ms. Simms and they proceed to discuss whether the computerized performance appraisal system Betty is selling will satisfy EverBright's needs. Ms. Simms leaves about 3:00 P.M. Satisfied with the meeting, Will takes a short break to discuss recent appointments in the organization with Sarah Tellitall, whose office in transmission and distribution is down the hall. Will returns to his office at 3:30 P.M. to find a note from Tim asking how he liked the design for the new goal-setting training package. Before calling Tim to say he couldn't get to it today, Will decides to finish opening the morning mail.

His support person calls to remind him of a departmental meeting which starts about 3:45 P.M. Will begins the meeting by suggesting that the group discuss the forthcoming Human Resource Conference in New York and who should attend. He indicates that the discussion and decision should only take a couple of minutes. Although the item is not on the agenda, the group agrees. Much to everyone's surprise, the discussion becomes quite heated; by 5:00 P.M. when the meeting ends they have not agreed who should go, and Will returns to his office to find that the president has called to ask whether he will receive the status report on the new performance appraisal program by 4:30 P.M. It seems that Will had promised him the report last week. Will digs out the report at 5:15 P.M. and hand delivers it to the president's office. Unfortunately, the president had already left for the day. Since it is 5:15 P.M., Will also decides to call it a day. He grabs Tim's report (Will never returned Tim's call), and John Crutch's material, determined he will get to both items this evening. Will figures he will finish the day on a positive note and can get a head start on tomorrow.

On the drive home, Will remembers that he has promised one of his trainers that he would pick up an overhead projector at a local camera shop. Both of the company's projectors were being repaired and the trainer had a session the first thing in the morning. However, the camera shop is already closed, so Will knows he will have to get up early tomorrow morning to pick up the projector on the way to work. Will has not called the shop beforehand to confirm that they even have an overhead projector available.

About 6:30 P.M., as Will walks through the front door of his home, he is met by his wife, Denise, who is upset about something. Will only then realizes that this is the night her firm is holding its annual benefits banquet. Denise tells Will that they have to leave in 15 minutes; the babysitter is already feeding the children. By the time Will and Denise return and Will has driven the babysitter home, it's midnight. He concludes that it is just too late to work on Tim's report or John's problem. Will calls it a day. The only problem is that he cannot get to sleep.

End Notes

1. R. Hendrickson, "Proactive approach to minimize stress on the job," *Professional Safety,* Vol. 34, No. 11, November, 1989: 29–32; T. A. Stewart, "Do you push your people too hard?" *Fortune,* Vol. 122, October 22, 1990: 121.

2. Hendrickson, November, 1989: 29–32;

3. H. L. Richardson., "De-Stress," *Transportation and Distribution,* Vol. 31, No. 6, June, 1990: 22–25.

4. C. K. Walker, "Stressed to kill," *Business and Health,* Vol. 9, No. 9, September 1991: 42–51.

5. A. Farnham, "Who beats stress best?" *Fortune*, Vol. 124, No. 8, October 7, 1991: 71–86. © 1991 Time Inc. All rights reserved.

6. Stewart, October 22, 1990: 121.

7. S. Reynolds and D. A. Shapiro, "Stress reduction in transition: Conceptual problems in design, implementation, and evaluation of worksite stress management interventions," *Human Relations,* Vol. 44, No. 7, 1991: 717–733.

8. J. E. Newman and T. A. Beehr, "Personal and organizational strategies for handling job stress:

A review of research and opinion," *Personnel Psychology,* Vol. 32, 1979: 1–43.

9. J. E. McGrath, "Stress and behavior in organizations," ed. M. D. Dunnette *in Handbook of Industrial and Organizational Psychology,* Rand McNally, New York, 1976: 1351–1395; H. Benson and R. L. Allen, "What chief executives can do to balance the value and dangers of stress in their organizations," *Harvard Business Review,* September–October, 1980: 86–92; J. M. Ivancevich and M. T. Matteson, *Stress at Work: A Managerial Perspective,* Scott, Foresman, Glenview, Ill., 1980; A. W. Riley, and S. J. Zaccaro, *Occupational Stress and Organizational Effectiveness,* Praeger, New York, 1987.

10. S. M. Puffer and J. T. Brakefield, "The role of task complexity as a moderator of stress and coping process," *Human Relations,* Vol. 42, No. 3, 1989: 199–217.

11. R. I. Sutton and A. Rajaeli, "Characteristics of work stations as potential occupational stressors," *Academy of Management Journal,* Vol. 30, 1987: 260–276.

12. McGrath, 1976: 1351–1395.

13. W. Gmelch, *Beyond Stress to Effective Management,* John Wiley & Sons, New York, 1982.

14. The model presented in Figure 5.2 reflects the authors' interpretation of current stress literature and stress models found in S. M. Puffer and J. T. Brakefield, 1989, and in S. Folkman and R. S. Lazarus, "Coping as a mediator of emotion," *Journal of Personality and Social Psychology,* Vol. 54, No. 3, 1988: 466–475.

15. T. A. Beehr and J. E. Newman, "Job stress, employee health, and organizational effectiveness," *Personnel Psychology,* Vol. 31, 1978, 665–699; S. Folkman and R. S. Lazarus, "If it changes it must be a process: Study of emotion and coping during three stages of a college examination," *Journal of Personality and Social Psychology,* Vol. 48, 1985: 150–170; S. M. Puffer and J. T. Brakefield, "The role of task complexity as a moderator of stress and coping process," *Human Relations,* Vol. 42, No. 3, 1989: 199–217; Reynolds and Shapiro, 1991: 717–733; P. J. Dewe, "Applying the concept of appraisal to work stressors: Some exploratory analysis," *Human Relations,* Vol. 45, No. 2, 1992: 143–165; S. Folkman, "Personal control and stress coping processes: A theoretical analysis," *Journal of Personality and Social Psychology,* Vol. 46, No. 4, 1984: 839–852.

16. T. J. Newton, and A. Keenan, Coping with work-related stress," *Human Relations,* Vol. 38, No. 2, 1985: 107–126; Folkman and Lazarus, 1988.

17. Beehr and Newman, 1978: 665–699.

18. Dewe, 1992: 143–165.

19. R. H. Miles and M. M. Petty, "Relationship between role clarity, need for clarity, and job tension and satisfaction for supervisory and nonsupervisory roles," *Academy of Management Journal,* Vol. 18, No. 4, 1975: 877–883; A. A. Abel-Halim, "Effects of role stress-job design-technology interaction on employee work satisfaction," *Academy of Management Journal,* Vol. 24, No. 2, 1981: 260-273; J. S. House, *Work Stress and Social Support,* Addison-Wesley Publishing, Reading, Mass., 1981: L. E. Tetrick and J. M. LaRocco, "Understanding, prediction, and control as moderators of the relationship between perceived stress, satisfaction, and psychological well-being," *Journal of Applied Psychology,* Vol. 72, No. 4, 1987: 538–543.

20. C. D. Fisher, and R. Gitelson, "A meta-analysis of the correlates of role conflict and role ambiguity," *Journal of Applied Psychology,* Vol. 68, 1983: 320–333; S. E. Jackson and R. S. Schuler, "A meta-analysis and conceptual critique of research on role ambiguity and role conflict in work settings," *Organizational Behavior and Human Decision Processes,* Vol. 36, 1985: 16–78; P. J. Dewe, "Primary appraisal, secondary appraisal and coping: Their role in stressful work encounters," *Journal of Occupational Psychology,* Vol. 64, 1991: 331–335.

21 D. J. Nelson and C. Sutton, " Chronic work stress and coping: A longitudinal study and suggested new directions," *Academy of Management Journal,* Vol. 33, No. 4, 1990: 859–869.

22. Folkman and Lazarus, 1988: 466–475.

23. Newton and Keenan, 1985: 107–126.

24. Puffer and Brakefield, 1989, 199–217.

25. McGrath, 1976: 1351–1395.

26. J. H. Howard, P. Rechnitzer, and D. A. Cunningham, "Coping with job tensions," *Public Personnel Management,* September-October 1975: 317–326.

27. Newton and Keenan, 1985: 107–126.

28. Newton and Keenan, 1985: 107–126.

29. S. E. Jackson, "Participation in decision making as a strategy for reducing job-related strain," *Journal of Applied Psychology*, Vol. 68, No.1, 1985: 3–19.

30. S. Cobb, "Social support as a moderator of life stress," *Psychosomatic Medicine*, Vol. 3, 1976: 300–314; A. Antonovsky, *Health Stress and Coping*, Jossey-Bass, San Francisco, 1979.

31. A. Bandura, "Social learning theory," *in Behavioral Approaches to Therapy*, ed. J. T. Spense, R. C. Carson, and J. W. Thibaut, General Learning, Morristown, N. J., 1975; A. Bandura, *Social Learning Theory*, Prentice Hall, Englewood Cliffs, N. J., 1977; C. C. Manz and H. P. Sims, Jr., "Vicarious learning: The influence of modeling on organizational behavior," *Personnel Journal*, January 1982: 58–65.

32. M. Friedman and R. H. Rosenman, *Type A Behaviors and Your Heart*, Knopf, New York, 1974; Newton and Keenan, 1985: 107–126; Tetrick and LaRocco, 1987; Puffer and Brakefield, 1989: 199–217; A. Newton, "Occupational stress and coping with stress: A critique," *Human Relations*, Vol. 42, No. 5, 1989: 441–461.

33. D. C. Glass, *Behavior Patterns and Coronary Disease*, Lawrence Erlbaum Associates, Hillsdale, N. J., 1977.

34. Howard, Rechnitzer, and Cunningham, 1975: 317–326; Newton and Keenan, 1985: 107–126.

35. C. R. Anderson and E. S. Craig, "Locus of control, leader behavior, and leader performance among management students," *Academy of Management Journal*, December 1978: 690–698; J. B. Rotter, "Generalized expectancies for internal versus external control of reinforcement," *Psychological Monographs: General and Applied*, Vol. 80, No. 1, 1966: 1–28; J. B. Rotter, "Some problems and misconceptions related to the construct of internal versus external control of reinforcement," *Journal of Consulting and Clinical Psychology*, Vol. 43, 1975: 56–67.

36. T. R. Mitchell, C. M. Smyser, and S. Weed, "Locus of control: Supervision and work satisfaction," *Academy of Management Journal*, September 1975: 623–631; E. Glogow, "Research note: Burnout and locus of control," *Public Personnel Management*, Spring 1986: 79.

37. B. A. Weiner, "A theory of motivation for some classroom experiences," *Journal of Educational Psychology*, Vol. 71, 1979: 3–25.

38. S. C. Kobasa, S. R. Maddi, and S. Kahn, "Hardiness, and health: A prospective study," *Journal of Personality and Social Psychology*, Vol. 42, No. 1, 1982: 168–177.

39. J. P. Campbell, M. D. Dunnette, E. E. Lawler III, and K. E. Weick, Jr., *Managerial Behavior, Performance, and Effectiveness*, McGraw-Hill, New York, 1970; D. T. Hall and R. Mansfield, "Relationship of age and seniority with career variables of engineers and scientists," *Journal of Applied Psychology*, Vol. 20, No. 2, 1975: 201–210.

40. Newton and Keenan, 1985, 107–126.

41. Sutton and Kahn, 1986; Tetrick and LaRocco, 1987, 538–543.

42. Tetrick and LaRocco, 1987: 538–543.

43. R. S. Lazarus and S. Folkman, "Coping and adaptation," in *The Handbook of Behavioral Medicine*, ed. W. D. Gentry, Guilford, New York, 1982; D. F. Parke and T. A. Decotiis, "Organizational determinants of job stress," *Organizational Behavior and Human Performance*, Vol. 32, 1982: 160–177; Folkman, 1984: 839–852; Dewe, 1991: 331–335.

44. Newton, 1989: 441–461.

45. Dewe, 1991: 331–335; Dewe, 1992: 143–165.

46. Dewe, 1991: 331–335; Dewe, 1992: 143–165.

47. W. Schonpflug, "Coping efficiency and situational demands," *Stress and Fatigue in Human Performance*, ed. G. R. J. Hockey, John Wiley & Sons, New York, 1983: 299–330.

48. I. L. Child and I. K. Waterhouse, "Frustration and the quality of performance: A critique of the Barker, Dembo, and Lewin experiment," *Psychological Review*, Vol. 59, 1952: 351–362; Folkman, 1984: 839–852.

49. Folkman, 1984: 839–852.

50. The items described in Table 5.3 are based upon a 63-item coping checklist developed by Dewe and Guest, 1989, and cited by P. J. Dewe, "Examining the nature of work stress: Individual evaluations of stressful experiences and coping," *Human Relations*, Vol. 42, No. 1, 1989: 993–1013.

51. Newton, 1989: 454.

52. Folkman, 1984: 839–852; Dewe, 1989: 993–1013; Dewe, 1992: 143–165.

53. Folkman, 1984: 839–852.

54. Newton, 1989: 441–461.

55. Dewe, 1989: 993–1013.

56. Dewe, 1992: 143–165.

57. Folkman and Lazarus, 1985, 150–170.

58. Folkman and Lazarus, 1985, 150–170.

59. Newton, 1989.

60. R. K. Spero, "Managing time horizons," *Journal of Quality and Participation,* Vol. 15, No. 2, 1992: 100–102.

61. D. T. Hall, *Careers in Organizations,* Goodyear Publishing, Santa Monica, Calif., 1976.

62. A. Deutschman, "The CEO's secret of managing time," *Fortune,* Vol. 125, No. 11, 1992: 135–146.

63. J. W. Lee and M. Pierce, *Hour Power,* Irwin Professional Publishing, Burr Ridge, Ill., 1980.

64. The steps being described reflect material presented in Lee and Pierce, 1980; W. R. Tracy, "Deft Delegation: Multiplying your effectiveness," *Personnel,* Vol. 65, February 1988: 36–38+; C. R. Leana, "Predictors and consequences of delegation," *Academy of Management Journal,* Vol. 29, No. 4, 1986: 754–774.

65. C. R. Hobbs, "Creative procrastination," *Executive Excellence,* Vol. 9, No. 2, 1992: 17–19; B. Farrar, "Beating procrastination," *Successful Meetings,* Vol. 41, No. 10, September 1992: 142–143; V. Reeves, "Break the chains of procrastination, *Manage,* Vol. 44, No. 1, September 1992: 34; K. L. Johnson, "Procrastination—putting off today what you can do tomorrow," *Broker World,* Vol. 10, No.7, July 1990: 78–82; J. A. Cox and R. L. Read, "Putting it off 'til later—procrastination: Causes and corrections," *Baylor Business Review,* Vol. 7, No. 3, 1989: 10–15.

66. Hobbs, 1992: 17–19.

67. K. H. Blanchard, *Leadership and the One Minute Manager,* Morrow, New York, 1985.

68. R. L. Weaver II, *Understanding Interpersonal Communication,* 6th ed., Harper Collins College Publishers, New York, 1993.

69. Weaver II, 1993.

70. A. Fisher, "Got a minute? The perils of an open-door policy," *Working Woman,* Vol. 16, No. 8, 1991: 44–45.

71. J. H. E. Tropman, *Effective Meetings: Improving Group Decision Making,* Sage Publications, Beverly Hills, 1980; K. Schabacker, "A short, snappy guide to meaningful meetings," *Working Woman,* Vol. 16, No. 6, June, 1991: 70–73.

72. Tropman, 1980.

NEGOTIATIONS I: THE MANAGER'S ROLE IN CREATING VALUE

Objectives

- Demonstrate the key role that negotiation plays in the level of success achieved by managers.

- Outline current negotiation theories that can guide managers when attempting to create value.

- Discuss strategies that will help managers face the negotiation dilemma.

- Articulate behaviors that facilitate interpersonal negotiations.

- Provide students with an opportunity to develop and fine-tune negotiation skills required for organizational success.

It is only recently that the study of negotiation has been recognized by management theorists and practitioners as an activity necessary for managerial success. The question that comes to mind is, "Why has negotiation only now attracted such attention?" Quite simply, this recognition reflects an increased environmental need to negotiate with others. Increased rates of change, and the proliferation of organizational agreements, increase the need for managers to negotiate effectively.

An important first step in any attempt to master this skill is an understanding of the underlying theory and concepts supporting the practice of negotiation. To facilitate the presentation of what is certainly a complex process, our discussion of negotiation theory is divided into two parts. *The present chapter emphasizes the general theory of negotiations and the desire to create value.* Negotiators create value by working together in an inventive and cooperative manner to create "joint gains."[1] *The following chapter addresses the issue of claiming value once it has been created.* Negotiators attempting to claim value seek to win, that is, maximize personal payoffs, at the expense of their negotiating counterparts.[2] These two elements of the negotiation process are often referred to as *the negotiating dilemma*. A dilemma exists for the negotiator because while both elements will be present during negotiations, the first element requires cooperative behaviors and the second requires competitive behaviors.

Negotiations: Some Basic Issues

Defining the Concept

To fully appreciate the importance of negotiations as a management tool, it is necessary to define the term and to articulate current conditions that make its managerial use necessary. However, before reading on, take a few minutes to list what comes into your mind when you hear the phrase *management or organizational negotiations*. List your responses in the space provided below.

The following comes to mind when I hear the phrase *management or organizational negotiations*:

_____

_____

_____

_____

_____

_____

If you used such descriptors as formal, collective bargaining, union–management conflict, contracts, behind-the-scene deals, win–lose confrontations, smoke-filled rooms, financial mergers, professional, etc., your views are consistent with those of many people who have completed this exercise. Without doubt, such descriptors reflect characteristics of one or more types of negotiation. However, such descriptors do not provide the basis for explaining why and how managers must negotiate on a day-to-day basis to help ensure personal success.

For purposes of our present discussion it would be more appropriate to define negotiation as *a process (either formal or informal) designed to produce mutual agreement and gain, where interpersonal differences exist between individuals*. Such a general definition implies that negotiating parties are likely to have a personal preference as to outcomes, and as a result, may engage in behaviors designed to ensure personal gain. Negotiation also represents the alternative of choice when other techniques are either inappropriate or ineffective, given the particular disagreement under consideration. This broader view of negotiation also supports the argument that the ability to negotiate effectively is rapidly becoming a necessary condition for managerial success. In short, managers must develop an effective negotiation style if they are to deal with an empowered work force within a dynamic and changing environment. At the same time, employees who are empowered must learn to deal with their own interpersonal differences without having to seek out others to solve their problems.[3]

Let us consider why managers will rarely succeed unless they learn to negotiate effectively. First, organizations are made up of a number of interpersonal agreements that allow the organization to continue to function. Without these agreements, contributing constituencies are likely to break off their association and as a result can threaten the viability of the organization. It therefore follows that managerial success will also rest upon the viability of the agreements negotiated and renegotiated by managers. The following are some of the partnerships within the organizational context that require supportable interpersonal agreements: superior–subordinate encounters, manager–customer encounters, manager–supplier encounters, management–union encounters, etc. Next, the belief that personal needs will be better served by working together rather than working independently is often necessary within North American firms. In other words, a negotiated solution will lead to a greater personal gain than one's **b**est **a**lternative **t**o a **n**egotiated **a**greement (**BATNA**).[4]

Trends of the 1990s (see Chapter 1) also indicate a number of factors that are likely to force managers into a negotiating mode. Without repeating our discussion, the command model of management (where managers can demand compliance) no longer fits organizational reality. Instead, today's employees are less likely to follow unilateral commands. Consequently, managers must find alternative methods to handle disputes and gain commitment. Similarly, given the dynamics and complexity of organizations, and the replacement of the segmented organization structures with integrated structures, managers must rely on individuals outside their department for information, resources, and support. However, managers increasingly find it difficult to use formal organizational relationships as an effective tool in building interpersonal consensus or commitment. This is especially true in the case of peers where there is no formal imbalance of power or authority. Last, as the rates of environmental change increase, we assume that managers will continually need to renegotiate existing agreements.

The list of activities presented in Table 6.1 reinforces the argument that negotiation is a critical management skill that will be used frequently by today's managers. Success in each of these areas will be a function of the manager's ability to negotiate effectively on a personal level and not necessarily within a formal or professional setting.

TABLE 6.1   Managerial Activities Requiring Personal Negotiating Skills

• Budget development	• Goal setting, both with top
• Performance appraisal and review	management and subordinates
• Counseling	• Conflict management
• Planned change	• Coaching
• Scheduling, (e.g., work, vacation,	• Disciplinary action
overtime).	• Customer complaints
• Obtaining agreement with suppliers	• Obtaining agreements with customers
• Salary reviews	• Resource allocation decisions
• Delegation	• Job sharing decisions
• Grievance resolution	• Strategic planning
• Team building	• Selection
• Problem solving	• Job design and redesign
• Mentoring	• Mediation

Management Responsibilities and the Role of Negotiations

Three major responsibilities facing managers are: goal consensus, implementation, and performance maintenance (see Figure 6.1). Only when managers achieve all three conditions (the intersections of the three circles) do they have the greatest probability of success. To be successful, managers must be able to obtain agreement from others. Once goal consensus is achieved, managers often face a second level of disagreement capable of derailing their efforts to succeed. Specifically, goal consensus does not ensure agreement on what behaviors and activities should be implemented to achieve agreed-upon goals. Here again, managers must rely on negotiation skills designed to gain constituency commitment for agreed-upon implementation strategies.

Last, performance maintenance activities will require appropriate management skills. Implementation often results in a complex set of relationships that themselves require administration. In addition, because environments change, managers must be alert to the possibility that performance may not be maintained at desired levels. This implies the ongoing administration of the activities and facilities required for production. When this occurs, managers often find themselves renegotiating with constituencies to regain operational momentum. The need for performance maintenance also implies that negotiated agreements must be managed after they have been reached.

The Negotiation Dilemma

There are two basic forces that produce the desire to negotiate effectively. The first is a belief that negotiating with others facilitates the identification of new alternatives that go beyond one's personal BATNA. Second, effective negotiations enhance the probability of increasing the level of personal gain or

Figure 6.1

Managerial responsibilities and managerial success

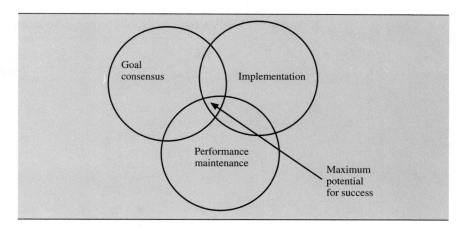

payoff by obtaining a maximum share of newly created alternatives. Unfortunately, the negotiator's desire to create alternatives and claim personal gains often results in interpersonal conflicts and dysfunctional negotiating behaviors. Because a negotiation encounter will involve both of the basic forces, negotiators are faced with the dilemma of balancing the two forces. The dilemma, if not adequately managed, will likely exacerbate the negotiation process and cause it to fail.

This conflict is reflected in the literature by such comparisons as: claiming versus creating value,[5] integrative versus distributive negotiation,[6] and position versus principled negotiations.[7] Similarly, Pruitt[8] argued that once the two parties have identified and stated their contradictory demands, there are basically two alternative approaches to removing the conflict. Either the two parties jointly work together to search for and identify new alternatives, or they make a sequence of concessions that will ultimately lead to an acceptable agreement.

The existence of an underlying conflict becomes more evident when we look at negotiating behaviors used to achieve the two types of goals (see Table 6.2). If negotiators attempt to create value, they will openly communicate personal interests, concerns, needs, preferences, resources, etc. Such behavior may be appropriate if the negotiators' counterparts have the same goal (that is, creating joint gains). Problems occur, however, if the negotiators' counterparts are more interested in claiming value, or when no new value can be created. In the first case, once the open or trusting negotiators expose themselves, their counterparts can exploit the situation for personal gain by using behaviors found on the right-hand side of Table 6.2. The likely result will be significant loss for the negotiator attempting to create value and maximum gain for the negotiator attempting to claim value.

Past negative encounters can cause future negotiations between individuals to break down. More specifically, the negotiation process represents an ongoing learning process. Negotiators develop their own implicit theory

TABLE 6.2   Negotiating Goals and Supportive Behaviors

Creating Value	*Claiming Value*
• Open communications	• Restricted communications
• Active listening	• Selective listening
• Conflict dampening behaviors (i.e., emphasis on facts rather than people)	• Conflict escalating behaviors (i.e., threats, demands, etc.)
• Emphasis on interests or issues	• Emphasis on position or distribution
• Strive for agreement	• Strive for victory
• Be open to influence	• Attempt to influence
• Refrain from manipulative ploys	• Manipulate one's counterpart through claiming, threats, resistance, exaggeration, partial disclosure, etc.

about the negotiation process and the particular individual(s) currently involved in the negotiations. Therefore, if the above scenario takes place, the negotiator attempting to create value would likely draw one of the following two conclusions, (*a*) the negotiation process itself is suspect and can no longer be perceived as an avenue of joint discovery, or (*b*) the negotiator's counterpart is someone who cannot be trusted. The consequence of either interpretation would be that during future negotiations the once-trusting individual would likely be less of a creator and more of a claimer.[9]

Depending upon the organizational partnerships being considered and the underlying relationship existing between the parties, it is possible for the negotiators to move back and forth between the two sides of the dilemma. For example, if we assume that the parties involved would like to maintain an existing positive relationship but have different interests, values, goals, or expectations, then they are likely to act out both sides of the dilemma. In this case, the parties involved would likely first express their contradictory demands. Once these were expressed, the parties would quickly move into a cooperative phase to create value. However, at some point it could become impossible to identify any *new* alternatives, and the parties would then have to decide which alternative should be selected. In other words, the parties would be faced with the problem of how to distribute value (that is, which individual gets what).

Alternatively, if the two parties are adversaries, it is likely that a different sequence will be followed. In this case, the parties will again state their positions, but because of the adversarial relationship, each will likely first attempt to claim value (that is, engage in behaviors associated with the right-hand side of Table 6.2). As a result, there is a reduced probability of cooperation or joint effort to create value. If one of the parties has greater power or more information, or is a skillful manipulator, he or she may claim value without ever moving into a value-creating mode. However, if the parties are equally powerful, have similar levels of information, and possess similar skills, then the two negotiators may continue to negotiate without any hope of success. When this occurs, the only alternative is either to break off negotiations or to cooperate and attempt to create value. When the latter condition occurs, it is possible for the negotiators to alter their style and begin to use behaviors that are likely to increase the probability of value creation. However, once a new set of alternatives has been identified, it is again necessary for the negotiating parties to attempt to distribute the created value.

As we will see shortly, the ability of managers to handle the "negotiator's dilemma" depends upon their effective integration of both theory and experience into an appropriate negotiation strategy.

Negotiation Strategies, Policies, and Tactics

When attempting to understand the negotiation process, it is important for readers to differentiate among negotiation strategy, policy, and tactics. Although the distinction among these terms often becomes blurred in practice, a theoretical structure can help readers organize their thoughts. The constructs of time and level of specificity can be used to help understand the differences among strategy, policy, and tactics.

Strategies
Negotiation strategies articulate the negotiator's overall game plan, which is designed to achieve desired or stated goals. In the case of integrative bargaining (i.e., where the negotiators cooperate to enlarge the pie), negotiating strategies would seek to (1) define the existing problem so that it is understood and accepted by both parties—this implies that the problem is stated in neutral, unbiased, terms; (2) define the problem statement in a clear and simple manner; (3) place emphasis on the primary problem under consideration; (4) place an emphasis on commonalities between negotiators rather than differences; and (5) take steps to build rapport between negotiators.[10] Strategies such as these are designed to create value and at the same time build a positive working relationship between negotiators. When involved in distributive negotiations (that is, negotiators want to get as much as they can), negotiating strategies attempt to (*a*) push for an agreement that maximizes personal gain at the expense of the other negotiator (as close as possible to the other's personal limits); (*b*) change the other's limits whenever possible; (*c*) create an acceptable range in which negotiations can occur; and (*d*) get the other party to believe that the agreement reached is the best one possible.[11]

Policies
Negotiation policies are designed to guide repetitive behaviors or activities that occur during the negotiation process (i.e., established rules, set procedures, and behavior or activity guidelines). If activities or behaviors do not occur frequently,

there is little reason to establish policy statements. During integrative negotiations it would not be uncommon for negotiators to follow a policy of open disclosure. There would also be procedural guidelines on how to carry out a brainstorming session when attempting to identify new alternatives and create value. In the case of distributive negotiations, policies would likely be established that sanction the use of threats, the frequent misleading of others for personal gain, and prevent the free and open sharing of information. Described in this manner, policies are more specific than strategies and are less concerned with long-term goals.

Tactics

Negotiation tactics, in contrast, are designed to increase the probability of success during a specific negotiation exchange. In other words, tactics are what the negotiator must do in the present (short term) to achieve overall strategies and stated policies. Therefore, before selecting a tactical approach to current negotiations, negotiators must diagnose the specific situation and select the course of action that gives them the greatest likelihood of success. As the component parts of the negotiation process are discussed below, tactical alternatives will be described for the reader.

The Nature of the Negotiation Process

A Basic Structure

Managers cannot effectively prepare for an upcoming negotiating encounter, carry out the negotiations themselves, and successfully manage the post-settlement environment, unless they have an understanding of the negotiation process. Figure 6.2 gives one interpretation of the various stages through which the negotiation process will pass. Such a structure is used because it accurately reflects how individuals should behave when involved in a negotiation encounter. The key to success in negotiations is to manage all stages effectively and to ensure that they are properly sequenced.

By listing the stages in a specific order, the authors do not intend to imply that there is only one proper sequence to the negotiation process, or that the stages will be acted out in a similar or like fashion each time the manager enters into a negotiation encounter. Nor is it implied that stages should be given equal time or have the same level of importance when assessing impact on the final agreement. The actual mix, with regard to these issues, will be affected by the distribution of power between the parties, the degree of familiarity between the parties, their experience with one another, the initial positions held by each party, and the perceived importance of personal interests for each individual involved in the negotiation encounter.

The bidirectional arrows between Levels 5 and 6 should be explained. Negotiators often proceed incrementally when attempting to create and distribute value. As a result, it is possible that negotiators may arrive at a list of alternatives that prove unacceptable as they attempt to select a final agreement.

FIGURE 6.2

Stages of the negotiation process

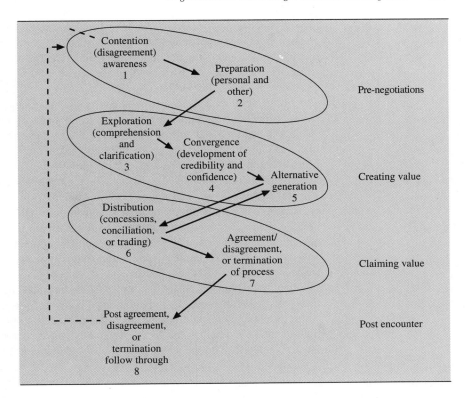

If this occurs, it will be necessary to revert back to the creation phase of the negotiation process and attempt to improve upon the initial list of alternatives. This iterative process will continue until an acceptable alternative is found, or negotiations break down.

Prenegotiation Activities

Managerial success is often a function of the level of preplanning and analysis carried out by the manager. This is especially true when attempting to negotiate effectively with others. Issues associated with overall climate, interpersonal perceptions, credibility, needs, and trust have a great impact on the ultimate outcome of any negotiation encounter. The proactive manager will engage in activities before the encounter that increase the probability of success when and if negotiations take place. Our model indicates that an important set of managerial activities is associated with the prenegotiation stage. The dashed line in Figure 6.2 leading to contention awareness indicates that the proactive manager has already taken steps to facilitate negotiations should they be required.

The following steps represent activities the manager should engage in prior to a negotiation encounter. The fewer of these steps brought on line by the manager, the less likely is it that required negotiations will produce personal gains.

Step 1. Create a Climate of Trust.   To make creating value an achievable goal, it is necessary for negotiators to trust one another. Trust implies that participants are willing to take a personal risk by putting their success in someone else's hands or by providing services to others without any guarantees of future benefits. The degree to which a trusting climate can be established and maintained is a function of activities, events, and behaviors that take place before, during, and after the negotiation encounter. As a result, it is our perception and assessment of others that determines the level of trust we are likely to afford them. Successes in building such a climate also reflect the intentions of each of the participants taking part in the negotiating encounter. If one of the participants is determined to make the negotiation encounter a win–lose proposition, and cannot be dissuaded from this position, then the encounter will cause others to distrust the individual's motive in the future. Finally, past behaviors that can be used to assess an individual's trustworthiness do not necessarily have to be associated with prior negotiations. Individuals will generalize from any past encounter that provides insight into the trustworthiness of another person.

It is possible to identify a number of factors that affect the level of trust likely to develop between individuals.[12] If an individual has demonstrated strength of character and competence in the past, we are more likely to place trust in the individual in the future. Let us consider each of these two building blocks to determine how managers should behave to stimulate trust in others.

• Managers can demonstrate strength of character by demonstrating a number of characteristics. They can demonstrate integrity by adhering to the moral code or values that are accepted within the organization. For example, in healthy organizations, managers would be expected to openly accept others, keep commitments, not promise what cannot be delivered or would compromise the integrity of others, and act in a manner that is consistent with what has been communicated. Next, strength of character implies that individuals will behave in a manner that is consistent and predictable. Such consistency occurs over time when similar situations appear, and between individuals who exhibit the same behavior or performance level. Consistency allows others to better predict how managers will behave in the future and will help create a feeling of trust in the manager. This is especially true when the manager's motives consider the needs and feelings of others. In other words, managers will not undertake a particular course of action unless they have first taken steps to ensure that it will not adversely affect others. Further, strength of character reflects a manager's willingness to be open and disclose information about himself or herself, feelings, and the situation, to others. Openness communicates to others that you are willing to be straight with them and thereby increases the probability that they will be open in return. Last, strength of character implies that individuals will have the presence of mind to be discreet when dealing with sensitive or personal issues, and it will increase the probability that others will be candid and trusting during future exchanges.

• An individual's willingness to place his or her trust in someone is also a function of the perceived competence of that other person. Therefore, the performance record of an individual will have an impact on how the individual is perceived. A manager's perceived competence can be assessed on three levels.[13] Central to successful performance is the manager's competency in the specific skill area for which he or she is responsible. If the manager is in charge of the accounts payable department, the human resource department, or thermal production in a public utility, he or she must be perceived as technically competent to be trusted. Interpersonal competency is a second area of competency that individuals assess before placing trust in another person. In other words, how well will they deal with the people problems likely to appear during future encounters? When this information is not readily available, others are likely to wait until they see the manager in action to assess his or her technical competence. Of particular interest in the area of negotiations is how well can managers handle conflicts, control personal anger and the anger of others, manage stress, actively listen, develop and maintain rapport, and be interpersonally sensitive. On a more general level, the basic business sense or judgment of others will also be assessed to determine how trustworthy they are likely to be. Thus we might expect to hear others refer to a manager's experience, common sense, wisdom, or insight. If others feel comfortable with the individual's general abilities and overall judgment, then they are more likely to trust that person in the future.

Finally, because trust takes time to develop, and often passes through a number of stages before complete trust is reached,[14] it is necessary for managers to develop prenegotiation strategies designed to create the proper organizational climate in which effective negotiations can take place. This can be accomplished if managers behave in a way that is consistent with the expectations and needs of others.

Step 2. Prepare for Upcoming Negotiations. For the manager to be a successful negotiator, it is important to engage in preparatory work before the negotiating encounter. Such activity should proceed on several distinct but related levels, that is, (1) organizational; (2) nature of the disagreement; (3) personal resources, interests and objectives; and (4) objectives and track record of relevant others likely to be encountered during the negotiation process. It is also important that managers clarify in their own minds (5) a preferred personal style and the underlying rules they would prefer to have guide the negotiation process. The information obtained about each of these levels will act as the manager's functioning database when developing an overall strategy to be used in the upcoming negotiation encounter. Let us consider each of these levels to determine what information the manager should collect and what behaviors should be engaged in to facilitate the process.

• **Organizational level.** At the organizational level, it is important that the manager understands the objectives and strategic intent of the organization. (For a detailed discussion of organizational considerations, and techniques for collecting this information, see Chapter 15.) If the manager is not part of the organization's strategic planning process, or it does not have such a process in place, then it is the manager's responsibility to collect a comparable set of information. The manager must understand both the organization's mission and where it wants to be within three to five years, and how this information can be translated into shorter-term objectives and goals. Answers to these questions will likely help managers to identify issues and directions important to their own well-being within the organization.

Having identified organizational long- and short-term objectives, the manager must also identify organizational SWOTs (strengths, weaknesses, opportunities, and threats). Knowledge of organizational and departmental SWOTs allows the manager to prepare for future negotiations. The manager so-equipped is better able to build on strengths, minimize losses or mistakes associated with weaknesses, take advantage of opportunities in a timely fashion, and buffer the organization against threats now and in the future. The alternative to a well-thought-out, flexible plan is a managerial response that is random and reactive and likely to lead to negotiation inefficiencies and failure.

• **Nature of the disagreement.** Negotiation is employed to overcome disagreements that cannot be effectively addressed otherwise. It is therefore in the interest of managers to ensure that they understand the nature of the current disagreement. Of particular interest is how it manifests itself, what events led up to its occurrence, who is actively and peripherally involved, what vested interests each constituency has associated with the disagreement, and what each could possibly lose, given the final agreement reached or not reached by the negotiators. This information will bring the disagreement into better focus and increase the probability that the strategies and tactics developed by the manager will facilitate a successful conclusion to the negotiation process.

• **Personal resources, interests, and objectives.** Before any negotiation, it is important for managers to understand themselves and what it is they would like to accomplish during the upcoming negotiation encounter. (Chapter 2 provides a detailed discussion of several issues covered below.) Knowledge of current resources available to managers allows them to better prepare strategies and alternatives likely to be used during the negotiations. Managers should know how much time they have available, and what authority they have to commit actual physical resources or spend additional organization dollars. Prior knowledge in this area also alerts managers to possible deficient areas and the opportunity to improve or clarify their position before the negotiation encounter. Such knowledge also allows the manager to bring into better focus differences that exist between departmental cultures and whether differences exist between his or her interests and the interests of relevant others. Considerable credibility can be lost if the manager cannot make expected decisions during negotiations.

A second area managers must consider is personal interests. Interests are determined by the individual's existing need structure and the likelihood that personal needs can be satisfied through a negotiated agreement. Needs themselves reflect the goals that individuals would like to achieve and the values that they bring to the situation. An analysis of personal goals and values must include an assessment of their importance and the degree to which they can be ranked by managers. It is necessary to rank both goals and values because it is unlikely that their full range will be satisfied by any negotiated agreement. Prior knowledge of these personal preferences facilitates negotiations through more rapid clarification and comprehension and increased flexibility by managers.

• **Objectives and track record of relevant others.** Because negotiations take place between two or more individuals, managers must make every effort to understand the relevant others involved in the negotiation process. If managers cannot put themselves in the others' shoes, it is unlikely they will be able to predict expectations, reservation points, firmness of commitments, sincerity of interests, concession rates, etc. (These points are detailed below.) Information about relevant others also allows managers to more accurately assess their values, goals, and trust level. Accuracy of information in this area is critical if managers are to correctly select a negotiating style (that is, how open they should be) or to appropriately counter, or expose, negotiating tactics used by others during negotiations.

It is also important for managers to review the track record of their counterparts in the negotiation process. In the preferred situation the managers will have dealt with the relevant others and therefore will have personal experience upon which to draw. If personal experience is not readily available, they must obtain their information through other sources. Through networking it is usually possible for them to find others, either internal or external to the organization, who have dealt with the individuals in question. There may also be written records of past negotiations others have had with the managers' counterparts. Whenever such material exists, every effort should be made to do an exhaustive search and review. When reviewing the information collected about negotiating counterparts, the following questions should be considered:

> "Are there any personal characteristics that I should know about the other negotiator? Is she or he dogmatic or open-minded, decisive or indecisive, flexible or rigid, a concrete or abstract thinker, a quantitative or feeling person, etc.?"

> "Who does the other negotiator represent, and does she or he have the authority to make decisions?"

> "Based upon who the other negotiator is, where she or he comes from, and whom she or he represents, what are her or his real interests and objectives?"

> "What moral or ethical code is the other negotiator likely to follow?"

> "How much does the other negotiator know about me and my unique interests?"

> "How is the other negotiator perceived by others within my organization, or by other organizations she or he has dealt with?"

The more frequent and recent the behavior observed or recorded, and the fewer external constraints placed on the studied individuals, the more comfortable should managers be in making predictions about their negotiating counterparts.

• **Preferred personal style and the underlying rules.** Managers' personal negotiating styles or rules often reflect their underlying value systems and personal beliefs about how the world around them works. Nevertheless, given the long-term relationships that typically exist between organizational members, and the desire to develop long-term positive relationships with those individuals with whom we frequently interact, managers should use behaviors consistent with those described in the left-hand column (creating value) of Table 6.2. However, this recommendation is based upon several assumptions. First, that prenegotiation analysis does not provide information likely to motivate the manager to exhibit a claiming style of negotiating. For example, if the manager learns that his or her negotiating counterpart cannot be trusted, is normally uncooperative, or seeks to maximize his or her payoffs at the manager's expense, then a more closed style may be appropriate. Similarly, if during negotiations the manager's counterpart demonstrates that he or she is not interested in creating value, but rather, claiming value and takes advantage of the manager's openness, it may be appropriate for the manager to also adopt the claiming behaviors found on the right-hand side of Table 6.2. Finally, if the consequences of planned negotiations are too important to chance failure, and little is known about the other negotiator, the manager may again prefer a more conservative or restrictive negotiating strategy.

It is also necessary for negotiators to consider rules that govern the number of issues, parties, and interests allowed during the negotiations. Lax and Sebenius[15] point out, "The game (the negotiation encounter) is that which the parties act as if it is." The implication of such a statement is clear: how the game is played is not determined until the participants decide. If participants abdicate their responsibility in this area, it is likely that their counterparts will unilaterally make the decision. Negotiators must, as part of their preparation work, unilaterally decide what issues, people, and interests are appropriate to them. The negotiators will then be prepared to negotiate jointly with their counterparts the rules governing the upcoming negotiations.

Once preparation work has been completed, negotiators are better prepared to enter into a joint effort with their counterparts to create value.

Creating Value

Lax and Sebenius[16] indicated that value can be created if one or more of the following conditions can be achieved. First, individuals can create value if they can jointly identify alternatives that are of greater value than nonagreement alternatives. In this case, both parties have benefited through the negotiation process. Next, negotiators create value if they can identify alternatives that all parties prefer over alternatives already known. Third, negotiators create value when they can identify a mechanism by which conflicting interests can be reduced or offset, that is, through trading, compensations, cost cutting, altered time schedules, etc. The present authors also believe that value can be created if an alternative is found which benefits one individual but does not reduce the benefit to his or her counterpart in the negotiation process.

The potential for creating value is reflected in Figure 6.3. For the purpose of our discussions, the *X* axis represents B's BATNA and the *Y* axis represents A's BATNA. Under most circumstances, B will not accept alternatives below the *X* axis and A will not accept alternatives to the left of the *Y* axis. Similarly, individuals will not accept newly identified alternatives that require them to lose value. (Exceptions to this rule may occur if either B or A seeks to forfeit value for political reasons, because one or the other is being compensated in some alternative manner, or because long-term benefit outweighs short-term losses, that is, to develop positive relationships or reciprocal obligations in the future, or prevent personal attack from someone with greater power.)

Negotiators can continue to create value by jointly identifying new alternatives not previously discovered. Moving from point *C* to point *D* represents a net benefit to both parties. In other words, both parties have gained more than they have given up by moving to the new alternative. However, if the negotiating parties did not engage in value-creating behaviors (see Table 6.2), it would be unlikely that the new, value-improved alternatives would have been identified.

The Pareto Frontier and Distribution of Claimed Value

At some point, however, the parties will have exhausted all possible options existing within the environment. When this occurs, the negotiating parties have reached the Pareto Frontier. (The Pareto Frontier delimits the full range of

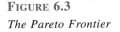

FIGURE 6.3

The Pareto Frontier

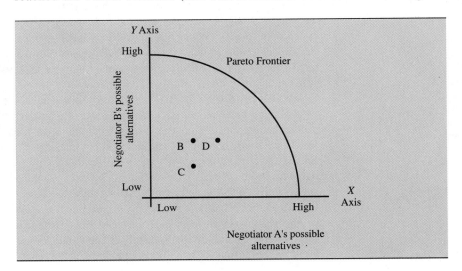

possible alternatives open to the negotiating parties.) Once all, or part, of the Pareto Frontier has been identified, the negotiators will no longer seek to create value but must turn their attention to the issue of distribution (i.e., claim value).

As argued above, it is possible to create value for one of the negotiating parties without taking away value from the negotiator's counterpart. For example, assume that Managers A and B have identified an initial agreement at point C. It is possible through cooperative efforts for Manager B to increase his/her satisfaction by getting Manager A to agree to alternative B. Such an agreement is possible because Manager A is likely to be indifferent to whether the final agreement is C or B; that is, they both produce the same level of satisfaction.

There are likely to be several important benefits for Manager A as a result of his or her cooperative, value-creating behavior. If the two managers are likely to work together in the future, and assuming that B's strategy is *not* to maximize his or her benefit at the expense of A, it is possible that Manager B may share the benefits created through B's open and honest behavior. Because the managers are likely to work together in the future, it is also likely that Manager B will remember A's cooperative behavior and seek to reciprocate such behavior in the future. The development of a long-term positive negotiating climate between two negotiators is a legitimate goal of any negotiation encounter.[17] Had Manager A been uncooperative, it would have prevented Manager B from realizing a personal gain, and if such behavior was recognized, the long-term relationship would suffer. (More will be said about this issue in Chapter 7 when discussing tactics of distribution.)

The Importance of Cooperative Behavior

The motivation behind joint effort to create value is the belief that working together is likely to produce greater benefit than working alone. Such interdependency exists when no one individual has sufficient resources, information, or authority; when one individual is physically unable to achieve the desired goal alone; when temporal constraints require sharing of task responsibilities; or when political or human resource considerations prevent the individual from taking unilateral action.

However, the ability for negotiators to create value is also important in establishing a positive relationship between negotiating parties. By creating value, managers help ensure that individuals with whom they deal receive a level of benefit capable of satisfying their interests. Individuals who perceive an increased likelihood of satisfying their own interests are more likely to agree to, and later support, identified alternatives. Such commitment also enhances the stability of the agreement as the negotiating parties move into the future. If one of the negotiators feels that he or she has been taken, it is unlikely that he or she will strive in the future to make the agreement work. The opposite is more likely. When individuals jointly create value, they are more likely to develop a mutual attraction for one another because of the positive feelings experienced.

For cooperative behavior to take place, the individuals involved must learn to trust one another. The existence of trust is primarily a function of the perceptions individuals have of their counterparts. Trust refers to the individuals' belief that the relevant others have concern for their interests, or otherwise have benevolent intentions toward the situation or the negotiating process. Trust is also a function of the individuals' perception of personal characteristics of the other individuals. Trust is enhanced when the relevant others are perceived as dependable, have abandoned competitive or punitive actions, perceive the environment in a similar or like manner, and indicate positive attitudes toward their counterparts. In those situations where trust is high, individuals are more likely to engage in the behaviors listed on the left-hand side of Table 6.2.

Building trust also appears to be a self-perpetuating process once it is started. The more individuals behave in a manner consistent with the behaviors on the left-hand side of Table 6.2, the higher the level of trust exhibited by the negotiating counterparts. Similarly, the more willing individuals are to match cooperative behavior, make concessions, and stay true to their stated interests, the greater the expressed trust by the individuals' counterparts.

Achieve Mutual Understanding through Comprehension and Clarification

When negotiators cooperate and can do so on the basis of trust, they are more likely to take the time to understand one another. Ultimately, it is the understanding of each other's interests, needs, values, expectations, resources, etc., that allows the negotiators to create value, and work toward the Pareto Frontier. For this to be accomplished, negotiators must be willing to engage in value-creating behaviors. If one or both of the individuals fail to play by the rules articulated in the left hand column of Table 6.2, there is little chance of creating value unless the noncooperative individuals are motivated to alter their position.

For the moment, let us assume that both parties are willing to play the value-creating game and that each negotiator wants to cooperate and can be trusted. It is also assumed that the negotiators have done their homework; that is, they know their own interests and objectives, recognize what their limits and expectations are, study their environment, and assess their counterpart's situation and personal characteristics. If this is the case, it is possible for the negotiators to apply some of the skills already covered in this text. Let us consider *two* areas of skill behaviors that allow negotiators to collect and process the needed information to produce the desired level of understanding and create value.

Importance of a Team Climate

Negotiators must first be able to create a team climate within the negotiation setting. To accomplish this, each negotiator attempts to build into the interpersonal exchange as many of the 12 team characteristics described in

Chapter 10 as possible. Clearly, if negotiators actively participate, develop a clear and shared purpose, listen, openly communicate, accept style diversity, engage in civilized disagreement, etc., the probability that each will begin to understand the other is greatly increased. Although there is no need to repeat what will be discussed in detail elsewhere in this text, several examples will reinforce the importance of negotiators building a team climate.

In the area of clear purpose, negotiators need to establish agreement as to why they are there and how they should proceed. When attempting to clarify these issues, it is recommended that negotiators start at a general level and then move on to specifics. Pruitt, synthesizing the work of others, identified six steps that negotiators might take when moving from the general to the specific in order to clarify the "why" and "how" questions of negotiations. They are:[18]

1. Agreement about the need to negotiate.
2. Agreement on a set of objectives and principles.
3. Agreement on certain rules of conduct, which occasionally leads initially to a protective contract.
4. Defining the issues and setting up an agenda.
5. Agreement on a formula (i.e., an agreement in principle).
6. Agreement on implementing details.

Moving from the general to the specific in this way increases the probability that negotiators can reach an early agreement on what it is that they want to accomplish, and how they might proceed. By defining the rules of the game in general terms, negotiators increase the probability that they can develop a framework that is capable of organizing negotiating activities and at the same time provide a "yesable" game plan that can be supported by all participants. Such early agreement allows participants to view themselves more as a team rather than as adversaries. On the other hand, to start at the specific level (step 6) significantly increases the likelihood that participants will become defensive and begin by protecting their positions rather than sharing interests.

Effective teams are also characterized by a climate of civilized disagreement. During negotiations, however, emotions can frequently run high, and if allowed to get out of control can threaten the negotiation process. To ensure that emotions remain at acceptable levels, participants can behave in an interpersonally sensitive manner, be assertive rather than passive or aggressive, and at the same time behave in an ethical manner. It is also recommended that participants be ready to apply the learning steps associated with how to handle an angry other (Chapter 12). Closely related is the negotiator's ability to effectively manage conflict (Chapter 12) and thereby ensure that the inherent disagreement that brought the negotiators together is not the cause of negotiation failure.

Data Collection and Rapport Building

To further increase the likelihood that negotiators understand each other, it is important that they actively seek out and collect data relevant to the issues under discussion. This can be accomplished if negotiators are willing to use active listening; observe nonverbal behaviors; and use stem questions, probes, reflecting statements, summary statements, and supportive statements. Effective integration of these skills in the exploration phase of the negotiation process fosters mutual understanding and interpersonal rapport (Chapter 4).

The key to success when attempting to explore and achieve understanding is the degree to which negotiators (*a*) can recognize that required managerial skills often interact to produce a cumulative effect, and (*b*) are willing to use these skills within the negotiation session. Success in this area allows participants to develop a feeling of perceived credibility and confidence in their counterparts. If negotiators are lucky enough to understand each other's expectations and interests, the environment and its existing cause and effect relationships, and have gained an acceptable level of perceived credibility and confidence in one another, it is time to create value.

Develop Multiple Options from Which to Choose

Negotiators are now able to create value by identifying new alternatives that have the potential to satisfy the interests of all parties. The objective is to identify a set of alternatives that are as close as possible to the Pareto Frontier. Unfortunately, when negotiators reach this stage, they often fall into six common traps that can short-circuit the value-creating process. The following text describes these six pitfalls that negotiators sometimes encounter when attempting to create value.

Common Pitfalls

1. Assuming that positions are the focus of the negotiation process. When positions become the primary focus during the value-creating phase, they often represent a major stumbling block. This is especially true when individuals become egoistically linked to a position that has been initially stated. If this has occurred, and a negotiator's position is attacked, the position holder will likely take the attack personally. Individuals resist such attack for two reasons. First, individuals are often afraid of backing away from a position because they may be perceived as weak or incompetent. This is especially true when the negotiator is representing a constituency not physically present during the negotiations. Second, once a negotiator backs away from a position, it is difficult to regain what is already given away. In essence, it is lost as a viable option. For example, once a car salesman drops his price to $20,000 from $22,000, and the offer is refused by the customer, it would be next to impossible for him to move back to the $22,000 price. Emphasis on positions rather than interests also increases the probability that negotiators will work toward a compromise rather than attempt to create value. A compromise typically results in agreements that satisfy each negotiator less than a hundred percent. The result is an agreement less likely to be supported in the post-negotiation environment. Therefore, positions should play a secondary role during the value-creation process. As Fisher and Ury pointed out, this can be accomplished by placing early emphasis on identifying and understanding each other's interests rather than arguing for a particular position.[19]

2. Assuming that participant interests are, by definition, in conflict. It is possible that even when attention is correctly directed at interests, negotiators can fall into a second trap if they make the assumption that interests themselves are in conflict. By turning their attention toward the interests rather than positions, it is often possible for negotiators to recognize that many other positions have the potential of satisfying each negotiator's interests—their goals and values. This information can help negotiators identify new positions that not only satisfy a particular negotiator's interests, but can simultaneously satisfy the interests of others involved in the negotiation process. Perceived in this way, interests are inherently not in conflict. Instead, conflict is a function of the interaction between interests and available alternatives. Find the right alternatives, when and where possible, and the conflict between interests disappears.

3. Assuming from the beginning that the pie available is fixed and cannot be expanded. Clearly, there is an upper limit to the number of new alternatives that can be identified by creative individuals. Negotiators are limited not only by reality, but by available time, energy, and resources. The existence of an upper limit is not in dispute. Instead, a premature decision that no new alternatives exist can cause the negotiators to miss opportunities to create value.

Many negotiators function as if what is known, or available, at the beginning of the negotiation process is all that exists. Therefore, if one individual is to gain, someone else must lose. Negotiators who view the process in this manner are assuming a win–lose exchange in all cases. When this occurs, negotiators automatically bypass the value-creating stage and jump directly to the claiming stage of negotiations. The net result is that no attempt is made to expand their understanding of interests, or environmental cause-and-effect relationships, or to jointly create new alternatives capable of satisfying more than one negotiator's interests. Negotiators must learn to alter their view of reality by recognizing the possibility of a win–win exchange where the identification of new alternatives can satisfy the interests of both negotiators.

4. Linking evaluation with creation. The identification of new alternatives often requires managers to engage in creative behaviors. As will be discussed in Chapter 7, creativity can be stifled if criticisms are allowed too early in the creative process. Repeated "Yes, but —" attacks quickly produce a negative climate between the individuals attempting to create value. When negotiators link either evaluation or the need to decide prematurely with the inventing efforts, excessive tension is often introduced into the negotiation process.[20]

To avoid this tension, or minimize personal attack, negotiators frequently reduce or eliminate their creative efforts. Instead, negotiators should attempt to separate creative activities and evaluation or decision making by separating these activities in time, by altering the individuals involved, or structurally altering the manner in which decisions are made. To separate the activities over time, the decision is made that individuals will be allowed to invent without any attempt by the parties involved to assess options or make decisions. Alternatively, it is possible to allow different individuals to attend to the different activities of inventing and evaluating or deciding. (This allows for a separation not only in terms of time but the individuals themselves. Such dual separation increases the perceived freedom to create without criticism.) Last, it is possible to alter the structure of the inventing/deciding process by allowing a third-party participant to mediate between the parties, or assess the creative input received from each negotiator.

5. Having a bias toward a sequential rather than a parallel search for alternatives. Because individuals are often pressured for time in which to act, and have limited resources, there is a natural bias to follow a sequential decision-making model. This error compounds the error of evaluating each of the new alternatives as it is identified. Sequential search implies that as each alternative is invented and evaluated, it is assessed relative to the choice criteria of the parties involved. As soon as an alternative is identified which satisfies the interests of the individuals involved, the decision is made to accept it. This often occurs even though the satisfaction each negotiator derives from the agreement may only be marginally acceptable. Sequential search prevents the search process from continuing, and closes the possibility that even better alternatives, which do exist, will not be identified and subsequently evaluated.

The more desirable approach is not only to separate inventing from evaluation and decision making, but also to ensure that available time and energy are applied to the parallel search. A parallel search attempts to identify the full range of alternatives before concluding the creative process. Negotiators will continue to invent alternatives until time, resources, or participant creativity are used up.

6. Viewing the problems facing others as their problems, not yours. A win-lose philosophy often causes negotiators to block out interests and issues that are important to their counterparts. Consequently, ineffective negotiators often take the position that problems faced by other negotiators are not their concern. The difficulty of such a view is that it acts to filter out the needs and expectations of others. Negotiators must learn that if it is important to the other parties, it must be considered important by them. If the others' goals are not met, or they feel threatened, they will likely become defensive. Similarly, if the other parties' goals or concerns are ridiculed as unimportant, they will respond in kind and treat the attacking parties' goals or concerns as unimportant. The net result of either scenario is a strained relationship that prevents creativity and joint effort.

Avoiding these common pitfalls increases the probability that negotiators will be able to jointly create value, thereby improving not only the content of the existing agreement but the interpersonal relationship as well. Both objectives should be goals of managers who find themselves negotiating more and more each day. What is needed, however, is a process that facilitates joint value creation. Brainstorming is a process that can satisfy these requirements and at the same time is easy to implement. The following is a brief description of how brainstorming works.

Brainstorming

Before creating new alternatives, negotiators must first have *(a)* achieved a mutual understanding of all participants' interests and expectations, *(b)* identified important cause-and-effect relationships that help explain how the environment works, and *(c)* developed trust in one another. If these building blocks are in place, it is possible for negotiators to attempt to jointly work together to create value. What is needed, however, is a process that facilitates joint value creation. Brainstorming is a procedure that can help managers avoid the common pitfalls described in the preceding section and at the same time improve the content of agreements, and the relationships developed between negotiators.[21]

The brief description of brainstorming given here represents only a "common" approach to brainstorming. In real-life encounters the steps may be modified to fit the particular needs of the situation, the negotiators' own style, and the policies established by each party involved. As a result, negotiators may vary the sequencing of steps and the time devoted to each step.

Brainstorming is typically described as an open, group-oriented, problem-solving process that can be used to enhance the creativity of negotiators. Although it is recommended that brainstorming involve 6 to 10 individuals, it can help small groups of any size to identify new alternatives. What is important is that the individuals involved are interested in jointly creating value, are supportive of some type of brainstorming technique, and have the interpersonal skills and sensitivity to facilitate free and open exchanges. If these conditions are reasonably met, it is possible to implement the five steps listed below and thereby enhance value-creating activities. These steps apply to brainstorming sessions among a single negotiator's group (assuming there is a constituent group supporting a single negotiator's activities) or to sessions among the negotiators themselves.

Step 1. Preparation

Negotiators should not proceed until all participants have a clear understanding of the objectives to be achieved and have a common understanding of problem parameters, participant interests and expectations, cause-and-effect relationships that define the environment, and what resources are available to support proposed agreements. Negotiators should also consider changing the location of the brainstorming session(s) from the previous discussion areas to facilitate the unfreezing of attitudes, judgments and positions.[22] It is also important to select, before the brainstorming session, an individual to act as facilitator who is respected and trusted by all participants. Such individuals should be perceived as fair, not locked into any one position, should have good interpersonal and communication skills, and should be able to assert themselves if the need arises.

Step 2. Warm-Up

As part of a warm-up to the brainstorming session, the facilitator should encourage participants to review the problem at hand and the knowledge base they are bringing to the session. Such a review can occur before the brainstorming session itself, or in the beginning moments of the session. Because brainstorming is a fluid process, it is possible that warm-up activities may lead to a redefinition of the problem under discussion or the information supporting individual creativity.

Step 3. Idea Generation

Idea generation is the heart of the brainstorming process and is designed to allow participants to suggest new alternatives without any criticism from other participants. To ensure that this occurs, the facilitator emphasizes the importance to members of making their ideas known, even if the ideas may at first appear crazy. Similarly, other participants are reminded that they should hold back any criticisms or concerns they may have until the appropriate time. The objective here is to ensure the required separation of inventing from evaluating. At this point, the facilitator writes down the ideas generated on some medium (e.g., flip chart, overhead projector, or computer display) visible to the remaining participants. Before and during the listing of participants' ideas, the facilitator encourages individuals to piggyback on alternatives already suggested. When this occurs, the ideas suggested and listed by other participants act to trigger new ideas from the remaining participants.

In most instances there is an initial flurry of ideas, but as time passes the number of new ideas coming from participants drops off. Periods of reduced participation can provide an opportunity for participants to consider ideas already mentioned and cognitively manipulate this information in the hope of creating additional ideas. However, if slumps become prolonged and clearly unproductive, facilitators can stimulate the group by asking provocative questions or introducing ideas of their own.

For those individuals who feel uncomfortable with such an unstructured approach, there are a number of more structured alternatives to the process just described. For example, the Nominal Group Technique (NGT) provides for an opportunity for participants, individually and without interruption, to create their own list of alternatives. After a stated period of time, participants present their ideas, one at a time, in round-robin fashion. The NGT alternative helps ensure that no one idea will dominate the process, and that less assertive people will not be ignored during the discussion. During the NGT, participants are again encouraged to piggyback on the ideas of others. The authors' own experiences have demonstrated that individuals often expand their initial list of ideas by 25 to 30 percent when piggybacking on the ideas of others.

Step 4. Idea Clarification

Once the idea-generation phase is completed, participants are given an opportunity to discuss the ideas generated to clarify the intent and meaning of listed ideas. The objective during this step is to explain new ideas and articulate their potential consequences. It is normally considered appropriate for idea clarification to take place only after all new ideas have been expressed. However, some negotiators prefer to integrate Steps 3 and 4 and discuss and clarify as each new idea is presented. Nevertheless, *evaluation of ideas is still considered inappropriate at this time*.

Step 5. Fine-Tuning

It is now possible to relax the nonevaluation rule of the brainstorming process to fine-tune the existing list of ideas. Negotiators begin by eliminating those alternatives that are clearly marginal in their relative ability to create value, or simply impractical, given environmental realities. As negotiators gain greater insight into the intent and meaning of listed alternatives, they are given the opportunity to improve the alternatives already listed. Effective screening and improvement activities increase the probability that the list of alternatives created by the negotiators represents a close approximation of the Pareto Frontier. Here again, the personal preferences of negotiators and the realities of the situation may result in Step 5 fitting better in the distribution phase of negotiation (Chapter 7).

Tactics for Creating Value

As stated earlier, tactics are situation specific and allow negotiators to adjust their style to the unique requirements of the current negotiations. Although the negotiator can apply a unique set of tactics during each step in the negotiation process, and at each sub-step of the creation phase, it is beyond the scope of this chapter to cover all possible areas. We will limit our discussion to the tactical alternatives open to negotiators when attempting to jointly create new alternatives with their negotiating counterparts. Tactical options associated with the value-creation phase often reflect the existence of *(a)* differences between negotiators, *(b)* complementary capabilities, *(c)* the practical limitations of the negotiators involved, or *(d)* common interests on single issues. Table 6.3 lists these conditions and the tactics likely to be used to create value. Once negotiators have come to understand these environmental conditions, they can situationally alter tactics to create value. The following examples will help clarify this process.

During a recent set of negotiations between a national union representing a newly certified group of employees and negotiators for a local nursing home, it was realized that the two sides placed different value on the multiple issues

TABLE 6.3   **Situational Tactics for Value Creation**

Observed Environmental Conditions	*Tactical Options*
Differences	
• Values	
• Interests	Exchanging or trading, bridging
• Expectations	Contingent agreements
• Risk aversion	Risk-sharing schemes
• Time preferences	Alternative payment schedules
Complementary capabilities	
Practical Limitations	Joint efforts or cooperative schemes
Personal Loss	
• Image	
• Content/Position	Cost cutting, compensation
Common interest on single issue	Unbundling, superordinate goals, education

Terms Defined:

Exchange or trading. Exchanging or trading interests or issues of lesser value for those of higher value.

Bridging. Developing new options that can satisfy both parties.

Contingent agreements. Agreements where benefits or payoffs are determined by actual results.

Risk-sharing schemes. Agreements where benefits or payoffs reflect risks taken.

Alternative payment schedules. Schedules designed to meet the needs or preferences of each negotiator.

Joint efforts or cooperative schemes. Agreements which define how the inputs of two or more negotiators can be dovetailed to produce value.

Cost cutting. Agreements designed to cut imposed costs incurred by the negotiator's counterpart. Cost may relate to personal image loss or future content loss (that is, anxiety over precedents set by current agreement).

Compensation. Benefits received to offset potential losses resulting from current agreement.

Unbundling. Separating issues which are in conflict or unrelated.

Superordinate goals. Goals of greater importance to the negotiating parties than contested issues.

Education. Attempts to inform negotiating counterparts of common interest or benefits.

being considered. Because the negotiations taking place were the first between the union and the nursing home's management, the union's negotiator had two objectives: he wanted to look good at the negotiation table and at the same time demonstrate the ability to get a number of concessions from management. Of primary interest to the union negotiator were process issues, such as work scheduling, grievance procedures, etc. However, he did not want to get into financial issues because of their current confused state and the likelihood that strong demands in this area would result in protracted negotiations. The nursing home's negotiator did not want to incur any significant new financial burdens resulting from significant salary gains and was less concerned with procedural issues that were already informally being carried out within the home. Given these differences in value, there was ample room to obtain an agreement. In effect, the union negotiator traded financial demands (low-value item for the union representative) for management's acceptance of clauses dealing with work scheduling, grievance mechanisms, etc. (high-value issues for the union representative). Such a trade was possible because management's value schedule was opposite to the union's value schedule.

When different value schedules do not exist between negotiators, or there is only one primary issue, it is impossible to reach an agreement through trading or exchange. It is possible to overcome this problem, however, by applying alternative value-creating tactics. For example, local negotiations between government and a group of nurses stalled because of an impasse over wage demands that were not considered affordable by government. To break the deadlock, and achieve its wage demands, the union offered government a number of incentives (e.g., compensation). Specifically, government was given a two-and-a-half-year pension holiday, an allowable reduction of 300 jobs over the life of the contract, and an interest-free loan from the national office. These incentives were sufficient to obtain government's agreement, and the contract was subsequently ratified by 70 percent of the union's members.

Summary

Thus far, our intention has been to leave you with an appreciation of the negotiation process and an understanding of how managers integrate the science and art of negotiation. The process of negotiation begins with a recognition that a disagreement exists and that negotiation is the alternative of choice when attempting to reach a workable agreement. It has also been our intent to demonstrate that managers negotiate every day, whether they are attempting to obtain goal consensus, implement agreed-upon goals, or ensure performance maintenance. The manager's ability to negotiate effectively is also a function of his or her success in managing the inherent dilemma that exists whenever negotiations take place. The dilemma facing managers is how to balance the conflicting needs to both create and claim value and to apply strategies and tactics that maximize the probability of success.

Success in creating value also reflects the manager's ability to explore and understand both his or her own needs and the needs of relevant others. Although such exploration requires the use of key support behaviors or skills, such as open communications, active listening, conflict-management skills, etc., it also requires that managers prepare themselves and their environment so that effective negotiations can take place. Preparation and understanding, however, only set the stage for value creation. Managers must also develop and use techniques capable of generating alternatives that bridge differences and satisfy common interests. In this way, managers create value and the potential to forge "yesable" agreements that last and at the same time build positive relationships with their negotiating counterparts.

Exercises

6.1 Exploring for Mutual Comprehension

Before managers can create alternatives or work toward an acceptable agreement, it is important to understand the interests, concerns and expectations of others. By making the effort to understand your negotiating counterpart, you increase the likelihood that you will achieve a convergence of thought and action. Unfortunately, many negotiators fail to take the time to understand the situation and the people involved. It is worthwhile to explore and to understand personal interests before identifying new alternatives. This exercise provides some practice in exploring a potentially explosive situation in order to produce understanding by all parties involved. Please follow the steps outlined below.

Step 1. The class will break up into groups of two to prepare for an approaching encounter between two individuals who wish to maintain a positive long-term relationship. Once groups have been formed, each should decide who will play the roles of Mary and Bob.

Step 2. Please read the Background material that follows Step 6. Additional information on the interests and expectations of Bob and Mary will be distributed.

Step 3. Develop a general script for each party whose objective is to understand your negotiating counterpart's interests, feelings, expectations, and goals prior to creating alternatives. Use skills already developed during earlier exercises, that is, probing, active listening, interpersonal sensitivity, assertiveness, and so on. (20 minutes)

Step 4. Each group should role-play the encounter between Bob and Mary. When you have completed your role play, you should share the additional information previously distributed with the other individual in your group. Make sure that all information is understood by both parties. At this point, switch roles and repeat the role play between Mary and Bob. (20 minutes)

Step 5. The class will assemble, and several volunteer groups will be asked to role-play the exchange between Mary and Bob before the class. (Step 5 is optional.)

Step 6. The class will assemble to discuss exercise results.

Background
The Unwanted Gun

Bob and Mary are distant cousins who have decided coincidentally to do their graduate work at Boston College. Before Bob and Mary went to Boston to find accommodations, their parents discovered that both children had been accepted by the same university and that both planned to live off campus. Both sets of parents suggested that the two cousins room together during their first year because they were unfamiliar with Boston. Also, it would be better to live with relatives than with total strangers. Bob's and Mary's parents feared that the children might get stuck with the wrong kind of people. Furthermore, no close friends of Bob and Mary were attending Boston College, so both would be alone in a big city. Although Bob and Mary had never met and had talked on the telephone only once, they agreed to their parents' suggestion.

Bob, a physical education major, is 24 years old. He is from a small town in northern Montana, where he grew up on a large ranch. Mary is 22 years old and working toward a MS in social work. She is an only child in a family which lives in a small town in western New Jersey. She has lived there all her life. Bob and Mary do not have any close relatives living in the Boston area.

When Bob and Mary moved into their apartment they signed a 12-month lease. The apartment was selected for its low rent, not its location, which has one of the highest crime rates in Boston. However, when they signed the lease, the landlord assured Mary and Bob that the area was not as bad as the news stories would have them believe.

The landlord was wrong. Since moving in, three robberies occurred in their apartment building alone. During one robbery, an elderly couple was beaten by an intruder and the husband spent a week in the local hospital. At one point, Bob and Mary discussed subletting the apartment, but no one was interested in taking it over.

While cleaning the apartment one afternoon, Mary found a large loaded gun in one of Bob's drawers. By the time Bob returned home from an evening class around 8:30 P.M., she had decided that if he did not get rid of the gun she would move out. Bob walked through the front door to find Mary with her coat on and bags in hand. She blurted out, "If you don't get rid of the gun this evening, I am not spending another night in this apartment."

You now have 30 minutes to plan your strategy and prepare your script.

6.2 Creating Value: Using the Nominal Group Technique (NGT)

In order to create value, it is often in the manager's interests to use a technique that allows for the generation of alternatives not yet considered. One such tool is the Nominal Group Technique (NGT). This exercise is designed to give students an opportunity to experience the use of NGT in addressing a problem. The following steps indicate how the student should proceed.

Step 1. Three days prior to the class, students will submit to the instructor one problem that they want solved. The problem should be relevant to the college or university they are attending. It also should be one that interests other students. (Option: to bypass Step 1, introduce the problem of how to increase the level of faculty involvement in student activities. This issue often generates considerable discussion and the output of the NGT can be used by students.)

Step 2. The class will break up into small groups of six to nine individuals. Each group will select a group leader.

Step 3. Group members should write down their suggested solution alternatives that relate to the issue being considered. (5 to 10 minutes)

Step 4. In round-robin fashion, group members will present one suggestion from their personal lists. This process will continue until members have no further items. The group leader will write each suggestion on a flip chart or chalkboard.

Step 5. Group members will discuss sequentially each suggested solution alternative on the group's flip chart or chalkboard. The purpose of this step is to clarify and evaluate objectively each alternative.

Step 6. The group leader will instruct members about how to rank each item on the list. The instructor will provide each group leader with ranking instructions.

Step 7. The total class will assemble and each NGT group leader will present the group's list of alternatives and ranks.

Step 8. The class will discuss individual alternatives and rankings. An open discussion reduces misunderstandings among members of the class.

Step 9. The class rates each of the listed alternatives from all NGT groups on a scale of 1 to 10, thus indicating the perceived importance or appropriateness of each alternative. Alternatives considered inappropriate would be given a 1 rating and alternatives considered highly appropriate would be given a 10 rating.

End Notes:

1. D. Lax and J. Sebenius, *The Manager as Negotiator: Bargaining for Cooperation and Competitive Gain,* The Free Press, New York, 1986.
2. Lax and Sebenius, 1986.
3. Lee Thompson, "Negotiation training: Win–win or what," *Training,* Vol. 28. No. 6, June 1991: 31–35.
4. R. Fisher and W. Ury, *Getting to Yes: Negotiating Agreement without Giving In,* Penguin Books, New York, 1986.
5. Lax and Sebenius, 1986.
6. N. W. Chamberlain and J. W. Kuhn, *Collective Bargaining,* 2nd ed., McGraw-Hill, New York, 1965; H. Raiffa, *The Art and Science of Negotiation,* Harvard University Press, Cambridge, Mass., 1982.
7. Fisher and Ury, 1986.
8. D. Pruitt, *Negotiation Behavior,* Academic Press, New York, 1981.
9. Lax and Sebenius, 1986.
10. R. Lewicki and J. Litterer, *Negotiation,* Irwin, Burr Ridge, Ill., 1985.
11. Lewicki and Litterer, 1985.

12. A. G. Athos and J. J. Gabarro, *Interpersonal Behavior: Communication and Understanding in Relationships,* Prentice Hall, Englewood Cliffs, N.J., 1978; W. Bennis, *On Becoming a Leader,* Addison-Wesley Publishing, Reading, Mass., 1989; R. L. Weaver, *Understanding Interpersonal Communications,* 6th ed., HarperCollins College Publishers, New York, 1993.

13. Athos and Gabarro, 1978.

14. Weaver, 1993.

15. Lax and Sebenius, 1986: 216.

16. Lax and Sebenius, 1986.

17. Fisher and Ury, 1986.

18. Pruitt, 1981: 15.

19. Fisher and Ury, 1986.

20. R. E. Walton and R. B. McKersie, *A Behavioral Theory of Labor Negotiations: An Analysis of a Social Interaction System,* McGraw-Hill, New York, 1965; G. F. Shea, *Creative Negotiating,* CBI Publishing Company, Boston, 1983; Lax and Sebenius, 1986; Fisher and Ury, 1986.

21. A. F. Osborn, *Applied Imagination,* Scribner's, New York, 1957; M. Martin, *Managing Technological Innovation and Entrepreneurship,* Reston Publishing, Reston, Va., 1984; Fisher and Ury, 1986.

22. Fisher and Ury, 1986.

CHAPTER

7

THE ART AND SCIENCE OF NEGOTIATIONS II: CLAIMING VALUE WITHOUT DERAILING THE NEGOTIATION PROCESS

Objectives:

- Demonstrate the role that claiming behaviors play in distributing value.
- Outline current negotiation theories that help to explain claiming behavior and where it fits within the negotiation process.
- Discuss strategies that will help in managing the second half of the negotiation dilemma: claiming without jeopardizing long-term relationships.
- Provide students with an opportunity to develop and fine-tune negotiation skills required for organizational success.

Once value has been created, the issue facing negotiators is how to distribute that value. In those situations where created value exceeds the needs of participants, the problem facing the manager is simple. Individuals are allowed to take what is required to satisfy their needs. Unfortunately, as we move deeper into the 1990s and are told to do more with less, such an option does not often exist. Therefore, managers must develop strategies and tactics that allow for distribution of value and at the same time maintain positive long-term relationships. This chapter specifically looks at the theory of claiming and what strategies are likely to work best for negotiators.

Claiming Value

At some point negotiators will no longer be able to identify new alternatives. Search activities will cease if the negotiators have reached the *Pareto Frontier*. In this case, there are simply no new alternatives to be identified. However,

259

termination of the creative phase can occur before reaching the Pareto Frontier. Premature termination occurs because negotiators have limitations in time, money, resources, or information, or because their personalities or abilities stand in the way of future efforts to create value. Whatever the cause, negotiators must determine how to distribute existing value. The task facing negotiators when attempting to distribute created value is to define the range of possible settlements and then arrive at an agreement as to how that value will be distributed. To facilitate our discussion of how the distribution, or claiming, phase works, we will assume a two-party, one-issue, negotiating encounter. Such a limited negotiation encounter is depicted in Figure 7.1.

For our purposes, we will refer to the two negotiators as the buyer and the seller. In the case of the buyer, the goal is to obtain some decision, goods, or services from the seller at a minimum cost. Conversely, the seller's goal is to extract the maximum value from the other party for the decision made, or goods or services given. Once this basic model has been discussed,

FIGURE 7.1

*The theoretical
settlement range*

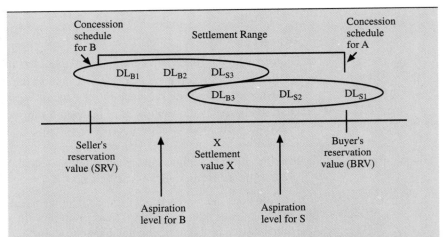

Seller's reservation point.   The minimum value sellers are willing to accept for their support, service, or product.

Buyer's reservation point.   The maximum value the buyer is willing to pay for the desired support, service, or product.

Settlement value.   The price at which the agreement or distribution of value is acceptable to both parties.

Demand level buyer (DL_B).   Stated position expressed by Buyer.

Demand level seller (DL_S).   Stated position expressed by Seller.

Aspiration level.   The negotiator's perception of what is attainable in the current situation.

Settlement range.   Range of alternatives that have the possibility of satisfying both individuals. If the buyer's reservation value is below the seller's reservation value no settlement range exists.

Concession schedule.   The speed at which demand levels decline over time (i.e., move from DL_{B1} to DL_{B3}).

attention will be directed to common negotiating tactics associated with claiming behavior. An understanding of negotiation theory and common tactics will provide insight into the claiming phase of negotiations and at the same time help to ensure that personal gain is maximized while maintaining a long-term positive relationship with all parties involved. Implied in this last statement is the authors' belief that, by understanding both theory and tactics, negotiators reduce the likelihood that they will be "taken" by others during a negotiation encounter.

Underlying Theory for Understanding the Bargaining Relationship

It is likely that the model presented in Figure 7.1 will be complicated by the realities of real world encounters (that is, more than two parties, different values held by members of each side of the negotiations, links between different negotiations, multiple issues, agreement or ratification requirements, the use of threats being possible, time limits, etc.).[1] Given such complicating factors, the negotiator will be forced to creatively link theory with the art of negotiation and to apply the resulting style to the situation. Success in both these endeavors will reflect the experience and maturity of the negotiator.

Reservation Values
As indicated above, the reservation value for the buyer or seller represents the limit beyond which either one will not go. In the case of the supplier of goods, services, or desired support, it is the value below which these items would not be offered. For the buyer, it is the upper limit above which he or she will not pay. The actual value for each negotiator will be largely determined by *(a)* the individual's best alternative should negotiations fail, and *(b)* the costs associated with failure.[2] If there are one or more alternatives to the present negotiations, and they have value, negotiators have greater freedom in setting reservation values. The greater the value of existing alternatives, the higher will be the limit. For example, if managers have a large pool of qualified job applicants who are willing to work for $50,000, it is unlikely that they will hire someone for more. The result is that $50,000 becomes the manager's reservation price when negotiating salary with others.

However, even when there are alternatives with favorable payoffs for the negotiator, there may be some hesitancy to set an extreme reservation value. This occurs when the perceived cost of failure is considered high regardless of the alternatives available. For example, negotiators are subject to political and interpersonal influences placed upon them by others. Within the organizational context, long-term survival often reflects the manager's ability to function within the political and social realities of the situation. Therefore, even though acceptable alternatives exist when negotiating with one's boss, it is not politically advisable to set one's limits so as to cause alienation or discourage future exchanges. Similarly, managers may be unwilling to jeopardize a long-term positive relationship for short-term gains. They may be willing to stay with a supplier even though the likely settlement value is higher than existing offers from known alternatives. Here again, managers are likely to lower their reservation value to reflect the social realities of the situation.

Unfortunately, real-world situations do not always reflect our simplistic model. As Raiffa[3] pointed out, negotiations differ to the degree to which individuals are aware of their counterpart's reservation value. If both negotiators know the other's reservation point and there is symmetry between the negotiators (that is, similar needs, wealth, power, personalities, etc.), research evidence indicates that negotiators will likely split the difference.[4] This is especially true if there are time pressures on one or both of the individuals. If symmetry does not exist, one's ability to predict the agreement's final location is significantly reduced. In such cases, the final agreement, if reached at all, will reflect the actual distribution of situational factors and the bargaining skills of each individual.

Alternatively, only one of the negotiators may know the other's reservation value. Then it is likely that the individual with the advantage will press to have the final agreement as close to the adversary's reservation value as possible. How successful the negotiator with the advantage will be is a function not only of his or her skill as a negotiator, but also the obstinacy levels of both parties. Also complicating the ability to predict is the likelihood of the disadvantaged negotiator finding out his or her counterpart's reservation value either during or after the negotiations. If the probability of either of these eventualities occurring is high, the ability of the advantaged negotiator to drive the agreement down to the adversary's reservation value is significantly reduced. For example, if the advantaged negotiator knows that his or her reservation value will be uncovered after an agreement is reached, and hopes to maintain a positive relationship with the other person, he or she is *less likely* to make full use of the information advantage.

In most instances, however, it is more likely that negotiators will not know with certainty what their adversary's reservation level is. Success in this case will be a function of several factors. First, the skill of the negotiators will play a significant role in constructing probability distributions for their adversary's possible range of reservation values. Critical here will be the negotiators' ability to collect and process information helpful in predicting where an adversary's reservation point actually rests. As we will see below, intimacy, or the state of the existing relationship between parties, will also play a role in determining whether the two parties will be able to find an existing settlement range. Finally, time plays a critical role in determining the ability of negotiators to find an existing settlement range. When time is abundant and trust is high, there is an increased probability that negotiators can work together to reach a settlement.

Settlement Range
Negotiations will only take place when a positive settlement range exists. This occurs when the buyers' reservation value is above the sellers' reservation

value. A positive range provides the motivation to continue negotiating because both parties have the potential of obtaining a net gain. The sellers' surplus would be represented by the settlement value minus their reservation value. The buyers' surplus would be represented by their reservation value minus the settlement value. The actual distribution of value will reflect the relative power, personality (e.g., obstinacy), needs, time constraints, and negotiating skills of the negotiators.

If no settlement range exists (that is, the buyer's reservation value is below the seller's reservation point), no negotiations are likely to take place unless one or both of the individuals are willing to alter their position. As a basis for developing strategies and tactics for changing the reservation points of one's negotiating counterpart, Lewicki and Litterer[5] developed the following four propositions:

1. The other parties' resistance point (reservation value) will vary directly with their estimate of the cost of delay or aborting negotiations to the first parties. Since a quick settlement is needed or a decision cannot be deferred, the other parties have the possibility of pressing for a more advantageous outcome. Therefore, expectations will rise and they will set a more demanding resistance point. The more they can convince the others that the costs of delay or aborting negotiations are low for them, the more modest will be the others' resistance point.

2. The others' resistance point will vary inversely with the cost to them of delay or aborting. The more needy they are of a settlement, the more modest they will be in setting a resistance point. Therefore, the more that they can do to convince the others that delay or aborting negotiations will be costly to them, the more likely the others are to establish a modest resistance point.

3. A resistance point will vary directly with the utilities that the others attach to the outcome. Therefore, the resistance point becomes lower or more modest as persons reduce the subjective utility for that outcome. If one can convince the other party that a present negotiating position will not have the desired outcome or that the present position is not as attractive because other positions are even more attractive, then the other's resistance point will be lowered or made more modest.

4. The other's resistance point varies inversely with the perceived utility the first party attaches to an outcome. Knowing that a position is important to the opposition, one will expect resistance, and therefore lower probability of a favorable settlement in that area. As a result, expectations will be lowered to a more modest resistance point. Hence, the more one can convince the other that one values a particular outcome, the more pressure is put on the other to set a more modest resistance point.

Aspiration Level

Whenever individuals enter into negotiation they bring to the encounter a set of aspirations as to hoped-for personal gains. The actual levels of aspirations are a function of *(a)* past encounters with the negotiators' counterparts, *(b)* perceived power within the situation, and *(c)* the level of the individuals' personal needs.[6] If negotiators have been successful in the past when dealing with other individuals, it is likely that they will raise personal aspiration levels in the current situation. Success in the past may have resulted from the negotiators' counterparts lacking experience, having excess resources, being nonassertive, or putting minimum weight on content issues and maximum weight on relationship issues. Regardless of the cause of past success, the negotiators will inflate their current expectations.

The negotiators will also consider the relative power between themselves and the other individuals. Although the actual source of power varies from situation to situation, it is generally assumed that the ability of individuals to influence others is derived from a number of key variables. These are: ability to reward, coercive power, position power, control over information, being the accepted expert, and referent power (resulting from the desire of individuals to associate with or emulate others). Although this list is not exhaustive, it gives the reader an idea of the basis upon which one individual can influence another. A more detailed discussion of power and the factors that determine how much influence one individual has over another is presented in Chapter 15. Power once having been legitimized, that is, where one individual allows another to influence him or her, the individual with the greater perceived power is likely to have higher aspirations as to personal gain.

The third factor likely to have an impact on aspirations is the specific needs of the individuals involved in the negotiation encounter. In this case, the higher the needs of the individual relative to the issue at hand, the higher will be the individual's aspirations. For example, if two individuals are negotiating the level of participation in future decisions, the individual who has a stronger need for participation is likely to set higher aspirations for the level of participation agreed to. Perceived in this manner, individuals with the greater participative needs are likely to be more highly motivated to argue on behalf of participation.

Research has also indicated that aspiration levels tend to decline over time.[7] This appears reasonable for the following reasons. Negotiators initially use incomplete information in determining their aspiration levels because future negotiation encounters are by definition uncertain. Temporally, individuals establish their aspirations before the actual negotiation encounter. As a result, the negotiator's aspirations are more likely to reflect the individual's own needs and experiences, rather than the realities of the current situation. When managers negotiate (assuming a free flow of information), they will update their information base. As the negotiators obtain more accurate information, aspirations should better reflect reality. The net result will likely be a dampening of personal aspirations. For example, the mere presence of rigidity on the part of the other negotiators can significantly reduce aspiration levels.

Demand Level

The demand level of negotiators is their stated position relative to the issue being discussed. For each stated position there will be a potential benefit for the negotiators. As was the case with buyer or seller surplus, the potential benefit for each negotiator is represented by the difference between his or her stated demand level and personal reservation value. The effective use of stated demands can fulfill several important functions for negotiators when dealing with other individuals. This is especially true when dealing with initial demands.

When dealing with distributive issues, negotiators often do not want their counterparts to know their reservation points or aspiration levels. Early knowledge of such positions may cause others to refuse to accept anything less than what the individual aspires to or has set as a fallback position. This often occurs because negotiators take an individual's initial demands to imply direction or end objectives. If negotiators start off low, then their goals must be low. Similarly, low initial demands may be taken as a sign of weakness or indifference and causes the negotiator's counterpart to expect significant concessions in the future. To prevent this from happening, negotiators use high initial demands to protect or camouflage actual reservation values or aspiration levels.[8]

High early demands are also used to protect negotiating positions or personal image. Stated positions make it difficult, if not impossible, to demand more in the future. Such behavior would most likely be considered unacceptable or in conflict with the norms of interpersonal bargaining. For example, if a salesperson offers to sell you the car of your choice at a stated price and you refuse, it is illogical for your rejection to be countered with a higher price. Not only is the salesperson less likely to get your business, you are likely to respond negatively to that individual. Initial low demands also increase the probability that the negotiator will be giving up gains that might otherwise have been achieved during the negotiation process. Low initial demands also reduce the ability to offer concessions in the future. Such concessions are often considered if there is any possibility of tracking or mirroring a counterpart's concessions.[9] The importance of leaving one's self room to offer concessions is also supported by Raiffa[10] in a laboratory experiment that required subjects to negotiate the sale price of a used car. Study results indicated that although a low but firm demand occasionally worked, it more often alienated the negotiator's counterpart. Raiffa's recommendation was not to embarrass the negotiating counterpart by requiring that he or she make all the concessions.

Image loss, resulting from low initial demands, can occur for several reasons. Low initial demands may cause the opponent to perceive the individual as weak or inexperienced. When the individual is so labeled, the opponent may become more aggressive than would have otherwise been the case. More damaging is the possibility that this negative personal image may be carried over into future negotiations or generalized to negotiations with a broad range of other individuals. Failure to negotiate effectively can also carry over to one's support constituency. Individuals who are perceived as externally weak or unable to obtain results lose support within their own groups.

Raiffa [11] found that initial demands or offers play a significant role in determining where the final agreement falls within the settlement range. His study results indicated that the best predictor of a final agreement was the midpoint between the two initial demands or offers put forth by the study subjects—provided that the resulting midpoint fell within the settlement range. Study results also demonstrated that by holding the buyer's opening bid constant, and on average adding $100 to the seller's opening bid, the seller nets an increase of $28. Conversely, when the seller's opening bid is held constant, and the buyer's bid is reduced on average by $100, the buyer nets a decrease in the final price of $15.

Claiming Tactics

It is now possible to turn our attention to a number of common tactics used, or encountered, by negotiators during the claiming phase of negotiations. The authors have selected *seven* tactical areas frequently listed as important in determining managerial success during negotiations. The ultimate success of managers during this phase will likely be a function of how well they use these tactics, as well as how they will respond to their use by others. The reader should remember, however, that the appropriateness of any tactic is a function of the unique characteristics of the particular situation being considered and the long-term objectives of the negotiator. Therefore, the negotiator has the responsibility of correctly diagnosing the situation, then making and applying tactical decisions, and after assessing the consequences, learning from the experience. One cannot be correct every time, but negotiators will hope to learn from each of their successes and failures.

1. The Importance of Interpersonal Relationships

Within organizations, it is important to view negotiations as a repetitive process taking place between managers and relevant others. This is especially true when dealing with subordinates, co-workers, one's immediate boss, and external stakeholders. In these instances, interactions tend to be of a forced-choice nature, on a day-to-day basis, and over a variety of task activities for which "yesable" agreements are the basis for success. Perceived in this way, the development and maintenance of strong positive relationships based upon trust, liking, or mutual respect, become important goals of negotiation encounters. Such a view has validity not only because of its compatibility with enlightened management principles but because positive relationships between negotiators have a positive impact on negotiation outcomes.

When individuals take the "we" rather than the "us versus them" view of the existing relationship, there is a greater likelihood that participants will attempt to help one another or, at the least, attempt to take the other's interests into account when making decisions.[12] Good interpersonal relationships also have a positive impact on the time it takes to reach an agreement, the number of unresolved issues, and the number of concessions each negotiator is willing to make.[13] Research in the area of liking, empathy, and mood can help us to understand why. Individuals tend to help those they like[14] and empathize with.[15] Similarly, individuals described as being in a good mood are more likely to help others. Therefore, it is not surprising to find that individuals who have had positive working relationships are more productive when attempting to negotiate.

The tactics capable of developing and maintaining positive relationships should be used before, during, and after a negotiation encounter. Before negotiations, the manager must take steps to open channels of communication, actively listen to others, treat others in a fair and equitable manner, be interpersonally sensitive, and where possible, explain actions taken. During the negotiation encounter, the manager must not only continue these prenegotiation behaviors, but expand upon them. Specifically, to build positive rapport with one's counterpart, it is necessary to apply a negotiation style that reflects the behaviors listed in the left-hand column of Table 6.2 and the far right column of Table 6.3. Such behaviors, when applied in an assertive but fair manner, greatly increase the likelihood of developing and maintaining a positive relationship with relevant others. Postnegotiation behavior can also affect the interpersonal relationship between individuals. Therefore, it is important for the negotiator to carry through with commitments, continually monitor and respond to changes in the postagreement environment, and devote time to listening to, communicating with, and supporting individuals affected by post-agreement activities. We will expand on these tactics in greater detail later in this chapter.

2. Openings

An appropriate starting point for our discussion is the question of how and what the negotiator should do to open a round of distributive negotiations. If a buyer's initial offer is too low, the relevant other may end negotiations because the offer is perceived to be so far below his or her reservation value. Conversely, if the buyer's offer is well above the seller's reservation or aspiration value, the offer may be accepted immediately. As a result, the buyer will pay a higher price than conditions would otherwise warrant. The same types of consequences occur if the seller made an offer that was too high or too low relative to the buyer's reservation value.

The following examples help demonstrate these issues. An acquaintance of one of the authors had two expensive homes and placed one on the market for sale. Unfortunately, the market was soft and he was having a difficult time selling the second house. An individual who had long shown interest in the house decided to make an offer. However, because of the soft market, and because the seller was carrying two expensive homes for two years, the would-be buyer made an offer far below the home's assessed value and far below an offer that had been made four years earlier when the house had once before been up for sale. The low offer so infuriated the seller that he refused even to counter the buyer's initial offer, and further indicated that he would not deal with this individual in the future. This was done in spite of the buyer's informal assurances that the offer was only a starting point for future negotiations. Consequently, negotiations were broken off, and the would-be buyer was denied an opportunity of buying a home he had sought for several years.

The next example deals with an issue commonly faced by graduating students looking for full-time employment. If a potential salary range is not evident and the applicant is asked what he or she expects as a salary, the burden of an opening offer is placed on the applicant's shoulders. However, if the applicant, because of ignorance or inflated self-worth, states a salary demand that is excessively high, this may cause negotiations to be broken off. The organization will then likely offer the job to a graduate who is not only qualified but realistic in terms of salary demands. Alternatively, if the applicant offers his or her services to the organization at an excessively low price, the organization may accept the salary demand without further discussion. In this case, the applicant is being hired at a salary below what he or she could have obtained from the future employer. In the latter case, if the applicant takes the job and subsequently finds out that he or she was, in effect, "taken" by the employer, it is not difficult to predict his or her future behavior. It is likely that the new employee will become dissatisfied with the salary and, if the shortfall is not corrected, will seek employment elsewhere.

Recognizing the inherent traps associated with opening bids, what tactics can negotiators use to help ensure that damaging errors are not made? Where time is available, an appropriate tactic is to undertake the necessary steps to collect accurate and relevant information about a relevant other's reservation level, its flexibility, and the likely consequences of exceeding it. Information can help negotiators set limits on the demands that are likely to be appropriate should they be forced to make an opening bid. In the case above, the house buyer had accurately assessed the need to sell, market conditions, and the expense of carrying two houses, but had failed to assess the seller's ability and willingness to carry the second house if need be. Also missed was the earlier offer which had acted to establish a psychological lower limit for the seller. Finally, the buyer failed to properly assess the seller's value system that played a role in determining actual behavior. As it turned out, the seller refused to deal with anyone who would take advantage of an individual's situation to obtain a better deal.

Many of these errors could have been avoided if the buyer had *(a)* more fully identified areas in which information could have been collected, and *(b)* identified and taken advantage of potential sources of usable information. The first recommendation could be operationalized by simply taking the time to list areas in which to collect information. If the buyer lacks the necessary expertise, then an attempt should be made to ask experienced others to recommend potential areas. Once areas needing exploration are identified, the buyer could use informal contacts to obtain the needed information. In this case the buyer could have used neighbors, mutual friends, or the real estate agents involved in the transactions. Informal procedures designed to "test the waters" could have been used by the buyer to obtain the needed information. Most negotiators and their constituents are willing to talk around issues without making formal offers. It is often the informal discussions and observations that provide the insight necessary to identify inappropriate initial offers.

In those instances where negotiators feel comfortable about the information obtained about their counterparts' needs, reservation and aspiration levels, personality, history, and back-home constituency, it may be desirable for them to make the first offer. In this case, negotiators are unlikely to obtain any additional information by allowing their counterparts to open first. If negotiators have accurate information, it is unlikely that they will make an offer that is either too high or too low. Finally, with accuracy of information, it is unlikely that the negotiators' opening offer will offend or anger the other individuals and thereby cause them to break off negotiations.[16] In addition, negotiators who act first can affect the counterparts' perceptions in a favorable direction. Buyers who open low, but not excessively so, may cause the sellers to lower their aspirations or reservation levels. By so doing, they may favorably restrict the settlement zone and achieve a better final price.

There is, however, no guarantee that efforts to collect needed information will be successful, or that one will have the time to engage in such behavior. Therefore, negotiators may still be faced with deciding what their opening offer will be or whether to wait for the other negotiator to make the first offer. It is recommended that when negotiators do not have the needed information to ensure an appropriate opening demand, they seek to have the other negotiator commit first. This tactic allows the negotiator to obtain information from the other's opening offer. It also prevents the negotiator from making an offer that is either too high or too low. Finally, it ensures that the negotiator will not offend or anger the other individual and thereby cause him or her to break off negotiations.[17]

As often happens, advantages gained through inaction also carry some offsetting risks. By giving control over to their counterparts, negotiators open themselves up to undue psychological influence. Let us now assume that the seller opens the negotiation process with a high bid. The bid is high but not unheard of, given the area in which the house is selling. In response to the bid, the buyer may raise his or her assessment of the seller's reservation or aspiration level. Unfortunately, if the seller was bidding high to drive up the final price of the house, the buyer may psychologically be reducing the settlement zone and thereby limiting his or her potential for gain.

Whatever the tactics used, negotiators must remember that the higher their opening offer, the greater will be the final benefits achieved from the agreement reached. Therefore, the negotiator must balance the availability of information, the possibility of contrast effect by making excessively high demands, and the need to maintain positive long-term relations. The negotiator's ability to balance these forces and still maximize personal gain is the essence of the art of negotiation.

3. Changing the Perception of Reservation Levels

It is possible to improve one's bargaining position by altering the perception others have of one's reservation level, or by changing the perceived value of alternatives available to others. By accomplishing the second objective the negotiator will change the other's reservation level. By changing perceptions of nonnegotiated alternatives that are open to each party, managers may change the settlement range to their advantage. Such tactical maneuverings also affect the level of aspirations held by negotiators and the demands they are likely to present during the negotiation process. Whichever tactic is used by negotiators, the desire is to cause the other negotiator to make greater concessions, while limiting the number of concessions they will be required to make to reach an agreement. The following are *two* common tactical maneuvers used to increase one's share of the created value by altering the perceived settlement range.

• **Making position commitments.** Position commitments are used by negotiators to demonstrate that their position is firm. Two important elements of this tactic are the ability of negotiators to (*a*) be first in committing to an irreversible position, and (*b*) present a logical argument as to why it is impossible for them to move from the stated position. Committing first is necessary to prevent the negotiators' counterparts from making a similar commitment. If they were to respond in kind, a deadlock is likely to occur with the resulting possibility the negotiations would break down. By preventing their counterparts from committing first, the negotiators also help ensure that they will not be denied the option of committing to a particular issue. Once the negotiators' counterparts commit, then their degrees of freedom are reduced.

Credibility is also necessary to successfully persuade others to make concessions based upon a position commitment. This can be accomplished by taking the time to gather support information and documentation. Documentation that is specific, relevant, and in sufficient magnitude adds considerable weight to one's argument. Failure to produce such documentation when challenged significantly reduces one's credibility. Negotiators can also increase credibility during current negotiations if they are willing to make their commitment public. If individuals publicly state their refusal or inability to move away from a stated position, they are less likely to reverse the stated position. To do so will cause negotiators to lose face, and will reduce their future credibility. A third technique of increasing commitment credibility is to link the stated position with a third party. The more influential or visible the third party, and the more realistic the link, the more credible the negotiators' position will become. Therefore, if the boss takes an unpopular position while negotiating with a subordinate, he or she can link the position to company policy or top management's preferred position. Such linking is often sufficient to alter the willingness of the others to make concessions, and the shape of the final agreement.

There are, however, dangers of acting precipitously or with excessive tenacity when making commitments. Negotiators may inadvertently lock themselves into an undesirable position that cannot be altered later. Such action reduces the negotiators' future flexibility to engage in trading behavior. Also, on the negative side, is the possibility that commitments will antagonize the negotiator's counterpart and reduce the likelihood of future cooperative behavior. These consequences can prevent negotiators from maximizing their returns from a given negotiation encounter. To offset the potential negative consequences of position commitment, it is sometimes desirable to build into one's position a loophole that allows for future modification if necessary.

To use this tactic effectively, it is sometimes necessary to keep one's counterpart uncommitted.[18] As noted above, commitment by the negotiators' counterparts severely reduces their degrees of freedom and increases the probability of negotiation deadlock. Consequently, it would be strategically desirable to prevent others from committing unless it is to one's advantage for them to do so, that is, you would like to hold those persons to their commitments at a later point in the negotiations. Negotiators have a number of tactics available that can be used to reduce the likelihood of others committing to a position.

By recognizing that individuals tend to commit when they are angry, threatened, or pressured, the following tactics can be used to reduce unwanted commitments. Negotiators must learn to use their observation and listening skills to become more sensitive to the emotional states of others. In those situations where there are signs of emotion overload, the negotiator must take the necessary steps to manage the emotions being expressed. Discussion material covered in Chapter 12 on conflict and anger would facilitate the negotiator's attempts to keep emotions at acceptable levels.

Effective commitment strategy also requires negotiators to spend time collecting the data and support necessary to defend their position. Good negotiators will not commit themselves until they have carried out the required back-up work, that is, done their homework. Therefore, if negotiators reduce the time available to their counterparts, they can significantly reduce the likelihood of commitment behaviors. This can be accomplished by keeping others busy doing research or number crunching, or simply building deadlines into the negotiation process.

Next, the negotiator may simply downplay stated commitments or even ignore their existence. The negotiator can make the following statement in an interpersonally sensitive manner, "Yes, I can understand your concern, but before I consider that issue, could you explain to me how you feel about—?" Lewicki and Litterer[19] go as far as stating that it may be a good tactic to defuse the issue by making a joke of the commitment: "You can't really be serious about going through with that!" Closely related to this approach is the use of social seduction or superordinate goals to stifle any attempt by one's counterpart to commit to an undesirable position. The following statements demonstrate such tactics: "As a good employee I know you don't really mean that" or "BMW owners don't question price" (social seduction) and "If you want our unit to win this year's competition, you'll have to forgo that point" (superordinate goal).

• **Altering the perceived or actual utility of relevant BATNAs.** In an attempt to manipulate the reservation level of relevant others, and ultimately the settlement range, negotiators can attempt to alter their perceptions of non-agreement alternatives. One tactic open to the negotiator is to persuade relevant others that the benefits likely to be derived from their BATNAs are not as high as they appear. Alternatively, the negotiator can persuade relevant others that the costs associated with their BATNAs are greater than initially determined. Perceptual changes caused by either technique will shrink the settlement zone and by so doing have an impact on aspiration levels, demand levels, and ultimately the distribution of value.

To be successful in any attempt to persuade others, negotiators must first get their facts straight about the other negotiators' environment, needs, and alternatives. Information often gives negotiators the ammunition to demonstrate why the relevant others' alternatives are not as attractive as they once thought. For example, during negotiations with a current customer for additional work, a manager discovered that staff within the customer's firm preferred to receive analytical sample data on an as-calculated basis, that is, as results were obtained they were faxed to the client rather than as a final report at the end of the project. In response to this preference, the manager's analytical staff were already faxing laboratory results at each step of previously contracted reports. A competitor with whom the customer was also negotiating could offer a better price on what were comparable core service characteristics. Although this was true, the customer was not fully aware of his own staff needs and the additional features already available from the vendor's analytical department. The vendor's analytic staff could tailor data delivery to fit the needs of their customers. Such service features were considered above and beyond core characteristics traditionally offered within the industry and were not being offered by the competitor. When the manager pointed out these facts, the customer's reservation level, and perception of a fair price, increased significantly. Eventually, the manager was able to close a deal with the customer at a higher price than offered by the competitor.

Similar results can be obtained if information can be used to show that *(a)* the costs associated with negotiation delays or failures are higher than first thought, *(b)* other alternatives can produce greater benefit than the one presently being considered by the relevant other, and *(c)* an agreement is of considerable importance to the negotiator. Item *(c)* requires clarification of how such information works to the manager's benefit. Assume that the manager communicates that the issue being negotiated is of considerable importance to him or her. If this information is accepted by the relevant other, there is a high probability that he or she would conclude that the negotiator is likely to fight hard for this issue and therefore put up considerable resistance when it comes to concessions. The relevant other would, in response to these conclusions, likely lower his or her resistance level to reflect the new reality of the situation. The impact would be a reduced settlement range that benefits the negotiator.

A more aggressive tactic for altering the reservation level of others is for an individual to actively take steps to remove or alter the alternatives available to others. For example, it is not uncommon for organizations to buy out competitors to reduce the alternatives open to customers. Similarly, individuals who cannot extract a reduced price for a parcel of land they are attempting to buy may attempt to reduce its market value by petitioning the city to change existing land use bylaws. The land's market value will be reduced if the changes in the bylaws reduce the number of activities for which the land could be used. If this occurs, the seller's expectations may also be reduced. The tactical options open to negotiators are limited only by their creativity and legal or moral codes. The difficulty with this second option is that it is classified a heavy tactic, while the first is classified a light tactic. Light tactics, while designed to enhance the negotiator's position, fall within the range of acceptable behavior as defined by the other negotiator's value system. Heavy tactics typically reflect behaviors that conflict with the other negotiator's value system. Once negotiators move from light to heavy tactics, they run the risk of triggering an emotional response from the other parties and escalating the encounter to a level of open confrontation. The impact of such confrontation could prove to be disruptive to long-term positive relations.

Negotiators can also change the effective settlement range by altering the perception others have of their reservation level. Altering the perception of others is often possible because they do not typically have access to complete information. The manager, by skillful manipulation of the environment, available information, or personal behaviors, can have a significant effect on how others assess alternatives and ultimately his or her perceived reservation level. A common tactic used by negotiators to alter the perception of others is to attempt to bluff their counterparts. The negotiators could flatly state that they had all the time in the world to reach an agreement or already had several alternatives from which to choose if current negotiations collapsed. When such statements are not true, or are exaggerations of reality, the negotiators are attempting to bluff their opponents. Negotiators have been known to produce fictitious documents, and even hire stooges to act out fictitious roles, in the hope of causing opponents to act. The danger is that others will call the negotiators' bluff or recognize their dishonesty. Both consequences can have a catastrophic impact on negotiations and relationships.

4. Promises and Threats

Individuals have the freedom to make two distinct choices when negotiating with others. The first is to choose between alternatives, and the second is whether to continue negotiating. If the intention of the negotiator is to motivate others to continue negotiating and to make concessions, then motivational theory provides a simple strategy for achieving agreement. To achieve these two objectives, the negotiator can seek to compensate or punish others for the concessions they make or fail to make. Threats represent statements of intent to behave in a manner that will produce negative consequences to another individual.[20] Promises, on the other hand, are statements of intention to behave in a manner that will benefit another individual. The combined impact of threats and promises is to alter the costs associated with the negotiators' inability to reach a joint agreement.

The tactical behaviors that support this strategy closely parallel the steps required for effective motivation (see Chapter 9). Negotiators must first determine the concessions (distribution) which will maximize their return. Once these are identified, the negotiators, based upon their understanding of the relevant others, inventory what is available to either compensate or punish other individuals within the current negotiations. Negotiators should then explicitly link the proposed compensation or threats with the desired behavior. The authors prefer explicit statements articulating the proposed links. Such explicit statements help to ensure understanding and at the same time eliminate the need to seek later clarification or testing of relationships. The use of explicit promises or threats also increases the flow of information during negotiations. By stating the potential links between desired behavior and consequences, the negotiators are communicating what is desirable. Furthermore, the actual level of reward or punishment indicated shows the importance the negotiators place on the desired concessions.

If the negotiators' counterparts fail to respond favorably to the compensation offered, it is possible to sweeten the pot, engage in open discussion to jointly identify reward substitutes, or unilaterally proceed by trial and error until the negotiators either run out of alternatives, switch to alternative tactics for obtaining concessions, or break off negotiations. Once agreement has been reached, it is important that the negotiators carry through with the promised behavior as soon as the relevant others have fulfilled their end of the bargain. Such carry-through is a necessary condition for maintaining credibility in the future.

In the case of threats, negotiators should always provide their counterparts with a clear understanding of alternative behaviors that will remove the threat. What is important, however, is that if the negotiators find it necessary to resort to threats to achieve desired results, they must carry out the threat if the relevant others do not alter their behavior. If threats are not carried out, then they lose relevancy in future exchanges. Perceived in this manner, threats are recommended by the authors as the tactic of last resort.

Before leaving the issue of threats and promises, it would be helpful to highlight the conclusions drawn by Rubin and Brown[21] after reviewing the relevant literature pertaining to their use.

- Promises and threats are likely to be used to the extent that bargainers believe they cannot successfully exert influence in other ways.

- Bargainers tend to transmit promises with greater frequency than they make threats.

- Threats, and to a lesser extent promises, tend to increase the likelihood of immediate compliance and concession-making by the other.
- Over the course of the bargaining relationship, the use of promises tends to elicit general liking for the transmitter, while the use of threats tends to elicit greater hostility.
- Over the course of the bargaining relationship, the use of promises tends to increase the likelihood of bargainers reaching a mutually favorable agreement, while the use of threats tends to reduce that likelihood.

5. Concession Rate

Concessions are traditionally perceived as a tactic designed to achieve the following four objectives: to speed up settlements, to encourage others to reciprocate in kind, to prevent others from withdrawing, or to misdirect one's adversary away from important issues on which the intent is to hold firm. The concession rate is the rapidity with which one concedes during the negotiation process. Willingness to alter one's position and the rate at which concessions are offered can have a significant impact not only on the likelihood that an agreement can be reached, but also on the time it takes to reach an agreement.[22]

The lower the initial demand levels are, and the faster the concession rate of one or both parties involved in the negotiations, the more quickly participants reach an agreement.[23] Under such conditions, the participants are more likely to approach the negotiations in a positive manner, that is, negotiators will reach an agreement if they try, and at the same time reach a "yesable" alternative in the time available. Concessions are important in demonstrating a willingness to cooperate or match concessions made by others. Raiffa[24] found that even reasonable initial demands not backed up by a willingness to offer additional concessions often lead to negotiation failure. The rationale for such a finding is that if negotiators attempt to force their adversaries to make most, if not all, of the concessions, the adversaries will reduce the level of cooperation or joint effort.

However, excessively low initial demands or rapid concession can have a negative impact on the negotiation process.[25] If negotiators concede too rapidly or begin with an uncharacteristically low initial demand, their counterparts may incorrectly conclude that they are weak or vulnerable. If this occurs, the negotiators' adversaries may refuse to make matching concessions or may demand even greater concessions from the negotiators in the future. Therefore, moderate demands and concession rates may have the greatest potential for resulting in a successful agreement, that is, reach a "yesable" agreement in the time available, and maximize the personal benefits of both negotiators.

6. Time as a Variable

Time also plays a significant role in determining the behaviors exhibited by negotiators. Its impact is magnified when specific deadlines are set, the opportunity cost of time spent on negotiations becomes prohibitive, or when negotiators classify time spent on negotiations as an investment rather than as a sunk cost. The net result is that the dynamics of the negotiation process change and thereby have an impact on the outcomes achieved by the negotiators. Furthermore, the response to these pressures can trap negotiators into actions that could otherwise have been avoided.

When the situation imposes hard deadlines on one or both negotiators, stated demands and concession rates change dramatically.[26] This is especially true when time begins to run out and the negotiators are faced with last-minute decisions. The typical relationship found between demand level and concession rate and time is depicted in Figure 7.2.

As deadlines approach, negotiators are likely to demand less and make faster concessions. The motivation behind such behavior appears to be to reach an agreement before time runs out and the recognition that there is insufficient time to engage in effective claiming tactics. Also, as mentioned above, negotiators often lower their demands over time as new information offers a more accurate reading of reality. In addition, a rapidly approaching deadline acts to moderate the effect of potential image or content loss. Personal criticisms directed at the negotiator can be offset with the statement, "It was the best that I could do with the little time we had left!"

The demand curve depicted in Figure 7.2 also shows a precipitous decline in the negotiators' demand level as the deadline is approached.[27] This is likely to happen during the final phase of negotiations if the negotiators' counterparts have ceased making concessions and there is a high probability of deadlock and failure. In addition, the negotiators have to have some room to move, that is, are sufficiently above their reservation value to allow for the reduction in demand level. When these conditions are present, the negotiators are likely to drop their demand level to closely approximate, or match, their counterparts' fixed demands.

FIGURE 7.2

Demand level and concession rate over time

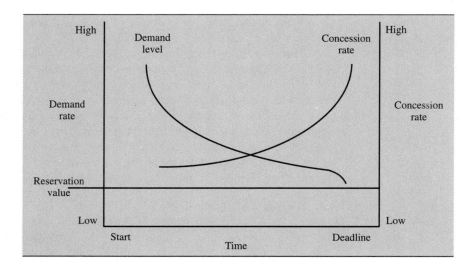

The effect of time on negotiations is amplified if negotiators consider time as an investment rather than as a sunk cost.[28] Such a view can cause individuals to trap themselves into negotiating for longer periods than they should, or to become more willing to lower their demands to achieve an agreement. In the first case, once this process starts, it becomes even more difficult to terminate the negotiations because the time investment cost continues to increase. Similarly, the more time one spends on negotiations, the more one is willing to give up, because the investment cost becomes part of the expense of termination.

The following story gives us a realistic view of how time can be manipulated to achieve desired results.[29] In the way of background, the story depicts an early negotiation encounter between an inexperienced Herbert Cohen (currently a management consultant) and a number of Japanese negotiators. It is described in the first person.

> I'm on a plane on my way to Tokyo. It's a 14-day negotiation. I've taken along all those books on Japanese mentality, their psychology. I'm really going to do well. Plane lands in Tokyo. I'm the first guy down the ramp. I'm raring to go. Three little Japanese guys [at one time, Cohen weighed in excess of 200 pounds; now 155] are waiting for me at the foot of the ramp and they're bowing. I liked that quite a bit. Then they help me through customs, they put me in this large limousine, sitting there in the rear all by myself, and they're sitting on those fold-up seats. I say "Why don't you guys join me?" They say, "Oh no—you're an important person. You need your rest." We're driving along and one of them turns around and says, "By the way, do you know the language?" I say, "You mean Japanese?" They say, "Right. That's what we speak. This is Japan." I say no. They say, "Are you concerned about getting back to your plane on time?" Up to that moment, I have not been concerned. They say, "Would you like this limousine to pick you up?" I say, "Oh, yeah." and hand them my ticket.
>
> Now, I don't realize it at the time, but what has happened? They know my deadline, but I don't know theirs.
>
> So we start negotiating, or I think we do. The first seven days, they send me to Kyoto to visit the shrine, they enroll me in an English-language course in Zen, they . . . I'm begging these guys to negotiate. They say, "Plenty of time."
>
> We finally start the 12th day. We end early, play golf. The 13th day, we resume. End early for the farewell dinner. The morning of the 14th day, we resume in earnest and just as we are about to get to the crux of things, the limousine pulls up to take me to the airport. We all pile in and just as we arrive at the airport, we consummate the deal.
>
> By the way—how well do you think I did?

Clearly, Cohen's hosts were manipulating time in their favor to maximize personal benefits. The following are common tactics employed by negotiators to claim a larger share of existing value.

- Make an effort to get your opponents to indicate the time they have available for negotiations, but keep your own time limits secret.
- Attempt to minimize progress until the opponents' deadline begins to approach and then apply pressure for concessions.

- If no deadlines exist, attempt to negotiate deadlines that favor you rather than your opponents.
- If no deadlines exist and they cannot be negotiated, unilaterally set an artificial deadline that places the opponents' needs in jeopardy.

As is the case with many distributive tactics, there are a number of downside risks associated with the use of time deadlines. It is possible that the negotiators' opponents will not respond to time pressures and subsequently refuse to be rushed. If this occurs and the negotiators want to save face, or remain credible, they may be forced to terminate negotiations without achieving an agreement. The use of time as a threat may also produce the opposite effects to the ones desired. Consequently, opponents may dig in their heels, make a position commitment, or break off negotiations immediately without making any concessions. At the very least, if the negotiators' opponents perceive themselves as being manipulated, long-term positive relations may be jeopardized.

7. Dealing with Uncooperative or Selfish Others

Much of our discussion has assumed that individuals involved in negotiations are interested in cooperating and can be trusted, or, at the very least, they are not attempting to take advantage of anyone. Put another way, negotiating parties are motivated by an underlying drive to find out what is right rather than who is right. If these assumptions were to hold, the environment in which negotiations occur would be a safer place, with agreements being fair to all parties involved.

However, as we have stated earlier, the world is not a perfect place, and as a result managers will on occasion be forced to negotiate with others whose negotiation stance is less than the ideal described above (see Figure 7.3). The negotiating stance has been described as a range so as to reflect the many possible levels of cooperation and trust that the manager may encounter. Each stance level will require some type of adjustment by the negotiator. Such adjustments are designed to help ensure success and at the same time protect the negotiator from being "taken" by others during the negotiation process. Because of the large variety of potential stance positions, our discussion of appropriate tactics will cover *two* common problems which new negotiators might encounter when dealing with uncooperative or selfish others, and how they might best be managed.

Increasing Value while Reducing Vulnerability When Negotiating with Uncooperative Others.   A common question asked by new negotiators is, "What do you do when someone will just not cooperate or is only interested in maximizing their own benefits and minimizing mine?" The matrix found in Figure 7.4, based upon the "prisoner's dilemma,"[30] can help answer this question and give the reader guidance when attempting to create value while at the same time reducing personal vulnerability. The matrix depicts a possible dilemma faced by two negotiators.

FIGURE 7.3
*Underlying
negotiation stance*

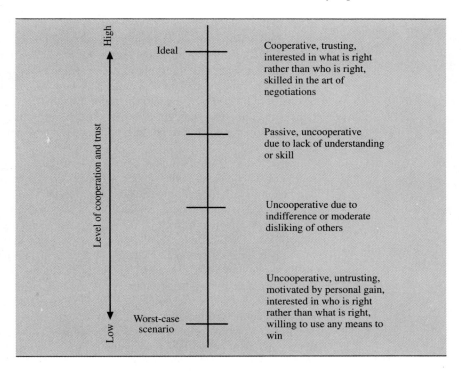

FIGURE 7.4
Prisoner's dilemma

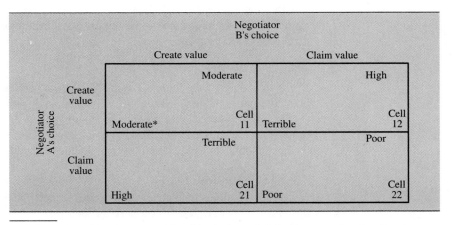

* Negotiator A's outcomes are found in the lower left-hand corner of each cell and
Negotiator B's outcomes are found in the upper right-hand corner of each cell.

If the two negotiators cooperate (both trying to create value—cell$_{11}$) then
both negotiators are likely to achieve moderate benefit from the exchange. At
the very least, neither negotiator will feel that he or she has been taken advantage

of. If both negotiators attempt to claim value (cell$_{22}$), it is likely that neither individual will achieve his or her goals. As a result, the outcome for each individual is likely to be poor. However, the worst-case scenario is when one negotiator naively attempts to create value and the second is only interested in claiming value (cells$_{12}$ and $_{21}$). When this occurs, one of the negotiators obtains high returns and the second negotiator obtains terrible returns. Unless the cooperative negotiator can change the stance of the claiming negotiator in some way, the exchange relationship between A and B is unlikely to continue.

Axelrod[31] offers a number of insights on how to reduce the probability that such a worst-case scenario does not occur and, if it does, what strategy can be employed to motivate the deviant negotiator to cooperate in the future. Axelrod's findings, although based on a negotiation tournament between computer programs, indicate that cooperative strategies (1) did not require a negotiator to defect first, (2) copied the opponent's action on the next round of the prisoner's dilemma, (3) gave the opponent the opportunity to correct his or her deviant behavior, and (4) were open and not too tricky, and produced the best results over a large number of plays. In other words, the benefits of such a strategy more than outweigh the potential loss associated with occasional defections (noncooperative behavior). It is also likely that during actual negotiations the impact of such a strategy would be enhanced when opponents, potential or actual, were made aware of one's willingness to employ such a strategy during the negotiation process. Here again, however, the authors assume that both parties are involved in an ongoing relationship and that they would prefer to cooperate rather than compete. If these assumptions do not hold, the negotiator must design new strategies or tactics capable of producing better results.

Protecting One's Self from Extreme Claiming Tactics of Others.   It is also possible that managers will enter into negotiations with others and encounter tactics used by others that are designed solely to claim value at their expense or designed to cause negotiations to break down. Dichtenberg[32] described five of these tactics and the ways their effect can be countered.

1. Good guy/bad guy—A common tactic is for two opponents to gang up on the negotiator in such a way that one plays a bad guy to set the individual up, and the second person, by playing the good guy, lulls the individual into demanding less or making a bad decision. When attempting to negotiate a salary increase, the individual's immediate boss may respond by saying the individual clearly deserves the money but the "big" boss wouldn't go for it. Another example given by Dichtenberg is when the car salesperson says, "I'll have to talk to the manager," and comes back complaining about how tough the manager is. In both cases, the negotiator backs away from his or her earlier demands and in effect gives up value to the opponent.

To counter the good guy/bad guy tactic, the individual can demand that the other individual come up with an alternative to offset the toughness of the bad guy. When the boss gives top management as the reason for the raise not being given, the individual can ask what the immediate boss can do to compensate for his or her high performance. In the second example, the individual could ask to speak to the sales manager directly and thereby negotiate directly with the person having the authority to make decisions. Both responses increase the probability that the individual will increase personal gain by holding firm or by calling the opponent's bluff.

2. The nibble—Once there is an agreement, negotiators often feel a surge of achievement and confidence. Dichtenberg argued that at this point individuals are vulnerable to external pressure to concede more or purchase more than they need. The office manager who just closed a large deal on computer hardware and software is pressured by the computer salesperson to buy nonessential peripherals. Confident from negotiating the deal, the manager may fall prey to the nibble and add to the final agreement. In fact, he or she may add items or services deemed unnecessary before the agreement was reached. An effective counter to the nibble is for the negotiator to remember that no agreement is final until all details are agreed to. Watchful, anxious, and analytical behavior that is used to protect the negotiator through the creating and claiming stages of negotiation should be maintained during the period immediately following the agreement. Such behavior counters the euphoria that results when an agreement is reached and helps to ensure that the negotiator will not be taken advantage of when his or her guard is temporarily down.

3. Limited or no authority—To stall negotiations and increase time pressures, one's opponent may complain of having limited authority, or being required to check with higher-ups before committing to current demands. When this occurs, the negotiation process is often derailed and the negotiator is likely to become frustrated and angry. Emotions and time pressures can affect the individual's analytical judgments and negotiating effectiveness.

If the negotiator has any doubt about the authority of others involved in the negotiations, he or she is well advised to address this issue before detailed negotiations take place. It is possible to ask directly, and in an interpersonally sensitive manner, whether the relevant other has the authority to make commitments and to agree to demands. If the relevant other's response is, "I don't know" or "No," the negotiator should not allow the discussion to continue beyond the exploratory phase. Instead, the negotiator should request permission to negotiate directly with the person having the required authority. If direct negotiations are not possible, the negotiator must be prepared for delays and be willing to control disruptive emotional responses.

4. Take it or leave it—Managers are likely to run across relevant others who are less interested in reaching an agreement than they are, or who have a style that is dogmatic and unyielding. In this case, the relevant other may use the take-it-or-leave-it tactic to force the manager into making concessions. For example, a building contractor was known for his hard-headed manner and a tendency to respond poorly to the negotiating ploys of others. During one sale, a would-be buyer made an offer for a home below the asking price. Given the seller's personality, and the fact that he was in no rush to sell, he responded with the following statement, "Two hundred and seventy-five thousand is the price today—tomorrow it will be three hundred thousand." In this particular case, the buyer paid the $275,000.

When confronted with the take-it-or-leave-it tactic, the negotiator must remember that even that statement is negotiable. If this fact is forgotten by negotiators, they significantly reduce the probability of negotiating successfully. It would be more effective for the negotiator, after reassessing the interests of both parties, to counter with an alternative to which the relevant other might respond favorably. Again, if the relevant other reverts to a position, it may be advisable not to respond to it directly. It is also important to keep one's self egoistically detached and to make sure that all options are known. Once the buyer in the above example decides that this is the house that he or she must have, and the seller makes a take-it-or-leave-it statement, negotiations are over.

5. The puppy dog—Manipulative negotiators recognize that one of the most effective ways to hook another person into a favorable negotiating position is to allow that individual to experience the goods or services prior to an agreement. Picture the pet shop owner saying to the parent, "Take the puppy home—if the kids don't like him, you can bring the dog back with no questions asked." Parents who allow themselves to fall into this trap significantly increase the probability that the pet will stay for life. Similarly, if a job applicant offers to work with you for a week at a reduced rate, there is a high probability that you will keep him or her after the week is up. In this case, you allow yourself to get to know the individual personally and as a result would find it more difficult to let the person go than to hire a stranger. Other common examples of this technique are when car dealerships offer a $150 award to try out their new cars, salespeople allow you to use their products free for a week, telephone companies offer to connect and disconnect the customer's telephone service for free, and record-, tape-, or book-of-the-month clubs allow prospective customers to try their items on a trial basis. Each offer is made in the belief that once the individual experiences the product, he or she will agree to the future terms of an unspecified agreement.

The first step in countering such traps is to be aware of their existence. Second, the negotiator should not accept the offer before first clarifying the other person's interests or demands, what the individual making the offer is likely to gain from the exchange, and what the future contents of any agreement would be. Last, Dichtenberg suggests that, if possible, involve a neutral third person in the negotiations who can offer an unbiased opinion as to the appropriateness of demands presented during negotiations.

Managing the Agreement: The Post-Agreement Experience

The final phase of the negotiation process deals with post-agreement behavior. More specifically, negotiators must ensure that the terms of the agreement are met, and that the agreement continues to satisfy the needs of the participants and the realities of the situation. Unfortunately, many managers fail to give enough attention to this phase and assume that once an agreement has been reached it will take care of itself. Such indifference by negotiators increases the probability that future disagreements will threaten the positive relations and perceptions that may have existed the moment the agreement was reached. Let us consider why future disagreements are likely to occur among interested, or affected, individuals once an agreement has been reached and moves into the implementation stage.

Why Manage the Post-Agreement Period?

Because the future is uncertain, and negotiators therefore often function with incomplete information, it is impossible for negotiators to construct an agreement that will always fit future realities. Negotiators are likely to make errors in predicting their own needs, the needs and expectations of others, the appropriateness of agreed-upon behaviors, and the direct and indirect consequences of future events. Even if decisions were correct when the agreement was reached, changes in the environment are likely to alter future realities so as to make past agreements inappropriate. At the same time, negotiators themselves also change as they move into the future. As needs and expectations change, organizations often alter their strategic plans, and major power brokers are often replaced. As a result, interested parties are likely to demand alterations in the agreement they once negotiated.

Future adverse consequences, resulting from unforeseen events or random errors, can also prove devastating to one or both negotiators. If this occurs, individuals will find the status quo unacceptable and demand that changes be made to the past agreement. Finally, the negotiators themselves complicate the negotiation process simply because they often want to be kept involved in things. Failure to keep one another informed can precipitate a crisis even when one does not exist. The authors therefore strongly recommend that managers become proactive and learn to manage the post-agreement period.

How to Manage the Post-Agreement Period

Negotiators can effectively manage the post-agreement period if they are willing to collect, process, and act on information available within their environments. The level of sophistication, formalization, and frequency of such activity should reflect the following key factors:

- Importance of agreement consequences.

- Dynamics and uncertainty of the future environment.
- Degree to which negotiators know and trust one another.

In those instances where the consequences of an agreement are important, the relevant environment is uncertain or dynamic, and negotiators do not know or trust one another, monitoring techniques are likely to be formalized, the responsibility of specific individuals, sophisticated, and frequent. Where these conditions do not exist, the monitoring techniques are likely to be informal or ad hoc in nature, poorly defined, and infrequently used.

To initiate this management process, the negotiator must first identify those areas likely to have an impact on the successful implementation and maintenance of the agreement, or the continued appropriateness of agreement terms. The areas likely to be of primary interest to negotiators are presented in Figure 7.5. Once areas of interest have been identified, it is the negotiator's responsibility to develop mechanisms by which he or she can collect the available information. The following are three examples of techniques that have proven useful in managing the post-agreement period and should be considered as standard operating procedures for proactive negotiators. The actual list developed by functioning negotiators should reflect the realities of their particular situation.

1. Open channels of communication. Negotiators should attempt to open and maintain clear channels of communication so as to enhance the information content available to all parties. Opportunities to express opinions, make appeals, give feedback, and reduce uncertainty greatly enhance the probability that the agreement will be maintained and supported. The key issue

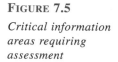

FIGURE 7.5

Critical information areas requiring assessment

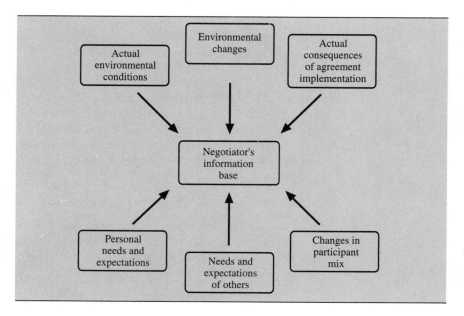

facing negotiators therefore is how to encourage open communications. The simple act of telling others what type of information you desire, why it is important to you, and how they may benefit from providing information, is a basic first step in attempting to open and maintain clear channels of communication. At the same time, it is desirable to indicate the actual channels that can be used to communicate. Failure to provide this information may produce a sufficient barrier to prevent the free flow of information.

The explicit scheduling of contact times can also significantly increase the flow of usable information between negotiators or their constituencies. A financial adviser (a personal acquaintance of one of the authors), who wants to ensure that his contractual relationships with clients are properly maintained, schedules a minimum of 18 contacts a year—12 by mail and 6 by telephone. The 18 scheduled contacts are in addition to any contacts that are initiated by the client. In the case of larger (more important) accounts, the number of contacts is increased. When asked, the financial adviser indicated that his intent is to tap into the needs and expectations of his clients and to ensure that environmental changes do not threaten existing or future contacts. Managers can develop similar contact schedules with subordinates, co-workers, and vendors whenever important agreements are being implemented. Actual scheduled contacts can occur during telephone conversations, site visits, conferences, as well as during formal and informal meetings.

Open channels can also be developed and maintained if the negotiator effectively uses active listening and observational skills, and applies stem questions, probes, reflective and support statements, to build rapport. Rapport often translates into a positive feeling being associated with the individual and open communications. At the same time, negotiators can reinforce senders verbally and nonverbally for providing useful information. By thanking an individual for information received, nodding one's head in an up-and-down motion, or vocalizing an "mmhmm" after desired communications, the negotiator can stimulate the flow of information.

2. Honor commitments. Managing the post-agreement period requires that the negotiator, or alternate, take steps to ensure that commitments are carried out when scheduled. The monitoring process should be designed to provide the greatest amount of lead time possible to allow the negotiator to take corrective action if necessary. The key is to guarantee that some individual has been given the responsibility of monitoring post-agreement activities. If commitments cannot be maintained, it will be necessary to correct the error or inform relevant others that required behaviors, services, or products cannot be provided as agreed. If timely corrections cannot be made and agreement cannot be met, the relevant other should be compensated for his or her loss. When such monitoring activities are carried out, the negotiator enhances the perception that he or she is dependable and can be trusted. The consequences of positive perceptions are obvious: continued positive relationships.

It is also critical that negotiators track the performance of their counterparts once an agreement has been reached. If this is not done, deficiencies may go undiscovered until it is too late for either side to take corrective action. This is especially important when goods or services are being supplied by others who cannot provide a past performance record.

3. Reassess goals.   Negotiated agreements are designed to facilitate personal goal achievement by maximizing personal benefits. As individuals develop and grow, are exposed to new information, respond to changing environments, and alter their basic need structure, their goal priorities may change. As a result, past agreements may require negotiators to behave in ways that are in conflict with current goal achievement efforts. To help prevent this conflict from reducing personal benefits, negotiators should periodically reassess their goals and determine whether past agreements are still functional. Frequent self-assessment increases the probability that the negotiator will be able to act in time to prevent serious loss or interpersonal conflict.

Where such conflicts have been identified, it is desirable to approach relevant others and attempt to renegotiate existing agreements. Renegotiations are much more likely when dealing with the informal or semiformal agreements that managers make on a day-to-day basis with subordinates, bosses, co-workers, etc. The willingness of others to renegotiate is also likely to increase when they value fair play and want to maintain long-term positive relations with relevant others.

In the case of formal contractual agreements, it may be necessary to wait until the existing agreement expires. Nevertheless, the insights gained through self-assessment can prove invaluable when preparing for the next round of negotiations.

Summary

We hope this chapter has sensitized the student to the importance and complexity of the negotiation process. We have attempted to demonstrate that as managers increasingly face dynamic and complex environments in which others are better educated and more demanding, there is a greater need to negotiate effectively. However, to be effective negotiators, managers must understand, accept, and be willing to apply the increasing body of theory that can guide future behavior. Over time, negotiating experiences will also strengthen managers' personal style and their capacity to fine-tune the art of negotiation. By integrating theory and practice, managers increase the likelihood of personal success, that is, to achieve an acceptable agreement and develop a positive, long-term relationship with others. To give this process a jump-start, we have included in Appendix A a set of questions managers can ask at each step of the negotiation process. By answering these questions, managers force themselves to assess whether they have devoted sufficient time and energies to the negotiation process to help ensure success.

Inherent in all negotiations is an underlying conflict between the need to create value and desire to claim value. If this dilemma is not managed effectively through the effective application of negotiating strategy, policy, and tactics, it is unlikely that long-term success will be achieved. Moreover, the unique situational requirements of each negotiating encounter complicate the manager's ability to apply developed strategies, policies, and tactics. Consequently, to be successful as a negotiator, the manager must respond to the unique requirements of each situation and alter his or her personal style as the situation changes.

The negotiation process also represents a time-integrating activity that links the past, present, and future. For example, the negotiator's current behavior and style reflect experiences and present needs. At the same time, the negotiator's current behavior will directly affect the type of agreements reached, and the attitudes and perceptions of the parties involved. Ultimately, the agreements reached, the attitudes formed, and the manager's post-agreement behaviors make up a new set of experiences that affect how individuals behave in the future. By developing an effective negotiating stance and making effective use of existing theory, managers can hope to increase the probability of long-term personal success.

APPENDIX

STEP BY STEP:
QUESTIONS TO BE ASKED BY NEGOTIATORS

1. Identify Relevant Issues

Are there others who have information, or other resources, that would enhance my well-being or organizational success? If so, are they willing to provide these resources freely, or must I negotiate an acceptable agreement of exchange?

Do I control resources that others want, and am I willing to share them? If so, would it be in my best interest to negotiate with others so as to increase the benefit I receive from controlling these resources?

Am I satisfied with the alternatives presently available to me? If not, can I create new alternatives through negotiations with others?

Do differences of opinion or authority exist between others and myself that I must rely on to achieve personal and organizational goals? If so, can they be better handled through a negotiated agreement, or should I use other conflict-resolution techniques such as forcing, accommodating, smoothing, or avoidance? (See Chapter 12 for a discussion of conflict-reducing techniques.)

Are there problems or complaints that others would like to resolve, but need my input to do so?

Do interpersonal roles or expectations need clarification?

Can I identify individuals with whom I interact that are adversaries? If so, do I have sufficient trust in their willingness to follow through on commitments to make negotiated agreements an alternative?

2. Gathering and Analysis of Relevant Information

Have I identified and talked to individuals, or parties, who are likely to be affected by any final agreement?

Have I collected sufficient information to define an acceptable agreement from the organization's point of view, my department's point of view, or my point of view? If so, are all levels compatible?

Have I used all available sources of information, that is, company records, formal contacts, informal contacts, observations, interviews, questionnaires, company files, public information, and correspondence from my counterpart?

Have I identified my best alternative if negotiations should fail?

Have I identified my aspiration level for the upcoming negotiations?

Have I considered or analyzed similar agreements negotiated in the past?

Have I assessed the environment in which the negotiations will take place and the agreement will be implemented?

Have I assessed my counterpart's track record in negotiations with others and me? In other words, is he or she fair, flexible, dependable (can be trusted to follow through on commitments) both during and after negotiations?

Where possible, have I made an effort to know my counterpart's position as well as or better than he or she does?

Have I clearly defined my power and authority? Similarly, have I clearly defined the power and authority possessed by my counterpart? In both cases, have I determined what environmental factors support existing levels of power and authority?

Do I know what behavioral or process norms are likely to be in place during the upcoming negotiations?

Are there any linkages between issues currently being considered and other issues existing within the organization or environment?

What alternatives are available if negotiations fail?

3. Planning for Upcoming Negotiations

Should the process be kept confidential? Alternatively, how much information should I communicate to others not directly involved in the negotiation process?

Have I clearly established my reservation point (e.g., the minimum I will take, the maximum I will give)?

Have I tried to identify the reservation point of my counterpart?

Should I follow behaviors and processes that are traditionally considered appropriate for this type of negotiation?

Have I anticipated my counterpart's concerns and questions and am I prepared to answer them?

Do I have sufficient insight into my counterpart, and his or her position, to take the initiative and make an opening demand? If insights into my counterpart's power, aspirations, and track record are insufficient, would it be better for me to allow him or her to state an opening position first?

Have I used the information available—that is, importance of decision, corporate policy, and counterpart's track record—to determine the appropriate level of openness with my counterpart in the negotiation?

On the basis of collected information, have I assessed the appropriateness of such tactical options as exchanging or trading, bridging, contingent agreements, risk-sharing schemes, joint efforts or cooperative schemes, and unbundling?

On the basis of collected information, have I established a set of rules designed to define the negotiation process, that is, number and type of issues to be discussed, who is to participate, how much time should negotiations be allowed to take, etc.?

Have I developed a strategy or set of tactics that will be useful should my counterpart refuse to negotiate in good faith or attempt to take advantage of my desire to cooperate or my openness?

Have I considered how such facts as time, power, and agreement importance impact on the speed at which concessions should be made?

Is ratification necessary, and if so, what will be the process?

4. Prenegotiation Contacts

Have I taken the time to develop an atmosphere of trust that is based upon personal character, competence, and overall work climate?

Have I taken the time to see my counterpart in action in an attempt to determine how he or she may behave when dealing with me?

Have I contacted others who have dealt with my counterpart in similar situations?

Have I informally approached my counterpart before formal negotiations to determine whether he or she believes that there is an opportunity to benefit from joint negotiations? (Informal contacts are most likely to occur during repetitive or ongoing relationships.)

Did I take time to communicate to my counterpart what I see as the rules that would guide negotiations between us, that is, number and type of issues to be discussed, who was to participate, how much time should negotiations be allowed to take, etc.?

5. The Act of Negotiating

Have I defined the problem as I see it in sufficient detail to ensure understanding by my counterpart?

Was my definition of the problem stated in a way designed not to alienate or anger my counterpart?

Did I take time to state my interests? Did I make an honest effort to understand the interests of my counterpart?

Did I initially take the time to identify commonalities between my counterpart and myself before dealing with differences?

Did I logically go from the general to the specific to ensure understanding by my counterpart?

Did I allow myself to be taken in by manipulative strategies such as time manipulation, threats and promises, good guy/bad guy routine, take-it-or-leave-it, and claims of limited authority?

Did I allow for sufficient time to jointly create alternatives? Did all parties refrain from evaluation of alternatives until brainstorming activities were complete?

Did I take time to work with my counterpart to develop agreed-upon criteria that could be used to assess the appropriateness of identified alternatives?

How is the general climate of the negotiating environment developing?

Is my counterpart opening up, becoming defensive or angry, losing interest, becoming impatient, etc.?

If the current climate is not conducive to an agreement, what steps can I take to create a more positive atmosphere—alter my tactics, change representatives, take a recess, etc.?

Am I allowing sufficient time to discuss and consider issues being presented by participants?

Have I maintained open channels of communications during the negotiation process? In other words, have I made myself available, been willing to listen, and shared all relevant information?

6. Finalizing the Agreement

Before accepting, or writing down, the final agreement did I review decisions or commitments made?

Did we confirm who is responsible for what?

Did we decide what specific action would take place first, and when such action would be taken, to ensure that the implementation of the agreement would successfully begin?

Did we agree as to how agreement success or compliance would be measured?

Did we discuss the consequences of implementation failure or of noncompliance?

Did we build in monitoring and feedback mechanisms to facilitate post-agreement changes should they be needed?

Before accepting the final agreement, did negotiating parties jointly assess potential adverse consequences resulting from the proposed agreement?

7. Follow-up

Did we notify all parties affected by, or interested in, the agreement in its final form?

Did negotiating parties monitor post-agreement behaviors, changes, and environmental consequences to ensure that successful implementation of the agreement took place or that participants followed through on commitments made?

Did negotiating parties maintain open communication channels to ensure the free flow of information?

Did negotiating parties periodically assess the continued appropriateness of the final agreement to current environmental conditions? In other words, have there been changes in environmental conditions, participant mix, needs and expectations of parties involved, etc.?

Is it necessary for me to educate others as to the terms of the agreement?

Exercises

7.1 Can We Make a Deal?

The following role play centers on a disagreement between two neighbors whose properties abut (see the chart below). Specifically, Ken Croft has recently put his 38-foot side yard up for sale at $150,000. Although land use bylaws normally require a minimum property width of 40 feet, Ken was given special approval by the city's developmental office to subdivide his property. Local residents had attempted to block the subdivision but failed in their efforts. The site currently has no structures, but a number of large trees grow on the property. His neighbor, Linda Johnstone, is upset because, if Ken's property is sold and a house is built on it, she will likely incur psychological and financial losses. Even though Linda does not own the property she will lose financially because the market value of her house is likely to decline if a house is built only eight feet from hers. Zoning laws allow residential homes to be built within four feet of the property line; because the property for sale next door is only 38 feet wide, this is likely to happen. The psychological consequences of a house directly next door are the loss of a green area, a pleasant view, and direct sunlight. Although Linda cannot afford the $150,000 price, she has asked to meet with Ken to see if there is some way he would sell the property to her. Linda is somewhat anxious about meeting with Ken because he has been a neighbor for only about two weeks and they have not met. Consequently, Ken and Linda know very little about each other.

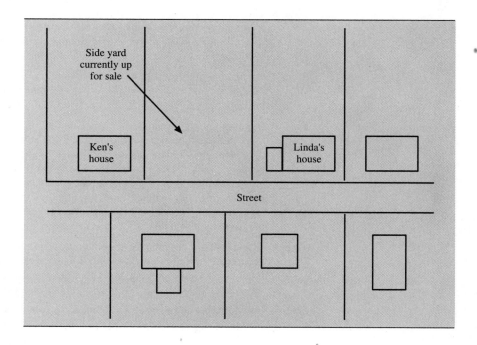

With these facts in mind, please follow the steps outlined below.

Step 1. The class will break up into small groups of five to six students. Each group will then assign members to play the roles of Ken and Linda.

Step 2. Through group discussion, develop a script for each of the two individuals during the approaching encounter. You will be provided with additional information that will help you better understand Ken and Linda, their personalities, and the expectations each has for the meeting. If time permits, practice your role. (Approximately 45 minutes)

Step 3. The class will assemble and groups will be selected at random to role-play the negotiating encounter between Ken and Linda.

Step 4. The entire class will critique the negotiators' behaviors and assess the quality of the agreement reached.

7.2 South Shore General: Is There Room for a Negotiated Agreement?

For the purpose of this exercise, you will play the roles of Harry Medcar or Janet Hill. Harry is South Shore General Hospital's medical director, and Janet Hill is the hospital's director of nursing. Janet and Harry have reached an impasse concerning a subject of considerable importance. To overcome this impasse, Harry and Janet will meet and, if possible, negotiate an alternative solution. To prepare for their meeting, please follow the steps outlined below.

Step 1. The class will form small groups of five to six individuals each. Each group will be assigned to play the role of either Janet Hill or Harry Medcar in a role play. Each group should then select a member of the group to role-play Janet or Harry. Read through the background information.

Step 2. Groups playing the role of Janet Hill will be given supplemental information to that presented in the background material. No additional information will be distributed to clarify Harry Medcar's role.

Step 3. Develop a script for the upcoming role play. Try to incorporate as many as possible of the negotiating dos and don'ts from a list distributed by the professor. (Option: instead of a list of negotiating dos and don'ts, the professor may prefer to verbally describe these points to the class.) To breathe life into your role, you can make any reasonable additional assumptions about the individuals involved and the environment at South Shore General Hospital. The only constraint is that your assumptions be consistent with the background information. (30 minutes)

Step 4. Groups should practice for the role play. To accomplish Step 4, a second group member must play the role of the negotiator's counterpart, that is, for the group role-playing Janet Hill, a second group member will play the role of Harry Medcar, but only during the practice session. (15 minutes)

Step 5. Individuals will be randomly selected to role-play Janet Hill and Harry Medcar in the negotiation encounter before the class.

Background

South Shore General is a 500-bed hospital on the south shore of New Jersey. During the past several months, the hospital has been increasingly aware of the need to devote more resources to the selection, development, and maintenance of staff. This is in keeping with the philosophy of the executive director, John Moore, and the value training the hospital has undergone over the past two years. Growing pressure has motivated the executive director to consider how the human resource function can best be structured. He would like all departments at South Shore General to make greater use of the human resource function and, at the same time, ensure continued quality services within the hospital.

Unfortunately, the decision appears to be more complex than originally stated and, as a result, requires input from the executive committee, a committee which reports directly to the executive director. In the past, the executive committee has set policy and considered structural issues. The executive director sees such involvement in the hospital's decision-making process as part of his effort to empower employees. Before any action is taken, the executive director wants the executive committee to evaluate all relevant information and make recommendations based on that information.

Five people presently sit on the executive committee: Paul Lucas, director of special projects; Mary Livingston, director of dietetics; Janet Hill, director of nursing; Robert Farr, administrative coordinator; and Harry Medcar, medical director. (See the attached organizational chart for details.) Paul Lucas is currently serving as the executive committee's official chairperson. The current meeting is the fifth and, the members hope, the last on this subject to be held by the executive committee. During the previous four meetings, the members discussed the committee's goals, terms of reference, the pros and cons of a decentralized versus centralized function, and several possible recommendations to make to John Moore, the executive director. However, the more often the committee meets, the more obvious it becomes that its members are not in agreement and that its efforts will fail to reach a decision.

During the current meeting, Harry Medcar suggests that the committee has spent sufficient time discussing how to structure the human resource function, and that all parties have had sufficient time to study the options and have adequately addressed the advantages and disadvantages of each. Harry strongly favors keeping a centralized human resource function. It makes sense to him for the following reasons.

- South Shore General is too small a hospital to warrant a completely decentralized function.

- Given the increased pressure for equality in pay and a desire to ensure the protection of individual rights, a high degree of centralization provides the needed coordination to achieve these objectives.

- Total decentralization tends to be considerably more expensive to operate and maintain. Most hospitals that have gone that route clearly state that the benefits must outweigh the real increases in cost, that is, increased staff, greater time spent coordinating a decentralized function, and so on.

- Given the increased importance of selection, personal rights, empowerment, and affirmative action programs, a centralized function tends to increase the credibility and visibility of the human resources management function.

Present organizational chart—South Shore General

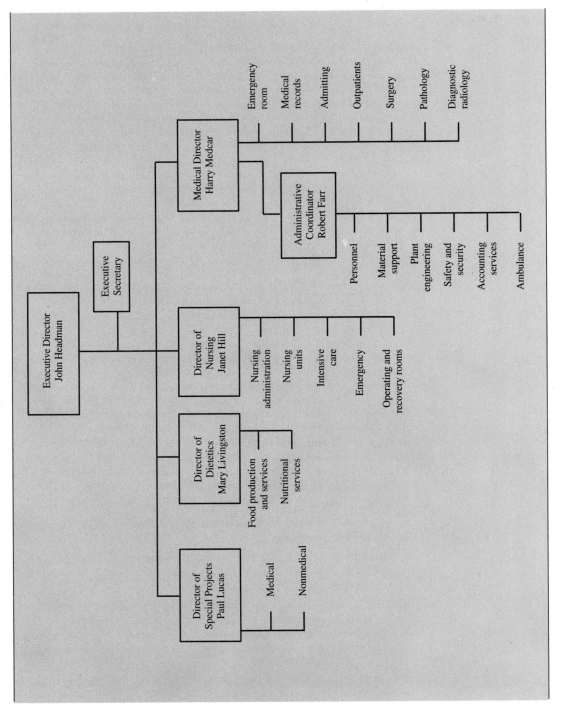

Harry believes that a majority of the committee agrees with him. In addition, the members are beginning to repeat themselves. Consequently, he has called for a vote. Much to his surprise, events did not turn out as he expected. Janet started the ball rolling by speaking out strongly in favor of a decentralized function. She went to great lengths to criticize Harry's assumptions and implied that Moore wants a decentralized function. Robert Farr chimed in to reflect Janet's sentiments. To emphasize his support for a decentralized human resource function, Robert said that he would be willing to give up control of the personnel function. Mary Livingston, however, agrees with Harry's arguments and favors a centralized function. Unfortunately, Paul Lucas indicates that at this time he is unable to make up his mind.

The impasse causes all parties involved to become increasingly emotional about the issue and their own positions. The remaining 20 minutes of the meeting turns into a shouting match between the leading proponents of opposing views, Janet Hill and Harry Medcar. Both sides are equally unhappy with Paul's inability to make up his mind. The committee adjourns without making a decision or even setting a time for the next meeting.

After the meeting, Harry reflects on the events that have led up to the current disagreement. He is clearly unhappy and believes that something should be done. Furthermore, John Moore wants a speedy decision, so Harry believes a way must be found to overcome the impasse. With pen in hand, Harry sits down with Mary Livingston and three close co-workers to develop a set of strategies that might lead to an agreement on a centralized or semicentralized human resource function.

7.3 Responding to Manipulation

When negotiating with others, it is not always reasonable to assume that the other parties will understand your interests. As a result, you will occasionally be forced to negotiate with people whose negotiating stance is designed to manipulate and take advantage of you. Proactive negotiators will try to identify the more common ways in which they can be manipulated and to develop techniques to counteract such behavior. This exercise allows you to practice behaviors capable of counteracting six manipulative ploys. Please carry out the steps outlined below.

Step 1. The class will break up into groups of two. One should be the negotiator, the other the counterpart, or person being manipulated.

Step 2. Prepare for the six mini role plays. Each will center on one manipulative ploy that a negotiator might encounter when dealing with a selfish person. The following ploys are used in this exercise:

Uncooperative defector. An individual who responds to a trusting open stance by taking advantage of the vulnerable person.

Good guy/bad guy routine. A common tactic in which two opponents gang up on a third person. One plays the bad guy and makes unreasonable demands to set up the third person. The good guy lulls the third person into demanding less or accepting a bad deal.

Limited authority. The negotiator's counterpart stalls, thereby increasing the time pressure by indicating that he or she does not have the authority to make the decision. As a result, the counterpart has to check with higher-ups before committing to current demands. Alternatively, a fictitious higher-up can be blamed for the counterpart's inflexible stand.

The nibble. A negotiator waits for a deal to be agreed upon. When the other person feels good about what has been achieved, the negotiator suggests additional items for the person to agree to. The problem is that the glow of achieving a recent deal may cloud the thinking of the person being manipulated.

Take-it-or-leave-it. This ploy typically occurs when the manipulator is less interested in reaching an agreement than is the counterpart. This behavior is designed to put pressure upon the other individual to concede more than would otherwise be warranted.

The puppy dog. Here the manipulator allows the counterpart to experience desired goods and services prior to reaching an agreement. The intent of the manipulator is to hook the other individual and subsequently negotiate better terms.

The instructor will either discuss or distribute a set of guidelines on responding to each manipulative ploy.

Step 3. Select a situation in which negotiations regularly take place. *Examples:* Buying a new car or house, buying a new piece of office equipment, leasing rental space, arranging a subordinate's vacation time, setting new production standards, and so on.

Step 4. Develop six dialogues of three or four sentences in length that incorporate one of the six types of manipulations. Use each ploy only once. Next, visualize (i.e., mentally walk through) the encounter, and write out your response to each of the six ploys.

Step 5. The two participants should take turns acting out their mini negotiating encounters. Individuals also should alternate role-playing the manipulator and the person being manipulated until all six exchanges have been acted out. Before role-playing each encounter, the person who developed the situation should explain it to the counterpart.

Step 6. The class will assemble and discuss group results.

End Notes

1. H. Raiffa, *The Art and Science of Negotiation,* Harvard University Press, Cambridge, Mass., 1982.
2. H. H. Kelley, L. L. Beckman, and C. S. Fisher, "Negotiating the division of reward under incomplete information," *Journal of Experimental Social Psychology*, Vol. 3, 1967: 361–398; D. Pruitt, *Negotiation Behavior*, Academic Press, New York, 1981; Raiffa, H., 1982.
3. Raiffa, 1982.
4. Raiffa, 1982.
5. R. J. Lewicki and J. A. Litterer, *Negotiation*, 1995, p. 81: Copyright Irwin; Reprinted by permission.
6. H. H. Kelley, "A classroom study of dilemmas in interpersonal negotiations," in *Strategic Interaction and Conflict,* ed., K. Archibald, California Institute of International Studies, University of California, Berkeley, Calif., 1966; Pruitt, 1981.

7. G. A. Yukl, "Effects of opponent's initial offer, concession magnitude, and concession frequency on bargaining behavior," *Journal of Personality and Social Psychology,* Vol. 30, 1974: 332–335.

8. Pruitt, 1981; P. H. Gulliver, *Disputes and Negotiations: A Cross-Cultural Perspective*, Academic Press, New York, 1979.

9. Pruitt, 1981.

10. Raiffa, 1982.

11. Raiffa, 1982.

12. H. A. Hornstein, *Cruelty and Kindness: A New Look at Aggression and Altruism*, Prentice Hall, Englewood Cliffs, N.J., 1976; E. Staub, "Social and personal influences," *Positive Social Behavior and Morality,* Vol 1, Academic Press, New York, 1978.

13. D. Druckman, "Dogmatism, prenegotiation experience, and simulated group representation as determinants of dyadic behavior in a bargaining situation," *Journal of Personality and Social Psychology* Vol. 6, 1967: 279–290; D. Druckman, "On concepts and methods in the study of international negotiations: Reflections on the 'state of the art'," unpublished manuscript, 1978; W. R. Fry, I. J. Firestone, and D. Williams, "Bargaining process in mixed-singles dyads: Loving and losing," paper presented at the annual meeting of the Eastern Psychological Association, Philadelphia, April, 1979; B. Mullick, and S. A. Lewis, "Sex-roles, loving and liking: A look at dating couples' bargaining," paper presented at the 85th annual convention of the American Psychological Association Convention, San Francisco, 1977.

14. R. A. Baron, "Behavioral effects of interpersonal attraction: Compliance with requests from liked and disliked others," *Psychonomic Science,* Vol. 25, 1971: 325–326.

15. J. S. Coke, C. D., Batson, and K. McDavis, "Empathic mediation of helping: A two-stage model," *Journal of Personality and Social Psychology,* Vol. 36, 1978: 752–766.

16. D. Lax and J. Sebenius, *The Manager as Negotiator: Bargaining for Cooperation and Competitive Gain*, The Free Press, New York, 1986.

17. Lax and Sebenius, 1986.

18. Lewicki and Litterer, 1985.

19. Lewicki and Litterer, 1985.

20. M. Deutsch, *The Resolution of Conflict,* Yale University Press, New Haven, 1973; J. Sawyer and H. Guetzkow, "Bargaining and negotiation in international relations," In *International Behavior: A Social-Psychological Analysis,* ed. H. C. Kelman, Holt Rinehart & Winston, New York, 1965; T. C. Shelling, *The Strategy of Conflict*, Harvard University Press, Cambridge, Mass., 1960.

21. J. Rubin and B. Brown, *The Social Psychology of Bargaining and Negotiation*, Academic Press, New York, 1975: 280–288.

22. A. A. Benton, H. H. Kelley, and B. Liebling, "Effects of extremity of offers and concession rate on the outcomes of bargaining," *Journal of Personality and Social Psychology,* Vol. 23, 1972: 73–83; D. L. Harnett and J. P. Vincelette, "Strategic influences on bargaining effectiveness," in *Contributions to Experimental Economics,* ed. H. Sauermann, Vol. 7, Mohr, Tubingen, Germany, 1978.

23. Pruitt, 1981.

24. Raiffa, 1982.

25. O. J. Bartos, *Process and Outcome in Negotiation*, Columbia University Press, New York, 1974; W. C. Hamner, "Effects of bargaining strategy and pressure to reach agreement," *Journal of Personality and Social Psychology*, Vol. 30, 1974: 458–467.

26. C. M. Stevens, *Strategies and Collective Bargaining Negotiations*, McGraw-Hill, New York, 1963; D. Pruitt and J. L.Drews, "The effect of time pressure, time elapsed, and the opponent's concession rate on behavior in negotiation," *Journal of Experimental Social Psychology,* Vol. 5, 1969: 43–60; D. F. Johnson and D. Pruitt, "Pre-intervention effects of mediation versus arbitration," *Journal of Applied Psychology*, Vol. 56, 1972: 1–10; J. Rubin and B. Brown, 1975.

27. O. J. Bartos, 1974; D. L. Smith, D. Pruitt and P. J. D. Carnevale, "Matching and mismatching: The differential effects of one's own limit," paper presented at the annual meeting of the Eastern Psychological Association, Philadelphia, April 1979.

28. A. Teger, *Too Much Investment to Quit*, Pergamon Press, New York, 1980.

29. Reprinted by permission of the Sterling Lord Agency, Inc. Copyright © 1980 by Andrew Tobias. Originally appeared in *Playboy* magazine.

30. R. D. Luce and H. Raiffa, *Games and Decisions,* John Wiley & Sons, New York, 1957.

31. R. Axelrod, "Effective choice in the prisoner's dilemma," *Journal of Conflict Resolution*, Vol. 24, 1980: 3–25; R. Axelrod and R. Mahoney, "More effective choice in the prisoner's dilemma," *Journal of Conflict Resolution*, Vol. 24, 1980: 379–403; R. Axelrod and R. Mahoney, *The Evolution of Cooperation,* Basic Books, New York, 1984.

32. G. Dichtenberg, "Exposing negotiating tactics," *Successful Meetings,* Vol. 39, No. 12, November 1990: 98–101.

USING THE INTERVIEW TO SELECT THE BEST POSSIBLE PEOPLE

Objectives:

- To familiarize students with the importance of selection and the role it plays in the manager's ultimate success.

- To explain the importance of basing selection decisions on behaviorally specific information.

- To describe the characteristics that make structured interviews an effective selection tool.

- To give students practice in preparing for, interviewing, and selecting staff.

The Importance of Selection

In growth organizations or departments, new employees are needed. Where there is the introduction of new technologies, new products, and procedures, the organization will likely have to replace or retrain existing personnel. Even if organizations or departments are not expanding or experiencing macro changes, there will still be the periodic need to replace existing personnel. Table 8.1 lists common reasons why employees must be periodically replaced.

In each of these cases, the ability of managers to select the most qualified individual from a pool of internal or external candidates is crucial to their long-term success. To appreciate the importance and value of selection decisions, one need merely consider the negative consequences of a poor selection decision (see Figure 8.1). Clearly, managers cannot hope to be successful if many of the negative consequences of poor selection decisions occur within their department.

TABLE 8.1   Factors which Require the Replacement of Existing Manpower

Voluntary termination
- Employee dissatisfaction with pay
- Lack of opportunities for employee advancement
- Employee dissatisfaction with work or workload
- Employee interpersonal problems — either with boss or co-workers
- More attractive employment opportunities elsewhere
- Spouse transfers

Involuntary termination
- Excessive tardiness and/or absenteeism by employee
- Low productivity or errors by employee
- Employee dishonesty
- Employee's inability to get along with others

Retirements
Need for new skills that existing employees cannot readily learn
Deaths
Accidents or health-related disabilities

FIGURE 8.1

Negative consequences of poor selection

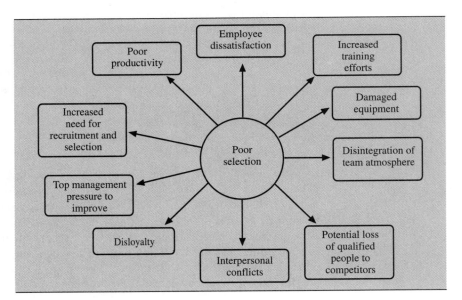

To further amplify the importance of selection as a first line of offense in obtaining desired performance from subordinates, it would be useful to describe how managers perceive the issue of selection. In management training workshops a question we often ask participants is: "As a manager, what problem or situation do you fear most?" The overwhelming response to this question is that they dread the possibility of inheriting a group of subordinates who are not qualified, or the possibility that through the selection process they will obtain a subordinate who cannot function at a satisfactory level. When asked, "What can you do to prevent these situations from occurring?" participants again overwhelmingly respond, "Better selection techniques, and if that fails, better training."

The Use of the Selection Interview and the Manager's Role in the Selection Process

In organizations having a centralized human resource function, the selection process (for either new hires or promotions) may offer a wide range of data collection techniques (e.g., work sample tests, ability tests, peer ratings, job knowledge tests, assessment centers, reference checks, biographical data). Even if this is the case, however, it is rare for managers not to have the opportunity to meet with and evaluate candidates who may be placed in their departments. In other words, managers often have the final say as to which candidate, from an externally generated short list, will be placed within their unit. At the very least, managers will have an opportunity to make a recommendation as to which candidate should be selected. This encounter is likely to take the form of a selection interview. The interview can be an effective tool in helping to collect and process the information necessary to make effective selection decisions. The employment interview is "an interpersonal interaction of limited duration between one or more interviewers and a job-seeker for the purpose of identifying interviewee knowledge, skills, abilities, and behaviors that may be predictive of success in subsequent employment."[1]

A survey conducted by the American Society of Personnel Administration[2] recorded that approximately 70 percent of firms use the interview most frequently as a selection decision tool for all jobs. The important role that managers play when using the interview for selection is reflected in the results obtained in a Bureau of National Affairs[3] survey of 245 firms. Survey data were broken down by job category and type of interviewer. A graphic representation of survey results is presented in Figure 8.2. Data confirm that the applicant's immediate boss will likely take part in some type of interview with the prospective employee. For professional/technical, commissioned employees, and manager/supervisors, it is also likely that managers will be involved in some type of selection interview, even when the applicant is not an immediate subordinate.

Our emphasis on the selection interview, however, should not be taken as a rejection of other sources of relevant information. In any selection decision (new hires, promotions, or certifications), managers should take advantage of all available information. Therefore, if managers are fortunate enough to work for

FIGURE 8.2

Percentage of firms indicating the required use of the selection interview, classified by job category and type of interviewer

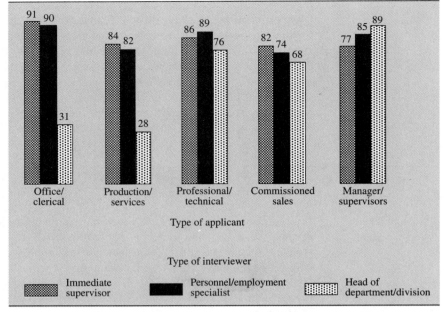

Source: Bureau of National Affairs, Inc. Reprinted with permission from *Recruiting and Selection Procedures: Personnel Policies Forum Survey* 146, p 7. Copyright 1988 by the Bureau of National Affairs, Inc., Washington, D.C.

organizations with a sophisticated selection process, they should take advantage of the information generated by that system, that is, assessment centers, personality testing, cognitive ability testing, biographical inventories, etc. The more valid the information used by decision makers, the more accurate their selection decisions. Unfortunately, in most organizations this information is not available, and it is unlikely that managers have the necessary time, energy, and resources to implement these techniques. Therefore, managers need an alternative that is easy to learn and use, yet capable of providing the necessary information. The structured selection interview is a technique that can satisfy this need.

Is the Selection Interview a Valid Technique?

Early research on the validity of the selection interview showed it was of questionable value. Wagner[4] found that inter-rater reliability, the extent to which two or more interviewers independently reach the same conclusion, ranged from .23 to .97 with an average of .57. In terms of validity coefficients,* the

---

* "Validity represents the accuracy with which a test, interview, etc., measures what it purports to measure or fulfills the function it was designed to fulfill."[5]

range was from .09 to .94 and a median of .27. Ulrich and Trumbo's[6] results were equally discouraging. Their review produced a range of validity coefficients of −.17 to .65 and a mean of .33. Reilly and Chao[7] reported a mean validity for the interview of .19. As late as 1984, Hunter and Hunter,[8] using a meta-analysis of cumulative research, demonstrated how poorly the selection interview (.14) compared to other selection techniques available to organizations (see Table 8.2). They also found that when selecting for promotion or certification, noninterviewing alternatives received higher mean validities, that is .54 for work sample tests, .53 for ability composites, .49 for behavioral consistency ratings, .48 for job knowledge tests, and .43 for assessment centers.

The net effect of these results caused people to question the use of interviews as a legitimate selection technique. However, Wiesner and Cronshaw,[9] in a study of interview format, found that the interview can be an effective selection instrument. In the case of the entire data set analyzed, Wiesner and Cronshaw obtained a mean corrected validity coefficient of $r = .47$, a figure that is much larger than those reported in earlier reviews. These authors do point out that "while interviews on average achieve acceptable validity coefficients, particular interviews can vary greatly in their predictive efficiency."[10] The largest validity coefficients were obtained for interviews that were structured, with a panel of interviewers, and where consensus was used to combine interviewer ratings. See Table 8.3 for a detailed description of the findings. In short, the negative criticisms of the interview are eliminated if a structured/panel/consensus format is used. (A detailed discussion of a structured interviewing format, and interviewing pitfalls, is presented below.)

TABLE 8.2   Mean Validities for Commonly Used Alternatives to Ability Tests*

| | Average Validities for Selected Criterion | | | |
| | Supervisory | | Training | |
Predictors	Ratings	Promotions	Success	Tenure
Peer ratings	.49	.49	.36	a
Biodata	.37	.26	.30	.26
Reference checks	.26	.16	.23	.27
College GPA	.11	.21	.30	.05
Interview	.14	.08	.10	.03
Strong interest inventory	.10	.25	.18	.22

* Hunter and Hunter argue that when cognitive ability tests are combined with psychomotor ability tests, the average obtained validity is .53 with little variance across job families. Hunter and Hunter argue that it is by this value that all alternative predictors should be judged.

TABLE 8.3   **Mean Predictive Validity of Interview Types**

Interview Source	Mean Validity Coefficients
All studies	.47
Unstructured individual	.20
Unstructured board	.37
Structured individual	.63
Structured board (total)	.60
Averaged ratings	.41
Consensus ratings	.64

Additional support for the structured interview is provided by Wright, Lichtenfels, and Pursell.[11] In reviewing unpublished and published validation studies of structured interviewing effectiveness, these authors concluded that the structured interview provides a promising alternative to the unstructured format. Analysis of review data demonstrated that the predictive power of the structured interview is significantly higher than that of the unstructured interview.[12]

The conclusion that can be drawn from recent research is that if the selection interview is designed and implemented correctly, it can indeed be used as an effective selection tool. Therefore, if a structured format is used, and the interviewer can be trained to avoid common interviewing pitfalls, managers can feel comfortable using the interview when making a selection decision. Before considering the difference between unstructured and structured interviews, let us first discuss a number of common interviewing pitfalls and how they might be prevented.

Common Interviewing Pitfalls

Considerable effort has been devoted to identifying moderator variables (other than structure) that can affect the accuracy of interviewer predictions. These efforts have helped researchers to identify numerous interactive pitfalls that can cause the interviewing process to fail. Space limitation precludes a complete listing of all such potential pitfalls so the authors will describe the most common ones likely to have an impact on interviewer performance. Summary recommendations will then be made on how to minimize their potential effect.

1. Temporal placement of information.   Temporal placement of information within the interview can adversely affect the interviewer's final rating. Order effect is viewed either in terms of recency (the most recent information presented has the greatest impact) and primacy (the first information presented has the greatest impact). Research evidence supports the view that primacy has the strongest impact in the interviewing process.[13] This is especially important if early decisions are likely to have a negative impact on the interviewer's subsequent behavior. If the individual is rated positively, or negatively, during the initial phase of the interview, it is likely the interviewer's behaviors will change toward the interviewee. Anderson[14] indicated that in those instances where the individual is evaluated positively, the interviewer will place greater emphasis on selling the company to the candidate than on collecting more information. As a result the interviewer would, in relative terms, do more talking than the candidate.

It is also possible that once a decision about the applicant's suitability has been reached, either before or at the beginning of the interview, the interviewer will alter the questioning to confirm that decision.[15] In other words, the interviewer will ask questions likely to generate negative information if the candidate has been assessed as unsuitable, or questions likely to generate positive information if the candidate has been assessed as suitable. Although support for a generalized confirmatory bias is weak, there is evidence that it is more likely to occur when interviewers have greater latitude in developing their own questions.[16]

Similarly, once interviewers have reached a decision, there is a tendency for them to perceptually distort, or filter, subsequent information.[17] In addition to perceptual distortion, or filtering, the actual behavior of interviewers can change. If the interviewers decide early in (or before) the interview that candidates are unsuitable, they may exhibit nonverbal behavior that indicates disapproval, dislike, or rejection. In response to this shift in the interviewers' behavior, interviewees may alter their answer content or nonverbal behavior. The consequence of the candidates' negative behavior is to confirm the interviewers' earlier decision. This tendency can be referred to as a self-fulfilling prophecy.

2. Negative information. Negative information can also have a significant dampening effect on the interviewer's final rating. Often, negative information will be assessed more heavily than positive information.[18] Webster proposed that because organizations tend to receive more feedback when they select bad candidates, there is a conditioned response in the future to screen out candidates, whenever similar negative factors are observed.[19] An anecdotal story will help demonstrate the potential impact of negative information, even when it is not related to on the job performance. We were involved in a national search for a vice president of personnel. The recruiting company was looking for an individual who could be best described as an independent self-starter. During an encounter between interviews, the candidate made the comment that his mother-in-law had seen the ad and suggested that he apply for the job. Once this statement was made by the candidate, we observed a change in the type of questions asked and the overall response to the candidate. This particular candidate was not offered the position.

3. Comparisons between candidates.   In most situations, the selection process involves a comparison between two or more candidates. When this occurs, the potential exists for contrast effects to take place. Contrast effects cause the interviewer to erroneously displace an individual's score away from the comparison person or persons.[20] Study results also indicate that the effect may lose its potency the wider the discrepancy between candidates or when professional interviewers are used. Where extreme comparisons exist (that is, highly qualified versus poorly qualified), it is possible that individuals are no longer perceived as comparable and as a result have a reduced impact on each other's rating. In the case of professional interviewers, either training or experience and feedback may condition the interviewer to anticipate and subsequently cancel out the effect of comparisons between candidates.

4. Misuse of knowledge.   A common error made by raters is the tendency for individuals to use knowledge (real or imagined) about a specific characteristic of an applicant to distort or affect the ratings of other unrelated characteristics.[21] When this type of error takes place, one characteristic or dimension is said to have a halo effect on all other characteristics or dimensions that require assessment. To tell if halo effects are present and if they are negatively affecting the interviewer's ratings, it is necessary to accurately assess each dimension separately. The likelihood of halo error taking place increases when the characteristics to be measured are ambiguous, poorly supported with behavioral data, or when dimensions are considered simultaneously.

Other common rater biases relate to leniency, severity, and central tendency.[22] In the case of leniency, the interviewer systematically rates candidates higher than reality would warrant. Bass offered a number of explanations for such behavior. Interviewers are likely to be lenient in applicant assessments if they believe poor ratings reflect poorly on their personal competencies, or will negatively affect future relations with the candidate, if they are conditioned to approve rather than to disapprove, and if they tend to respond positively to others so that they will reciprocate in kind. Severity is more likely to occur when no such attitudes exist, and when the interviewer has been conditioned by the organization to emphasize negative characteristics or behaviors. Severity also occurs when the interviewer establishes unrealistic standards or has been punished for poor decisions in the past. Severity errors result in the applicant being given a lower rating than reality would warrant. Central tendency occurs when interviewers are unwilling to use extreme values found on the rating schema used by the organization. Unfortunately, when central tendency errors predominate, decision makers do not adequately differentiate among candidates because there is insufficient variance within the collected data.

5. Individual differences.   Individual differences can play a significant role in determining how interviewers behave during the selection interview, and what characteristics or dimensions they will assess.[23] For example, when interviewing, interviewers are more likely to pay attention to those dimensions they consider important in assessing their own self-concept or worth. If interviewers use intelligence as a self-defining dimension, they are more likely to use this dimension to assess candidates. Conversely, interviewers who define who and what they are in terms of sensitivity and interpersonal warmth, are likely to emphasize these dimensions more than intelligence. Inexperienced or unsure interviewers are more likely to rate in a favorable light candidates who are similar to themselves.[24] Such encounters are likely to be more rewarding, or less threatening, and as a result motivate interviewers to rate the candidates favorably.

Individual differences also play an important role in determining what implicit theories of personality and stereotypes the interviewers bring to the selection interview.[25] Such differences will reflect the cognitive structures or schema that each individual brings to the situation. In the case of a particular job, or position, individuals are likely to have mental schema of what constitutes an ideal or a typical job incumbent.[26] Similarly, individuals use mental schema to classify applicants. For example the following five dimensions are frequently used to describe others: extrovert–introvert, agreeable–disagreeable, conscientious–careless, emotionally stable–unstable, and cultured–crude.[27] Furthermore, once an individual has classified a relevant other, the next step is to link, through implicit theories of personality, other behavioral characteristics. If individuals are characterized as agreeable, they may also be described as good-natured, not jealous, mild, and cooperative. The perceived fit between perceived applicant characteristics or behaviors and job stereotypes is likely to affect the interviewer's rating of the applicant.

6. Nonverbal behaviors. Nonverbal behaviors can also affect the behaviors and perceptions of both parties in the interview. For example, candidates who maintain straight-ahead eye contact are assessed as more alert, dependable, responsible, assertive, confident, and demonstrating more initiative.[28] Similarly, individuals who use great amounts of eye contact, head gestures, and smiles receive higher ratings than those not demonstrating these behaviors.[29]

Equally important is the realization that the interviewer's nonverbal behavior can alter the interviewing climate and ultimately interviewee perceptions and behavior.[30] Interviewers who demonstrate positive nonverbal behaviors, that is, good eye contact, approval behaviors (nodding of the head, smiles, etc.), and lean toward the applicant are generally perceived as competent and relaxed. Interviewers demonstrating positive nonverbal behaviors also make the job applicant feel comfortable and increase the interviewee's willingness to talk or express opinions.

Overcoming Interviewing Pitfalls

To be successful interviewers, managers must identify and implement those strategies and behaviors designed to prevent or offset the pitfalls just described. The following summary of recommendations should help the manager achieve these objectives. The recommendations listed have a side benefit in that, when implemented, they increase the probability that a structured interviewing format will be followed by the manager.

An important first step is for the interviewer to determine what *knowledge, skills,* and *abilities* (KSAs) are needed for success on the target job. As described below, this will require that the interviewer (manager) undertake a detailed job analysis to define which KSAs are likely to lead to success.

Before scheduled interviews, an interviewer should construct a set of predetermined questions that can be asked of all candidates. These should have the effect of allowing the interviewee to do most of the talking during the interview, and should specifically be designed to draw out information about past performance in situations similar to the target position, behavioral intentions if faced with situations similar to those likely to be experienced by job incumbents, and content knowledge necessary to perform the target job effectively.

In the area of selection, one often hears the terms "screening out" or "selecting in." In many cases, there is greater reliance on the process of screening out because it is easier to identify those individuals who are likely to be failures than it is to select in by identifying those individuals who are likely to succeed. Unfortunately, by screening out the failures, there is still no guarantee that those who are hired will perform well. It is therefore recommended that interviewers direct their energies to the identification of KSAs likely to support success on the job rather than failure.

The candidates are the richest source of information about their abilities, the situation in which their skills have been applied, and future intentions. To obtain relevant and objective information during the selection interview, it is important that the interviewer develop a climate in which the candidate will do most of the talking by maintaining a friendly, attentive, and openly communicative style. This can also be accomplished by asking open-ended questions and refraining from critical or threatening statements.

Interviewers should refrain from rating the candidate until after the interview is completed. By delaying evaluation, the manager reduces the probability of making a premature decision. Furthermore, interviewers should base their evaluations on behaviors or stated intentions about future action rather than on the traits or interests of candidates. The primary purpose of the interviewing session should be the asking of questions and the recording of behaviorally specific, or content information, relevant to performance on the target position.

Recorded behaviors obtained during the selection interview should be compared to a predetermined evaluation scale or standard. The criteria for success, or range of success, should be based upon the job description information obtained before the start of the interviewing process. When developing evaluation scales, behavioral illustrations should be used to define scale values. Behavioral illustrations facilitate the interviewer's ability to distinguish between different levels of performance, job knowledge, or skill acquisition.

Research has demonstrated that note taking can enhance interviewer recall and accuracy.[31] Therefore, to ensure accuracy of information, interviewers should take notes during the interview.

The manager should attempt to establish a panel of interviewers who interview the candidate and then pool their personal ratings to obtain an overall rating based on consensus. At a minimum, the manager should use a structured format based on a detailed job analysis. However, because the effect of each recommendation on decision accuracy is additive, it would be desirable to do both.

The manager must make a conscious effort to understand and accept the existence of interviewing pitfalls and be willing to avoid them wherever possible. For inexperienced managers, this will require that they seek out training in key areas of the interviewing process and integrate other skills covered in this text into the interviewing encounter. Specifically, managers must be willing to listen, probe, engage in active listening, control and respond to nonverbal behaviors, while at the same time asserting themselves in an open and interpersonally sensitive manner. This recommendation cannot be considered fully implemented unless they are willing to practice newly acquired skills.

The Selection Interview: The Need for Structure

Several basic errors in the way in which the traditional unstructured interview is conducted help explain its questionable reliability and validity.[32] Interviewers frequently do not ask the same questions of interviewees; when interviewees are asked the same questions, the questions often are not job related; when job-related questions are used, the interviewers frequently cannot agree what is an acceptable answer; and when interviewers can agree, the questions are usually transparent. Transparent questions increase the likelihood that the interview will be adversely affected by issues of social desirability (that is, interviewees giving answers they believe the interviewer wants to hear), and thereby minimize the likelihood that true intentions will be expressed.[33] Structuring the selection interview can help managers overcome these weaknesses and help ensure that multiple interviewers will reach the same accurate conclusion of an applicant's suitability. Two approaches to structuring the selection interview dominate the literature. They are the situational interview,[34] and the patterned behavioral description interview (PBDI).[35] An essential difference between these two approaches is their time orientation. The situational interview emphasizes future behavior and focuses on what the applicant "would do if," whereas the PBDI emphasizes past behavior and focuses on "what did you do when." To facilitate our discussion of how to use the structured interview, we will first describe each in greater detail.

The Situational Interview

The situational interview is one of the few, if not the only interview technique, grounded in theory. Specifically, goal-setting theory "states that intentions or goals are the immediate precursor of a person's behavior."[36] By asking questions that are not transparent, the interviewer forces the interviewee to express his or her true intentions. Research evidence supports the proposition that stated intentions correlate with future behavior.[37] When used correctly the situational interview results in concurrent and predictive validities ranging from .33 to .46.[38] Such results compare favorably with the mean validity of .14 associated with the traditional unstructured interview.[39] Research has also demonstrated that interobserver reliability for the situational interview ranges from .76 to .96.[40] In other words, the situational interview achieves the stated goals of the selection interview.

To understand why the situational interview is effective, we can consider how it is developed (see Figure 8.3).[41] First, the appraisal instruments, performance criteria, and "what would you do if" questions are based on a detailed job analysis. Thus the interviewing and evaluation processes are behaviorally based, and have content validity (representatively samples significant aspects of the job) and face validity (test is perceived as a fair and good test of required skills and ability). Second, by using experts or knowledgeable employees to develop a behavioral scoring guide for interviewers to use to evaluate interviewee answers, it is possible to have an agreed-upon measuring stick against which to compare applicant answers.

FIGURE 8.3

Steps for developing the situational interview

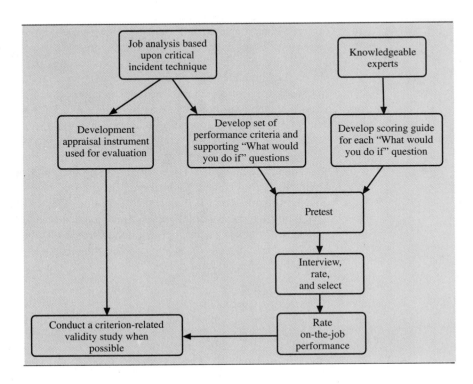

Table 8.4 provides an example of a critical incident, a "what would you do if" question, and the scoring guide to rate the applicant's response.[42] Third, the situation posed to applicants contains a dilemma. It is the dilemma that taps the interviewee's true intentions.

Two additional examples may help indicate the range of situations that can be covered by using situational questions developed from critical incidents. While interviewing candidates for the position of director of personnel and labor relations, the interviewer might ask, "You have just spent a weekend totally cut off from work. You return to work on Monday morning to find a wildcat strike in progress. Management believes in dealing swiftly and severely with illegal strikers. You believe in developing a mutually beneficial working relationship with the union. What would you do?" It should be noted that the hiring organization believed that the relationship between management and labor could be developed into a working partnership designed to maximize benefit to both parties. Therefore, ratings given to candidate responses were assigned with this standard in mind. If candidates indicated that they would first fire all the illegal strikers, they were given a low score on the evaluation scale for that question. If the candidates' response indicated that they would (*a*) first collect relevant information, (*b*) then meet with the union president and attempt to negotiate an acceptable agreement, and (*c*) take more aggressive action only if (*a*) and (*b*) failed, they would be given a high rating.

Alternatively, when hiring sales or counter clerks at a bowling alley, the interviewer might ask candidates the following question: "A parent and son have just come in and asked for a lane to bowl several strings. The parent and son are frequent patrons. There are few bowlers in the alley because the bowling

---

TABLE 8.4 **Example of Critical Incident, a Question, and Scoring Guide for the Situational Interview**

An example of a critical incident describing ineffective behavior of an hourly worker :

The employee is a new parent and is devoted to his or her family. Unfortunately, the employee uses any excuse possible to stay home. One day it's a problem with the new baby, the next time it's the spouse that has some minor illness. If it's not the spouse who is ill, it is the employee who has a cold or personal problem that must be attended to. As a result, the employee does not come to work. Making matters worse, the employee does not even call.

"What would you do if" question :

Your spouse and two teenage children are sick in bed with a cold. There are no relatives or friends available to look in on them. Your shift starts in 3 hours. What would you do in this situation?

Scoring guide

Score:

(1) I'd stay home—my spouse and family come first.

(3) I'd phone my supervisor and explain the situation.

(5) Since they only had colds, I'd come to work.

leagues are about to begin their games in 20 minutes. The leagues have reserved all lanes for their games. What would you do in this situation?" Candidates are also told that there are very few patrons in the bowling alley. If the job applicants indicate that they would merely tell the father to "buzz off" and not explain why, then they would receive a low rating in terms of customer service or sensitivity. However, if the candidates indicate that they would explain the problem, allow the father and son to bowl for free until the leagues start, and then give them a complimentary pass for having made the trip, they would be given a high rating.

During the pretest step, managers review the performance criteria and develop questions to ensure that the criteria adequately cover the material discovered during the job analysis and are already incorporated into the appraisal instrument. It is also necessary to pilot-test the questions and scoring guide to ensure that items are unambiguous, questions elicit a range of good and poor answers (e.g., remove those questions that all applicants in the pilot study answer correctly), and agreement on the scoring of answers is high with use of the scoring guide.

At this point, interviewers are able to begin using the situational interview. It is worth noting that training beyond minimal instructions on how to use the situational interview is not necessary to improve interobserver reliability.[43] At the same time, the situational interview has also been found to be resistant to rater errors such as similar-to-me, positive and negative leniency, first impressions, and contrast effect. A more detailed discussion of how to use the situational interview will be given below.

The Patterned Behavioral Description Interview (PBDI)

The PBDI is "not based upon theory but rather on the well-founded empirical truism that past behavior predicts future behavior."[44] The effectiveness of past-oriented questions is based upon a number of assumptions.[45] They are:

- Past performance/behavior, under similar conditions, is an effective predictor of future performance/behavior.
- The predictive validity of past performance/behavior increases, the more current the past performance/behavior that is being assessed.
- The predictive validity of past performance/behavior increases, the more frequently that past performance/behavior occurs.[46]

As was the case with the situational interview, research evidence supports the proposition that past behavior can be effective in predicting future behavior (e.g., validity coefficients of .54 and .61).[47] Again, such results compare favorably with the mean validity of .14 associated with the traditional unstructured interview. However, it should be noted that interobserver reliabilities were found to be lower for the PBDI than for a standard unstructured interview.[48] Figure 8.4 describes the steps typically associated with the PBDI.

FIGURE 8.4

The patterned behavioral description interview (PBDI)

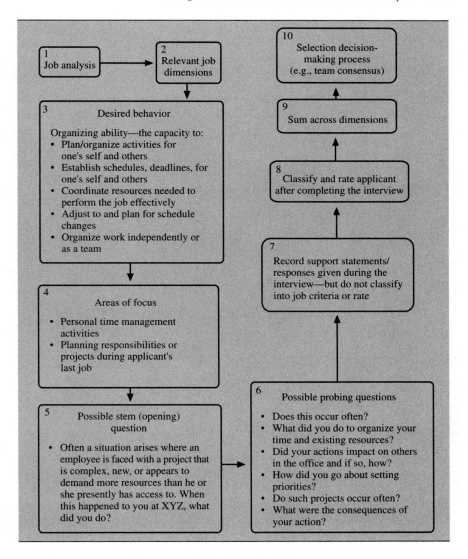

A Comparison between the Situational Interview and the PBDI

As reflected in Table 8.5, there are a number of similarities between the situational interview and the PBDI. As noted, both techniques use a detailed job description to build a structured interview format. Similarly, the situational interview and the PBDI both place a heavy emphasis on the use of

TABLE 8.5   **Similarities and Differences between Situational Interviews and Patterned Behavior Description Interviewing (PBDI)**

	Situational	*PBDI*
1. Characteristics based on theory	X	-
2. Job Analysis: CIT (critical incident technique)	X	X
3. Client/customer writes and asks questions	X	-
4. Psychologist or trained interviewer prepares and asks questions	-	X
5. Same questions asked of all applicants	X	-
6. Probing allowed/encouraged	-	X
7. Scoring guide for interviewers	X	-
8. Questions emphasize past	-	X
9. Questions emphasize future	X	-
10. Emphasis on behavior	X	X
11. Check for social desirability	X	-
12. Evidence of reliability	X	X
13. Evidence of validity	X	X
14. Evidence of test fairness	X	-
15. Evidence of practicality	X	-
16. Evidence of utility	X	X

Source: G. P. Latham, "The reliability, validity, and practicality of the situational interview," *The Employment Interview*, ed. R. W. Edler and G. R. Ferris, Sage Publications, Beverly Hills, Calif., 1989: p. 181.

behaviors and behavioral descriptions when assessing the suitability of applicants. Third, both techniques appear to have achieved the objectives of increasing the likelihood of multiple interviewers independently arriving at the same true ratings. Last, both techniques have demonstrated utility in minimizing the cost and liabilities associated with selection.

Nevertheless, there are a number of important differences associated with the two techniques. As noted above, while the situational interview is future oriented, the PBDI is past oriented. The emphasis on past behavior increases the risk that the PBDI may inadvertently discriminate against applicants who have not had the opportunity to demonstrate the criterion support behaviors in the past. Although there are ways to minimize such problems (e.g., ask an applicant who does not have significant work experience, for example, a graduating student, to relate the "what did you do when" questions to a university situation), the lack of experience puts that applicant at a disadvantage. The same disadvantage does not apply to the situational interview because the emphasis is on what you would do rather than on what have you done.

Another major difference between the situational interview and the PBDI is that the situational interview does not allow for probing questions. In other words, each applicant is asked the same questions. Repeating the question is allowed. The PBDI, however, strongly encourages the interviewer to actively probe the applicant once a stem question has initiated discussion in a focus area. As a result, the number and types of questions an interviewer asks during the PBDI will be a function of the applicant's responses. This can introduce bias into the interview as different interviewees receive different questions.

A third major difference between the PBDI and the situational interview is the use of the scoring guide. As noted earlier, the guide is intended to provide the structure and interobserver reliability that is necessary to overcome the difficulties of the unstructured interview. We should also point out that the term *guide* is used to imply that an applicant does not have to state exactly what is on the scoring guide to receive a specific rating.

Problems occur when applicants perceive that different applicants are being asked different questions or when they are asked the same questions but their responses to the questions are being evaluated differently. An established scoring guide minimizes the latter problem. As we will discuss below, when a scoring guide is not provided, the interviewer must record all behavioral responses, classify them under a job dimension or criterion, and then rate the applicant based upon his or her interpretation of poor, average, or above-average performance.

Finally, for a selection instrument to be used, it must be perceived as practical. In other words, it must satisfy the user's needs. It appears that managers perceive the situational interview technique as more practical than either the unstructured interview or the PBDI. In a study designed to assess the relative practicality of the unstructured interview, PBDI, and the situational interview, managers preferred the situational interview. They found that the situational interview made them appear better organized and prepared, and made it easier to assess the applicant's ability to perform. In addition, the situational interview effectively compares the applicants on an objective basis, and appropriately hires or rejects applicants for purely job-related reasons.[49] It is also worth noting that in the same study, attorneys rated decisions resulting from the situational interview the easiest to defend relative to other interview techniques.

Although there appears to be sufficient evidence to recommend the use of the situational interview, research is still needed to clarify the relative advantages of the situational interview and the PBDI, and the conditions in which each works best. Therefore, one's choice of technique must consider the philosophy of the organization, the strengths of the individuals being asked to apply the selection tool, the support likely to be provided by the human resource department, and the time available to the managers designing and implementing selection strategies.

Using the Structured Interview

The following material is presented to provide the reader with greater insight into how to prepare for, and carry out, a structured selection interview. Figure 8.5 describes the three phases of the process required to effectively carry out a structured interview. When discussing the activities supporting each phase, we will attempt to point out areas in which implementation differences exist between the situational interview and the PBDI. (It should be realized that you may not be able to implement as detailed an interviewing procedure as the one described. Nevertheless, an attempt should be made to build into the interviewing process as many of these behaviors and techniques as possible. What is important is that you incrementally improve the interviewing process, and that you base your decisions on a structured procedure that emphasizes behavior.)

FIGURE 8.5

The structured interview

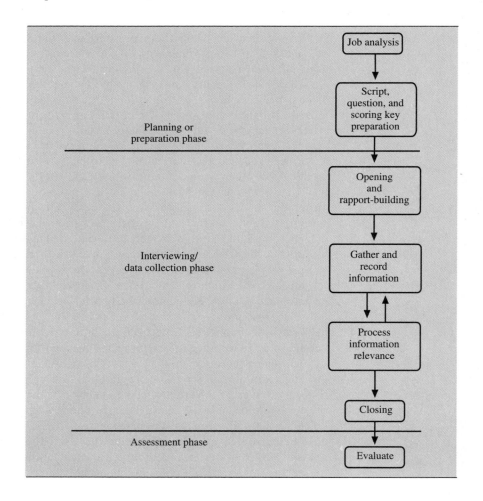

Planning or Preparation Phase

The success of this phase depends upon the completion of three distinct but related activities. Managers must make the effort to obtain a detailed understanding of the target position. Next, they must familiarize themselves with the candidate. Specifically, knowledge of the applicant's past gives the manager direction when asking questions that are past oriented (tap into past job experiences), and future oriented (situational questions capable of assessing behavior intentions). It is also possible to supplement these two types of questions with job knowledge, work requirements, and job sample and simulation questions.[50] A broadened option set affords the manager the greatest opportunity to collect data relevant to the evaluation and decision-making processes. Last, managers must take the time to design a structure and general script that will facilitate the interviewing process. The following discussion considers each of these areas in greater detail.

Analyzing the Target Position

The key to successful selection interviews is the ability of managers to understand and articulate what they want a job incumbent to be able to do. The actual process is briefly described in Figure 8.6. As indicated, the interview process cannot be completed (planned and prepared for) unless managers have a thorough understanding of the job for which they intend to select a candidate. Managers must determine what constitutes success on the job and what behaviors or skills are necessary for the prospective employee to achieve and maintain successful performance. Moving from the general to the specific, this first definition of success will be general in nature and reflect the organization's goals (i.e., mission, stated strategic intent, and action plans). Next, employee performance must satisfy the manager's own personal goals, standards and expectations. Last, employee performance must take into consideration the physical realities of the situation (i.e., technology, resources, and labor pool available to the organization and manager).

FIGURE 8.6

Analyzing the target position

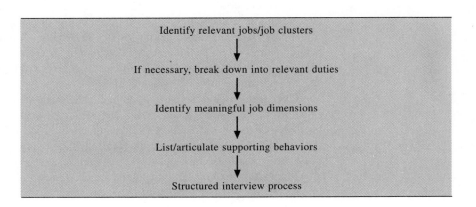

Identify relevant jobs/job clusters

↓

If necessary, break down into relevant duties

↓

Identify meaningful job dimensions

↓

List/articulate supporting behaviors

↓

Structured interview process

To demonstrate how this process works, consider the following example of a public utility. Assume for discussion purposes that one of the goals of the utility is excellent customer service. Managers in charge of cashier clerks would have to build into their standards or expectations the customer service goal. Further, assume that a particular manager, who has actively supported good customer relations in the past, must now hire a new cashier clerk for that department. With the information just presented, let us follow through the process and activities the manager might employ when carrying out the above process.

Knowing the job that is to be filled, and recognizing the importance of good customer service, the manager quickly moves into an analysis of what the job incumbent does. One of the responsibilities and duties of the cashier clerk is to handle customer complaints. The manager must now collect and process the information needed to define the appropriate job dimensions and support behaviors when handling such an encounter.

The critical incident technique (CIT) is an effective means for collecting job-related information that is behaviorally based.[51] The CIT requires that individuals who are familiar with the target position describe, or write out, an incident of either effective or ineffective behavior that they have observed over the past 6 to 12 months. The CIT should include a description of the general circumstances in which the incident took place, what the focus person did in terms of actual behaviors, and the incident's consequences, that is, why was the employee's behavior ineffective or effective, and how did it affect the task being performed.

Let us assume, therefore, that the manager has identified handling stress and pressure as an important job dimension of the cashier clerk position. More specifically, the job incumbent must be able to remain calm when confronted with conflict or personal attack, be able to cope and adapt to situational stressors as they appear in his or her environment, and be able to take the necessary steps to remove or offset existing stressors. The manager might use the following example of specific behavior needed to handle a stressful encounter with a customer: when verbally attacked by a customer, the cashier clerk is able to remain calm, acknowledge the customer's feelings and then ask, in a normal voice, how he or she might help the customer solve his or her problem. When dealing with specific support behaviors, the manager is likely to list several representative examples of the types of situations that might be faced by the typical cashier clerk. The lists of support behaviors for each job dimension are not to be considered exhaustive, but merely representative of what is central to job effectiveness.

Once this process has been completed, the manager is now ready to engage in script and question development, as well as construction of an objective scoring key to be used when evaluating candidates' responses to the questions asked. Table 8.6 provides a detailed list of steps that can be followed to develop a situational interview.

For example, Mary, a candidate for a collections clerk position, might be presented with the following situation: "It is 8:30 A.M. and a large

TABLE 8.6   Steps for Developing a Situational Interview

1. Conduct a job analysis, using the critical incident technique (CIT).
2. Develop an appraisal instrument such as behavioral observation scales (see Chapter 13).
3. Select one or more incidents that formed the basis for the development of the performance criteria (e.g., cost consciousness), which constitute the appraisal instrument.
4. Turn each criterion incident into a "what would you do if—" question.
5. Develop a scoring guide to facilitate agreement among interviewers on what constitutes a good (5), acceptable (3), or an unacceptable (1) response to each question. If a 2 and a 4 anchor can also be developed, do so.
6. Review the questions for comprehensiveness in terms of covering the material identified in the job analysis and summarized on the appraisal instrument.
7. Conduct a pilot study to eliminate questions where applicant/interviewees give the same answer, or where interviewers cannot agree on the scoring.
8. Conduct a criterion-related validity study when feasible to do so.

Source: G.P. Latham, "The reliability, validity, and practicality of the situational interview," in *The Employment Interview: Theory, Research, and Practice* ed. R. W. Edler and G. R. Ferris, Sage Publications, Newbury Park, Calif., 1989: p. 171.

gentleman is waiting to see you. He has money tightly grasped in both hands. As you walk into the collections area, you hear him yelling to one of the other clerks that he wants to see you—the person who had threatened to turn off his power, if he didn't come in first thing in the morning to pay his overdue bill. Your company expects you to deal directly with all customers. However, last week, another clerk was physically assaulted by an angry customer when the clerk tried to assist the customer. If you were the clerk, what would you do in this situation?" In terms of scoring, if Mary indicated she would not enter the office until the angry customer left, she would warrant a low evaluation. Alternatively, if she indicated that she would enter the office, position the counter between herself and the customer, and then in a calm and even voice introduce herself and then ask how she might be of assistance, she would receive a high score on handling stress and pressure.

Familiarizing One's Self with the Candidate

The ability of managers to ask past-oriented questions requires that they be familiar with each candidate's background and experiences. Recall the three underlying premises associated with the use of past-oriented questions:

- Past performance/behavior, under similar conditions, can predict future performance/behavior.
- The predictive validity of past performance/behavior increases, the more current the past performance/behavior that is being assessed.

- The predictive validity of past performance/behavior increases, the more frequently that past performance/behavior occurs.

With these premises in mind, the manager reviews the candidate's file and identifies areas of interest he or she will emphasize during the interview. If interviewing an individual who must interact with customers, the manager will look for and identify those areas of recent experience where the candidate frequently interacted with others, preferably customers. If such experiences do not exist, the manager must search for situations where the individual would have been required to use similar skills or behaviors. This knowledge represents a second factor necessary for the effective design of a structured interview.

If managers intend to limit themselves to situational interview questions, then it becomes less critical to engage in behaviors that result in a detailed understanding of the applicant's past work history. Instead, managers would spend their time developing future job-related questions and the scoring guide used to rate applicants' responses to each question. For example, one of the authors recently carried out a job search for a director of personnel for an organization of 2,200 employees. As recommended above, he carried out a job analysis that identified seven job dimensions or criteria considered necessary for success. From the pool of critical incidents generated during the job analysis, the author then developed 23 questions to be used in the situational interview with each applicant.

Next, the manager developed a scoring guide to ensure consistency in rating applicants' responses. This was accomplished by first developing a number of descriptive anchors for the appropriate rating levels on the guide (i.e., 1 for low, 3 for satisfactory, 5 for outstanding). Next, the author asked five knowledgeable organizational members to allocate his list of unclassified behavioral anchors to each of the three scale positions. In those cases where four or five individuals correctly classified a behavior, the statement was considered reliable.

Alternatively, managers could meet with knowledgeable employees and ask them to independently benchmark each of the scale levels on the scoring guide. Once participants have developed their anchors, they could be asked to read them to the other group members. Through the process of group discussion, the group would then be given the responsibility of reaching consensus on which statements best anchored the scoring guide.

Preparing an Appropriate Design

At this point, the manager is ready to design a structure and script that can be used during the upcoming interview. Of primary importance to any design will be the interviewer's opening, collecting and processing behaviors, rapport-building and controlling behaviors (including how to deal with problem candidates), and closing.

1. Opening and Rapport-Building Behaviors

The critical first element of the structured interview is the opening statements made by the manager. The opening statements are designed to explain to the candidate what will happen during the interview and at the same time help reduce candidate anxiety. More specifically, the manager's opening statements should communicate the following information:

- Explain as briefly as possible what will be happening over the course of the interview.

- Explain to the candidate that you would prefer to deal with questions relating to company or administrative issues at the end of the interview.

- Describe the type of questions you will be asking and why, that is, future oriented, past oriented or both.

- Clearly indicate your own name and position within the organization so that there is no misunderstanding in the applicant's mind.

- Clearly indicate the position for which the candidate is applying.

- Mention that you will be taking notes.

The following represents a typical structured opening that incorporates many of the points described above.

> "Why don't we get started, my name is Pat Smith and I'm the manager of this district office. As such, I am responsible for conducting the final interview with all candidates. As you know, you are on the short list of three remaining candidates for the sales clerk position. What I would like to do is spend about 40 to 50 minutes discussing with you your background and work experience. There will be time at the end of our meeting for you to ask me questions about Ever-Bright Electric. I should mention that, because I will be meeting with the remaining two candidates, and because I want to make sure that I can accurately recall what we talk about, I will be taking notes. It helps me to keep my facts straight. Do you have any questions? (pause) Many of the questions I will be asking require that you either respond to situations that might happen on the job you are applying for or to recall specific events or situations from your past. However, I realize that this is often difficult to do on the spur of the moment and that it may take you some time to bring your thoughts together. Don't worry about it. Most candidates have the same difficulty. Just take your time. Also if you don't understand a question I will be more than happy to repeat it. The important thing is that I obtain an accurate idea of your strengths and how you are likely to perform as a cashier clerk. Do you have any questions?"

When dealing with openings, the issue is often raised whether the interview should engage in social chit-chat as a form of interview icebreaker, or instead limit the opening to information of the type presented above. Social openings often heighten candidates' anxiety level as they wait for the "real" questions, thus a social opening should be eliminated or curtailed.[52] An alternative solution is to replace the social opening with a number of simple questions that the candidate should be able to answer comfortably. A danger of social chit-chatting is that it can foster similar-to-me and first impression errors.

An alternative to social chit-chat is for the interviewer to ask warm-up questions that are job related yet nonthreatening.[53] Such questions can deal with issues of experience, education, willingness to do shift work or travel, or general knowledge about the job being applied for. Warm-up questions not only get the applicant used to talking but can also serve as realistic job previews. For example, when situational interview questions are used, the interviewer typically explains how they were developed and that they describe situations that the person will encounter on the job. Thus, they serve as a realistic job preview for the applicant. The interviewer may also ask "practice" questions so that the applicant gains a feel for what is required during the interview period.

Managers should use the opening, and their general demeanor throughout the interview, to build rapport with the interviewee. Such a climate can help ensure that candidates will feel comfortable openly discussing their experiences. Although rapport-developing behaviors are many, and can be easily applied, many managers fail to assess the degree to which they are carried out. Table 8.7 provides a quick method by which managers can rate their own performance.

TABLE 8.7   Rapport-Building and Communication-Maintenance Techniques Evaluation Form

	Behavior				
	Acceptable			*Unacceptable*	
1. Meets candidate at the door	5	4	3	2	1
2. Demonstrates acceptance (e.g., shakes candidate's hand, smiles, etc.)	5	4	3	2	1
3. Appropriate use of verbal approval (e.g., "interesting," "mm-hmm," "excellent point")	5	4	3	2	1
4. Appropriate nonverbal response (e.g., varies vocal intonation, leans forward, good eye contact, shakes head to demonstrate approval)	5	4	3	2	1
5. When necessary uses small talk to put applicant at ease	5	4	3	2	1
6. Verifies (questions) whether applicant understands or has any questions	5	4	3	2	1
7. Responds in full to candidate's questions	5	4	3	2	1
8. Use of open-ended questions	5	4	3	2	1
9. Allows applicant to respond in full	5	4	3	2	1

2. Data Collection and Processing Behaviors

The goal of the structured interview is to collect sufficient information to make an accurate predictive decision as to which applicant will perform the best in the target position. The structured interview facilitates accurate data collection by using the same procedure and process with all applicants. The result is that all applicants are treated in a uniform manner. Once you have made your opening comments, and have established a positive interviewing climate, it is time to direct your attention to the task of data collection and processing. (Processing in this context refers to assessment as to whether the manager has collected sufficient data to rate a candidate on a particular job dimension.) By asking the applicant to respond to future job-related questions that contain a dilemma, the interviewer forces the applicant to express intentions.

A number of processing alternatives are available to the interviewer. It is possible for interviewers to conduct the interview without any assistance. When this format is followed, the interviewer has the responsibility of both asking the questions and recording the applicant's responses. Given the dynamics of the interviewing situation, however, it is not recommended that the interviewer attempt to rate responses until after the interview. Simply put, there is just insufficient time for the interviewer functioning alone to ask questions, record answers, and assess the applicant's responses.

Given the findings reviewed earlier by Wiesner and Cronshaw, it is wise to have more than one individual involved during the interview session. When this occurs, one individual might have the responsibility of asking the situational questions while one or two other individuals record the applicant's responses. If more than one interviewer is to be present during the session, the individual making the opening statement should explain why this is necessary and what the others will be doing.

When dealing with past-oriented questions, managers must develop "stem" questions that will get the candidates talking about their performance in a particular past situation. (Refer to cell #5 of Figure 8.4) Although stem questions can vary to reflect the applicant's background and experience, their primary purpose is to bring out past behaviors that relate to a particular job dimension. It is the job dimensions and the set of questions that are used to collect behavioral support from the applicant that act as the common element across applicants.

On a general level, the stem question asks the candidate to articulate a very favorable or unfavorable situation (which relates to a particular job dimension) and explain what occurred. For example, to assess an applicant's organization and planning skills, the interviewer could ask the following questions: "Often situations arise where an employee is faced with a project that is complex, new, or appears to demand more resources than he or she presently has access to. Could you describe a situation when this happened to you and what you did?" In this case, the interviewer does not focus on a particular job or time period but rather allows the candidate to select the time and place. Alternatively, the manager could have focused on a particular job or experience that stood out in his or her review of the applicant's background material and that could have required behaviors similar to those deemed necessary for the target position (e.g., "While you were working at Southshore General as training coordinator, what was the most difficult project you were assigned?") Once the candidate begins to describe the situation, it is the manager's responsibility to process the information received; to probe, reflect, and summarize. In so doing, the manager collects the needed support to document an applicant's strengths or weaknesses for each job dimension.

It is at this point that the processing of the data becomes crucial to the success of PBDI. Specifically, it is unlikely that in response to a stem question, candidates will give perfect information that makes the transfer of understanding complete on the first try. The managers must therefore continually attend and respond to the candidate to ensure complete and accurate information has been obtained. The manager must probe for greater detail. This helps to ensure that a sufficient behavioral support is obtained to rate the candidate accurately on each of the job dimensions. Of particular interest are the answers to such questions as: Who else was involved? Where and when did this happen? What specifically did you do? What were the consequences of your actions? What did other people say and do? There are many different probing questions that can be asked by interviewers. This process of stem question, probing, and information processing is continued until the interviewer believes sufficient information has been collected to allow for accurate candidate rating. The diagram depicted in Figure 8.4 should help you to understand better (*a*) the central role of the collection and processing phase, (*b*) the type of information collected, and (*c*) the importance of attending and responding behaviors. Cells 5, 6, and 7 are the activities directly associated with the information collection and processing phase of the structured interview and will take the greatest amount of time to complete.

It is also not uncommon to have an applicant interviewed several times by different interviewers. Multiple interviews can be used for the PBDI; it's rarely done with the situational interview because a panel is used. Multiple interviews can increase accuracy by pooling several independent ratings on each job dimension. This process will be described below in greater detail.

Given the differences just described between the situational interview and the PBDI, it becomes clear that when the PBDI approach is used, the interviewer must rely more heavily upon his or her rapport building and data collecting skills, that is, active listening, probing, reflecting, summarizing, and the use of supportive statements (see Chapter 4). The situational interview minimizes the need for rapport-building and data-collecting skills because of its greater emphasis on a structure that asks the same questions of all applicants and does not encourage probing. It also reduces the need to cognitively assess applicants' responses by providing a scoring guide.

Before leaving our discussion of data collection and processing it is important to consider two common errors often made by interviewers. The first occurs when the interviewer records personal inferences or conclusions rather than behavior, and the second occurs when the interviewer asks questions that should not be asked during a selection interview.

Behavioral Specificity versus Inference and Conclusions. During the processing phase, the interviewer is expected to record the data necessary to support the evaluation process. Unfortunately, this is a point at which many interviewers fail to perform effectively. Improper recording can result from two common errors made by the interviewer during the processing phase of the interview. The first error is that managers frequently do not record statements of behavior but rather record inferences and conclusions resulting from behavioral observation or the content of the applicant's responses to questions asked by the interviewer. For example, the following observation represents a behaviorally based statement, "The applicant indicated that he informed the boss whenever required tasks could not be performed as planned." Whereas, the following statement is inferential because it fails to provide any behavioral support,"The applicant is dependable."

In terms of the interview process, behavioral statements are the result of direct observation (e.g., what candidates wear, how they speak, what they do), or the response content to the interviewer's questions. The difficulty with inferences and conclusions is that they are too general to function effectively when attempting to differentiate between candidates, make a decision, or defend one's selection choice to those around you. Similarly, if the interviewer records only inferences and conclusions, it is very likely that soon after the interview he or she will be unable to recall specific information that caused him or her to draw a specific inference or conclusion.

There is also another difficulty with the manager drawing conclusions or inferences about the candidate during the interviewing process. Conclusions and inferences by their very nature often imply a value judgment by the manager. At the very minimum it requires a cognitive process that would best be carried out after the interview is completed. Recall the issue of premature closure; the interviewer makes a decision before all information is available. If this occurs, it is highly probable that the manager will begin to color or distort subsequent information on the basis of established inferences and conclusions. In addition, once the interview reaches a conclusion, it is less likely that managers will dig and probe, because they believe that sufficient information has already been obtained.

Pre-employment Questions. Efforts to collect and process information will require the interviewer to ask a broad range of questions. Inappropriate questioning can reduce the overall effectiveness of the interviewing process and potentially expose the interviewer to charges of discrimination.[54] Areas of questioning that courts find particularly troublesome deal with issues that relate to gender, race, religion, color, age, marital status, physical disabilities, and national/ethnic origin. Although state and provincial guidelines vary as to what are appropriate questions in these areas, there is sufficient overlap to discuss this issue on a general level.

Pre-employment questions that allow interviewers to form subjective judgments make it difficult for organizations to defend their selection decisions should they be challenged. To minimize the role subjectivity plays in the interviewing process, interviewers should use (*a*) questions that reflect proper job analysis and thereby ensure that questions are job related, (*b*) same questions to ensure consistency across candidates, (*c*) questions that tap information relevant to predetermined standards, and (*d*) questions that reflect a predetermined weighting scheme based upon job relevancy. These steps will help ensure that one candidate can be objectively assessed as being more qualified than all others and that this assessment is based upon differences in job relevant knowledge, skills, and abilities.

The following examples will clarify this point.[55]

When asking questions about a candidate's name, it is acceptable to ask the individual his or her name or the name used at a previous job, but it is unacceptable to ask the person's maiden name.

To avoid legal problems with the issue of age, the interviewer should not ask for the candidate's date of birth or age. However, it is acceptable to ask candidates if their age is within a given range.[56]

It is illegal to probe issues regarding marital status and family relationships. It is unacceptable to ask a candidate's marital status, number or age of children, person with whom he or she resides, or are there any dependents that can be contacted in a case of an emergency.

Discrimination based upon physical disabilities or characteristics is legally prohibited unless they can be shown to impact on job performance. As a result, it is illegal to simply ask if the candidate has any physical disabilities. Instead, the interviewer should ask whether there are any physical conditions or disabilities that would affect the candidate's ability to perform the job for which he or she is applying.

Concerning religion, organizations must make a reasonable effort to accommodate the religious beliefs of their employees. In other words, organizations cannot use religion to exclude a candidate unless such exclusion can be justified by business necessity. Therefore, it is inappropriate to ask the candidate his or her religious affiliation or religious faith. However, the interviewer can indicate the shift that must be worked and whether such a schedule is manageable.

In reviewing these examples, you should realize that they represent only a sample of the possible areas and area alternatives open to the interviewer. As such, they were given to sensitize the reader to the types of problems likely to be encountered when addressing questions to the job applicant.

3. Controlling Behaviors

For structured interviews to be reliable and valid, managers must be prepared to maintain control during the interview session itself. Control allows them to ensure that all relevant dimensions will be covered during a predetermined amount of time and at the same time allows them to handle problem situations if they occur. From a purely administrative point of view, managers should follow the guidelines presented below.

- Keep track of time and how interviewing time is being utilized.
- Move from one dimension/focus area to the next as each is adequately dealt with.
- Skip topics/areas that have already been adequately dealt with.
- Keep the candidate from getting off on an unrelated (unimportant) tangent.
- Keep the candidate from rambling on about a point already explained.
- Follow up on earlier topics/areas if new information is offered.

When managers apply these guidelines they must ensure that they follow two important corollary principles. The first guideline deals with the interpersonal style of the manager as an interviewer. In all transactions within the selection interview, managers must ensure that they are interpersonally sensitive to the needs, feelings, and emotions of the candidates being interviewed. Interpersonal sensitivity helps ensure that the channels of communication remain open and that the candidates continue to transmit meaningful and relevant information about themselves. The second principle deals with the level of assertiveness employed by the interviewer. Passive managers may miss opportunities to respond to appropriate openings while aggressive managers may alienate the candidates. (Refer back to Chapter 2 for attitudes associated with both interpersonal sensitivity and assertiveness.)

Part of the preparation needed for effective control is to sensitize oneself to specific candidate problems likely to occur during the interview. By preparing for such problems, the manager develops strategies on how to handle difficult or problem candidates. The following are the four most frequently identified problems that can interfere with the smooth flow of the patterned behavior interview: (*a*) the silent candidate, (*b*) the candidate who attempts to bluff, (*c*) the candidate who attempts to evade questions asked, and (*d*) the candidate who rambles. Let us consider what the manager can do to overcome these problems.[57]

The Silent Candidate.   The candidate may not talk openly, because he or she is anxious, insecure, intimidated by a potential future boss, or lacks experience in interacting during a selection interview. If the candidate will not talk, the manager cannot hope to obtain the desired information needed to make a sound decision. New managers rarely see this as a potential problem until they have experienced live encounters with such candidates. Inexperienced managers often argue that "if they (the candidates) really want the job, then they will talk—if they don't, they're not worth hiring." This type of faulty logic causes the manager to make early and negative decisions about the candidate. Instead, interviewers must recognize that silence is a symptom of many different problems.

Early evaluation of the candidate often causes managers to distort what takes place during the remainder of the interview and thereby prevents them from collecting accurate and complete information. Therefore, if silence is perceived as an unwillingness to cooperate, or a lack of ability, the manager is likely to rate the candidate poorly. The following flow diagram describes one possible response sequence that can help stimulate the candidate to talk openly with the manager. (This sequence assumes that small talk designed to put the candidate at ease has already taken place—for example, How did you find your flight into Halifax? I see from your resume that you received your MBA from Toronto.)

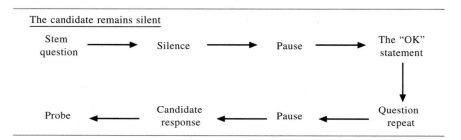

Before reaching a negative conclusion about a candidate it is important that the manager attempts to draw him or her out. Silence by the candidate occurs most frequently at the beginning of the selection interview. At this point the candidate will experience the greatest anxiety and uncertainty about, or distrust toward, the interviewer. At other points during the interview the candidate may not respond because he or she does not understand the question, or cannot think of a situation that satisfies the interviewer's questions. If the candidate does not respond to a question, the manager should follow several steps designed to stimulate an appropriate response.

1. Do not respond too quickly to the candidate's silence. It would be preferable to give the candidate 10 to 15 seconds to collect his or her thoughts and overcome the difficulty him/herself. Self-correction is likely to decrease the probability that future silences will occur. In addition, too quick an attempt by the manager to force the candidate to talk may cause him/her to perceive the manager as aggressive or domineering.

2. If the candidate remains silent the manager must act. At this point, it would be desirable for the manager to introduce some type of "It's OK" statements to help dissipate the candidate's anxiety or confusion about what is expected from him/her.

3. Once the "It's OK" statement has been made, the managers should restate the original question. To help reduce any remaining confusion in the candidate's mind it would be desirable to repeat the question in a slightly modified form.

This sequence, if made tactfully by interviewers, should elicit the desired response from candidates. Once the candidate begins to talk, managers are in a position to probe for further clarification. Below is an example of such an exchange.

Manager: "Often situations arise where an employee is forced to leave work for several hours. Could you tell me about the last time this happened to you, and you knew about the situation ahead of time?"

Candidate: "_____"

Manager: (10 to 15 second pause)—"I realize that it is difficult to come up with specific examples—that's OK. Most candidates have a difficult time in the beginning when they try to think of past experiences.—What I am really trying to get at is a situation where you knew you had to be away from your job during regular hours and what you did about it?"

Candidate: "Well—there have been times where I had a doctor's appointment and I had to take time off from work."

Manager: "Could you tell me when this happened and what you did to prepare yourself and others for the time you were going to be away?"

The information that can be obtained from discussing this situation is likely to go beyond the job dimension that the stem question was directed toward, that is, organization and planning. Behaviors the candidate is likely to talk about could be related to such job dimensions as dependability, handling stress and pressure, interpersonal sensitivity. Nevertheless, to ensure the success of the structured interview, managers should devote their time only to probing, recording, and ensuring that all relevant job dimensions are covered adequately. The actual detailed classification and evaluation should take place after the interview is completed.

The Bluff.   In an effort to present a favorable image of themselves, candidates may attempt to bluff when difficult or unfamiliar questions are asked. In this way the candidate attempts to maintain a positive self-image by deceiving the manager through pretense or an unsupported show of competence.

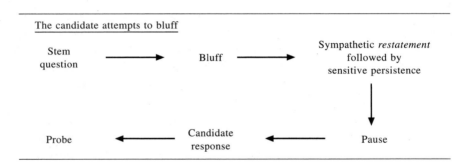

(concluded)

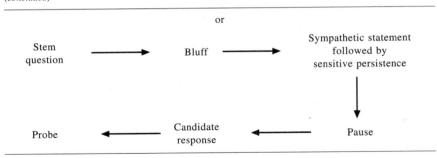

When attending and responding to the candidate, the manager must be alert to such attempts, and if bluffing behavior is observed, take the necessary steps to overcome the problem.

The two response sequences described above are alternative solutions to this problem. In the first sequence, the manager restates the candidate's answer to the stem question and in a sensitive manner restates his or her original statement. The intent is to redirect the candidate, and in so doing, gently persuade him or her to give a more relevant and informative answer to the stem question asked. The alternative sequence does not directly restate the candidate's answer but instead allows the manager to respond in a sympathetic manner and at the same time engage in sensitive persistence. Let us consider how such an exchange might work.

> *Manager*: "When dealing with customers, we don't always have the answer just when the customer wants to know something. Could you tell me about a recent situation where you just didn't have an answer and how you responded?"
>
> *Candidate:* "I can't think of any situation where I didn't have the ability to solve the customer's problem."
>
> *Manager:* "I can appreciate the fact that you have always been able to solve customer problems, but have there been any specific situations where, at the time of the exchange with the customer, you were unable to completely solve the problem or satisfy the customer?"
>
> *Candidate:* "Well I guess there were times where I had to collect additional information before I could act on a customer's behalf."
>
> *Manager:* "Could you tell me about a particular situation? For example, when did this happen and what specifically was the customer's request?"

The object of the exchange is not to confront the candidate, or attack him or her personally. Rather, the manager is using his or her perceptiveness and interpersonal skills to ensure a complete exploration of the candidate's recent past and specifically those behaviors that directly relate to the target position.

The Evade.   Because the candidate wants to be successful, and because there are likely to be questions asked which are difficult to answer or potentially threatening, he or she may attempt to evade the specific question being asked. The "evade" short-circuits the information gathering process by redirecting the flow of the interview. The manager cannot be sure whether this is a conscious effort on the part of the candidate to avoid the question, or an unconscious act resulting from anxiety and lack of experience. It is the manager's responsibility to be alert to the presence of responses that evade, and to take the appropriate steps to keep the information collecting and processing phase of the selection interview on track. Successful information collection and processing are also the only way in which the manager can determine whether the "evade" was a conscious manipulative response by the candidate, or an unconscious response to an internal emotional state. A popular technique for achieving this objective, and at the same time maintaining a positive rapport with the candidate, is for the manager to use the "assumed responsibility" statement (see below).

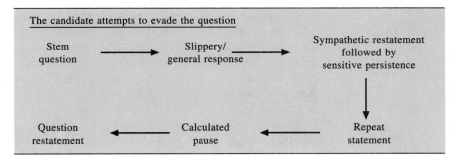

The underlying premise behind such a statement is that the manager is not attempting to dominate, win, or demonstrate superiority over the candidate. Rather, the manager's objective is to collect all relevant information from the candidate to help ensure a high-quality selection decision. Following this logic, it is acceptable, and desirable, for managers to accept the possibility that they may have been at fault. In other words, managers have little to lose but a lot to gain by demonstrating sensitivity, openness, and a willingness to accept partial blame if a communication is not accurately received. Furthermore, such an approach reduces the amount of potential stress on the candidate—an individual who is already under considerable emotional pressure to perform well. For example:

Manager: "When dealing with customers, most of them would be considered reasonable people. However, every now and then you'll run into one who for whatever reason is looking for a fight. Could you describe a recent situation where you encountered an extremely angry customer and how you handled the situation?"

Candidate: "At Southshore, we always follow the guidelines set out by the company's policy manual."

Manager: "I apologize, I guess I didn't make myself clear as to the type of answer I was looking for. I appreciate the fact that there is a company policy on how to handle an angry customer, but what I was hoping you would tell me is what you specifically did the last time you were confronted with an irate customer."

Candidate: "I'm not sure I understand how much detail you want."

Manager: "Well, why don't you start by describing what caused the customer to get upset in the first place?"

Candidate: "It was the third time this customer had come back to the store with the same VCR to be fixed and it still didn't work. The customer started yelling at me personally as if it was my fault, and told me in no uncertain terms that he wanted his money back."

Manager: "How did you respond to his personal attack?"

The Rambler.   Unfortunately, some candidates believe that they have to do all the talking to impress the interviewer. Consequently, when these candidates hit upon a topic they feel comfortable with, they may continue to talk even when sufficient information has already been transmitted. If interviewers allow this "rambling" behavior to continue, they become pressured because of time constraints, and because they are giving up control to the interviewee. To control ramblers, managers must be perceptive, assertive, and sensitive. Perceptiveness is needed to determine when sufficient information has been obtained so as to go on to a new topic or focus area. Assertiveness is needed to ensure that the manager will act soon enough so as not to waste valuable interviewing time. Last, interpersonal sensitivity is required so that when the manager attempts to regain control, the candidate is not alienated or made to feel inconsequential. Therefore, it would be helpful for the manager to follow the steps outlined below.

The "polite interrupt," the "repeat," and the "redirect," represent the core elements in any attempt to control the rambler.

1. In the case of the polite interrupt, the manager waits for a natural pause and then, in an interpersonally sensitive way, interrupts. Fortunately, natural pauses will always occur because speakers eventually have to take a breath, or will occasionally pause to assess the impact they are having on the receiver.

2. The repeat is a statement that summarizes what the candidate has been saying. This demonstrates to the candidate that the manager has been listening, despite the interruption.

3. The "stem question redirect" is a technique designed to move the interview in a new and more productive direction.

Each of these core elements is represented in the following exchange.

Candidate: "Last week when the store wasn't busy and a customer I recognized couldn't find what he was looking for, I personally took him to where the item was. The way I see it, that is the least you

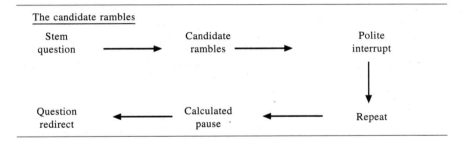

could do for a regular customer who prefers to be shown rather than told where things are. If you work for a place long enough, you get to know the regulars and whether they want to be shown or just told where the product is. It's like anything else, you treat customers right and they will treat you right — (breath, but no sign of stopping or giving up control)."

Manager: (interrupting) "I see, during slow periods you would be willing to show regular customers where the product is, rather than just telling them, especially when they have indicated a past preference to being personally shown. Clearly, I would consider that good customer service, but could you tell me what you do when the store is busy?"

The ability, therefore, to be able to recognize potential candidate problems, and have in place a strategy to overcome these problems, can greatly facilitate the manager's success as an interviewer.

4. Closing

The ultimate decision to hire should not play a role in the manner in which the candidate is treated during the interview's closing. If the steps outlined above are followed, the actual hiring decision will not be made until the interview is completed, the candidate has left, and the evaluation process is completed. Therefore, even the interview's closing must be considered an important and integral part of any selection interview. As such, the closing must be planned for.

The final moment of the interview plays a critical role in providing closure for the candidate and maintaining the positive rapport that has been developed during the interview. Furthermore, candidates, whether they are current employees from other departments or "walk-ins" from the local community, represent important vehicles of good-will. Therefore, candidates who are treated well will likely communicate to others their positive perceptions of the interviewing experience and the manager involved. At the organizational level, well-treated candidates (even ones who have not been selected) will likely communicate their positive experiences to others within the community, thus producing a positive community reputation. Similarly, internal candidates will communicate their positive experiences to others within the organization and thereby enhance the manager's reputation. Both outcomes are themselves creditable objectives for the organization and its managers.

When closing the interview, the manager should do the following to ensure that the overall atmosphere remains neutral and factual.[58]

- Indicate your personal appreciation for the candidate's cooperation.

- Explain the sequence of steps that will follow after the interview and when the candidate is likely to hear from the organization, that is, relevant dates, contact person, remaining steps to be completed before a final decision (reference checks, police checks, physicals, etc.).

- Ask the candidate if he or she has any questions, and answer each fully.

- In those instances where requested information cannot be provided, indicate if and when it will be provided to the candidate.

- Indicate that if the candidate should think of any questions in the next few days, he or she should feel free to give you a call.

- Thank the applicant again for his or her cooperation and time, and escort him or her to the door.

Having thought through and prepared for the selection interview, managers should now have a flexible script that will help guide them during the initial structured interview.

The Assessment Phase

Once the structured interview is over, managers must deal with the raw objective data they have collected on each candidate. Applicant responses generated from the situational interview should be compared to the pre-established scoring guide and a rating obtained for each question. Total scores are obtained for each of the job dimensions obtained, and a global rating can be obtained by summing across dimensions. Typically, more than one recorder is used during an interview session. Each interviewer or recorder independently rates the applicant's answers. Once this has been accomplished, the individuals read their recorded answers and through group consensus arrive at one agreed-upon rating. This process is continued until all questions have been considered.

In the case of the PBDI, the assessment process revolves around the manager's ability to classify behavioral support statements collected during the interview into correct job dimensions and then rate the applicant on each job dimension (see Figure 8.7). The ability to perform this task rests on three factors:

1. First, managers are in a better position to classify if they have played an active role in the development of the job dimensions and the articulation of examples of the types of behaviors likely to be considered supportive

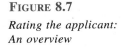

FIGURE 8.7

Rating the applicant: An overview

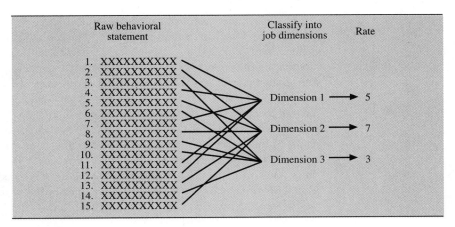

of each dimension. In other words, managers must have a clear idea beforehand what behaviors and dimensions they are looking for and the behaviors that support them.

2. Next, they must make every effort to record as many behavioral statements as possible made by the candidate during the interview. These statements must be behaviorally specific and not conclusions or inference. Also, they should be detailed enough to ensure that the manager will understand the context in which they occurred. Understanding the context in which a behavior occurs is essential in determining the actual value of the behavior, that is, whether it contributes positively or negatively to a particular dimension.

3. Last, managers must make the effort to fine-tune their ability to record, classify, and as we shall see shortly, rate behaviors. This is accomplished by practicing these skills whenever the opportunity arises. If one is prepared to undertake these activities, the probability of success is greatly increased.

The following discussion is intended to help readers to understand how they should go about rating a dimension once behavioral support statements have been classified. Managers should first review what they consider poor, satisfactory, and above average behavior for each job dimension. This mental image will reflect managers' own standards and expectations of what they want from a job incumbent. One way to accomplish this is for managers to picture all the employees they have observed in the target position and to visualize those individuals and instances where behavior was poor, satisfactory, and above average. It is against this internal cognitive map that individuals compare the profile or mix of classified behaviors supporting a particular dimension.

If a particular job dimension has 20 behavioral support statements, they will first be individually evaluated to determine the degree to which they support the dimension being considered. Managers will then compare the 20 support statements as a whole with what they would expect from job incumbents who are poor, satisfactory, or above-average performers. Based upon this comparison, they should be able to rate the candidates on that dimension.

For demonstration purposes, assume that the rater is using a 7 point rating scale, with 1 indicating poor performance, 4 indicating satisfactory performance, and 7 indicating above-average performance. Also assume that after comparing the collected data with performance standards the manager has rated the applicant as a satisfactory performer. In this case the interviewer could then rate the applicant a 4 on that dimension. If challenged, or in doubt, managers have the necessary behavioral support information to defend or reassess their rating. Such ratings are as close as managers can get to an objective assessment of the candidate's potential to perform well on the target position. This process will be carried out for all relevant dimensions. Ultimately, the manager's intention is to compare the ratings of all candidates to determine (in conjunction with other available information, e.g., performance tests, personality tests, and references) who is most likely to succeed on the job.

When using the PBDI, it is also possible to have multiple raters assessing the suitability of each applicant. This occurs if more than one interviewer is involved in each interview session, or if the applicant is interviewed sequentially by different individuals. To arrive at a single rating for each job dimension, it will again be necessary to pool individual ratings. Such a process involves a team meeting in which the interviewers present their individual rating for each dimension and the behavioral support statements used to arrive at each rating. Should disagreements between the individual raters occur, group discussion is used to reach consensus on a single rating.

Summary

Clearly, if managers want to perform well, the first line of offense is to select the best people possible. Managers cannot fully abdicate their responsibility to the human resource management department. The ultimate decision in most instances will be left up to the department head. It is therefore important that managers develop an ability to assess the potential performance of available candidates. The techniques used by managers must be easy to apply, behaviorally based, require minimum resources, and at the same time have predictive validity. The structured interview technique described in this chapter appears to satisfy these criteria.

Exercises

8.1 Classifying Behavior into Behavioral Categories and Rating Its Consequences

An important skill required of all managers is the ability to correctly classify observed behavior into appropriate job dimensions. This skill is critical to activities such as goal setting, performance evaluation, feedback, counseling and motivation, and so on. Only by observing, recording, and correctly classifying behaviors can managers effectively assess and discuss the strengths and weaknesses of others within the organization. Please follow the steps outlined below.

Step 1. Read the descriptions on the Job Dimension Definition List. Be sure that you understand the types of behaviors or actions that support each dimension.

Step 2. Assume that the statements on the *Statements* list represent actual recorded observations. After reading each statement, indicate the job dimension to which you believe it belongs. It may appear that a particular statement belongs to more than one dimension. Although this is possible, one job dimension is of primary importance and the others are of secondary importance. You may refer back to the Job Dimension Definition List. Next to each statement, place your answer in the column marked *Dimensions*.

Step 3. After you have classified an observed behavior into a job dimension, indicate in the *Consequences* column whether the behavior is likely to have a positive (desired) or negative (undesired) consequence.

Step 4. The instructor will lead an open discussion of student results.

Job Dimension Definition List

Organization and Planning. Ability to establish courses of action for self and/or others to accomplish specific results; to make effective use of personnel and other resources; to establish objectives, schedules, and priorities.

Decision Making. Ability to use logical and sound judgment in using resources, determining courses of action, and defining solutions to problems. Also critical to the decision-making process is the ability to collect and use available information.

Interpersonal Sensitivity. Ability to be sensitive to and perceive the needs, feelings, and emotions of others; to deal effectively with others regardless of their status or position; to accept interpersonal differences and to develop rapport with others.

Behavior Flexibility/Managing Stress and Pressure. Ability to alter one's normal posture when presented with additional information, to appropriately change courses of action in response to changes in the environment, to have the presence of mind to remain calm when confronted with conflict or personal attack, to be able to adapt to or cope with stressful situations.

Perception. Ability to identify, assimilate, and understand the key elements of a situation; to recognize the implications of alternative courses of action.

Decisiveness. Ability to make decisions, take action, make commitments, and remain firm in one's position when challenged.

Honesty. Ability to carry out one's responsibilities/commitments in a sincere, straightforward, and truthful manner; to fulfill one's organizational roles without the existence of hidden agendas.

Leadership. Ability to take charge, to direct and coordinate the activities of others, to maintain control in terms of the overall situation and others, to obtain desired results through delegation and follow-up.

Statements	*Dimensions*	*Consequences*
1. When in doubt on the job, I would probe my subordinates to determine the performance goals for each subordinate.	_____	_____
2. If a colleague failed to respond to such a deadline (deadline had been buried in a report), I would make that person aware of the fact that unless we meet with representatives of the finance department by the Dec. 15th deadline, there is little hope of changing budgetary limits.	_____	_____
3. When arranging budgetary meetings, the candidate always schedules such meetings for her office.	_____	_____
4. "I keep three day-planners going at the same time, one on the computer, one at home, and one I carry on my person. At the beginning and end of each day I update the three to make sure that they all had the same information."	_____	_____
5. "The other day we were ahead of schedule and one of the men wanted to take the day off for personal reasons—so I said OK. A day later a big order came in and we were behind the eight ball—just then another subordinate made a similar request and I said no."	_____	_____
6. I would first try to prevent arguments with co-workers. But if someone came in and said that to me, I would keep my cool and state that we hve to work together in a small office and that when he takes his anger out on me, it only makes me angry. Then I would point out that when I am angry at a coworker, I find it harder to work with that person. I would finish by saying that I hoped that this did not happen between us and suggesting we start working on the problem at hand.	_____	_____

8.2 Group Activity: Overcoming Difficult Candidates

The purpose of this exercise will be to give you experience handling the four problem encounters discussed in this chapter, (the silent applicant, the bluff, the evade, and the rambler). You will be asked to break up into groups of three. Each group will be given a set of interview questions which might be asked during a typical selection interview. It will be the responsibility of one of the group members to respond to the interviewer's questions by using one of the four "difficult responses"—these will be referred to as response strategies for the purpose of this exercise. During the exercise each group member will have an opportunity to ask and respond to the four questions provided by the instructor. Please follow the steps outlined below.

Step 1. First identify each group member as either A, B, or C. This will be your classification throughout the exercise.

Step 2. Each participant will be given a set of four interview questions likely to be used during a selection interview. Each group member should take 10 to 15 minutes to plan a response strategy for each question. When planning your strategies, use all four of the possible responses discussed earlier. In other words, there will be no repeats.

Step 3. During round 1, "A" will be the interviewer, "B" will be the applicant, and "C" will act as an observer. "A" will begin by asking Question 1. In response to "A's" question, "B" will respond by choosing the response strategy he or she has selected for that question. It will be "A's" responsibility to overcome the difficulties presented by "B." During round 1, "C" will play the role of an observer. It will be his or her responsibility to assess which response strategy "B" is using and how well "A" deals with the difficulties caused by "B's" behavior. Before discussing "A's" performance, "A" should work through all four questions. At that point "C" will provide feedback to the group. At this point all group members should make whatever comments they believe appropriate. Step 3 should take approximately 15 to 20 minutes to complete.

Step 4. During round 2, "B" will be the interviewer, "C" will be the applicant, and "A" will be the observer. Once these roles have been clarified proceed by asking and responding to the four questions in the manner outlined in Step 2. Again, when the four situations have been acted out, the observer will give his or her observations. Step 4 should take approximately 15 to 20 minutes to complete.

Step 5. During round 3, "C" will be the interviewer, "A" will be the applicant, and "B" will be the observer. Once these roles have been clarified, proceed by asking and responding to the four questions in the manner outlined in Step 2. Again, when the four situations have been acted out, the observer will give his or her observations. Step 5 should take approximately 15 to 20 minutes to complete.

Step 6. The total class will reassemble to discuss group results.

8.3 Selecting the Director of Personnel

You are the city manager for Harbortown, a city with a population of about 500,000. Last month your director of personnel informed you that he planned to return to the University of Toronto to complete a two-year MBA program. To be completely up front with you, he resigned because he did not plan to return to Harbortown afterwards. You believe it is in your best interest to undertake an in-depth search for a new director of personnel. To ensure the selection of the best possible candidate, you decide to use a structured interview as one element of the selection process.

In response to a national advertisement you received over 50 applications, which you reduced to a list of six candidates with about the same qualifications. You, of course, want to ensure that you select the best one. Larry Benton is the first applicant you will interview. In preparation for your interview, you have developed a set of behavioral dimensions that reflect the types of behaviors (both good and bad) expected of the director of personnel. The job dimensions and the applicant's résumé follow the steps in the exercise.

Before you meet with Larry Benton, you want to develop a set of interview questions to help you assess his background. The answers to these questions should help you determine whether his past behavior and performance will support a decision to hire him. Please follow the steps outlined below.

Step 1. The class will break up into small groups of five or six students each. Each group will select one member to play the role of interviewer.

Step 2. Option 1—Through group discussion, use the behavior-observation scales described on the following pages to develop a set of situational questions (future oriented) that could be used to collect the needed behavioral data to make a sound selection decision. (When selecting option 1, students may find it helpful to review Table 8.6.)

Option 2—Through group discussion, develop a set of structured questions (past oriented) that can be used to collect the needed behavioral data to make a sound selection decision.

Step 3. Develop a script of how the interviewer should run the forthcoming selection interview. You will run the interview from the time the candidate enters your office to the moment he leaves. In Steps 2 and 3 you can make additional assumptions about Harbortown, but they must be reasonable and consistent with the information presented in this exercise. Your instructor will indicate whether the interview structure should follow a situational or patterned approach or some combination. (30 minutes)

Step 4. Practice the interview within your group. Time will not permit you to go through all the questions. Become familiar with the interview process so that you are more comfortable using it. (15 minutes)

Steps 2 to 4 may be completed prior to class.

Step 5. The class will assemble and a group will be selected randomly to interview Larry Benton. The role of Larry Benton will be played by the instructor.

Résumé

Larry Benton
1842 Main Street
Centerville, New Jersey
212–456–7810

Male
Canadian and U.S. Citizen
West Long Beach, New Jersey
Born March 21, 1952

<u>Education</u>

1968–1972   South Shore High School
West Long Beach, New Jersey
Graduated June 1972

1977–1981   Fulton University
Harrison, New Jersey
Graduated June 1981—BComm

<u>MBA Courses Taken</u>

Organizational Behavior
Training and Development
Labor Relations
Personnel Functions
Organizational Theory Program

<u>Workshops Taken</u>

Training for the Trainer
All There Is to Know about Personnel
15-Day Midmanagement Training Program

<u>Experience</u>

1972–1975   LTA Industries, Centerville, New Jersey
Shipping Clerk

1975–1977   United States Army—Supply Terminal
Rank—Captain

1982–1991   Centerville Power Corporation
Centerville, New Jersey
Staff Training Coordinator

1991–present   South Shore General Hospital
Personnel Manager

<u>Professional Organizations</u>

New Jersey Personnel Association
Atlantic Society for Human Resource Development

<u>Current Salary</u> $52,000

<u>References upon Request</u>

Key Behavior

A. Decisiveness—The ability to make decisions quickly, take action, make commitments, and not change one's position when challenged.

1. When given sufficient information on an important issue, makes decisions within allotted time.

   Almost never   1   2   3   4   5   Almost always

2. Able to make up mind and does not change position unless presented with new and contrary information to the position taken.

Almost never   1   2   3   4   5   Almost always

3. In response to an employee's single request for a preferred vacation schedule (or work schedule) and one that is consistent with company policy and supervisory needs, immediately accepts or rejects.

Almost never   1   2   3   4   5   Almost always

4. When allocating resources, able to quickly make "yes" or "no" decisions.

Almost never   1   2   3   4   5   Almost always

5. When confronted with multiple pieces of information, easily selects the information he or she will use to make decisions.

Almost never   1   2   3   4   5   Almost always

6. When asked by a subordinate for instructions, does not hesitate to give him or her directions.

Almost never   1   2   3   4   5   Almost always

B. Leadership—The ability to take charge; to direct and coordinate the activities of others; to maintain control, to delegate where appropriate and follow up when required on a subordinate's progress.

1. During meetings, is able to maintain control, complete the agenda as stated, and keep side conversations from disrupting the meetings' rhythm

Almost never   1   2   3   4   .   5   Almost always

2. When assigning a new, difficult, or important task, follows up on employee's performance.

Almost never   1   2   3   4   5   Almost always

3. Varies his or her level of monitoring of employees progress in response to their level of experience, past performance, and importance of the task.

Almost never   1   2   3   4   5   Almost always

4. Before delegating work, ensures that the subordinate is interested, has the ability, will learn from the experience, has the time, or (to ensure equity) is next employee scheduled to do the task.

Almost never   1   2   3   4   5   Almost always

5. If the team becomes sidetracked or appears unwilling to perform, steps in to give direction or sets group goals.

Almost never   1   2   3   4   5   Almost always

C. Organization and Planning—The ability to establish courses of action for both one's self and others in order to accomplish desired goals; to make proper use of available resources; to be able to establish timely schedules and goals; and to set priorities when and where appropriate.

1. When making presentations, comes prepared, follows agenda, and is able to find material as needed.

Almost never   1   2   3   4   5   Almost always

2. Before acting (that is, attending meetings, making important telephone calls, assigning work to subordinates) collects appropriate support information to ensure their availability if needed.

Almost never   1   2   3   4   5   Almost always

3. Makes information and schedules available to others before asking them to participate in meetings.

Almost never   1   2   3   4   5   Almost always

4. Manages his or her time effectively by establishing schedules and setting aside time for both crises and quiet times.

Almost never   1   2   3   4   5   Almost always

5. Sets aside sufficient amounts of time to carry out planned activities or to account for environmental constraints (e.g., sets realistic time-tables).

Almost never   1   2   3   4   5   Almost always

6. Informs relevant others of his or her activities so as to keep them aware of what is happening.

Almost never   1   2   3   4   5   Almost always

D. Dependability—To be willing to accept tasks and responsibilities that are within one's authority and abilities zone; to provide the required time and energy to accomplish accepted tasks; to finish the tasks on time; and if unable to complete the tasks as assigned, inform the appropriate other of this fact and explain why.

1. Carries out responsibilities and attends meetings as scheduled or assigned.

Almost never   1   2   3   4   5   Almost always

2. If work cannot be completed as assigned, informs affected individuals, and explains why as well as what are the likely consequences.

Almost never   1   2   3   4   5   Almost always

3. Shares all relevant information with others to ensure high levels of performance from all staff.

Almost never   1   2   3   4   5   Almost always

4. When the individual says something will get done, it gets done.

Almost never   1   2   3   4   5   Almost always

5. Stands behind his or her staff and effectively represents their interests to top management.

Almost never   1   2   3   4   5   Almost always

6. Carries out personal work and activities in the time allotted.

Almost never   1   2   3   4   5   Almost always

E. Interpersonal Sensitivity—The ability to respond to and perceive the needs, emotions, and feelings of others; to deal openly with others regardless of their status, power, or position; to tolerate individual differences; and to develop positive relations with others.

1. Willing to listen and respond to the concerns of others.

Almost never   1   2   3   4   5   Almost always

2. Before acting or making decisions, takes into consideration the interests and schedules of others.

Almost never   1   2   3   4   5   Almost always

3. Willing to share information that will directly affect the performance of others.

Almost never   1   2   3   4   5   Almost always

4. Does not attack others in public.

    Almost never   1   2   3   4   5   Almost always

5. Gives recognition and support to employees when needed or expected.

    Almost never   1   2   3   4   5   Almost always

6. When responding to others, takes into consideration their needs and value system.

    Almost never   1   2   3   4   5   Almost always

8.4. Rating the Applicant

This exercise is designed to give students an opportunity to observe, record, and rate behavior. You will be asked to rate the applicant who is interviewed for the position of director of personnel (see Exercise 8.3). Information obtained during this interview will serve as the raw data for your final rating of the applicant. For this exercise to have maximum impact, please follow the steps outlined below.

Step 1. During the forthcoming role-play, each participant will have the responsibility of recording relevant examples of behavior described or discussed by the applicant; in other words, each participant will act as the interviewer taking notes during the interview. This is the only way you will be able to remember all the details covered in your meeting with the applicant. The person role-playing the interviewer will also take notes. You are to look for behaviors that will allow you to rate the candidate on the dimensions described in your text.

Step 2. Each individual will review his or her notes after the role-play and classify recorded behaviors into relevant job dimensions. Do not attempt to classify behaviors as you record them; you will run the risk of missing something important during the selection interview. (*Option:* Steps 2 through 5 can easily be completed at home in preparation for the next class.) (20 to 30 minutes)

Step 3. The class will form small groups of five to six individuals to develop a rating of the applicant on each of the job dimensions. First, a list of all the relevant support statements for the first skill dimension must be developed. Each member reads in a round-robin sequence his or her support statements to the group. The rater list is then formed from the individual statements.

Step 4. Through group consensus, the groups will arrive at a rating for the job applicant for job dimension 1.

Step 5. Repeat Step 3 and Step 4 in sequence for each skill dimension.

Step 6. The class will assemble and each group will present their ratings. Group ratings will then be compared with the instructor's ratings. (1 hour 15 minutes for all steps)

End Notes

1. W. A. H. Wiesner and S. F. Cronshaw, "A meta-analytic investigation of the impact of interview format and degree of structure on the employment interview," *Journal of Occupational Psychology,* Vol. 61, 1988: 276.

2. American Society for Personnel Administration, ASPA–BNA *Survey No. 45: Employee Selection Procedures,* Bureau of National Affairs, Washington D.C., 1983.

3. Bureau of National Affairs, *Recruiting and Selection Procedures: Personnel Policies Forum Survey 146,* Bureau of National Affairs, Washington D.C., 1988.

4. R. Wagner, "The employment interview: A critical summary," *Personnel Psychology,* Vol. 2, 1949: 17–46.

5. G. Dessler and J. F. Duffy, *Personnel Management,* Prentice Hall, Canada, Scarborough, Ontario, 1984.

6. L. Ulrich and D. Trumbo, "The selection interview since 1949," *Psychological Bulletin,* Vol. 63, 1965: 100–116.

7. R. A. Reilly and G. T. Chao, "Validity and fairness of some alternative employee selection procedures," *Personnel Psychology,* Vol. 35, 1982: 1–61.

8. J. E. Hunter and R. H. Hunter, "The validity and utility of alternative predictors of job performance," *Psychological Bulletin,* Vol. 96, 1984: 72–98.

9. Wiesner and Cronshaw, 1988: 275–290.

10. Wiesner and Cronshaw, 1988: 281.

11. P. M. Wright, P. A. Lichtenfels, and E. D. Pursell, "The structured interview: Additional studies and meta-analysis," *Journal of Occupational Psychology,* Vol. 62, 1989: 191–199.

12. Wright, Lichtenfels, and Pursell, 1989.

13. J. L. Farr, "Response requirements and primacy-recency effects in a simulated selection interview, *Journal of Applied Psychology*, Vol. 58, 1973: 228–233; J. L. Farr and C. M. York, "Amount of information and primacy–recency effects in recruitment decisions," *Personnel Psychology,* Vol. 28, 1975: 233–238; R. L. Dipboye, C. Stramler and G. A. Fontenelle, "The effects of the application on recall of information from the interview," *Academy of Management Journal*, Vol. 27, 1984: 561–575.

14. C. W. Anderson, "The relation between speaking times and decision in the employment interview," *Journal of Applied Psychology,* Vol. 44, 1960: 267–268.

15. M. Snyder, "When belief creates reality," in *Advances in Experimental Social Psychology,* ed. L. Berkowitz, Academic Press, Orlando, Fla., 1984; P. H. Eccher, T. A. Sheskey, T. A. Lavelle, and J. F. Binning, "Confirmation of preinterview impressions: Differential use of biased versus bidirectional questions," paper presented at the Society of Industrial and Organizational Psychology, Dallas, Tex.; P. S. Radefield, K. B. Williams and J. F. Binnings, "Preinterview impressions and recruiter's questioning in same- and opposite-sex interviews," paper presented at the 1990 Annual Meeting of the American Psychological Society, Dallas, Tex., 1990.

16. R. L. Dipboye, *Selection Interviews: Process Perspectives,* South-Western Publishing Co., Cincinnati, Ohio, 1992; T. M. Macan and R. L. Dipboye, "The effects of interviewers' initial impressions on information gathering," *Organizational Behavior and Human Decision Processes,* Vol. 42, 1988: 364–387; J. F. Binning, M. A. Goldstein, M. F. Garcia, and J. H. Scattaregia, "Effects of preinterview impressions on questioning strategies in same- and opposite-sex employment interviews," *Journal of Applied Psychology,* Vol. 73, 1988: 30–37.

17. R. Merton, *Social Theory and Social Structure,* The Free Press, Glencoe, Ill., 1957; R. L., Dipboye, "Self-fulfilling prophecies in the selection recruitment interview," *Academy of Management Review,* Vol. 7, 1982: 579–587; S. T. Fiske and S. L. Neuberg, "A continuum of impression formation from category-based to individuating processes: Influences of information and motivation on attention and interpretation," in *Advances In Experimental Social Psychology,* Vol. 23, ed. M. P. Zanna, Academic Press, New York 1990: 1–74.

18. B. M. Springbett, "Factors affecting the final decision in the employment interview," *Canadian Journal of Psychology,* Vol. 12, 1958: 13–22; T. D. Hollman, "Employment interviewers' errors in processing positive and negative information," *Journal of Applied Psychology,* Vol. 56, 1972: 130–134; L. H. Peters and J. R. Terborg, "The effects of temporal placement of unfavorable information and of attitude similarity on personnel selection decisions," *Behavior and Human*

Performance, Vol. 13, 1975: 279–293; Dipboye, Stramler, and Fontenelle, 1984: 561–575.

19. E. C. Webster, *Decision Making in the Employment Interview,* Eagle Publishing Co. Ltd, Quebec, 1964.

20. M. D. Hakel and M. D. Dunnette, *Checklists for Describing Job Applicants,* Minnesota Industrial Relations Center, University of Minnesota, Minneapolis, Minn., 1970; K. N. Wexley, G. A. Yukl, S. Z. Kovacs, and R. E. Sanders, "Importance of contrast effects in employment interviews," *Journal of Applied Psychology,* Vol. 56, 1972: 45–48; F. J. Landy and F. Bates, "Another look at contrast effects in the employment interview," *Journal of Applied Psychology,* Vol. 58, 1973: 141–144; J. C. Burkhardt, D. Weider-Hatfield, and J. E. Hocking, "Eye contact contrast effects in the employment interview," *Communication Research Reports,* Vol. 2, 1985: 5–10; S. J. Cesare, A. Dalessio, and R. J. Tannenbaum, "Contrast effects for black, white, and female interviewees," *Journal of Applied Social Psychology,* Vol. 18, 1988: 1261–1273.

21. W. H. Cooper, "Ubiquitous halo," *Psychological Bulletin,* Vol. 90, 1981: 218–244.

22. B. M. Bass, "Reducing leniency in merit ratings," *Personnel Psychology,* Vol. 9, 1956: 359–369; W. F. Cascio and E. R. Valennzi, "Relations among criteria of police performance," *Journal of Applied Psychology,* Vol. 63, 1978: 22–28, 50.

23. S. M. Dornbursch, A. H. Hastorf, S. A. Richardson, R. E. Muzzy, and R. S. Vreeland, "The perceiver and the perceived: Their relative influence on categories of interpersonal perception," *Journal of Personality and Social Psychology,* Vol. 1, 1965: 434–440; N. Lemon and M. Warren, "Salience, centrality, and self-relevancy of traits in construing others," *British Journal of Social and Clinical Psychology,* Vol. 13, 1974: 119–124; H. Markus and J. Smith, "The influence of self-schema on the perception of others," in *Personality, Cognition, and Social Interaction,* ed. N. Cantor and J. F. Kihlstrom, Lawrence Erlbaum and Associates, Hillsdale, N. J., 1981.

24. L. L. Frank and J. R. Hackman, Jr., "Effects of interviewer–interviewee similarity on interviewer objectivity in college admission interviews," *Journal of Applied Psychology,* Vol. 60, 1975: 356–360.

25. M. D. Hakel, T. W. Dobmeyer, and M. D. Dunnette, 1970: 65–71; M. E. Heilman, "Sex bias in work settings: The lack of fit model," in *Research in Organizational Behavior,* Vol. 5, ed. B. M. Staw and L. L. Cummings, JAI Press, Greenwich, Conn., 1983; P. M. Rowe, "Decision processes in personnel selection," *Canadian Journal of Behavioral Science,* Vol. 16, 1984: 326–337.

26. M. D. Hakel and A. J. Schuh, "Job applicant attributes judged important across seven diverse occupations," *Personnel Psychology,* Vol. 24, 1971: 45–52; D. N. Jackson, A. C. Peacock, and R. R. Holden, "Professional interviewers' trait inferential structures for diverse occupational groups," *Organizational Behavior and Human Performance,* Vol. 29, 1982: 1–20; J. L. Holland, *Making Vocational Choices: A Theory of Careers,* Prentice Hall, Englewood Cliffs, N. J., 1985.

27. M. D. Hakel, "Normative personality factors recovered from ratings of personality descriptions: The beholder eye," *Personnel Psychology,* Vol. 27, 1974: 409–421; M. D. Botwin and D. M. Buss, "Structure of act–report data: Is the five-factor method of personality recaptured?" *Journal of Personality and Social Psychology,* Vol. 56, 1989: 988–1001; J. M. Digman, "Personality structure: Emergence of the five-factor model," *Journal of Personality and Social Psychology,* Vol. 41, 1990: 417–440; R. L. Dipboye, 1992.

28. J. G. Amalfitano and N. C. Kalt, "Effects of eye contact on the evaluation of job applicants," *Journal of Employment Counseling,* Vol. 14, 1977: 46-48.

29. I. P. Yound and E. G. Beier, "The role of applicant nonverbal communication in the employment interview," *Journal of Employment Counseling,* Vol. 14, 1977: 154–165; T. V. McGovern and H. E. Tinsley, "Interviewer evaluation of interviewee nonverbal behavior," *Journal of Vocational Behavior,* Vol. 13, 1978: 163–171.

30. A. Keenan and A. A. Wedderburn, "Effects of nonverbal behavior of interviewers on candidates' impressions," *Journal of Occupational Psychology,* 1975: 129–132; A. Keenan, "Effects of nonverbal behavior of interviewers on candidates' performance," *Journal of Occupational Psychology,* Vol. 49, 1976: 171-176; S. Rynes and H. E. Miller, "Recruiter and job influences on candidates for employment," *Journal of Applied Psychology,* Vol. 68, 1983: 147–154; R. A. Fear, *The Evaluation Interview,* 3rd ed., McGraw-Hill, New York, 1984;

J. D. Drake, *Interviewing for Managers: A Complete Guide to Employment Interviewing,* rev. ed., AMACOM, New York, 1983.

31. LIMRA (Life Insurance Marketing and Research Association), *Face to Face,* LIMRA, Hartford, Conn., 1974; A. J. Schuh, "Effects of early interruption and note taking on listening accuracy and decision making in the interview," *Bulletin of the Psychonomic Society,* Vol. 13, 1978: 263–264.

32. G. P. Latham, L. M. Saari, E. D. Pursell, and M. A. Campion, "The situational interview," *Journal of Applied Psychology,* Vol. 65, No. 4 1980: 422–427; G. P. Latham and L. M. Saari, "Do people do what they say? Further studies on the situational interview," *Journal of Applied Psychology,* Vol. 69, 1984: 569–573.

33. G. P. Latham, "The reliability, validity, and practicality of the situational interview," in *The Employment Interview,* ed. R. W. Edler and G. Ferris, Sage Publications, Beverly Hills, Calif., 1989: 169–182.

34. Latham, Saari, Pursell, and Campion, 1980; Latham and Saari, 1984.

35. T. Janz, "Initial comparisons of patterned behavior description interviews versus unstructured interviews," *Journal of Applied Psychology,* Vol. 67, 1982: 577–580; C. Orpen, "Patterned behaviour description interviews versus unstructured interviews: A comparative validity study," *Journal of Applied Psychology,* Vol. 70, 1985: 774–776; T. Janz, *Behavior Description Interviewing,* Allyn & Bacon, Newton, Mass.; 1986; T. Janz, "The selection interview: The received wisdom versus recent research," in *Canadian Readings in Personnel and Human Resource Management,* ed. S. Dolan and R. Schuler, West Publishing, St. Paul, Minn., 1987.

36. Latham, 1989: 171.

37. Latham, Saari, Pursell, and Campion, 1980; Latham and Saari, 1984; M. A. Campion, E. D. Pursell, and B. K. Brown, "Structured interviewing: Raising the psychometric properties of the employment interview," *Personnel Psychology,* Vol. 41, 1988: 25–42; Latham, 1989.

38. Latham, 1989.

39. J. E. Hunter and R. H. Hunter, 1984.

40. Latham, Saari, Pursell, and Campion, 1980; Latham and Saari, 1984; Campion, Pursell, and Brown, 1988; Latham, 1989.

41. Figure 8.3 is based upon material presented in Latham, 1989.

42. Table 8.4 based upon material presented in Latham, Saari, Pursell, and Campion, "The situational interview," *Journal of Applied Psychology,* Vol. 65, No. 4, 1980: 422–427.

43. S. D. Maurer and C. Fay, "Effect of situational interviews, conventional structured interviews, and training on interview rating agreement: An experimental analysis," *Personnel Psychology,* Vol. 41, 1988: 329–344.

44. Latham, 1989: 180.

45. Janz, 1982: 577–580; C. Orpen, 1985, 774–776.

46. Janz, Allyn & Bacon, Newton, Mass., 1986.

47. Janz, 1986; Orpen, 1985.

48. Janz, 1986.

49. G. P. Latham and B. J. Finnegan, "The practicality of the situational interview," paper presented at the annual meeting of the Academy of Management, August, 1987, New Orleans.

50. Campion, Pursell, and Brown, 1988.

51. J. C. Flanagan, "The critical incident technique," *Psychological Bulletin,* Vol. 51, 1954: 327–358; G. P. Latham and K. N. Wexley, *Increasing Productivity through Performance Appraisal,* 2nd ed., Addison-Wesley Publishing, Reading, Mass., 1994.

52. C. J. Stewart, and W. B. Cash, Jr., *Interviewing Principles and Practices,* 2nd ed., Wm. C. Brown, Dubuque, Iowa, 1974.

53. Campion, Pursell, and Brown, 1988.

54. C. M. Koen, "The pre-employment inquiry guide," *Personnel Journal,* Vol. 59, 1980: 825–829; R. D. Gatewood and H. S. Feild, *Human Resource Selection,* The Dryden Press, Chicago, Ill., 1987; T. L. Leap and M. D. Crino, *Personnel/Human Resource Management,* 2nd ed., Macmillan, New York, 1993.

55. The examples being used have been taken from Gatewood and Feild, 1987: 284–289 and 103–107.

56. R. D. Gatewood and H. S. Feild, *Human Resource Selection,* The Dryden Press, Chicago, Ill., 1987.

57. The following material dealing with problem candidates is based upon the material presented in Janz, 1986.

58. Stewart and Cash, Jr., 1974.

GOAL SETTING: A MOTIVATIONAL TOOL THAT TRULY WORKS

Objectives:

- To review the characteristics of effective motivation and demonstrate how the goal-setting process satisfies each characteristic.
- To articulate the behaviors necessary to effectively implement the goal-setting process.
- To provide an opportunity to practice behaviors critical to the goal-setting process.

Introduction

What is needed for an individual to be an effective manager? Clearly, there is no simple answer to this question. To be effective as a manager you must possess the full range of management skills presented in this text. However, there are three major lines of offense for the manager (i.e., selection, training, motivation). If these three building blocks are in place, then the probability that the manager will do well is relatively high.

Imagine being in charge of a work unit that you had no role in bringing together, that had never been exposed to any type of training, and whose members were unwilling or unable to perform the job that you assigned them. You would not have to strain your imagination to recognize this as an unfavorable situation and one that you would like to avoid at all costs. Even the best manager would be unable to obtain high levels of output unless major changes were introduced to the unit. To overcome these problems, a proactive manager would take the necessary steps to correct the situation.

Selection procedures described in Chapter 8 could be put in place. A needs analysis could be performed to implement training and development activities designed to correct employee deficiencies. To overcome a lack of employee willingness, managers could create an environment designed to motivate subordinates to perform at, or near, their peak capabilities. Here the value of effective goal setting becomes apparent. Locke and Latham[1] articulated the central role of effective goal setting when they stated:

> The practicing manager does not have to understand all the intricacies of the human psyche in order to have highly motivated employees. There is a technique that does not depend on knowledge of the employee's subconscious. This technique is not another fad or a seductive gimmick. It has been used successfully, in various forms and guises, by managers for more than seventy years. This technique is not management by objectives, although it is the basis for MBO. It is not job enrichment, a job design strategy that motivates by building challenge, responsibility, authority, autonomy, etc., into the job, but it may be the hidden element in job enrichment that is responsible for the motivational effects derived from it. The technique is not an incentive plan, but it is often associated with incentive plans and may vastly increase their effectiveness. It is not behavior modification in the historical meaning of that term, but behavior modification advocates often employ its technique successfully while using their own special terminology to describe it. It is not organizational development, but it may very well be the key to making OD interventions effective. It is not Theory X, Theory Y, or Theory Z, although it is explicitly or implicitly assumed by all three. It is goal setting, a motivational technique that works!

Goal Setting: Some Basic Assumptions

The increased popularity of goal setting as an effective motivational tool rests primarily on two factors. It is relatively simple to understand and apply, and it works. Many traditional motivational models or techniques that base their structure on concepts such as instincts, drives, and conditioning, attempt to be all-encompassing. Consequently, they fail to give the detail necessary to translate theory into usable steps designed to increase a subordinate's effort and persistence. Goal-setting theory limits its objectives by dealing with specific behaviors and practices that can be applied directly to the organizational setting and, more specifically, to self-management and the manager–subordinate interface. As a result, both laboratory and field studies consistently demonstrate the success of goal setting as an effective way of increasing productivity.

Empirical results clearly support the positive effect goal setting has on employee productivity. In a review of goal-setting studies between 1969 and 1980, Locke and his associates found that 99 out of the 110 studies demonstrated that "specific, hard goals produced better performance than medium, easy, do-your-best, or no goals. This represents a success rate of 90 percent."[2] In terms of specific productivity increases, Locke and Latham[3] described 10 studies in which the percentage change in performance ranged from 16 percent to 27 percent, with an average increase of 19.3 percent. Companies represented in the sample came from a wide range of industries. More recently, Mento,

Steel, and Karren[4] evaluated published research from 1966 to 1984 and concluded that the average expected percentage increase in productivity above baseline data ranged from 8.88 percent for specific and hard goals, to 17.46 percent when specific hard goals were coupled with feedback. The actual percentage increase reflected the degree of goal specificity and difficulty, as well as performance feedback regarding goal attainment. Mento, Steel, and Karren's positive evaluation of goal setting is reflected in the following statement:

> Goal difficulty and goal specificity–difficulty were found to be strongly related to task performance across a variety of tasks and in both laboratory and field settings. If there is ever to be a viable candidate from the organizational sciences for elevation to the lofty status of a scientific law of nature, then the relationships between difficulty, specificity–difficulty, and task performance are most worthy of serious consideration. Certainly, if nothing else, the evidence from numerous studies indicates that these variables behave lawfully.[5]

Basic to understanding how goal setting works to increase employee productivity is that goals are the immediate regulators of individual behavior. A goal is "what an individual is trying to accomplish: it is the object or aim of an action."[6] Having said this, however, there is not always a one-to-one mapping between a specific goal and actual behavior. This is because individuals make mistakes, function on incomplete information, vary in terms of self-confidence, and may face environmental constraints beyond their control. Nevertheless, as pointed out in Chapter 1, the world is not a perfect place, and one cannot expect to be able to accurately predict subordinate performance a hundred percent of the time. What you want is to be a better manager tomorrow than you were yesterday. Effective goal setting is a technique that can do this for you.

Goal Mechanisms

When a goal is *(a)* perceived as important, and *(b)* is a standard against which actual performance will be measured and feedback given, then goal setting will have a positive effect on one's behavior. Goal setting works because of its positive effect on the following four mechanisms: *(a)* behavioral direction, *(b)* the individual's effort, *(c)* behavioral persistence, and *(d)* the development of strategies to achieve the goal (see Figure 9.1).

At the most basic level, goals help a person focus their attention and behavior.[7] They clarify what it is the person is to accomplish within a specific time frame. It is this focus that increases the probability of goal achievement. The actual degree of focusing achieved is a function of goal specificity, perceived consequences, perceived legitimacy of the stated goal, and the perceived likelihood of success. As we will see shortly, each one of these components will be built into an effective goal-setting process.

Furthermore, if individuals focus their attention in the direction of a particular goal, and accept its appropriateness or desirability, they will exert a great deal of effort to attain it. The actual amount of effort expended

FIGURE 9.1

Why goal-setting works: Four basic mechanisms

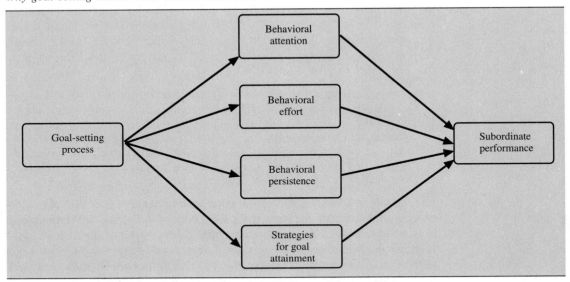

Source: E. A. Locke, K. N. Shaw, L. M. Saari, and G. P. Latham, "Goal setting and task performance: 1969–1980," *Psychological Bulletin* Vol. 90, 1981, pp. 125–152 and G. P. Latham and E. A. Locke, "Self-regulation through goal setting," *Organizational Behavior and Human Decision Processes,* Vol. 50, 1991, pp. 212—247.

will reflect the level of goal specificity and goal difficulty.[8] The greater the specificity and difficulty, the greater the amount of effort expended by the individual.

Goals also affect an individual's persistence (duration of effort) in attempting to achieve desired goals.[9] In situations where time constraints exist, individuals are likely to work harder and faster. If no time constraints exist, desired goals induce individuals to work longer.

In those instances where attention, effort, and persistence are insufficient to achieve a desired goal, it may be necessary for individuals to develop new strategies to be successful. When faced with specific and challenging goals, individuals generally plan more and develop plans of higher quality.[10] Such cognitive activities increase the probability of improved performance as individuals devote more time to analyzing, evaluating, and identifying potential adverse consequences that may take place in the future. In other words, individuals facing specific challenging goals are likely to spend time developing and applying their creative problem-solving skills. Furthermore, when employees are allowed to participate in strategy formulation, they produce a larger pool of suitable task strategies.[11] Ultimately, the development and use of suitable strategies by subordinates facilitate the achievement of complex tasks and increases perceived self-efficacy.[12] For the manager, this means a greater likelihood of success for subordinates.

The Role of Commitment

The effectiveness of any goal-setting process requires that participants are committed to the goals that have been established.[13] Commitment refers to "the degree to which the individual is attached to the goal, considers it significant or important, is determined to reach it, and keeps it, in the face of setbacks and obstacles."[14]

When high commitment exists, the individual's performance level increases as the goal level increases.[15] This occurs because committed individuals are likely to do what they say they will do, whereas less committed individuals are likely to replace difficult goals with easier ones. In the case of easy goals, high commitment has a negative effect on performance. Individuals who become locked into easy goals are likely to refuse to replace them with more difficult goals. Uncommitted individuals, when faced with easy goals, may set more difficult goals to increase the task challenge. Both of these effects are shown in Figure 9.2.

Behavioral scientists have identified a number of determinants that affect the level of goal commitment.[16] Determinants of commitment can be classified into three general categories: (1) external factors (e.g., authority, peer group influence and models, publicness, external rewards and incentives), (2) internal factors (e.g., expectancies, self-efficacy, internal rewards), and (3) how goals are set (e.g., assigned, participative, and self-set). We will briefly consider the factors associated with each category.

FIGURE 9.2

Main and interaction effect of goals and commitment

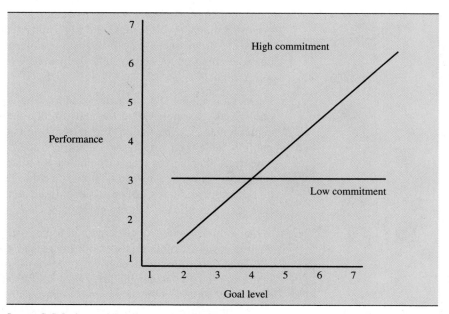

Source: G. P. Latham and E. A. Locke, "Self-regulation through goal setting," *Organizational Behavior and Human Decision Processes,* Vol. 50, 1991, p. 217.

External Factors:

- Employee commitment is increased when assignments are made by a person perceived as having legitimate authority.[17] In other words, individuals try to do what is asked of them. Increased commitment to assigned goals may also reflect the fact that assigning a goal implies the recipient is competent, and by accepting an assigned goal without objection, the subordinate implies consent.[18] On the basis of their review of available research, Locke and Latham argued that assigned goals are most effective when:[19]

  1. The authority figure is seen as legitimate.
  2. The assigned goals imply associated rewards and punishments.
  3. Goal assignment conveys (positive) self-efficacy information.
  4. Goal assignment fosters a sense of achievement.
  5. The assigned goals imply opportunities for self-improvement.
  6. The assigned goals challenge people to prove themselves.
  7. The authority figure is physically present, supportive, trustworthy, provides a convincing rationale for the goal, exerts reasonable pressure, and is knowledgeable and likable.

- The effect of peer pressure on employee behavior is well established within the behavioral science literature.[20] Although the view of peer pressure is that it often restricts performance, group commitment to high performance can be facilitated if there is support from management, congruence exists between externally set standards and group members' own desires, and high importance is placed on group goals and group success.[21] It is also possible that peers may have a positive effect on an employee's performance by acting as positive role models.[22]

- Research evidence also indicates that making a public statement about one's goals can motivate individuals to take the necessary action to achieve them.[23] The underlying assumption is that individuals who publicly state their intentions will expend the necessary effort to not embarrass themselves later or demonstrate a lack of personal integrity.[24] However, research supporting the link between publicness and commitment does not necessarily indicate that individuals who set their goals in private will not commit or cannot be effective.[25]

- When goal achievement is perceived to be instrumental in obtaining desired rewards, individuals exhibit increased goal commitment.[26] However, when linking incentives or rewards to goal achievement, managers must consider the level of goal difficulty. For example, bonus pay linked to the achievement of goals of moderate difficulty can be quite effective. However, in the case of hard or unreachable goals, greater commitment can be obtained if bonus pay is linked to performance rather than goal achievement. The rationale here is that as goals become increasingly difficult or unreachable, there is a reduced probability of success. Therefore, if incentives and rewards are given for goal achievement, rather than performance or partial success, there is likely to be a reduction in employee motivation. In other words, when incentives and rewards are linked to hard or difficult goals, employees may move from a "get as close as you can" mental set to a "succeed or nothing" mental set.

Internal Factors:

• It has been demonstrated that increased levels of objective goal difficulty, especially when arbitrarily set, lower employee commitment.[27] This is likely to result from employees lowering their effort–performance expectancies, that is, "If I try I am likely to fail." When such a conclusion is reached, there is an increased likelihood of individuals rejecting difficult goals. Conversely, when individuals demonstrate a high subjective expectancy of success, goal commitment is significantly increased.[28]

• Closely related to an employee's effort-performance expectancy is the concept of self-efficacy—a concept that is broader in scope. As you will recall from our earlier discussion (Chapter 2), self-efficacy refers to the full range of capabilities that an individual draws upon to perform a task.[29] In those instances where an individual's self-efficacy is increased, either by receiving positive feedback about performance capabilities, having access to relevant information, or being able to develop suitable strategies, there is a comparable increase in commitment.[30]

• Self-administered rewards have also been found to increase commitment.[31] To increase commitment within an organizational setting, employees could be required to complete and submit periodic self-assessments, or be trained to self-administer feedback in the form of such statements as, "I did a very good job." It is possible that self-administered rewards increase commitment by increasing self-efficacy, or because self-generated feedback is more meaningful to the individual than feedback received from others.[32]

Methods of Setting Goals

• Managers have at least three ways of setting goals when interacting with subordinates. They can assign the goals, allow subordinates to participate in the process, or give subordinates the authority to set their own goals. Although there may be a North American bias in favor of a participative style, empirical evidence demonstrates that no one approach is more effective than others in increasing goal commitment or performance.[33] More important than technique is whether managers or employees actually set goals, and the level of goal difficulty and specificity.[34] Managers can also enhance subordinate goal commitment and performance by using a tell-and-sell style rather than a tell style alone, communicating the importance of the goal, and demonstrating support for their subordinates.[35]

It is worth noting that support for participative decision making has historically reflected the belief that participation increases employee motivation. Such an emphasis by behavioral scientists has unfortunately deflected attention from the more important cognitive benefits of participative decision making. Participation increases the amount of information available to subordinates and facilitates strategy development.[36] As a result, participation has a positive effect on commitment and subordinate self-efficacy.

Nine Key Characteristics of Goal Setting

Managers who are trained in the goal-setting process, and correctly implement the goal-setting steps described below, increase the probability of reaping the benefits of effective goal setting. The steps described below expand upon the **SMART** approach to personal goal setting described in Chapter 2. As you will see, the required steps in the manager-subordinate goal-setting process are not difficult to understand, but they will require managerial commitment if implementation is to be successful. Our discussion outlines the nine steps that are most frequently used to describe effective goal setting. First, we will discuss a number of issues relevant to effective implementation.

The issue of allowing subordinates to participate in goal setting is an administrative decision. Any decision about participation must be based upon the managers' personal knowledge of subordinates and the situation. Therefore, managers must address such issues as subordinate ability, knowledge, interest, willingness, the compatibility of manager–subordinate goals, and time. For example, if the subordinates lack ability, knowledge, interest, or time, the level of participation may be very limited or nonexistent. Conversely, if the subordinates have clearly demonstrated these characteristics and have available time, then many of the steps outlined below may be bypassed, with total responsibility delegated to the subordinates. Such a response by managers is consistent with the underlying philosophy of situational leadership.

Before choosing the level of subordinate involvement, managers must also consider the nature of the problem, including degree of confidentiality required, desirability of sharing control of such issues, ability to unilaterally make decisions in the future, and whether managers can effectively monitor subordinate behaviors as part of an ongoing goal-setting and evaluation process. Last, managers must consider whether available time allows for employee participation and whether participation is in keeping with the overall managerial philosophy of the organization.

A situational response will also determine the actual number of steps included in the goal-setting exchange between the manager and a particular subordinate. Furthermore, certain goal-setting steps can be considered more critical than others in determining the ultimate success of the effort. Therefore, certain characteristics may not always be necessary when dealing with a particular subordinate in a specific situation.

From a motivational standpoint, participation in goal setting is no more effective than self-set or assigned goals. But employee participation in goal setting can be extremely valuable from a cognitive standpoint when the task is complex. Through participating in the goal-setting process, employees' understanding of what is required to attain the goal is increased. Moreover, participation in the goal-setting process can increase the person's self-efficacy when a challenging goal is indeed attainable. This occurs when through the participation process the person discovers ways of attaining the goal.[37]

We may now consider nine key characteristics of effective goal setting.

1. Articulate the Specific Objective or Task to Be Done

Inherent in the goal-setting process is the activity of articulating and clarifying the general, or broad objectives, of the department or organization so that they are specific. This allows employees to put the specific agreed-upon goals into perspective and to translate the organization's vision into concrete action steps. The number of possibilities is quite large and may relate to such issues as size, quality, market share, customer relations, volume, etc. Employees, through specific goals, must understand how to implement the strategy necessary for the organization to move toward its vision.

Goal specificity relates to the degree that goals are objectively quantified. The importance of goal specificity can be seen when comparing the following two goal statements made to a brokerage account executive:

"Pat, you've done well this year and I would like you to increase your gross sales again next year."
"Pat, you've done well this year and I would like you to increase your gross sales by 30 percent in the next six months."

The first statement is too ambiguous and allows Pat to define his own quantitative goal. In the extreme case, Pat could set the desired increase at one dollar. A one dollar increase would likely lead to a reprimand and conflict between Pat and the boss. Such ambiguity and potential for conflict do not exist for the second goal statement. In this case, Pat clearly knows "what" is expected and "when" it is expected. If a 30 percent increase is perceived as not possible, it is Pat's responsibility to discuss this issue at the beginning of the evaluation period and not at the end.

2. Assess Goals in Terms of Difficulty

Goals can range from the very easy to the impossible. The level of difficulty experienced by an employee, however, reflects the relationship between that individual and the particular task or goal being faced.[38] Central to this relationship is the level of ability and experience that the employee brings to the situation. As a result, what one employee finds easy another may find difficult. Nevertheless, the higher the absolute level of the goal, the more difficult it will be for the employee to achieve it.

It is also generally recognized that there exists a linear relationship between the degree of goal difficulty and performance.[39] Such a relationship reflects the fact that individuals generally adjust their effort and persistence to the level of goal difficulty being experienced.[40] In addition, difficult goals will require individuals to increase performance to obtain self-satisfaction. If individuals are able to perform, and remain committed, their performance increases as goal difficulty increases. Thus "higher goals produce higher performance than lower goals or no goals because people simply work harder for the former."[41]

There is obviously an upper limit to the positive effect of goal difficulty on performance. Performance will first level out as individuals reach the limits of their ability (see Figure 9.3a). If the goal becomes so difficult that the employee no longer believes it can be achieved, effort and performance will drop off precipitously. The willingness to expend effort on a difficult task is also related to the degree to which rewards are given for partial completion of the task. If the reward is conditional on total success, then the subordinate's willingness to expend effort decreases as the levels of difficulty increase (see Figure 9.3b).

FIGURE 9.3

Goal difficulty and performance

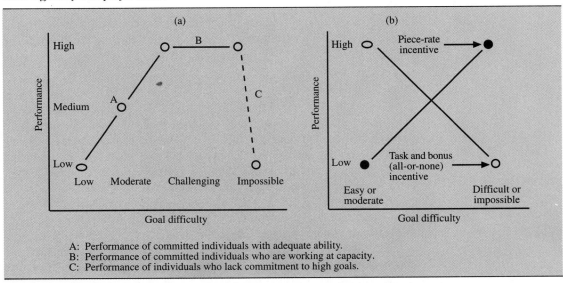

A: Performance of committed individuals with adequate ability.
B: Performance of committed individuals who are working at capacity.
C: Performance of individuals who lack commitment to high goals.

Source: E. A. Locke and G. P. Latham, *Goal Setting: A Motivational Technique That Works,* © 1984, pp. 3, 22–24, 29. Reprinted by permission of Prentice Hall, Englewood Cliffs, New Jersey.

3. Specify How Subordinate Success Will Be Measured

To guide the subordinate's attention and energies in the desired direction, it is important to articulate how the employee will be measured. That which gets measured gets done. This is because the act of measurement conveys cogently exactly what the organization considers to be important to the attainment of its vision. Measurement allows the employee to track progress toward goal attainment, and to take steps to minimize discrepancy between the goal and actual performance. Without measurement, the setting of a goal becomes relatively meaningless.

Employee performance can be measured by results as well as behavior. In the case of results, work outcomes associated with a particular subordinate can be measured by physical units, quality, time, or dollar units. Measurement of results is typically easier to obtain for jobs at lower levels within the organization, as well as for production and technically oriented jobs.

The measurement of results for a particular subordinate is not always possible. Jobs that do not produce a measurable physical output, or produce output that cannot be linked to the activities of one individual, do not lend themselves to end result measurement. In such cases, goals can be set in terms of behaviors critical to the goal difficulty and performance attainment of end-results (e.g., profits). Once the behaviors are identified, goals can be set in terms of demonstrating these behaviors. (Chapter 13 deals with performance management and discusses the mechanics of this process in detail.) An example of how to overcome resistance to change is given in Figure 9.4. A job analysis was completed, identifying ways of being effective in this area. The manager sets a goal as to the score to be achieved on these behavioral observation scales.

4. Specify the Criteria or Standard of Success and Follow-Up Procedures

Closely linked to the communication of what is to be measured is the criterion or standard used to measure success either for end-result or employee behavior. It is not enough to indicate to the subordinate that you will be measuring dollar sales, or that you will measure whether one listens to subordinates. Effective managers must specifically articulate an objective target to be reached, that is, letters typed by a secretary, number of new accounts obtained by a stock broker, deliveries for a truck driver, or a desired objective score on a number of behavioral dimensions considered necessary for success. In other words, during the next relevant time period, the manager must specify what must be accomplished by the subordinate so that the manager can determine that a goal has been successfully reached.

For example, in a large brokerage firm the target for a first-year account executive was $100,000 in gross sales. This fact was clearly communicated to new account executives upon entry into the business. If this gross figure was reached or surpassed, a new target was set for the next year. In this particular organization the incremental increase for the next year was set between 20

FIGURE 9.4

*Example for
measuring managerial
behaviors designed
to reduce subordinate
resistance to change*

Overcoming Resistance to Change					
(1) Gives the details of the change to the employee.					
Almost Never	0	1	2	3	4	Almost Always
(2) Explains why the change is needed.					
Almost Never	0	1	2	3	4	Almost Always
(3) Explains how the change will affect the employee.					
Almost Never	0	1	2	3	4	Almost Always
(4) Listens to the employee's concerns.					
Almost Never	0	1	2	3	4	Almost Always
(5) Asks the employee for assistance in making the change work.					
Almost Never	0	1	2	3	4	Almost Always
(6) If necessary, specifies the date for a follow-up meeting to discuss/resolve the employee's concerns.					
Almost Never	0	1	2	3	4	Almost Always

Total = _____

Below adequate	Adequate	Full	Excellent	Superior
0–5	6–10	11–15	16–19	20–24

Source: E. Locke and G. Latham, *Goal Setting: A Motivational Technique That Really Works,* Prentice Hall, New Jersey, 1984, p.29.

and 30 percent. The actual figure was a function of the overall environment and the characteristics of the particular account executive. Alternatively, if job behavior is to be the measure, one uses behavioral observation scales similar to the ones in Figure 9.4 to establish a desired level of performance. If a performance review system has been in place and the manager has knowledge about a subordinate's behavior, this information can be used to establish baseline data about the employee. Assume for the moment that after a relevant evaluation period the employee is given a total score of 5 on the six behaviors designed to overcome employee resistance to change. Since the score is unacceptable, it is possible to establish a target of 9 for improvement during the next evaluation period. In both cases, the subordinate not only knows on what he will be measured but also what target must be achieved to be considered successful.

No goal-setting process would be complete unless there was agreement as to the follow-up procedures to be used by the manager. One of the most effective techniques for directing subordinates' attention and efforts toward a particular goal is to make them aware that performance will be evaluated and that some type of time-specific follow-up will take place. Here again, however, managers' use of follow-up techniques must reflect their knowledge of the subordinates' past performance, and levels of experience, the subordinates' personalities and levels of self-confidence, as well as the overall importance of the goal under consideration. Depending upon the mix of these factors, follow-up and monitoring techniques may range from very formal and obtrusive to virtually no follow-up at all.

In keeping with such theories as situational leadership, if a subordinate is inexperienced, and unable or unwilling to function independently, the follow-up and monitoring procedure employed should be quite severe. This would be especially true if the goal is critical to the overall success of the department or if the goal's success or failure could significantly affect other departmental members. Conversely, if a subordinate is experienced, able to unilaterally carry out the goal, if the goal has limited impact on the department or others, and the subordinate places significant value on personal autonomy, then follow-up and monitoring techniques should be informal and limited. In some instances, if managers never hear from the subordinate again, they will assume that the goal has been achieved.

Associated with the measurement of performance, and the assessment of whether standards have been met, is the need to provide employees with meaningful feedback about their performance. Locke and Latham analyzed the results of 33 studies and concluded "that goals and feedback together are more effective in motivating high performance or performance improvement than either one separately."[42] Feedback, however, will not have a positive effect on performance unless the employee receiving it *(a)* has high self-efficacy, *(b)* is dissatisfied with existing performance levels, and *(c)* sets higher goals for the next evaluation period.[43]

5. Clearly Articulate the Consequences of Successful Performance and Ensure that the Consequences Are Acceptable to the Subordinate

Motivation is affected by an employee's outcome expectations, that is, their anticipation of consequences to their actions.[44]

Employees offer their services to the organization with the expectation that they will receive something positive in return. It is this implicit psychological contract between the organization and the individuals that motivates them to join and then remain with the organization. If perceived equitable rewards are not forthcoming, then the individuals will, at the very minimum, restrict effort, and at the extreme, leave the organization. Therefore, the manager must accept the position that an important question in the minds of most employees is, "What is in it for me?" Such a need to know should not be considered as a sign of employee selfishness but rather of normal behavior.

Just as dissatisfaction and turnover can be significantly reduced by giving realistic job previews to prospective employees,[45] management–subordinate conflict can be reduced and motivation increased if employees receive realistic reward previews. It is better to be candid and discuss rewards early in the goal-setting process than to wait until performance is measured and then offer a reward, only to find that it is unacceptable to the employee. At that point a manager may be unable to meet the expectations of high-performing subordinates.

Let us consider why an early discussion of the linkage between rewards and performance is desirable. First, if managers realize that such a discussion will likely take place, they will more likely make the effort to identify what rewards are under their control. Furthermore, by discussing the performance–reward link during the early stages of goal setting, managers are more likely to know whether they can satisfy employee needs. Moreover, employees will be able to *(a)* anticipate what specific rewards are linked to performance, *(b)* assess whether contingent rewards are likely to satisfy their dominant need structure, and *(c)* assess the equitability of the managers' proposed reward structure before performance occurs.

6. Specify the Time Span Involved

Time deadlines activate cognitive processes by which subordinates rank order goals in terms of perceived priorities and expend mental and physical effort to attain them. (Refer back to Figure 5.3 in Chapter 5.) Goals without stated time frames are likely to be pushed off into the future as they are continually being replaced with those goals that are time specific or are of personal importance to the subordinate.

7. Jointly Set Goal Priorities

Employees at all levels in an organization have multiple goals. The existence of multiple goals sometimes means there is insufficient time to complete all goals identified during the goal-setting process. Consequently, the manager and the subordinate must establish goal priorities. These priorities are based upon a discussion of importance and difficulty, and hence their time frame.

To appreciate the importance of clarifying goal priorities, consider the following scenario. Assume for the moment that a manager and a subordinate have met and discussed a number of goals that would generally improve the subordinate's performance and the overall productivity of the department. However, even though agreement as to measurement, criteria of success, and difficulties has been reached, the issue of goal priorities has not been addressed. Some managers argue that because other issues have been considered, priorities will automatically be understood. Unfortunately, this assumption does not appear to hold up in practice. The parties leave the goal-setting meeting with their own interpretation of what are the goal priorities. Consequently, what subordinates rate as a high priority, and devote their time to, may be considered a relatively low priority by the manager. The result of such a situation is poor subordinate performance, at least in the manager's mind, conflict as placement of blame is attempted, and a negative interpersonal relationship that is carried over into future goal-setting encounters. These negative outcomes can be minimized by openly discussing and agreeing upon goal priorities. Such a discussion is especially critical when the environment is dynamic and ambiguous, the subordinate is new and inexperienced, or certain goals are of particular importance to the manager.

8. *Specify Strategies and Tactics for Goal Attainment*

The degree of detail explored during a goal-setting meeting is, as indicated above, a function of environmental factors. Consequently, it is often useful to discuss ways to achieve the stated goal. In this way, goal-setting not only clarifies goal direction but also acts to facilitate goal attainment by identifying key behaviors. Furthermore, assuming subordinate participation, this process also becomes developmental. Coordination requirements and future adverse conditions are two areas in which it is often necessary to develop detailed strategies and tactics.

As discussed in Chapter 1, many organizations are designing their structures around an open-system philosophy. Open environments increase the number of interactions required of employees as they attempt to achieve their goals. Strategies and tactics necessary to facilitate such interactions must be integrated into the goal-setting process. For example, subordinates can consider the coordination requirements of any project or program that is likely to affect other people or departments. They must answer the who, what, where, and when questions before designing a detailed implementation plan. The following sample questions are to be considered.

> "Who is likely to be affected by my efforts to achieve my goals, and what is likely to be their response?"
> "Whom should I network with to collect and share relevant information?"
> "Who has the authority, influence, and resources necessary for successful goal achievement?"
> "What do I have to offer to others within the organization?"
> "What is the worst thing that could happen if I don't coordinate my efforts with XYZ department?"
> "What information, help, or support do I need from others?"
> "When is it necessary to inform others of my plans and actions?"
> "When should I expect help, support, or information from others?"
> "Where within the organization do I find the information, help, or support that I need?"

Once the manager and subordinates have developed their plans for the future, it is important that they consider potential problems that may occur in the future as the plan, support activities, and personal initiative of the subordinate are brought on line. Put another way, you are attempting to guard against becoming a victim of Murphy's three laws:

- Nothing is as simple as it seems.
- Everything takes longer than you think it should.
- If anything can go wrong, it will.

The actual steps you should take to guard against future adverse consequences are quite simple. The hard part for most managers is an unwillingness to take the time to do a needs analysis and planning to successfully bring one's goals into the future. Figure 9.5 outlines the process by which a manager and subordinate can increase the likelihood of successfully attaining their goals. The first step taken by the subordinate (with support from the manager) is to identify a list of potential adverse consequences that might occur in the future. For example, if you were a soccer coach setting up the first indoor evening practice of the season, what could go wrong to prevent you from achieving your goals? One possible adverse consequence is that when you arrive at the gym the doors are locked and all the lights are out. To ensure that such an adverse consequence does not interfere with the goals of having a successful practice, you would have to consider next what might have caused the adverse consequence. On the basis of your knowledge of the situation, you identify as many potential causes as time, energy, resources, and other practical issues allow. In response to such an analysis you might identify the following:

- Janitorial staff were not informed.
- Janitor was delayed on way to the gym.
- The wrong date was listed on the work order.
- The wrong location was listed on the work order.

Having listed potential causes of an adverse consequence, the logical next step is to determine the probability of the cause occurring and the impact on goal achievement if such an adverse consequence occurred. Clearly, if the probability of occurrence is low or the impact on goal achievement is minimal, then it is unlikely that the subordinate would want to devote significant time or energy to prevent or buffer against the adverse consequence. If, however, the probability and consequence are high, then the subordinate may want to develop action plans designed to prevent or buffer against the potential adverse consequence and its causes. In the case above, the coach may reduce the likelihood of failure by getting written notification from the janitorial staff of the day, time, and location of the gym that they will open (prevention), or the coach may pick up his own set of keys, or have an alternative site selected, just in case no one shows up to open the door (buffering). What is important is that the subordinate is trained to bring his or her plan into the future.

FIGURE 9.5

Bringing one's goals into the future

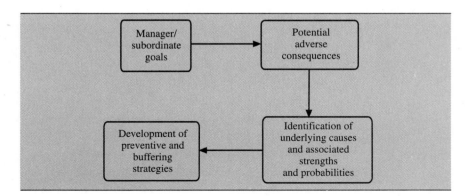

9. Clearly Articulate the Conditions under Which Performance Will Be Required

A lack of clarification of conditions under which goals must be carried out can leave an employee confused about how to act when the situation changes. This is especially true for new and inexperienced employees, or employees who have not been exposed to effective goal setting in the past. Therefore, the effective manager may want to map out the conditions under which performance or desired behavior must be carried out. Clearly, it would be impossible for the manager to define all future states. However, some attempt must be made to identify major conditions that must be considered if success is to be achieved.

In the past several years we have worked with a number of organizations that wanted to improve service to customers. Although the desired goal varied from organization to organization, for example, reduce the number of customer complaints, be rated in the top three within the industry for customer service, or coax customers away from competitors because of better service, the training emphasis was always at the employee–customer interface. One of these organizations went so far as to indicate that the customer must always be right and must always leave the store satisfied. Because of the extreme nature of the objective, considerable time had to be spent outlining the conditions under which this objective had to be achieved. Consequently, the following statements were often heard during the practice goal-setting meetings: "Even if you are angry, you have to keep smiling and not offend the customer"; "Even if you have been up all night, as long as you are on the job the customer receives quality service, that is, the time and attention necessary to make him or her feel like our only customer"; "If the customer is wrong when returning an item, but it is under $100, he or she leaves the store with either a refund or a new item." In each of these cases, the statement is defining the conditions under which employees must keep the customer happy. If these conditions are not explicitly stated, employees can interpret the goal–environment according to their own standards.

Self-Regulation through Goal Setting

As organizations continue to downsize, flatten their structures, reduce the number of middle managers, and move in the direction of self-managed employees and teams, there is a need to train employees on how to use self-regulation techniques. Although self-regulation has been shown to be an effective technique in teaching individuals to stop smoking, overcome drug abuse, reduce weight, improve study habits, and enhance academic achievement,[46] it has only recently received attention in the human resource literature.[47] Research has demonstrated that the benefits of self-regulation apply both to blue-collar and management levels.[48]

As you recall, research has demonstrated that self-set goals are as effective, but not consistently more effective, in producing employee commitment and increases in performance than assigned goals or goals resulting from participation. It is also important to note that goal-setting facilitates self-regulation because "people must choose to discover what is beneficial to their welfare, they must set goals to achieve it, they must choose the means for attaining these goals, and they must choose to act on the basis of these judgments."[49] In other words, goals establish what is an acceptable level of performance.

Important to the success of any effort to introduce a self-regulation program within organizations is the willingness to provide training to employees.[50] Training has been demonstrated to be effective in teaching employees such self-regulation behaviors as identifying problems, setting specific and difficult goals necessary for self improvement, identifying environmental factors that hinder or facilitate goal achievement, monitoring personal success and failures in achieving short-term goals, and self-administering rewards and punishments.[51] The training provided must cover the full range of component behaviors necessary to ensure that subordinates will succeed in their self-regulation efforts.

Effective leadership also plays a role in establishing the climate in which self-regulation by employees works.[52] Effective leaders first develop a long-term vision that gives employees a cause to rally around. Such a vision will only be management rhetoric unless the leader translates it into short-term goals. The purpose of short-term goals is to make the vision concrete in the employee's mind. Next, the effective leader must model the types of behavior he or she wants employees to exhibit. Specific areas of concern are problem solving, decision making and taking action-steps designed to achieve short-term goals. Consistent with the need for managers to be supportive, effective leaders must make themselves available to employees by listening to their ideas and concerns. Finally, effective leaders must ensure that employee behavior is measured and that feedback is provided to strengthen and regulate goal commitment.

Our conclusion is that although self-regulation can be an important management tool, most employees are not inherently self-regulators. The skills necessary to ensure success can only be achieved though experience, training, and effort.

The High-Performance Cycle

Effective organizations must take steps to ensure high levels of employee motivation and satisfaction to maintain desired levels of performance. It is now possible to use goal-setting theory to describe a high-performance cycle that helps us to better understand the phenomena of employee motivation and satisfaction (see Figure 9.6).[53] The cycle begins with high demands or challenges set for the employee and is operationalized in the form of specific and difficult

FIGURE 9.6

The high-performance cycle

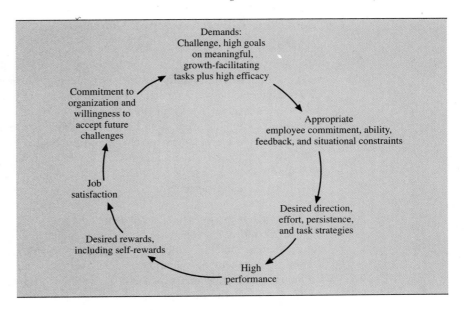

goals plus high self-efficacy. If appropriate levels of employee commitment, ability, feedback, situational constraints, and task strategies result in behavior direction, effort, persistence, and task-specific strategies, then high performance will occur. Next, if measured performance results in desired rewards (including self-rewards), the employee will experience high satisfaction.

The consequence of high satisfaction is increased employee commitment to the organization and an increased propensity to remain on the job.[54] Such employees are likely to accept future challenges or demands, and by so doing, cause the cycle to repeat itself. In work environments where the components of the cycle are not present, the result is a low-performance cycle. For example, employees experiencing dissatisfaction may *(a)* quit their jobs, *(b)* avoid work, *(c)* engage in psychological defenses such as drug abuse, *(d)* protest, *(e)* become defiant by refusing to do what is asked, and *(f)* exhibit aggressive behavior in the form of thefts and assault.[55] The most likely effect of dissatisfaction is turnover.

It is important to note that the high-performance model does not imply a direct link between satisfaction and productivity. However, the model does demonstrate two ways in which these variables are related. First, when equity exists, that is, rewards are commensurate with performance, high performance leads to satisfaction. Second, satisfaction only leads to future high performance if it results in commitment to specific and challenging goals that are supported by goal mechanisms and moderators such as ability, feedback, appropriate levels of task complexity, and situational constraints.

Supporting Characteristics of Motivation

As we have seen, goal-setting should be considered a motivational technique designed to increase a person's productivity. To fully appreciate the effectiveness of goal setting, it is necessary to understand how a properly designed and implemented system satisfies the requirements of effective motivation. The following characteristics represent those which must be present if managers are going to motivate their subordinates to perform at peak levels. Clearly, the more of these characteristics the manager builds into the motivational process, the greater will be the probability of success. The following represent nine factors generally considered critical to successful implementation of any motivational program.[56]

1. Motivation Is Not an All-or-Nothing Process

Figure 9.7 indicates that there is an upper and a lower limit to the practical range of subordinate productivity. A minimum to employee performance must be set by management to help ensure long-term organizational survival within an industry and a manager's own survival within the organization. In the private sector, if the quality or price of products and services offered are not competitive, organizations will increasingly find it difficult to compete. Management, through the evaluation process (see Chapter 13), continually monitors results and behaviors to ensure that employees maintain desired standards.

In government organizations, employees must function above a set lower limit. If they do not, then public officials are unlikely to be re-elected. Even in the case of monopolies, a minimum level of performance must be achieved. If not, then customers and clients will seek out substitutes. For example, if the price of electric heat becomes too high because of a poorly managed organization, customers will look for substitute sources of heat (i.e., wind, oil, wood, solar, etc.).

FIGURE 9.7

Understanding the limits of motivation

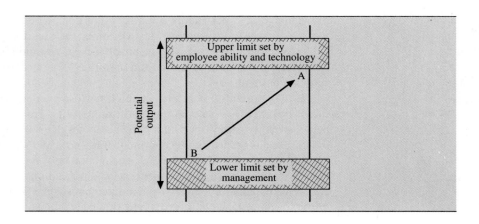

Situational constraints interact directly with an employee's ability to produce an upper limit to performance.[57] Specifically, situational constraints such as *(a)* job-related information, *(b)* tools and equipment, *(c)* materials and supplies, *(d)* budgetary support, *(e)* required services and help from others, *(f)* task preparation (i.e., previous experience, training and education), *(g)* time availability, and *(h)* work environment (i.e., noise level, temperature, etc.) are likely to directly determine the upper limit to performance and the employee's motivation to perform. Furthermore, because situational constraints directly affect the top end of the potential performance distribution (that is, of highly able and motivated employees) their effect is to reduce the range between low performers and high performers.[58]

Situational constraints also play a role in determining affective reactions of employees toward their work environments.[59] The effect of situational constraints on frustration, stress, and job satisfaction levels is likely to be greatest when employees perceive that they cannot control or manipulate their environment[60] and when employees are highly able and motivated.[61] Employees who work in environments where severe situational constraints limit their performance and result in prolonged periods of frustration and stress, are likely to lower their expectancies of future success. Individuals who have been conditioned to expect severe constraints may continue to perform poorly even when constraints are removed.[62] In other words, they have learned to believe that increased effort will not lead to increased performance.

In less severe settings, removal of constraints may result in increased performance. In this case, however, the increase is likely to result from two factors. Increases in productivity will first reflect a better utilization of existing abilities. Second, as employees increase their expectancies, that is, the perception that effort will lead to success, increased motivation will result in further performance improvements. The first type of increase is likely to occur immediately and the second type of increase will occur over time.

Situational constraints must also be considered when attempting to improve performance through training, job redesign or goal setting.[63] Such efforts are likely to fail if managers do not first consider and manage existing environmental constraints. Unless the upper limit is raised by removing situational constraints, an employee's desire to increase performance may only result in increased frustration and dissatisfaction. The employee has the ability and motivation, but environment prevents him or her from reaching desired goals. Therefore, one of the first steps to any successful change program should be the early identification and removal of situational constraints.

If managers do not know where the upper limit is, they run the risk of setting goals or standards of performance that are beyond the individual's ability or motivation to achieve. In either case, it is unlikely that employees will activate the four basic mechanisms of goal setting outlined in Figure 9.1: attention, effort, persistence, and strategic planning. Managers must accept that if they cannot answer yes to the questions, "Is it possible for my subordinates to achieve this goal?" and "Is there something in it for my subordinates?"

they should not expect standards or goals to be reached. Expectations and standards that are set above the upper limits are likely to produce conflict and frustration rather than an increase in productivity.

2. Incremental Improvement without Frustration

To maintain high levels of motivation, and cause incremental improvement over time, managers must be able to incrementally improve employees' performance without frustration. This can be accomplished by setting goals just beyond subordinates' present abilities. Such goals are likely to be perceived as difficult, but **if** subordinates experiment, observe, and copy successful others; undertake personal research or self-development; and receive support and encouragement from their immediate boss or co-workers, they are likely to maintain motivation and improve personal abilities over time. These "ifs" remind us that motivation cannot be taken for granted. Rather, managers must make a conscious effort to create an environment that fosters and maintains high levels of subordinate motivation and results in high self-efficacy.

Figure 9.8 demonstrates how the process of incremental improvement can be linked to the goal-setting process. Performance curve A represents the existing performance range for a particular subordinate given different levels of task difficulty. The relationship between task difficulty and performance is represented by a curvilinear relationship for the following reasons. Levels of task difficulty below X fall short of the subordinate's current ability level and as such do not challenge the individual. Consequently, there is little intrinsic motivation to perform (i.e., the job itself does not challenge, provide opportunities for achievement, growth, etc.). Furthermore, task difficulty levels below X do not take advantage of the employee's existing skill base, and as a result do not adequately tap his or her abilities. Closely related is the psychological response of subordinates who ask, "Why work hard to produce an outcome that

FIGURE 9.8

Understanding the concept of stretch

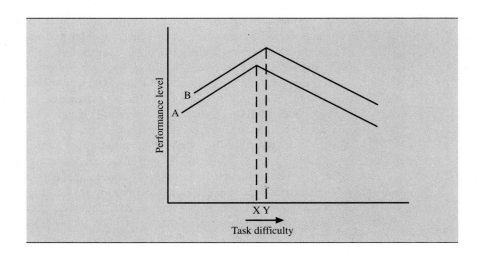

is by definition easy?" This last point can best be understood by considering the children's story about the race between the tortoise and the hare. The hare believed there would be no contest between himself and the tortoise, and therefore did not put out the required effort to win. Consequently, performance for the hare was low and he lost the race.

At some point, X, there is a maximum match between task difficulty and ability that will result in maximum motivation and performance. If task difficulty exceeds this level, the subordinate's abilities become taxed, and the perceived "expectancy" of being successful declines. As the subordinate's expectancy of success declines, so does motivation and, eventually, performance. However, if the goal is set just beyond the existing optimum level, motivated employees will seek to develop and grow. As indicated above, they will experiment, engage in self-development, ask questions, etc. Where subordinates are not at their peak theoretical level of performance, the process of stretch, coupled with managerial support, should result in a new optimum level of task difficulty, that is, Y. This results from a movement of the performance curve upward and to the right; that is, the employee's performance curve A changes to performance curve B. This shifting of the performance curve upward and to the right can be continued until individuals approach their theoretical upper limit for personal performance.

Assigning goals that are difficult (just above the employee's current abilities) also affects the employee's self-efficacy. The act of assigning challenging goals communicates to the employee that he or she is considered competent by the manager. In other words, the manager has confidence in the employee's ability to perform. Self-efficacy is also increased when the manager shares task information with the employee and allows the employee to participate in the development of usable task strategies. Finally, by providing positive feedback as the employee incrementally improves, the manager strengthens the subordinate's confidence in achieving the next level of difficulty.

Problems will appear when the manager does not know where the upper limit is for each subordinate and inadvertently sets goals beyond it. Similarly, attempts to make incremental shifts that are beyond the subordinate's ability to learn in the short run will also prove unsuccessful. Problems can also occur if managers do not recognize existing situational constraints that prevent successful goal achievement, or if they fail to develop a supportive environment designed to facilitate and encourage subordinate development. If any of these conditions exists, then the employee will experience excessive frustration. It is this excessive frustration that leads to unproductive employee behavior (see Figure 9.9).[64]

The key to managing subordinate frustration is to ensure that it remains within an acceptable range for the subordinate. Successful managers must be able to recognize when situational constraints or personal barriers block their subordinates from achieving an accepted goal. If subordinates are not initially successful (arrows 1–3), they will attempt to achieve the desired goal through alternative means. However, for each subordinate, a point will be reached where continued positive attempts to overcome existing barriers will be replaced with

FIGURE 9.9

*Managing
subordinate
frustration*

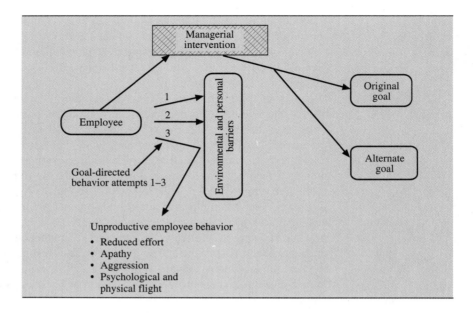

unproductive behavior (i.e., reduced effort, apathy, aggression, and psychological or physical flight). The effective manager must be able to determine
when to act and what to do to prevent this from happening.

If managers intervene too soon, they may become a crutch to their subordinates. In the worst case scenario, whenever subordinates have a problem,
they will come to the manager for a solution rather than solving it themselves.
Multiply this by the total number of subordinates reporting to a manager and
the effective work day will be reduced significantly. However, if the manager
waits too long, the subordinate reaches a point at which frustration becomes
debilitating and unproductive.

The type of management intervention employed will reflect the unique
requirements of the situation, the resources available to the manager, and the
subordinate's personality. Simple encouragement and support will work in some
situations, while sophisticated modeling and training activities will be required
in others. In still other situations, it may be necessary to alter the goals being
sought or even the physical environment in which the employee functions. To
make timing and content decisions about interventions effectively, managers
must have the requisite knowledge about their staff and their environment.

3. Recognize the Existence of Subordinate Needs

One of the most basic conditions necessary for subordinate motivation is the
existence of unsatisfied subordinate needs (see Figure 9.10). Any process
designed to create a motivational environment must facilitate need satisfaction at the subordinate level. This requirement applies whether you are an internalist (one who believes that the actual needs profile of the subordinate must

FIGURE 9.10

The relationship between unsatisfied needs and motivation

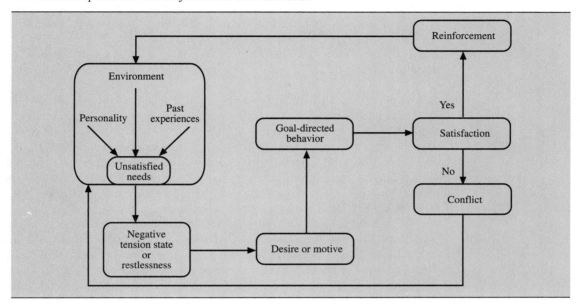

be identified and articulated) or an externalist (one who believes that the only variables that should be considered are those that can be observed (that is, behavior and consequences). In other words, for a motivational system to work, it must facilitate goal satisfaction. If not, employees will significantly reduce personal effort.

For example, consider the following situation described during a training workshop and the resulting overall motivational climate it implies. One of the organization's plant managers would meet all new employees on their first day of employment. The plant manager would then request the new employee to roll up his shirt sleeves and put the exposed fist and forearm into a bucket of water. The plant manager would then tell the employee to take out his hand, and then he would ask, "Do you see any difference in the bucket?" Invariably, the new employee would respond no, to which the plant manager would reportedly reply: "Well, that's the difference you'll make to this organization—screw up once and you're out of here!" The fact that this particular plant was located in an area of high unemployment gave the manager's threat added weight. Given such a motivational climate, it is questionable whether any higher order needs could be satisfied. Nor could employees feel secure about their jobs. As a result, they were described as doing just enough to keep their jobs and nothing more. In addition, several participants also indicated that as soon as they could find alternative employment they would quit.

Implied in this example is the argument that motivation will not occur unless there is a high probability that meaningful rewards will follow performance of desired behaviors. For this to take place, managers must *(a)* identify consequences under their control, *(b)* make the subordinate aware of an existing link between performance, or behavior, and consequences, and *(c)* ensure that a match between the subordinate's need profile and the consequences is made available.

4. Managers Must Identify Rewards under Their Control

To manage the motivational process effectively, it is important for managers to identify all potential rewards over which they have control. This knowledge is crucial to managers' ability to reward subordinates differentially, that is, reinforce high performers or subordinates who demonstrate incremental improvement. Unfortunately, many managers fail to take the time to identify the full range of rewards over which they have control. As a result, they frequently limit their search to what we refer to as the "big three," that is, money, promotion, and job enrichment. When such tunnel vision occurs and the "big three" are not available, managers give up on motivation because, they argue, there is nothing they can offer. As Figure 9.11 indicates, creative managers have many reward options open to them when attempting to motivate subordinates.[65] The key is for managers to take the time to develop an inventory of rewards that are under their control and, based upon knowledge about subordinates, and past successes and failures, identify those which are most likely to act as reinforcers, that is, act to increase or maintain desired behavior.

5. Match Reward Opportunities with Subordinate Needs

Critical to any successful motivational climate is the ability of the manager to match available rewards with the unique needs profile of each subordinate. Figure 9.12 indicates that if an employee's dominant set of unsatisfied needs originates at one level, maximum motivation will occur when the available goals and motivational programs match that level of emphasis. For example, if subordinates' dominant set of unsatisfied needs can be described as growth-oriented, one would expect minimum motivational change by offering them more money. Conversely, if the employee's dominant set of unsatisfied needs can best be described as existence-oriented, one would not expect job enrichment to increase motivation. In short, only when the employees believe that their needs will be satisfied is it likely that internal motivation will occur.

This matching can be accomplished in at least three general ways. First, from an internalist's point of view, managers can attempt to explicitly identify the unique needs profile for each of their subordinates and then introduce the motivational programs likely to satisfy the employees' needs. Some researchers and practitioners, however, would argue that this is not possible, given the complexity of human personality, or not necessary,

FIGURE **9.11**

Identifying available rewards

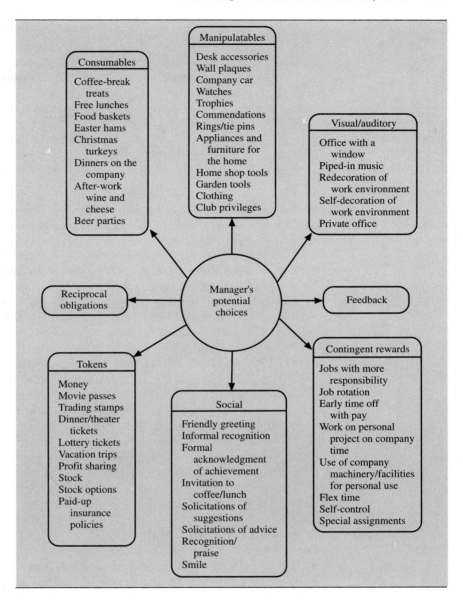

given the availability of a simpler alternative. Critics of the internalist's approach would argue that managers need only deal with observable behaviors, consequences, and resulting changes in behavior to ensure matching. If matching is taking place, then the desired performance or behavior remains steady or increases. If matching is not taking place, then the motivation program must be modified to ensure that it does. There is a third alternative, which combines these two approaches in such a way as to take advantage of

FIGURE 9.12

*Matching
consequences and
employee needs*

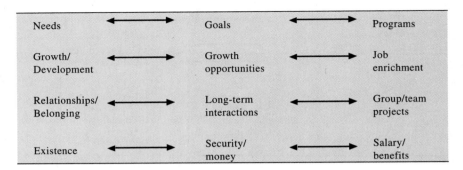

the benefits of both. Alternative three allows the manager to take advantage of all available information, that is, information about both internal needs and observable behaviors.

6. Link Desired Behavior and Performance with Appropriate Rewards

To obtain maximum employee motivation, it is important to make explicit the link between desired performance, or behavior, and desired rewards. If employees fail to see this link, then it is less likely that they will perform or behave in a manner consistent with the manager's goals. Failure to make employees aware of this link causes the motivational climate to become too informal, unstructured, and random, with the consequence being undirected motivation. But this link, when made explicit and carried through in operational terms, becomes the basis for differential reward. Without differential rewards, poor performers will be treated in the same manner as high performers or employees demonstrating incremental improvements. Failure to differentially reward occurs when everyone in the organization receives a Christmas turkey or ham regardless of performance or when merit increases are replaced by across-the-board salary increases and as a result both high and low performers receive the same raise. Such a condition is one of the quickest ways to destroy employee motivation.

7. Ensure Justice When Motivating

Organizational justice has long been recognized as an important requirement for effective organizational performance and employee satisfaction.[66] Behavioral scientists have also identified two key dimensions of organizational justice. They are distributive justice and procedural justice.[67] (See Figure 9.13.)

Employees who believe that outcomes received do not appropriately reflect their inputs (effort, experience, education, etc.) are likely to experience feelings of distributive injustice.[68] Management must recognize that subordinates are continually assessing the degree to which personal outcomes are fair and equitable. This evaluation process will occur on two levels. The first level (arrow 1, Figure 9.13), occurs when employees compare their inputs (time,

FIGURE 9.13

Perceived inequity and its impact on motivation

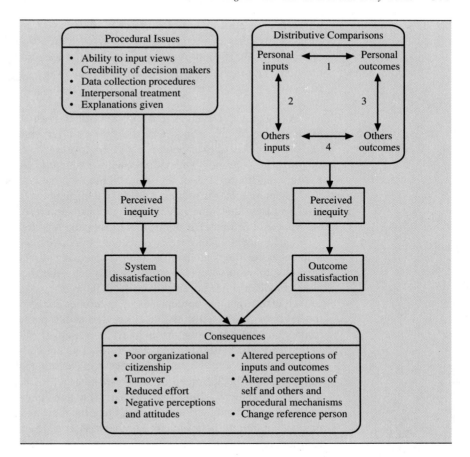

energy, resources, opportunity costs, etc.) and the rewards or outcomes they receive. If the perceived value of the employees' inputs is greater than the perceived value of the rewards received, then perceived inequity occurs. However, because employees do not work in a vacuum they also engage in other comparisons (arrows 2–4). Therefore, an individual may be satisfied with the ratio of personal outcomes to personal input. However, this satisfaction can quickly become reversed if the employee's personal ratio compares unfavorably to the output–input ratio of others (relevant others receive greater rewards for the same level of input or receive the same rewards even though they input less).

Employees who believe that procedures supporting distributive decisions are unfair will likely perceive procedural injustice.[69] The procedures supporting distributive decisions become suspect if employees believe they cannot adequately input their views, or believe they have no control over how the process works.[70] For example, employees are more likely to be satisfied with performance appraisal and reviews if they have had an opportunity to express their views during their reviews.[71] Perceived procedural injustice can also occur if employees question how decision makers were selected, methods for collecting information, the available avenues of appeal, ground rules for evaluating rewards, or the built-in safeguards for avoiding abuse of power.[72]

Along with the formal sources of procedural injustice just described, research evidence has demonstrated that the type of interpersonal treatment received and the adequacy of explanations given employees can also affect their perception of procedural justice. Individuals who are treated honestly, courteously or politely, and with respect are more likely to perceive the process leading up to outcome decisions as fair.[73] Similarly, a manager's willingness to explain how and why distributive decisions were made increases the likelihood that employees will perceive distributive procedures as fair.[74]

As Figure 9.13 indicates, perceived injustice can have catastrophic consequences for the organization and the manager in particular. The employee's response to such perceived injustice may be either behavioral or psychological.[75] For example, an employee who believes rewards are inadequate can reduce effort or alter perceptions or outcomes received or personal inputs. If the level of perceived injustice is great, and the perception occurs often, the impact on employee behavior is likely to be significant. The consequences are varied and will likely reflect the individual's personality and the dynamics of the situation.[76] Nevertheless, the evidence is clear that subordinates who believe that they have been treated unfairly will attempt to redress the imbalance. As a result, managers should not be surprised to meet with higher levels of subordinate dissatisfaction, poor organizational citizenship (that is, unwillingness to cooperate, help others, or otherwise engage in any behavior designed to improve the quality of work life for others), high turnover, reduced effort, and expressed negative perceptions toward the managers, their unit, and the organization. To prevent such negative consequences, any motivational process must ensure perceived justice.

The following example will demonstrate the importance of perceived justice. During a workshop, a participant related the following story. The comments made were in response to an overhead diagram similar to Figure 9.12. As it turned out, the company had in the past given out turkeys as a Christmas bonus. However, because of cost-cutting measures the company had discontinued the practice approximately 12 years ago. A new president had recently been appointed, who set up a series of presidential meetings throughout the organization to meet the staff. As it turned out, one of the most frequently asked questions was, "When will the company bring back the turkeys?" This question so annoyed the president that he soon began all future question-and-answer periods with the statement that Christmas turkeys would not be reinstated and therefore it would be inappropriate to ask questions about them. Indeed, the turkey question became a companywide joke— at least for nonmanagement personnel.

However, the turkey story did not end there. Another workshop participant indicated that while working 40 feet off the ground on a high voltage tower he dropped a large bolt used in its construction. Each of these bolts was worth between three and four dollars. From that distance, the bolt lying on the ground reminded him of a turkey wing, and everyone knows a turkey has two wings. Therefore, he took another bolt out of his pouch and threw it to the ground. Since the first episode, this particular lineman has periodically dropped many metal turkey wings around the countryside as he works on the company's towers. From a personal point of view, he indicated such behavior made him feel good by offsetting the company's refusal to provide turkeys at Christmas time. A second revelation was that this particular employee was hired several years after the company had stopped distributing Christmas turkeys but still felt that the company was being unjust.

Why did such unproductive behavior occur? This employee felt that a turkey was his right even though he had never received one in the past. In addition, management had never clearly explained why the practice of distributing Christmas turkeys was stopped. Compounding the problem was management's failure to recognize the importance of a reward that was not one of the "big three." Clearly, in this organization, the Christmas turkeys, or lack of them, continued to play a role in its motivational climate.

8. Facilitate Performance

Another central element in any attempt to maintain high levels of motivation is the degree to which the manager facilitates subordinate performance or the subordinates' carrying out of desired behaviors. The consequence of effective facilitation is an increased subordinate expectation that if they try, success is possible. Without positive expectations, the subordinates will significantly curtail effort. Employees reflect this sentiment when they make the following statement: "Why break your back when you're not going to be successful anyway?" or "If you're going to fail and be punished anyway, why not just enjoy yourself and do what you want to do?" Therefore, it is in the best interest of managers to create an environment that facilitates subordinate success.

In keeping with the philosophy of this text, one of the best ways to accomplish this is to be an effective manager, that is, master all relevant knowledge, skills, and attitudes. More specifically, however, managers must learn to encourage subordinates, clarify subordinate role responsibilities and means–ends relationships. Where possible, they should train to reduce existing deficiencies, redesign jobs and where necessary simplify, buffer subordinates from environmental fluctuations, minimize the negative effects of situational constraints, provide meaningful feedback, and create an environment in which subordinates can learn from their mistakes. This brief list is not intended to be exhaustive, but rather only a sample of the types of activities that can be used to increase the "expectancy" component of subordinate motivation.

9. Build in Motivational Maintenance

The eight characteristics of effective motivation just described are crucial to any manager's attempt to motivate employees. The greater the number built into a motivational program, the greater the probability of success. This is especially true if the first two lines of offense, selection and training, have been successful. However, there remains one last component that, if ignored, may wipe out the gains of the first eight. We are referring to the issue of maintenance. Many managers make the error of assuming that once subordinates are motivated they will remain motivated. Put another way, once you have employees working at or near their peak capabilities, you can turn your attention to other motivational problems. Unfortunately, what happens is that the productive employee is ignored. These events may be described as supporting the "squeaky wheel syndrome."

In reality, however, if steps are not taken to maintain the high performer's existing motivational level, it too will begin to deteriorate. Simply put, it must be maintained. To do this, the manager must provide periodic rewards, feedback, stroking, or recognition to ensure that the subordinate's needs are being satisfied. If the implicit psychological contract between the subordinate and manager is not maintained (the subordinate provides loyalty, effort, skills, and experiences in return for security, rewards, opportunities for growth and development or challenging tasks) then the subordinate's performance will likely decline.

Assessing the Motivational Value of Goal Setting

The value of goal setting as a motivational tool is a function of its ability to facilitate the requirements of effective motivation. Table 9.1 summarizes the relationship between goal-setting characteristics and the requirements of an effective motivational program. Motivational requirements are listed on the horizontal margin, and goal-setting characteristics are listed on the vertical margin. If a particular goal-setting characteristic supports or facilitates a motivational requirement, an **X** is placed at the point of intersection. As indicated, all motivational requirements are supported or facilitated by one or more goal-setting characteristics. The net effect is that goal setting is a motivational tool that truly works.

The Goal-Setting Encounter

The goal-setting process involves a number of interactions between managers and their subordinates. Such interactions may be formal or semiformal meetings, or may be informal encounters designed to facilitate the monitoring,

TABLE 9.1   Matching between Goal-Setting Characteristics and Motivational Requirements

GOAL SETTING \ MOTIVATION	Motivation Is Not an All-or-Nothing Process	Incremental Improvement without Frustration	Recognize Employee Needs	Identify Available Rewards	Match Reward Opportunities with Employee Needs	Link Performance with Consequences	Ensure Justice	Facilitate Performance	Build in Maintenance
Articulate the specific objective or task to be done	X	X			X	X		X	
Assess goals in terms of difficulty	X	X						X	
Specify how employee success will be measured									X
Specify the criteria or standard of success and follow-up procedures		X			X	X	X		X
Clearly articulate consequences			X	X	X	X	X		
Specify the time span involved		X						X	
Jointly set goal priorities		X	X					X	
Specify strategies and tactics for goal attainment		X				X		X	
Clearly articulate the conditions under which performance will be required	X	X						X	

evaluation, and feedback activities critical to the success of the goal-setting process. Alternatively, the components of an effective goal-setting process may also be incorporated into broader management techniques including management by objectives (MBO) and performance appraisal and review (PAR). In the case of integrating the goal-setting process with PAR, the two activities become two halves of the PAR interview. Assuming an ongoing process, the evaluation component occurs during the first half of the PAR interview when the manager and the subordinate assess the subordinate's performance over the past evaluation period. Having completed the evaluation of the past review period (i.e., achievements, short falls, appropriate and inappropriate behaviors) attention can be turned to setting new goals for the upcoming period. Newly established goals will become the benchmarks for evaluation at the end of the new assessment period. More will be said about this integrated process in Chapter 13 when the process of performance appraisal and review is discussed in detail.

Whichever direction the process follows, however, a key element is the quality of the meeting between managers and their subordinates. Therefore, managers should ensure that the meeting's format is designed to achieve desired results. For greater detail refer to Appendix A at the end of this chapter. After the goal-setting meeting (or sequence of meetings) has been completed, the manager and the subordinate both should have a clear understanding of what is to be achieved by the subordinate. It is crucial that subordinates be committed to attaining the goals and thus be willing to devote time, energy, and resources to accomplish success.

Summary

Goal setting has been described as a motivational technique designed to improve subordinate performance. It achieves higher productivity by incorporating the key components of effective motivation, and by so doing *(a)* directs employee attention, *(b)* stimulates effort, *(c)* maintains perseverance and *(d)* causes the employee to analyze and plan future behavior. It was also pointed out that the actual structure of any goal-setting process must consider the employee's self-image, ability, and personality, as well as goal importance and organizational norms. Finally, goal-setting can be initiated internally within any department or can be infused into other ongoing programs such as a formalized MBO program or a performance appraisal and review program.

Appendix A
The Goal-Setting Meeting: Relevant Steps and Behaviors

Step 1

Effectively prepare for the interview:

- Select and establish an appropriate interviewing environment, when both parties have the time and have been forewarned, and are psychologically prepared for the encounter, in a location likely to be comfortable to both parties.
- Develop, as best as possible, pre-session understanding of the subordinate to be interviewed, his or her strong points and weak points; review behaviorally specific support material if available; familiarize yourself with the subordinate's performance track record.
- Identify the appropriate aids to be used during the interview (i.e., department/ organizational goal statement, production/service data for the department, subordinate's personal file, etc.).
- Develop your interview strategy before the actual interviewing session, especially for initial interviews (i.e., prepare a flexible script).
- Review good interviewing habits and attitudes as an interviewer (see step 2).
- Complete your own planning/goal-setting activities prior to the meeting, as well as reviewing those for your immediate boss and the organization as a whole.
- When appropriate, review subordinate's progress during the last review period.

Step 2

Establish rapport:

- Meet the employee at the door.
- Say hello, be sincere, and show enthusiasm.
- Address the employee by name, preferably by first name.
- If necessary (to desensitize), conduct small talk such as asking him or her how things are going on the job.
- Reinforce the subordinate's cooperation both verbally and nonverbally.
- Attempt to put to rest any early concerns the subordinate may have.
- Where appropriate, allow the individual to vent his or her emotions/negative feelings (much of what has been described in Step 2 can be built into a structured opening statement).

Step 3

Establishing two-way communication:

- Encourage the interviewee to express whatever he or she feels.

- Indicate how he or she and the department will benefit from the two of you working together.
- Ask the subordinate if there are any questions.
- Respond in full to all the subordinate's questions.
- Nod in agreement where appropriate.
- Use good eye contact when the subordinate is talking.
- Ask open-ended questions rather than those permitting simple yes or no answers.
- Allow the subordinate to respond fully, without cutting him or her off.
- Demonstrate empathic listening.

Step 4

Control the interview:

- Keep track of time.
- Move from one topic/issue to the next as each is adequately dealt with.
- Skip goals/issues that have already been adequately dealt with.
- Keep the subordinate from getting off on an unrelated (unimportant) tangent.
- Keep the subordinate from rambling on about areas already examined.
- Follow up on earlier goals/issues if new information is offered.
- Probe/repeat to ensure the subordinate's understanding and agreement, and that all information has been processed.

Step 5

Identify and articulate relevant goals. Step 5 has been built around the nine characteristics of effective goal setting. In this step attempt to obtain the desired level of specificity, clarity, understanding, and commitment necessary to help ensure employee motivation.

Step 6

Close the interview:

- Indicate your personal appreciation for the subordinate's help, time, and cooperation.
- Repeat agreed-upon goals and objectives as well as relevant attainment steps/behaviors.
- Repeat the benefits to him or her and to the organization.
- Indicate the type of follow-up, if any.
- Ask for any final questions, concerns, or comments.
- If it appears that this employee is especially a "problem employee" it may be necessary to write down the agreed-upon attainment steps.
- Thank the interviewee again for the cooperation and escort him or her to the door.

Exercises

9.1 Developing Job Skills and Supporting Work Standards

To ensure your success as a manager, it is important that you determine relevant job dimensions and supporting behavioral standards for your subordinates. These are necessary to give direction to the subordinate and useful for you later as a basis for evaluation and development. This exercise will help you understand the process by which managers establish relevant job dimensions and behavioral standards—goals, objectives, attainment steps or behaviors—for their subordinates.

Step 1. The class will form groups of five to six individuals each. It will be the responsibility of each group to construct a set of relevant job dimensions and behavioral standards for a particular job. (These behavioral standards must be behaviorally specific to be effective.) Select from within each group a particular job to use as a basis for discussion. The job should be one that is currently performed or has been performed by one of your group's members. Be sure to select a job that provides sufficient variety and detail to ensure a good discussion within the group. It is also helpful if the job selected is one with which other group members are somewhat familiar.

(*Option:* the instructor may ask the class to consider a job with which all students are familiar.) (5 minutes)

Step 2. The individual whose job is selected for discussion should provide a general description of what the work entails or what the worker is responsible for. The individual describing the job may consider the following points:

- Tasks performed.
- Procedures used.
- Personal responsibilities.
- Actual job behaviors required such as decision making, physical actions, communications.
- Machinery/equipment used.
- Products made.
- Services rendered.
- Nature of supervision.
- Working conditions/physical environment.
- Formal interaction required.
- Informal interactions likely to occur.
- Knowledge needed on the job.

Nonreporting members of each group should actively participate during this step by asking questions for the purpose of clarification. Their questions will ensure that all relevant information about the target job is covered. In addition, nonreporting group members are strongly advised to take notes to ensure active participation during Step 3 and Step 4. (5 to 10 minutes)

Step 3. Each group will construct a list of job dimensions that it believes must be present if the person performing the job is to succeed. Job dimensions relate to general skills, abilities, and behavioral categories which, when taken together, largely determine the degree of success or failure achieved by the jobholder. When deciding on the relevance of a particular job dimension, consider how that dimension relates to overall performance. If no relevant link is found, that particular job dimension should not be listed.

In addition to the job dimensions listed in Exercise 8.3 the following additional examples are frequently used.

- Assertiveness and enthusiasm.
- Clerical ability.
- Intellectual/cognitive ability.
- Manual skills.
- Physical ability.
- Responsibility and maturity.
- Technical knowledge.

This list is not exhaustive and is intended only as a guide to help your group construct its list. Although certain job dimensions can be generalized across jobs, each job frequently has unique requirements. Feel free to consider and list whatever job dimensions you believe are relevant. (15 minutes)

Step 4. Each group will identify at least three examples of job-specific behaviors that can be used to document whether an employee is performing at an acceptable level. Only through the identification and observation of job-specific behaviors can a supervisor assess employee performance objectively and give meaningful feedback. Time constraints limit your discussion to two relevant job dimensions. (20 minutes)

Step 5. The class will assemble to review and discuss selected examples from each group's list.

(Less than one hour for all steps.)

9.2 The Goal-Setting Meeting

For the purpose of this exercise, the class will break up into small groups of five to six individuals to prepare for the forthcoming goal-setting meeting with a new executive secretary. In this case, the role of the new executive secretary will be played by the professor. You are to role-play Bob D. Manding, the director of planning for a municipality located in the Northeast. You have a number of important behavioral standards that you want the person who fills the position of executive secretary to meet, particularly with regard to the problems you had with your last executive secretary, Mary Loseit. Today you plan to meet with L. Benton, who has been hired to replace Mary. Mary had been hired one week after you were promoted to the position of department head. Mary was fired after only three months on the job. You now have had some time to clarify in your own mind what should be expected from an executive secretary.

L. Benton was not hired because of his experience but because he was bright, had a college degree in English, and came with great references. Because of your experience with Mary, who had been a secretary for many years, you want to hire someone with limited experience whom you can mold to your standards. In this way, you will make sure that L. Benton knows what you want, is committed, and understands the basis upon which he will be evaluated in the future.

You believe that the following are the job (skill) dimensions required for any executive secretary.

- Clerical skill and competence.
- Dependability.
- Interpersonal skill and competence (with both co-workers and the public).
- Works steadily.
- Maintains a clean work area.
- Ability to handle stress and pressure (from co-workers, children, and the public).
- Well-organized leadership (the executive secretary is responsible for the supervision of all clerical personnel in the planning department).
- Honesty.

Each group is responsible for developing a script for the forthcoming meeting. Please follow the steps outlined below.

Step 1. Select one of the group's members to role-play Bob D. Manding.

Step 2. The group should decide upon the appropriate goals and standards for each job dimension listed above. What specific behaviors would you like to see in the new executive secretary so that the candidate can be given a high rating for each?

Class time constraints will limit your use of all the dimensions. However, you should use at least three. You may also add one appropriate dimension of your own. (20 to 30 minutes)

Step 3. Work as a group to develop a script for handling the meeting with the new executive secretary. In preparing your script, pay particular attention to the learning points (discussed or distributed by the professor) on what to do during a goal-setting meeting. All steps should be incorporated into your script.

Step 4. Once your script is developed, take 10 to 15 minutes to practice the planned meeting within your own group. One group member should play the role of the new executive secretary, one should play Bob Manding's role, and the remaining members should act as observers.

To gain a better understanding of Bob D. Manding and the problems he faced with Mary Loseit, you should review the excerpts from her personnel file listed below. It was Mary's behavior that caused Bob to seek her dismissal.

(You now have one hour and 15 minutes to prepare for the role play.)

Excerpts from Mary Loseit's Personnel File

1. During May, June, and July, she came to work late 19 times despite repeated warnings.

2. Mary was frequently unable to tell others where Bob was, even after Bob told her about fixed appointments.

3. When assigned work by Bob, she rarely, if ever, delegated any of this work to other secretaries who reported to her for work assignments.

4. On at least three occasions, Mary did not call in to inform Bob that she was ill. Bob had to call her to find this out.

5. She frequently made personal telephone calls on office time.

6. Mary was often criticized for extended coffee breaks in the cafeteria. When this occurred, Mary was usually talking with John Busybody.

7. The inventory under Mary's control was frequently out of stock (e.g., toner for the copier, 11-inch by 14-inch envelopes, overhead felt-tip pens, etc.). Mary's solution was to borrow what she needed from another department.

8. When giving typing or reports for Mary to complete, Bob frequently had to return the work to her for corrections. A typical error: When asked to make 25 copies of a single sheet and one copy of a 50-page report, Mary made one copy of the single sheet and 25 copies of the 50-page report.

9. When Bob returned work for corrections, Mary complained about working conditions in the department and the excessive pressure Bob placed on her. No one else in the department made similar complaints.

10. When attending meetings in Bob's place, Mary was often late or unprepared; she had not reviewed the agenda or support material. Mary also found it difficult to explain to Bob what major decisions had been made at these meetings.

11. Bob often received complaints about the abusive language and behavior Mary demonstrated when interacting with co-workers and employees outside the planning department.

12. Before Mary was hired, Bob was able to find whatever he wanted in the departmental files. Within two months of hiring Mary, he had difficulty finding anything.

13. During slack periods, Mary would manicure her nails or read a book rather than take the initiative to start a new project or help a fellow employee.

14. On several occasions, Mary was overheard criticizing the planning department, Bob, and the municipality.

This list does not represent a complete documentation of the problems Bob had with Mary. Therefore, when attempting to understand what is important to Bob, you should make any additional assumptions you believe are consistent with the material provided and that represent how an executive secretary should act.

9.3 Planning for Contingencies

Once a manager has developed meaningful goals for the future, it is also important to consider potential problems that may occur as the project, support activities, and personal initiatives are brought on-line. The key is to anticipate problems that may occur in the future; you are attempting to guard against becoming a victim of Murphy's three laws:

Nothing is as simple as it seems.

Everything takes longer than you think it should.

If anything can go wrong, it will.

The actual steps you should take to guard against Murphy's laws are quite simple. For managers, the hard part is a willingness to take the time to analyze their goals within the context of existing and future environments. This exercise is designed to help you overcome this problem.

You are asked to consider a particular decision presently facing a manager working for a large organization. Consider the following steps.

Step 1. In the case presented, you will first develop a list of possible adverse situations that might occur some time in the future as you work toward the attainment of your goal(s). For example, if you are organizing a practice for a soccer team you are coaching, and it is the first indoor, after-school practice, one possible adverse situation is that you and your team cannot get into the gym because the doors are locked. In Step 1, the list of adverse situations represent potential problems of a general nature. When constructing your list, be as thorough as possible. (10 to 15 minutes)

Step 2. The class will assemble to compare the output of each group with the instructor's list.

Step 3. List the causes of each adverse situation listed in Step 2. Causes are events that, if they occur, produce the adverse situation. There are many possible causes, and it is in the best interest of effective managers to identify them before they occur. In the soccer practice case, you might ask "What is likely to occur in the future to cause the gym door to be locked?" In response, you might jot down the following:

- Janitorial staff was not informed.
- Janitor is delayed on his way to the school.
- The wrong date was listed on the work order.
- The wrong school was listed on the work order.

(15 minutes)

Step 4. Assess each cause in terms of its risk (i.e., its likelihood of occurring and its seriousness). In the "Likelihood" column of your work sheet, you should indicate on a scale of 1 to 10 the probability (1 being low and 10 being high) that a particular cause will occur. In the "Seriousness" column, you should indicate on the same scale of 1 to 10 the seriousness of a particular adverse consequence. Because you are dealing with an uncertain future, you will be guessing as to the likelihood and seriousness of each cause. Nevertheless, it is the manager's responsibility to make an educated guess—based upon past experience and knowledge—about what these values will be. Use the work sheets provided.

(Approximately 15 minutes)

Step 5. Consider each cause and come up with a course of action that will prevent or offset the cause. In the soccer practice case, to prevent the cause that the janitorial staff was not informed by a third party requires that you get written verification from the janitorial staff when they were or were not informed about the gym door, or contact the janitor yourself. An action designed to offset the cause is to bring your own set of keys. In either case, you reduce the probability that such a cause will occur again. This in turn increases the probability that you will achieve your goal(s).

(30 minutes)

Step 6. After all the small groups have completed their tasks, they will assemble to discuss each group's decisions.

(Please begin by reading the following case. You can make whatever assumptions you want to breathe more life into your discussion. The assumptions you make must be reasonable and consistent with the facts presented in the case.)

PLANNING THE CONVENTION

You are Jim Turner, an assistant program manager, newly hired by the Midland Software and Hardware Association (MSHA). Your job is to plan and manage several annual conferences and conventions that MSHA sponsors. Your first project assignment is a large computer and software convention (CSC) scheduled in two months. You were put in charge of the CSC because your predecessor unexpectedly gave Midland a month's notice and then left to work for another organization. Although you have scheduled conferences before, past conferences were small compared to this assignment. When you were hired, no one at MSHA was aware that your predecessor was planning to quit.

Your immediate superior is Susan Lipton, whom you have found to be very demanding and, even worse, a perfectionist. Furthermore, she loves detail and appears to enjoy finding other people's mistakes. She is also considered one of the most influential individuals in MSHA and is known for her long memory.

The schedule of sessions and evening activities, exhibitors, and presenters for CSC have been in place for over 18 months. One of the largest cities in the Southwest will host the convention, and the exhibition area will be housed in the city's largest hotel. However, given the large number of expected registrants, 25 to 50 percent of the rooms in three other hotels have been booked to provide overnight accommodations during the three-day convention. The closest of these hotels is five blocks away from the main hotel and the furthest is approximately 20 blocks away.

More than 300 exhibitors are scheduled to set up booths during the convention. The average space rented by exhibitors is about 400 square feet. The largest exhibitor demanded over 1,000 square feet. Several of the exhibits are ambitious and will take considerable time to construct because of their complexity and extensive structural or electrical requirements. All exhibit drawings and artwork have been received and filed, but your predecessor failed to verify many of the details with exhibitors. Susan apologized for your predecessor's oversight but has indicated that it is now your problem to work out the details with exhibitors.

The hotel maintains a busy schedule and has informed you that CSC will have three days to complete the full setup of exhibition cubicles. Exhibitions will be located on the sixth and seventh floors. Below the sixth floor are dining rooms, administrative offices, shops, an open-air lobby, and a second conference that is starting on the same day. This group is the International Association of Geography Teachers; the theme of their conference is computer-assisted instruction.

In addition to the exhibits, several hardware and software theory sessions that go on throughout the day are a major part of the CSC. A minimum of three sessions will take place at the same time. Sessions will be offered more than once to ensure that participants have an opportunity to attend all of them. Fortunately for you, the schedule of sessions has been completed. In addition to the daily sessions, two major dinners will be held during the exhibition. Although organizers estimate that approximately 3,500 people will attend the exhibits, only 1,000 are likely to attend the sit-down dinners. After each dinner, a well-known person in the computer industry will give a keynote speech. One speaker is best known for his research application packages in CBT (computer-based training), and the second is a world-renowned visionary in computer applications.

Although MSHA conferences and exhibitions are noted for their content, they are also given high marks for planned after-hours activities. This year's major event is a massive outdoor barbecue and rodeo. This activity has been successful at several other conventions, but it has never been tried by MSHA. MSHA has advertised its plans to roast sides of beef and whole lambs for the barbecue, and it has booked the arena for the rodeo.

You have an internal staff of 15 (excluding hotel and arena staff and municipal support) to use to complete all the tasks necessary to make CSC a success. Your job is complicated, however, by the unorganized condition in which your predecessor left things and the short time that now remains before the first exhibitors show up with their equipment. You cross your fingers and begin to plan.

End Notes

1. E. A. Locke and G. P. Latham, *Goal Setting: A Motivational Technique that Works,* Prentice Hall, Englewood Cliffs, N. J., 1984: 4.
2. E. A. Locke, K. N. Shaw, L. M. Saari, and G. P. Latham, "Goal setting and task performance," *Psychological Bulletin,* Vol. 90, No.1, 1981: 131.
3. Locke and Latham, 1984: 15.
4. A. J. Mento, R. Steel, and R. Karren, "A meta-analytical study of the effects of goal setting on task performance: 1966–1984," *Organizational Behavior and Human Decision Processes,* Vol. 39, 1987: 52–83.
5. Mento, Steel, and Karren, 1987: 74.
6. Locke, Shaw, Saari, and Latham, 1981: 126.
7. E. A. Locke and J. F. Bryan, "The directing function of goals in task performance," *Organizational Behavior and Human Performance,* Vol. 4, 1969: 35–42; E. A. Locke, N. Cartledge, and C. S. Kneer, "Studies of the relationship between satisfaction, goal setting, and performance," *Organizational Behavior and Human Performance,* Vol. 5, 1970: 135–138; J. R. Terborg, "The motivational components of goal setting," *Journal of Applied Psychology,* Vol. 61, 1976: 613–621; E. Z. Rothkoph and M J. Billington, "Goal-guided learning from text: Inferring a descriptive processing model from inspection times and eye movements," *Journal of Educational Psychology,* Vol. 71, 1979: 310–327.

8. J. F. Bryan and E. A. Locke, "Parkinson's law as a goal-setting phenomenon," *Organizational Behavior and Human Performance,* Vol. 2, 1976: 258–275; J. R. Terborg and H. E. Miller, "Motivation, behavior and performance: A closer examination of goal setting and monetary incentives," *Journal of Applied Psychology*, Vol. 63, 1978: 29–39; A. Bandura and D. Cervone, "Self-evaluation and self-efficacy mechanisms governing the motivational effects of goal systems," *Journal of Personality and Social Psychology*, Vol. 45, 1983: 1017–28; M. A. Brickner and P. A. Bukatko, "Locked into performance: Goal setting as a moderator of the social loafing effect," University of Akron, unpublished manuscript; S. M. Sales, "Some effects on role overload and role underload," *Organizational Behavior and Human Performance*, Vol. 5, 1970; 592–608; G. P. Latham and G. Yukl, "A review of research on the application of goal setting in organizations," *Academy of Management Journal*, Vol. 18, 1975: 824–845; G. P. Latham and J. J. Baldes, "The practical significance of Locke's theory of goal setting," *Journal of Applied Psychology,* Vol. 60, 1975: 187–191.

9. R. E. LaPorte and R. Nath, "Role of performance goals in prose learning," *Journal of Educational Psychology,* Vol. 68, 1976: 260–264; J. Bavelas and E. S. Lee, "Effect of goal level on performance: A trade-off of quantity and quality," *Canadian Journal of Psychology,* Vol. 32, 1978: 219–240; Locke, Shaw, Saari, and Latham, 1981; V. L. Huber, "Effects of task difficulty, goal setting, and strategy on performance of a heuristic task," *Journal of Applied Psychology,* Vol. 70, 1985: 492–504; H. K. Hall, R. S. Weinberg, and A. Jackson, "Effects of goal specificity, goal difficulty, and information feedback on endurance performance," *Journal of Sport Psychology,* Vol. 9, 1987: 43–54; E. A. Locke and G. P. Latham, *A Theory of Goal Setting and Task Performance,* Prentice Hall, Inc., Englewood Cliffs, N. J., 1990; G. P. Latham and E. A. Locke, "Self-regulation through goal setting," *Organizational Behavior and Human Decision Processes,* Vol. 50, 1991: 212–247.

10. Latham and Locke, 1991.

11. G. P. Latham, D. C. Winters, and E. A. Locke, "Cognitive and motivational effects of participation: A mediator study," *Journal of Organizational Behavior,* Vol. 15, 1994: 49–63.

12. Latham, Winters, and Locke, 1994.

13. E. A. Locke, G. P. Latham and M. Erez, "The determinants of goal commitment," *Academy of Management Review,* Vol. 13, No. 1, 1988: 23–39; Locke and Latham, 1990; Latham and Locke, 1991.

14. Latham and Locke, 1991: 217.

15. Locke and Latham, 1990; Latham and Locke, 1991.

16. Locke, Latham, and Erez, 1988; Locke and Latham, 1990.

17. H. Garland, "The influence of ability, assigned goals, and normative information in personal goals and performance," *Journal of Applied Psychology,* Vol. 68, 1983: 20–30; E. A. Locke, E. Frederick, E. Buckner, and P. Bobko, "Effects of previously assigned goals on self-set goals and performance," *Journal of Applied Psychology,* Vol. 69, 1984: 694–699; G. P. Latham and T. W. Lee, "Goal setting" in *Generalizing from Laboratory to Field Settings,* ed. E. A. Locke, Lexington Books, Lexington, Mass., 1986: 101–117;

18. G. R. Salancik, "Commitment and the control of organizational behavior and belief," in *New Directions in Organizational Behavior,* ed. B. M Staw and G. Salancik, St. Clair, Chicago, 1977: 1–54.

19. Locke and Latham, 1990: 135.

20. Locke, Latham, and Erez, 1988; Locke and Latham, 1990.

21. Locke, Latham, and Erez, 1988; E. A. Locke and G. P. Latham, 1990.

22. A. Bandura, *Social Foundations of Thought and Action: A Social Cognitive Theory,* Prentice Hall, Englewood Cliffs, N. J., 1986.

23. S. C. Hayes, I. Rosenfarb, E. Wulfert, E. D. Munt, Z. Korn, and R. D. Zettle, "Self-reinforcement effects: An artifact of social standard setting?" *Journal of Applied Behavioral Analysis,* Vol. 18, 1985: 201–214; K. D. McCaul, V. B. Hinsz and H. S. McCaul, "The effects of commitment to performance goals on effort," *Journal of Applied Social Psychology,* Vol. 17, 1987: 437–450; J. R. Hollenbeck, C. R. Williams, and H. J. Klein, " An empirical examination of the antecedents of commitment to difficult goals," *Journal of Applied Psychology,* Vol. 74, 1989: 18–23.

24. Bandura, 1986; I. L. Janis, and L. Mann, *Decision-Making: A Psychological Analysis of Conflict, Choice and Commitment,* The Free Press, New York, 1977.
25. G. R. Ferris and J. F. Porac, "Goal setting as impression management," *Journal of Psychology,* Vol. 117, 1984: 33–36.
26. Locke, Latham, and Erez, 1988; Locke and Latham, 1990.
27. Locke, Latham, and Erez, 1988; Locke and Latham, 1990.
28. A. J. Mento, N. D. Cartledge, and E. A. Locke, "Maryland vs. Michigan vs. Minnesota: Another look at the relationship of expectancy and goal difficulty to performance," *Organizational Behavior and Human Performance,* Vol. 25, 1980: 419–440; R. L. Oliver and A. P. Brief, "Sales manager's goal commitment correlates," *Journal of Personal Selling and Sales Management,* Vol. 3, No. 1, 1983: 11–17; V. L. Huber and M. A. Neale, "Effects of cognitive heuristics and goals on negotiator performance and subsequent goal setting," *Organizational Behavior and Human Decision Processes,* Vol. 38, 1986: 342–365.
29. M. E. Gist, "Self-efficacy: Implications for organizational behavior and human resource management," *Academy of Management Review,* Vol. 12, 1987: 472–485.
30. Locke, Latham, and Erez, 1988; Locke and Latham, 1990; Latham, Winters, and Locke, 1994.
31. J. C. Masters, W. Furman, and R. C. Barden, "Effects of achievement standards, tangible rewards, and self-dispensed achievement evaluations on children's task mastery," *Child Development,* Vol. 48, 1977: 217–224; I. Kirsch, "Tangible self-reinforcement in self-directed behavior modification projects," *Psychological Reports,* Vol. 43, 1978: 455–461; J. M. Ivancevich and J. T. McMahon, "The effects of goal setting, external feedback, and self-generated feedback on outcome variables: A field experiment," *Academy of Management Journal,* Vol. 25, No. 2, 1982: 359–372; Locke and Latham, 1990.
32. Locke, Latham, and Erez, 1988.
33. Locke and Latham, 1990.
34. Locke and Latham, 1990.
35. Locke and Latham, 1990.
36. Latham, Winters, and Locke, 1994.
37. Latham, Winters, and Locke, 1994.
38. Latham and Locke, 1991.
39. Locke and Latham, 1990; Latham and Locke, 1991.
40. Latham and Locke, 1991.
41. Locke, Shaw, Saari, and Latham, 1981: 132.
42. Locke and Latham, 1990.
43. Latham and Locke, 1991.
44. Bandura, 1986.
45. J. P. Wanous, "Effects of realistic job preview on job acceptance, job attitudes, and job survival," *Journal of Applied Psychology,* Vol. 58, 1973: 327–332; J. P. Wanous, "Organizational entry: Newcomers moving from outside to inside," *Psychological Bulletin,* Vol. 84, 1977: 601–618; J. P. Wanous, *Organizational Entry: Recruitment, Selection, and Socialization of Newcomers,* Addison-Wesley Publishing, Reading, Mass., 1980; S. L. Premack and J. P. Wanous, "Meta-analysis of realistic job preview experiments," *Journal of Applied Psychology,* Vol. 70, 1985: 706–719.
46. F. H. Kanfer and J. S. Phillips, *Learning Foundations of Behavior Therapy,* John Wiley & Sons, New York, 1970; F. H. Kanfer, "Self-regulation: Research, issues, and speculations," in *Behavior Modification and Clinical Psychology,* ed. C. Neuringer and J. Michaels, Appleton-Century-Crofts, New York, 1974; M. J. Mahoney, N. G. Moura, and T. C. Wade, "The relative efficacy of self-reward, self-punishment, and self-monitoring techniques for weight loss," *Journal of Counseling and Clinical Psychology,* Vol. 40, 1973: 404–407; E. L. Glynn, "Classroom applications of self-determined reinforcement," *Journal of Applied Behavior Analysis,* Vol. 3, 1970: 123–132.
47. Locke and Latham, 1990.
48. C. A. Frayne and G. P. Latham, "Application of social learning theory to employee self-management of attendance," *Journal of Applied Psychology,* Vol. 72, 1987: 387–392; C. A. Frayne and M. Geringer, "Self-management practices and performance of international joint venture general managers," paper presented at the annual meeting of the Academy of Management, San Francisco, 1990; Latham and Locke, 1991.
49. Latham and Locke, 1991: 213.
50. Frayne and Latham, 1987; Latham and Locke, 1991.
51. Locke and Latham, 1990; Latham and Locke, 1991.
52. Locke and Latham, 1990.

53. Figure 9.6 based upon material presented in Locke and Latham, 1990; E. A. Locke and G. P. Latham, "Work motivation: The high performance cycle," in *Work Motivation,* ed. U. Kleinbeck, H. Quast, H. Thierry, and H. Hacker, Erlbaum, Hillsdale, N. J., 1990; Latham and Locke, 1991.

54. Locke and Latham, 1990.

55. Locke and Latham, 1990.

56. R. M. Steers and L. W. Porter, *Motivation and Work Behavior,* McGraw-Hill, New York, 1987; F. Luthans, *Organizational Behavior,* 5th ed., McGraw-Hill, New York, 1989; J. L. Gibson, J. M. Ivancevich, and J. H. Donnelly, Jr., *Organizations: Behavior, Structure, Process,* Irwin, Burr Ridge, Ill., 1994.

57. L. H. Peters and E. J. O'Connor, "Situational constraints and work outcomes: The influences of a frequently overlooked construct," *Academy of Management Review,* Vol. 5, No. 3, 1980: 391–397; L. H. Peters, E. J. O'Connor, and C. J. Rudrof, "The behavioral and affective consequences of performance-relevant situational variables," *Organizational Behavior and Human Performance,* Vol. 25, 1980: 79–96.

58. Peters and O'Connor, 1980.

59. Peters and O'Connor, 1980; Peters, O'Connor, and Rudrof, 1980; O'Connor, L. H. Peters, C. J. Rudrof, and A. Pooyan, "Situational constraints and employee reactions: A partial field replication," *Group & Organization Studies,* Vol. 7, No. 4, December 1982: 418–428; J. S. Phillips and S. M. Freedman, "Situational performance constraints and task characteristics: Their relationship to motivation and satisfaction," *Journal of Management,* Vol. 10, No. 3, 1984: 321–331.

60. Peters, O'Connor, and Rudrof, 1980.

61. Peters and O'Connor, 1980.

62. Peters and O'Connor, 1980.

63. Peters, O'Connor, and Rudrof, 1980; Peters and O'Connor, 1980.

64. P. E. Spector, "Relationships of organizational frustration with reported behavioral reactions of employees," *Journal of Applied Psychology,* Vol. 60, 1975: 635–637; P. E. Spector, "Organizational frustration: A model and review of the literature," *Personnel Psychology,* Vol. 31, 1978: 281–297.

65. Figure 9.11 is based upon material presented in Luthans, *Organizational Behaviors,* 5th ed., McGraw-Hill, New York, 1989: 303.

66. J. Greenberg, "Organizational justice: Yesterday, today, and tomorrow," *Journal of Management,* Vol. 16, No. 2, 1990: 399–432.

67. G. C. Homans, *Social Behavior: Its Elementary Forms,* Harcourt, Brace, & World, New York, 1961; J. S. Adams, "Toward an understanding of inequity," *Journal of Abnormal and Social Psychology,* Vol. 67, 1963: 422–436; E. Walster, G. W. Walster, and E. Berscheid, *Equity: Theory and Research,* Allyn & Bacon, Boston, 1978; R. Vecchio, "Predicting worker performance in inequitable settings," *Academy of Management Review,* Vol. 7, 1982: 103–110; R. C. Husemann, J. D. Hatfield and E. W. Miles, "A new perspective on equity theory: The equity sensitivity construct," *Academy of Management Review,* Vol. 12, 1987: 222–234; J. Greenberg, "A taxonomy of organizational justice theories," *Academy of Management Review,* Vol. 12, No. 12, 1987: 9–22; J. Greenberg, "Equity and workplace status: A field experiment," *Journal of Applied Psychology,* November 1988: 606-613; Greenberg, 1990.

68. Homans, 1961; Adams, 1963; Walster, Walster, and Berscheid, 1978; J. Greenberg, " Approaching equity and avoiding inequity in groups and organizations," in *Equity and Justice in Social Behavior,* ed. J. Greenberg and R. L. Cohen, Academic Press, New York, 1982: 389–435; Greenberg, 1987; Greenberg, 1990.

69. J. Thibaut and L. Walker, *Procedural Justice: A Psychological Analysis,* Lawrence Erlbaum Associates, Hillsdale, N. J., 1975; E. A. Lind and T. Tyler, *The Social Psychology of Procedural Justice,* Plenum, New York, 1988; Greenberg, 1987; Greenberg, 1990.

70. Thibaut and Walker, 1975; J. Greenberg and R. Folger, "Procedural justice, participation, and the fair process effects in groups and organizations," in *Basic Group Processes,* ed. P. B. Paulus, Springer-Verlag, New York, 1983: 235–256; Lind and Tyler, 1988; Greenberg, 1990.

71. R. L. Dipboye and R. de Pontbraind, "Correlates of employee reactions to performance appraisals and appraisal systems," *Journal of Applied Psychology,* Vol. 66, 1981: 248–251; J. Greenberg, "Organizational performance appraisal procedures: What makes them fair?" in *Research on Negotiation in Organizations,* ed. R. J. Lewicki,

B. H. Sheppard, and M. H. Bazerman, Vol. 1, JAI Press, Greenwich, Conn., 1986: 25–41.

72. G. S. Leventhal, "What should be done with equity theory?" in *Social Exchange: Advances in Theory and Research,* ed. K. J. Gergen, M. S. Greenberg, and R. H. Willis, Plenum, New York, 1980: 27–55; G. S. Leventhal, J. Karuza and W. R. Fry, "Beyond fairness: A theory of allocation preferences," in *Justice and Social Interaction,* ed. G. Mikula, Springer-Verlag, New York, 1980: 167–218.

73. R. J. Bies, "Identifying principles of interactional justice: The case of corporate recruiting," in *Moving Beyond Equity Theory: New Directions in Research on Justice in Organizations,* R. J. Bies (Chair), symposium conducted at the meeting of the Academy of Management, Chicago, 1986; R. J. Lewicki, "The management of classroom justice: Instructor evaluations and concern for fairness," in *Procedural Fairness Theory and Research: Applications to Human Resource Management,* C. Martin (Chair), symposium conducted at the meeting of the Academy of Management, Washington, D.C., 1989; Greenberg, 1990.

74. R. J. Bies, "The predicament of injustice: The management of moral outrage," in *Research In Organizational Behavior: Vol. 9,* ed. L. L Cummings and B. M. Staw, JAI Press, Greenwich, Conn., 1987; R. J. Bies and D. L. Shapiro, "Interactional fairness judgments: The influence of causal accounts," *Social Justice Research,* Vol. 1, 1987: 199–218; T. R. Tyler and R. J. Bies, "Beyond formal procedures: The interpersonal context of procedural justice," in *Advances In Applied Social Psychology: Business Settings,* ed. J Carroll, Lawrence Erlbaum Associates, Hillsdale, N. J., 1989: 77–98; J. Greenberg, "Looking fair vs. being fair: Managing impressions of organizational justice," in *Research in Organizational Behavior: Vol. 12,* ed. B. M. Staw and L. L. Cummings, JAI Press, Greenwich, Conn., 1990: 111–157.

75. E. Walster, G. W. Walster and J. Thibault, *Equity: Theory and Research,* Allyn & Bacon, Boston, 1978.

76. Greenberg, 1990.

BUILDING AN EFFECTIVE TEAM

Objectives:

- To clarify the role that managers can play in developing and maintaining effective teams.
- To familiarize students with the stages commonly associated with team formation and management.
- To articulate a set of managerial behaviors necessary to operationalize the team process within any department.
- To provide students with an opportunity to practice their newly acquired skills.

The Importance of Teams[1]

"Subordinates carry the boss but effective teams lighten the load."

Managerial success is primarily built upon the accomplishments of subordinates. Consequently, successful managers are, in a manner of speaking, carried by subordinates who are motivated, know what is expected of them, have access to appropriate resources and technologies, and are well trained. Managers who create such a work force increase the probability that they will achieve high performance results. However, to state that successful managers are carried by their subordinates does not tell the entire story. As we move further into the 1990s, successful managers are increasingly turning their energies to team building to regain the competitive edge.[2] The team phenomenon, however, is not limited to large manufacturing organizations. It is alive and growing in both small and large organizations and has spread to health care organizations, government agencies, and other service-related organizations.[3]

397

Teams, once formed, act to focus subordinates' efforts and help to ensure subordinates' commitment through employee involvement, creativity, and mutual support. At the very least, team involvement increases employee satisfaction, acceptance of change, and facilitates creative problem solving.[4]

The importance of teams can be best understood by considering the following high-performance equation: performance = ability (A) $\times$ effort (E) $\times$ support (S).[5] Perceived in this manner, individual performance can only be maximized when these three conditions are met. The likelihood of this occurring reflects the degree to which organizations select the right individuals, train and develop employees, create a motivational climate, and, finally, transform a group of employees into a functioning team. Each of these activities directly affects one, or more, of the independent *variables* listed in the performance equation: "A", "E", and "S". While the variables of ability and effort (motivation) need no additional explanation, the concept of support does need further clarification.

Within the work group, individual performance is enhanced when support comes from two sources, namely, from the manager responsible for the work group and from other group members. In the traditional sense, managerial support occurs when managers fulfill their role as leader, administrator, coach, and adviser (see Table 10.1).[6] When these roles are

---

TABLE 10.1   Managerial Behaviors Linked to Supportive Climates

Leader Behaviors
- Sets goals
- Directs and controls
- Delegates
- Ensures follow-up

Administrative Behaviors
- Establishes plans and organizes all resources
- Coordinates activities, schedules, and data
- Ensures availability of materials and resources
- Maintains records
- Distributes all relevant information
- Buffers group from external pressures

Coaching Behaviors
- Trains and develops
- Monitors developmental progress
- Encourages and supports
- Gives meaningful and timely feedback

Advising Behaviors
- Provides personal expertise and insight
- Trains others to take over advising function
- Facilitates group problem solving

not adequately carried out, it becomes increasingly difficult for subordinates to effectively perform their job responsibilities. Managers who do not clearly set goals and state expectations increase the probability that subordinates will behave in ways inconsistent with preferred behaviors. Managers who fail to bring together the correct equipment, resources, and people cannot expect subordinates to perform at peak levels. Last, managers who do not coach, encourage, and advise are likely to limit the growth and development of their staff.

The second area of support comes from the other members of the individual's work group. When a work group develops into an effective team, this type of support is maximized. Table 10.2 compares characteristics of teams versus groups.[7] The key difference between the two conditions is that when a group becomes a team a bonding and integration takes place among group members—that is, a "we-feeling" develops. When this occurs, members of the team begin to act as one, sharing a common set of goals, attitudes, values and beliefs. Effective teams allow members to draw on the strength of others within the group. When a group becomes an effective team, each member is sensitive to the needs and feelings of other members and responds to help them wherever and whenever possible. This allows the team to achieve commitment, and at the same time, gives focus and direction to their efforts. The team appears to have a natural rhythm or flow as it moves toward a common goal. When a team's energies are in direct support of the manager's goals, high productivity will be achieved.

TABLE 10.2   Differences between Groups and Teams

Groups	*Teams*
• Convenience-based	• Intentional and purposeful
• Product of environment or task	• Product of member preferences/desires
• Conformist driven/norm-based behavior	• Consensus-driven/goal-based behavior
• Interpersonal awareness	• Interpersonal awareness plus sensitivity
• Task leadership	• Principled and shared leadership*

(*) As discussed by Larson and Lafasto, a team leader is principled and will not use short cuts to achieve the appropriate task performance.[8] At the same time, the effective team leader will develop a supportive or shared decision-making environment to ensure maximum team creativity.

The Benefits of Team Building

The decision to expend time, energy, and resources to develop effective teams must be based upon the belief that the manager or organization will likely obtain a net benefit from the effort. According to Beckhard, team building can play a significant role in increasing group effectiveness on the following four levels:

- Clarifying/setting the goals and priorities of the work unit.

- Analyzing the work situation and clarifying the roles and responsibilities of group members.

- Analyzing group processes (such as communications and decision making), and making corrections where necessary.

- Assessing the existing relationships between group members, measuring their impact on goal achievement, and taking corrective action where necessary.[9]

The absence of any one of these levels can lead to a general breakdown and render a group inoperative as a team.

If the group does not have shared goals, the members are unlikely to pull together to work toward a common end. Each group member should be able to answer the following questions: "Where do we want to be in 'X' number of years?" "Where are we now?" "What interim accomplishments would indicate successful movement toward desired goals?" "What is the appropriate period in which to achieve these goals?" Unless group members give the same answers to these questions there can be no consensus.

Shared common goals, however, are insufficient to ensure success. In addition, the group's members must be able to personalize these goals by articulating their roles and responsibilities. In other words, as a group member what must **"I"** do to keep the total group moving in the direction of our shared goals? Without this clarification, there is likely to be duplication of effort and, possibly, conflict. Furthermore, if group members do not effectively internalize the need to carry out critical tasks or behaviors, these are likely to be left undone. The relevant questions at this level are; "How do **I** fit within this group?" "What must **I** specifically do to fulfill my responsibilities to the group?" "When should **my** roles and responsibilities be completed?" "What else could **I** be doing to make this group work more effectively?" "What can **I** do to help others do their jobs better?" By each one openly answering these questions in the group, others have the opportunity to agree or disagree with the stated perceptions.

Team building can also help to ensure that the underlying processes and procedures that help facilitate team operations are in place. Process and procedure issues are important because they can mediate input/output relationships within a group. How group members communicate, make decisions, share authority, establish and maintain norms, reward one another, identify and solve problems, and how the group is led greatly affects the likelihood of group success.

To ensure success at this level, each member, and the group collectively, should be able to answer the following questions: "How do group or team processes and procedures relate to group behavior?" "Do the processes we have in place help or hinder group operations?" "How might existing processes and procedures be changed to enhance group performance?" "Does the group spend sufficient time considering process issues, and if not, why not?"

Last, unless group members can relate to one another in an open and sensitive manner there is little likelihood that the team will be effective. Here, again, team building plays a critical role in creating a climate in which the team will develop and grow stronger. To achieve success at this level, it is generally accepted that group members must be open and honest with one another. This requires a certain level of trust and intimacy that can only be achieved if the group has been functioning as a unit for some time. The team building process can be used to identify, clarify, and then remove those interpersonal behaviors or environmental barriers that prevent the group from reaching the needed level of intimacy and trust. Critical at this stage is the members' ability to give and receive feedback.

Feedback, either one-on-one, or within a group context, is the lubricant that facilitates the development of trust and intimacy. To provide the needed feedback on interpersonal relationships, group members must be able to answer such questions as: "How do I relate to others and how do my behaviors affect others in the group?" "Do I trust or otherwise feel comfortable with other group members, and if not, why not?" "Do others feel comfortable with me, or otherwise trust me, and if not, why not?" "What behaviors exhibited by others within the group motivate me to either open up or withdraw during interpersonal exchanges?" "What are the interpersonal strengths and weaknesses of other members and what changes, if any, would I like to see?"

Team building can clearly play an important role in making the group an effective team. When attempting to engage in a team-building intervention, however, managers must realize that to maximize the impact of their efforts, some consideration should be given to which level of the process needs attention. Each level requires a different type of intervention and only when there is a match between the intervention and the environmental needs is the manager likely to be successful. If he or she attempts to improve interpersonal relationships within the group but agreement has not yet been reached on goals, member responsibilities, or appropriateness of process, little progress is likely to be achieved.[10]

Problems with the Traditional Team-Building Approach

As more and more managers attempt to create effective teams, the demand for team-building workshops and material continues to grow.[11] Unfortunately, the traditional technique for building organizational teams is for managers to seek the help of outside professionals. Once selected, these outside professionals typically take the natural work group off-site, and engage in some type of intensive team-building experience. Carried out in this manner, team-building experiences often take employees away from the job for two and three days at a time. The desired outcome of such an experience is for the group to leave the session as a functioning team and then to transfer the newly learned skills and insights to the work environment.[12]

Such efforts can sensitize organizational members to the importance of team characteristics. Problems occur, however, when the traditional approach is used at all organizational levels. Let us consider some of the potential difficulties in using the "professional, off-site" technique.

A Problem of Cost

First, managers are increasingly being asked to do more with less. Faced with this reality, it is unlikely that all managers will have the budget to take their staff off-site for a two- or three-day team-building experience. This is especially true for smaller organizations and managers near the bottom of the management hierarchy.

A recent team-building intervention carried out by one of the authors dramatizes this point. To facilitate team problem solving, senior management undertook, with the help of an outside facilitator, a three-day retreat to identify the organization's strategic intent and to assess the appropriateness of the existing corporate culture. The retreat was held off-site at a convenient training facility. At the end of the experience, all managers indicated that not only had significant progress been made toward defining corporate strategy and culture but that the group also had a new feeling of camaraderie and openness. Follow-up team-building sessions were planned for senior management, with the outside facilitator still involved, but on the company's premises.

After several team-building sessions, over a six-month period, the decision was made to (*a*) continue the senior team meetings on a regular basis, (*b*) involve the next level of management in the team-building and problem-solving process, and (*c*) continue moving the process down into the organization until all employees were part of the process. Due to cost constraints, however, a decision was also made to continue the process without the external facilitator. All future team-building experiences would be carried out by line personnel and, if needed, the organization would supplement line expertise with internal human resource management staff. The rationale given for this decision was simple: the organization could not justify the expense of having an outside consulting group carry out a companywide intervention.

A Problem of Logistics

Managers facing tight budgets, reduced staff, and increased pressure to produce are likely to be reluctant to release employees for off-site team-building sessions. An alternative is to arrange for the team-building session to be held on weekends or evenings. This solves the problem of direct work interference but requires employees to give up their personal time to attend to organizational business. Such a sacrifice, although reasonable in the eyes of senior management, is often perceived as being in conflict with family responsibilities, leisure needs, and an emerging work ethic that calls for a balance between organizational demands and personal activities.

A Problem of Transfer

Important to the success of any team-building experience is the degree to which the skills and openness acquired during the team-building retreat are transferred to the employee's day-to-day performance on the job. At one level, off-site experiences help to unfreeze the employee by removing the environmental stimuli that frequently define power relationships, appropriate behavior, and emotional responses between individuals. Under these conditions, participants are more likely to respond positively to the team-building experience. Therefore, it is not uncommon for participants to leave such an experience with a "we-feeling," but at the same time be psychologically unwilling to attempt to transfer team behaviors back to the real world.

It is at the point of transfer that difficulties most frequently arise. Central to the concept of transfer is the concept of identical elements.[13] Simply put, the more similar the elements of the training environment to the on-the-job environment, the greater the likelihood of transfer. As indicated above, this is not the case with off-site team-building experiences. It is at best an artificial environment designed to psychologically unfreeze the participant. When participants return to their respective departments it is often "business as usual." Consequently, the impact of this type of experience is significantly diluted back on the job.

To offset the problems of cost, logistics, and transfer, it is desirable for managers to become personally involved, on a day-to-day basis, in the creation and maintenance of a team climate within their own departments. Such an approach, though, must be considered only a partial solution to the problems associated with the traditional approach to team building and must be applied only when appropriate to the situation, namely, when participant ability, environmental support, and participant motivation are high.[14]

The Manager's Role

Critical to the development and maintenance of any work team is the behavior and the general philosophy managers bring to the manager–subordinate relationship. This fact was reflected in the performance equation presented earlier. Moreover, for managers to effectively contribute to the team-building process they must be able to influence group members. Rosen describes four factors likely to result in the manager having influence over subordinates. They are as follows:

- They (managers) have superior knowledge about the group's task and how it ties in with the larger organization.
- Group members feel the manager has a right to tell them what to do.
- The group members think the manager is just like them, only better.
- Group members find both the manager's apparent personal motives for being in the job and the process by which he or she was selected acceptable.[15]

Although each of these factors plays an important role in determining the level of managerial influence, it is to the perceived motives of the manager that we now turn our attention. The following characteristics are important elements of the manager's personal motive and style base and, as such, should be given careful consideration when he or she is interacting with subordinates.[16]

1. The manager has the will to manage. The manager's enthusiasm for his or her personal vision or the group's goals clearly reflects a willingness to be responsible for other people. If the manager has been forced by circumstance to fill his or her current position—if no one else was available and the position was accepted because of loyalty to the organization and not because of a personal desire to manage and the job is providing the only way out of one's current situation—it is unlikely that the manager will be highly motivated to perform at or near his or her peak capabilities. When this lack of enthusiasm and effort is observed by the group, the consequence is a reduced desire to follow the manager or be part of his or her team. **Therefore, managers must want to manage for the right reasons. When performing the job, managers must demonstrate enthusiasm, energy, and commitment, and must act as a model for their subordinates.**

2. Looks out for more than "number one." Managers who are only interested in making themselves look good, fail to share the benefits of their successes, or otherwise use subordinate efforts for personal gains, will soon find that they have no grassroots support. In other words, subordinates are just as happy to see the manager stumble and fall rather than carry him or her to higher levels of performance. **Therefore, a manager must ensure that subordinates are given credit for the successes they had a role in creating.**

3. Balances internal and external pressures. As group goals and organizational goals do not always coincide, and because the manager acts as the linking or buffering agent between internal and external pressures, the manager must be perceived as having a balanced and fair perspective. Similarly, the manager cannot be perceived as having external obligations that run counter to the interest of the group, such as prior obligations to an external mentor. For if this is perceived to be the case, the manager's credibility is greatly diminished, and so is his or her influence over the group. **The manager must**

therefore approach all boundary-spanning conflicts with an open mind and a balanced perspective.

4. A manager acts like one. Subordinates like to have their bosses act like managers. Managers must establish a vision, facilitate group performance, and protect and buffer the group from external threats. Unfortunately, some managers, when promoted up through the ranks, are unable to relinquish what they had been doing before the promotion. Other managers believe they cannot gain the respect of their subordinates unless they work side by side with them. Neither of these views is correct. Successful managers gain respect by effectively planning, organizing, buffering, coaching, developing, networking, and making hard decisions when needed. **Therefore, it is better to be a good manager than a good co-worker.**

5. Uses power judiciously. Internally, it is in the manager's best interest to gain acceptance through his or her track record of personal successes and negotiated participative agreements. This allows the manager to obtain subordinate agreement and commitment. If managers rely on position power or coercive force, they run the risk of triggering a contrast effect from subordinates. In other words, the subordinate's response will be opposite to the one desired. This is not to say, however, that during a crisis, when the situation requires a fast decision, or when the manager must make an unpopular decision, the manager cannot act unilaterally. The only caveat that we would place on such action is that managers be honest with themselves; that is, such action must be appropriate, and when possible, managers must explain their action to subordinates. **Managers must attempt to gain cooperation through participation, sharing, and principled negotiations rather than through forcing.**

6. Treats staff as a group rather than as individuals only. The manager will always have some discretion in how he or she manages. In other words, the manager's department, although immersed in a larger culture, or system, is still unique within some acceptable range. Within this range, the manager should begin to treat his or her subordinates as a team rather than as a collection of independent employees. This can be accomplished through team meetings, group projects, group objectives, group rewards or incentive systems, collective learning, and through the application of the concept of an open work force.

For example, collective learning can be achieved if subordinates are allowed to learn the jobs of their co-workers or encouraged informally to share knowledge, expertise, and experience with other group members. Similarly, in an open work environment, employees are encouraged to meet informally and without following a predetermined schedule to solve unit or organizational problems. Here again, managers must strike a balance between group and individual responses to their staff. **Groups cannot become teams unless they are treated as a team.**

The success of any on-the-job team building effort will also be a function of the leadership behaviors of the manager facilitating the process. A critical first step in this area is the manager's ability to create a clear and engaging vision that unites the members of the group.[17] To create a shared vision with subordinates, managers must be able to effectively communicate ideas; listen to the views of others; effectively probe, summarize, and reflect the feeling of others; and establish interpersonal relationships built on trust.[18] Vision alone, though, is insufficient to cause a group to become a team. The leader must also be able to cause needed changes to occur, and to ensure that group members are involved.[19] Such a leader transforms the group and its members into something more than the sum of its parts. Burns defines a transforming leader as an individual who looks "for potential motives and followers, seeks to satisfy higher needs, and engages the full person of the follower. The result is a relationship of mutual stimulation and elevation that converts followers into leaders and may convert leaders into moral agents."[20]

Managers who transform groups into teams must also develop a cooperative leadership style designed to produce employee change.[21] Cooperative leaders inspire commitment and trust by sharing personal resources and expertise with group members. They also facilitate goal achievement by acting to integrate group members into the problem solving process, thus ensuring that participants have had an opportunity to share their views, discuss issues, and work together to develop problem solutions.[22] What is important is that cooperative leaders are able to direct their power into constructive activities, such as providing assistance and support to others.[23]

It may be helpful to view leaders' behavior as reflecting a number of skill levels that allow them to carry out the activities needed to produce an effective team.[24] Table 10.3 describes three general skill levels that support on-the-job team building efforts. If managers want to become successful team builders, they must move beyond the traditional skills associated with control and direction. That is, they must move in the direction of level three skills. As we will discuss below, level three skills are necessary for effective development of self-directed teams.

TABLE 10.3   Three Skill Layers for Managers

A	B	C
When used alone, these skills are suited only to a rigidly traditional workplace	*With Column A skills, these are needed in today's more progressive workplace*	*With Column A and B skills, these are needed to build and maintain a team environment*
Direct people	Involve people	Develop self-motivated people who set their own goals and evaluate their own efforts
Get people to understand ideas	Get people to generate ideas	Get groups of diverse people to generate and implement their own best ideas

TABLE 10.3   Three Skill Layers for Managers (concluded)

Manage one-on-one	Encourage teamwork	Build teams that manage more of their own day-to-day work
Maximize the department's performance	Build relationships with other departments	Champion cross-functional efforts to improve quality, service, and productivity
Implement changes imposed from above	Initiate changes within the department	Anticipate, initiate, and respond to changes dictated by forces outside the organization

Source: J. H. Zenger, E. Musselwhite, K. Hurson, and C. Perrin, "Leadership in a team environment," *Training and Development Journal,* October 1991, p. 48.

Prerequisites for Team Success: A General Overview

The model presented in Figure 10.1 incorporates input, process, and output variables to fully demonstrate how the team process fits within the organization context.[25] The first three blocks are overlapped to indicate that the variables listed interact to determine the degree of "focus" and "buy in" achieved within the team. Let us first consider the role each of these three blocks plays in creating an effective team climate.

Culture

As indicated by the model, an organization's culture reflects the set of underlying, and often subconscious, assumptions held by organizational members; existing values or norms; and behavioral patterns that define preferred employee behavior. (A detailed discussion of culture and its impact on the employee can be found in Chapter 15.) Each organizational member is affected by the existing culture and will attempt to behave in an acceptable manner. Consequently, the overall organizational culture will affect the degree of team supporting behaviors likely to be exhibited either by managers or their subordinates. For example, if some of the generally accepted norms of the organization are to compete for scarce resources, or to withhold information from others, it becomes more difficult for a particular manager to motivate his or her subordinates to exhibit team supporting behaviors.

Organizational Context

When attempting to predict behavior within an organization, it is important to consider contextual variables likely to impact on employees and team supporting behaviors. A number of such contextual variables must be considered by the manager seeking to cultivate a team climate within his or her unit. Three such variables have been listed in block 2. They are the reward system, educational system, and the information system.[26]

FIGURE 10.1

Prerequisites for team success: General overview

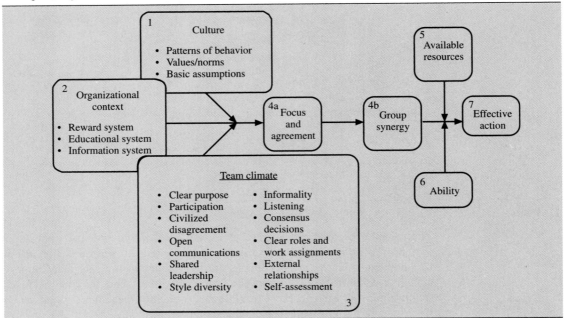

1. The reward system. One of the more important contextual variables associated with employee support for team development is the reward system existing within the organization. Simply put, the employee will ask, "What's in it for me?" If, after analysis, the employee determines that the consequences are negative, support for the team building activity is likely to decline. In the example given above, if the employee determines that the team building activity is likely to impinge on personal time that he or she values more, or that co-workers are unlikely to support team activities, then low levels of personal effort will result. The consequence for the manager is that the team building efforts are likely to fail.

After an effective team has been established, rewards are also necessary to maintain employee support for team efforts. At the individual level, employees must believe that by behaving in a manner consistent with team membership, personal benefits will result. This can be accomplished by providing both individual and group rewards. Rewards at this level may deal with feelings of personal achievement, belonging, acceptance and support from co-workers, and recognition from the employee's immediate boss. At the formal level, the organization's reward structure must be designed to reward team performance through bonus or merit plans, promotions, and profit sharing, for example.

Managers who fail to adequately reward team efforts run the risk of reducing employee support for their team building efforts. Before beginning a team building effort, therefore, managers should determine what rewards are available and how much control they have in their distribution. If such rewards are not available, the manager's primary objective should be to develop strategies by which they can be achieved.

2. The educational system. For teams to form and function effectively, it is important that members have the technical skills necessary to contribute to team goals, and the interpersonal skills necessary to facilitate and maintain interaction. Competency at the technical and interpersonal levels is not only important because of its direct impact on group performance but also because it generates a necessary condition for group development: trust. Member trust is critical to the development of open and supportive relationships and the maintenance of the "we feeling." Managers cannot assume that the required levels of competency exist within their departments or within themselves. It is the organization's educational system that helps ensure that the necessary skills are in place.

When assessing the organization's educational system, one must recognize that learning takes place on several levels. At the formal level, the organization provides both in-house and external programs designed to improve the technical and interpersonal skills of managers and subordinates. The manager cannot assume, however, that the formal structure, namely, the human resource department, will provide all the training necessary to ensure effective team performance.

At a semiformal level, managers have the responsibility of considering the training and development needs of their subordinates and of creating a climate in which learning can occur. Included at this level is the manager's willingness to act as a role model for his subordinates. If the manager is willing to be open and share information, then subordinates are more likely to follow his or her lead. If the manager demonstrates effective behaviors in handling interpersonal conflict, there is an increased probability that subordinates will demonstrate similar behaviors. Similarly, the manager must continually engage in evaluation, coaching, counseling, and interpersonal feedback.

At the informal level learning takes place as employees gain experience and interact with others within the organization. The learning that takes place at this level is the least controlled by management, but frequently has the greatest impact on employees. Therefore, it is important to ensure that the formal and informal learning environments are compatible and that both support effective team development. The manager can help ensure that the learning at this level is positive from a team building perspective. For example, predetermining a group's structure can help managers create teams with an appropriate mix of skill, personalities, and internal climate. At the same time, the manager can ensure that the group is the correct size to handle the task at hand. Last, much can be gained by matching up senior, well-skilled employees with new inexperienced employees to help stimulate positive learning.

3. The information system. As we look to the next decade and the increased turbulence existing within organizations, the importance of information becomes increasingly apparent. Appropriate and timely information allows organizational members to make quality decisions, better understand their environment, feel comfortable with what is happening around them, and feel that they are part of the solution and not the problem. Furthermore, without appropriate and timely information, subordinates are unlikely to be motivated to perform at peak levels. A perception of having incomplete information frequently leads to a reduced expectancy of successful performance in the subordinate with this perception. If this occurs, then subordinate motivation is reduced.

Here, again, the manager plays a critical role in ensuring that subordinates have the information necessary to increase their expectations that they will be successful, and, at the same time, feel part of the process and ultimately part of a team. By providing clear information to the subordinate, the manager helps to answer key questions frequently asked by most subordinates. For example, during workshops with managers, we often ask the following questions: "Do you want to know what you are supposed to do?" "Do you want to know the terms of reference, limits, or constraints under which you will perform?" "Do you want to know the conditions under which you will perform?" "Do you want to know what resources and material you will have to work with?" "Do you want to know your boss's standards and how they will be used to evaluate your performance?" "Do you want to know the consequences of performance and non-performance?" "Do you want to know how to improve on the job?" In every instance, the managers respond with a resounding **"YES!"** At that point we typically ask one last question—"Would your subordinates answer any differently?" After some hesitation, and, sometimes, intense soul searching, typically 90 percent or more of the managers indicate that their subordinates would also respond with a "yes." The moral of the experience is simple—most individuals within the organization want access to relevant information.

Unfortunately, access to information is not always possible. For one thing, the desired information may not exist within the organization. Second, given the technologies used (e.g., software programs, accounting systems, scanning mechanisms, etc.), it may be impractical to collect, process, and distribute the information demanded by subordinates. Next, based upon political or psychological reasoning, other managers within the organization may not be willing to provide the manager with data he or she believes should be shared with subordinates. Last, the manager may withhold certain information from subordinates to prevent information overload. Barriers to the free flow of information represent another opportunity for managers to build information links with their subordinates. When the manager takes time to explain why needed information is not forthcoming, subordinates are more likely to understand and accept these deficiencies, and, at the same time, work with the manager in the future to increase accessibility. The net impact of such managerial behaviors will be a greater feeling of team membership by subordinates.

Team climate

At this point we are ready to consider the internal group characteristics necessary for an effective team to develop and be maintained. Building on the works of McGregor[27] and Likert,[28] Parker[29] articulates 12 characteristics or behaviors that he believes differentiate ineffective and effective teams. These 12 characteristics or behaviors are listed in block 3 and fit well with the set of attitudes and skills being discussed in this book.

1. Clear purpose. As discussed in Chapter 6, the effective manager builds into his or her work unit a mechanism by which clear and jointly agreed upon goals can be established. Goals or visions that become jointly shared by group members act as the spark that ignites team effort and the glue that bonds group members together.

2. Participation. One of the key attitudes described in Chapter 3 for dealing with employees in the 1990s relates to the manager's willingness to allow subordinates to participate. Without the effective use of participation, the probability of subordinate "buy in" and motivation is significantly reduced. As you will recall, participation facilitates strategy development and the sharing of relevant information among team members. The sharing of information and the availability of an increased number of solution strategies will also have a positive effect on the perceived self-efficacy of participants.

3. Civilized disagreement. When groups form and develop into a team, it is common for conflicts to occur. Such conflict must be effectively managed if the "we-feeling" is to take root within the group. To do so, groups must develop the internal mechanisms and interpersonal sensitivities that allow conflict to be discussed and resolved in a civilized manner. Here the techniques discussed in Chapter 12 will prove most helpful to the manager.

4. Open communications. Trust is the key ingredient that develops among group members as they interact over time. Once trust is established and once the group members have bought into a common goal or vision, open communications are likely to follow. Open communications will also depend upon the ability of group members to handle conflict in a civilized manner and upon the degree to which the overall working climate can be characterized as informal in nature (see below). Effective teams actively engage in and openly use informal opportunities to communicate with other group members. For example, some organizations have tables and flip charts strategically placed within the organization so that groups can have impromptu meetings whenever the urge strikes them.

5. Listening. Communications that are ignored do little to develop and maintain effective teams. As discussed in Chapter 4, effective listening is necessary if individuals are to achieve interpersonal understanding and empathy and at the same time maintain open channels of communication. Parker considers it the single most important element in developing a team climate.[30]

6. Informal climate. Informality represents the degree to which the group's environment can be characterized by a comfortable and relaxed atmosphere. Under these conditions, interpersonal interactions are sought out and maintained because members feel comfortable with each other. Furthermore, when informality is the accepted mode of operation, the group's members are more willing to appropriately bypass the formalized structure to achieve shared goals. Flexibility, resulting from informality, appears to better reflect the needs of the 1990s and at the same time is supportive of Peters' concept of bureaucracy bashing.[31]

7. Consensus decisions. Shared goals, participation, informality and effective communications should help the group achieve consensus decision making. Without it, there is little hope that members will agree on decisions. Critical to consensus decision making is the acceptance that a consensus decision requires unity but not unanimity. The group allows all members to express their opinions and preferences openly and to discuss any disagreements that might exist. Within the consensus-building process, alternatives that are at least partially agreed upon by all group members are identified. In other words, some members may still believe that their alternative is better, but can accept the position being supported by other group members. Parker states this principle as follows: "A consensus is reached when all members can say they either agree with the decision or have had their 'day in court' and were unable to convince the others of their viewpoint. In the final analysis, everyone agrees to support the outcome."[32]

Managers must recognize, however, that consensus building takes time and can dilute the manager's authority. Forcing, or unilateral decision making, although saving time and preserving one's authority, can prevent "buy in" and often increases the probability of employee resistance. Ultimately, the actual decision to use consensus decision making should be based upon the manager's assessment of existing conditions within his or her department. These conditions include the experience and competency level of subordinates, time availability, subordinates' interest and motivation, importance of the decision, interpersonal climate, and history, to name a few.

8. Clear roles and work assignments. For any group to function effectively there must be internal agreement on the roles, responsibilities, and assignments of group members. Ambiguity in this area will likely produce conflict and prevent the group from achieving consensus regarding the group's appropriate direction. This is especially true in the early stages of group development when uncertainty and tension can often be used to describe the group's environment. It is the manager's responsibility to ensure that the work group has addressed this issue and that the roles, responsibilities and assignments of group members are understood, accepted, and fair.

Important, also, is the manager's willingness to negotiate (Chapters 6 and 7) with subordinates regarding the importance, content, and allocation of roles, responsibilities, and assignments. Depending on the level of team maturity, managers can begin the clarification process by either stating their expectations to subordinates, or asking subordinates to articulate their perceptions of what they believe their roles, responsibilities and assignments should be. However the process is initiated, managers and subordinates will, through negotiations and consensus decision making, eventually agree upon and articulate what should be done and by whom.

9. Shared leadership. The concept of shared leadership is closely linked to the concept of team. To foster a team climate, the manager must reject the "hero" approach to leadership where he or she is primarily responsible for directing, controlling, coordinating, advising, supporting, and problem solving for the group. Instead, the manager must be willing to share his or her leadership responsibilities with others within the group. In the extreme case, the work team functions as a self-directed group in which most of the day-to-day leadership responsibilities are shared among the subordinates. At the same time, the manager's time is freed up to address issues of long-term planning and development of his or her team.[33]

10. Style diversity. As the rate of organizational change quickens, the level of employee education increases, and as the demographic characteristics of the North American work force change, managers will face increased work group diversity. From this perspective, work groups are likely to reflect greater differences in experience, cultural backgrounds, and ethnic origins. Work group diversity will be accompanied by style or behavior diversity. Consequently, to be successful in the 1990s, managers must not only become more tolerant of style diversity but also learn how to effectively manage it. When managed correctly, style diversity is likely to result in *(a)* a broadened idea or information base available within the group, *(b)* an increased probability of critical thinking, which can prevent "group-think", *(c)* reduced response times when adjusting to changing environments, and *(d)* increased overall creativity in the work group. In this way, the team will be strengthened.

11. External relationships. To be effective the team must look beyond departmental boundaries and must network with relevant constituencies. Hastings, Bixby, and Chaudry-Lawton describe the "invisible team" that can be drawn upon to enhance the performance of the team.[34] This "invisible team" is made up of other groups internal and external to the organization that might be of use to the team under study. Invisible teams can provide information, support and resources necessary for team success. Internally, the team may draw upon the support of other functional areas to form an appropriate coalition. Once formed, the coalition gives the team greater power and influence within the organization. Similarly, other groups within the organization can provide information necessary for critical evaluation during upcoming decision-making sessions. Conversely, the team can use its contacts in other groups to lobby for its point of view.

External to the organization, the work team may draw upon customers, vendors, and political groups to gain information, relevant feedback on products or services, influence, and resources. Failure to develop contacts with such groups often causes groups to become myopic. Such tunnel vision is likely to result in poor decision making and reduced creativity. The ultimate, likely result is an increased probability of failure.

By networking, the group expands its influence and visibility and increases the likelihood of success. This, in turn, builds pride in the work group and increased commitment to the team. Therefore, it is the responsibility of all team members to network to help their team.

12. Self-assessment. No team can survive unless it periodically assesses how well the group is doing. Self-assessment allows the team to ask important questions about its own performance, such as, "How well are we doing?" "What are we doing right, and can we continue to behave in this manner?" "What are we doing wrong, and is it possible to change our behavior?" "What could we be doing differently to improve the overall performance of our team?" "Are we satisfying the interpersonal needs of our group members?" "Are we taking advantage of all our member strengths?" If these questions are not asked, the answers will not be heard. Without hearing the answers the team cannot be sure whether it is achieving its goals, is performing optimally, or is just satisficing.

Focus and Agreement

When conditions described in blocks 1 through 3 (Figure 10.1) support a team climate, there is an increased probability that group members will exhibit a desired level of focus and agreement (block 4a). In other words, the members will jointly agree on where they want to go, understand what needs to be done to get there, understand and accept who is responsible for what, and are committed to the group's goals.

There is, however, a higher level that the group must reach to be considered a true team (block 4b). When group synergy is reached, group members move in concert and the group becomes more than the sum of its parts. At this point, the "we-feeling" is maximized as members tune in to the feelings, needs, strengths and weaknesses of each other. If a fellow group member is in need, other members rally in support. If another group member has a weakness, other members seek to compensate for and develop the weaker member. If conflicts arise, the members openly discuss and attempt to create a solution in which all members are winners. That is, no one leaves an exchange in which he or she feels victimized. Hackman describes positive group synergy as a condition where the group dampens "the negative impact of performance conditions (e.g., a badly designed group task or a nonsupportive reward system): perhaps transcending their effects for a limited period of time." Hackman adds that a synergistic group makes "full exploitation of favorable performance conditions."[35]

Ability and Environmental Constraints

Our normative model indicates that the performance level reached by a group will primarily be a function of three factors: *group synergy, existing abilities of group members*, and *environmental constraints*. Therefore, although group synergy plays a critical role in determining actual performance levels, managers cannot ignore the remaining two variables.

Managers often inherit a work group, such as when they have been promoted to a new unit, or have little influence in shaping its makeup because top management makes selection and transfer decisions. As a result, managers must, in the short run, accept ability levels as given. Consequently, they cannot expect more out of their work group than existing abilities allow. As discussed in Chapter 6, managers who attempt to do so will only frustrate subordinates and, ultimately, reduce motivation and performance. In the long run, managers have the responsibility to train and develop their staff and thereby attempt to increase the overall ability of the existing work group. In addition, the group's overall ability level may increase over time as staff turnover occurs and as the manager is able to select new employees.

Environmental constraints also determine the performance level achieved by work groups. Such constraints relate to the technologies used, the employee's physical surroundings, the quality and quantity of resources available, and the level of environmental change. In each case, the existing conditions can either support or hinder the group's effort to reach its shared goals. Here, again, the manager must be aware of these constraints in order not to set unreasonable expectations for his or her work group.

Effective Performance

At some point the manager must evaluate the performance of his or her team. Hackman describes three criteria of team effectiveness that can be used by the manager to assess his or her group's effectiveness.[36] The three levels deal with the group's actual output, the group processes, and the impact of the team experience on individual members. Specifically, Hackman describes his criteria in the following manner:

1. The productive output of the work group should meet or exceed the performance standards of the people who receive and/or review the output. If a group's output is not acceptable to its "clients" and/or to managers who are charged with evaluating or are responsible for its performance, then it cannot be considered effective.

2. The social processes used in carrying out the work should maintain or enhance the capability of members to work together on subsequent team tasks.

3. The group experience should, on balance, satisfy rather than frustrate the personal needs of group members.[37]

When these three criteria are satisfied, not only does the team achieve its goals in the short run, but member behaviors, attitudes, and need satisfaction also help to guarantee continued existence and growth in the long run.

A Simple Test of the Theory

As indicated above, groups that demonstrate the 12 characteristics of effective teams should outperform groups that do not demonstrate these characteristics. That is, teams scoring high on these dimensions are more likely to satisfy Hackman's criteria of success. To test this hypothesis one of the authors asked 133 of his students and colleagues to complete a 60-item questionnaire measuring the 12 characteristics of effective teams.[38] Each of the 60 items was measured on a 1 to 5 point scale with 5 indicating a high agreement. There were five items supporting each dimension. Consequently, the range of scores for each team characteristic was 5 (low presence of team characteristics) to 25 (high presence of team characteristics).

Approximately half of the respondents were asked to think of a group that satisfied Hackman's criteria for a successful team. The remaining respondents were asked to think of a group that did not satisfy these criteria. Respondents were allowed to select a group to which they currently belonged or one in which they had been a member sometime during the past year. With this group in mind, individuals were asked to complete the 60-item team questionnaire. Results presented in Figure 10.2 indicate that, as predicted, high-performing groups reflect a characteristics profile that is significantly higher on these scales than the low-performing groups. Analysis of the data demonstrated that *(a)* the profiles were not parallel, and *(b)* there was a significant difference in means between the low- and high-performing means for each of the pairs of measurements.[39] In other words, groups that were perceived to have satisfied Hackman's success criteria reflected more of each team characteristic.

Self-Directed Teams (SDTs)

The use of teams to enhance an organization's efficiency is not a recent phenomenon.[40] The term "team," however, does not have an accepted definition unless it is linked with a set of adjectives that better defines the sender's meaning.[41] For some, the term is used to describe quality circles, cross-functional groups, or project teams. We have been using the term to refer to any intact group of employees that might have different backgrounds, interests, experiences, and needs, which has been transformed into a highly integrated and effective work team. Others used the term to describe the current phenomenon known as self-directed teams.

It is this concept of self-directed teams that appears to be the center of much of the North American discussion about work teams.[42] In a recent study done by *Training Magazine,* 82 percent of responding firms classified some employees as belonging to a group identified as a team.[43] Of these organizations, an average of 53 percent of all their employees were classified as team

FIGURE 10.2

Mean scores for high and low groups

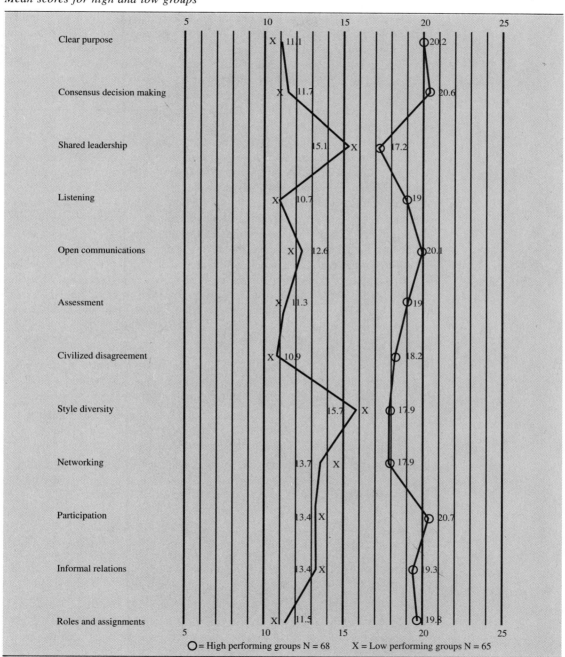

	Clear purpose	X 11.1	O 20.2
Consensus decision making	X 11.7	O 20.6
Shared leadership	15.1 X	O 17.2
Listening	X 10.7	O 19
Open communications	X 12.6	O 20.1
Assessment	X 11.3	O 19
Civilized disagreement	X 10.9	O 18.2
Style diversity	15.7 X	O 17.9
Networking	13.7 X	O 17.9
Participation	13.4 X	O 20.7
Informal relations	13.4 X	O 19.3
Roles and assignments	X 11.5	O 19.8

O = High performing groups N = 68   X = Low performing groups N = 65 members. The same study found that 35 percent of responding firms had at least one group classified as a self-directed team. Of these firms, the average percentage of all employees who were participating in self-directed teams was 32 percent. In the case of organizations with 10,000 or more employees, the proportion was 42 percent. A second survey done by Development Dimensions International for *Industry Week Magazine* found that 25 percent of companies in the United States have implemented self-directed groups in their organization.[44] Although a third survey of 476 of the *Fortune* 1,000 firms found that only 7 percent of the work force of responding firms were currently in self-directed teams, half the companies indicated that they would rely more heavily on them in the coming years.[45]

The increased use of self-directed work teams reflects, in part, a desire by North American firms to become more competitive. These companies recognize that the traditional pyramid no longer gives organizations the ability to respond rapidly to their changing environments.[46] Others would argue that, although the work ethic is alive and well, employee productivity does not reflect its presence as employees have become increasingly alienated in the workplace.[47] One alternative to help counterbalance such trends is for organizations to increase the level of employee self-management.[48] Therefore, organizations are using self-directed teams to improve the quality of product and services offered, increase productivity, increase organizational flexibility, reduce operating costs, and improve employee job satisfaction.[49] In many cases, the introduction of self-directed teams appears to achieve these objectives.

- After introducing self-directed teams, Northern Telecom experienced an increase of 63 percent in revenue, 26 percent in sales, 46 percent in earnings and 60 percent in employee productivity. It had a 63 percent decrease in scrap resulting from its manufacturing process.[50]
- Gate Rubber Co. reduced its lead times, improved product quality, and reduced work in progress by 300 percent after empowering employees by introducing self-directed teams.[51]
- With self-directed teams, Pitney Bowes reduced inventories by 60 percent, and space requirement by 25 percent, while improving its cycle time by 94 percent.[52]

Characteristics of SDTs

Self-directed work teams are defined as "an intact group of employees who are responsible for a 'whole' work process or segment that delivers a product or service to an internal or external customer."[53] Self-directed teams have the following characteristics:

- Members of SDTs normally work together and interact with one another on a day-to-day basis.

- SDTs are specifically given ownership of a distinct product or service, thus requiring a broadening of job categories and sharing of work responsibilities.

- SDTs are **formally** given control over activities traditionally assigned to the boss or manager of a particular work unit or department.[54]

It is this last characteristic, reflecting a corporatewide strategy, that clearly distinguishes self-directed teams from other types of teams or work groups. In other words, organizations are consciously changing their structure and processes to empower employees. Therefore, as teams are empowered by increasing their responsibility level, they increasingly take on activities traditionally associated with the management function rather than with the traditional role of follower or subordinate (see Figure 10.3).

Level 1 teams represent new teams that have not yet taken over many of the responsibilities of the traditional manager. At this level, team members do not have the necessary skills, experience or training to implement the full

FIGURE 10.3

Team empowerment continuum

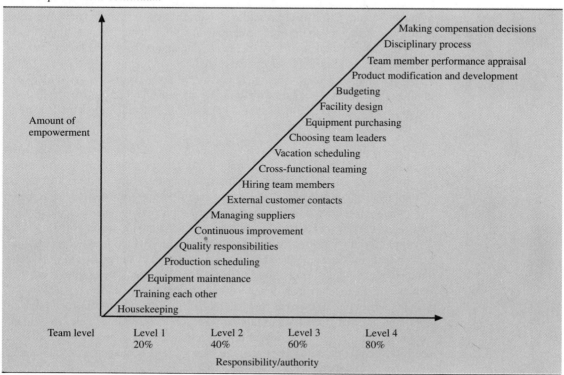

Source: R. S. Wellins, W. C. Byham and J. M. Wilson, *Empowered Teams,* Jossey-Bass Publishers, San Francisco, California, 1991, p.26.

SDT model. This is why many successful self-directed organizations intentionally devote 20 percent of the team members' and leader's time to training in the first year.[55] Three critical areas of training during the early phase of SDT development are job skills, interaction skills, and quality/action skills.[56]

Job skill training is necessary to give team members the depth and breadth of behaviors necessary to effectively carry out the broadened range of activities they will be asked to perform. Team and interaction skills become critical as SDT members prepare to take on higher-order empowerment activities, such as dealing with suppliers, problem solving, self-assessment, and so on. Quality and action skills are necessary to allow team players to effectively participate is such activities as trouble shooting, problem identification, decision making, and implementing improvements.

A New Role for Managers

Managers who become facilitators and coordinators within empowered organizations will likely need additional training if SDTs are to succeed.[57.] These activities are significantly different from the traditional behaviors (directing and controlling the behaviors of others) required of managers who function within traditional organizations. In addition, there is traditionally one manager responsible for a particular department or unit. In empowered organizations, managers are likely to facilitate and coordinate the activities of three or more self-directed teams. As a result, the supervisory role as an independent position is gradually being eliminated.

Carr has identified five new trainable roles that are critical to the manager's success in a team organization managing: (1) alignment, (2) coordination, (3) the decision process, (4) continuous learning, and (5) creating and maintaining trust.[58]

Role 1. Managing Alignment—As stated earlier, it is important for managers to communicate a vision and to create a climate in which all team members are united in a common effort. For the team organization to move effectively toward desired goals, managers must ensure that there is "vertical alignment" from the senior level of management to team players of self-directed groups. In traditional organizations, the initiative and controls designed to achieve alignment come from senior management. In empowered team organizations, however, team players at all levels must be involved in the goal-setting process. Therefore, managers must act to ensure that the goals of empowered team players are aligned with the goals of the organization.

To achieve alignment in team organizations, it is important to have (*a*) open channels of communications between organizational levels, (*b*) organization levels that are clear about their goals, (*c*) employees who believe that proactive behaviors are more productive than reactive behaviors, and (*d*) employees who believe that organizations must engage in renewal and continual improvement. Managers can play an important role in ensuring that these conditions exist with the team organizations. By networking across levels, scanning the organization and its environment, asking appropriate questions, and sharing relevant information with others, the manager can open communication channels.

Regarding clear goals, managers can lead through example. That is, they can place a high value on goal setting and devoting the needed time to set personal and team goals. Along with making goal setting and continual improvement necessities during the early stages of team formation, managers can also provide the needed guidance and information necessary to facilitate goal setting within self-directed groups.

Managers must also decide just how much empowerment is appropriate. They will have to assess teams and determine to what level each team should be developed. Level 1 teams will be given much less freedom in making important unit or organizational decisions because they are newly formed. As team players are trained, gain experience, and demonstrate their ability to perform well, managers will grant greater decision-making autonomy. In addition to being able to diagnose the situation, managers must also be skilled in determining whom to develop to higher levels.

Role 2. Managing Coordination—Employees within a team organization do not work in a vacuum. Instead, they frequently find themselves interacting with others within their own units, crossing departmental boundaries, and working with individuals outside the organization. Furthermore, as unit boundaries disappear and activities are integrated, the behavior of one group is likely to affect the performance of other groups. Interdependency also relates to how scarce resources are distributed within the organization. To successfully carry out the coordination role, managers must ensure that (*a*) teams are satisfying internal and external customers, (*b*) resources are appropriately distributed to maintain the desired work flow, (*c*) teams take responsibility for their product, service, and goals, (*d*) problems are resolved, and (*e*) team players share all relevant information, as well as their best practices.

The manager, again, needs a set of skills to facilitate coordination. How well managers negotiate (Chapters 6 and 7) and handle conflict (Chapter 12) will affect their ability to create value and maintain positive relations with and between others. Managers must also be able to facilitate the negotiations and conflict management efforts that take place among others within the organization. This can be accomplished through managing by example, influencing rather than directing, and by creating an open and trusting environment in which interested parties can be brought together to jointly create value.

Coordination efforts can succeed only if managers also have the prerequisite skills necessary to carry out the required negotiations and conflict management interventions. Specifically, managers must be able to actively listen to others, use personal influence rather than positional power, and be able to empathize with others by considering their views and interests.

Role 3. Managing the Decision Process—At the heart of team empowerment is the team player's ability to make decisions. The role of the manager is to ensure that the best ideas of team players are effectively integrated into a decision-making process that can maintain continued performance improvement. What is important is that team managers ensure that (*a*) team players make the decisions rather than having the manager make decisions for them, (*b*) team players are exposed to and understand how to make effective decisions, and (*c*) decisions are consistent with organizational goals.

The team's decision-making effectiveness will reflect its ability to identify a wide range of action alternatives to any given problem or issue it faces. Therefore, to support this role, managers must be able to develop a creative or innovative climate within each self-directed team. Related to the establishment of a creative environment is the manager's ability to build confidence and employee self-efficacy. As a manager it is easier to communicate the steps of effective decision making than to motivate employees to risk taking control and making decisions. To build confidence, the manager must effectively set goals for, develop and train, provide feedback, coach, and counsel employees. Last, because decision making involves exploration and the identification of action alternatives, conflicts may occur. When this occurs, the manager must be able to manage this conflict and effectively negotiate with the conflicting parties. Each of these skills is discussed elsewhere in the text.

Role 4. Managing Continuous Learning—We have already stated that the world is changing at an increasing rate. To survive in such an environment, managers and team players must continually learn. It is the manager's responsibility not only to take steps to remain personally current but also to create the climate and opportunities in which team players want to learn and do learn. It is important to recognize that in an empowered organization each team player is responsible for his or her own learning. It is the manager's role to facilitate this learning. As a result, Carr argues that managers are not merely change agents; they are learning agents.[59]

As with the previous three roles, managers must possess certain skills if they are to be successful as learning agents. Learning agents must have the skills necessary to introduce change and manage the transition from the old to the new (see Chapter 11). They must have the skills necessary to act as counselors and coaches who provide the support and direction to maintain the employee's willingness to learn (see Chapter 14). Fostering learning in an empowered organization will also require that managers are able to relinquish activities and responsibilities traditionally associated with the management function. Such yielding implies that managers will pass these tasks and responsibilities down to team players, thereby giving them the needed experience to develop and learn. Finally, managers must be effective trainers to convey the required skills to team players.

Role 5. Creating and Maintaining Trust—Trust is one of the most important elements of an empowered organization. Team players must believe that (*a*) management will back them when controversial decisions are made, (*b*) new freedoms are real, (*c*) they will share in the benefits and improvements they create, and (*d*) new responsibilities and activities will not be taken back in the future. Such trust is a prerequisite for team players to take risks.

As discussed in Chapter 6, managers develop a trusting environment by demonstrating strength of character—integrity, acceptance of others, and a willingness to fulfill commitments. The manager's perceived competence and performance track record also facilitate team players' trust in management. Perceived competence reflects the manager's technical expertise, interpersonal competencies (that is, the OLAF skills—observing, listening, asking, and feeling[60]—and willingness to consider the interest of others), and demonstrates business sense or judgment. Finally, managers must recognize that trust takes time to develop.

Potential Errors

Although organizations can benefit from the introduction of self-directed teams, management should be aware of potential errors that can be made and take steps to prevent them from occurring or to minimize their impact. Any attempt to introduce self-directed teams can fail because management has not made an effort to understand the process and ensure that the organization and employees can support such an effort.[61] To prevent *this first error* from occurring, management can review the growing literature on self-directed teams. What is more important, however, is the identification of a group of individuals who will act as a steering committee responsible for assessing the appropriateness of SDTs in the organization. Such a committee would be collecting data about SDTs, visiting organizations that have had successful and unsuccessful experiences with self-directed teams, and determining the receptivity of organizational members. This team would also organize self-directed teams if a decision were made to introduce SDTs and would manage the transition to a team-based organization.

As indicated above, there are a number of critical skills that must be in place if self-directed teams are to function effectively. Therefore, note that a *second error* that can reduce the effectiveness of SDTs is management's failure to provide the needed training for team players and the managers responsible for their operation. Training efforts can also fail if they are rushed.[62] Therefore, management must be patient and allow team players to master the required skills. The importance of training is reflected in the efforts of Chrysler when they opened their Jefferson Avenue plant in Detroit. To ensure that self-management succeeded, Chrysler provided workers with over a million hours of training before the plant opened.[63]

A *third error* can occur if management becomes too far removed from the activities of self-directed teams.[64] Managers, in their enthusiasm to yield control and empower employees, risk removing themselves from the process. This in turn prevents effective monitoring and assessment of team activities. The end result is a team that wanders without direction, hence the likelihood of failure is increased.

Punishing employees for helping each other is a *fourth error* that quickly reduces the creativity of self-directed teams.[65] If employees learn that the fruits of their efforts result in fewer employees or provide solutions that put them out of work, then they will cease to be creative. If management ignores this possible outcome, the potential benefits of SDTs are reduced. The key is to recognize this problem and then ask the team to come up with a workable alternative. For example, teams faced with too many members may identify the following alternatives: use attrition to solve the problem; identify individuals who seek either paid or unpaid leaves, reduced work weeks or benefits; implement job-sharing arrangements among group members; and assign group members to special projects elsewhere in the organization.

To nurture SDTs, it is important that management establishes a reward system which emphasizes team as well as individual efforts.[66] If managers only assign problems to individuals, selectively share information, or reward individual effort, they may fail to effectively model team behavior or set the stage for team rewards. It is necessary for management to consider alternatives such as group bonus plans or some type of gain-sharing. Gain-sharing is a system that allows team players to gain from the improvements resulting from their efforts. It is different from a companywide profit sharing plan as it is based upon the improvements within a particular unit. In other words, team players have control over the factors that affect productivity, quality, cost savings, and so on. Organizations also find it helpful to introduce a pay-for-skill system that motivates team players to expand their skill base, which in turn increases their value to the team and the organization.[67] When a pay-for-skill system is introduced, employees typically receive an increase in pay each time they demonstrate mastery of a new skill important to team success.

As indicated above, the state of team development plays an important role in the degree of autonomy or control the team can handle. If too much autonomy is given too soon, then the team will have more freedom than they know how to handle. The *fifth error* managers make is to rush the transfer of responsibility as they become frustrated with the rate of change. Therefore, the transfer of decision-making authority must be managed and allowed to continue in stages. Orsburn and his colleagues indicate that such a transition may take two to five years to accomplish.[68] Figure 10.4 provides a hypothetical schedule for a gradual transfer of responsibility to team players.

The introduction of SDTs as a major organizational intervention requires a shift in management style and is likely to result in significant structural changes. Consequently, organizations frequently convert to self-directed teams on a trial basis. It is also during the early stages of implementation that the greatest likelihood of team member ambiguity and frustration are likely to occur. Unfortunately, in an effort to introduce the next new team, or because of a motivational let down after the design and implementation phase of team development, managers may fail to adequately monitor and evaluate the functioning SDT.[69] This *sixth and last error* prevents management from fine-tuning the process and learning from its mistakes.[70]

FIGURE 10.4

A planning framework: The transfer of decision-making authority

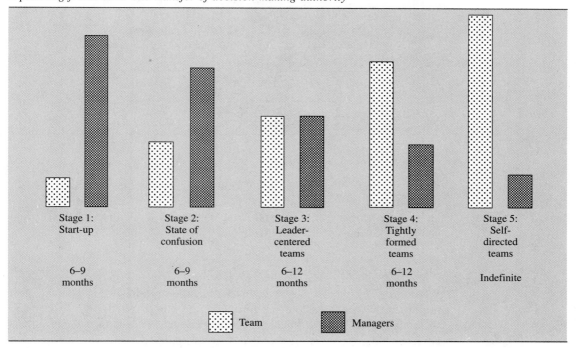

| Team | Managers |

Source: J. D. Orsburn, L. Moran, E. Musselwhite, J. H. Zenger, with C. Perrin, *Self-Directed Work Teams: The New American Challenge*, Business One Irwin, Burr Ridge, Illinois, 1990, p.62. Used with permission.

Stages of Team Development

Important to any effort to introduce teams within an organization is an understanding of the various stages through which groups pass before becoming a highly integrated and effective work team. Keep in mind that the six stages described below apply whether we are discussing quality circles, cross-functional teams, an intact work group, or a self-directed team.

Tuckman argued that there are four stages through which a group passes as it becomes an effective team.[71] The four stages are *forming*, *storming*, *norming*, *performing*. Along with Tuckman's four stages we have also included a *preparation stage* and *maintenance stage* (see Figure 10.5).[72] The model itself is intended to act as a guide in helping managers understand how groups function. When considering a particular group, the observer may find the group functioning at any one of the levels. Groups may also fail to pass through stages 2 through 5 in a linear fashion. That is, they may skip stages or revert to earlier stages once passed. Finally, stages are not linked with specific lengths of time. In fact, it is possible for a group to experience all four stages during a

FIGURE 10.5

Stages of group development

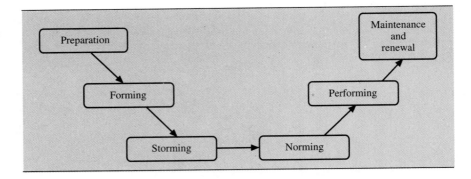

single meeting. What should be obvious, however, is that maximum performance is likely to occur when the group has reached the performance stage and has become a team. The following represents the authors' interpretation of these six stages of development.

Stage One: Preparation

When considering the use of teams within the organizational context, it is important that managers prepare for their team-building activities. It is during the preparation stage that managers collect relevant information, analyze their environments, and develop strategies that will guide them through subsequent stages. During the preparation stage there are a number of questions managers can ask to focus their efforts.[73]

Question 1. Will the organization's environment support my team-building efforts? Not all organizational environments support team-building efforts. As indicated in our basic model, the organization's culture and context may support or hinder the manager's attempt to build a strong team. By assessing the organization's environment, the manager can determine the availability of resources, likelihood of support from other departments, potential rewards associated with successful team efforts, level of discretion afforded managers within their own departments, and whether organizational values and norms will support an open trusting climate, characterized by the free flow of timely and relevant information. The greater the number of organizational road blocks, the greater the need for managers to buffer team-building efforts from the department's external environment. Road blocks also increase the likelihood that managers will be forced to act unilaterally to build effective teams within their units. Perhaps the successful effort in one department will motivate others to follow the manager's lead. When working independently, the manager should only expend the effort when long-term benefits offset long-term costs. If not, the manager is better off directing his or her efforts into more productive endeavors.

Question 2. What tasks must be performed within my department to ensure departmental success, how do they relate to one another, and how do they relate to departmental success? It is important for managers to accurately assess the task activities that must be performed by departmental staff. When assessing task activities, the manager must determine what he or she believes are the critical behaviors necessary to support task performance. Such information is critical when making decisions about work assignments, the degree of interdependence required among subordinates, effort levels required, and the skill and interest levels needed by subordinates to maintain high levels of motivation.

Question 3. What are the interests, expectations, strengths, and weaknesses of my staff? Before making any decision about staff, managers need to have some understanding of their subordinates' interests, expectations, strengths, and weaknesses. Specific staff information facilitates decision making in such areas as group mix (that is, who works with whom), what can and cannot be delegated, how much freedom and autonomy can be given to subordinates, and how fast structural and interpersonal changes can be made.

Question 4. What are the interpersonal dynamics within my work group? Synonymous with effective teams is the ability of team members to interact effectively with one another. How well do the group members fit together in terms of individual personalities, needs, expectations, strengths and weaknesses? If the desired fit does not exist, then the manager must take the necessary steps to ensure that it does.

Question 5. What are my personal needs and abilities? The manager must determine just what it is that he or she wants to accomplish before acting. Given the organizational context, culture, task, and work group characteristics, what type of team structure does the manager want to create? For example, should it be manager-led, self-managed, or self-designed? Managers must also be honest with themselves in assessing current personal abilities and whether they are sufficient to handle potential group problems in the future. For example, can the manager deal with intragroup conflict, coach and counsel subordinates, set goals and negotiate with subordinates, and act as a group facilitator? Here, again, if these skills are not already in place, the manager must determine the best ways to overcome personal deficiencies.

During the preparation stage, managers also want to consider the behaviors and strategies that will ensure each of the remaining stages are successfully completed. Behaviors and strategies should relate to the composition of the team, the roles and responsibilities of the manager and team players, and the training that will likely be needed to facilitate team performance.

Group members, throughout the team development process, will actively be seeking information that will increase their likelihood of success (see Table 10.4).[74] The data collection process and strategy development activities initiated during the preparation stage will help the manager create an environment in which the questions and concerns of team players can be answered.

TABLE 10.4   Questions Relevant to Team Members at Different Stages of Team Development

Forming:

Do I want to belong to this group?

What am I doing here?

Will I fit into the group?

What does the leader expect from group members?

What will be expected of me?

Do I want to be here?

What will be expected from other group members?

Storming:

Who has the real power around here?

Should I worry about who is right or what is right?

Are people fair and reasonable around here?

In this department, do you get what you want by forcing or by being willing to negotiate, compromise, listen, etc.?

How does my position compare with the position of others?

How do my interests compare with the interests of others?

What role does organizational politics play in this department?

Is my position really worth fighting for?

Will people in this group ever work together?

Norming:

What should we be doing?

Which way do we go from here?

Are group standards reasonable and maintainable, given group interests and resources?

Do group norms allow for critical thinking and self-evaluation?

What must we accomplish as a group?

What are our roles and responsibilities in implementing agreed-upon action plans?

Can the group maintain focus and buy in?

Do expressed norms fit our environment and do they support group goals?

Performing:

Can the group keep up this pace?

Are we using team member skills to the fullest?

Are we taking full advantage of existing technologies?

Do we need to evaluate ourselves?

Are group members sufficiently independent of the boss?

Is there anything we can do to make ourselves more productive?

Maintenance and Renewal

Are we beginning to rely on our past successes?

Is our group maintaining sufficient flexibility to change if necessary?

Are we staying current on environmental issues, technologies, user demands, etc.?

Do we have any members that have become stagnant?

Are we paying enough attention to what tomorrow will bring?

Are there any internal signs of burnout?

Stage Two: Forming

Although most managers will face work groups that have already passed through the forming stage, there are circumstances where already-established groups will experience the same internal dynamics. This occurs when some major change disrupts the status quo and forces the group to redefine who and what it is. For example, if the group experiences significant turnover, influx of a large number of new members, the introduction of a new major technology, or a significant change in its accepted mandate, then the group will have to go through some type of reforming process. It must also be noted that when a manager is put in charge of a new group, or is given the responsibility of creating a new group, the forming stage will likely take center stage. The issue to consider is just what must the manager do to ensure that group members successfully pass through the forming stage.

It is during the forming stage that group members define who they are, what the group is, and define in their own minds what everyone else is supposed to be doing. The group's ability to pass through this stage is determined by the degree to which members adequately answer the questions associated with forming. If the manager can facilitate the defining process, the group's passage through this stage will also be facilitated. Consequently, managers must play an active role in creating the environment in which group members can obtain a clear picture of what is expected of them and why. Managers can accomplish this by carrying out a number of activities designed to transfer critical information, and at the same time shape subordinates' behavior. These activities include orientation programs, one-on-one goal setting, group discussions, and team pairing.

1. Orientation programs. In the case of new employees joining the group, significant time can be saved during the forming stage if the manager has an integrated orientation program within his or her department. This may be in addition to, or in place of, an organizationwide orientation through which many employees are processed. It is through the orientation process that the manager transfers general information about the department and the expected role of subordinates. Orientation activities are often the employee's first formal interaction with the department and are often viewed as an indication of things to come.

2. One-on-one goal setting. Once the manager has clarified personal perceptions and expectations of what constitutes desired subordinate behavior, he or she should initiate an ongoing goal-setting process with the employee (review Chapter 9). As part of this process, the manager articulates his or her desire for the subordinate to behave in a manner consistent with the 12 dimensions associated with effective teams. In doing so, the manager gives specific examples of the types of behavior that support each dimension. If the manager wants the subordinate to share in the leadership of the group, he or she should give examples of what would be expected of the employee. A subordinate who acts as a group leader would be expected to exhibit behaviors such as controlling disruptive co-workers during departmental meetings, following up on work performed by another group member, initiating and leading group discussions designed to improve departmental performance, encouraging others to become more involved in departmental issues, and so on.

By initiating the goal-setting process, the manager helps ensure that subordinates have a clear picture of what is expected of them and allows them an opportunity to clarify or alter such expectations by using, for example, the process of principled negotiations. Furthermore, effective goal setting is a critical step in the evaluation and feedback process necessary to facilitate employee development (see Chapter 13).

3. Group discussions. To clarify goals and behavioral expectations, it is often desirable for the manager to bring subordinates together and give the total group the responsibility of discussing, clarifying, or establishing departmental goals. The actual level of responsibility given to the group is determined by their experience, interest, commitment, and the importance of the goal area being considered. What is important is that the manager begins to involve subordinates as a group in some level of the goal-setting process. This involvement not only facilitates passage through the forming stage but also creates the environment in which group members can begin to experience and develop the "we-feeling."

As the group is at an early stage of development, it is likely that the leader will have to take a very active role in leading such a meeting. Four "member" roles articulated by Parker (1990) help clarify which managerial behaviors would be appropriate during early group attempts to identify departmental goals.[75] The four roles the manager will play are:

- **Contributor**—provides the group with the best information, opinions, insights, or expertise at his or her disposal. Information, opinions, and expertise are used to initiate group discussions and motivate the group to set high standards. This is possible because the contributor has a clear personal idea of group priorities. Ultimately, the contributor will attempt to mentor and train others to fill this and other team roles.

- **Collaborator**—helps the group clarify and establish long-term goals, establish milestones, and, at the same time, helps integrate short-term activities and behaviors with long-term goals. Part of the collaborator's responsibility is to ensure that the group periodically reassesses its action plans and goals. The collaborator is also willing to help others through personal effort to help ensure short-term success.

- **Communicator**—facilitates the team process by helping to open channels of communication and actively listening to the position of others. The communicator also engages in rapport-building activities by using probing, summarizing, reflecting, supporting, and feedback statements. The communicator will also step in, when appropriate, to resolve interpersonal conflicts.

- **Challenger**—fulfills the role of group critic or devil's advocate. As such he or she will freely disagree with group decisions, criticize statements made, and ask "How?" and "Why?" questions designed to motivate the group to analyze and reflect on what they are doing. Ultimately, the challenger acts as the conscience for the group to ensure that actions taken are ethical and legal.

The authors would also add the role of **Controller** to Parker's four roles. During each stage of team building, managers may find it necessary to control, take charge, or direct group activities to facilitate the development of a "we-feeling." As the team develops, the controller role should become less important, and when needed, will be shared among the team's members. In fact, members of a successful team will share the responsibility of carrying out each of the roles outlined above. Again, the ultimate goal is a self-managed or self-designed group.

In early attempts to clarify group goals through the process of group discussion, managers are likely to find themselves engaged in the following behaviors. As a *Contributor*, the manager would take the initiative and call a group meeting to discuss departmental goals. The same would be true if the manager wanted to call a meeting to discuss goals in a specific area or in terms of a specific project. The manager would also give direction to group members by indicating how each participant could prepare for the upcoming discussion and, at the same time, articulate a process to be followed during the upcoming meeting.

As a *Collaborator*, the manager shares his or her views about what the goals of the group should be. The manager can also outline his or her view of how stated goals might be translated into measurable milestones for the group in order to integrate short-term activities with long-term goals. This is done in a manner designed to communicate that such preferences are not irrevocable and that there is room for negotiation. The manager can specifically ask group members to either state their views or critically comment on their views. If group members do not yet feel comfortable in stating their views in the larger group format, the manager may find it necessary to divide the group into smaller discussion groups that will independently discuss the goal area under consideration and report back to the larger group. Alternatively, it is sometimes effective for the manager to have group members independently write down their views and then, in round-robin fashion, read their views to the total group.

To ensure a free flow of information, the manager will often find it necessary during early group discussion to play the role of *Communicator*. Realizing the need to stimulate open communications, the manager will often meet subordinates before the planned group discussion and explain the importance of each member's willingness to talk openly within the group. If this cannot be done before the planned meeting then one of the first priorities of the manager is to state the necessity for each member to speak openly. It is important for the manager to model this principle through his or her own behavior. As a communicator, the manager will also act as group facilitator by ensuring that all members have an equal opportunity to talk and that interpersonal conflict or dominant personalities do not stifle open communications. To keep channels of communication open, managers will be expected to summarize, probe, and support the communications of other group members.

Last, the manager must also act as a model for the group as a *Challenger*, asking questions and openly criticizing, in an interpersonally sensitive manner, positions taken by members or the group as a whole. This can be accomplished by specifically asking if the members are (*a*) happy with what they have accomplished, (*b*) happy with the statement of the group's goal, or (*c*) in any way uncomfortable with the group's accomplishments or progress. The manager must attempt to instill the belief that it is each group member's responsibility to become group critic to ensure that nothing important is missed and that "group think" does not prevent the group from engaging in self-assessment.

4. Team pairing. An effective technique for integrating new members into a functioning group is team pairing. Here, the manager pairs the new employee with one of his or her senior subordinates. The intention is to use the senior subordinate as a role model for the new employee. The new employee is expected to define his or her role within the department and determine appropriate departmental goals and behaviors by vicariously observing and interacting with the seasoned co-worker. The most common example of this process occurs when a veteran police officer is paired with a rookie who is just out of the police academy.

Stage Three: Storming

As individuals define who and what they are, what they want from a particular situation, what they believe is expected of them by others, and become more comfortable with the idea of expressing themselves, guarantees that the group will remain harmonious no longer exist. Conversely, the reverse is often the case when groups are relatively young, the situation is ambiguous, or the membership is diverse. Therefore, it is not surprising for both theorists and practitioners to envision a period of storming within the group's developmental process. The process of storming may be important to the development of an effective team. The reasoning for such a statement is that conflict indicates that stress exists within the system. As indicated in the conflict chapter, the group that learns to effectively handle conflict is often better off for its efforts. The conflict resolution process often draws the group together as a team by clarifying goals and member roles and responsibilities. If conflict is not openly addressed, it often becomes covert, resulting in passive resistance by group members.

When groups are young and members are inexperienced, the burden for conflict management rests on the shoulders of the manager. It is only when the group matures and members share in its leadership that members lighten the manager's burden. The behavioral guidelines articulated in Chapter 12 on conflict would help the manager fulfill this role. It is also possible to discuss the manager's appropriate response to conflict at the storming level by considering how he or she carries out the roles of contributor, collaborator, communicator, and challenger. (Since one individual is fulfilling all four roles, it is likely that the manager will alternate between the roles as he or she *attempts to help the group manage the conflict.*)

Even before conflict occurs, *Contributors* educate their subordinates about the positive and negative effects of conflict and the value of civilized disagreement. When conflict does occur, contributors, while remaining neutral, use their expertise, insight, and influence to help the group overcome problems. If the conflicting parties are present, the manager requests that they take the time to consider available information, and group or member interests in an attempt to develop an acceptable solution through joint problem solving. During such a discussion, the manager facilitates the process by asking conflicting parties to support their position with specific points.

As *Collaborator*, managers immerse themselves in the discussion of issues, interests, and supporting information. The manager's objective is to ensure that the group relates material discussed with long-term goals, intermediate milestones, and short-term activities. In so doing, the manager hopes to motivate the group to keep the conflict in perspective and to arrive at solutions that are consistent with team success. Managers also act as models by demonstrating a willingness to alter their position relative to group goals in response to information presented during the discussion.

The manager fulfills the role of *Communicator* by ensuring that all interested parties have input into the conflict-management process. This can be accomplished by ensuring that the discussion is not dominated by one or two individuals or that quiet or withdrawn members are not ignored during a heated or emotional confrontation. The manager can also maintain open channels of communication through the appropriate use of probes, summarization, and nonverbal reinforcement of other communicators within the group. If emotions are high, the manager may decide that the interpersonal dynamics of the situation are such that the conflicting parties should be separated. That is, interactions should be postponed until all sides are ready for open and candid discussions. Once communications have been concluded, the situation may require a form of shuttle diplomacy with the manager functioning as a communications link between the conflicting parties.

As *Challenger*, the manager must ensure the authenticity of the information provided by the conflicting parties and that each has been candid. In an interpersonally sensitive manner, the manager may find it necessary to ask others to defend their motives, information sources, and even the accuracy of the information presented. Furthermore, the manager must ensure that all statements relate to substantive issues being considered and do not reflect personal attacks between group members. Conflicting parties may also be challenged to explain how their position supports the group's or team's goals and why the issue was raised.

Often, however, it is possible to avert, or shorten, the storming stage by acting in a proactive manner. One of the main areas in which conflict arises is in the assignment or allocation of roles and responsibilities to group members.[76] Recognizing this fact, many managers reduce the likelihood of future conflict by taking the time to have the group openly discuss the allocation of roles and responsibilities for a particular goal or project. Three techniques one of the authors has found to be effective for managers are *group discussions* facilitated by the manager (or another group member), *role negotiations*, and *responsibility charting*.[77]

1. When using **group discussions** to achieve consensus on work allocation, the manager will find it desirable for one individual to act as group facilitator. If the group is newly formed, or significant conflict exists, the manager will most frequently fulfill this role. We have also found that this technique works best when discussing an agreed-upon sequence of action plans designed to achieve a desirable end goal. For example, a group seeking to reorganize its departmental structure to better service other organizational units may identify data collection as the necessary first step in the action plan sequence. The group, with guidance from the facilitator, would first identify those organizational units most in need of the department's services. Such external departments would provide the richest source of information during the data collection process. The group then considers member interests, contacts, time, and areas of expertise to identify the most appropriate individual to contact a particular department. This process would continue until all data collecting responsibilities were assigned. During this process the group may also find it helpful to articulate and list the types of data that should be obtained from each department and the questions most likely to elicit this information. The use of group discussions to allocate work responsibilities requires that (*a*) the group has achieved an acceptable level of "we-feeling", (*b*) the manager feels comfortable facilitating such a meeting, and (*c*) the manager believes his or her subordinates can openly communicate with one another.

2. **Role negotiations** work best after task/behavior responsibilities have been allocated and the group has been functioning for some time. This process also assumes that members are able to give effective feedback to one another and are willing to openly discuss the allocation of work responsibilities. During personal team-building sessions we have used the techniques with only 2 individuals who are experiencing a disagreement or with groups as large as 18 members. The process requires that participants write down for other group members their response to the following questions: What could the other person do more often to make the group more successful? What could the other person do better? What could the other person do that they are not doing now to make the group more effective? What tasks, activities, or behaviors could the other person do less often, or stop altogether, to make the group perform more effectively? Once participants have individually written out their responses, the group openly discusses their answers.

The group reviews member responses to ensure a complete understanding of what has been written by each participant. This is done without any attempt to negotiate or evaluate what has been stated. Once group understanding has been reached, members identify those areas in which disagreement exists. Changes designed to overcome disagreements are negotiated, using the process of principled negotiations and group discussion, among the group members. Output from this process acts as a basis for group member behavior in the future and represents the new standards against which they will be assessed. This process can be repeated whenever the manager, or other group members, believe disagreements about work allocation exist within the group and are of sufficient magnitude to reduce the group's effectiveness.

3. **Responsibility charting** is a more structured process that attempts to answer the following questions: Who has the responsibility to make certain decisions and take certain actions? Who has the right to approve or veto these decisions and actions? To achieve group success, who must support (provide information, resources, etc.) these decisions and actions? Once made, or carried out, who should be informed of these decisions and actions? To facilitate the process, the manager can use a chart, or grid, that group members are asked to fill out individually (see Figure 10.6).[78] This would require group members to individually list the names of group members across the top of the responsibility chart. Next, group members would identify, for each decision or action, who has "R"—primary responsibility, "A-V"—approval power or right to veto, "S"-provides support in terms of resources, and "I"—should be informed.

Next, group members would discuss individual perceptions to assess the level of agreement among each other. For each decision or activity, members

FIGURE 10.6

Responsibility chart

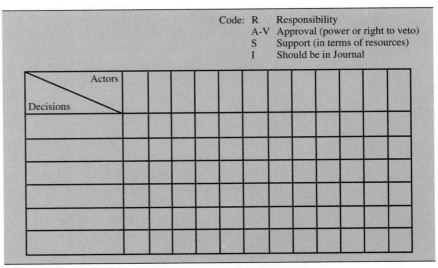

Code: R   Responsibility
A-V   Approval (power or right to veto)
S   Support (in terms of resources)
I   Should be in Journal

Source: R. Beckard and R. T. Harris, *Organizational Transitions: Managing Complex Change*, Addison-Wesley Publishing Company, Inc., Reading, Massachusetts, 1977: p. 78.

would indicate how they distributed their R's, A–V's, S's, and I's. One way the group could continue would be to present individual perceptions in a round-robin fashion. In those instances where disagreement existed, the group would attempt to achieve group consensus by discussing possible reasons for the disagreement, the implications of such disagreement, and possible alternatives designed to overcome existing conflict. Here again the process of principled negotiation and group consensus can be used as a mechanism to achieve desired results.

Clearly, the manager plays an active role in helping the group to successfully pass through, or avoid, the storming stage of group development. It is conceivable, however, that groups will periodically revisit this level. To lighten their load, managers want to ensure that through modeling, training, coaching, and so on, group members are motivated to share the leader's responsibility in managing conflict in the future.

Stage Four: Norming

Norms, within the group setting, act as an internalized guide when determining acceptable behavior. More specifically, norms reflect the individual's belief that certain behaviors are appropriate, will lead to both individual and team success, and that such success will result in positive payoffs for both the individual and the team. Sequentially, norming partially results from the group's successful passage through the first three stages of group development. In other words, the learning that has been taking place throughout the development process helps the individual to create his or her normative structure.

For example, at some early stage in the team's development, it may have been determined that the group's interpersonal interactions would follow an open work group design. Such a design would allow all members to freely access any group meeting that took place within the group, to stop work at any time to discuss progress directly relating to performance or process issues, and to have a group meeting anywhere to address issues of concern. Once such behavior is internalized and accepted as a behavioral norm, group members will routinely carry out their daily tasks in a manner consistent with the internalized norm.

The steps that managers take to create an internalized set of norms at their subordinates' level are many and can occur at all levels of the team development process (see Figure 10.7).

As subordinates interact with their environment, they learn what is expected of them. Energizing this process is the individual's desire to be successful within his or her environment. The manager can play an active role in activating each of the identified building blocks of the norming process.

We have already determined that one-on-one goal setting is a critical step when attempting to obtain high levels of performance. Similarly, managers ensure further goal clarity by ensuring that their subordinates unite to jointly discuss what should be the team's goals. The focus and acceptance resulting from these *goal setting* activities play an important role in determining the direction in which the subordinates' normative structure will develop.

FIGURE 10.7

*Understanding the
norming process*

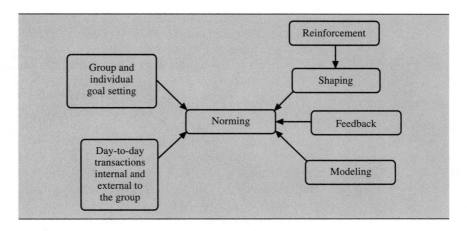

Figure 10.7 indicates that *day-to-day transactions* within the organization also play a role in determining the subordinates' normative structure. Through vicarious learning, the subordinates copy the dominant behaviors that appear to work within the existing environment. If co-workers are behaving in a particular way and this new behavior is not in conflict with the subordinate's existing system of values and attitudes, there is a high probability that the subordinate will copy this behavior. In other words, the relevant others in the subordinates' environment are acting as a model for them.[79] Copied behavior that is further reinforced when carried out by the subordinates will likely become part of those individuals' normative structure.

At a more structured level, the manager can take an active role creating specific models designed to influence the behavior of subordinates. Due to the manager's position, formal power, and visibility, he or she often acts as the model for subordinates. Therefore, the manager must be aware of his or her own behaviors and how they shape the normative expectations of subordinates. If the manager wants his or her staff to engage in open communications, then the manager must freely share information with others within the organization. If the manager wants his or her staff to network with others internal and external to the department then he or she must do the same. For example, a manager for whom one of the authors provided process consultation was often hearing complaints that his staff did not attend professional conferences on a regular basis. Such behavior was important to the success of his department because of the opportunity to share ideas with fellow professionals and hear new ideas in the field. Through the process of interviewing subordinates, it quickly became apparent that the manager himself never attended scheduled professional meetings. This occurred even though such trips were part of the manager's job responsibilities. The manager's failure to attend professional conferences was the main reason given for the lack of attendance by subordinates.

Managers also create a *modeling* environment when they use team pairing. As indicated earlier, the manager may pair an inexperienced subordinate with a more experienced team member so the more senior individual can act as a model. The subordinate is expected to copy the behavior of the senior individual and thereby internalize an appropriate normative structure.

Shaping is another strategy the manager can use to cause subordinates to change personal behaviors and internalize new norms. Shaping works well in those areas where the desired terminal behavior is unlikely to occur even after instructions have been given or the employee has been shown a model. If the manager waits for an employee to reach a pre-established standard of behavior before some type of reinforcement is given, the subordinate may never be reinforced. The likely result is that the employee will not improve. By engaging in shaping, the manager reinforces closer and closer approximations of a desired terminal behavior and thereby increases the probability of change by the subordinate. In this way, the manager is *reinforcing* improvement.

When used by itself, the process of shaping may prove to be a tedious and time-consuming experience. It is therefore recommended that the manager combine the processes of modeling and shaping to reduce the time and effort needed to produce behavior change.

The process of *feedback* can also be used effectively by the manager to affect the behaviors and expectations of subordinates. To fine tune subordinate behaviors, managers must provide accurate and timely feedback to each of their staff. Subordinates must also be educated on how and when they can give feedback to one another. Team members cannot be expected to appropriately maintain or alter their behavior unless they understand that their behavior is either acceptable or unacceptable. Such global assessments must also be backed up by specific examples. The process of feedback requires that the manager know what behavior he or she desires, monitors actual behavior exhibited by subordinates, records and classifies observed behavior, and, finally, rates behavior.

Stage Five: Performing

The difference between earlier stages of group development and the performing stage is one of degree. Group activities and individual behaviors during the earlier stages are intended to bring the group to the performing level. During the performing stage, the group is focused, committed, and taking advantage of team synergy. The team also does not face any threatening issues or problems that could divert the group's attention from stated goals. When this stage occurs, the manager and his or her staff should be performing at desired levels. The team's performance can then be evaluated on the effectiveness criteria discussed earlier, namely the achievement of stated goals, continued improvement of the team's social and process components, and the satisfaction of individual needs.

At the performing level, tasks and group members fit well together. Consequently, the group exhibits rhythm, flow, and oneness. When this occurs, there is a noticeable change in the climate of the group, which members can feel. The following represent visible signs of such a climate:

- Group members anticipate the actions and feelings of others and subsequently act in a manner designed to maximize group performance.
- Group members begin to anticipate future problems and crises, and act in a proactive manner to prevent such problems/crises from occurring.
- Group members don't wait for co-workers to ask for help; rather, they help before being asked. In fact, members often anticipate a future need and act to prevent the problem from arising.
- Creativity and innovation occurs frequently and without external pressure. Consequently, change is a natural process within the group and results in minimum, or no, resistance.
- Problem solving reflects an intuitive quality, thereby reducing the time devoted to data collection, analysis, and alternative generation.
- Group members activate informal channels of communication more frequently than formal channels.

To ensure success at the performing stage, the manager has two key responsibilities. First, the manager must ensure that a system has been established which effectively processes performance information and must use this information to reward high performance (For a detailed discussion of this issue, see Chapter 9). Second, the manager must ensure that the team is buffered and protected from resource, information, and political fluctuations that might threaten high performance.

1. The manager must take steps to reward behaviors consistent with the 12 characteristics of effective teams and the actual results achieved by teams. This will require that the manager, in concert with his or her subordinates, has first established the set of behaviors, tasks, and responsibilities necessary for employee success and the result desired. Such initial steps are, as we have discussed, directly linked with the goal-setting process, either on a one-to-one basis, or on a group basis. Success at this level provides the manager with direction when attempting to monitor individual behaviors and team results. The monitoring stage is designed to provide the information necessary to make correct decisions when rewarding either individuals or groups. The manager must take the time to observe, record, classify, and rate performance. Having gone through this process, the manager now has sufficient information to determine the appropriate allocation of rewards.

The manager now allocates rewards in a manner designed to bring maximum reinforcement for results and behaviors associated with team and individual success. To accomplish this, some balance must be reached between rewards based upon individual efforts versus rewards based upon group efforts. If managers rely exclusively on an individually based reward system, they run the risk of dampening cooperative efforts because group members must compete among themselves for scarce resources—in this case, rewards distributed by managers.[80] The objective is to motivate employees to start thinking in "we" terms: "What is in it for **us**?" Conversely, if there is no clear mechanism to measure the contribution of individuals to the team activity, and some rewards do not reflect individual contributions in expertise, knowledge, or skill, then individual employee efforts may again be reduced. Achieving a workable balance between individual and team rewards may be one of the most difficult tasks facing the manager when cultivating a team climate.

2. High performance in the group can be facilitated if managers take steps to support, buffer, and protect their staff. The manager must ensure that subordinates can move effectively toward desired goals. If such movement is threatened, or perceived as unlikely, the employee will reduce personal efforts or seek out other less desirable goals. The logic behind this view is firmly rooted in process motivation theories, goal setting, and the path-goal theory of leadership. The following are specific examples of supporting, buffering, and protecting behaviors.

- The manager ensures that subordinates have sufficient information and resources to achieve desired results. This can be accomplished through personal networking, negotiating, bargaining or trading with other departments or units to obtain the information and material necessary to support high performance.
- The manager can absorb pressure and criticism from more senior managers and thereby prevent his or her staff from being affected by such negative behavior.
- The manager can actively fulfill his or her directive role when subordinates face ambiguous or rapidly changing task environments.
- During periods of rapid change or high environmental stress, or when dissatisfying tasks must be performed, the manager can act to coach, counsel, and support subordinates' efforts.
- The manager effectively represents subordinates' views to power brokers external to the unit.

Stage Six: Renewal

Self-assessment by the team allows its members to determine whether renewal is desirable to maintain high levels of performance. Members may ask, "Should we continue in the same direction, as a group, or at the current level of performance?" When the answers to these questions are negative, the team must make a clear choice regarding its future. The team can allow itself to disintegrate, or seek renewal. In the case of temporary work teams, self-assessment may indicate there is no defensible reason for continuance. That is, stated goals have been achieved, there is nothing else for the team to do, and team disintegration is appropriate. When the temporary team has not yet achieved its objectives but is experiencing entropy, or when the team is permanent, renewal is the desired alternative.

When dealing with his or her staff, it is the renewal alternative that must be the primary concern of the functioning manager. Without actively ensuring renewal it is likely that managers will find themselves directing groups that have become stagnant or otherwise unproductive. To be successful, the manager must ensure that this does not occur.

Three conditions appear to be associated with successful team renewal. They are self-assessment, shared leadership, and action-oriented renewal strategies.

1. Self-assessment. Timely renewal most often occurs when the team assesses its own performance. Self-assessment begins with the team asking key questions about team performance: Are we beginning to rely on our past successes? Do we have any members that have become stagnant? Is our group maintaining sufficient flexibility to change if necessary? Are we paying enough attention to what tomorrow will bring? Are we staying current on environmental issues, technologies, user demands, etc.? Are there any internal signs of burnout?

The frequency of self-assessment must reflect the underlying conditions existing within the team's environment. Situational factors such as environmental dynamics, environmental uncertainty, and task importance are likely to play a critical role in determining the appropriate rate of self-assessment. Teams that face dynamic and uncertain environments and are engaged in tasks central to the department or organization increase the probability of success when self-assessment is carried out frequently. The further a team's environment moves toward certain, predictable, and low task importance the less frequently it needs to engage in self-assessment.

2. Shared leadership. The next issue of concern facing the manager is the question of who is responsible for the team's self-assessment process. It is possible for the manager to unilaterally to assess the group's performance. Such a tactic, however, is inconsistent with the management style needed for the 1990s and the characteristics of an effective team. In the authors' experience, the most effective teams are those that rely on shared leadership to ensure that self-assessment occurs. Shared leadership again allows for group acceptance, employee empowerment, maximum information sharing, leader style and environmental congruence, and the lightening of the manager's load. Each one of these conditions increases the probability that self-assessment will have the desired result. In other words, the team will recognize that something must be done to revitalize the team and its members.

It is also possible to use the roles of collaborator, contributor, communicator, challenger and controller to explain how shared leadership works within the effective team. The following are examples of how these roles might be acted out during the self-assessment process.

- **Challenger**—The challenger acts to point out to the group that all is not well. He or she may be responding to information originating internally or externally to the group, nonverbal behaviors, or even a gut feeling on his or her part that the group is losing steam. What is important is that the challenger asks the right questions at the right time to confront the group with evidence of stagnation.

- **Collaborator**—The collaborator works with others to review standards and expectations and compare these with actual performance levels. This individual is willing to work with other members to collect and process information so that useful information has been made available to all team members.
- **Contributor**—The contributor is willing to share all of his or her perceptions of what has, is, and should be taking place within the team. He or she also plays an active role in pointing out what should be considered if the group is to openly and honestly assess its performance.
- **Communicator**—During the self-assessment process, the communicator ensures that all members have had an opportunity to present their views.
- **Controller**—The controller can help ensure that side conversations or dominant figures do not prevent the group from carrying out the self-assessment process. The controller also ensures that, while time is not wasted, forward momentum is maintained.

3. Action-oriented renewal strategies. Knowing that the team has a problem does not automatically produce a solution to that problem. Action strategies are needed which, when implemented, will act to revitalize the team. Whatever steps are taken to ensure team renewal, its result will be to provide the answers to questions such as, "Are we the best that we can be?" "Are we living up to our potential?" "Have we taken advantage of all existing opportunities in our environment?" "Have we identified our weaknesses and are we, as a team, taking the necessary steps to correct them?" "Is there a reason for the team to continue?" Here again, the richest source for such alternatives can be found within the team itself.

Team enthusiasm may decline as the individuals involved in group activities lose interest in what they are doing. This can occur when the excitement of the new project is replaced by repetitiveness. As problems are solved or revisited, activities become routine. To revitalize such teams, scanning and prospecting activities designed to uncover new opportunities can be encouraged. The group may establish scanning and prospecting activities as normative behaviors to be carried out by all team members. Should such an alternative prove unproductive, the team can assign such activities to specific individuals. In both cases, the carrying out of such activities should be supported by the manager by establishing renewal as a goal, allocating time and resources to assessing, scanning, and prospecting activities, and by rewarding results— both individually and as a group.

The manager must also take steps to ensure that team members are exposed to new ideas. Funds can be made available for training opportunities that are likely to expose the employee to new ideas, processes, or new technologies. Similarly, the manager can encourage team members to network with other individuals either internally or externally to the organization. Alternatively, group members can be encouraged to join associations, attend conferences, and even put on their own brown-bag lunches to facilitate cross-fertilization of ideas. By opening up channels of communication with similar others, who are facing similar problems or have access to important information, the potential exists to stimulate team renewal.

There are also situations where the manager, or another team member, recognizes that the group is not exhibiting normal levels of output or enthusiasm. This may occur even though other renewal strategies are in place and operative. When this happens it is often desirable for the manager (or other group members) to request that the team stop what it is doing and turn its attention to the issue of why it is not performing at desired levels. At this point, team members have the potential to provide the needed insight, information, and action alternatives to revitalize the team. Team members frequently come up with a greater variety of action alternatives than a single manager who may be a linear thinker, committed to a particular course of action, or less familiar with the day-to-day activities of each individual.

Summary

Trained and motivated subordinates who do not function as a team are likely to limit the performance levels achieved by the manager. Traditionally, managers have turned to others off-site to create the team performing within their departments. Such an alternative is often not viable for managers who have limited funds or want to create an on-the-job environment conducive to long-term team building. To facilitate on-the-job team building, managers must recognize the six states of team development and design and implement a set of strategies necessary to bring the group successfully through each stage.

We have also discussed the concept of self-directed teams. Although SDTs are built upon the same theory as teams developed by managers, they represent a formalized organizational intervention that goes beyond the manager's own department. As such, SDTs require structural changes within the organizations and some type of steering committee capable of implementing and assessing the SDT program.

Exercises

10.1 Evaluating Team Climate and Its Role in Determining Team Success

It has been argued that groups that demonstrate team characteristics will be more effective than groups that do not. To assess the validity of this statement, a small experiment will be run. Please follow the steps outlined below.

Step 1. The class will be broken into two groups. Members of Group 1 will be asked to think of an organization to which they now belong or have belonged in the past that has the following characteristics: (*a*) work was always late or poorly done, (*b*) criticism came from individuals both inside and outside the organization, and (*c*) members expressed low satisfaction. Members of Group 2 will be asked to think of an organization to which they now belong or have belonged in the past that has the following characteristics: (*a*) work was always of good quality and completed on time, (*b*) few internal or external criticisms were directed at the group, and (*c*) members expressed high satisfaction.

Step 2. Visualize this organization and some of the events that took place while you were a member. (5 minutes)

Step 3. Complete the evaluation questionnaire distributed to the class by the instructor. You should answer the 60 items with reference to the organization you were thinking about in Step 2. Once you have completed the questionnaire, score it by using the answer key on the last page. Do not look at the scoring key until after you have finished. To do otherwise may distort your score. (15 minutes)

Step 4. The instructor will distribute overhead transparencies and markers. Once you have yours, please plot your group profile. (Refer to the example shown on the overhead projector.) Group 1 will use red markers. Group 2 will use blue markers.

Step 5. Transparencies will be collected and results will be discussed. Selected transparencies will be projected on the overhead and results will be discussed.

10.2 Allocating Roles and Responsibilities

Once a group has identified its goals and objectives, it is critical that its members agree on the internal allocation of activities necessary for group success. Unfortunately, many groups function with members uncertain about their roles and responsibilities. This uncertainty reduces group effectiveness through conflict and an unwillingness to act quickly or by allowing important activities to go unattended. This exercise is designed to help your group identify and gain consensus on the allocation of such activities.

Assume that it is the first week of a business policy course in the School of Business Administration. You are in the last year of your program. The policy professor has just informed you that the school has entered a national case competition. Entering the competition is a course requirement. The competition requires that policy students form teams to analyze specific cases. Each team will compete with other teams. During the first round of competition, teams from the three sections of the policy course compete against one another. The winner moves on to the next level of competition. Please follow the steps outlined below.

Step 1. The class will break up into small groups of five to six individuals each.

Step 2. Each group will list activities (decisions and actions) it believes must be performed to compete effectively in the first round of the case competition. The activities listed may be a combination of formal activities necessary for goal achievement, process activities, and team maintenance activities. List the identified activities on the right-hand side of a blank 8-1/2 x 11 sheet of paper. Label this your Role/Responsibility Chart. (The instructor will draw an example of the chart on the chalk board.) (Approximately 20 minutes)

Step 3. Each group member should work alone and list other group member names across the top of the Role/Responsibility Chart. Next, for each activity (decision or action) indicate who has primary responsibility with a P, approval power with an A, veto power with a V, provides support in terms of resources with an S, and who must be informed with an I. Output from Step 3 should reflect each individual's personal perceptions of how the group should function. If you are unfamiliar with members of the group, make assumptions or random allocations. If you feel uncomfortable about making allocations at this time, leave the space blank. (Approximately 15 minutes)

Step 4. Each group assembles to discuss individual perceptions and assess the level of agreement among group members. For each activity, individual members should indicate how they distributed their P's, A's, V's, S's, and I's. One way to do this is through a round-robin discussion. Where there is disagreement, the group should discuss reasons for the disagreement and their implications, and then attempt to reach a consensus. For those activities that do not have a complete allocation, groups should assign missing responsibilities/roles. This can be accomplished by group members volunteering, indicating preferences, accepting workloads, and so forth. (Approximately 45 minutes)

Step 5. The class will assemble to consider the implications of obtaining both agreement and commitment.

End Notes

1. Throughout this chapter, the authors will be discussing the team concept at the department level. Described in this manner, the team should be considered relatively permanent and involving all members of the manager's staff. The team concept can also be used to describe temporary work groups formed to handle a particular problem or issue. Although many of the points covered in the following pages apply to both types of teams, there may be application and process differences.

2. J. Gordon, "Work teams: How far have they come?" *Training,* Vol. 29, No. 10, 1992: 59–65.

3. Gordon, 1992.

4. J. R. Schermerhorn, Jr., "Team development for high performance management," *Training and Development Journal,* Vol. 40, No. 11, 1986: 38–41; S. L. Perlman, "Employees redesign their jobs," *Personnel Journal,* Vol. 69, No. 11, 1990: 37–40; D. Tjosvold, *Team Organization: An Enduring Competitive Advantage,* John Wiley & Sons, New York, 1991; D. Hitchock, "Overcoming the top ten self-directed team stoppers," *Journal for Quality & Participation,* Vol. 15, No. 7, December 1992: 42–45; B. McKee, "Turn your workers into a team," *Nation's Business,* Vol. 80, No. 7, July 1992: 36–38; L. Jones, "We need to re-expand

our organizational brains," *Journal for Quality & Participation,* Vol. 16, No. 3, June 1993: 28–31.

5. Schermerhorn, Jr., November 1986.

6. H. R. Jessup, "New roles in team leadership," *Training and Development Journal,* Vol. 44, No. 11, 1990: 79–83; J. H. Zenger, E. Musselwhite, K. Hurson, and C. Perrin, "Leadership in a team environment," *Training and Development Journal,* Vol. 45, No. 10, 1991: 47–52.

7. F. D. Barrett, "Teamwork—How to expand its power and punch," *Business Quarterly,* Winter 1987: 24–31.

8. C. E. Larson and F. M. J. LaFasto, *Team Work: What Must Go Right/What Can Go Wrong,* Sage Publications Inc., Newbury Park, California, 1989.

9. R. Beckard, "Optimizing team building efforts," *Journal of Contemporary Business,* Vol. 1, No. 3, 1972: 23–32.

10. W. W. Burke, "Team Building," in *Team Building: Blueprints for Productivity and Satisfactions,* ed. W. B. Reddy with K. Jamison, co-published by NTL Institute for Applied Behavioral Sciences, Alexandria, Va., and University Associates, San Diego, California, 1988: 3–14.

11. B. Newman, "Expediency as a benefactor: How team building saves time and gets the job done," *Training and Development Journal,* Vol. 40, No. 2, 1986: 26–30.

12. Newman, 1986.

13. I. L. Goldstein, *Training in Organizations: Need Assessment, Development, and Evaluation,* 2nd ed., Brooks/Cole Publishing, Monterey, Calif., 1986.

14. Schermerhorn, Jr., November 1986.

15. N. Rosen, *Teamwork and the Bottom Line: Groups Can Make a Difference,* Lawrence Erlbaum Associates, Hillsdale, N.J., 1989.

16. Rosen, 1989; R. Hackman, "The Design of Work Teams," in *Handbook of Organizational Behavior,* Jay W. Lorsch, Prentice Hall, Englewood Cliffs, N. J., 1987: 315–342.

17. D. Tjosvold and M. M. Tjosvold, *Leading the Team Organization,* Lexington Books, New York, 1991.

18. W. Bennis and B. Nanus, *Leaders: The Strategies for Taking Charge,* Harper & Row, New York, 1985.

19. Larson and LaFasto, 1989.

20. J. M. Burns, *Leadership,* Harper & Row, New York, 1978.

21. D. Tjosvold, I. R. Andrews, and H. Jones, "Cooperative and competitive relationships between leaders and their subordinates," *Human Relations,* Vol. 36, 1983: 1111–1124; Tjosvold and Tjosvold, 1991.

22. D. Tjosvold, " Interdependence and power between managers and employees: A study of the leader relationship," *Journal of Management,* Vol. 15, 1988: 49–64.

23. D. Tjosvold, "The effects of attribution and social context on superior's influence and interaction with low-performing subordinates," *Personnel Psychology,* Vol 38, No. 2, 1985: 361–376; "Power in cooperative and competitive organizational contexts," *Journal of Social Psychology,* Vol. 130, 1990: 249–258; D. Tjosvold, I. R. Andrews, and J . Struthers, "Power and interdependence in work groups: Views of managers and employees," *Group & Organization Studies,* Vol. 16, No. 3, 1991: 285–312.

24. J. H. Zenger, E. Musselwhite, K. Hurson and C. Pervin, 1991.

25. The model described in Figure 10.1 reflects the authors' interpretation of material presented in G. H. Varney, *Building Productive Teams: An Action Guide and Resource Book,* Jossey-Bass, San Francisco, 1990; N. Rosen, 1989; R. Hackman, 1987.

26. Hackman, 1987.

27. D. McGregor, *The Human Side of Enterprise,* McGraw-Hill, New York, 1960.

28. R. Likert, *New Patterns of Management,* McGraw-Hill, New York, 1961.

29. G. M. Parker, *Team Player and Teamwork: The Competitive Business Strategy,* Jossey-Bass, San Francisco, 1990.

30. Parker, 1990.

31. T. Peters, *Thriving on Chaos,* Harper & Row Publishers, New York, 1988.

32. Parker, 1990: 44.

33. Jessup, 1990: 79–83.

34. C. Hastings, P. Bixby, and R. Chaudry-Lawton, *The Superteam Solution: Successful Teamworking In Organizations,* University Associates, San Diego, 1987.

35. Hackman, 1987: 332.

36. Hackman, 1987.

37. Hackman, 1987: 323.

38. The questionnaire used was developed by one of the authors for organizational team-building activities and reflects the material presented in Varney, 1990.

39. Data was analyzed using SPSS MANOVA profile analysis and resulted in significant differences at $p \leq .001$.

40. W. G. Dyer, *Team Building: Issues and Alternatives,* Addison-Wesley Publishing, Reading, Mass., 1977.

41. Gordon, 1992.

42. Gordon, 1992.

43. Gordon, 1992.

44. R. S. Wellins, "Building a self-directed work team," *Training and Development Journal,* Vol. 46, No. 12, 1992: 24–28.

45. J. Schilder, "Work teams boost productivity," *Personnel Journal,* Vol. 71, No. 2, 1992: 67–71.

46. J. D. Orsburn, L. Moran, E. Musselwhite, J. H. Zenger, and C. Perrin, *Self-Directed Work Teams: The New American Challenge,* Business One Irwin, Burr Ridge, Ill., 1990; P.A. Galagan, "Beyond Hierarchy: The search for high performance," *Training & Development Journal,* Vol. 46, No. 8, 1992: 21–25; R. S. Wellins, 1992.

47. Orsburn, Moran, Musselwhite, Zenger, and Perrin, 1990.

48. Galagan, 1992.

49. R. S. Wellins, W. C. Byham, and J. M. Wilson, *Empowered Teams: Creating Self-Directed Work Groups that Improve Quality, Productivity, and Participation,* Jossey-Bass, San Francisco, 1991.

50. Schilder, 1992.

51. N. A. Hitchcock, "Can self-directed teams boost your bottom line?" *Modern Materials Handling*, Vol. 48, No. 2, February 1993: 57–59.

52. Anonymous, "How Pitney Bowes establishes self-directed work teams," *Modern Materials Handling,* Vol. 48, February 1993: 58-59.

53. Wellins, Byham, and Wilson, 1991: 3.

54. Wellins, Byham, and Wilson, 1991: 4.

55. Wellins, 1992.

56. Wellins, 1992.

57. C. Carr, "Managing self-managed workers," *Training & Development Journal,* Vol. 45, No. 9, 1991: 36–42; Wellins, Byham, and Wilson, 1991; Wellins, 1992.

58. Carr, 1991.

59. Carr, 1991.

60. Carr, 1991.

61. Orsburn, Moran, Musselwhite, Zenger, and Perrin, 1990; Wellins, 1992.

62. T.E. Benson, 1992.

63. Galagan, 1992.

64. T.E. Benson, "A braver new world," *Industry Week,* August 3, 1992: 48–54.

65. Galagan, 1992.

66. Orsburn, Moran, Musselwhite, Zenger, and Perrin, 1990; S. Horton, "Team effort," *American Printer,* Vol. 209, 1992: 30–32.

67. Orsburn, Moran, Musselwhite, Zenger and Perrin, 1990.

68. Orsburn, Moran, Musselwhite, Zenger and Perrin, 1990.

69. Wellins, Byham, and Wilson, 1991; Wellins, 1992.

70. Wellins, 1992.

71. B. W. Tuckman, "Developmental Sequence in Small Groups," *Psychological Bulletin*, Vol. 65 No. 6, 1965: 384–399.

72. Hackman, 1987; Parker, 1990; Varney, 1990.

73. Hackman, 1987.

74. Questions appearing in Table 10.4 reflect material presented in Hackman, 1987; Parker, 1990; and Varney, 1990.

75. Parker, 1990. When integrating these four roles into our discussion of team development, we draw upon Parker's material and our own consulting experience.

76. The following discussion assumes that the group has reached consensus on desired goals and a sequence of supporting action plans. If conflict in these areas exists, the manager must revisit one-on-one negotiations and group discussions in an attempt to reach a consensus.

77. R. Harrison, "Role negotiation: A tough-minded approach to team development," in *The Social Technology of Organization Development,* ed. W.W. Burke and H.A. Hornstein University Associates, San Diego, Calif., 1972: 84–96; R. Beckhard and R. T. Harris, *Organizational Transactions: Managing Complex Change,* Addison–Wesley Publishing, Reading, Mass., 1977; W. W. Warner Burke, 1988: 3–14.

78. Warner Burke, 1988.

79. A. Bandura, *Social Learning Theory,* Prentice Hall, Englewood Cliffs, N.J., 1977

80. E. E. Lawler, *Pay and Organizational Development*, Addison-Wesley Publishing, Reading, Mass., 1981.

11

CREATIVITY AND THE PROBLEM OF EMPLOYEE RESISTANCE TO CHANGE

Objectives:

- To sensitize the student to the importance of employee creativity in maintaining an organization's competitive edge.
- To describe the factors that relate to employee creativity and how these factors can best be used by effective managers.
- To articulate the important role that learning plays in determining the level of employee resistance found within the organization.
- To give students an opportunity to analyze and apply techniques designed to overcome employee resistance to change.

Employee Creativity and Organizational Success

Managerial successes have become increasingly difficult to achieve as organizations increasingly face environments characterized by rapidly changing technologies, increased competition, and declining resources.[1] Also limiting managers' ability to achieve organizational, departmental, and personal goals is their continued reliance on rigid organizational structures that reflect a hierarchical or military model.[2] Although such a structure may have been appropriate during the early part of this century when American manufacturing firms were introducing the assembly line, relying on a work force that was primarily made up of uneducated immigrant workers, and specialization and large size provided financial and operational benefits, it fails to provide the necessary flexibility to overcome today's environmental threats.[3]

A strategy designed to revitalize North American businesses and overcome these challenges is management's encouragement and use of employee creativity. The *Encyclopaedia Britannica* defines creativity as "the ability to make or otherwise bring into existence something new, whether a new solution to a problem, a new method or device, or a new artistic object or form."[4] Creativity extends the employee's experience and knowledge. In other words, it takes employees "from the known and the familiar to the novel and the what might be."[5]

By encouraging and using employee creativity, managers provide benefits to both the innovators and their companies. Environments that allow for creativity tend to provide employees the opportunity for increased involvement, personal satisfaction, growth, and intrinsic rewards.[6] Organizations benefit because employee creativity is likely to result in improved or new work techniques, products, and services; reduced production and marketing costs; proactive decision making; better market penetration and product differentiation; rapid adjustment to environmental changes; and finally, improved profits.[7] Unfortunately, the track record of American firms attempting to encourage and use employee creativity does not compare well with that of other countries. For example, Table 11.1 compares the number of suggestions put forth by several Japanese companies and a typical leading United States company.

Clearly, these figures do not bode well for North American firms that are attempting to become more competitive. This is especially true if one considers what is considered a bona fide suggestion. An employee's idea is not considered a suggestion until he or she has demonstrated that it works. Before an idea is classified a usable suggestion, it must successfully pass through three stages. They are, problem finding, problem solving, and solution verification or implementation.[8]

TABLE 11.1   Average Number of Suggestions per Organizational Employee

Company	Number of Suggestions	Number of Employees	Suggestions per Employee
Matsushita	6,446,935	81,000	79.6
Hitachi	3,618,014	57,051	63.4
Mazda	3,025,853	23,927	126.5
Toyota	2,648,710	55,578	47.6
Nissan	1,880,686	48,849	38.5
Nippon Denso	1,393,745	33,192	41.6
Canon	1,076,356	13,788	78.1
Fuji Electric	1,022,340	10,226	99.6
Tohoku Oki	734,044	881	833.2
JVC	728,529	15,000	48.6
Typical leading U.S. company	21,000	9,000	2.3

Source: M. Basadur, "Managing creativity: A Japanese model," *Academy of Management Executive*, Vol 6, No. 2, 1992, p. 32.

North American managers, however, are beginning to recognize the need for employee creativity. This increased recognition is demonstrated in part by the priority given creativity training.[9] A recent survey found that 25 percent of all organizations with more than 100 employees provide creativity training for their staff.[10] This represents a 540 percent increase in four years. The increased value being placed on creativity training is also demonstrated by a *Business Week* report that indicated that "over half of the Fortune 500 companies send their chief executives as well as employees from all other levels of the organization for creativity training."[11] The increased popularity of creativity training also reflects the growing belief that creativity can be taught, and that the ability to create is not restricted to a select few.[12]

Innovation: How It Relates to the Concept of Creativity

Closely related to employee creativity is the concept of innovation. A typical dictionary describes an innovator as someone who introduces change and new things. Kanter reflected this view when she stated, "Innovation is the generation, acceptance, and implementation of new ideas, processes, products and services. It can thus occur in any part of the corporation, and it can involve creative use as well as original invention."[13] Drucker gave the following narrow definition of innovation, "Innovation is an act which endows resources with a new capacity to create wealth—a means by which an entrepreneur exploits change as an opportunity."[14] Defined in this way, the result of innovation is the creation of something new (i.e., a process, method, or device transformation designed to improve performance).

However, in reviewing the literature on innovation it also becomes clear that many individuals use the term to describe macro changes that move the organization in a new direction. In these instances, the emphasis is not on the manager–subordinate level but rather the organizational level. Delbecq and Mills were clearly describing this macro aspect of innovation when they stated, "Innovation is a significant change within the organization or its line of services or products that (*a*) requires a substantial adjustment in function and or structures, and (*b*) is successfully introduced, decided upon, and incorporated into the organization. As such, it differs from 'incremental change' (involving minimum disruption, usually within current tradition) and 'invention' (which might not become institutionalized)."[15]

As so often happens with the use of terminology, its meaning is shaped to fit the needs and perspective of a particular writer. Reflecting this diversity, innovation can be used to describe behavior on several levels. On the micro level it can be used to describe the act of an individual who introduces new ideas, methods, and devices to improve performance. Described in this manner, innovation can be incremental in nature and be used interchangeably with the term *creativity*. At the macro level it is used to describe major changes that significantly alter structure and process and move the organization in new directions. Given the authors' personal philosophy, and the emphasis of this book on the manager–subordinate interface, it is the micro perspective of innovation that is most useful. When innovation is defined in this manner, the terms *innovation* and *creativity* can be used interchangeably. To be consistent and minimize confusion, we will use the term *creativity* to denote a situation where an employee introduces something new into his or her work environment and where the net result of the transformation on employee productivity will be positive.

Creativity as an Individual Process

Every problem, process, artifact, or social encounter can be perceived as an opportunity to create something better. What is needed is only the desire to improve on something that already exists and then engage in behaviors that increase the likelihood of a creative outcome. This implies that the full range of daily activities experienced by the employee is ripe with opportunities for creative behavior. In other words, many creative ideas that significantly improve subordinate and organizational performance represent the restructuring and reorganizing of what already exists. Often, however, the outcome of such a transformation is known or predictable. Therefore, it does not constitute a creative outcome. For a transformation to be creative, "it must expand the experience or knowledge of the creator."[16]

Creativity should not be equated with bold, earthshaking change. To view creativity and its consequences in this manner dampens the individual's motivation to try to create. The lament we often hear from individuals is, "How can I be creative without the time, education, or resources to do it right?" Our response is, "Never, if you are looking for the 'Big One.'" However, we quickly add that because employees are right there on the job, interacting with their work environment every day, they are the richest source of information and insight into how the job can be improved. This is especially true for employees who function within environments and a management system supportive of creative activity. (Environmental characteristics of creative environments are discussed below.)

Similarly, the "out-of-the-blue" model of creativity is also in conflict with the more realistic position that there are identifiable stages associated with the process of individual creativity.[17] The premise behind the "stages" model is that there is an underlying sequence of identifiable steps associated with creativity. Preparation, incubation, illumination or insight, and verification or working out, are frequently identified as the four basic phases that individuals pass through as they create something new.[18]

1. The preparation phase. In the preparation phase, the individual must first be confronted with a problem to be solved or goal to be achieved. In other words, there must be some event that triggers the process. The triggering event may come from inside individuals themselves in the form of a personal goal or belief that things can be improved, or from an outside source that identifies a problem or establishes a new goal to be achieved. Regardless of the direction, there must be a belief that the status quo is unacceptable. The preparation phase also includes an attempt by individuals to become intimately knowledgeable about the problem and its environment or the desired goal and its environment. Therefore, the preparation phase can involve observation, literature searches, review of past practices, policies, and action, etc. It is also at this step in the creative process that the individual should actively seek out advice from knowledgeable others within the environment. The preparation phase is therefore likely to produce a state of over-learning by individuals and ultimately result in some of the relevant material becoming automatic in their conscious state.

Unfortunately, individuals can subconsciously accept a set of assumptions that do not apply to the current situation or problem even after they have collected information. If this occurs, it is unlikely that these individuals will break new ground or come up with an original problem. To prevent this from happening, individuals must attempt to articulate relevant assumptions and then test their validity. For example, assume that you have been requested to cut a round birthday cake into eight equal pieces and in so doing can only make three cuts. Before reading on, take a minute or so to solve this problem.[19]

The solution to this dilemma requires you to test and then reject one of the key assumptions individuals often make when faced with this problem. Specifically, there is no requirement that the three cuts have to be made in the vertical plane. The solution to this dilemma is to make one horizontal cut and two vertical cuts at right angles. The result is eight slices with only three cuts.

The preparation phase also requires that individuals explore trial solutions and similar situations or problems experienced in the past. It is possible that such a review can help individuals identify solutions for the current problem. Although it is possible for a final solution to be identified in this way, explorations of past or similar situations are primarily designed to help lay the foundation for subsequent steps in the individual's efforts to be creative. When both of these conditions have been met, the individual is prepared to move into the next phase of the creative process.

Before leaving our discussion of the preparation phase, it is necessary to mention a potential error that can be made at this point. Specifically, individuals can become impatient and move on to subsequent steps. When this occurs, they are likely to spend insufficient time on preparation, thereby damaging the creative process.

2. The incubation phase. This phase can best be described as occurring at the subconscious level. It represents mental activities that cannot be controlled or consciously managed by the individual. It is a period during which individuals subconsciously manipulate, test, and reorganize what they know in order to gain structure and understanding of the problem faced. It is at this level that the individual is testing new combinations of the multiple bits of information stored within his or her mind. Creativity occurs when a new combination is arrived at which satisfies the needs of the individual.

Although the incubation phase is accepted as a critical component of the creative process, it is not yet well understood. However, Rowan recommends that the individual attempting to be creative engage in the following behaviors:

- Continue thinking about the problem to allow it to simmer at the cognitive level. However, while attending to the problem under consideration, the individual cannot ignore other issues or problems that may also exist within the environment.
- Redefine the problem in as many new ways as possible. This allows you to look at the problem from multiple directions and thereby increase your understanding of the total problem domain.
- Brainstorm a list of alternatives without discounting any possibilities.
- Allow the child, or unsophisticated self, free expression. Such behavior often allows the individual to find a simpler, or more varied, solution than would otherwise have been possible.
- Proceed by trial and error.
- Clearly discriminate between real and imagined obstacles. Too many obstacles can stifle creativity.
- Be willing to spend the time.[20]

The incubation phase can also be active when the individual has turned his or her attention away from the problem at hand by considering unrelated problems or issues. Specifically, the individual who temporarily leaves a problem is more relaxed, has turned off the conscious struggle with the problem, and is more likely to have tuned out the frustration involved. In this way, the unconscious mind is free to reorganize and restructure all relevant information obtained during the preparation phase or the more active incubation phase.

3. Illumination. Hopefully, the result of the incubation phase will be a new and fresh idea (i.e., behavior, activity, method, device, process, etc.). In an instant the individual may experience insight into a problem that until then has remained unsolved. This sudden insight is often referred to as the "aha!" phenomenon.

4. Verification. The individual must verify that the new creative idea will work or be accepted by others. Therefore, there must be an opportunity to determine the degree to which the new process, method, or device will fit the problem as initially envisioned. It must be determined that the creative idea is valid, reliable, and cost effective, and that it will be accepted by relevant power brokers within the organization and eventually by the individuals who may be asked to implement and use it. Because of the complexity and time sometimes required to complete the verification stage, it is not always practical, or desirable, for the individual who carried out the first three phases of the creative process to also complete the verification phase. He or she may be given help from others within the organization, may be given administrative and or technical support, or may even turn over the last phase to another individual or group.

Creativity as an Interactive Process

Many individuals perceive creativity as a magical process where in a flash of insight, or out of the blue, they come up with new behaviors or environmental changes that will make them more successful. Still others erroneously equate creativity with dramatic discoveries that significantly alter the direction of human existence (e.g., Salk vaccine, splitting of the atom, or microchip technology). Unfortunately, while most individuals would quickly define what is meant by creativity if asked, there still remains little agreement among behavioral scientists as to its precise meaning.[21]

This paradox results in part because creativity cannot be controlled or predicted. When attempting to assess creativity, behavioral scientists cannot guarantee in advance that individuals will act creatively or produce a creative outcome. As a result, much of the research dealing with creativity has been essentially retrospective in design. Making matters worse, behavioral scientists continue to disagree on what constitutes a creative outcome.[22] The result is often a state of confusion and conflict that makes it difficult for practitioners to transfer theory into practice.

By looking at creativity as an interactive process, it is possible to gain a better understanding of key variables that impact on employee creativity and which, if mastered, facilitate a creative environment and the effective use of employee potential. Such a process is described in Figure 11.1.[23] Before discussing the model, it is necessary to describe several assumptions upon which the model is based. First, the level of creative behavior obtained reflects the interaction between individuals and their environments. Second, both individuals and their environments are changing over time. A third assumption is that current behavior

FIGURE 11.1

An interactionist model of creative behavior

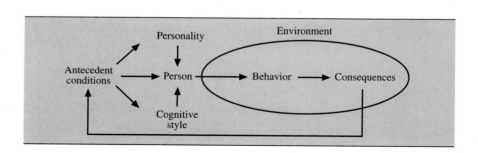

is not only a function of the individual and the environment in the present but also a function of what has taken place in the past. Last, the behaviors and consequences that occur in the present will affect the individual's future behavior.

Antecedent Conditions

Antecedent conditions relate to an individual's past reinforcement history, training, early socialization and background characteristics, such as gender, family position, or birth order.[24] In other words, experiences shape how employees interpret or respond to their current work environments. Employees who have been allowed to experiment and learn from mistakes in previous work environments, or have had senior management listen to their ideas, are more likely to exhibit these behaviors during current work assignment.[25] Similarly, a creative team climate is difficult to nurture if the organization's culture is based upon 30 or 40 years of bureaucratic control and hierarchical decision making.[26]

Personality

Behavioral scientists have also recognized personality as an important area of study when attempting to understand and predict creativity.[27] Research attempts to explain creativity through personality differences have considered comprehensive global theories, an identifiable set of characteristics or traits associated with creative individuals, or specific personality dimensions linked to creative behavior.[28] The following represent the dominant characteristics typically associated with creative individuals.[29]

1. Independence of judgment—highs (highly creative individuals) are able to function independently of others, resist subtle group pressure designed to influence them, and are able to maintain their position when confronted with disagreement.
2. Deviance—highs perceive themselves as being different from others, and the acceptance of these differences allows the creative individual to again resist external pressures.
3. Acceptance of authority—highs are less likely to accept autocratic and dogmatic uses of authority. They would more likely view authority as a transient state situationally defined by the unique characteristics that currently exist. Authority would have to be won and would likely be a function of the individual's proven track record.
4. Impulse acceptance—highs are quicker to express and follow personal whims and impulses. Creative individuals are also less likely to hold on to the realistic and often prefer to embrace that which is at the forefront of their field.

5. Motivation—highs tend to be driven by the internal need to achieve rather than the existence of extrinsic rewards that may be provided by the organization. Consequently, when highs buy into a project, task, or idea, in order to be successful they will persist longer and work harder than low creative individuals.

6. Orientation—highs tend to be cosmopolitan in orientation while lows tend to be more local in their orientation. Highs are therefore more likely to respond to, and be linked with, information and occurrences outside the organization. Highs also look beyond the obvious. Conversely, lows tend to be more directly tied into what happens within the organization and less concerned with external events or groups. Orientation differences tend to make highs, compared to lows, less loyal to the organization and more likely to move from organization to organization as they pursue personal accomplishments.

7. Impressionable—highs are open-minded and willing to listen. They tend to respond positively to events and information found within their environment.

Having identified the personal characteristics of creative individuals, two additional questions must be considered by managers. The first question asks whether such characteristics are desirable, given the requirements and culture of the existing department. The second question asks how to select such individuals once you know you want them.

In response to the first question, it must be realized that not all organizations require highly creative, independent, cosmopolitans. There exists the potential for conflict between the dominant personality characteristics of the creative individual and the desired organizational structure. Managers may also find creative behavior threatening both to themselves and to the existing status quo found within the organization. Thus, Shapero states:

> Highly creative people are attracted by the work, by the problem being worked on, which is good from an organizational viewpoint, but they don't respond in satisfactory ways to the political or organizational constraints that are involved in every problem. Creative people are nonconformists. They are jokers. They have little reverence for authority or procedures. They are short on apparent loyalty to the organizations they work for. They don't respond to the kinds of incentives that stir others. They are not moved by status. High creatives don't seem to care about what others think, and they don't easily become part of a general consensus. In short, creative people can make most managers very uncomfortable. (Teachers and even parents are far more comfortable with students and children with high IQs than with those who are highly creative.)[30]

A case can always be made for creativity, but managers should carefully consider and honestly think about whether they truly need more creativity and can live with it.[31] Specifically, managers may want to ask, "Is employee creativity, and the environment required to support it, consistent with the existing corporate culture?" "Am I willing to give up the level of control necessary to support a creative personality?" "How many risks am I willing to take or will others allow me to take?" "How many mistakes am I, and others within the organization, willing to take?"[32]

Cognitive Style

Cognitive style also plays a role in determining the level of creative behavior likely to be exhibited by employees. Cognitive style refers to the habitual and consistent manner in which individuals perceive their environment and respond to stimuli within that environment.[33] An individual's cognitive style determines how the environment is analyzed, information is used, and problems solved.

Three cognitive styles thought to have important links to creativity are field independence/dependence, fixity–mobility, and formal thought. Individuals who are field independent are individuals who can respond to their environment independent of external environmental cues. When compared with field dependent individuals, they are more independent of social relations, have greater self-awareness, express impulses directly, have a high level of incidental learning, and actively self-strive in their environments.[34] Fixity–mobility relates to the degree to which individuals can function both on global and focused levels. Individuals classified as mobile, when compared to fixed counterparts, are able to regress to more primitive cognitive development. In other words, they can apply both complex and simple or more relaxed cognitive strategies when attempting to solve environmental problems.[35] Formality refers to an individual's ability to deal with the abstract and hypothetical as well as the concrete. As a result, formal thinkers would be able to develop and test solutions without concrete examples.[36] By integrating these three cognitive styles, Noppe found that individuals who were field independent, formal, and mobile scored highest in symbolic logic, perceptual insight, and uncommon uses of verbal association.[37] He also found that individuals classified as field dependent, concrete, and fixed scored lowest on these creativity measures.

Research has also indicated that high creative individuals tend to use a more systematic approach when organizing their approach to problem solving.[38] The following responses from individuals classified as creative on a word association test clearly demonstrate this tendency.

- First I read the three words and sometimes a word would immediately be associated in my mind with the word. Most times there wouldn't be a word so then I would read two of them and at the same time add words to the beginnings and ends of words. The last thing I did was think—I mean I just sat and visualized the places where the word would be.
- For the more obvious answers, it seemed that repeating the words a couple of times helped me reach an answer. I also tried to make compound words out of each word using common prefixes. For the

real tough ones, I tried to visualize each noun object and think of its varied uses and try to draw a correlation between the functions of the three words.[39]

It is useful to compare these two statements with two typical responses from individuals who demonstrated low creativity on the same word association test. Besides demonstrating differences in organizational style, the comparison also gives us an idea of how mobility and formal operations affect creativity.

- I just thought about what the words had in common.
- I groped for any association I could possibly think of.[40]

Ideational fluency has also attracted considerable attention as a cognitive style that relates positively to creative potential.[41] "Ideation is defined as idea generation without evaluation (putting aside the judgment capability)."[42] The increased interest in ideation also reflects the belief that such a cognitive style can be developed through training.[43] Ideation, when linked with evaluation, energizes the creative problem solving process (see Figure 11.2). At each stage of the process, ideation is the critical first step before evaluation can take place and allows employees to successfully complete all three stages.[44]

FIGURE 11.2

Creative problem-solving process

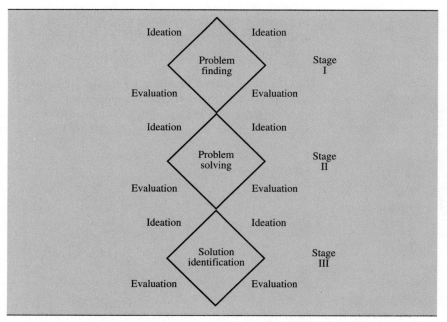

M. Basadur, G.B.Graen and G. Green, "Training in creative problem solving: Effects on ideation and problem finding and solving in an industrial research organization," *Organizational Behavior and Human Performance*, Vol . 30, 1982, p. 45.

However, when attempting to increase ideation through training, managers should keep in mind three important assumptions.[45] The first is that most individuals find ideation a more difficult behavior than evaluation. This occurs in part because "our society, general training, and school systems tend to reward and hone our evaluation capabilities and preferences and promote their use virtually to the exclusion of ideation."[46] Second, it is important to recognize that individuals will differ in terms of their preferences and abilities in the two-step process of ideation and evaluation. Therefore, not all individuals will require the same level of training or need the same level of training in both areas. Third, training is likely to have the greatest effect on the aspect of the ideation–evaluation process that is the weakest.

Environment

Even when managers have employees with the personality and cognitive characteristics described above, they must accept that creativity behavior cannot be dictated as can be work hours, organizational policies, production sched-ules, etc. Managers should also not expect subordinates to unilaterally take the initiative to create. To do so causes the creative process to become random and informal, a condition that significantly reduces the likelihood of success. If managers want creative subordinates then they must make a conscious effort to cultivate an environment in which employees will be able and will-ing to create.[47] Figure 11.3 indicates that an environment that encourages creativ-ity is built upon a number of key factors. The greater the number of these factors managers build into their departments, the greater the likelihood that employee creativity and innovation will occur.

1. Organizational Culture
As defined in Chapter 4, culture represents the collective programming of the mind. It represents the social legacy passed down from one generation to the next of what has been found to work best for a particular group. Managers

FIGURE 11.3

Building a creative environment

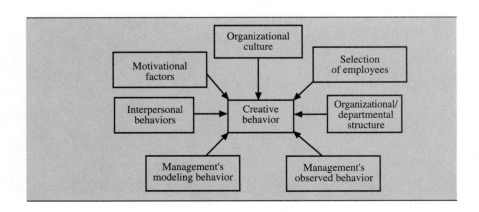

performing in organizations with cultures supporting employee creativity are likely to state that: R&D is every one's business; problems are golden eggs or opportunities for improvement; the goal is for all employees to demonstrate the spirit of never-ending improvement; it is important to encourage employees to think for themselves, speak out, and say "no;" and instead of saying "if it works don't fix it," employees should be encouraged to find faster, better and easier ways of doing things. However, statements alone will not ensure employee creativity. Managers must back up their statements with the appropriate assumptions, values, and behavior. The following are a number of cultural assumptions or values that encourage employee creativity.[48]

- *A winning attitude*—Employee creativity must reflect a positive attitude toward winning. The desire to win motivates employees to find alternatives that work. However, the drive toward winning must not incorporate the value of winning at all costs.

- *Employees buy into change*—Creativity only occurs when organizational members buy into the belief that change is necessary for organizational excellence to be achieved. Change must be perceived as a new way of life and that the alternative (i.e., entrenchment) will lead to marginal performance in a changing environment.

- *A sense of optimism*—The organization's culture must make employees believe that they can influence their environment and make things happen. This does not mean that employees can rest on their laurels or assume that needed skills are already in place. Instead, the organization represents a team with untapped potential. By working together, experimenting, and proceeding by trial and error, employees can overcome many obstacles. The key is for employees to believe in themselves and the organization.

- *Desire to add value*—Organizational members must believe that it is in their best interests to pack as much value as possible into their products or services. Such behavior satisfies customer demands and creates a competitive edge for the organization.

- *Self-questioning and assessment*—Constructive feedback is likely to stimulate the desire to create or change one's behavior. An effective way for individuals to stimulate such feedback is to engage in self-questioning and assessment. Individuals who continually ask the questions "Are we the best that we can be?" or "Are we doing all that can be done?" are more likely to create and innovate than those individuals who bury their heads in the sand and accept the status quo.

- *Success based on sharing and collective effort*—Creative behavior is enhanced when organizational members recognize that no one individual possesses all the needed expertise to handle complex problems. Instead, organizational members must recognize the importance of sharing information across departmental and organizational boundaries in increasing decision-making efficiency. Equally important is the belief that collective action (team behavior) significantly enhances the chances that creativity will occur and take hold. (Authors' addition to Morgan's list of five cultural characteristics.)

Ultimately, these assumptions and values must be translated into managerial behavior. It is this behavior that will be discussed in the next six building blocks.

2. Selection of Employees

There are a number of alternatives open to the organization when trying to select highly creative subordinates. The organization can attempt to measure the degree to which individuals possess the traits associated with creativity. The organization would then select those applicants who most closely match the desired trait profile. To make the test organizationally specific, an attempt must be made to validate the instrument within the organization by undertaking predictive or concurrent validity testing.[49] For concurrent validity testing, an attempt is made to correlate test scores with on-the-job performance scores (i.e., creative output). In the case of predictive validity testing, test scores are obtained and correlated with future on-the-job performance scores (i.e., creative output). During predictive validity testing no attempt is made to select employees on the basis of test scores, and as a result the organization doing the testing is being asked to do worse in terms of selection before they can do better—something many organizations are unwilling to do.

Unfortunately, considerable criticism has been directed toward the use of personality tests during the selection process.[50] Simply put, many argue that they are neither valid nor reliable in predicting on-the-job creativity. Another negative aspect of personality testing is that many organizations do not have the internal talent needed to administer the test or correctly interpret test results. The issue then becomes: what is the alternative? As was argued in Chapter 8 (Selection), one alternative is to use past performance as a predictor of future performance. In other words, has the individual demonstrated frequent creative behavior during recent on-the-job performance? If so, the applicants would score high on this particular selection criterion and thereby have a higher probability of being selected.

For some applicants, the identification of their contribution to creative results is not always directly measurable. In those instances, it may be necessary to ask the applicant what new changes he or she has introduced in the past. If such changes can be identified, then it is the manager's responsibility to probe to determine just how the applicant went about developing a new idea, evaluating its appropriateness, and how it was implemented. To corroborate this information, managers can contact others who are familiar with the applicant's past job record. Finally, if the organization has the resources, it may have access to assessment center technologies and can build the creative dimension into the assessment center simulations.

Although employee selection reflects the needs of the organization, that is, its financial resources, and its culture,[51] the selection process should attempt to ensure balance within a particular work team. For example, "a balance of professional and nonprofessional generalists and specialists can be very helpful in increasing productivity."[52] Behavioral scientists also recognize that individuals may differ in their preferred approach to problem solving.[53] Some individuals may prefer to scan their environments to collect data and identify problem areas. Others may prefer to conceptualize or define the problem, and subsequently generate ideas. Still others would prefer to evaluate and assess the appropriateness of ideas or solutions. Finally, some individuals may prefer to implement, that is, take solutions and make them reality. If all four types of behavior are not found within a team, it is likely that the creative process will suffer.[54]

3. Organizational/Departmental Structure

To support creativity, a structure must first be developed that encourages free and open communication.[55] This can be accomplished in part by creating a flat design in which all departmental members are considered equal members of a team. Flat structures, as indicated earlier, have fewer organizational levels and thereby facilitate communications between employees and upper management. This implies equal access to information and access to top management when needed. One of the easiest ways to stifle creativity and innovation is to force the new idea to travel through many levels before it is acted upon. In other words, the more levels through which employee ideas have to pass, the more individuals there are who can criticize, question, or demean the employee's new idea. Such multiple roadblocks can be devastating to new ideas because of the psychological impact they can have on the creative person. In the early phases of creativity the employee is vulnerable and insecure. Consequently, even the slightest negative feedback can cause him or her to terminate future creative activities.

Structurally, there should also be a mechanism designed to facilitate access to top management and others within the organization. Amoco formally identifies individuals who can act as connectors. Connectors work with the originator of an idea to ensure that it receives a fair hearing and that resources are made available to move it beyond the idea stage.[56] Similarly, Kodak assigns facilitators to departments to work with employees. Their responsibility is to help people turn an idea into a usable form.[57] This requires that the facilitator act as an ally and advocate. As an ally, the facilitator attempts to work with the employee to discuss the strengths and weaknesses of the idea, to develop presentation material should the idea go beyond the informal stage, and to lend encouragement and support at the earliest stages of idea development. As an advocate, facilitators can help the employee find internal resources, free up time, or locate a sponsor or champion who would be willing to lend the necessary support to ensure that the idea is implemented.

Structurally, organizations can take steps to establish ad hoc or formal committees to assess the merits of employee ideas and allocate available resources.[58] Committees provide employees with a forum at which to present their ideas. Committees can also be used to evaluate ideas and make suggestions where appropriate. Should both the presenter and committee want to pursue an idea, the committee, facilitators or connectors, or a committee member can take steps to find funding or encourage support from top management. In those instances where ideas are outside the department or expertise of the original presenter, a champion from an appropriate department can be chosen.

To ensure that appropriate teams are formed, and open channels of communications exist between relevant departments, organizations can require that the originator of an idea find co-champions in those departments likely to contribute to the idea and its implementation.[59] Such action is often required to ensure that innovators do not work in isolation or wait too long to involve key functions or departments. Crossing of departmental boundaries broadens the knowledge base available to creative employees. By forming cross-functional partnerships early in the creative process, managers can help identify fatal flaws, and reduce the likelihood of future resistance.

Creativity is significantly increased when organizational participants are exposed to what others are doing, and are willing to share information. This can be partially accomplished by improving the lateral interaction that exists within the organization, by cross-functional teams, project groups, and task forces. Unfortunately, many organizations foster a segmented rather than an integrative structure.[60] Under a segmented structure, departments and units build barriers around themselves that prevent the free flow of information within the organization. Segmentation also reinforces the "we versus them" mentality. Organizations built upon a segmental structure also increase the probability of interdepartmental conflict.[61] Conflict further reduces the flow of information needed to stimulate problem identification and creativity. (More will be said about conflict in Chapter 12.)

To stimulate creative activity, organizations must also be designed to provide the appropriate level of freedom of movement.[62] David Hills from the Center for Creative Leadership, Greensboro, North Carolina, defines freedom of movement as "the degree to which the environment provides adequate resources, support and encouragement, and reasonable targets and goals."[63] Employees who are denied support funds, who are forced to work at 110 percent or are given unreasonable deadlines, are unlikely to find the time or desire to create. To help ensure freedom of movement, 3M has taken steps to free up as much as 15 percent of its employees' time for personal projects; Akzo allocates 1 percent to 2 percent of net investment capital to fund embryonic projects; and Amoco has established a risk fund from which employees can easily get up to $20,000 to develop a personal idea.[64]

Unfortunately, there appears to be a conflict between management's desire to control others and the need for an open, free, and supportive environment needed to stimulate employee creativity.[65] Such a structure also conflicts with the creative person's need to function within an environment characterized by organizational freedom or departmental democracy.[66] This desire for control reflects a North American bias toward the bureaucratic or military model when designing organizational structures.[67] Under such a model, employees might identify problems but their immediate supervisor would identify the solution or desired course of action. The implication is that creativity comes from the top and that creative solutions are then passed downward. Furthermore, bureaucratic or military type structures minimize employee participation. Lack of participation makes it difficult for employees to contribute to strategy formation when setting goals or to interact with others to facilitate the distribution of relevant job information.

Within their own departments, managers can stimulate employee creativity by designing a structure that offers freedom of movement, opportunities for joint goal setting, freedom to question, and stimulates open communications.[68] Managers must therefore design departmental structures that facilitate broad-based support for employee participation and provide follow-through on employee participation, commitment, and creativity, in that order.[69] Managers can also stimulate employee creativity by giving employees freedom to initiate ideas and minimize personal interference in their subordinates' creative efforts.[70]

One such technique that demonstrates a manager's ability to take action within his or her own department is the "Lions Den" technique.[71] As a creative technique, the Lion's Den can be easily introduced into any department's structure to simulate employee creativity, to establish norms of cooperation and information sharing, and encourage collaborative problem-solving. Table 11.2 outlines the key steps associated with the Lion's Den technique.[72] The technique works for a number of basic reasons.[73] It provides a structure that motivates employees to prepare for a creative problem solving session as well as share experiences and ideas that relate to the problem or issue being discussed. Next, the Lion's Den can easily be integrated into an existing meeting structure that already exists within the department. In fact, the technique can be used to give structure to

---

TABLE 11.2   Characteristics of the Lion's Den

- Plan to run the Lion's Den during the last 30 minutes of a scheduled departmental meeting.
- Form subgroups along logical or natural divisions within the department, (e.g., functions or job clusters).
- Select a group to present a problem for which they want a solution but are having difficulties solving or need the cooperation/input from other groups. Presenting group is called the Lambs and the nonpresenters are the Lions. To ensure that all groups within the department have a chance to present, subgroups can rotate as Lambs into the Lion's Den during subsequent meetings.
- Before entering the Lion's Den the Lamb group prepares a visual presentation of their problem and potential solutions.
- The Lambs then ask the Lions (nonpresenting groups or individuals) to give input on the problem, solutions, and recommendations.
- After the Lambs listen to the Lions, they are ultimately responsible for choosing what course of action to take. They do not have to accept any of the recommendations made by the Lions.

and revitalize meetings that fail to generate the desired level of employee input or creativity. The Lion's Den also balances the group's desire to solve problems quickly and the need to obtain relevant input from others. Last, the Lion's Den does not require consensus since the presenting group can accept or reject the solutions identified. The net result according to Robert Bookman, "The Lion's Den gives credibility to those hollow words: 'Our employees are the most important assets of the organization.' "[74]

4. Management's Observable Behavior

Managerial behavior plays an important role in determining whether a creative environment is established.[75] Managers must be especially careful not to behave in a way that discourages subordinate efforts to break new ground and move in new directions. All it takes from the manager is a raised eyebrow, inaction, poorly timed feedback, personal criticisms, or a request for tangible proof before any further action can be taken, for the subordinate to stop what he or she is doing. Adams specifically argued that managers who become impatient with employees, criticize employee efforts by nitpicking during early stages of idea formation, dominate, threaten employees to stimulate creativity, or behave in a negative or pessimistic manner are likely to reduce employee creativity.[76]

Leonard Silk adds to Adams' list by stating that managers who fail to respond personally to employee ideas, only encourage creativity in groups rather than make it everyone's responsibility, expect creative behaviors from only a few highly gifted employees, or criticize innovators for not being team players, also run the risk of reducing employee efforts to improve or innovate.[77] Basadur further argued that when managers come up with problems to be solved, or preliminary ideas for improvements, they should not become directly involved.[78] Instead, they should find a champion among the rank and file and by so doing build employee commitment and ownership of the creative process. Managers who engage in negative behaviors are likely to cause employee resentment, rebellion, or submissiveness that results in employee stagnation.

The key is to replace negative behaviors with behaviors that stimulate employee creativity. An important first step is the manager's willingness to be permissive or democratic in those areas suitable for subordinate creativity or in areas in which subordinates have the interest, time, and ability to make a contribution.[79] Managers must demonstrate that they accept divergent ideas and alternative points of view. Ultimately, managerial behavior must communicate to employees that they have permission to be creative.[80] It is also important that managers are willing to share all relevant information with the subordinate. In this way, managers demonstrate personal trust in their subordinates and continue to build employee self-confidence.

Subordinates who are attempting to create something new are, by definition, traveling down an unexplored path. Managers can encourage employee efforts by removing existing bottlenecks and providing interpretive assistance to the subordinate. In other words, managers should act as facilitators or coaches to their subordinates.[81]

During the early stages of employee creativity, managers must watch out for negative phrases that can creep into their discussion with subordinates. During its infancy, creativity can be killed by the use of such phrases as: "It will likely cost too much," "We have never done it that way before," "If your idea is so good why hasn't anyone else thought of it before," or "Yes, but — ." Instead of using these negatively oriented statements, the manager can support creative efforts by rephrasing his or her statements in the positive mode—by being supportive and constructive. For example, the "Yes, but—" statement can be restated as follows: "Yes, that is a possibility, and if we can get the cost down it would have broader appeal." This statement is less likely to turn the subordinate off and may motivate him or her to work even harder. Last, feedback that is relevant, constructive, and timely, can play an important role in maintaining and guiding the subordinate's creative behaviors.[82] Managerial feedback should also be designed to help employees assess the appropriateness of ideas to ensure that they begin to self-manage their own creativity.[83] Feedback from one's immediate boss also demonstrates continued interest and thereby helps to maintain subordinate confidence.

How managers assign work can also have an impact on employee creativity.[84] When setting goals, managers can explicitly set their expectations as to the level of employee creativity desired. For example, 3M explicitly states that "25 percent of sales in any given year has to be based on products that were not in the marketplace five years before."[85] When consulting, we often hear of cases where managers fail to communicate the need for employee creativity. The most common scenario is where a subordinate has created an improved way of doing something but does not pass it on to his or her immediate boss or co-workers. When asked why, the employee responds in the following ways: "The boss doesn't really want us to change anything," "The boss's only interest is to maintain the status quo," or "He or she just never asked me."

When work is being assigned to subordinates, managers must also ensure that two-way communications are encouraged. Two-way communications permit the opportunity to ask questions and clarify areas of misunderstanding should they occur. While assigning the work, managers must demonstrate confidence in the employee's ability to improve on what already exists. However, to be creative, employees must have the necessary time to engage in the creative process. Therefore, managers should make sure that work assignments are scheduled in such a way that it ensures promising people some free time in their work schedule. Last, the manager must communicate that although the standards are firm, the employee has the freedom to determine how they will be achieved or maintained.

5. Management Modeling Behavior

Creativity will not occur unless managers, at all levels, but especially employees' immediate bosses, engage in creative and innovative behavior themselves. When managers are willing to experiment, stray from tradition, act quickly to take advantage of opportunities, create permissive and open relationships with others, and remove the constraints of bureaucratic rules, then subordinates will feel comfortable engaging in similar behaviors. For example, Peters and Waterman concluded that innovative organizations and their managers were able to overcome inertia and conformity by demonstrating a bias toward action, that is, do it, fix it, or try it.[86]

Similarly, managers who call together their staff for a brainstorming session signal to others that they not only value creativity, but also value employee input. When such behavior becomes the norm, rather than the exception, subordinates are more likely to see creativity as a personal goal. The manager can also engage in the practice of "**M**anagement **B**y **W**alking About."[87] By wandering through the department and asking the right questions, or pointing out problem areas that might be opportunities for improvement, the manager acts as a stimulus to the creativity of others. MBWA can also act to prepare managers for their own creative efforts. Specifically, by being more familiar with workplace activities, subordinate behaviors, relationships, preferences, and ideas, the preparation or data collection phase of the creative process is made active.

On a general level, managers become models for their subordinates by effectively carrying out the four phases of the individual creative process. When managers prepare themselves by collecting data and testing assumptions, successfully pass through the incubation phase, gain insight, verify or successfully test creative ideas, and thus improve the organization by implementing creative ideas, they help employees recognize that creativity is more than just a flash of inspiration.[88] They learn that creativity must be nurtured within a supportive environment, and that all phases are of equal importance.[89]

6. Interpersonal Behaviors

Because subordinates function within a sociotechnical environment, the state of interpersonal relationships is a critical variable in determining the level of individual creativity.[90] As already mentioned, creative individuals must have access to information, the ideas and opinions of others, and perceive that relevant others support what they are doing. If these interpersonal factors are not in place, it is unlikely that creative efforts will be fully developed.

Basic to positive interpersonal relationships is the feeling of trust and openness between organizational members. This allows individuals to feel comfortable in expressing their ideas, overcome defensive behaviors, and be willing to approach others for information or help. Similarly, co-workers must demonstrate a willingness to tolerate deviant behavior. Such tolerance fosters individual self-expression and ensures that early attempts to be creative will not be criticized. Early criticism is a highly effective means of stifling an individual's desire to experiment with new ideas.

Relevant others must also be willing to listen to the creative individual to provide him or her with a mechanism for sounding out new ideas. Empathic listening by relevant others can be further enhanced if the interpersonal environment is friendly, cooperative, and open. Similarly, organizational members must recognize that all participants have rights. Recognizing the rights of others increases the probability that employees will be assertive in their interpersonal stance. These conditions are critical if there is to be any hope for open confrontation and problem solving within the organization.

7. Motivational Factors

Employees will only be creative if their work environments motivate them to do so. The issue for managers desiring creative employees is how to establish an organizational climate that incorporates the motivational principles discussed in Chapter 9. Much of what is needed has been discussed in the previous six points. We will, however, briefly review these points and discuss several areas not already covered.

- Goals—Although creative employees want freedom, they also need guidance.[91] Therefore, managers can increase employee creative efforts by explicitly stating that such behavior is desired and working with them to identify problem areas and to provide a general structure to their activities. This will require that managers incorporate the characteristics of effective goal setting when assigning work to employees.[92]

- Job Design and Content—In simplest of terms, if employees love what they are doing, they have the motivation to create on the job.[93] Intrinsic rewards have been found to stimulate creative effort by employees.[94] Specifically, employees who have the autonomy to initiate ideas, control their own behavior, and minimum interference from supervisors are likely to find their jobs intrinsically satisfying and will likely demonstrate greater creativity.[95] Given the increased education of employees, and their increased desire to participate, it is likely that organizations that do not provide their employees intrinsic rewards may find it hard to retain the most creative of them.[96]

  In the case of extrinsic rewards there is some controversy whether such rewards increase or decrease the likelihood of employee creativity.[97] Our view is that extrinsic rewards can have a positive effect on employee creativity if extrinsic rewards are specifically linked to creative effort, are part of a motivational program that incorporates broad management support and follow-up to employee efforts, and take into consideration individual differences. Specific examples of extrinsic rewards will be described below in Consequences.

- Work Climate—As indicated above, the existing work climate can have a significant effect on creative effort. Behavioral scientists indicate that climates that facilitate creative efforts are likely to increase the employee's willingness to innovate. Facilitating climates permit free flow of information, allow for internal and external networking, have slack resources, are staffed with managers with favorable attitudes toward change and a tremendous tolerance for failure, and have a higher proportion of managers capable of facilitating innovation.[98]

- Management Support—To maintain employee motivation, managers must support employee efforts. Managers who help identify problem areas, ensure needed resources are available, help prepare presentations, provide constructive feedback and emotional support, buffer innovators from external threats, and create teams made up of interested employees with complementary skills, do increase their employees' perceived expectancy that if they make an effort to create there is a high probability they will succeed.[99] The net result is increased employee motivation.

- Consequences—Important to any motivation strategy is the clear indication of what are the consequences of being creative. The link between consequences and creativity can be communicated during the goal-setting process (see Chapter 9) or can be learned vicariously as employees observe what takes place within their work environment. What managers must ensure is that creativity results in positive consequences for employees. Positive consequences signal management's interest in and support for creative effort and thus sensitize employees to its importance.

  For example, Federal Express grants awards up to $25,000 to employees who come up with creative and innovative suggestions.[100] The company also provides what it calls "Five Star" awards for the five most creative and innovative executives of the year. Five-Star awards range from $5,000 to $25,000 each year. Awards do not have to be presented on a yearly basis, or have to be so large. Instead, they can be as small as $5 to reward small incremental improvements and can be given on the spot by the employee's immediate supervisor.[101] Peters also recognized the need to link consequences with creativity when he stated that managers should "seek out and celebrate innovators; establish a hall of fame in every unit—and insist that it be full; reward small innovations as well as large ones, and make sure that those in the support functions who help the innovators get about as much credit, in both fanfare and dollars, as the hotshot software engineer or children's wear merchant."[102]

  What managers must realize is that they can be creative in the manner in which creative subordinates are rewarded. Other potential reinforcers are:

  > Making participation real and not symbolic.
  >
  > Demonstrating that promotions can come from anywhere within the organization and that seniority is not the only game in town.
  >
  > Building creativity dimensions into the performance appraisal and review process.
  >
  > Linking profit sharing/incentives to market value of creative outputs.

Ensuring that individual efforts are acknowledged through celebrations and rituals.

Removing the anonymity of group rewards.

Employee Resistance: The Other Side of the Coin

A recent survey of 100 chief executives indicated that although organizations are attempting to develop strategies that will allow them to compete more effectively, improve productivity, and ultimately increase profits, employee resistance and a static corporate culture often prevent managers from reaching these objectives.[103] To overcome the conflict between the desire for a stable organizational environment and the desire for employee creativity, managers must learn to "acknowledge and validate employees' concerns about change, particularly the feelings of 'riskiness' that they will experience."[104] Unfortunately, when 700 managers were measured on their knowledge of 25 key issues on how to deal with organizational change, they scored lowest in their understanding of how individuals respond to change, that is, the distinction between change that is resisted and change that is accepted.[105]

To create a positive response by employees to change, managers must (*a*) recognize the potential for resistance, (*b*) understand how and why resistance occurs, and (*c*) develop a set of strategies or options designed to prevent or buffer its occurrence.[106] The following discussion addresses the last two points. The authors will first attempt to explain the process by which employees learn to resist change. Once this process is understood, it is then possible to articulate what managers can do to prevent or eliminate the potential negative consequences of employee resistance to change.[107]

Relevant Needs of Employees

Individuals seek to evaluate changes that occur within their environment. The conceptual model described in Figure 11.4 assumes that the key to an individual's positive or negative response to change is his or her own self-interest.[108] In other words, how will the proposed change impact on personal needs and need satisfaction? Changes that are favorable and satisfy employee needs are rarely resisted, while those considered unfavorable (that is, fail to satisfy employee needs and result in fear, anxiety, and frustration) are likely to be resisted.[109] Let us briefly consider each of the needs listed in our model.

1. Need for relevant information—Employees need information specific to their environment, that is, why changes are necessary, how the proposed changes will affect them, what their responsibilities will be, what skills will be valued in the future, degree of top management support, and the roles of others functioning within the same system.[110] Filley, House, and Kerr also argue

FIGURE 11.4

Overcoming employee resistance to change

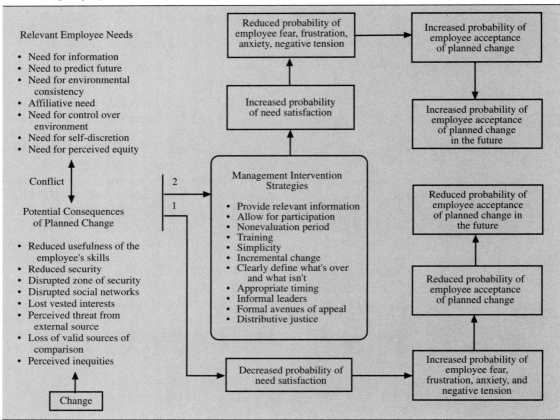

that information in the form of feedback "aids the learning process by serving as a correction device, furnishing individuals with the ability to improve and serving as a powerful positive reinforcer, which increases motivation and thus affects the individual's willingness to learn."[111]

2. Need to predict future—Employees want to be able to effectively predict the future.[112] Such a need reflects their basic need for security. Employees who are forced to replace relatively certain futures with ones that are uncertain must re-educate themselves about how the new systems will likely work in the future. This will require employees to expend time and energy collecting data and experimenting with the new system to reach the same level of knowledge achieved before the change. At the same time, they must cope with the anxiety and frustrations of functioning within a system they do not fully understand.

3. Need for environmental consistency—The ability of the employee to successfully predict, and thereby plan for, future contingencies is also dependent on the degree of consistency built into the employee's job environment. Change that disrupts the continuity between the past, present, and future has the potential of causing employees to incur loss.[113] Changing work environments may threaten employees' job security, rewards, friends and social contacts, and the relevancy of current skills.

4. Affiliative need—Behaviorist scientists have long argued that individuals generally possess a high need to interact with others. As indicated in Chapter 2, such a need results from the individual's desire to (*a*) define who and what he or she is, (*b*) achieve common goals, (*c*) reduce anxiety and/or fear, and (*d*) engage in social contacts as an objective in and of itself.

5. Need to control environment—Behavioral scientists have also indicated that individuals need some degree of control over what takes place within the organization.[114] Control relates to the ability of employees to affect the social and physical aspects of their work environments. For example, Kenneth Rinehart found that individuals who perceived themselves as having control over their work environments demonstrated lower levels of resistance to change than did their counterparts who perceived themselves as having limited control.[115]

6. Need for autonomy—Closely related to employees' need for control is the need to exercise personal autonomy when performing role responsibilities. Autonomy applies to personal behavior and relates to the degree of personal freedom, independence, and discretion provided by the employee's job.[116] In those situations in which the employee is not allowed discretion, he or she is unlikely to develop a positive attitude toward his or her own competencies and future personal development.

7. Need for perceived equity—We have already discussed the importance of distributive justice when attempting to motivate employees to behave in a desired manner. (See Chapter 9.) In the case of change, employees also assess the effect of implementation of a proposed change on the perceived equity for the self, distribution of benefits between the organization and self, and impact of equity on self as compared to others within the organization.[117] For example, changes that are considered equitable to the individual on each of the three levels are less likely to be resisted. Alternatively, changes that are considered inequitable or unfavorable for the individual are likely to be resisted.

Potential Consequences of Planned Change

Our intention is not to imply that only these seven needs are relevant to understanding employee resistance to change. They do, however, provide insight into why employees might resist change and what managers can do to reduce the probability that resistance occurs. Furthermore, we do not assume that all individuals are high on these seven needs.[118] However, employees high on these needs are likely to experience negative tension, anxiety, fear, or frustration if change is introduced in such a way as to prevent need satisfaction.

To demonstrate how this might happen, let us consider the potential effects of change when not introduced by employees themselves. First, change, by definition, produces a situation that is in some way different from the past (i.e., it introduces new tasks, procedures, methods, technologies, structures, and work flow). Some type of transformation has taken place within the work environment. When this occurs, employees may find that their present skills are no longer of value to the system. If this is true, they will be forced to upgrade old skills or develop new ones. However, the upgrading of old skills or the acquisition of new skills may not be feasible because of (*a*) time constraints, (*b*) lack of support facilities, or (*c*) inability of the employee to learn the new required skills. Employees may ultimately be forced to change positions if they cannot adjust to the changes brought about by management.

Even when employees learn new skills or remain current after a planned change, they may still question their job security. Good performance no longer guarantees job security when such programs as Total Quality Management, downsizing, or rightsizing are introduced by organizations.[119] Marginal or poor performers have already been removed during past restructuring. As a result, future efforts to restructure or downsize organizations will likely result in the loss of jobs for employees who are productive.[120] Under these conditions, change will be perceived as a threat to one's existence within the organization.

Organizations that function within a stable environment develop rules, policies, and procedures that act as guides to the employee. This is even true for highly turbulent environments as the organization oscillates between stable states and change states. Such rules, policies, and procedures take on significance when one considers the tendency for individuals to develop habits to guide future behavior. Such habits are relied upon by employees for both guidance and protection (i.e., they act as a zone of security for the individual).

When introduced, change typically disrupts this zone of security by reducing the applicability of established habits. The employee must now face a changed and unfamiliar job environment without a zone of security to facilitate his or her task performance, interactions with others, and planning for future contingencies. The removal of the employee's zone of security is likely to increase a feeling of vulnerability and thereby reduce his or her feeling of control and understanding of the job environment.

The employee performing within a sociotechnical system frequently develops numerous social relationships. As indicated earlier, these relationships are important to the individual for several reasons. First, day-to-day interactions with familiar others serve to satisfy the employee's affiliative needs. Second, the interaction with familiar others affords the employee an emotional outlet for the reduction of anxiety that may develop on the job. Third, by interacting with familiar others, the employee has a constant reference point against which to assess and define his or her own behavior. When change is introduced, these social relationships are frequently disrupted or destroyed. This disruption can only be interpreted by employees as a further threat to their well-being.

Individuals performing within complex organizations develop, over time, what they perceive to be vested interests. Specifically, employees may perceive that they have a right, given their position and personal status within the organization, to (*a*) make decisions, (*b*) direct others, (*c*) control resources, and (*d*) use a high degree of self-discretion when fulfilling their responsibilities. These rights, whether real or imagined, take on an air of normalcy. Consequently, to the degree that change appears to endanger these vested interests, employees feel threatened.

Finally, change is frequently introduced from a power center outside one's department or by someone other than oneself. Behavioral scientists have long argued that individuals possess a rather high propensity to distrust that which is initiated by an external source, as well as the external source itself.[121] This means that an employee tends to feel threatened, irrespective of the quality of the change program, when change is introduced by an external source.

Interactional Consequences of Change and Basic Needs

The process by which individuals learn to resist change is described in this section. (The conceptual model presented in Figure 11.4 assumes that employee resistance to change is not an innate but a learned response.) It has generally been accepted that unsatisfied needs are the primary motivators of human behavior. Specifically, when individuals have an unsatisfied need or set of needs, they experience a negative tension state that they will attempt to reduce. This attempt will be accomplished by redirecting their full range of behaviors, as well as psychological outlook, in a way consistent with need satisfaction.[122]

The importance of employees who are high on the seven needs discussed above becomes evident when one considers the consequences of change. Change has the potential for producing an environment that prevents the fulfillment of these needs, that is, lack of information; reduced security; disruptions of social networks; removal of previously relied upon rules, regulations, and policies, etc. Therefore, employees faced with repeated change situations may find it impossible to satisfy their dominant needs profile, a situation that results in a continued state of negative tension. Such a tension state produces other negative consequences (i.e., frustration, anxiety, fear). Because of these negative consequences, employees learn to resist change by linking negative consequences with change. Because of what employees have experienced in the past, and because employees learn to associate (link) these negative consequences with change, they learn to resist change in the future. This process of learning to resist is summarized in Figure 11.4, path 1.

How to Reduce Employee Resistance to Change

Using the strategies in Figure 11.4, managers can act to reduce the probability of employee resistance. The key is to break the perceived link between change and employees' inability to satisfy their dominant needs.[123] Before this can happen, however, managers must understand that the potential for employee resistance exists whenever change is introduced. Managers must also recognize the importance of planning as a critical first step when attempting to introduce change.[124]

The following material represents a set of 11 possible change strategies that, if used, will help facilitate the introduction of change into an organization and thereby weaken the perceived link between negative consequences for employees and change.

1. Provide relevant information. Where possible, managers should describe the objectives of the proposed change, why it is needed, and clearly outline the consequences.[125] This information should include both the benefits and the potential negative consequences. The effect of full disclosure is to communicate that it is "business as **unusual**."[126] Full disclosure also satisfies employees' need to know where they are going and why; prevents rumors, misunderstandings, and resentments; and it gives management the opportunity to explain what steps will be taken to ensure an employee's continued success on the job, that is, training programs, nonevaluative periods (discussed below), avenues of appeal (discussed below), etc.

Information should be dispersed early in the change process to ensure complete understanding by affected employees. Early dispersal also provides employees with time to express their views, provide input, and for management to respond.[127] Early dispersal of information also gives the employee more time to plan for and adjust to potential adverse consequences of the change program.

Full dispersal of information also implies that managers should communicate their own feelings toward the proposed change.[128] Communicating feelings of discomfort about a particular issue or aspect of the change program allows managers to open up a dialogue with employees about possible future problems early in the change program and at the same time humanizes the situation. Such behavior on the part of managers must be consistent with the recommendations pertaining to self-disclosure discussed in Chapter 2; that is, a positive relationship currently exists between the manager and his or her subordinates, subordinate's goals are compatible with the manager's, appropriateness of disclosure, etc.

2. Allow for participation. When the affected employees are knowledgeable, interested, and likely to affect ultimate success of the change program, managers should allow employee participation in planning of the proposed change.[129] Participation will help ensure (*a*) input of all relevant information into the decision-making process, (*b*) dispersal of all relevant information after the decision has been made, and (*c*) personal commitment by employees to the successful introduction of change.

To maximize the benefits of participation, it is recommended that employees be involved in all stages of the planning process, and that they be included early in the process.[130] To gain employee commitment, it is desirable to involve employees in joint diagnosis of existing business problems. Similarly, employee involvement in solution generation or solution selection can significantly reduce future resistance. The assumption here is that changes and problem solutions initiated or selected by employees are less likely to be resisted than those forced upon them by others.[131]

For example, an auto part manufacturer was forced into a severe cost-cutting program due to declining sales.[132] As part of its cost-cutting program it was decided that salary expenses had to be trimmed by 20 percent. However, it was also decided that the company would not take the easy way out by laying off 20 percent of its employees. Instead, the company identified six alternatives that would accomplish their objectives and then allowed employees to decide which solution best fit their unique needs. The six alternatives provided by management were, "five months of Fridays without work or pay, one month off without pay, 10 percent reduction in salary for one year, elimination of vacation pay and all holiday pay for one year, half days of work and pay for two months, or two and one half months (June 15–August 31) of Fridays and Mondays without work or pay."[133] The company's employees agreed to decide for themselves, and most selected the last alternative. The net result was additional work for the personnel department, but no resignations, complaints, or reduction in morale or productivity by employees.

3. Nonevaluative period. Where possible, management should build into its change program a period during which the employee's performance cannot have a negative impact on income, rank, or other perceived benefits already being received from his or her present position.[134] The purpose of a nonevaluative period is to allow the employee to adjust and to develop new skills in an atmosphere free of perceived threats to need satisfaction. Also critical to the success of a nonevaluative period is the amount of constructive feedback or training that management gives the employee when attempting to upgrade his or her skills.

4. Training. Employee fears about making mistakes on the job are likely to increase when faced with the threat of a changed work environment.[135] These fears increase because most changes require employees to learn new skills, develop new methods, learn new concepts, or expand their knowledge base in some way.[136] However, in those instances where employees are fully informed as to the consequences of change and what skills will be needed to perform effectively within the changed environment, and where threats to the employee are minimized by building in a nonevaluation period, management is provided with a key opportunity to develop their employees through training. Under ideal conditions, employees will recognize the need for learning new skills and request that management provide the training.[137] By making relevant training available to employees, management further reduces the likelihood of resistance.

5. Simplicity. The ability of an employee to adjust to a changed environment is frequently a function of the complexity of the change program itself.[138] This becomes a problem when managers, trying to demonstrate their expertise, develop a change program that is more complex than is necessary to achieve organizational or departmental goals. The more complex the change program, the greater the probability that it will exceed employees' adaptive capabilities and thereby cause them to fail. A more desirable course of action would be to introduce a change program with only the complexity required to achieve existing objectives and no more.

6. Incremental change. Closely related to the concept of simplicity is the concept of incremental change.[139] The ability of an employee to effectively adjust to change is also a function of the amount of change introduced within a given period of time. Managers who introduce too much change within a limited time span increase the probability of failure of the change program and the likelihood of future employee resistance. It is often more desirable to recognize that large or bold changes can be divided into digestible steps that can be introduced sequentially. Peters reflected this sentiment when he stated, "the most efficient and effective route to bold change is the participation of everyone, every day, in incremental change. Most bold change is the result of a hundred thousand tiny changes that culminate in a bold product or procedure or product."[140]

The importance of incremental change is also demonstrated by the model presented in Figure 11.5.[141] Organizations increase the probability of success if they behave in a manner consistent with environmental demands—time periods A and D.[142] When environmental changes do occur (that is, changes in

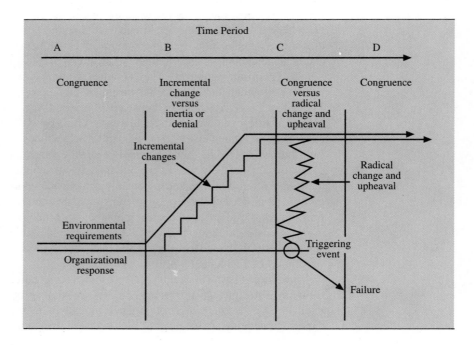

FIGURE 11.5

Importance of incremental change

customer demands, government regulations, work force, corporate mission, etc.), proactive or change-sensitive managers initiate incremental changes designed to track changes in the environment—time period B. Such behavior allows managers to maintain congruence without experiencing radical changes or organizational upheavals and minimizes the potential of employee discomfort. Change-resistant managers take a reactive approach to environmental change and allow organizational inertia or denial to prevent timely adjustments to the environment.[143] The potential consequence is that at some point in the future, a triggering event will cause organizations to initiate major change or organizational upheavals to survive—time period C. If these changes are successful, congruence will again be obtained but at a significant cost to the organization and its employees. Employees will again learn to associate change with significant personal loss.

7. Clearly define what's over and what isn't. Change represents an end to how things were done in the past and the introduction of new ways to do things in the future. Change, however, rarely requires a total rejection of past practices. This is especially true when change is introduced incrementally to adjust to changes in the environment and to avoid radical change and upheaval.[144] To minimize confusion, managers must define what activities are no longer appropriate and which are to be continued, and communicate this information to employees.[145] Failure to do so is likely to cause employees to (*a*) continue doing both the old and the new, and burn out in the process, (*b*) make their own decisions about what to reject from the past and increase the probability of organizational chaos, and (*c*) reject the past in total and as a result, discontinue activities still critical for success.[146]

Clearly defining what activities stay or go also facilitates managerial attempts to make changes compatible with past practices. The better the fit between proposed changes and the existing system, the more likely that subordinates will accept present and future change.[147]

8. Appropriate timing. Also critical to the ultimate success of any change program is the timing of its introduction.[148] Before introducing change, management must consider the environment in which the employee is functioning. Only by being sensitive to the employee's unique situation is management likely to introduce change at an optimal time period and with a minimal threat to the employee. For example, management should not (unless forced to by time constraints or external pressures) introduce new purchasing procedures during a peak work period. Such a change would likely be resisted by employees who, when performing under the pressure of a peak period, are likely to rely on behaviors proven to be successful in the past. It would be more appropriate to introduce change during a slack period to ensure minimum pressure and maximum probability of acceptance.

Managers should also attempt to build in as much lead time as possible to the implementation of any change program. This allows employees to think the changes through, get mentally prepared, and make adjustments which will minimize personal loss or discomfort. Kanter echoed this point when she stated, "Time is one of the first requirements for significant long-term organizational changes. There has to be sufficient calendar time to make it work, as well as enough available participant time to engage in planning, communication, and reflection about the appropriateness of job and project activities."[149]

The following example demonstrates the importance of timing.[150] A computer software company in response to rapid growth decided to close its original facilities and move to a site 60 miles away. The decision was made not to inform employees of the move until one week before the grand opening. As a result, employees did not have sufficient time to plan for the change. When the move was announced, 941 out of 3,710 of the company's employees resigned.

9. Informal leaders. It is generally accepted that within any formal organizational structure, there will also exist an informal social structure which management can frequently identify. Such informal structures will typically have one or more informal leaders. Managers can expedite change by working through these informal leaders.[151] This is especially true when managers cannot effectively deal with all the employees involved in the change program. Involving informal leaders in the development and implementation also gives the change program credibility when being evaluated by other employees and thereby reduces the probability of employee resistance.

10. Formal avenues of appeal. As indicated above, a major source of anxiety is an employee's perceived inability to control his or her environment. The negative feelings associated with not being in control can occur during the implementation phase of the change process. To help alleviate anxieties in this phase, it is desirable to build into the process formal avenues of appeal.[152] This facilitates upward communication from dissatisfied employees and offers them a mechanism to share their ideas with senior management.

Formal avenues of appeal are especially important because change, by its very nature, will have its greatest impact in the future—when the effects of the change program permeate throughout the organization. The problem, however, is that the future is uncertain, and as a result the planned change may be inappropriate because of unforeseen events. Therefore, feedback from those employees who are implementing the change is a critical factor in determining the ultimate success of any change effort.

There may, however, be a hesitancy by employees to communicate their dissatisfaction about current changes.[153] Employees may fear attack or ridicule for speaking out against changes supported by top management. Similarly, individuals who question changes designed to improve the total organization may be criticized for not being team players. It is therefore critical that managers be receptive to the feedback they receive, guarantee employee confidentiality, and take steps to ensure that there are no negative repercussions for those employees appealing senior management's actions.[154]

11. Distributive justice. The key to any attempt to ensure that inequities are not built into a change program is to take the time to analyze the likely consequences of change on employees' payoffs and outcomes.[155] In instances where inequities are identified, managers can make adjustments to the affected employees' outcomes or inputs to bring the equity equation back in balance. Table 11.3 lists a number of alternatives when dealing with equity issues following the introduction of a change in MIS technology.

TABLE 11.3

Strategy	Objective	Actions
Altering actual inputs and outcomes	Reduce users' inputs	• Well-designed training programs to reduce learning effort and frustrations • Help line/on-demand help • Extra temporary staff or overtime help during implementation
	Increase users' outcomes	• Positive equity through "royal/plush treatment," in training programs, design reviews, or briefing sessions • Praise, recognition, awards • Salary/grade increase • Job reclassification • Alleviate concerns about loss of employment, future prospects
Altering perceptions of inputs and outcomes (through suitable training, communication, and fair procedures)	Reduce users' inputs	• Emphasize learning new skills as outcomes rather than inputs
	Increase users' outcomes	• Emphasize the status and prestige of working in a modern environment with latest technology/innovation • Emphasize the outcomes on account of learning market skills
	Employer's input	• Explain employer's inputs and deservingness (e.g., risk, investment, R&D effort) • Explain the need to pass on the benefits to customers on account of competition
	Others' inputs and outcomes	• Explain better-treated users' deservingness
	Users' perceptions of procedural fairness	• Fair procedures for user involvement, bargaining and negotiations with user representatives

Source: K. Joshi, "A model of users' perspective on change: The case of information systems technology implementation," *MIS Quarterly*, June 1991, p. 237. Reprinted with permission from the *MIS Quarterly*.

If changes in an employee's inputs or outputs are appropriate, managers must give employees an opportunity to state their views, explain why such a distribution schedule was established, and explain why change is appropriate given the changes occurring in the environment.[156]

By helping to destroy the perceived link between planned change and negative consequences for employees, these 11 strategies facilitate the development of an atmosphere in which management is seen as (*a*) receptive to the needs of employees, (*b*) willing to listen and respond to the concerns of employees, and (*c*) desirous of working with employees to develop an environment beneficial to both management and employees. Of course, the incorporation of all the above strategies may not be possible because of environmental constraints. Nevertheless, the more closely management approaches the ideal, the greater will be the probability that its change programs will succeed (see Figure 11.4, path 2). The implication for management is clear: if you ignore employee needs, especially the needs of those who will be asked to implement a proposed change, the probability of employee resistance soars. Conversely, develop a change strategy that considers the needs of employees and the probability of employee resistance diminishes.

Summary

Although not all organizations require the same degree of creativity and innovation, to be successful, many contemporary organizations must develop strategies that encourage and maintain such activities. The level of creativity and innovation occurring within a given organization will primarily be a function of the selection decisions made by management and the internal climate which management creates. In selecting subordinates, management has several options open to it, i.e., personality testing, structure selection interviews, assessment center technology, and personal reference checks. Similarly, when developing an organizational climate that supports creativity and innovation, management must take steps to ensure that managers set an example for their employees; support, encourage, and reward employee efforts; and create an internal structure that facilitates employee efforts.

Innovation, however, by its very nature produces changes within the organization. For a change program to be considered successful, it must have both content quality and employee acceptance. To help ensure that employees accept a proposed change program and do not learn to resist change, management should take steps to ensure that employee needs are considered. Management strategies designed to ensure need achievement should ensure full disclosure, employee participation, nonevaluative periods, training, simplicity, divisibility, reasonable compatibility with past, appropriate timing, use of informal leaders, avenues of appeal, and justice.

Exercises

11.1 Words: How Do Interaction and External Cues Affect Creativity?

You are asked to participate in a brief experiment to demonstrate the impact of social interaction and external cues on group creativity. Target, a common word game, will be used as a focal point of this exercise. The game requires that you make as many four-letter words as possible from the letters provided in a three-by-three matrix. The rules are simple. You can use each letter only once. Next, each word must contain the letter in the center of the matrix, the darkened cell. There must be at least one nine-letter word in the list. Finally, do not use plurals, foreign words, or proper names in your word list. Please follow the rules outlined below.

Step 1. The class will break up into small groups of five to six members each. Groups will be assigned to one of three conditions: A, B, and C.

Step 2. Members of A groups must work on their list independent of other Group A members. Members of B groups will be able to interact openly. C group members will not only be able to interact but also will receive a number of suggested words. (10 minutes)

Step 3. Group output will be collected and assessed.

Step 4. Each group list of words will be listed on a flip chart, or chalkboard, and the results will then be discussed by the class.

11.2 Case Analysis and Group Discussion: Alternative Strategies for Innovation and Change

When managing change within an organization, it is important to assess the appropriateness of specific actions that you might take as a manager. Less effective managers spend too much time, energy, and resources on activities that are not likely to facilitate change and ultimate acceptance by others. This exercise allows you to practice the skill of assessing the appropriateness of alternative actions available to a manager who wants to introduce needed change. Please follow the steps outlined below.

Step 1. Read individually the case about Computer Soft Corporation. The information will familiarize you with the company, its history, and why changes are being considered. (10 minutes)

Step 2. Next, you will be provided with 16 possible actions open to a manager bringing about change in an organization. Individually rate each option in terms of its appropriateness; that is, whether or not it should be implemented by the manager. When rating each alternative, use the four-point rating scale provided on the Available Action Alternatives Sheet. You will be assigned to discussion groups after you have completed the alternative sheet. (Approximately 10 minutes)

Step 3. Through group discussion, each group will establish a consensus on the ratings for each action alternative. Each group should articulate a rationale for each rating. (Approximately 40 minutes)

Step 4. The class will assemble and discuss group results.

COMPUTER SOFT CORPORATION[157]

The success of Computer Soft Corporation is owed to the massive growth in customer demand for tailor-made computer software. Computer Soft began as a small unit within a larger university in the Northeast. The rationale behind its creation was a desire to take advantage of excess capacity existing within the computer and business departments of the university. In addition, it was hoped that this venture would generate funds to offset the increasing shortfall of government funding for universities. Within three years, Computer Soft grew from the idea of five talented academics to a thriving business employing 250 workers and generating $65 million in gross sales.

Key to the success of any software company is its ability to service its clients and work the bugs out of the software packages. Since it started operations, Computer Soft has stratified its service to customers. For example, questions received over the telephone are handled first by the least-experienced group of programmers. If the first level of programmers cannot solve the customer's question, it is then referred to a second level of more talented and experienced programmers. Finally, if the second level of programmers cannot solve the client's problem, it is redirected to Computer Soft's most experienced group of programmers. If the problem still cannot be solved over the telephone, the senior programmer can make a personal trip to the customer and, if necessary, rewrite the program. The logic behind this system is that experienced and highly paid programmers should not waste their time solving simple problems. At the same time, the procedure will help less-experienced programmers develop their skills.

Computer Soft's stratified system is initiated by a client's service call, which is randomly directed to the first level of programmers. The same randomized process is used each time a problem is referred to a higher level within the service sequence. Consequently, customers are unlikely to talk to the same programmer more than once. To ensure that programmers in the service sequence are not disturbed while talking to customers, they are required to work in cubicles separated by movable partitions. Finally, programmers for each level are grouped together to facilitate interaction between individuals with the same level of expertise. Given the numbers involved, the company has been forced to locate each level of programmers on a different floor within the company building.

Programmers have become accustomed to the system and have expressed satisfaction with the level of personal independence, control, and ability to interact with programmers at the same level of expertise. Unfortunately, the disadvantage of the Customer Service Department's physical layout is that little interaction takes place between levels. Indeed, when the programmers are in their cubicles, there is little interaction between them at any level.

At first, Computer Soft's service system worked smoothly with few customer complaints. However, as sales grew, the complexity of the company's software packages increased as did the level of service from competing firms. The result was an increase in the number of customer complaints. The following represent some of the complaints directed toward Computer Soft and the services they provide:

- Service is impersonal with no consistency among programmers.
- Customers are often put on hold for long periods of time when referred to a higher level.
- Customers are often referred to several programmers before they find one that can help with their problem.
- If for some reason customers are disconnected or hang up while on hold and call back later, they have to start the entire process over again.
- Because individual programmers are evaluated on the number of calls they handle on a given day, they appear in a hurry either to solve the problem or to refer the customer to another programmer. This often results in a software program recommendation that does not work and the customer is forced to call back a second or third time.
- Complex problems that should be handled from the beginning at the third level of expertise often bog down at lower levels as junior programmers make recommendations that do not work.

In response to these complaints, and pressure from top management to streamline the system, Tim Crafton, manager of the Customer Service Department, changed the structure of the department. The old system was scrapped and in its place a system of work-teams capable of solving customer problems was introduced. Each team consisted of one representative from each of the three programming levels. The company was also able to relocate all programmer teams on one floor, a move that required relocating some other departments. However, after the change, programmers continued to work in their own cubicles. Finally, to ensure ownership, customer identification, and equitable work distribution, top management assigned customers to specific service teams after contracts had been signed. The plan was introduced at a general meeting to all the programmers, who appeared to be in broad agreement that the change would address their most pressing problems.

Unfortunately, when the change was brought on-line, results were less than had been hoped. Customer complaints remained high, team identities did not develop, and interaction remained within levels and did not grow between levels. In response to this apparent failure, Tim constructed a list of 16 possible actions that might make the new system work.

Available Action Alternatives
Computer Soft Corporation

Rating Scale

1 = Best choice. Implement immediately.
2 = Desirable, but will take time and planning.
3 = Appropriateness likely to be determined by manager's alternative actions.
4 = Worst choice. Likely to make matters worse.

_____ 1. Network with other similar organizations that have successfully implemented a team-based service department.

_____ 2. Determine how affected employees' attitudes must change to facilitate a changeover to a team-based system.

_____ 3. Establish a bonus system to reward programmers who process more than the set number of calls each day.

    _____   4. Ask affected programmers to articulate problems they have encountered since the changeover.

    _____   5. Determine the personal losses likely to be experienced by each programmer.

    _____   6. Change individual cublicles to areas large enough to accommodate programmers with their three desks, work units, telephones, and so forth.

    _____   7. Ask the group to come up with a workable solution.

    _____   8. Assign coordination responsibilities to one manager to ensure that the change is carried out correctly.

    _____   9. Determine the losses and threats that programmers associate with the change.

    _____   10. Threaten to take disciplinary action if programmers do not support the change.

    _____   11. Use your best people to establish one, or two, model teams to demonstrate how well teams can work together when given the chance.

    _____   12. Ask programmers to contact dissatisfied customers and personally assess their complaints.

    _____   13. Create a pay-for-performance system that will reward group/team performance rather than individual performance.

    _____   14. Hold daily meetings among the three group members to build a "we" feeling.

    _____   15. Bring programmers together and give them a pep talk about teams and the importance of making the change work.

    _____   16. Bring the group of three programmers together and sell the changes that have been introduced.

11.3 CFC Case Analysis: Understanding Resistance to Change

Very often managers are faced with the need to introduce some type of planned change into their units. The degree of success of these changes is a function of the quality of the change program and the degree of acceptance by subordinates. The case presented with this exercise explains how one manager went about introducing change within his department. Unfortunately, many errors were made in introducing what the manager believed were insignificant changes. Errors that prevent the satisfaction of employee needs are likely to increase the future level of employee resistance. Your task will be to identify the errors made and explain their significance. Please follow the steps outlined below.

Step 1. Individually read the Canadian Furniture Corporation Case. (10 minutes)

Step 2. The class will break up into small groups of five to six individuals each.

Step 3. Through group discussion, list the errors you believe were made by the main character and other members of the organization when they introduced their changes. Be as specific as you can and list as many mistakes as you can. (30 minutes)

Step 4. The class will assemble and discuss each group's list of errors. (30 minutes)

Step 5. After all errors have been identified, the class will identify a set of management strategies to prevent such errors from occurring.

CANADIAN FURNITURE CORPORATION[158]

Canadian Furniture Corporation (CFC) is a manufacturer of household furniture located in southern Ontario. It has been in business since the early 1950s and has always experienced steady growth, even in periods of economic downturn. This steady growth appeared to explode as the Canadian and U.S. economy came out of the 1990–1993 recession. At present, CFC has an assembly plant in 8 of the 10 Canadian provinces. Because of Canada's geography, the unique provincial differences in consumer preferences, and early transportation problems, CFC has traditionally given local assembly plants considerable freedom of action in all aspects of the business. This is especially true in purchasing.

In 1993 the business was purchased by Centrex, a manufacturer of office furniture headquartered in Toronto, that wanted to expand into household furniture. Shortly after the takeover, Mr. Benton, president of Centrex, decided that CFC's operations should be brought more in line with those of Centrex. These included introducing a new position at CFC—Vice President of Purchasing. To fill the position, Benton selected John Speedman, who had been with Centrex for seven years. Benton assured Speedman that he had the authority to make whatever changes he wanted, to bring the CFC operations into line with Centrex. Speedman's appointment was announced through formal channels and CFC's newsletter. In addition, Benton assigned Bob Hestent as Speedman's assistant. Hestent had been with the CFC purchasing group since 1984 and was familiar with the assembly plant managers. The new Purchasing Department was to be located in CFC's Toronto home office.

Speedman decided there was no reason to delay efforts to restructure CFC. As far as he was concerned, that is what Benton and the board of directors of Centrex wanted and that's what they would get. His first move was to centralize the purchasing practices of CFC. All assembly plant purchases over $50,000 would be made through the Toronto office. Speedman thought the coordination of assembly plant purchases would ensure a standard quality of furniture and allow the company to obtain quantity discounts when purchasing high-demand items. He presented his plan to Benton and the Board and they gave it their complete backing.

At the time Speedman enacted his changes, CFC experienced a major increase in demand for furniture. This was likely to have a major impact on future purchases. Nevertheless, Speedman prepared the following letter to be sent to assembly plant managers in order to explain his position.

Before mailing the letters, Speedman asked Hestent (his assistant) for his opinion. Hestent thought the letter was good and clearly made its point. However, he suggested that Speedman first meet with some of the assembly plant managers. Speedman was quick to say no because he was too busy and, as Hestent said, the letter was clear and to the point. There would be no wasteful field trips.

In the weeks that followed, Speedman's office received positive replies from all assembly plant managers. The following is one such response (see below).

Although the anticipated increase in sales did occur over the next four months and reports from the field indicated a high level of activity, Speedman's office did not receive any purchase information from the assembly plant managers.

Dear _____:

The home office has recently authorized a change in the way CFC obtains its resources. Starting immediately, all purchases over $50,000 will be sent first to my office for approval. This should be done well before the material is actually needed so that quantity purchases can be made where possible. I am sure that you will agree that such a move will improve the quality of CFC's product and help CFC save money. By accomplishing both these objectives, CFC will be better able to compete in what appears to be a very aggressive industry.

Sincerely yours,

(signed) John Speedman

Dear Mr. Speedman:

In response to your letter of the 13th, I see no problems in meeting your request. We at South Shore will do our best to inform you of all purchases over $50,000 and will give you the required lead time.

End Notes

1. E. J. Zelinski, "Creativity training for business," *Canadian Manager,* Summer 1989: 24–25; C. M. Solomon, "Creativity training," *Personnel Journal,* May 1990: 65–71; L. S. Silk, "The great freedom of corporate life: To question," *Business Month,* April 1989: 11; M. Basadur, "Managing creativity: A Japanese model," *Academy of Management Executive,* Vol.6, No. 2, 1992: 29–42.

2. R. Mitchell, "Nurturing those ideas," *Business Week,* 1989: 107–118; R. S.Wellins, W. C. Byham, and J. M. Wilson, *Empowered Teams: Creating Self-Directed Work Groups that Improve Quality, Productivity, and Participation,* Jossey-Bass, San Francisco, Calif., 1991.

3. Wellins, Byham and Wilson, 1991.

4. *Encyclopaedia Britannica,* Vol. 3: 227.

5. E. Pickard, "Toward a theory of creative potential," *The Journal of Creative Behavior,* Vol. 24, No. 1, First Quarter 1990: 1–9.

6. M. Gates, "Managing creativity," *Incentive,* September 1989: 181–185; D. V. Brazeal and K. M. Weaver, "Differential motivating factors among interpreneurial and traditional managers? A look at the influence of reward systems and structures on performance among intrapreneurial and traditional managers," *The Journal of Creative Behavior,* Vol. 24, No. 4, Fourth Quarter 1990: 263–74; Basadur, 1992; K. F. Gretz and S. R. Drozdeck, *Empowering Innovative People,* Probus Publishing, Chicago, Ill., 1992.

7. Zelinski, 1989.

8. Basadur, 1992.

9. Zelinski, 1989.

10. Solomon, May 1990.

11. Zelinski, 1989: 24.

12. M. Basadur, G. B. Graen, and S. G. Green, "Training in creative problem solving: Effects on ideation and problem finding and solving in an industrial

research organization," *Organizational Behavior and Human Performance,* Vol. 30, 1982: 41–47; M. Basadur, G. B. Graen, and T. A. Scandura, "Training effects of attitudes toward divergent thinking among manufacturing engineers," *Journal of Applied Psychology,* Vol. 71, No. 4, 1986: 612–617; Zelinski, 1989; Solomon, May 1990.

13. R. M. Kanter, *The Change Masters*, Simon & Schuster, New York, 1983.

14. P. F. Drucker, *Innovation and Entrepreneurship: Practice and Principles*, Harper & Row, New York, 1985.

15. A. L. Delbecq and P. Mills, "Managerial practices that enhance performance," *Organizational Dynamics*, Summer 1985: 24–34.

16. Pickard, 1990: 2.

17. S. G. Asthana, "The creative profile and organizational values," *Indian Psychological Review,* Vol. 14, No. 2, 1977: 16–23; Gates, 1989; P. Russell and R. Evens, *The Creative Manager,* Unwin, London, 1989.

18. Asthana, 1977; A. Shapero, "Managing creative professionals," *Research Management,* March–April, 1985: 23–28; R. Rowan, *The Intuitive Manager*, Berkley Books, New York, 1986; Russell and Evens, 1989.

19. The following problem and solution is taken from Russell and Evens, 1989: 50.

20. Rowan, 1986.

21. R. W. Woodman and L. F. Schoenfeldt, "An interactionist model of creative behavior," *The Journal of Creative Behavior,* Vol. 24, No. 1, 1990: 10–20; Gretz and Drozdeck, 1992; Pickard, 1990.

22. Pickard, 1990.

23. The model depicted in Figure 11.1 is based upon material presented in Woodman and Schoenfeldt, 1990.

24. Woodman and Schoenfeldt, First Quarter 1990.

25. S. Wilkinson, "Insight into in-house innovation," *Chemical Week,* December 20/27, 1989: 56+.

26. Mitchell, 1989.

27. R. Helson and V. Mitchell, "Personality" in *Annual Review of Psychology,* Vol. 29, 1978: 555–585, ed. M. R. Rosenzweig and L. W. Porter.

28. Woodman and Schoenfeldt, 1990.

29. S. G. Asthana, 1977: 16–23; Rowan, 1986.

30. Shapero, March–April, 1985: 26.

31. Shapero, March–April, 1985.

32. J. Katz, "The creative touch," *Nation's Business,* Vol. 78, March 1990: 42–43; W. F. Sturner, "Maximizing success by work setting diagnosis," *The Journal of Creative Behavior,* Vol. 24, No. 2, Second Quarter 1990: 132–139.

33. G. A. Kimble and N. Garmezy, *Principles of General Psychology,* 3rd ed., The Ronald Press, New York, 1968: 695.

34. Kimble and Garmezy, 1968; M. Bloomberg, "Creativity as related to field independence and mobility, *Journal of Genetic Psychology,* Vol. 118, 1971: 3–12; A. C. Del Gaudio, "Psychological differentiation and mobility as related to creativity," *Perceptual and Motor Skills,* Vol. 43, 1976: 831–841; L. D. Noppe, "The relationship of formal thought and cognitive styles to creativity," *The Journal of Creative Behavior,* Vol. 19, No. 2, Second Quarter 1985: 88–96.

35. K. Gamble and J. Kellner, "Creative functioning and cognitive regression," *Journal of Personality and Social Psychology,* Vol. 9, 1968: 266–271; Bloomberg, 1971; C. Golden, "The measurement of creativity by the Stroop color and word test," *Journal of Personality Assessment,* Vol. 39, 1975: 502–506; Noppe, Second Quarter 1985.

36. P. K. Arlin, "Cognitive development in adulthood: a fifth stage," *Developmental Psychology,* Vol. 11, 1975: 602–606; C. I. Saarni, "Piagetian operation and field independence as factors in children's problem-solving performance," *Child Development,* Vol. 44, 1973: 338–345; Noppe, Second Quarter 1985; J. P. Dworetzky, *Psychology,* 4th ed., West Publishing, St. Paul, Minn., 1991.

37. Noppe, Second Quarter 1985

38. L. D. Noppe and J. M. Gallacher, "A cognitive style approach to creative thought," *Journal of Personality Assessment,* Vol. 41, No. 1, 1977: 85–90.

39. Noppe and Gallacher, 1977: 88.

40. Noppe and Gallacher, 1977: 89.

41. M. Basadur, G. B.Graen, and G. Green, "Training in creative problem solving: Effects on ideation and problem finding and solving in an industrial research organization," *Organizational Behavior and Human Performance,* Vol. 30, 1982: 41–70; M. Basadur and R. Thompson, "Usefulness of the ideation principle of extended effort in real world professional and managerial creative problem

solving," *Journal of Creative Behavior,* Vol. 20, No. 1, First Quarter, 1986: 23–34; J. B. Carroll and S. E. Maxwell, "Individual differences in cognitive abilities," In *Annual Review of Psychology, Vol. 30,* 1979: 603–640, M. R. Rosenzweig and L. W. Porter.

42. Basadur, Graen, and Green, 1982: 44.
43. Basadur, Graen, and Green, 1982.
44. S. Farnham-Diggory, *Cognitive Processes in Education,* Harper & Row, New York, 1972.
45. Basadur, Graen, and Green, 1982.
46. Basadur, Graen, and Green, 1982: 44.
47. T. Richards, *Stimulating Innovation,* Frances Pinter Publishers, London, 1985.
48. G. Morgan, *Riding the Waves of Change,* Jossey-Bass, San Francisco, 1988.
49. W. F. Casci, *Applied Psychology in Personnel Management,* 2nd ed., Reston Publishing Co. Inc., Reston, Virginia, 1982. R. D. Gatewood and H. S. Field, *Human Resource Selection,* Dryden Press, Hinsdale, Ill., 1987.
50. For a discussion of the types of personality tests available for selection purposes and their limitations see Gatewood and Field, 1987: 419-450.
51. Gretz and Drozdeck, 1992
52. Gretz and Drozdeck, 1992: 25.
53. M. Basadur, G. Graen, and M. Wakabayashi, "Identifying individual differences in creative problem solving," *The Journal of Creative Behavior,* Vol. 23, No. 2, 1990: 111–131.
54. Basadur, Graen, and Wakabayashi, 1990.
55. Gretz and Drozdeck, 1992; Mitchell, 1989; J. H. Carter, "When work needs to be assigned," *Supervisory Management,* Vol. 35, No. 4, 1990: 7–9.
56. S. Wilkinson, "Insight into in-house innovation," *Chemicalweek,* December 20/27, 1989: 56.
57. Gates, 1989.
58. Gates, 1989; Wilkinson, 1989; Delbec and Mills, 1985.
59. Wilkinson, 1989; T. Peters, "Get innovative or get dead," *California Management Review,* Vol. 33, No. 2, 1991: 9–23.
60. Kanter, 1983.
61. Kanter, 1983.
62. Gates, 1989.
63. As quoted in Gates, 1989: 181.
64. Wilkinson, 1989.
65. Silk, April 1989.
66. S. G. Asthana, 1986; Shapero, 1985; Silk, 1989.

67. Mitchell, 1989.
68. A. G. VanGundy, "How to establish a creative climate in the work group," *Management Review,* August 1984: 24–38.
69. D. Plunkett, "The creative organization: An empirical investigation of the importance of participation in decision-making," *The Journal of Creative Behavior,* Vol. 24, No. 2, 1990: 140–148.
70. F. M. Andrews "Social psychological factors which influence the creative process," in *Perspectives in Creativity,* ed. L. A. Taylor and J. W. Getzels, Aldine, Chicago, Ill., 1975.
71. R. Bookman, "Ignite team spirit in tired lions," *HR Magazine,* June 1990:106–108; R. Bookman, "Rousing the creative spirit," *Training & Development Journal,* November 1988: 67–71.
72. The steps described in Table 11.2 represent the authors' interpretation of material presented in R. Bookman, Vol. 35, No. 6, 1990; Bookman, November 1988.
73. R. Bookman, November 1988.
74. R. Bookman, June 1990: 107.
75. J. L. Adams, *The Care and Feeding of Ideas: A Guide to Encouraging Creativity*, Reading, Mass., Addison-Wesley, 1986; E. Raudsepp, "101 ways to spark your employees creative potential," *Office Administration and Automation,* September 1985: 38–56; Russell and Evens, 1989; Katz, March 1990; Carter, April 1990; Gretz and Drozdeck, 1992.
76. J. L. Adams, *The Care and Feeding of Ideas: A Guide to Encouraging Creativity,* Reading, Mass., Addison-Wesley, 1986.
77. Silk, April 1989;
78. Basadur, 1992.
79. Katz, March 1990; Gates, 1989; Raudsepp, September 1985; VanGundy, August 1984.
80. Katz, March 1990.
81. Basadur, 1992; Gates, 1989; Wilkinson, 1989.
82. Basadur, 1992; Gates, 1989.
83. Basadur, 1992.
84. Basadur, 1992; Carter, April 1990; Wilkinson, 1989; Raudsepp, September 1985.
85. Wilkinson, 1989: 58.
86. T. J. Peters and R. H. Waterman, Jr., *In Search Of Excellence,* Warner Books, New York, 1984.
87. Rowan, 1986; J. MacPherson, "Inspiring creativity by wandering around," *International Management,* April 1984.

88. Gates, 1989.
89. Russell and Evens, 1989.
90. VanGundy, August 1984.
91. Silk, April 1989.
92. For a detailed discussion on how this can be accomplished, review Chapter 9.
93. Solomon, May 1990.
94. T. M. Amabile, *The Social Psychology of Creativity,* Springer-Verlag, New York, 1983; Plunkett, 1990; M. Basadur, 1992.
95. Andrews, 1975.
96. Solomon, May 1990.
97. Plunkett, 1990.
98. F. Damanpour, "Organizational innovation: A meta-analysis of effects of determinants and moderators," *Academy of Management Journal,* Vol. 34, No. 3, 1991: 555–590.
99. VanGundy, August 1984; Delbecq and Mills, 1985; Wilkinsin, December 20 1989; Carter, April 1990; M. Basadur, 1992.
100. Silk, 1989.
101. Basadur, 1992.
102. T. Peters, *Thriving on Chaos,* Harper & Row, New York, 1987: 310.
103. J. F McKenna, "Change must be managed," *Industry Week,* Vol. 242, No. 2, 1993: 50.
104. S. R. Quinn, "Supporting innovation in the work place," *Supervision,* Vol. 51, No. 2, 1990: 3-5.
105. W. W. Burke, J. L. Spencer, L. P. Clark, and C. Coruzzi, "Managers get a 'C' in managing change," *Training and Development Journal,* Vol. 45, No. 5, 1991: 87-90.
106. P. E. Connor and L. K. Lake, *Managing Organizational Change*, Praeger, New York, 1988: 117-118.
107. The following discussion is based in part on the material presented in L. Mealiea, "Learned behavior: The key to understanding and preventing employee resistance to change," *Group & Organizational Studies,* Vol. 3, No. 2, 1978: 211–223.
108. Ibid.
109. J. Kailash, "A model of users' perspective on change: The case of information systems technology implementation," *MIS Quarterly,* Vol. 15, No. 5, 1991, 229–242.
110. J. F McKenna, 1993; L. P. Steier, "When technology meets people," *Training & Development Journal,* Vol. 43, No. 8, 1989: 27-29; E. A

Kazemek and R. M. Charny, "Managing change at the front line," *Health Care Financial Management,* Vol. 54, No. 4, April 1991: 103; Kailash, 1991; Marks, "Preparing for recovery: How HR can add value by confronting employee fear and burnout," *Employment Relations Today,* Vol. 20, No. 2, 1993: 175–185.
111. A. C. Filley, R. J. House, and S. Kerr, *Management Process and Organizational Behavior,* Scott, Foresman, Glenview, Ill., 1976: 83.
112. J. Lawrie, "The ABCs of change management," *Training and Development Journal,* Vol. 44, No. 3, 1990: 87–89; Burke, Spencer, Clark, and Coruzzi, May 1991.
113. D. Kirkpatrick, *How To Manage Change Effectively,* Jossey-Bass, New York, 1985.
114. D. Rosenberg, "Eliminating resistance to change," *Security Management,* Vol. 37, January 1993; S. R. Quinn, "Supporting innovation in the workplace," *Supervision,* Vol. 51, No. 2, 1990: 3–5; Marks, Summer 1993; L. Morris, "Research capsules," *Training and Development Journal,* Vol. 46, No. 4, 1992: 74–76.
115. Morris, April 1992.
116. J. R. Hackman, "Work design," in *Improving Life At Work,* ed. J. R. Hackman and J. L. Suttle, Scott, Foresman, Glenview, Ill., 1977: 129; J. R. Hackman and G. R. Oldham, "Motivation through the design of work: Test of a theory," *Organizational Behavior and Human Performance,* August 1976: 250–279.
117. K. Joshi, "A model of users' perspective on change: The case of infomation systems technology implementation," *MIS Quarterly,* June 1991: 229–242.
118. Mealiea, 1978.
119. Marks, 1993.
120. Marks, 1993.
121. G. Watson, "Resistance to change," in *The Planning of Change,* ed. W. G. Bennis, et al, Holt, Rinehart & Winston, 1969; D. Klein, "Some notes on the dynamics of resistance to change: The defender role," in *The Planning of Change*, ed. W. G. Bennis, et al, Holt, Rinehart & Winston, 1969.
122. R. M Steers and L. W. Porter, *Motivation and Work Behavior,* 4th ed., McGraw-Hill, New York, 1987.
123. Mealiea, 1978.

124. R. D. Elliott, "The challenge of managing change," *Personnel Journal,* Vol. 69, No. 3, 1990: 40–49.

125. Kazemek and Charny, April 1991.

126. Marks, 1993.

127. Steier, 1989.

128. Kazemek and Charny, April 1991.

129. S.R. Quinn, 1990; Steier, 1989; Marks, 1993; Morris, 1992; Burke, Spencer, Clark, and Coruzzi, 1991.

130. M. Beer, R. A. Eisenstat, and B. Spector, "Why change programs don't produce change," *Harvard Business Review,* November–December, 1990: 158–166.

131. Lawrie, 1990.

132. The following example appeared in D. Rosenberg, 1993.

133. Rosenberg, January 1993: 21.

134. Mealiea, 1978.

135. Rosenberg, January 1993.

136. Steier, 1989; J. L. Hunsucker, and J. Martinez, "Industrial transition: The view from top-level managers," *Industrial Management,* Vol. 33, No. 3, 1991: 11–14; Beer, Eisenstat and Spector, 1990.

137. Beer, Eisenstat and Spector, 1990.

138. Mealiea, 1987.

139. Mealiea; T. Peters, *Thriving on Chaos,* Harper & Row, New York, 1987; R. M. Kanter, *The Change Masters,* Simon & Schuster, New York, 1983.

140. Peters, 1988: 565.

141. The model described in Figure 11.5 is based upon material presented in M. Hennecke, "Toward the change-sensitive organization," *Training,* May 1991: 54–59.

142. L. Mealiea and D. Lee, "An alternative to macro-micro contingency theories: An integrative model," *Academy of Management Review,* Vol. 4, No. 3, 1979: 333-345.

143. Hennecke, May 1991.

144. Hennecke, May 1991.

145. W. Bridges, *Managing Transitions: Making the Most of Change,* Addison-Wesley Publishing, New York, 1991.

146. Bridges, 1991.

147. L. Mealiea, 1978.

148. Kanter, 1983; Lawrie, March 1990; Bridges, 1991; Rosenberg, January 1993.

149. Kanter, 1983: 122.

150. Rosenberg, January 1993.

151. Mealiea, 1978 ; Kazemek and Charny, April 1991.

152. L. Mealiea, 1978.

153. Marks, 1993.

154. Marks, 1993.

155. K. Joshi, 1991.

156. For a detailed discussion of how best to deal with equality issues, you should refer to our discussion of distributive justice in Chapter 9.

157. This case and accompanying questions are based on material from Bridges, 1991: 7–16.

158. The following case is based on the "Dashman Company" case by J. D. Glover, R. M. Hower, and R. Tagiuri, *The Administrator: Cases on Human Aspects of Management,* 5th ed., Irwin, Burr Ridge, Ill.: 1973: 499–500.

CONFLICT AND ANGER

Objectives:

- To familiarize students with the nature of conflict and its causes.
- To differentiate between functional and dysfunctional conflict.
- To describe the alternatives open to managers when attempting to deal with organizational conflict.
- To sensitize students to the different levels of anger.
- To describe the steps necessary to effectively manage the anger of others.

The Nature of Conflict

Managers are likely to lead full and active careers, if there is any truth to the expression "conflict is the spice of life." An American Management Association study indicated that 24 percent of middle- and upper-level managers' time is spent dealing with conflict.[1] Gordon Lippitt argued that while corporate managers may spend a quarter of their time dealing with conflict, managers performing in schools, hospitals, and government may spend nearly 50 percent of their time dealing with conflict.[2] The potential for conflict within organizations is likely to grow as environments become more turbulent, demographics of the North American work force continue to change, and organizational structures become more fluid and open.

The importance of change within today's organizations is also reflected in the comments made by Louis Pondy when asked to reflect on his classic 1967 *ASQ* paper "Organizational conflict: Concepts and models."[3] The 1967 paper described conflict as an episodic aberration that would periodically disrupt the harmony and stability of an effective organization. While reflecting on his model, Pondy stated, "The central flaw in the 1967 model is, I believe, the assumption that organizations are cooperative, purposeful systems that occasionally experience conflict or breakdowns in cooperation."[4] The alternative is that conflict "is the very essence of what an organization is. If conflict isn't happening, then the organization has no reason for being."[5] Conflict must therefore be considered a natural phenomenon within organizations and a natural result of human interaction.[6] Robbins has gone as far as to say that conflict is necessary if organizations are going to survive.[7]

Although there are likely to be as many definitions of conflict as there are conflict situations, there appears to be agreement as to key elements that should be included when defining organizational conflict. In reviewing the research on conflict, van de Vliert identifies a number of important elements that should be included or implied by any working definition of conflict.[8] They are, (*a*) conflict occurs when at least one party in the conflict episode experiences frustration, (*b*) recognition that frustration can be both affective and cognitive, (*c*) frustration is subjective and does not necessarily reflect objective reality, and (*d*) conflict and an individual's reaction to feeling frustration are independent events. Such a list implies interaction and dependence between conflicting parties, the blockage of at least one party's concerns or interests (i.e., goals, values, behavior, etc.), the perception of incompatibility of individual concerns or interests, and the ability to manage conflict by applying appropriate conflict-handling behaviors.

Conflict definitions often reflect the research interests of the particular behavioral scientist providing the definition. For example, the following three definitions view conflict as either a process, state, situation, or type of behavior. It is our view that all three components must be integrated if managers are going to understand and manage conflict.

- Conflict is "the process which begins when one party perceives that another has frustrated, or is about to frustrate, some concerns of his or hers"[9] (a process).

- Conflict is "an interactive state in which behavior or goals of one actor are to some degree incompatible with the behaviors or goals of some other actor or actors"[10] (a situation—underlying structure), or is "a situation in which the conditions, practices, or goals for the different participants are inherently incompatible"[11] (a situation—underlying structure).

- Conflict is "a type of behavior which occurs when two or more parties are in opposition or in battle as a result of a perceived relative deprivation from the activities of or interacting with another person or group."[12]

The manager's ability to understand and handle conflict has also been affected by the research and theories provided by behavioral scientists.[13] What follows in the next several paragraphs is a simplified look at the evolution of conflict theory. It does not attempt to describe all the fads and cycles associated with conflict, or address the full complexity of the theory, but will provide an understanding of how the field has evolved.

Before 1900 the discussion of conflict was primarily the domain of philosophers, political scientists, and anthropologists. In the early 1900s, classical theorists such as Fayol,[14] Gulick and Urwick,[15] Taylor,[16] and Weber[17] described how to make organizations effective, and find the "one best way" of doing things so as to ignore conflict.[18] If you correctly designed and managed the organization, that is, followed classical principles, rules, work procedures, division of labor, clear lines of authority, etc., there would be no conflict. As a result, it was not necessary to explicitly develop a theory of conflict management.

During the 1950s and 1960s behavioral scientists recognized conflict as a natural organizational phenomenon that threatened organizational effectiveness.[19] By explicitly accepting conflict as a natural part of organizational life, managers had the responsibility of eliminating it. Resolution models developed during this period placed emphasis on the normative benefits of collaborative behavior or joint problem solving.[20] The underlying assumption was that collaborative or joint problem-solving behavior would heal strained relations, correct injustices, and strengthen the relationships between conflicting parties.

The next major shift in the evolution of conflict theory begins in the late 1960s and reflects an increased acceptance that conflict can have both positive and negative consequences for the organization.[21] With the acceptance that conflict can result in positive or negative consequences, one notices subtle changes in the literature. No longer are behavioral scientists discussing conflict resolution, but instead are turning their attention to issues of conflict management. In other words, behavioral scientists and practitioners recognized that whether conflict has constructive or destructive consequences is a function of how it is managed.[22]

The issue of conflict management, however, relates to both reactive and proactive behaviors by managers. Initially, conflict management related to those activities designed to ensure that episodes of conflict resulted in positive consequences for the organization. Soon, however, it was argued that conflict management also included proactive behaviors designed to create conflict in those situations where existing levels were insufficient to ensure innovation or organizational survival.[23]

Currently, there appears to be agreement on several key issues relating to conflict management and its role in determining organizational effectiveness. Conflict, reflecting environmental dynamics and complexity, as well as individual differences, must be considered the normal state for organizations. Furthermore, conflict should not be exclusively associated with discrete public events linked with formal negotiations. It also relates to the ongoing disputes associated with day-to-day organizational life, and as a result, conflict is frequently not visible. Conflict management may require managers either to promote conflict when conflict levels are too low, or reduce conflict when it threatens organizational effectiveness. Next, there appears to be agreement that the collaborative approach to conflict management or resolution is not necessarily the most appropriate choice in all conflict situations. Finally, a contingency approach is likely to produce the greatest benefit to managers attempting to deal with conflict situations.

Understanding the Basics

By accepting that conflict is inevitable, and in certain instances desired, the issue becomes how to manage conflict effectively so that positive consequences outweigh negative consequences. Table 12.1 presents a summary of the functional and dysfunctional consequences associated with conflict.[24] It is our view that if conflict is managed effectively, it is possible to limit its consequences to the left-hand side of Table 12.1. When this occurs, the result of conflict can be increased productivity, improved intrapersonal relationships, increased employee creativity, and an increased likelihood of organizational success.

To effectively use available conflict management techniques, managers must understand, accept, and be willing to follow a contingency approach. Such an approach integrates process, situational, and behavioral variables. However, *before* discussing an integrated model, we will first discuss a number of conflict basics. Specifically, what are the most common sources and levels of conflict within organizations, what is meant by the inverted "U" relationship between conflict and performance, who are the beneficiaries of successful conflict management and are their interests compatible, and what are the types of conflict that can occur within organizations.

Sources of Conflict

Pondy referred to potential causes of conflict that exist within the environment as antecedent conditions or latent conflict.[25] He identified three broad

---

TABLE 12.1   **Consequences of Conflict**

Positive Consequences	*Negative Consequences*
• Opens up an issue in a confronting manner	• Diverts energy from the real task
• Develops clarification of an issue	• Destroys morale
• Improves problem-solving quality	• Polarizes individuals and groups
• Increases involvement	• Deepens differences
• Provides more spontaneity in communications	• Obstructs cooperative action
• Initiates growth	• Creates suspicion and distrust
• Strengthens a relationship when it is resolved creatively	• Decreases productivity
• Helps increase productivity	

Source: G. Lippitt, "Managing conflict in today's organizations," *Training and Development Journal,* Vol. 36, 1982, pp. 68–69. Copyright © 1982, *Training and Development.* American Society for Training and Development. Reprinted with permission. All rights reserved.

categories of latent conflict. These are, (*a*) competition for scarce resources, (*b*) individuals' drive for autonomy, and (*c*) incompatibility of sub-unit goals. However, while no one argues with Pondy's list of potential causes of conflict, other behavioral scientists have added to it.[26] The following represents an expanded list of conflict sources:

• Different employee interests have the potential of producing conflict if individuals must compete for scarce resources. If two managers both need an additional staff member but are told by senior management there are only sufficient funds to hire one individual, there is a high probability that one or both managers will experience frustration.

• The need for autonomy is a potential source of conflict when individuals within the organization attempt to control other employees. This is particularly relevant when considering the superior and subordinate relationship. As indicated in our discussion of creativity, there is an inherent conflict as managers seek to control and subordinates seek autonomy to try out new ideas.

• Substantive conflict can occur when employees or departments have incompatible goals. Individual and departmental goals reflect the unique needs, reference base, and perceptions of the individuals involved. Given this uniqueness, the possibility exists for each party's goals to be different. For example, sales personnel want to promise early delivery even if such promises disrupt production schedules. At the same time, production wants to keep schedule changes to a minimum to keep production costs low.

• Incompatibility of feelings and emotions can lead to conflict if employees openly express themselves. Employees who become angry and attack fellow employees may produce long-term hostility or residual emotions resulting from hurt feelings or personal attacks.

• Value differences among employees result in organizational conflict when employees attempt to translate values into actions. For example, individuals may place different values on the importance of affirmative action and the amount of time, energy, and resources devoted to affirmative action programs. More specifically, one employee may seek some type of quota system when hiring minority groups, while another may be strongly opposed to such a practice.

• Cognitive differences in the interpretation or perception of events have the potential of precipitating a conflict episode. For example, two employees attending the same meeting may interpret the boss's statements differently. One subordinate may interpret the president's statements as supporting a quick decision on a particular project, while a second hears a recommendation to go slow. If these differences are not clarified during the meeting, they can result in conflict between two employees who must work together on the project.

• Failure in communication also increases the potential for employee conflict.[27] Employees who fail to communicate their position clearly, or function within an environment that blocks the free flow of information, are more likely to misunderstand the goals, values, and interests of others.

However, while semantic conflicts can be eliminated by open communication, conflicts that reflect real differences between parties may be exacerbated by open communication.

The Many Levels of Conflict

To understand the complexity of conflict it is necessary to recognize the multiple levels at which conflict may occur.[28] Figure 12.1 identifies six levels of conflict relevant to organizational effectiveness. The six levels of conflict may be described as follows.

  • *Intrapersonal conflict* can represent "a situation in which a person is motivated to engage in two or more mutually exclusive activities."[29] Individuals faced with such conflict may find it difficult to choose between different courses of action. Intrapersonal conflict can reflect three different situations.[30] In the case of approach–approach conflict, individuals must choose between two equally attractive choices. A manager who must delegate a popular assignment to two equally qualified subordinates is experiencing approach–approach conflict. Approach–avoidance conflict occurs when employees are faced with a single alternative, situation, or object that has both positive and negative consequences. The manager who wants a promotion but recognizes it will put strains on his or her family is facing this type of conflict. Last, avoidance–avoidance conflict results when an individual is being forced to choose between two undesirable choices. Managers who are told by top management to fire a good friend and trusted employee or be fired themselves face such a dilemma.

FIGURE 12.1

Levels of conflict

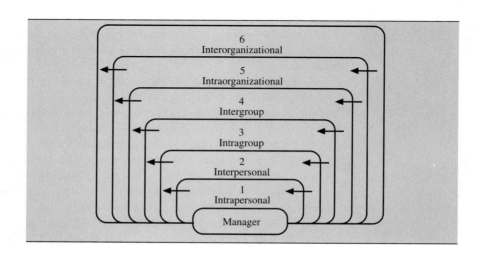

Intrapersonal conflict can also occur when employees experience dissonance between two conflicting cognitions.[31] In response to such conflict, managers may attempt to distort information or change their behavior to regain balance. A manager may expect a newly hired MBA to be successful because in the past other employees graduating from the same university have performed well. If the new employee fails to perform at acceptable levels, the manager will attempt to balance the situation. He or she may rationalize the conflict by blaming the individual's poor performance on a new training program put on by the Human Resource Department. As a result, the manager can continue to maintain his or her positive attitude toward both the new MBA and his or her alma mater. Alternatively, the manager may accept that his or her decision was a poor one and subsequently alter his or her attitude and behavior. In this case, the manager is also likely to take action against the new MBA (i.e., terminate or transfer).

Role conflict or ambiguity can also result in intrapersonal conflict.[32] Role conflict occurs when employees are confronted with divergent role expectations.[33] Role ambiguity occurs when employees are unclear as to the rights, privileges, and obligations relating to their jobs.[34] If a manager accepts the role of a parent (e.g., going to a daughter's piano recital) and manager (e.g., completing a report for the boss), he or she will likely experience conflict. To achieve internal balance, and remove the role conflict, the manager may attempt to rationalize not going to the recital. By arguing that he or she has been to several others in the past month, the manager can minimize the negative consequences of missing the daughter's next recital. Alternatively, the employee could downplay the report by arguing internally that the report is not really important to the boss or that the boss will be unable to read it until after he or she returns from holiday.

Unfortunately, actions taken to balance or remove internal conflict can spill over to other conflict levels. In the above example, a decision not to go to the recital may result in conflict between the employee and his or her child or spouse. If the employee decides not to complete the report, he or she may trigger a conflict episode with the boss or other employees who are waiting for the report. (The potential interactions between conflict levels are demonstrated by the arrows in our model.) Similarly, conflict at the institutional level may trigger intraorganizational or intergroup changes that are perceived as threatening by organizational members, and the result may be interpersonal or interdepartmental conflicts.

- *Interpersonal conflict* occurs when **two** individuals find themselves at odds, in disagreement, or in opposition when dealing with goals, behaviors, allocation of resources, feelings, emotions, and values.[35] The key to understanding interpersonal conflict is the manager's ability to identify and deal with the antecedent or latent conditions that place two individuals on a collision course. If antecedent factors cannot be removed, or are being engineered by management to stimulate change, managers' efforts to deal with conflict must reflect the unique characteristics of each situation. The goal for managers is to ensure a fit between behavior and situational requirements, and to ensure that conflicts do not escalate to the point at which they become dysfunctional. (More will be said about escalation, emotions, and the appropriateness of conflict management styles later in the chapter.)

• If the two individuals involved in conflict are members of the same group, and the conflict involves group-related issues, then it is more appropriate to classify this situation as *intragroup conflict*.[36] The intragroup classification also holds if the two individuals attempt to form coalitions within the existing group structure. Coalitions are formed to politically strengthen one's position and thereby increase the chances of winning. Finally, if a number of subgroups already exist psychologically, and find themselves with different goals, needs, roles, ideas, or are vying for the same scarce resources, then it is at the intragroup level that conflict occurs. The danger is that the original group may break apart as a result of the internal conflict. There is, however, evidence that by preventing groups from becoming complacent, or engaging in *groupthink,** intragroup conflict can result in improved group performance.[37]

• If the observed conflict is between two existing groups, it makes greater sense to talk about *intergroup conflict* rather than interpersonal conflict. The underlying antecedent conditions that can produce interpersonal and intragroup conflict also work at this level. The only difference is the focus of attention. At this level, the manager should be concerned with the impact of conflict on intergroup relationships. Here again, the consequences may be either positive or negative. The ultimate direction that intergroup conflict takes will be a function of how it is managed and its magnitude.

Much of what has been written about conflict emphasizes the changes that take place "within" and "between" groups. The following summarizes generally accepted consequences of intragroup and intergroup conflict:[38]

Consequences of Conflict *within* Groups

1. *Increased cohesiveness*—External threats motivate group members to ignore minor differences and close ranks. As Korten has indicated, this represents a high goal situation in which the status quo is no longer acceptable.[39] In fact, individuals are willing to forgo individual needs so that the group can achieve its objectives.

2. *Emphasis on loyalty*—It follows that once the group is perceived as the primary vehicle through which the individuals achieve their long-term objectives, then group loyalty intensifies. This is especially true when the threat to the group is perceived as external to the group. Similarly, as the group's goals become more important in the short term than need satisfaction of the individual members, there is less tolerance of deviant behavior.

---

* *Groupthink* refers to situations where "congruence-seeking becomes so dominant in a cohesive in-group that it tends to override realistic appraisal of alternative courses of action."[40]

3. *Acceptance of autocratic direction*—Under conditions of high stress the status quo is no longer acceptable, and social mechanisms are often insufficient to move the group effectively in one direction (i.e., the overall goals are agreed to, but the means are still ambiguous). Under these conditions, autocratic direction becomes more acceptable.

4. *Focused activity*—Once the status quo is no longer acceptable, goal achievement takes precedence over personal, short-term satisfaction, and if the threat producing the conflict is external, the group places greater emphasis on task-oriented behavior. For example, as the football team gets ready for the big game, there is greater emphasis on task behavior preparing the team for the game.

5. *Taking extreme positions*—Research also indicates that groups, when compared to individuals, tend to take on extreme positions.[41] Therefore, when pressed about delivery dates, the production group is likely to take a more extreme position than would individual production employees making the decision alone.[42]

Consequences of Conflict *between* Groups

1. *Decreased interaction*—As opposing groups draw together internally, and as they become more cohesive and demand greater loyalty from their members, the level of interaction between opposing groups declines significantly. Group members not only reduce social and professional contacts but they also reduce the number of attempted communications directed toward the other group. The impact of such behavior is to further strengthen the We versus They perception and to reduce the likelihood of information being exchanged that is designed to facilitate creative problem solving or principled negotiations.

This also reflects a tendency for groups to judge their own members more favorably than nonmembers and at the same time give members preferential treatment.[43] Such discriminating behaviors also occur when group members have not met one another and have not yet met members of competing groups.[44] These behaviors are likely to increase the distance between groups and increase the probability of misunderstanding and future conflict.

2. *Distorted perception*—When conflict produces an emotional rather than a rational response (fear rather than problem solving, or anger rather than critical thinking) and groups reduce the level of interaction, it is not surprising to find that groups begin to distort the perceptions they have of one another. The We versus They perception quickly leads to the I'm OK, You're Not OK perception. Once this occurs, group members begin to rationalize why they are right and develop negative stereotypes of their opponents to explain when they are wrong. In organizations we hear the following statement used to stereotype different groups: "Salespeople are only interested in volume, not quality or the customer's ability to pay." "Production people are only interested in getting the product out at the least cost and in the shortest time." "All accountants are bean counters and have no feelings for people."

• Intraorganizational conflict—When studying organizations, the four conflict levels just discussed can all be classified loosely as intraorganizational conflict.[45] However, to fit neatly within this classification the conflict being considered should be structurally based, or have a significant impact on the total organization. Using these guidelines, conflicts between managers and subordinates can fit within this category if they are structurally based or are likely to affect a large number of individuals. When a manager and his or her subordinate disagree on departmental goals, the conflict often arises because of structural (level) differences between the two individuals. Conflicts between departments and divisions are likely to fit into this category because they are structurally based and because they will likely have a significant impact on the total organization. This type of conflict also occurs when line personnel interact with staff personnel. The potential for conflict between these two groups often reflects the differences in basic orientation. Table 12.2 outlines some of these differences.[46]

• Interorganizational conflict—The final level of organizational conflict considered deals with the relationships between organizations.[47] At this level, the underlying antecedent conditions that produce conflict remain the same, but the focus of analysis changes. Instead of assessing individual or group needs, roles, attitudes, demand for scarce resources, etc., the unit of study becomes the organization.

Traditionally, the study of the relationship level has dominated the conflict literature, with behavioral scientists paying primary attention to interpersonal, intragroup, intergroup, and intraorganizational conflicts.[48] Recently, however,

---

TABLE 12.2   Role Differences between Line and Staff Personnel

Line Personnel	*Staff Personnel*
• Highly action oriented	• Concerned with studying a problem in depth before making recommendations
• Highly intuitive, in contrast to being analytical	• Highly analytical, in contrast to being intuitive
• Often short-sighted	• Often too long-range oriented
• Often ask the wrong kinds of questions	• Have the answers, and therefore spend their time looking for questions
• Want simple, easy-to-use solutions	• Complicate the situation by providing esoteric data
• Accustomed to examining some of the available alternatives and choosing one them	• Interested in examining all the possible alternatives, weighing them, analyzing them, and then choosing the "best" one regardless of time or cost restraints
• Highly protective of the organization	• Highly critical of the organization

Source: R. Hodgetts, *Management: Theory, Process, and Practice,* 3rd ed., Dryden Press, Hinsdale Ill., 1982.

the general acceptance of the open systems theory, globalization, the large number of mergers and takeovers, and concerns about the environment have stimulated additional interest in the interorganizational, or the institutional, level of conflict.[49] Nevertheless, given our emphasis on employee productivity, manager–subordinate interactions, and interactions between managers and relevant others, our discussion will deal with conflicts at the relationship level.

The Inverted U Relationship between Conflict and Performance

A helpful vehicle for visualizing the relationship between conflict and productivity is the inverted U function of stress. Recall the discussion in Chapter 5 of the inverted U function that described the relationship between stress and performance. Given that conflict produces significant stress and pressure within any system, it can be substituted for the stress variable.[50] The resulting relationship is depicted in Figure 12.2. As the curve indicates, both high and low levels of conflict will produce low levels of productivity. Such a view is consistent with the activation or arousal theory of performance,[51] motivation theory,[52] and the interactionist approach to conflict.[53] The interactionist philosophy states that (*a*) functional conflict is absolutely necessary for organizational survival, (*b*) functional opposition is desirable, (*c*) both conflict stimulation and resolution are part of conflict management, and (*d*) conflict management is the responsibility of all managers.[54] Let us consider the mechanics of this relationship.

Low levels of conflict result in low performance because there are insufficient stimuli to motivate individuals to change, grow, or develop. In Zone 1 of Figure 12.2, employees are either unaware of, deny, or bury conflict, and as a result fail to take the necessary steps to correct underlying problems that exist in the system. The open expression of conflict acts as a signal that something is wrong within the organization. Conflict and its accompanying stress motivate managers to seek out and implement constructive solutions that will ultimately improve the system. If insufficient conflict is present in the

FIGURE 12.2

Inverted U function of conflict

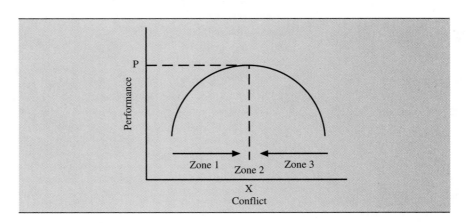

system, the result will be slow adaptation, few constructive changes, reduced innovation, and ultimately organizational stagnation.[55] Table 12.3 lists a number of stimulating techniques that can be used to increase the level of functional conflict within the organization. Clearly, the items presented do not represent an exhaustive listing but only indicate that managers can creatively manipulate their environment to stimulate functional conflict.

The degree to which the relationship between conflict and performance takes on a U-shaped function also reflects the response of management to perceived conflict. As will be discussed below, management's approach to conflict must be situationally based. If managers do not take the correct action in response to perceived conflict, it is likely that the negative consequences of conflict will outweigh the positive consequences and performance will decline.

Figure 12.2 also implies that for each situation there is an optimum level of conflict. Once this level has been surpassed (i.e., management has moved in Zone 3), increasing levels of conflict will have a negative impact on performance. Excessive or poorly managed conflict will increase the level of stress and pressure within the system. This increased level of stress and pressure is likely to cause individuals to (*a*) narrow their attention and thereby increase the probability of poor judgment, (*b*) commit an increased number of errors, (*c*) revert to well-learned dominant behaviors that are inappropriate in the new situation, (*d*) be unable to distinguish between trivial and important environmental factors, and (*e*) exhibit inappropriate emotional or psychological behavior (i.e., anger).

TABLE 12.3   Stimulation Techniques

Manipulate communication channel
  • Deviate messages from traditional channels
  • Repress information
  • Transmit too much information
  • Transmit ambiguous or threatening information
Alter the organization's structure (redefine jobs, alter tasks, reform units or activities)
  • Increase a unit's size
  • Increase specialization and standardization
  • Add, delete, or transfer organizational members
  • Increase interdependence between units
Alter personal behavior factors
  • Change personality characteristics of the leader
  • Create role conflict
  • Develop role incongruence

Source: S. P. Robbins, "'Conflict management' and 'conflict resolution' are not synonymous terms," *California Management Review,* Vol. 21, No. 2, Winter 1978, p. 71. Copyright © 1978 by The Regents of the University of California. Reprinted from the *California Management Review,* Vol. 21, No. 2. By permission of The Regents.

The Question of Functionality (Beneficiaries)

The issue of functionality of conflict is determined by the outcome criteria chosen.[56] If conflict results in positive consequences as defined by these criteria, then it is said to be functional. Pondy in his 1967 article indicated that we can measure the functionality of conflict and the behaviors used to manage it if there is a positive effect on the quantity and quality of productivity, organizational stability, and organizational adaptability.[57] Pondy's emphasis, however, was on the benefits for the organization and not the individual. He stated that the functionality of intrapersonal conflict was only of concern if it had an effect on organizational performance.

It is also possible to measure the functionality of conflict by assessing the degree to which it results in those outcomes listed in the right-hand column of Table 12.1. If positive outcomes outweigh the negative consequences, then conflict is classified as functional. Here again, there is no explicit effort to balance the interests of the organization as opposed to the individual's interests.

Thomas and his co-authors provided a list of criteria that take into account organizational and individual needs (see Table 12.4). Their list is not exhaustive, but it does give the reader an appreciation of the range of criteria that can be used for each interest group. Although the choice of who is to be the *beneficiary* of conflict management efforts is a value judgment, we believe managers must consider both. In those instances where joint benefits can be achieved, managers must make an effort to satisfy the interests of both. For example, by integrating employees into the decision-making or creativity process, managers can increase the intrinsic satisfaction of employees who want to participate. Similarly, employees can use the accomplishments of the organization to improve personal self-esteem or reputation.

Where joint employee–organizational gains cannot be obtained, it will be necessary for participants to make the appropriate decisions and trade-offs. When this occurs, it is still possible to consider both the employee and the organizational needs. Recall the example provided in Chapter 11 on creativity, where the organization had to reduce payroll expense by 20 percent. The organization's gain would clearly result in a financial loss for its employees. However, by giving the employees control over how the reduction would be achieved for each individual, the potential negative effects of the conflict situation were reduced.

An Integrative Model

The conflict definitions provided above indicated that conflict can be studied on three distinct levels, that is, process, underlying environmental structure and behavioral levels. Unfortunately, by studying each level separately, behavioral scientists fail to accurately communicate the true complexity and dynamics of organizational conflict, or the need to integrate these three

---

TABLE 12.4   Criteria for Evaluating Conflict Outcomes

Organizational Welfare	*Personal Welfare*

1. Quality of decisions
  • creativity of decisions
  • commitment to implementing decision
  • feedback and information
  • organizational adaptability and viability
	1. Power and effectiveness variables
	  • using behavioral strengths
	  • maintaining/augmenting one's allocation of organizational resources
	  • obtaining/controlling strategic information
	  • favorableness of reputation
	  • husbanding time and energy for key personal concerns

2. Effect upon human resources
  • intellectual and physical resources
  • absence and turnover rates
  • individual productivity
  • trust (relationship resource)
	2. Satisfaction variables
	  • self-esteem
	  • frustration
	  • job satisfaction
	  • using familiar behaviors
	  • perceived equity of resource share
	  • exhilaration
	  • fatigue

3. Expenditures of organizational resources
  • time and energy spent on conflict issues
  • training costs for collaborative skill
  • goal displacement from organizational concerns to personal battles
  • disruptions (disorder, protest, violence)	

Source: K. W. Thomas, D. W. Jamieson, and R. K. Moore, "Conflict and collaboration: Some concluding observations," *California Management Review,* Vol. 21, No. 2, Winter 1978: p. 92. Copyright © 1978 by The Regents of the University of California. Reprinted from the *California Management Review,* Vol. 21, No. 2. By permission of The Regents.

levels. Segmentation also increases the possibility that managers will miss the full range of options available when attempting to deal with organizational conflict and the importance of time when selecting a conflict management strategy.[58] Our intention, however, is not to develop a new model of conflict but to integrate the three major thrusts that are found within the conflict literature. The model in Figure 12.3 represents our interpretation of existing models and is designed to integrate process, situation, and behavioral variables.[59]

1. Structural Characteristics

The environment in which a conflict episode takes place represents the relatively stable structural characteristics that cut across conflict episodes.[60] Furthermore, it is the environment's underlying structure that helps shape each conflict episode. The following discussion considers five structural components that are likely to impact on the occurrence and intensity of organizational conflict.

FIGURE 12.3

Integrative model of organizational conflict

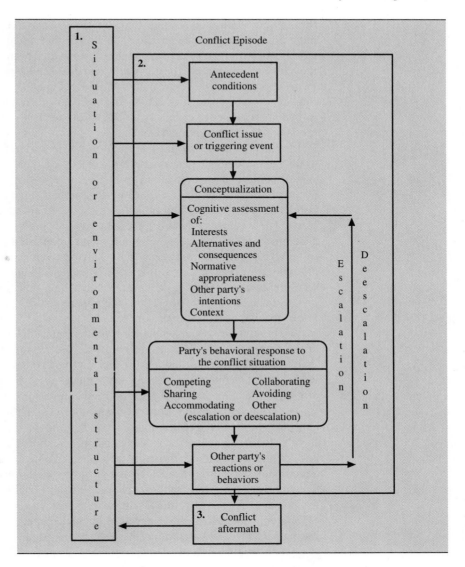

• **Behavioral predispositions**—Employees' behavioral predispositions reflect their personalities, habits, and preferred styles of interacting with the environment. As a result, these predispositions are relatively fixed. What is important to recognize is that predispositions have the potential of affecting the initiation, intensity, and persistence of conflict.[61] For example, research has indicated that Type A individuals are more likely to behave aggressively or in a hostile manner than Type B individuals, should their concerns be threatened.[62] Characteristics that are likely to make Type A individuals more prone to experience conflict than Type B individuals are their impatience, irritability when not in control, desire to work alone, and the ease with which they lose their temper.[63] As a result, Type A managers were found to have more conflicts with subordinates than did Type B managers.[64] Similarly, individuals who exhibit a high need for power or dominance are more likely to become competitive than individuals low in these needs, and thereby set the stage for organizational conflict.[65]

Predispositions also play an important role in determining the behaviors used by employees when attempting to resolve organizational conflict. Type A individuals have been found to be less likely to handle conflict through accommodation than their Type B counterparts.[66] Individuals with high affiliation needs preferred to smooth over conflicts rather than engage in confrontations.[67] Introverts, however, prefer to avoid and collaborate rather than accommodate or compete.[68] Individuals with a high need for control were found to be less likely to compromise when experiencing conflict.[69] Last, individuals who are classified as self-monitors (high self-monitors are individuals who are socially sensitive, keenly aware of how others react to their behavior) preferred to use collaboration as compared to compromise when attempting to resolve organizational conflicts.[70]

Demographic variables such as gender, age, tenure, and education also affect an employee's response to conflict.[71] For example, when compared to males, females reported having less conflict with others. In addition, females were found to demonstrate a strong preference to resolve conflict through collaboration and avoidance rather than through competition.[72]

• **Organizational structural design**—The likelihood of organizational conflict will also reflect the organization's structure. At the most basic level, there is the issue of interdependence of organizational parties.[73] (Parties may refer to either individuals or identifiable units within the organization.) Dependence implies that the success of one party is a function of some other party. Consequently, the greater the level of organizational interdependence, the greater the potential for organizational parties to experience conflict.[74]

Figure 12.4 describes four levels of interdependence.[75] In the case of pooled interdependence, organizational parties are not required to interact. At level two, sequential interdependence, one party's success is dependent upon the success of a second party whose activities precede it in some way. Reciprocal interdependence represents a structure where two parties exchange both inputs and outputs. Finally, team interdependence occurs when more than two parties exchange inputs and outputs. Such a structure is characterized by organizational members freely crossing organizational boundaries to improve organizational success.

New structural designs that are being introduced into organizations to make them more competitive and responsive also affect the level of employee interactions. Matrix designs, by simultaneously incorporating functional and product components into the organization's structure, increase the likelihood

FIGURE 12.4

Types of interdependency

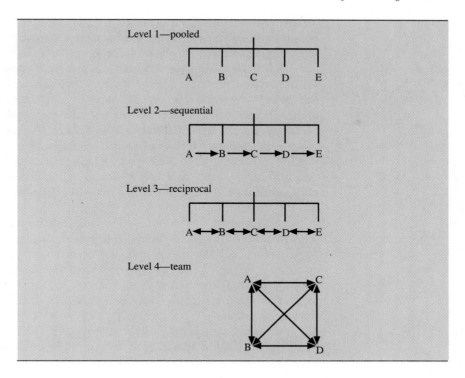

of interdependence and organizational conflict.[76] For example, under a matrix structure, employees are reporting to two bosses, one from a functional area and the other from a technical or product area. In addition, the employees themselves are forced to interact and communicate with peers with different interests and backgrounds. The result is an increased likelihood for conflict and the need to devote time and energy to its management. The assumption, however, is that the conflict stimulated by the matrix design can improve organizational performance by increasing the employee's information base, improving organizational response time to environmental changes, and fostering a confrontation–problem-solving approach to conflict management.[77]

To become more competitive and adjust quickly to environmental changes, organizations have moved away from bureaucratic type structures to designs that reflect a certain level of "adhocracy."[78] Paralleling this move toward a more ad hoc and open structure is the increased use of task forces, cross-functional teams, and project teams. Such structures imply conflict because specialists, professionals, and employees from different disciplines are required to work together.

Finally, in Chapter 10 we described one of the phenomena of the 1990s and its potential for conflict: specifically, as more organizations attempt to integrate self-directed teams into their structures, the potential exists for increased levels of organizational conflict. The potential for conflict exists not only within teams as the members attempt to manage themselves and their resources, but between teams as the levels of inter-team interactions increase.

• **Social pressures**—Employees can face two types of social pressures.[79] The first type comes from the constituency they represent or the group to which they belong. When representing a group, employees are expected to act on the group's behalf.[80] Employees who act out their own preferences or judgments are likely to be evaluated and treated as traitors. As group members, employees are also expected to act out roles that consist of group-supporting behaviors.[81] Similarly, groups establish standards of behavior (norms) that group members are expected to follow.[82] Group members who fail to act out their roles, or deviate from group norms, will likely be pressured by the group's majority to conform.

The second source of group pressure comes from third party individuals who do not directly belong to the constituencies or groups specified above.[83] Nevertheless, because of the potential negative effects associated with any employee's behavior, these individuals have a vested interest in applying social pressure within the system. Bystanders may act because of a perceived threat to their personal interests, values, or because of threats to the well-being of the larger system.[84]

• **Incentive structures**—As noted above, the potential for conflict increases as the levels of interdependence among organizational members increase. This phenomenon is partially explained by what Thomas refers to as inherent incentive structures within organizations.[85] Specifically, dependency implies that parties have a stake in organizational relationships, and that each party's desired outcomes resulting from organizational relationships may, or may not, be compatible. In the latter case, the issue is whether there exists an inherent conflict of interest.

A party's stake in organizational relationships reflects the degree to which his or her success or satisfaction is dependent upon what some other party does. Other things being equal, employees will increase personal assertiveness and sensitivity to what others do as their own perceived stakes in relationships increase.[86] If two employees are dependent upon each other for successful job performance, but differ in their perception of personal stakes in the issue, there is potential interpersonal conflict. Take for example a situation where two co-workers are working on a common problem. The employee perceiving a high personal stake in solving the problem may request frequent meetings on the issue. However, if the co-worker perceives a low personal stake in the issue, he or she may refuse to meet altogether.

Conflicts of interest occur when there are fundamental incompatibilities between the concerns of employees.[87] Such situations are likely to result in competitive or avoidant behavior by employees.[88] Conversely, where concerns associated with an issue are compatible, employees are said to have common problems. When faced with common problems, employees are more likely to cooperate.[89] The choice between cooperative and competitive strategies may also be affected by other environmental constraints. In updating his 1976 paper, Thomas recognized the importance of a short-term perspective.[90] In the short term it is possible that organizational incentives that favor a competitive style (that is, lack of employee problem-solving skills) and the need to make quick decisions, may force managers into a competitive or forcing style. And, therefore, while managers may want to work toward a collaborative style in the longer term, short-term conditions may force them into a more noncollaborative mode. Table 12.5 summarizes the differences between short-term and longer-term issues and supports the use of a contingency-based response to organizational conflict.[91]

- **Organizational rules and procedures**—A simple, but effective, technique for handling organizational issues is to develop a set of rules and procedures to cover recurring situations.[92] Well-designed rules and procedures can facilitate decision making, organizational negotiations, and the coordination of employee efforts. However, to be effective, rules and procedures have to be known, clear, and unprejudiced.[93] When rules and procedures have been accepted, they can act to minimize the appearance and intensity of conflicts, because they are impersonal, perceived as legitimate, and transcend both employees and issues. Over time, it is possible for rules and procedures to elicit spontaneous behavior by employees, thereby building automatic conflict-prevention techniques into the system.[94]

Along with positive characteristics, the reliance on rules and procedures has a number of drawbacks.[95] Rules and procedures can overshadow the unique aspects of each situation, and as a result, cause employees to generalize across events. Second, rules and procedures can cause employees to develop a win/lose or yes/no orientation, thereby creating a competitive environment. Environmental ambiguities force employees to interpret rules to fit the situation. If employee interpretations are different, then the likelihood of conflict

---

TABLE 12.5   Comparison of Short-Term and Longer-Term Theories of Conflict Management

Properties of Theory	Short-Term	Longer-Term
Focus	Coping with the here and now	Building desirable futures
Context assumptions	Contextual variables are given	Contextual variables are changeable
Goal	Local optimum: best achievable in present situation	Global optimum: excellence
Recommendations	What actions to take in present circumstances	What circumstances to create
Type of theory	Contingency theory	'Normative' theory
Flavor	Pragmatic/realistic	Idealistic/visionary

Source: K. W. Thomas, "Conflict and conflict management: Reflections and update," *Journal of Organizational Behavior,*" Vol. 13, 1992, p. 272.

increases. It may also be difficult to construct a set of rules and procedures that will cover all situations. However, in an attempt to do so, organizations allow rules and procedures to proliferate to the point where they become too complex and unmanageable. Last, rules and procedures can cause managers to ignore the attitudes, needs, and feelings of employees.

To overcome these drawbacks, behavioral scientists argue that it is possible to build some flexibility into organizational systems that rely on rules and procedures. Kanter argued that, given the dynamics of environments and the need for flexibility, managers should engage in selective rule-changing, -bending, and -breaking.[96] Similarly, Peters refers to the need for managers to engage in bureaucracy-bashing.[97] Both authors believe that managers must take the initiative to determine the appropriateness of rules and, where necessary, be willing to act in a proactive manner to ensure rules and procedures do not stifle organizational success.

2. *Conflict Episode*

Having recognized the importance of situational variables in initiating, controlling, and determining conflict intensity, it is now possible to describe the sequence of events that make up a conflict episode. This aspect of conflict theory is most frequently categorized as the *process model of conflict.* "The process aspect of any system is the temporal sequence of events that occur as the system operates—the mental and behavioral activities of the conflicting parties."[98]

• *Antecedent conditions*—The process model begins with the existence of antecedent or latent conditions that exist within the system. As discussed in a previous section, "Sources of conflict," antecedent conditions can be scarce resources; incompatible needs, goals, feelings, values, and roles; cognitive differences; and poor organizational communications. Also, recall that underlying structural variables affect the likelihood that a conflict episode will occur and the intensity of conflicts that do occur. For example, if pooled interdependencies exist, if rules and procedures are in place to guide behavior, if the organization's work force is homogeneous, if employees perceive low personal incentives to act against the interests of others, and if there is minimum social pressure to act, it is unlikely conflict will occur, or, if it does, the conflict is likely to be trivial.

• *Triggering event*—Antecedent conditions will remain benign unless some triggering event occurs within the system.[99] In other words, individuals with different values or feelings do not have conflict unless they are asked to work together or one of them breaks an accepted norm; scarce resources do not produce conflict unless employees simultaneously make demands on them; and subordinates do not resist the boss's power unless he or she tries to apply it by restricting employee freedom. By design, or accident, triggering events do occur causing a conflict episode to manifest itself within the system. It is at this point that the emotional component (frustration) of the conflict episode occurs, and the nonpleasurable experience is transferred to an individual's conscious level.[100]

• *Conceptualization*—Parties within the organization are now aware that some of their interests are being, or are about to be, threatened.[101] This felt frustration is sufficient motivation for employees to attempt to conceptualize (understand) what is happening, how relevant systems work, and thereby determine how best to respond.[102] The individual's motivation is to regain control over his or her environment. Conceptualization involves the cognitive assessment of interests, available alternatives and their consequences, the normative appropriateness of alternatives, the intentions of others, and the context in which the conflict occurs. Such information creates the backdrop against which behavioral intentions are formed and conflict-handling strategies are developed.

1. Conflicting parties must consider both their own interests and the interests of others involved in the conflict episode.[103] Failure to assess personal interests makes it almost impossible for individuals to define what is important, rank outcomes, determine what personal resource to use when dealing with conflicts, or what are minimum acceptable outcomes should compromise of negotiation be necessary. Similarly, knowledge of the other parties' interests allows for interpersonal comparisons and helps determine what is right rather than who is right. In other words, the assessing party's interests may be outweighed by the interests of others, or the needs of the larger system. Such a position is consistent with our earlier discussions of assertive behavior, distributive justice, and principled negotiations.

2. It is also important that individuals contemplating action in response to conflict identify the options available and their likely consequences.[104] It is at this level of cognitive assessment that the rational-economic model has the greatest relevance.[105] Simply put, individuals attempt to assess potential valences (payoffs) and instrumentalities (usefulness of proposed actions in obtaining valued outcomes) before selecting a preferred course of action. Although individuals cannot identify, with certainty, all available options, they can, based upon personal experience, knowledge of others, and organizational familiarity, identify a set of reasonable alternatives and likely payoffs.

Having insight into the likely behavior of other parties is also helpful in developing an appropriate behavior strategy for dealing with an existing conflict. It is therefore desirable to determine what behavioral options are likely to be used by others in the conflict situation and what are the probabilities that such options will be used. Here again, past knowledge of other parties and existing organizational constraints, rules, and policies provides the backdrop for shaping personal expectations.

3. Normative considerations are a third factor that appears to be gaining recognition as an important reasoning component in determining behavioral intentions.[106] Here, individuals are attempting to assess the goodness, or fairness, of potential courses of action rather than the value of consequences. It

is our belief that individuals are more than rational-economic thinkers and that the issues of fairness and goodness also enter into their strategies for handling conflict. This is especially true if managers want to establish long-term positive relationships with other organizational members.

4. If we assume that behavior is nonrandom and therefore has a cause, it is important for conflicting parties to determine whether the cause of behavior rests within the individuals involved or the environment in which they act.[107] Understanding the intent of others helps individuals locate cause and helps determine how they should respond to the behavior of others. If individuals believe that others want negative consequences to occur, their response is likely to be anger and retribution. However, if others have no choice, that is, are forced by their boss or organizational rules to behave as they do, or are unaware of potential negative consequences from their behavior, anger and retribution are less likely.[108] In other words, the manager's ability to assign intent increases, the fewer the number of environmental forces causing a person's behavior.[109]

Unfortunately, research indicates that the perceptions of individuals are negatively biased against others and positively biased toward themselves. For example, when asked to compare conflict-handling styles for themselves and others, 74 percent of responding executives described their own behavior as cooperative, while indicating that only 21 percent of their counterparts were cooperative. At the same time, only 21 percent of the executives described themselves as competitive, while 73 percent described their counterparts' behavior as competitive.[110] Since executives used in the survey were not considered different from their counterparts, survey results indicated a positive bias toward the self and a negative bias toward others.

5. Finally, it is necessary to consider the context in which conflict takes place.[111] The importance of contextual understanding is implied by inclusion of long-term structure considerations in our model. Assessment of each of the previous areas requires the conflicting parties to assess the total environment. It is the context that defines reality for participants in the conflict episode. Therefore to conceptualize or interpret behavior, it is necessary to consider both the behavior and the environment in which it occurs.

Considering personal interests without comparing them to the interests of others and the organization makes it impossible to assess the level of organizational justice achieved or the appropriateness of actions already taken or planned. Conflicting parties cannot be successful in determining the consequences of behavior, or their likelihood, unless one compares the present context (that is, people, rules, policies, activities, interdependencies, personal stakes, etc.) as compared to similar situations in the past. For example, to determine if aggressive behavior will be rewarded right now, it is necessary to consider similar past situations and whether aggressive behaviors resulted in positive consequences. Alternatively, the relative power of conflicting parties often determines the appropriateness of conflict-handling behaviors. To force one's interests on others, it is necessary for the individual to have the power to do so. Last, intentions cannot be assigned unless one assesses the constraints placed on others, their personalities, and past performance.

• *Behavioral response*—The process model next deals with the party's behavioral response to the conflict situation. Figure 12.5 depicts nine response behaviors that can be used to handle a conflict episode.[112] (Definitions are provided in Table 12.6.) The party's choice of a particular response behavior reflects his or her dominant behavioral orientation and the conclusions reached during the conceptualization phase of our process model. Behavioral orientation reflects the party's position on the two underlying dimensions depicted in Figure 12.5. The first is the party's desire to satisfy the concerns or interests of others. The second is the party's desire to satisfy personal concerns or interests. The descriptive characteristics of such a dual-concerns model have withstood empirical examination.[113]

As indicated earlier, behavioral scientists have come to accept the view that a contingency approach is needed when selecting an appropriate behavioral response. Therefore, it is critical that the conclusions resulting from the conceptualization phase are an accurate representation of environmental conditions. Furthermore, individuals must be willing to adjust their style to reflect the realities of the situation. By applying a contingency perspective, managers seek to maximize the benefits of conflict without triggering its negative consequences. A detailed discussion of strategies designed to achieve these objectives is presented in Figure 12.5.

FIGURE 12.5

Conflict-handling styles

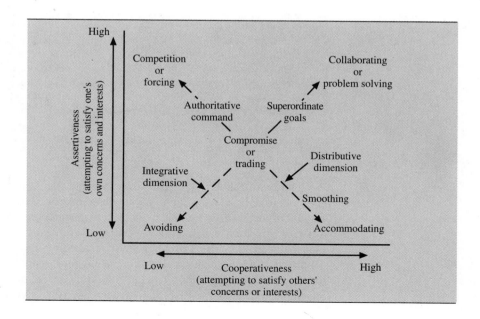

TABLE 12.6   Conflict Management Techniques

- **Competition or forcing**—A situation where one of the conflicting parties tries to satisfy personal needs at the expense of others. This style is aggressive, relies on power, and resembles the I'm OK, You're Not OK life position.
- **Authoritative command**—A technique used when conflicting parties cannot resolve their conflict or have equal power. Under such circumstances, one or more of the conflicting parties may seek out the help of a more powerful individual (e.g., a common boss) to resolve the conflict. Unfortunately, when this technique is used, parties often do not focus on the underlying issues and only remove the conflict in the short run.
- **Collaborating or problem solving**—A situation designed to maximize the need satisfaction of both conflicting parties. This style is based upon data collection and analysis, principled negotiations, and an I'm OK, You're OK life position.
- **Superordinate goals**—A style that introduces an objective that is desired by both conflicting parties, but can only be achieved if they cooperate.
- **Avoiding**—A passive style that requires that at least one of the conflicting parties withdraws. Where joint action is needed, avoidance will prevent the satisfaction of either party's needs.
- **Accommodating**—A style where one of the conflicting parties acquiesces to the needs of others so as to satisfy the other's needs. This tends to be associated with an unassertive style.
- **Compromising**—This style represents a balance between assertive and cooperative behaviors. Conflicting parties tend to split the difference with the consequence that neither the individual nor the group maximizes need satisfaction.
- **Trading**—A style that allows the conflicting parties to exchange services, obligations, objects, etc., of like value to remove the conflict. Part or all of the proposed exchange may take place in the future (i.e., you agree with me now, I'll support you next time.)
- **Smoothing**—A style that plays down the differences between conflicting parties while emphasizing interests that the two parties have in common.
- **Mediation**—A process by which a third party attempts to persuade the conflicting parties to accept a position likely to satisfy their needs.
- **Arbitration**—A process by which the conflicting parties present their position to a third party. Typically the decision of the third party is binding.
- **Altering people**—A situation in which specific individuals who are involved in the conflict are replaced to remove the conflict.
- **Altering structure**—Altering reporting relationships, job design, organizational design, procedures, plans and goals, etc., to remove the factors causing conflict.

The two dashed-diagonal arrows indicate that behavioral responses can be integrative or distributive in nature. The integrative diagonal represents the amount of total satisfaction received by both parties combined. Response behaviors that fall along the integrative diagonal are designed to satisfy the interests of all parties, with maximum benefit obtained when collaboration or problem solving is used. The distributive dimension represents how value is divided. In the case of competing or forcing behavior, parties are attempting to win a greater share at the expense of other parties. As you move along the distributive diagonal toward accommodating, one party gives up some value so that others will gain value. Integrative responses can be viewed as win/win alternatives, while distributive responses represent win/lose alternatives.

• *The other party's reaction, and closing the interactive loop*—Our model assumes that for every action there is likely to be a reaction; that is, one party's behavior is likely to trigger a response from his or her counterpart. Once the other person responds, the individual initiating the exchange must update his or her conceptualization of the situation and respond accordingly. Ongoing exchanges of this type can result in deescalation or escalation of the conflict. Such interactive sequences continue until the conflict episode ends. Unfortunately, it is difficult to predict whether deescalation or escalation will occur without considering the form that initial behaviors take, the other party's response, and the underlying structural characteristics found in the situation.

For example, an employee may repress feelings of frustration because his or her stake in the conflict's outcome is small. In other words, the threat to personal interests is minor. The frustrated employee may also alter his or her perception of the situation, thereby eliminating the felt frustration. The frequency of these two responses reflects the personality of the employee and the actual intensity of the conflict.[114] Alternatively, existing rules and policies, or a powerful other, may prevent the employee from acting.

The frustrated employee's outward behavioral response to this situation is therefore one of avoidance or accommodation. However, if the other person perceives such behavior as a sign of weakness, or acceptance of the behavior causing the employee to feel frustrated, he or she may repeat, and even intensify, the behavior that initially caused the employee's frustration. In response to such escalation, the passive employee may become more aggressive (e.g., personally attack the other person) or assertive (e.g., openly explain the consequences of the other's behavior) to protect personal interests. Here again, the employee's behavior can deescalate or escalate the existing conflict.

3. Conflict Aftermath

Once a conflict episode ends, managers must consider its outcomes.[115] Outcomes relate to the content of agreements reached; what parties have learned about themselves, others, and their environments; impact on interpersonal relationships; and residual feelings such as degree of liking or responsiveness, hostility, and trust. By becoming part of the underlying situational structure, these outcomes set the stage for future conflict episodes. More specifically, they can act to alter latent conditions, decrease or increase the intensity of future conflicts, affect goal achievement, and help determine the appropriateness of conflict-handling techniques during subsequent conflicts. Therefore, managers are responsible for the management of conflict episodes and the longer-term conflict environment or climate.

Strategies for Managing Conflict

As managers build their knowledge base, gain experience, and develop skills necessary to be successful on the job, they should take the necessary steps to create an environment in which functional conflict flourishes and dysfunctional conflict is minimized. This is the proactive side of conflict management. However, because of environmental dynamics, because proactive strategies are unlikely to be one hundred percent effective, and because conflict can deescalate or escalate, managers must also be able to react to organizational developments. The goal for managers is to ensure that conflicts result in desired changes, successful organizational adaptation, and ultimately organizational survival.[116]

Proactive Techniques

Proactive efforts designed to manage conflict can occur on a number of levels. At one level, managers can attempt to remove the latent conditions that set the stage for conflict to occur. Second, managers can establish routine mechanisms to manage conflict when and if it appears. Last, managers must assess their environments to determine whether sufficient conflict exists to motivate organizational members to challenge the status quo, analyze their environments, and change when needed.

Level 1—Managing Latent Conditions

It is possible to reduce the occurrence of conflict by reducing the likelihood that latent conditions that lead to dysfunctional conflict exist or will become active. If conflict arises because of personality and need differences, then management can make an effort, through selection, to select those individuals who will have personalities and needs that are compatible with the culture and objectives of the organization. When taking such steps, however, the organization must ensure that mind-guarding does not occur (i.e., so isolating the organization that new ideas or critical views are not allowed). If role ambiguity is likely to produce conflict when two individuals interact, then it is important that duties, responsibilities, and goals be clearly communicated to relevant individuals. At the departmental level, strategic plans, schedules, budgets, and procedures can be established and clearly communicated to the interested parties. The interested parties should actively participate in any decision-making process used to produce these plans, schedules, budgets, etc. Participation allows all interested parties to buy into the plans, procedures, etc. If limited resources are the potential problem, then managers should attempt to increase the level of supply. If this cannot be accomplished, they should develop a plan for the distribution and/or rationing of scarce resources. Last, if departmental conflict occurs because of sequential or reciprocal interdependence, managers should build in mechanisms to cushion or buffer interdepartmental transactions (e.g., stockpiling of inventories).

Level 2—Routine Mechanisms for Managing Conflict

Although it is impossible to remove all latent conflict conditions, there are types of conflict that frequently and routinely occur within organizations. Typical flash points occur between subordinates and their supervisor, management and labor, production and sales, line and staff, lower and upper management, etc. Along with Table 12.2's description of underlying differences between line and staff, Table 12.7 lists a number of underlying differences between marketing and other departments.

TABLE 12.7   Summary of Organizational Conflicts between Marketing and other Departments

Other Departments	Their Emphasis	Marketing Emphasis
Engineering	Long design lead time	Short design lead time
	Functional features	Sales features
	Few models	Many models
	Standard components	Custom components
Purchasing	Standard parts	Nonstandard parts
	Price of material	Quality of material
	Economical lot size	Large lots to avoid stockouts
	Purchasing at infrequent intervals	Immediate purchasing for customer needs
Production	Long production lead time	Short production lead time
	Long runs with few models	Short runs with many models
	No model changes	Frequent model changes
	Standard orders	Customer orders
	Ease of fabrication	Aesthetic appearance
	Average quality control	Tight quality control
Inventory	Fast-moving items, narrow product line	Broad product line
	Economical level of stock	High levels of stock
Finance	Strict rationales for spending	Intuitive arguments for spending
	Hard and fast budgets	Flexible budgets to meet changing needs
	Pricing to cover costs	Pricing to further market development
Accounting	Standard transactions	Special terms and discounts
	Few reports	Many reports
Credit	Full financial disclosure by customers	Minimum credit examination of customers
	Low credit risks	Medium credit risks
	Tough credit terms	Easy credit terms
	Tough collection procedures	Easy collection procedures

Source: D. W. Organ and T. Bateman, *Organizational Behavior,* 3rd ed., Business Publications, Inc., Plano, Tex., 1986, p. 519.

If managers realize that these flash points exist, but cannot remove the latent conditions, it is in their best interests to formalize routine mechanisms capable of managing the conflict. Management can set up monthly labor–management meetings, appeal systems to resolve superior–subordinate conflicts, quality circles and focus feedback groups to solve departmental issues, temporary or permanent cross-functional problem-solving groups, as well as a vast set of rules and policies designed as decision tools when conflict arises. The alternatives open to managers are only limited by their imagination, and the time, money, and resources provided by the organization.

Two qualifiers must be considered when attempting to build in formalized routine mechanisms to deal with conflict. First, the effective manager will only incorporate such mechanisms when the benefits outweigh the costs. Critical to this decision are the frequency and importance of the conflicts the manager is attempting to control for. The less frequent and important the conflict being considered, the less useful such techniques become. Second, given the dynamics of any situation, it is again impossible to cover all situations and flash points where conflict may occur. Consequently, managers cannot assume their job is done when proactive mechanisms are put in place. There will always be a need for reactive responses to conflict.

Stimulating Conflict

As conflict theory evolves, behavioral scientists increasingly argue that "managers should continue to resolve those conflicts that hinder the organization, but stimulate conflict intensity when the level is below that which is necessary to maintain a responsive and innovative unit."[117] Unfortunately, the demarcation between functional and dysfunctional conflict is unclear and reflects in part the issue of who is the beneficiary of conflict management, the organization or its members. While this issue is an important one (refer to our earlier discussion), we will assume that a U-shaped function does exist between the level of organizational conflict and performance. Therefore, managers must continually scan their environments for those situations in which lack of organizational conflict threatens organizational innovation and growth.

Robbins provides a number of helpful questions that managers might ask themselves to assess existing conditions.[118] They are: Am I surrounded by "Yes men"? Are my subordinates afraid to admit ignorance and uncertainties? Does the emphasis on compromise cause decision makers to lose sight of my goals, long-term objectives, or the organization's overall welfare? Do organizational members seek organizational peace at any price? Are organizational members excessively concerned with not hurting the feelings of others? Do decision makers place excessive emphasis on consensus? Do employees typically resist change? Are there too few new ideas or innovations to keep up with environmental changes? Is there too little employee turnover? The implication is that the more "yes" answers managers give to these questions, the more likely is functional organizational conflict to be too low. When this is the case, proactive managers take steps to stimulate a healthier level of conflict. (Review Table 12.3 for techniques for stimulating organizational conflict.)

Level 3—Managing Conflict from a Contingency Perspective

Table 12.6 listed the most frequent response behaviors available to managers. The first nine alternatives are often described as intentions and are assessed in terms of their assertiveness and cooperative components (see Figure 12.5 and Table 12.6). Although early normative models argued that the appropriate conflict-resolution style is one that places emphasis on collaboration and problem solving, the approach taken here is that the correct style will be a function of the situation. Such a contingency perspective now appears to be generally accepted as the most appropriate course of action to follow. Therefore, any one of the nine styles presented may be appropriate, at least in the short run. In the long run it may be desirable to work toward a situation where the collaborative/problem-solving style dominates the corporate culture.[119] As indicated in Chapter 10 on team building, a collaborative or problem-solving approach is critical for managers' efforts to build a viable work team. Should these nine management styles fail to address the issues raised by the conflict situation, it will be necessary for the manager to consider several other reactive options. The last four options listed in Table 12.6 (mediation, arbitration, altering people, and altering structure) also represent reactive alternatives.

The key to the success of a third party attempting to mediate a conflict is the perception by the two opposing sides that the mediator is personally unbiased and qualified. The selected mediator must also be skilled in facilitating social interactions and have the professional expertise to always maintain control, yet at the same time stimulate content creativity. Borisoff and Victor* articulate the following nine abilities and characteristics the mediator must possess if he or she is to be effective in the art of persuasion.[120]

- Establish and maintain credibility.
- Assure both sides that he or she will address all concerns fairly and openly.
- Demonstrate neutrality toward both sides.
- Manage effective contact and communication between the parties.
- Help both parties determine, analyze, and understand all the facts.
- Listen for clues to a settlement.
- Accurately convey information from and to both sides.

---

*D. Borisoff and D. A. Victor, *Conflict Management: A Communication Skills Approach,* Englewood Cliffs, N.J., Prentice Hall (1989), p. 18. Copyright © 1989 by Allyn & Bacon. Reprinted/Adapted by permission.

- Try to keep the channels of communication open between the parties.
- Maintain discretion about what is said and how it is communicated.

Should mediation be inappropriate, or fail, managers can use arbitration as a third-party intervention to achieve the results desired. In this case, the groups must abide by the arbitrator's final decision. When arbitration is the preferred route, the conflicting parties are charged with the responsibility of proving their case. One of the benefits of such an approach is that groups are unable to compromise and are therefore forced into a final decision. Once a decision has been made, it is hoped the opposing sides can get back to a cooperative relationship. For arbitration to be successful, the two parties must be willing to accept the decision of the arbitrator. Acceptance is typically agreed to before the initiation of the process, or is a function of the structural relationships already established within the organization. In the latter case, a common superior may act as an arbitrator when a departmental conflict gets out of hand.

If the conflicts still remain unresolved, it may be necessary to change the components of the two conflicting subsystems. This can be accomplished by changing either the people involved or the structure in which they function. Therefore, if a group cannot function because of conflicting personalities or needs, then it may be necessary to change or replace specific individuals to achieve the required cooperation. Similarly, reporting relationships can be changed, activities relocated, and work flows altered to alleviate a conflict that cannot be managed in any other way.

A contingency perspective assumes that the strategies used by managers to handle conflict must be a function of the situational factors operating within the environment at that moment in time. Table 12.8 describes a sample of reactive response behaviors† available to the manager, and the situational factors that must be considered before selecting the appropriate course of action.[121] It is the authors' position that although the ideal scenario might be the collaborative/problem-solving mode, real-world constraints and limited availability of time may require managers to apply one of the other styles. For example, in those instances where quick action is required, when the manager has all the needed information and knows that he or she is right, and it is unlikely that others are likely to support the action in the time required, then the manager may resort to a forcing mode of conflict management.

When selecting a particular mode of conflict management, the manager must also be aware that any action he or she takes may have negative consequences. Here again, the manager must do a cost–benefit analysis to assess the appropriateness of his or her action. Managers who use excessive force on a frequent basis run the risk of turning their people into "yes people."

---

† We have only discussed in Table 12.8 the five response behaviors most frequently cited in the behavioral literature. The remaining four shown in Figure 12.5, while important, have not been as well reviewed in terms of situational appropriateness or potential negative consequences.

TABLE 12.8 Situational Factors to Be Considered When Selecting a Conflict Management Style

Conflict Style	Where Appropriate	Where Inappropriate	Potential Negative Consequences
Collaborating or Problem Solving	• When both sides of concerns are too important to be compromised. • When the objective is to test one's own assumptions or better understand the views of others. • Where there is need to merge insights from people with different perspectives on the problem to come up with a better solution, or when one party alone cannot solve the problem. • When commitment can be increased by incorporating others' concerns into a consensus decision. • When long-term relationships are important. • When the problem is complex. • When time is available.	• Task or problem is simple. • Immediate decision is required. • Other parties are unconcerned about the outcome.	• Too much time spent on insignificant issues. • Ineffective decisions made with input from people unfamiliar with the situation. • Goal failure because of unfounded assumptions about trust.
Competing or Forcing	• When quick, decisive action is required. • On important issues for which unpopular action needs implementing. • On issues vital to company welfare and when one knows one is right. • When protection is needed against people who take advantage of noncompetitive behavior. • Where the issue is trivial and others are not interested in it. • Where it is necessary to overcome assertive or aggressive subordinates. • Where subordinates lack the expertise to make quality decisions.	• Issue is complex. • Issue is not important to the manager. • Both parties are equally powerful.	• Eventually being surrounded by "yes people." • Fear of admitting ignorance or uncertainty. • Distorted perceptions. • Reduced communications. • Damaged relationships. • No commitment or buy-in from the other person. • Having to keep selling or policing the solution during implementation.

TABLE 12.8 (continued)

Conflict Style	Where Appropriate	Where Inappropriate	Potential Negative Consequences
Avoiding	• When the issue is trivial. • When there is no chance of getting what you want. • When the potential damage of confrontation outweighs the benefits of resolution. • When the need is to cool down, reduce tensions, and regain perspective and composure. • When there is a need to gather more information. • When others can resolve the conflict more effectively. • When the issue seems symptomatic of another more fundamental issue.	• Issue is important to the manager. • It is the manager's responsibility to make the decision. • Where parties are unwilling to defer and the issue must be resolved. • Prompt action is needed to avoid negative consequences.	• Decisions by default. • Unresolved issues. • Energy and morale sapped by sitting on issues. • Self-doubt created by lack of self-esteem. • Creative input and improvement prevented. • Lack of credibility.
Accommodating	• When the manager realizes he or she is wrong. • When the issue is much more important to the other person. • When "credits" need to be accumulated for issues that are more important. • When continued competition would only damage the cause or relationship. • When preserving harmony and avoiding disruptions are especially important. • When subordinates need to develop and to be allowed to learn from mistakes. • When the manager is dealing from a position of weakness.	• Issue important to manager. • Manager believes that he or she is right. • Temporary resolution may provide more time to reach an agreement in the near future.	• Decreases influence, respect, or recognition by too much deference. • Laxity in discipline. • Frustration as own needs are not met—emotions build over time. • Self-esteem undermined. • Relinquished or ignored better solution.
Compromising	• When goals are moderately important but not worth the effort or potential disruption of more assertive modes.	• One party is more powerful.	• No one fully satisfied. • Short-lived solution.

TABLE 12.8   *(concluded)*

Conflict Style	Where Appropriate	Where Inappropriate	Potential Negative Consequences
Compromising *(continued)*	• When two opponents with equal power are strongly committed to mutually exclusive goals. • When temporary settlements are needed on complex issues. • When expedient solutions are necessary under the pressure of time. • If a back-up mode is needed when collaboration or competition fail. • When consensus cannot be reached.	• Problem is complex or important enough to warrant a problem-solving approach.	• A cynical climate through perception of a sellout. • Losing sight of the larger issues, principles, long-term objectives, values, and the company welfare by focusing on practicalities.

Unfortunately, "yes people" often fail to communicate important information, or withdraw, or develop negative perceptions of the manager. The long-term consequence is a destruction of the team atmosphere needed to ensure full participation by all group members. Tom Peters gives an excellent example that demonstrates this point.[122] The example centers on a manager who considered himself to have a participative management style. The manager had a consultant sit in on a staff meeting during which the issue of where to locate a new facility was considered. After all information was discussed, the vote was 5 to 1 against the boss. The boss at that point indicated that his choice would be implemented. After the meeting when the consultant was alone with the manager he asked for an explanation for what had happened. The manager's response was simply: "Sometimes we tally the votes, sometimes we weight them—in this case we weighted them." It would not be long before the subordinates understood the manager's true style (his way or no way—i.e., forcing). The consequence would be subordinate withdrawal from any future debates of substantive issues.

The key to successful conflict management is for managers to use each style when and if it is appropriate. This can be facilitated if managers (*a*) take the time to understand the organization's environment, systems, and people, and (*b*) are willing to be honest with themselves when processing this information. Clearly, managers will not always be correct in their choice, but nevertheless must seek to increase the average number of times a correct choice is made.

The Problem of Anger

Emotions are a by-product of conflict episodes.[123] They can result from the simple fact that an employee's interests or concerns are being blocked by others.[124] Strong emotions can result when employees believe that others have intentionally set out to cause them harm.[125] Even the perception that one's personal self-esteem or intelligence is under attack can provoke an emotional response. The likelihood of an emotional response also increases as parties engage in escalating behaviors such as exaggeration, personal attacks, restricted communications, competing for the sake of competing, and looking for allies to enhance one's position.[126]

Anger is an intense emotional state that is often associated with conflict.[127] Therefore, managers should not be surprised to find themselves confronted by others who are angry. Bosses can become angry over failed assignments, co-workers over office procedures or schedules, subordinates over decisions being made without their input, customers over poor products, and vendors over canceled orders.

Like conflict, anger can have both positive and negative consequences. Anger can be healthy for employees and organizations because it warns us that something is wrong with the system and that the status quo is unacceptable. At the very least, controlled anger can cause others to explain their actions and thereby improve understanding. Anger also directs our attention toward injustices perceived to exist within the organization, and at the same time prevents complacency. However, uncontrolled anger can have negative consequences for organizations by disrupting interpersonal relationships, intensifying existing conflicts, producing residual emotions that are carried into the future, and triggering verbal or physical attacks.

Steps for Effective Management of Anger

Managers can effectively handle the anger of others if they are willing to learn and apply a number of basic skills. The following discussion outlines a set of behaviors that can be useful in managing angry "others" and ensuring that those conflict situations involving anger do not become dysfunctional.[128]

Step 1. Determine the level of anger.
When confronting an angry person, it is important that managers determine the intensity of anger being experienced by that individual. Different intensities of anger require different managerial responses. To identify the intensity of anger being experienced by others, managers can assess verbal and nonverbal cues of individuals they are dealing with. Managers should tune into what the relevant other is saying, how he or she is saying it (e.g., intonation, speed, volume, etc.), facial expressions, and body movement or positioning. Important

in any attempt to assess available cues is the manager's ability to assess changes in the verbal and nonverbal behaviors of relevant others. It is often the changes in such behaviors that signal the existence of an emotional response.

During our present discussion we will consider three levels of anger, that is, controlled, expressed, and irrational anger. *Controlled anger* represents a situation in which individuals experiencing anger are in control of themselves and refrain from personal attacks on others. Individuals experiencing controlled anger are likely to vocalize in even, deep tones, stand with arms crossed, and clench their teeth. Individuals at the controlled level may also distance themselves from others or withdraw from the situation altogether. In terms of verbal behavior, individuals experiencing controlled anger may either refrain from speaking or in a factual manner explain their concerns about events taking place.

Expressed anger represents a more intense level of anger that is characterized by verbal attacks on others. At this level, vocalizations become loud and forceful, accompanied by physical actions such as finger pointing or fist pounding. Individuals, however, are still in control of their behavior.

Irrational anger occurs when individuals lose personal control. Individuals no longer assess or understand the consequences of their actions. Vocalization at this level becomes shrill and uncontrolled. In extreme situations, individuals will physically attack their environment or others within the environment.

Step 2. Select the appropriate initial response.

Once managers have identified the intensity of anger being exhibited by another person, it is important that they adjust their response to that level. It is during Step 2 that managers make the decision how to respond to each level. Controlled anger is the simplest level to respond to. Managers must simply remember that when two people interact and one is exhibiting symptoms of anger, it is the one who is not angry who manages the situation. When confronted with controlled anger, managers must respond in a nonhostile, nondefensive manner. In other words, they should be receptive, open, and empathic. If this is done correctly, and the relevant other does not move to a higher level of anger, then the manager can go directly to Step 3.

For example, assume that a salesman, after receiving a poor route for the third straight week, asks the boss "Why?" but also remains at a controlled level of anger. The manager should recognize this fact and not antagonize the subordinate by responding in a demeaning, defensive, or critical tone. The following statement, reinforced with negative nonverbal behavior, would likely drive the subordinate to a higher level of anger: "Because you deserve it and I'm the boss!"

If the angry person is at the expressed level of anger, the manager must adjust his or her style accordingly. In this case, a simple nonhostile, nondemeaning, or nondefensive manner is insufficient to control the situation. In this instance, it is important to inform the angry salesman of the impact his behavior is having on you. The normal visceral response is to respond in kind to the angry salesman. In other words, if he calls you a S.O.B., you call him the same thing plus a little to redress the insult. Unfortunately, such behavior increases the probability that the angry person will remain expressive or, even worse, move to the irrational level. Returning to the example above, assume that the salesmen made the following statement:

> "You bigoted S.O.B.—you've had it in for me ever since I've transferred in from the Western zone. Where the *&^% do you get off giving me the South Shore route for the third week in a row?!!!"

To handle this level of anger the manager must remain calm and explain the impact the angry person's behavior is having. The following statement would be an appropriate response:

> "Clearly you're upset, Bob—but when you use that type of language I get angry and as a result won't discuss the issue. Why don't we just look at the facts and come up with either an explanation or a solution?"

If the angry person responds well to this statement and moves down to the controlled anger level, the manager can again go on to Step 3.

There will, however, be that rare instance where the angry person has moved beyond the expressed level and has become irrational. Irrational anger is the most difficult to manage because the angry person has, in essence, lost self-control. In those instances where physical or personal harm is likely to occur, the only course of action is to remove yourself from the situation and seek help. The rationale here is that most managers are not paid extra for interpersonal combat and, therefore, it should be avoided at all costs. If the angry person is irrational only at the verbal level, and is unlikely to cause personal or physical damage, then it may be desirable to allow the individual to vent his or her emotions. At some point, the individual will tire and move back down to the expressed (rational) level. When this occurs, the manager treats the situation as expressed or controlled anger.

Step 3. Request a full description of the individual's problem and listen openly.

The likelihood of reaching Step 3 is dependent upon the manager's success in moving the angry person to the controlled level of anger. If this has been accomplished, the manager's next step is to use a stem question and ask the angry person to explain the facts or the problem as he or she sees it. The key to success at this point is to effectively listen, probe, reflect, and summarize so that the manager ensures that he or she has complete and accurate information. (You can review the rapport-building section in Chapter 4 for more detail.) It is during this step that the manager must make an effort to keep an open mind (that is, guard against premature closure) and be prepared for surprises. At the same time, the manager must refrain from critical or evaluative statements that are directed toward the angry person.

Step 4. Recognize and acknowledge the employee's point of view.

It is often desirable to respond to the angry person's position in an empathic or understanding manner. This step is designed to communicate to the other person that the manager understands and appreciates his or her problem. The following statements are typical of those made during this step:

> "I understand why you are upset—if I had to wait for two weeks before receiving a response I would have been angry also."
>
> "I can see why you reacted the way you did—having someone give you false information that I needed for an important decision is serious indeed."
>
> "I can appreciate your concern—you shouldn't have to put up with those types of comments from anyone."

What the manager should not do is go off on a tangent by telling about one of his or her own experiences that is similar to what the other person is going through, but which does little to solve the other person's problem.

Step 5a. If the employee is correct (i.e., a legitimate victim), apologize for the mistake.

Once the manager has collected and verified all relevant information, the correctness of the angry person's position should be assessed. (If managers believe that they do not have sufficient information to assess the stated position, this fact should be made clear, but then indicate how needed information will be collected.) If the angry person is a legitimate victim, then it is in the manager's best interest to openly recognize this fact. At this point, the manager must determine whether he or she has the authority to take action on the angry person's behalf. If the manager does not have the authority, the angry person should be informed of this fact and be directed to individuals with the needed authority. If the manager has the authority, he or she should move on to Step 5b.

Step 5b. Indicate the corrective action that will be taken.

Step 5b is designed to inform the angry person what action will be taken on his or her behalf. The manager must provide the information necessary to clearly answer the what, when, where, why, and by whom questions likely to exist in the angry person's mind. In the example above, Bob the salesman would like to know the answers to such questions as "Will I get this route again next week or sometime soon?" "Why did I get it three weeks in a row anyway?" "Where will I be assigned next time?" "Who made the decision?" "What steps will be taken so that this doesn't happen again?" Answering these questions and promising corrective action will significantly reduce the angry person's emotional level. During Step 5a, however, the manager must never promise more than he or she can deliver. Similarly, the manager should not make promises that can only be carried out by others. This is the quickest way to raise the level of expressed emotion in any relationship. The manager who makes the simple statement, "I will get John to send you that information by Friday," runs the risk of being proven wrong when John cannot deliver. Consequently both individuals look bad.

Step 6. If the employee is incorrect, state your position nonaggressively but be willing to share all relevant information and if possible give the individual a choice.

When a manager is attacked by an angry person, and subsequently determines that the attack was unjustified, he or she may attempt to redress the situation by becoming aggressive toward the other individual. Such behavior can act to move the once angry person to higher levels of anger even though he or she understands the initial emotion was unjustified. Similarly, failing to provide an adequate explanation why the employee is wrong, when such does exist, is also likely to drive the individual to higher levels of anger. The manager should instead be assertive but yet supportive. An assertive or supportive stance implies that the manager is willing to explain why the angry person was wrong, and clearly communicates the consequences of his or her behavior, but whenever possible gives the individual a choice.

The process of discipline without punishment closely parallels what is currently being described. If an individual—who has been counseled and coached before—continues to come to work late, produces substandard work, lies, or is interpersonally aggressive or hostile toward others, it is recommended that the individual be presented with the performance data, be educated as to the consequences if such behavior continues, but then be allowed to make up his or her own mind about remaining on the job. In this way, the employee is given the opportunity to make the decision. If the employee stays, he or she is accepting the organizational standards. If the individual does not accept these standards, then he or she is advised to resign or otherwise leave the organization. The emphasis here is that the choice is the employee's. If the employee is unwilling to take control of his or her own life, then the performance appraisal process is in place to document and remove the problem employee (see Chapter 13).

Step 7. Before leaving the situation, repeat what has been decided and, where appropriate, indicate the follow-up that will take place. Again, do not promise anything that cannot be delivered.

To communicate effectively, it is often necessary to build in a certain level of redundancy. This is especially true when one of the communicators is in a heightened emotional state. It may also be possible that the actions promised during the exchange require some type of follow-up. To reduce the probability of future emotional encounters, it is important to articulate clearly the manner and timing of any proposed follow-up. The time to question the desirability, appropriateness, manner, and timing of follow-up is before the two parties go their separate ways, and not after.

To handle angry others effectively, managers must internalize and practice each of the steps outlined above. The list, although easy to describe, represents a set of complex behaviors that managers must be willing to implement immediately. They cannot say to the angry person, "Hold on a few minutes while I figure out what level of anger you're on and then review how I should respond." Managers must be prepared to respond without thinking about it.

Summary

Conflict is inevitable in today's complex and changing organizations. To manage conflict effectively, and to ensure that it does not prove dysfunctional for the organization, the manager must understand the multiple levels at which it occurs and the stages through which it moves. The manager must also recognize the need for both proactive and reactive components to any strategy designed to manage conflict. Critical to the manager's personal success in controlling conflict is a knowledge of the antecedent causes unique to the situation. This implies that, to be successful, any managerial response to organizational conflict must be situationally specific.

During personal encounters designed to manage conflict, the manager may find it necessary to deal with the emotions of conflicting individuals. Anger is one of the most common emotional consequences of organizational conflict. When conflicting members move from controlled anger to expressed or irrational anger, it becomes increasingly difficult to manage conflict. To defuse anger, the manager can apply the preceding seven steps for keeping anger at a workable level. Controlling the level of anger allows the manager to create a climate in which organizational participants can work together to find a solution to manifest conflict.

Exercises

12.1 Understanding How and Why Conflicts Escalate[129]*

Any conflict within an organization can lead potentially to a major confrontation between the disagreeing parties. When this occurs, the disagreeing employees, the organization, and third-party individuals run the risk of incurring significant loss. It

---

*This exercise is based on material presented in the video "Escalation of a Conflict," Video Lecture Series, Program on Negotiation and Dispute Resolution, Harvard Law School, Cambridge, Mass.

is important for managers to understand why and how this occurs and to identify the transformations that can take place during any confrontation. Managers who understand the escalation process are more likely to be able to prevent it from occurring.

The purpose of this exercise is to present you with a familiar situation. You are to identify the transformations that take place and explain why they occur. Please follow the steps outlined below.

Step 1. The class will break up into smaller groups of five to six individuals each.

Step 2. Quickly read, individually, the father–son scenario presented following these steps. Consider the many transformations that have taken place, but do not write down any of your impressions or in any way try to interpret what took place. (Approximately 5 minutes)

Step 3. Using group consensus, consider the various transformations that have occurred and why they have occurred during confrontation. A transformation is any change that takes place either consciously or unconsciously, and which takes the parties to a higher level of conflict. Most groups find 8 to 10 transformations. (Approximately 30 minutes)

Step 4. The class will assemble to discuss their findings. Group lists will then be compared with the instructor's list.

MINI CASE: THE FATHER/SON CONFRONTATION

The following exchange takes place between Harry and his 18-year-old son, John. The dialogue centers around what Harry at first believes is a minor event, but one which nonetheless should be brought to the attention of John. Harry frequently allows his son to borrow the family car at night to go out, either on a date or with his friends. The only requirements are that John return the car where he found it and with the same amount of gasoline.

When John took the car last night it had three quarters of a tank of gasoline. When Harry got in the car to go to work this morning, he discovered the gas gauge on empty. Harry has to drive 30 miles to work in heavy traffic, so he was forced to find an open station and fill up. It took him an extra 20 minutes to find a service station and fill the tank with gas. The extra 20 minutes caused Harry to get caught in rush hour traffic. Consequently, he was 15 minutes late to work. Fortunately, he gets along quite well with his superior who also has an 18-year-old son and can identify with Harry's problem. Harry decided that when he got home he would bring today's event to his son's attention.

Harry arrives at home to find John watching dance videos on the large-screen TV set in the family room. The following exchange takes place between Harry and John.

Harry: John, I thought you might want to know that because you didn't leave any gas in the car this morning, I was late for work. When you borrowed the family car, I thought you had agreed to replace the gas you used.
John: [*Still watching television and without turning around*] Yeah, Dad. No problem.
Harry: No problem! I think it was inconsiderate of you not to fill the gas tank. The least you could have done is told me so that I could have left for work earlier than I did.

John: [*Grunts an inaudible response as he munches on pizza and then washes that down with a soft drink.*]

Harry: I would like an apology that I can understand!

John: Chill out, Dad! I said "no problem." The next time I am out with the car, you'll get your gas.

Harry: What kind of apology is that? Your attitude is getting worse rather than better. As far as I can see, you just don't carry your weight around here. Your room is a mess. I don't know how you can tell which clothes are dirty and which are clean. You don't do your chores unless you're told 10 times, and the lawn hasn't been cut in a month.

John: Just who do you think you are? I don't think you have any rights to tell me to clean up my act. If anyone around here needs change, it's you. When was the last time you helped Mom with anything around here? She asked you to hang the shutters months ago and they're still not hung. In fact, when was the last time you smiled around here? The way I see it, you would rather complain about others and make us feel like dirt than be part of this family!

Harry: Betty! [*calls Betty, his wife*] Listen to the garbage that is coming out of your son's mouth. We have to do something about it before he ruins his life. We have to teach him the meaning of respect.

John: Respect? Ha! You're lucky if you can spell the word, much less understand its relevance to getting along with people. Ask anyone around here. If they're honest, they'll tell you it isn't me who lacks respect.

Harry: You don't care about anyone but yourself, young man. You can forget about using the car for your big date this weekend. In fact, you'll be lucky if you get behind the wheel all summer. You had better start thinking about getting a real job and earning some money so you can get your own car. And while I am at it, you can forget about your allowance. Maybe then you'll learn some respect rather than mooching off your parents.

Harry and John continue to trade insults until John gets up to leave. As John is walking out the front door, he tells his father to "go to hell" and then slams the door.

12.2 Conflict Management: South Shore General Hospital

This exercise is designed to give you practice in analyzing a particular conflict and developing effective strategies to manage conflict. Please follow the steps outlined below.

Step 1. The class will break up into small groups of five or six individuals each.

Step 2. Read individually the material relevant to the South Shore General Hospital (see Exercise 7.2).

Step 3. Through group discussion, construct a list of potential strategies open to Harry Medcar to overcome the conflict that has developed at South Shore General. Be as creative as possible; there are many options open to Harry. (Approximately 45 minutes)

Step 4. The class will assemble to discuss the appropriateness of each group's identified strategies. Student suggestions will be compared with the instructor's list of conflict resolution techniques.

12.3 Handling an Angry Employee: The Case of Gloria Madly

The purpose of this exercise is to practice strategies for managing an angry employee. To prepare for an encounter between Bob Busybody and Gloria Madly, follow the steps outlined below.

Step 1. The class will form small groups of five to six individuals each.

Step 2. Select one of your group's members to play the role of Bob Busybody.

Step 3. Prepare a script that will guide Bob Busybody during his encounter with Gloria Madly. Incorporate into your script all strategies previously discussed or distributed which are designed to control the angry employee and simultaneously maintain a positive relationship between the two participants. In developing your script make whatever additional assumptions you believe are consistent with the facts of the case. (The instructor will distribute a list of behaviors that you can use to successfully handle an encounter with an angry employee.) (30 minutes)

Step 4. Practice how you will deal with Gloria Madly. During this step, one of the group's members should play the role of Gloria Madly and the remaining members should act as observers. (15 minutes)

Step 5. The class will assemble and groups will be selected at random to role-play the planned meeting between Bob Busybody and Gloria Madly. The role of Gloria Madly will be played by the instructor.

You now have 45 minutes to prepare for the role play.

Background

THE CASE OF GLORIA MADLY

Gloria Madly is the chairperson of the Salary Review Committee set up by Evercare Nursing Home. This committee reviews requests for salary adjustments from employees who believe that their salaries are lower than they should be. Gloria is a sensitive, totally honest, and conscientious person, but she tends to be highly emotional and has been known to openly express her anger toward others. The committee was established after the last round of negotiations with the union and has been in operation for about two months. It currently has five members, including Gloria. Although the committee has heard only three cases, it has met on numerous occasions to clarify policies and guidelines likely to be used during deliberation on individual cases.

Bob Busybody is another committee member. Gloria was disappointed when she learned that Bob was going to be on the committee because the two tend to disagree. As it turned out, their relationship did not improve on the Salary Review Committee. As Gloria sees it, the following are typical problems concerning Bob.

- Bob is one of the few committee members who is always late for meetings.
- In the three individual cases heard, Bob and Gloria were on opposite sides of all points discussed.
- Bob has openly stated that Gloria should be replaced as chairperson.

Surprisingly, Gloria has kept cool for two months but the most recent situation upset her.

The appeal being heard by the committee involves an employee named "Linda in Demand." As part of her appeal, Linda has included a written job offer from a competing nursing home. Although the correspondence was initiated by the competing organization, the salary offered Linda is significantly higher than what she is earning now. Linda has requested that this information stay within the committee and that her supervisor, Tom Suspicious, not be told of the offer. The committee is split over holding back such information, because any salary increase awarded Linda would have to be explained to Tom. The committee ended its last meeting without establishing a clear position on confidentiality.

When Gloria got to work this morning she found Linda, apparently upset, sitting in her office. She explained that Tom had somehow found out about her job offer and now questioned her loyalty to him and the organization. He suggested that she transfer to another unit. Gloria called Tom to try to alleviate his concerns and set the record straight. During her conversation with Tom, Gloria learned that Bob Busybody had been at Tom's house the night before and had brought up Linda's job offer during a discussion of job market conditions.

Hearing this, Gloria lost control of herself. She hung up the telephone and went directly to Bob Busybody's office.

End Notes

1. K. W. Thomas and W. H. Schmidt, "A survey of managerial interests with respect to conflict," *Academy of Management Journal*, Vol. 19, No. 2, 1976: 315–318.
2. G. Lippitt, "Managing conflict in today's organizations," *Training and Development Journal*, Vol. 36, No. 7, 1982: 66–72.
3. L. R. Pondy, "Organization conflict: Concepts and models," *Administrative Science Quarterly*, Vol. 12, 1967: 296–320.
4. L. R. Pondy, "Reflections on organizational conflict," *Journal of Organizational Behavior*, Vol. 13, 1992: 259.
5. Pondy, 1992: 259.
6. E. van de Vliert, "Conflict—prevention and escalation," in *Handbook of Work and Organizational Psychology*, ed. P. J. D. Drenth, H. Thierry, P. J. Willems, and C. J. de Wolf, John Wiley & Sons Ltd., Chichester, England, 1984: 521–551; C. B. Derr, "Managing organizational conflict," *California Management Review*, Vol. 21, No. 2, 1978: 76–83.
7. S. P. Robbins, "'Conflict management' and 'conflict resolution' are not synonymous terms," *California Management Review*, Vol. 21, No. 2, 1978: 67–75.
8. van de Vliert, 1984.
9. K. W. Thomas, "Conflict and conflict management: Reflections and update," *Journal of Organizational Behavior*, Vol. 13, 1992: 265; K. W. Thomas, "Conflict and conflict management," in *Handbook of Industrial and Organizational Psychology*, ed. M. D. Dunnette, Rand McNally, Chicago, 1976: 891.
10. J. T. Tedeschi, B. R. Schlenker, and T. Bonoma, *Conflict, Power and Games: The Experimental Study of Interpersonal Relations*, Aldine, Chicago, 1973.
11. C. G. Smith, "A comparative analysis of some conditions and consequences of intraorganizational conflict," *Administrative Science Quarterly*, Vol. 10, 1966: 511.
12. J. A. Litterer, "Conflict in organizations: A re-examination," *Academy of Management Journal*, Vol. 9, 1966: 180.
13. R. J. Lewicki and G. Spencer, "Conflict and negotiation in organizations: Introduction and overview," *Journal of Organization Behavior*, Vol. 13, 1992: 205–207; M. A. Rahim, *Managing Conflict in Organizations*, Praeger, New York, 1986; T. Kochan and A. Verma, "Negotiation in organization: Blending industrial relations and

organizational behavior approaches," in *Negotiating in Organization,* ed. M. Bazerman and R. J. Lewicki, Sage Publications, Beverly Hills, Calif., 1983; Robbins, 1978.

14. H. Fayol, *General and Industrial Management,* Pitman, London, 1949 (originally published, 1916).

15. L. H. Gulick and L. Urwick, eds., *Papers on the Science of Administration,* Institute of Public Administration, Columbia University, New York, 1937.

16. F. W. Taylor, *The Principles of Scientific Managment,* Harper, New York, 1911.

17. M. Weber, *The Theory of Social and Economic Organization,* Oxford University Press, New York, 1947 (originally published, 1929).

18. Lewicki and Spencer, 1992.

19. Lewicki and Spencer, 1992; Rahim, 1986; Robbins, 1978.

20. R. J. Lewicki, S. E. Weiss, and D. Lewin, "Models of conflict, negotiation and third-party intervention: A review and synthesis," *Journal of Organizational Behavior,* Vol. 13, 1992: 209–252; Lewicki and Spencer, 1992; R. Blake and J. Mouton, *The Managerial Grid,* Gulf Publishing Co., Houston, 1964; R. Likert, *New Patterns of Management,* McGraw-Hill, New York, 1961.

21. Pondy, 1967: 296–320; Thomas, 1976; S. P. Robbins, "Conflict can be stimulating," *International Management,* 1973: 50–54; S. P. Robbins, *Managing Organizational Conflict,* Prentice Hall, Englewood Cliffs, N. J., 1974; T. T. Herbert and R. W. Estes, "Improving executive decisions by formalizing dissent: The corporate Devil's advocate," *Academy of Management Review,* October, 1977: 662–667; G. Lippitt, 1982; R. R. Blake and J. S. Mouton, "Overcoming group warfare," *Harvard Business Review,* Vol. 62, No. 6, November–December, 1984: 98–108; D. Tjosvold, "Making conflict productive," *Personnel Administrator,* Vol. 29, 1984: 121–130.

22. Thomas, 1976.

23. Robbins, Winter 1978; L. D. Brown, *Managing Conflict at Organizational Interfaces,* Addison-Wesley, Reading, Mass., 1983; Rahim, 1986.

24. Lippitt, 1982.

25. Pondy, 1967.

26. L. Gibson, J. M. Ivancevich, and J. H. Donnelly, Jr., *Organizations: Behavior, Structure, Process,* 8th ed., Irwin, Burr Ridge, Ill., 1994; Lewicki,

Weiss, and Lewin, 1992; Rahim, 1986; van de Vliert, 1984; R. A. Cosier and G. L. Rose, "Cognitive conflict and goal conflict effects on task performance," *Organizational Behavior and Human Performance,* Vol. 19, 1977: 378–391.

27. D. Borisoff and D. A. Victor, *Conflict Management: A Communication Skills Approach,* Prentice Hall, Englewood Cliffs, N. J., 1989; G. R. Miller and M. Steinberg, *Between People: A New Analysis of Interpersonal Communication,* Science Research Associates, Chicago, 1975.

28. B. H. Sheppard, "Conflict research as scizophrenia: The many faces of organizational conflict," *Journal of Organizational Behavior,* Vol. 13, 1992: 325–334; J. R. Gordon, *Organizational Behavior,* 3rd ed., Allyn & Bacon, Boston, 1991.

29. E. J. Murry, "Conflict: I. Psychological aspects," in *International Encyclopedia of the Social Sciences,* ed. D. L. Sills, Crowell and Macmillan, New York, 1968: 220–226.

30. G. A. Kimble and N. Garmezy, *Principles of General Psychology,* 3rd ed., The Roland Press, New York, 1968.

31. L. Festinger, *A Theory of Cognitive Dissonance,* Stanford University Press, Stanford, Calif., 1957; L. Festinger and D. Bramel, "The reactions of humans to cognitive dissonance," in *The Experimental Foundations of Clinical Psychology,* ed. A. Bacharach, Basic Books, New York, 1962: 254–279.

32. Rahim, 1986.

33. Gibson, Ivancevich, and Donnelly Jr., 1994.

34. S. P. Robbins and M. C. Butler, *Organizational Behavior,* 5th ed., Prentice Hall, Englewood Cliffs, N. J., 1991.

35. Gordon, 1991; Rahim, 1986.

36. Rahim, 1986.

37. M. A. Rahim, *Rahim Organizational Conflict Inventories: Professional Manual,* Consulting Psychologists Press, Palo Alto, Calif., 1983; D. C. Pelz and F. M. Andrews, *Scientists in Organizations: Productive Climates for Research and Development,* John Wiley & Sons, New York, 1976; J. W. Julian and F. A. Perry, "Cooperation contrasted with intra-group and inter-group competition," *Sociometry,* Vol. 30, 1967: 79–90.

38. The findings presented reflect the classic work of M. Sherif and C. Sherif, *Groups in Harmony and Tension,* Harper & Row, New York, 1953, and

as summarized in J. L. Gibson, J. M Ivancevich, and J. H. Donnelly, Jr., 1994.

39. D. C. Korten, "Situational determinants of leadership structure," in D. Cartright and A. Zander, *Group Dynamics,* Harper & Row, New York, 1968: 351–361.

40. I. L. Janis, "Groupthink," *Psychology Today,* November 1971: 43.

41. As quoted in E. van de Vliert, 1984.

42. van de Vliert, 1984.

43. As quoted in E. van de Vliert, 1984; J. B. Rijsman, "Group characteristics and individual behavior," in *Handbook of Work and Organizational Psychology,* ed. P. J. D. Drenth, H. Thierry, P. J. Willems, and C. J. de Wolf, Vol. 1, John Wiley & Sons Ltd., Chichester, England, 1984: 451–480; H. Tajfel, M. Billig, R. Bundy, and C. Flament, "Social categorization and intergroup behaviour," *European Journal of Social Psychology,* Vol. 1, 1971: 149–175.

44. W. Doise and A. Sinclair, "The categorization process in intergroup relations," *European Journal of Social Psychology,* Vol. 3, 1973: 145–153; H. Tajfel and M. Billig, "Familiarity and categorisation and intergroup behavior, *Journal of Experimental Social Psychology,* Vol. 10, No. 2, 1974: 159–170.

45. Gordon, 1991.

46. R. Hodgetts, *Management: Theory, Process, and Practice,* 3rd ed., Dryden Press, Hinsdale, Ill., 1982.

47. Gordon, 1991.

48. L. D. Brown, "Normative conflict management theories: Past, present, and future," *Journal of Organizational Behavior,* Vol. 13, 1992: 303–309.

49. Brown, 1992.

50. Gibson, Ivancevich, and Donnelly, Jr., 1994; Lewicki, Weiss, and Lewin, 1992; Rahim, 1986; Brown, 1983; A. Rahim and T. Bonoma, "Managing organizational conflict: A model for diagnosing and intervention," *Psychological Reports,* Vol. 44, 1979: 1323–1344; Robbins, 1978.

51. W. E. Scott, "Activation theory and task design," *Organizational Behavior and Human Performance,* Vol. 1, 1966: 3–30.

52. V. H. Vroom, *Work and Motivation,* John Wiley & Sons, New York, 1964.

53. Robbins, Winter 1978; S. P. Robbins, *Managing Organizational Conflict: A Nontraditional Approach,* Prentice Hall, Englewood Cliffs, N. J., 1974.

54. Robbins, 1978; Robbins, 1974.

55. Gibson, Ivancevich, and Donnelly, Jr., 1994; Robbins, 1978.

56. K. W. Thomas, D. W. Jamieson, and R. K. Moore, "Conflict and collaboration: Some concluding observations," *California Management Review,* Vol. 21, No. 2, 1978: 91–95; Pondy, 1967.

57. Pondy, 1967.

58. van de Vliert, 1984; Thomas, 1976.

59. Our model reflects material presented in M. A. Rahim, 1986; E. van de Vliert, 1984; Thomas, 1976; Pondy, 1967.

60. Thomas, 1992; Thomas, 1976.

61. R. L. Daft, *Organizational Theory and Design,* Addison-Wesley Publishing, Reading, Mass., 1986.

62. G. W. Evans, M. N. Palsane, and S. Carrere, "Type A behavior and occupational stress: A cross-cultural study of blue-collar workers," *Journal of Personality and Social Psychology,* Vol. 52, No. 5, 1987: 1002–1007; D. S. Holmes and M. J. Will, "Expression of interpersonal aggression by angered and nonangered persons with Type A and Type B behavior patterns," *Journal of Personality and Social Psychology,* Vol. 48, No. 3, 1985: 723–727.

63. Holmes and Will, 1985; S. M. Miller, E. R. Lack, and S. Asroll, "Preferences for control and the coronary-prone behavior pattern: I'd rather do it myself," *Journal of Personality and Social Psychology,* Vol. 49, No. 2, 1985: 492–499; D. C. Glass, *Behavior Patterns, Stress, and Coronary Disease,* Erlbaum, Hillsdale, N. J., 1977.

64. R. A. Baron, "Personality and organizational conflict: Effect of the Type A behavior pattern and self-monitoring," *Organizational Behavior and Human Decision Processes,* Vol. 44, No. 2, 1989: 281–296.

65. B. Kabanoff, "Predictive validity of the MODE conflict instrument," *Journal of Applied Psychology,* Vol. 72, No. 1, 1987: 160–164.

66. Baron, 1989.

67. R. E. Jones and B. H. Melcher, "Personality and the preference for modes of conflict resolution," *Human Relations,* Vol. 35, 1982: 649–658.

68. J. Mills, D. Robey, and L. Smith, "Conflict-handling and personality dimensions of project-management personnel," *Psychological Reports,* Vol. 57, 1985: 1135–1143; M. N. Chanin and J. A. Schneer, "A study of the relationship between

Jungian personality dimensions and conflict-handling behavior," *Human Relations,* Vol. 37, 1984: 863–879; R. H. Kilmann and K. W. Thomas, "Developing a forced-choice measure of conflict-handling behavior: The MODE instrument," *Educational and Psychological Measurement,* Vol. 37, 1977: 309–325.

69. Kabanoff, 1987.

70. Baron, 1989.

71. A. Rahim, "Some contingencies affecting inter-personal conflict in academia: A multivariate study," *Management International Review,* Vol. 20, No. 2, 1980: 117–121.

72. Baron, 1989.

73. Gibson, Ivancevich, and Donnelly, Jr., 1994; R. L. Daft, *Organization Theory and Design,* West Publishing Company, St. Paul, Minn., 1983.

74. R. E. Walton and J. M. Dutton, "The management of interdepartmental conflict: A model and review," *Administrative Science Quarterly,* Vol. 14, No. 1, 1969: 73–84.

75. The first three levels reflect material presented in J. D. Thompson, *Organizations in Action,* McGraw-Hill, New York, 1967. The fourth level reflects the flexible, porous, adaptive organization described by T. Peters, *Thriving on Chaos,* Harper & Row, New York, 1987.

76. Daft, 1983; S. M. Davis and P. R. Lawrence, *Matrix,* Addison-Wesley Publishing, Reading, Mass., 1977.

77. Davis and Lawrence, 1977.

78. D. M. Kolb and L. L. Putnam, "The multiple faces of conflict in organizations," *Journal of Organizational Behavior,* Vol. 13, 1992: 311–324; P. Drucker, "New organizational forms," *Harvard Business Review,* January–February 1988; T. J. Peters and R. H. Waterman, *In Search of Excellence,* Harper & Row, New York, 1982.

79. Thomas, 1992; Thomas, 1976.

80. R. R. Blake and J. S. Mouton, *The Managerial Grid,* Gulf Publishing, Houston, Texas, 1964.

81. D. W. Organ, *Organizational Citizenship Behavior: The Good Soldier Syndrome,* Lexington Books, Lexington, Mass, 1988.

82. D. C. Feldman, "The development and enforcement of group norms," *Academy of Management Review,* Vol. 9, No. 1, 1984: 47–53.

83. Thomas, 1976.

84. Thomas, 1976.

85. Thomas, 1976.

86. Thomas, 1976.

87. Thomas, 1976.

88. K. W. Thomas and R. E. Walton, "Conflict-handling behavior in interdepartmental relations," Research Paper #38, Division Research, Graduate School of Business Administration, UCLA, 1971.

89. Thomas, 1976.

90. Thomas, 1992.

91. Thomas, 1992.

92. A. D. Szilagyi, Jr., *Management and Performance,* 3rd ed., Scott, Foresman, Glenview, Ill., 1988; van de Vliert, 1984; Thomas, 1976.

93. van de Vliert, 1984.

94. van de Vliert, 1984.

95. van de Vliert, 1984; Thomas, 1976.

96. R. M. Kanter, *The Change Masters,* Simon & Schuster, New York, 1983.

97. Peters, 1987.

98. Thomas, 1992: 266–267.

99. Lewicki, Weiss, and Lewin, 1992; Thomas, 1976; R. Walton, *Interpersonal Peacekeeping,* Addison-Wesley Publishing, Reading, Mass., 1969.

100. M. R. Louis, "How individuals conceptualize conflict: Identification of steps in the process and the role of personal/developmental factors," *Human Resources,* Vol. 30, No. 5, 1977: 451–467.

101. Thomas, 1992.

102. Thomas, 1976.

103. Thomas, 1992; R. Fisher and W. Ury, *Getting to Yes,* Penguin Books, New York, 1983; J. W. Eiseman, "Reconciling incompatible positions," *Journal of Applied Behavioral Science,* Vol. 14, 1978: 412–460; Thomas, 1976; A. C. Filley, *Interpersonal Conflict Resolution,* Scott, Foresman, Glenview, Ill., 1975.

104. Thomas, 1976.

105. K. W. Thomas, "Norms as an integrative theme in conflict and negotiation: Correcting our 'Sociopathic' assumptions," in *Managing Conflict: An Interdisciplinary Approach,* ed. M. A. Rahim, Praeger, New York, 1989: 265–272; E. E. Lawler, *Motivation in the Work Environment,* Brooks/Cole, Monterey, Calif., 1973; V. H. Vroom, *Work and Motivation,* Wiley, New York, 1964.

106. Thomas, 1992; Thomas, 1989; I. Ajzen and M. Fishbein, *Understanding Attitudes and Predicting*

Social Behavior, Prentice Hall, Englewood Cliffs, N. J., 1980.

107. K. W. Thomas and L. R. Pondy, "Toward an 'intent' model of conflict management among principal parties," *Human Relations,* Vol. 30, No. 12, 1977: 1089–1102; M. R. Louis, "How individuals conceptualize conflict: Identification of steps in the process and role of personal/developmental factors," *Human Relations,* Vol. 30, 1977: 451–467.

108. Thomas and Pondy, 1977.

109. H. H. Kelly, *Attribution in Social Interaction,* General Learning Press, New York, 1971.

110. Thomas and Pondy, 1977.

111. Louis, 1977.

112. Thomas, 1992; Rahim, 1986; K. W. Thomas, "Introduction," *California Management Review,* Vol. 21, No. 2, 1978: 56–60; S. P. Robbins, 1978; Thomas, 1976; R. L. Thomas and K. W. Thomas, "Support for a two-dimensional model of conflict behavior," *Organizational Behavior and Human Performance,* Vol. 16, No. 1, 1976: 143–155; R. R. Blake and J. S. Mouton, "The fifth achievement," *Journal of Applied Behavioral Science,* Vol. 6, No. 4, 1970: 412–426; Blake and Mouton, 1964

113. Lewicki, Weiss, and Lewin, 1992.

114. van de Vliert, 1984.

115. Thomas, 1976; Pondy, 1967.

116. Robbins, 1978.

117. Robbins, 1978: 69.

118. Robbins, 1978.

119. Thomas, 1992.

120. D. Borisoff and D. A. Victor, 1989: 18.

121. Material presented in Table 12.8 has been taken from S. L. Philips and R. L. Elledge, *The Team-Building Source Book,* University Associates, Inc., San Diego, Calif., 1989; and Rahim, 1986: 28–29.

122. Peters, 1987.

123. Thomas, 1992; A. J. Dubrin, *Effective Business Psychology,* 2nd ed., Reston Publishing Company, Reston, Va., 1985.

124. Thomas, 1976; Louis, 1977.

125. Thomas and Pondy, 1977; Louis, 1977.

126. Thomas, 1976; van de Vliert, 1984.

127. R. G. Ensman, Jr., "When tempers flare," *Manage,* Vol. 43, No. 1, 1991: 21–22.

128. L. Grensing, "A five-stage approach to defusing emotional outbursts," *Manage,* Vol. 43, No. 4, 1992: 26–29; Ensman, Jr., August 1991; R. Dawson, "Resolving angry disagreements," *Supervisory Management,* Vol. 34, No. 2, February 1989: 13–16.

129. The following exercise is based upon material presented in the video "Escalation of a Conflict," Video Lecture Series, Program on Negotiation and Dispute Resolution, Harvard Law School, Cambridge, Mass.

PERFORMANCE APPRAISAL AND REVIEW

Objectives:

- To describe the performance appraisal and review process and articulate the behaviors required for successful implementation.
- To integrate the goal-setting and performance appraisal and review process.
- To describe the characteristics of effective feedback.
- To give students an opportunity to apply the behaviors necessary to carry out effective behaviorally based performance appraisal review.

Introduction

To be effective, organizations must have an internal assessment mechanism designed to provide feedback on performance. Such feedback allows for the maintenance of the status quo when goals are being achieved, and corrective change when goals are not being achieved. Similarly, managers cannot be certain that employees are performing at, or near, their peak capabilities unless they are willing to engage in effective assessment of employee performance. A properly designed and implemented performance appraisal and review system allows managers to communicate what is expected of employees, assess the contribution of each subordinate to organizational goals, and take corrective action when employee contributions are less than desired (see Figure 13.1).

Employee development can be facilitated through effective feedback, coaching and goal setting, employee self-management, and the identification of employees likely to gain from formalized training. For example, one of the most important roles for managers is their ability to train subordinates to effectively perform current tasks, and at the same time develop subordinates for future tasks. It is the well-trained and developed employee who is able to

FIGURE 13.1

*Assessing the value
of performance
appraisal*

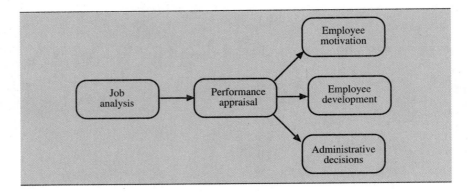

perform at levels necessary to help ensure managerial success. Performance appraisal pin-points the areas where subordinates are deficient. Armed with this information, the manager is in a better position to design those training and development experiences required to improve an employee's performance. At the very minimum, performance evaluation can sensitize subordinates to areas in which self-development is needed.

Performance appraisal can also have a positive effect on a subordinate's motivation. That which gets measured gets done. This is especially true when that which gets measured is linked to desired, or valued, consequences. In addition, performance evaluation and review can help produce a better fit between subordinates and their job environments.[1] By increasing the fit, the manager increases an employee's willingness to perform effectively. At the same time, performance appraisal can provide the manager with the data necessary to justify differential rewards between high and low performers. When differential rewards are based upon data, they are more likely to be perceived as fair and just by subordinates. Perceived equity increases the probability that employee motivation will be maintained or increased as a result of the manager's action.

Because managers are responsible for a broad range of activities, they will often be called upon to make key administrative decisions about departmental staff. At the very least, they will be asked to provide information to other decision makers within the organization. The information obtained through performance appraisal will act as the raw input to any such administrative decision (i.e., promotions, demotions, merit increases, transfers, termination, work assignments, delegation decisions, etc.). The importance of these decisions is further amplified by the legal implications of a wrong decision in North America. This is especially true given the findings of a recent study indicating employees were three times more likely to sue their employers in 1988 as they were in 1980.[2]

The probability of legal action taken against a manager or organization (and the probability of losing such legal action) is significantly reduced if decisions are backed up by objective support.[3] Many wrongful dismissals, arbitration, and discrimination cases have been won by using well-documented evidence. Effective performance evaluations can provide this evidence. Performance evaluation is also necessary for explaining the rationale underlying administrative decisions such as promotions, training and development, differential rewards, termination, and the validation of selection instruments.

It is not surprising, therefore, that 94 percent of the organizations responding to a recent survey indicated that they conducted formal performance appraisals.[4] The same survey also indicated that the proportion of organizations using performance appraisals for more than one purpose increased from 11 percent in 1977 to 30 percent in 1988.[5] Latham and his co-authors identified eight common purposes for which performance appraisals are used:

1. Ensuring mutual understanding of effective performance.
2. Building confidence between employer and employees.
3. Clarifying any misunderstandings regarding performance expectations.
4. Establishing developmental procedures.
5. Allocating rewards.
6. Sustaining and enhancing employee motivation.
7. Career planning.
8. Fostering communication and feedback.[6]

Unfortunately, many managers leave the appraisal process to chance observations, evaluate performance so infrequently that there is insufficient time to correct an employee's behavior, allow political considerations to distort the accuracy of their assessments, or go through the process but then fail to use the results.[7] Thus, it is not surprising that only one out of three surveyed employees felt that the appraisal process was effective in telling them where they stood.[8] Similarly, International Survey Research in Chicago reported that after surveying 6,000 managers and 24,000 employees, only 40 percent of the respondents were satisfied with the level of feedback they were receiving about their performance.[9]

The primary purpose of performance appraisal is to coach and counsel employees in a way that inculcates their desire for continuous improvement. The secondary purpose is to provide a means and a rationale for determining who should be promoted, demoted, transferred, laid off, terminated, given or denied a salary increase or bonus. Defined in this manner, there are several implications for the manager who attempts to implement a performance evaluation system. To effectively conduct performance evaluations, the manager must have clearly established agreed-upon standards of performance. To accomplish this, the manager must ensure that a job analysis has been conducted to identify and articulate the knowledge, skills, and behaviors that are critical to attaining the organization's strategic goals. The above definition also implies that the manager must ensure adequate observation and recording of an employee's behavior. Observing and recording behavior must be carried out for the entire review process to ensure that a fair and representative sample of subordinate behaviors has been collected. Finally, the performance evaluation process will require ongoing interactions between the manager and subordinates. This is necessary to ensure not only the representative observations but to ensure timely and meaningful feedback to each subordinate.

The success of a performance appraisal system depends on the degree to which the manager understands and accepts the process, the system is fully integrated with the goal-setting process, the manager is trained, and the operational components of performance evaluation are integrated into the manager's department. Ultimately, a performance evaluation system must answer the following five questions for the subordinate: "What is expected of me?" "How am I doing?" "Where am I going?" "How can I improve?" and "What will be the reward for me improving?" The answers to these questions determine whether subordinates will commit to attaining the organization's strategic goals.

The Performance Appraisal and Review (PAR) Process

Figure 13.2 depicts the various steps that must be built into an appraisal system if it is expected to work. As the process is described below, the student should recognize that the process acts to integrate a number of activities that have already been discussed. This overlap should be perceived as desirable as it reflects the integrative nature of management, and reinforces the argument that to be effective the manager must master a broad range of behaviors.

Before discussing the various steps in the performance appraisal and review (PAR) process, the student should understand the importance of the outer and inner loops described in Figure 13.2. The outer loop represents the traditional view of a formalized end-of-period evaluation of a subordinate's performance. It leads directly to an end-of-period review and a number of administrative decisions. Its primary emphasis is on results (that is, whether goals and objectives were achieved by the subordinate), including job behaviors and activities. The inner loop represents ongoing, day-to-day, coaching between the manager and subordinates. The inner loop is informal in that it emphasizes the behaviors and activities that are necessary for goal achievement.

Research on the structure of appraisal systems also supports the value of a strong inner loop.[10] Specifically, performance reviews that are done intermittently throughout the review period increase employees' belief that they understand their job assignments and that the appraisals are fair.[11] The need for frequent interaction with employees to facilitate development and growth is supported by the finding that once-a-year appraisals result in only small improvements in performance.[12]

The inner loop also facilitates the process of incremental change and helps prevent feedback overload. By building in frequent, informal interactions, managers are less likely to retain negative feedback until the formal,

Figure 13.2

The performance appraisal and review (PAR) process

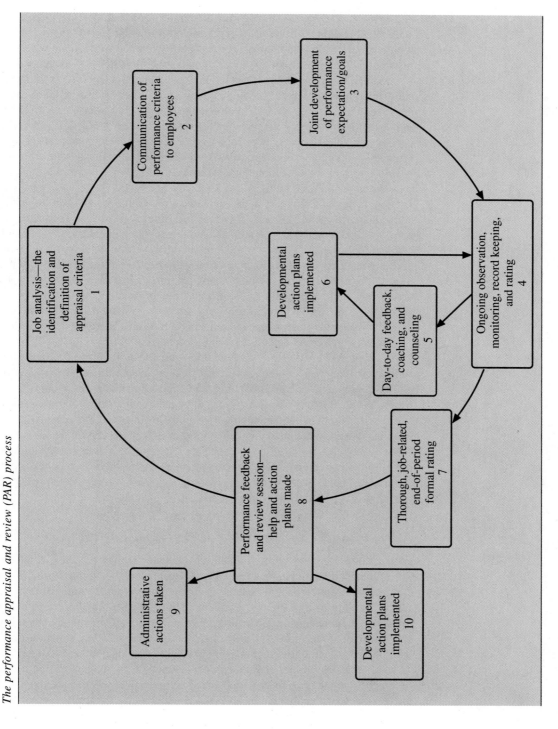

end-of-period review.[13] In addition, the inner loop reduces the likelihood of subordinates being surprised by a negative review. Negative surprises, linked with feedback overload, increase the probability that the subordinate will become resistant to change rather than continuously seek ways to improve performance.

Finally, by recognizing the importance of the inner and outer loops, managers can effectively deal with the controversy of whether both administrative and developmental issues should be discussed during the formal appraisal meeting. Proponents on the separation side of the controversy argue that when administrative and development decisions are considered at the same time employees are likely to place greater emphasis on administrative issues (e.g., raise or promotion) than on developmental issues (e.g., comments, coaching tips, problem solving, and goal setting).[14]

In support of this view, researchers have found that when supervisors administer financial rewards, they are less likely to provide feedback on an employee's competence.[15] Survey evidence has also demonstrated that employees prefer appraisals where administrative and developmental issues are considered separately.[16] In contrast, Prince and Lawler found that employees prefer to discuss administrative issues during appraisals because decisions in these areas clearly communicate that employee performance is valued by the organization.[17] Similarly, Dorfman, Stephan, and Loveland demonstrated that employee satisfaction with the appraisal is likely to increase when a discussion of pay and advancement are included.[18]

The question becomes, "How do managers reconcile these contrasting positions?" The answer, we believe, must reflect the manager's willingness and ability to provide feedback, coaching, and counseling on an ongoing basis (inner loop). When this occurs, the formal appraisal (outer loop) serves only as a summarization of what has been taking place throughout the appraisal period. In other words, when a strong inner loop exists, there should be no surprises at the end-of-the-period review. Therefore, "when researchers find that combining administrative and developmental aspects in the formal interview is inappropriate, it is because ongoing coaching has not taken place; when researchers find that it is appropriate, ongoing coaching has taken place."[19]

1. Identification and Definition of Appraisal Criteria

Before any attempt to communicate performance standards or expectations to subordinates, it is critical that managers determine both the behaviors and results that are required from employees to implement the organization's strategy. Step 1 is an attempt to link the organization's strategy with the appraisal process.[20] Such a link increases the probability that when a PAR process is used, it will result in employee understanding of organizational and departmental goals.

One of the potential errors at this step is for managers to focus primarily on desired results rather than behavior. When results become the cornerstone of the PAR process, the required level of specificity is threatened. A new, inexperienced, or problem employee, faced only with the results to be achieved, is unwittingly being given total discretion of the means used to achieve the desired result. Such ambiguity is inconsistent with the principles of sound management and good performance appraisal and review.[21] This fundamental error is reflected in the following vignette.[22]

> To facilitate the turn around of a failing operation the company's president directed a senior executive to "Get the operation in the black." After two years the senior executive had taken a deficit operation and turned it into a money maker. Gaining confidence from these results, the senior executive applied for a promotion. Unfortunately, the president did not share the senior executive's enthusiasm. Instead the president criticized the individual for single handedly bringing the change about, not considering others, and replacing good employees with submissive employees. In other words, the president believed that the senior executive had achieved the results through personal efforts alone and in the process had weakened the organization. The president also indicated that there would be no further promotions if the senior manager's autocratic style did not change.

The basic error indicated by this vignette was a failure by the president to accurately indicate appropriate behaviors. Compounding the problem is the president's apparent failure to give meaningful and timely feedback to the senior executive. This story also implies another strong argument for clearly articulating desired behaviors. Even when managers indicate that they will measure results, in actual practice they will at some point assess behavior. This is especially true in those areas where results cannot be directly linked to a particular individual. If behavior is what the manager will eventually assess when evaluating subordinate performance, he or she owes it to the subordinate to communicate what constitutes acceptable behavior. When this is not done, and the subordinate fails, the typical employee response is, "You never told me that!"

A focus on results rather than behavior is deficient in that it excludes factors for which an employee should be held accountable. It can also be excessive in that results measures are affected by factors beyond the employee's control. For example, employees in forest product companies may be erroneously rewarded or penalized in the quarterly bonus they receive due to the value of the exchange rate between the dollar and the yen that affects the value of log exports to Japan. A focus on results can also encourage a "results-at-all-cost" mentality that in turn can lead to ethical or legal complications. Consider NASA's drive to control costs by getting the space shuttle, the Challenger, launched on time. This emphasis had tragic consequences. Finally, an emphasis on results does not tell employees what they are to start doing, stop doing, or consider doing differently to continuously improve the results that the organization wishes to attain.

A second error at this point is for managers to deal with traits (e.g., loyalty and attitude) rather than behaviors. Although appraisals using traits are the most often used by organizations, are easy to develop, and facilitate use across multiple jobs or organizational levels, they fail to provide the detail needed to achieve desired organizational behaviors, namely, goal setting, feedback, counseling, and motivation. At best, traits only refer to potential predictors of performance and not performance itself.[23] As a result, trait-based systems produce little agreement among raters as to what these traits mean.[24] Furthermore, managers often refuse to give negative feedback on traits for fear of criticizing personal qualities.[25] Finally, trait-based appraisals are likely to be considered suspect by the courts because of their lack of specificity or behavioral support.[26]

Employee evaluations should be based upon observable behavior. Long supported by industrial psychologists, behaviorally based evaluations provide the needed detail to articulate indexes of excellence.[27] Behavioral criteria that are based upon an appropriate job analysis clearly articulate what employees must do to be productive. When these behaviors are understood, accepted, and followed by employees, and this fact is accurately measured by the appraisal process, managers can provide accurate feedback, set goals, motivate, and eventually make relevant administrative decisions.

Figure 13.3 outlines the steps the manager must take to reach the required level of specificity before communicating behavioral standards to the subordinate. First, managers must identify the jobs, or job clusters, for which they are responsible. Once that is accomplished, managers must then determine in their own minds the general job dimensions employees must perform high on to be considered successful. Job dimensions relate to general skills, abilities, traits, and responsibilities that, when taken together, largely determine the degree of success or failure achieved by the job holder. When deciding upon the relevance of a particular job dimension it is necessary for the manager to consider how that dimension relates to overall job performance. If no link is found to exist between a particular job dimension and overall employee performance, the manager should not list that particular job dimension.

FIGURE 13.3

Establishing behavioral standards

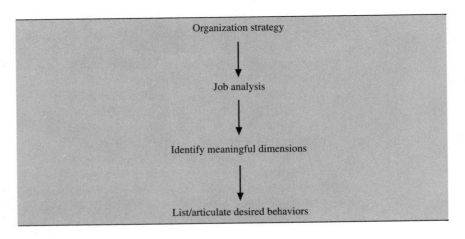

Organization strategy

↓

Job analysis

↓

Identify meaningful dimensions

↓

List/articulate desired behaviors

The manager, however, cannot be satisfied with the identification of desired job dimensions. Merely informing a subordinate that he or she must be dependable is insufficient to ensure desirable behavior. No matter how relevant the dimension, or how clearly defined, the behavioral response by the subordinate remains open to interpretation or subjective manipulation. Under ambiguous conditions, the typical subordinate will behave in a manner that parallels his or her own needs and goals, is easiest, or is implied by the situation. All three alternatives increase the risk that subordinates will behave in a manner inconsistent with the manager's own behavioral expectations. It is therefore necessary to articulate examples of behaviors that are consistent with the manager's expectations. In the case of dependability, the following examples come to mind.

- If you are unable to come into work on a given day, you are to inform me several days in advance—if this is not possible, please do so as soon as you know. If you do not know until that day, inform me a minimum of one hour before the start of the work day. On those days you are out, please inform me of what is to be accomplished (here is where a to-do list is helpful), and who is responsible or involved.

- If you cannot return within 20 minutes after your rounds, I would like you to page me so that I can assign your work to other group members.

- If you cannot complete an assignment as agreed, and the consequences are likely to have a negative impact on yourself or others in the department, please alert me to this fact.

Behaviorally specific examples will clarify in the subordinate's mind what the manager means by dependability. At this step, the manager must indicate that any behavioral examples given to the subordinate are just that—examples. It would be impossible for the manager to articulate all behaviors and situations supporting the dependability dimension. In other words, the subordinate must be able to generalize across a broad range of situations by employing personal discretion.

Two approaches that attempt to build behavioral statements into the performance appraisal instrument are Behaviorally Anchored Rating Scales (BARS)[28] and Behavior Observation Scales (BOS).[29] Table 13.1 provides an example of a standard BARS appraisal instrument. Figure 9.4 (Chapter 9) provides an example of a standard BOS appraisal instrument. Both BARS and BOS have distinct advantages over instruments that are not behaviorally based.[30] Both instruments are based upon a detailed and systematic job analysis that incorporates employee input. As a result, behavioral statements use terminology familiar to employees. Furthermore, behavioral statements that are based upon systematic job analysis increase the content validity of the appraisal instrument. Next, the behavioral statements used in the BARS and BOS remove much of the uncertainty or ambiguity that is often

TABLE 13.1   Example of a Behavioral Expectation Scale for Work Habits

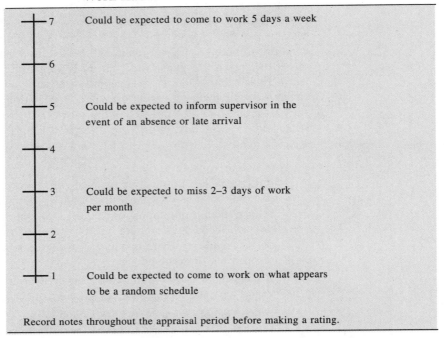

—7   Could be expected to come to work 5 days a week

—6

—5   Could be expected to inform supervisor in the event of an absence or late arrival

—4

—3   Could be expected to miss 2–3 days of work per month

—2

—1   Could be expected to come to work on what appears to be a random schedule

Record notes throughout the appraisal period before making a rating.

Source: G.P. Latham and K. N. Wexley, *Increasing Productivity through Performance Appraisal,* 2nd ed., Addison-Wesley Publishing, Reading, Mass.,1994: 80.

associated with trait-based rating scales. Last, job specific, behavioral statements facilitate employee feedback and coaching designed to improve on-the-job performance.

When compared to the BARS, the BOS avoids several of the operational problems associated with the BARS.[31] When the BARS is developed, a large pool of behavioral statements is obtained from critical incidents used in its construction. Unfortunately, the BARS only uses a small percentage of these statements (e.g., seven per job dimension) and discards the remaining. In contrast, the BOS uses the complete set of valid statements. Simply put, the BOS does not waste useful information. As a result, the BOS can be used to replace or supplement existing job descriptions by making explicit what behaviors are required for successful performance on the job.

The listing of actual job behaviors rather than a limited number of examples also makes it easier for the rater to assess and rate actual performance. In the case of the BARS the rater must select the anchor he or she believes best fits the observed behavior or incident. Difficulties arise when the raters cannot discern the similarlity between anchors and observed behavior. Such a step is not necessary with the BOS because required job behaviors are listed on the instrument.

When using BARS, the rater is required to make one rating for each job dimension. This rating is based upon the recorded and classified information he or she has observed over the full evaluation period. The BOS considers the same job dimensions but requires the rater to rate the employee on each behavior. The ability to rate the employee on multiple behaviors for each dimension is likely to increase the reliability of the BOS instrument. This may also help to minimize rater bias as the raters do "not have to extrapolate from what they have observed to the placement of a check mark beside an example on the scale that may or may not be appropriate."[32]

As Wiersma, van de Berg, and Latham have pointed out, "user reactions to the appraisal system affect perceptions of and willingness to utilize the system."[33] Managers will use an instrument if it is understandable, plausible, and acceptable.[34] Research evidence demonstrates that employees and managers generally prefer the BOS over the BARS.[35] More specifically, when considering such key aspects of appraisal as: ability to give feedback, ability to differentiate among employees, objectivity, ability to account for position differences, ability to provide training, setting corporatewide standards, and overall ease of use, the BOS is preferred over the BARS. In addition, BOS instruments have been found to be effective in achieving goal clarity, acceptance and commitment, increased work satisfaction, and increased employee feelings of control.[36]

We believe that organizations and managers can greatly facilitate their performance appraisal efforts if they use BOS-type instruments when evaluating employees and giving employee feedback. Where the human resource departments have already developed BOS instruments, managers need only be trained in their use and be willing to use them.[37] In organizations where this has not occurred, managers can take steps to analyze the jobs they supervise and develop behavioral statements (BOS-type statements) that describe the behaviors and actions they believe determine employee success on the job. For example, assume that a supervisor working within a power-generating plant believes that it is important that the safety coordinator inform him or her when a crew member needs ear plugs. Such basic equipment is required to prevent long-term ear damage. As a result, the supervisor has requested the safety coordinator to inform him or her when a worker needs a set of ear plugs. The BOS statement would be:[38]

Immediately informs supervisor of crew members who need ear plugs.

Almost never   1   2   3   4   Almost always

Crew members who exhibit the desired behavior 0–64 percent of the time are given a rating of 1; 65–74 percent of the time, a rating of 2; 75–84 percent of the time, a rating of 3; and 95–100 percent of the time, a rating of 4. The actual percentage used is determined by the manager and reflects the supervisor's expectations in each situation. Therefore, if the behavior being assessed by the supervisor is critical to success and should occur frequently, then the percentage range used would be higher.

2. Communication of Measures of Performance

The usefulness of behavioral standards is a function of the degree to which subordinates understand, accept, and implement them. Similarly, goals give subordinates the understanding of where they are going and why they are being asked to behave in a particular way. Managers who educate subordinates to the relationship between organizational goals and appropriate subordinate behaviors, are likely to have productive and satisfied work groups.[39]

As indicated in our discussion of effective goal setting, the communication of behavioral requirements and desired results also sensitizes the subordinate to how his or her performance is evaluated. The subordinate who understands and accepts the standards as stated is more likely to be monitoring his or her own behavior during the upcoming evaluation period and take the necessary action to match actual behavior with the organization's strategy.[40]

Self-evaluations can be extremely useful when they are part of the formal performance appraisal system.[41] Self-evaluation can enhance employee dignity and self-respect, change the manager's role from judge to counselor, increase employee commitment, enhance self-motivation, reduce employee defensiveness, and facilitate the integration of self-development into the appraisal process. Furthermore, subordinates should bring their personal ratings and accompanying support statements to the formal review session (Step 7). In addition, the manager should encourage the employee to review self-assessments with peers.[42] By engaging in self-evaluation, subordinates can satisfy their personal need for feedback, as the process can be performed as often as the subordinate desires or believes necessary.

If subordinates have not been sensitized to the behavioral standards and goal expectations being used for evaluation, and yet are eventually criticized for the failure to exhibit such behaviors, they are likely to become defensive. To defend themselves, subordinates usually attack the appraisal instrument and the person who used it. They attack the instrument by arguing that it fails to provide a comprehensive measure (deficiency) of what they have accomplished, or that it measures them on the wrong things (excessive). They attack the appraiser by arguing that the person is not qualified to assess performance. Such hostility from employees can lead to subsequent cowardice by the appraiser. The appraisor "learns" to inflate performance ratings in the future as a means of avoiding conflict with subordinates.

3. Joint Development of Performance Expectations

Rarely will there be total initial agreement between the appraisers and subordinates on either the means or ends of achieving departmental or organizational success. They usually have different reference bases, access to different information, and even different values. As a result, managers and subordinates develop differences of opinion about what the job is, and what behaviors and knowledge are needed to perform effectively.[43] The manager must, therefore, be willing to negotiate with subordinates to achieve commitment and buy-in by subordinates.[44] The objective of this process is mutually agreed-upon expectations about which behaviors are and are not acceptable for attaining departmental goals. This is why a job analysis includes input from managers, job incumbents, and customers. The involvement of all three parties ensures comprehensive measures, the rationale for which is understood by all three groups. Thus, the "rules of the game" make sense. They do not reflect the whim or capriciousness of a manager alone, an employee alone, or a customer alone.

4. Periodic Observation, Record Keeping, and Rating

Steps 1 to 3 are best completed before the start of the evaluation period. The required activities necessary to carry out effective evaluations are indicated in Figure 13.4. To obtain an accurate rating, the manager must spend the time developing his or her data base by recording observed behavior.[45] This requires appraisers to interact with subordinates on an ongoing basis to ensure that a representative sample of subordinate behavior is observed and recorded over the full evaluation period. Unfortunately, many managers fail to obtain a representative sample of an employee's behavior. Instead, managers succumb to the necessary effect of recalling only what the employee has "done for me lately." If the employee has a good two–three week period before the formal appraisal, the rating is likely to be high; if the subordinate has a poor two–three week period, the rating tends to be low.

FIGURE 13.4

Periodic observation, recording, and rating

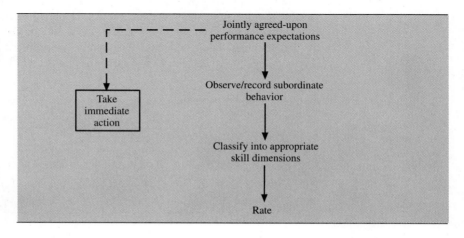

To develop an accurate assessment of the subordinate's performance, the manager must make a conscientious effort to observe and record behavior over the full evaluation period. The manager, to ensure the perception of fairness, must allow employee and customer input.[46] The evaluation should not be based solely on one source or input, especially if it is only the manager's. Getting multiple perspectives, which include the employee's, not only ensures appraisal accuracy, but also increases feelings of fairness in the person who is being appraised.

5. Day-to-Day Coaching, Counseling, and Feedback

The inner loop requires the manager to give feedback, coach, and counsel subordinates. (For a discussion of counseling see Chapter 14.) This should be done on an ongoing basis. Doing so only once a season would guarantee that an athletic coach would be fired. The same fate should hold true in nonathletic organizations. Most behaviors cannot be changed by once-a-year goal-setting and feedback sessions. It is through ongoing feedback, coaching, and counseling (FCC) encounters that the manager shares perceptions about performance and behavioral observations of the subordinate. Although such encounters can vary widely in terms of time spent and depth of material covered, they are mini-versions of the thorough end-of-period review session.

A candid discussion of an employee's strengths, weaknesses, and their consequences is an essential step in creating an environment in which the subordinate will alter behavior and ultimately acquire other behaviors. The first part of any feedback, coaching, and counseling session is intended to sensitize the subordinate to how well he or she has been doing the job. Because we are functioning within the inner loop, this period may be as short as one day or as long as several weeks. Once discussions of the performance level achieved and the behaviors observed have taken place, the second half of the FCC encounter can be devoted to setting goals and specifying the behaviors necessary for attaining them. Again, this period may vary in length from a day or less to several weeks. The structure of FCC encounters is depicted in Figure 13.5.

To overcome a subordinate's deficiency, it may be necessary to link several FCC encounters. The result will be an employee who is functioning at desired levels or an employee who is demonstrating sufficient improvement as he or

FIGURE 13.5

FCC (Feedback, Coaching, and Counseling) encounters and their structure

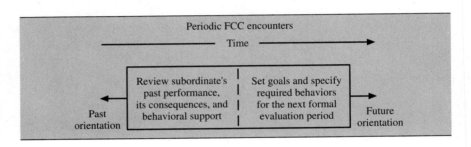

she moves toward this goal. Also recall that, for FCC encounters to be effective, they must result in the establishment of specific goals toward which the employee can strive. By providing feedback, setting specific goals, coaching, and measuring performance (employees can do the measuring themselves), it is possible to turn otherwise meaningless activity into a challenging activity.[47] When managers link these behaviors with managerial support and employee participation, the result is improved performance. Support facilitates and encourages the employee to perform effectively, and participation increases the employee's understanding of how to achieve desired goals.

To help ensure that FCC encounters are productive, the manager must develop positive relationships with subordinates before carrying out the inner loop of the PAR process.[48] Without a positive relationship between the manager and subordinates, it is unlikely that the manager will carry out the inner loop or that the employee will respond positively. Instead, the manager is likely to engage in avoidance behaviors designed to minimize the number of confrontations experienced with subordinates. Similarly, unless a positive relationship has been developed before the FCC encounter, subordinates are likely to remain defensive and resist all but the most aggressive attempts to change them.[49]

The actual number of FCC encounters with any one subordinate will be a function of the existing performance deficiency. It must also be remembered that the FCC encounters are part of the inner loop described in Figure 13.2 and as such represent a separate sub-level of the traditional PAR process (i.e., the outer loop).

Before leaving our discussion of the appraisal model's inner loop, we should again mention the importance of developing the employee's perceived self-efficacy. Employees with the same skills can perform below average, at satisfactory levels, or well above average, depending upon how they assess their own capabilities.[50] Such performance differences result from differences in perceived self-efficacy. Employees with high self-efficacy are likely to believe that "they can learn; they can do what is required; and they can be successful." Conversely, employees with low self-efficacy are likely to make up their minds that they cannot learn or to seek ways to escape activities they believe are beyond their present abilities. Therefore, when coaching, counseling, and providing employee feedback, managers must find ways to increase the individual's feeling of self-efficacy.

As indicated in Chapter 2, managers can take steps to increase the employee's perceived self-efficacy. The following actions give some idea of how managers can build positive self-efficacy when attempting to give feedback, coach, and counsel employees.[51]

- Managers can educate employees in the practice of self-talk. Because what people say to themselves affects their performance, it is desirable to tell oneself that success is possible. Constructive self-talk also requires that employees replace inaccurate self-deprecating statements with accurate statements of what has caused, or is likely to cause, difficulties. When this occurs employees are more likely to articulate past situations in which such difficulties were overcome.

- Managers can educate employees in the practice of visualization. Instead of visualizing failure, employees should visualize what can be done to increase the probability of success. In this way, employees are motivated to think of ways of overcoming potential problems rather than accepting failure as the likely outcome of their efforts.

- Managers can clearly indicate the belief that employees can succeed if they try. In other words, employees who believe that respected others have faith in their capabilities are likely to develop positive self-efficacy and, as a result, exhibit increased performance.

- Managers can increase self-efficacy by providing positive feedback and recognition when employees perform well. Not only is such recognition rewarding, but it reinforces the employee's belief that he or she has have the capability to perform well.

- Managers can provide positive or successful experiences for their employees. This can be accomplished through training or by giving them progressively more difficult tasks to complete. However, the more difficult tasks are only given to employees who have been successful on the less difficult or intimidating activities. Simply put, little successes lead to bigger successes.

- Managers can increase self-efficacy by providing models (i.e., individuals similar to employees) who exhibit desired behaviors and successful task performance. The most successful modeling occurs when the model exhibits only correct behavior rather than showing the employee incorrect behavior leading to failure.

- Managers can educate employees to the fact that initial feelings of tension and anxiety about task performance are natural and not a sign of incompetence. Such negative feelings can be overcome by self-talk, visualizing, relaxation exercises, and recognizing that it is possible to learn from one's mistakes.

6. Developmental Action Plans Implemented

Out of each FCC encounter comes a set of action-oriented sub-plans designed to improve the employee's performance. It is implementation of these interim action plans that acts as the focal point of future observations, recordings, and ratings. The action plans are interim because the resulting data become the input for the next FCC encounter. This process is repeated throughout the formal review period of the traditional PAR process (i.e., outer loop) and should result in the incremental improvement of the subordinate.

7. Thorough End-of-Period Rating

Given the interim data collected and the incremental improvement demonstrated by the subordinate, the manager is in a strong position to make an accurate, objective, and fair final rating of the subordinate on each of the relevant job dimensions. It is this final rating that will be discussed during the formal review meeting between the manager and the subordinate. In those instances where subordinates have been asked to assess themselves, and customer input has been received, the manager and subordinate can discuss the different rating perspectives.

8. Performance Appraisal and Review Session

The final PAR session between the manager and subordinate is designed to generate an agreed-upon end-of-period rating for each subordinate. It is at this time that the manager and subordinate resolve differences and formalize goals and objectives for the next appraisal period (cell 9). Final ratings are also recorded for present or future administrative decisions (cell 10).

The data generated during the inner loop need not become part of the employee's permanent file within the human resource department. It is the output of the final review meeting and the relevant behavioral support for the subordinate's final rating that become part of an employee's permanent file. Manager–subordinate agreement is easier to achieve if ongoing FCC encounters have taken place throughout the appraisal period. Separating developmental data from information kept in the employee's permanent file increases the probability that the subordinate will be open and receptive to behavioral change during the inner loop.

In those instances where final agreement cannot be reached between the manager and a subordinate, the subordinate should be encouraged to attach a written explanation as to the rationale or basis for the disagreement. Organizations that have appraisal systems, and encourage employees to use them, not only ensure perceptions of organizational justice, but also ensure the likelihood that the organization will win if the decision is challenged in court.[52]

Alternate Sources of Appraisal

In 1977 a Conference Board survey indicated that 95 percent of U.S. organizations relied upon appraisals carried out by an employee's immediate supervisor. A more recent survey of Fortune 100 companies found that only two companies used self-appraisals, fewer than 3 percent used peer assessments, and none of the reporting organizations used subordinate appraisals. The implication, therefore, is that North American companies continue to rely upon supervisory assessments when evaluating employee performance. Neverthe-less, it is our belief that by using multiple sources of information, managers can increase the accuracy and usefulness of employee appraisal.

Before discussing alternate sources of performance appraisal let us consider why supervisory assessment (*a*) continues to dominate the appraisal process and (*b*) may not be the best alternative available.[53]

Supervisory Appraisal

A traditional or formal organizational structure implies that managers are respon-sible for their staff. As part of their formal responsibilities, managers set goals and assess each employee's performance to ensure that departmental and organizational goals are achieved. Traditionally, managers also have the responsibility of rewarding those individuals who successfully carry out their duties and achieve the goals they were assigned. Similarly, many individuals continue to believe that an employee's immediate supervisor is the best person to assess his or her performance. Finally, by moving away from super-visory appraisals, organizations run the risk of weakening managerial power. Given these perceptions, we should not be surprised by the survey results presented above.

Such perceptions, however, may obscure other facts that, if known, would encourage managers to collect assessment data from the full range of available sources of information. In many organizational settings, managers may spend as little as 1 percent of their time observing employee performance.[54] For example, in electrical generating facilities, instrumentation, maintenance, and operation supervisors often do not directly observe their subordinates. Subordinates are out in the plant carrying out their assigned jobs while the supervisor is at another location carrying out his or her responsibilities. As a result, these supervisors rarely observe what the employee is doing.

Managers who carry out performance appraisals know that they may have to take into account the responses of dissatisfied employees or others within the organization to appraisal results. As a result, managers who carry out performance appraisals often find the experience an emotional one.[55] Super-visors can also contaminate employee ratings by allowing personal views of how work should be performed, rather than how well the task is done.[56] In both cases, the result can be subjective or biased ratings rather than objec-tive employee assessments.

The following are three alternatives to supervisory assessment.[57]

Peer Assessment

Peer appraisals have been found to be more reliable and valid predictors of job performance than supervisory assessments.[58] Equally important is that accu-rate peer appraisals can be made after only short periods of time[59] and even when employees have been transferred between organizational groups.[60]

Additionally, the effectiveness of peer assessments does not appear to be affected when co-workers are aware that their ratings could be used to allocate future rewards.[61] Peer appraisals may also have an advantage in the courts as they are "in alignment with the North American judicial system, namely, a judgment by one's peers."[62]

The effectiveness of peer appraisal reflects three key factors.[63] First, peers have the benefit of daily interactions during which time they can effectively observe and assess the performance of co-workers. As a result, peers often have greater access to job-relevant information. Next, multiple raters increase the number of independent ratings. When multiple ratings are possible, the average of such ratings is often more accurate than a single evaluation. Third, when done correctly, peer assessments are anonymous and thus maximize rater honesty.

A potential criticism of peer appraisals is that in large groups it becomes too time-consuming for co-workers to rate one another. To overcome the problem of excessive time and effort needed to complete the process, managers can work with team members to identify a reduced number of peers who would be asked to rate a particular individual.

Self-Appraisal

Along with peer assessments, managers can also draw upon the subordinate's own assessment of personal performance. Two major benefits are obtained when managers build self-assessment into the appraisal system. It effectively integrates the employee into the appraisal process and allows for self-management or self-regulation.[64] As a practice, self-appraisal requires employees to set their own performance and improvement goals, monitor their own on-the-job behavior, and engage in self-reward and punishment.

For example, once the supervisor and employees have met to discuss performance criteria (e.g., the BOS instrument), employees monitor their own behavior over the full evaluation period. Because employees clearly know the standards against which their performance will be measured, they can engage in self-development or correction. Therefore, when employees meet with their boss to evaluate performance, they usually have already improved, and are well prepared for the assessment meeting with their manager. Such preparation and self-development facilitate joint problem solving during the appraisal meeting. Self-appraisals also increase the subordinate's dignity, change the manager's role from judge to counselor and coach, and increase the employee's understanding of what is expected of him or her.[65]

Critical to the success of any attempt to make self-appraisals work is the manager's ability to ensure that the employee's self-appraisals are objective. This can be accomplished by first telling employees that their appraisals will be compared to other performance measures.[66] Managers can also provide employees with information about how co-workers are, in general, performing.[67] Such information gives employees benchmarks against which to rate their own performance. Finally, managers can increase accuracy of self-appraisals by requiring employees to document their ratings.[68] For example, the manager can require that all self-ratings discussed during an appraisal meeting be supported with behavioral support statements or critical incidents.

Subordinate Appraisals

A third alternate source of information that can be used when evaluating performance is the employee's own subordinates. Subordinate input enhances the appraisal process in three ways.[69] First, because subordinates observe managerial performance from below, they provide a valuable and unique perspective on how well the manager is performing. At the same time, subordinates represent multiple sources of information that can help offset the organization's traditional reliance on one rater—the boss. Finally, by allowing subordinates an opportunity to assess their boss, the organization is demonstrating its commitment to employee empowerment.

While there are few systematic assessments of the effectiveness of subordinate appraisal, anecdotal reports from such companies as IBM, RCA, Syntex, Weyerhaeuser Company, and Libbey-Owens-Ford offer support to the argument that it can help improve managerial effectiveness, develop staff, select and promote employees, change the organization's culture, and further corporate strategic plans.[70] For example, 1975 and 1985 survey data at RCA demonstrated that when compared to the traditional supervisor-only approach to performance feedback, managers preferred feedback from multiple sources, including input from subordinates.[71] At Weyerhaeuser, a study by Latham, Fay, and Saari demonstrated that when a composite of supervisory and subordinate ratings was used, subordinate appraisals were more accurate on some BOS items.[72] When comparing subordinate appraisals with assessment center results, the personnel manager of a highway patrol organization found that subordinate assessments were better predictors of future supervisory success and cost only one-twentieth of their current appraisal system. Last, a recent survey indicated that although less than 8 percent of responding companies used subordinate appraisals, those that did considered their appraisal system to be highly effective.[73]

It is also noteworthy that survey evidence suggests managers may be receptive to the use of subordinate appraisals, especially in the area of development.[74] In a recent survey of eight different organizations, ranging from retail to aerospace, two-thirds of responding managers indicated that they would approve or strongly approve of the use of subordinate appraisals. Only 17 percent of the responding managers disapproved or strongly disapproved. When asked if they would find subordinate appraisals useful for development, three-quarters of the managers responded definitely to extremely definite. Only 6 percent of the managers indicated that subordinate input would be of limited or no value. Acceptance dropped off significantly when subordinate appraisals were used for administrative decisions or when given equal weight with supervisory ratings.[75] Table 13.2 indicates those areas in which managers would be most/least receptive to subordinate appraisals.[76]

The Problem of Rater Error[77]

In our discussion of a well-designed PAR system, it was argued that there is a logical set of skills that must be applied if performance appraisal is to work well (see Figure 13.6.). The two final skills necessary for effective PAR are the manager's ability to rate subordinates based upon objective behavioral observations and his or her ability to give meaningful and timely feedback. Unfortunately, errors can occur when individuals are asked to assess the performance of others. For our purpose, we will define a rating error as "a difference between the output of a human judgment process and that of an objective, accurate assessment uncolored by bias, prejudice, or other subjective, extraneous influences."[78] The following six errors frequently occur when a manager appraises a subordinate's performance.

Positive and Negative Leniency

Positive leniency occurs when a subordinate is rated higher than is justified. If managers make the assumption that by the time subordinates get to their department all the marginal performers have already been eliminated, then they are likely to exhibit positive leniency. Research has also indicated that where managers anticipate the need to give face-to-face feedback to subordinates, they will inflate employee ratings.[79] Positive leniency can also occur when the rater believes that poor performance has been a result of external or

TABLE 13.2   Appropriateness of Subordinate Ratings

Most Appropriate	*Least Appropriate*
Leadership	Planning and organizing
Oral communications	Budgeting
Delegation	Goal setting
Coordination of team efforts	Decision making
Interest in subordinates	Creativity
Performance feedback ability	Quantity of work
Providing work guidance	Quality of work
Composure and self-control	Analytical ability
Interpersonal relations	Technical ability
Written communications	Developing subordinates

Figure 13.6

Skill sequence for effective performance evaluation

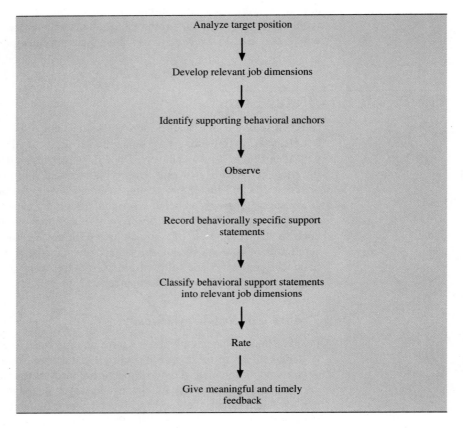

Analyze target position

↓

Develop relevant job dimensions

↓

Identify supporting behavioral anchors

↓

Observe

↓

Record behaviorally specific support statements

↓

Classify behavioral support statements into relevant job dimensions

↓

Rate

↓

Give meaningful and timely feedback

environmental factors (e.g., a death in the family or the need to take care of dependents).[80] Positive leniency, however, inappropriately raises the expectations of employees and increases demands for raises, promotions, increased responsibility, or more challenging work.

Negative leniency occurs when a subordinate is rated lower than is justified by actual performance. If the rater holds to the assumption that "if I have to suffer so do all my subordinates," then it is likely that the rater will lean in the negative leniency direction. The consequence of negative leniency is that subordinates give up trying because they expect negative ratings regardless of their efforts or output. Negative leniency is also likely to adversely affect the relationship between the manager and his or her subordinates.[81]

Central Tendency

A seemingly safe approach to rating subordinates is for managers to rate all subordinates close to average. If a subordinate does well in the future the manager can state, "See, I told you the employee wasn't that bad."

Conversely, if the subordinate does poorly in the future, the manager can state, "What did you expect?"[82] Unfortunately, by refusing to use the extremes of the rating scales, the manager is failing to effectively differentiate between subordinates and thereby threatens the principle of differential reward. In other words, the manager is limiting his ratings to a narrow range and by definition reducing rating variance.

By defining job dimensions behaviorally, the rater finds it more difficult to rate all subordinates as average. This is especially true when the manager is forced to defend his or her rating with behavioral data collected over the total evaluation period.

Halo

A common rater error is the tendency for one overall impression or dimension to inappropriately influence all remaining job dimensions. Such rater bias is likely to occur when the rater's job knowledge is limited, when job dimensions are poorly defined, or when observational support is unavailable. Halo error may also reflect the rater's tendency to place new performance information in a categorization schema that has already been established.[83] If a manager has already categorized an employee as outstanding or above average, he or she is likely to cognitively recall this classification when assessing performance in the future.

When considering the issue of halo error, it is important to differentiate between halo error and true halo or halo effect.[84] True halo occurs when the abilities needed to perform well on several job dimensions are either identical or highly correlated. Under such conditions it is possible for true halo to improve rater accuracy.[85] As a result, employees who perform well, or poorly, on their jobs should be expected to receive similar ratings across job dimensions.

First-Impressions Error

This error occurs when the rater allows initial events to distort the overall rating given to the subordinate at the end of an evaluation period. The probability of a manager making this error increases the less frequently the manager observes employee behavior and when the manager limits observations to the end of the review period. There is also evidence to suggest that a primacy error can affect the rater's appraisal of performance even when managers collect information over the entire review period.[86] Managers pay attention to early information collected about an employee's performance and then pay less attention to performance information received later in the appraisal period. When this occurs, employees who do outstanding work during the first month on the job but then produce mediocre results for the next five months may continue to receive outstanding appraisals.

Similar-to-Me Error

Similar-to-me error relates to the tendency for individuals to rate those individuals who are similar to themselves on non-job-related factors higher than those individuals who are different. Conversely, the dissimilar-to-me error occurs when the rater lowers the rating because the employee is different. The actual characteristic(s) selected to assess the degree of similarity or dissimilarity will be unique to each individual rate and will reflect his or her needs and value structure.

Upon reviewing the literature relating to the similar-to-me error, Latham and Wexley concluded that "it would appear that when employees make their work visible to appraisers, when appraisers and appraisees together clarify objectives and task responsibilities, and when the appraiser uses behaviorally based appraisal scales, ratee characteristics, such as age, race, and sex, have negligible effect on the resulting performance appraisal."[87]

Contrast-Effects Error

The contrast-effects error occurs when the rater bases his or her rating on differences between employees rather than assessing the employee's performance relative to some predetermined standard. For example, a manager who has supervised only poor performers may, when faced with average performance, rate the employee outstanding. When comparing the employee's performance to how well he or she fulfilled the requirements of the job, the manager would rate the employee average. However, when compared to the past performance of below-average employees, he or she comes across as outstanding.

Efforts to Reduce Rater Error

It is possible to attempt to correct the problem of rater error on several levels. By using a behaviorally based system that reflects a detailed job analysis, it is possible to reduce rater error. The result is a set of clear, specific, and non-overlapping performance criteria.[88] Such a system also requires that the rater become familiar with relevant job dimensions and supporting behaviors that are considered critical to employee performance. Knowing what to look for makes it easier for the manager to recognize relevant behavior, if it occurs. A behavioral system also sensitizes the manager to the fact that generalized statements about employees are not acceptable, unless there is sufficient evidence to document these statements.

As indicated above, it is also important that employees make certain that their performance is visible to the manager. Employees must also ensure that the goals and expectations against which they will be compared are clearly understood. Should this not be the case, employees should work with their boss to clarify both expectations and job responsibilities.

It is also possible to reduce rater errors by exposing managers to rater training. This training can emphasize the actual ratings given subordinates,[89] or the process by which the manager goes about collecting and processing the data used to develop his or her ratings.[90] For training to have the desired effect of reducing rater errors, it must allow trainees to actively participate in applying the behaviors during the training session, provide feedback on trainee performance, provide structures so as not to waste trainee time, ensure that trainees see the relevance of training material to on-the-job performance, allocate sufficient time to each rater error, and give trainees an opportunity to practice newly acquired skills on the job.[91]

Training alone, however, can not be expected to eliminate all rater errors. First, rating errors reflect habits that are difficult to overcome. Second, the effects of training may be outweighed by political, emotional, or situational considerations. For example, managers may be more concerned about a negative employee response to a harsh appraisal, or prefer to downplay employee deficiencies or development and instead use the process to reward or motivate employees.

Feedback: Its Role in Maintaining Effective Performance Appraisal and Review

Feedback can be defined as the process of data sharing by which individuals communicate back to others their perceptions of, or affective response to, behaviors that have taken place or are in the process of taking place.[92] Behavioral scientists have demonstrated the importance of performance feedback on goals designed to maintain and improve on-the-job performance.[93]

Unfortunately, managers reduce the benefits of performance feedback by being less willing to give feedback when subordinates fail to meet performance standards than when they succeed in meeting these standards.[94] Such reluctance by managers can adversely affect both the content and frequency of performance feedback.[95] For example, managers may distort the feedback given subordinates to minimize the number of interpersonal conflicts. The manager's reluctance to give negative feedback, however, is likely to reflect situational characteristics, e.g., pressure from top management to provide negative feedback, relevance of subordinate performance on the manager's own payoffs, and whether the subordinate's poor performance represents a downward trend.[96] To help ensure that PAR has the desired effect on employee performance, it is important that managers develop an effective feedback style.

Characteristics of Effective Feedback

Managers must take the necessary steps to open up channels of communications to facilitate meaningful and timely feedback. The following represents a list of characteristics associated with effective feedback. The more of these characteristics the manager builds into the feedback process, the greater the likelihood that feedback will have its intended impact.[97]

Develop an Atmosphere of Trust

For feedback to be effective, the atmosphere in which it takes place must be characterized by a feeling of trust between the manager and the subordinate. Put another way, the subordinate must believe that the feedback is designed to be helpful.[98] If these conditions are not met, the subordinate will block or ignore the feedback.

Management can win the subordinate's trust by being fair, not acting on incomplete information, disclosing all possible information, by trusting subordinates and protecting their interests, and above all else, by exhibiting behavior that is consistent with subordinates' values and beliefs. Trust can also be facilitated if management attempts to explain why some actions that are in conflict with the subordinate's values and beliefs were taken. Ultimately, subordinate trust and openness increase the likelihood that feedback will be requested from the boss.

Feedback Should Be Specific Rather than General

For feedback to have its intended impact on the subordinate, it should be specific. As indicated above, if management allows communications to remain ambiguous, subordinates are free to interpret the message in a way that satisfies their needs, allows them to do what's easiest, or to do what is implied by the situation. In all three of these cases, the probability is that the intended message will be lost and the positive impact of the feedback attempt will be minimal. Consider the following two statements and choose the one you believe will have the greatest impact on the receiver.

"If you don't improve your attitude in the next three weeks I will be forced to discipline you."

"The last three times I asked you to do something, you refused. Instead, you told me why it couldn't be done that way. In the future when I ask you to do something, and I tell you it has to be done that way, I'd appreciate it if you just did what you were told. If you don't, you'll have to be disciplined."

Clearly the second statement is much more behaviorally specific than the first. The undesirable behavior occurred three times, the subordinate continues to tell the manager why a request cannot be carried out, he or she is told why this is an unacceptable behavior, and then is told the consequences if such behavior continues in the future. By being behaviorally specific there should be no doubt in the subordinate's mind what you are attempting to communicate.

Feedback Should Be Descriptive Rather than Evaluative

Subordinates frequently become egoistically involved with what they are doing, with artifacts within their work space, and with processes that they may have had a hand in developing. Subordinates also tend to ignore communications that challenge their self-concept. Subordinates who have a high propensity to respond in this way are likely to resist, or block out, any feedback that is evaluative. Evaluative feedback assesses the goodness or badness of the events that have been taking place within the work environment or the individuals themselves.

To ensure that the subordinate does not tune out the incoming feedback, the manager should rely on descriptive feedback rather than evaluative feedback (that is, describe what events took place within a particular situation while at the same time informing the subordinate of the impact these events have had on the manager and others within the situation). For example, if a subordinate has offended someone within the department, it is ill advised for the manager to attack the person, with "John, you are truly an insensitive S.O.B.! I think you should stop acting toward people that way." Not only are these statements too general, they are likely to attack John's self-concept. Consequently, they will have little positive impact on John. A descriptive statement such as, "During our staff meeting yesterday, it was only after you described Mary's work as sloppy that she refused to participate in the discussion," is less likely to result in a negative reaction from the receiver because it is specific and does not directly attack John's self-concept.

Feedback Should Be Well Timed

During the subordinate's day there are multiple pressures that affect receptivity to incoming messages. Managers must ask themselves, before attempting feedback, whether it is a good time to do so. More specifically, is the subordinate in a state of readiness to respond positively to incoming feedback?

What factors must the manager consider before giving feedback? Clearly, the emotional state of the subordinate should be considered. The manager must also consider the time of day. It is unwise to attempt to give feedback just before the individual leaves for home. Also, certain times of the day are likely to be busier than others. Where possible, the manager should select those time periods that are the least active for the subordinate. There will also exist individual differences concerning the level of personal readiness. The key is to know your subordinates, their schedules, stress levels, emotional states, and their overall personalities to ensure maximum benefit from your timing.

There is a rule managers should follow whenever possible. That is, feedback should be given as soon after the precipitating event as possible. The "ASAP" principle helps ensure that the subordinate will make the appropriate link between the positive or negative feedback and the event that triggered the need for feedback.

Select an Appropriate Location

The level of subordinate readiness is often affected by the environment in which the feedback is attempted. To ensure maximum impact, the manager must assess the relative impact of the location in which the feedback is attempted. The location should be considered nonthreatening to the subordinate. If the manager's office intimidates the subordinate, then it may be necessary to relocate to a neutral location. Disruptions are also likely to affect the level of subordinate receptiveness. Therefore, the manager should make every effort to minimize the number of disruptions (i.e., inform the secretary that you do not want to be disturbed, or that he or she should hold your calls).

Site selection should also be affected by the nature of the feedback being given. In general, negative feedback should be given privately. As soon as co-workers know that feedback is to occur they are all ears. This occurs because co-workers want to be successful in their environment. By listening to feedback being given to a co-worker, employees can learn how to be more effective in the future. Unfortunately, the employee also knows that others will be listening and will become defensive. The subordinate does not want to lose face in front of his or her co-workers. Positive feedback should be given in public. Because the manager realizes that others will listen, he or she can educate co-workers about what should be considered appropriate behavior. If others within the department also want to receive positive feedback and recognition they will know the behaviors that will elicit positive feedback from the boss.

When the manager makes a decision on the location for giving positive or negative feedback, the above guidelines do not always apply. There may be situations where the manager is forced to give negative feedback in public because of timing considerations or because the subordinate has not responded positively to feedback in the past and has opted for a confrontation. Similarly, the manager may be dealing with a sensitive subordinate who finds public recognition embarrassing. If this is the case then it may be more appropriate to give positive feedback in private.

Feedback Should Be Appropriate to the Receiver

Managers must continually be alert to individual differences when dealing with subordinates. Differences in personality, needs, values, expectations, perceived self, etc., will affect the subordinate's response to any attempt to provide feedback. Effective managers will take the necessary steps to know their subordinates well enough to predict how they might respond to different feedback strategies. Based on this knowledge, managers alter their feedback strategy to ensure the maximum impact and the greatest probability that personal goals will be achieved.

If a subordinate is emotional, or insecure, the manager's strategy must reflect this fact. Such individuals will require a more subtle, limited, and sensitive feedback style to ensure that the subordinate does not withdraw or block out the feedback message. Conversely, if a subordinate is dogmatic and close minded, the manager should again alter his or her strategy to adjust to these characteristics. Feedback under these conditions is more likely to be direct, forceful, and repetitive. If the feedback strategy does not accurately consider idiosyncratic differences between subordinates, it is likely to fail. At the very least, its impact will be diminished.

Avoid Feedback Overload

When exposed to negative feedback, individuals differ as to the amount of feedback tolerated. Perceptive managers adjust their style to the subordinate's unique ability to absorb negative feedback. It is as if each subordinate has a certain amount of psychological cushion that allows him or her to accept and respond to the negative feedback being received. When this cushion is used up, the subordinate becomes defensive and will often refuse to accept any further attempts by management to provide negative feedback. The subordinate may also withdraw psychologically or physically from the situation, thereby adversely affecting the manager–subordinate interface. This interface may be threatened directly if excessive negative feedback causes the subordinate to develop a negative perception of his or her boss, moving to an "I'm OK, You're Not OK" life position.

Make Certain the Receiver Has Understood What You Have Said

In every feedback exchange the possibility exists for the subordinate to engage in half listening or fake listening. When this occurs, the subordinate gives verbal and nonverbal cues that indicate the feedback has been received and understood. Unfortunately, in reality the message has not been correctly received.

To prevent half listening or fake listening from occurring, the manager must verify that the subordinate has received and understood the message. This can be achieved by asking how the subordinate might go about implementing the changes called for by the feedback message and the time table for implementing it.

Realize That Feedback Will Improve with Practice

During early attempts to practice, the manager should select situations in which the receiver is likely to be receptive and supportive. It is also suggested that during initial efforts the manager devote considerable time preparing for the upcoming feedback encounter. Preparation should include the writing out of a flexible script and pre-session practice. A well thought out, flexible script does not require any memorization, but rather provides a general guide for giving feedback. As such, it allows the manager to vary both content and style to fit the situation. Throughout the learning process, managers must also be willing to learn from their mistakes. Ultimately, the manager will gain confidence in his or her ability to give timely and meaningful feedback (i.e., the manager's effectiveness and comfort level should increase with practice).

Benefits of Giving Feedback

To the degree that feedback helps correct undesirable behavior, reinforces desired behavior, helps the employee develop an accurate self-image, satisfies employee needs, and improves informational content, it will enhance organizational performance. Let us briefly consider these benefits of giving meaningful and timely feedback.

1. Opportunity for Needed Change or Behavior Maintenance. Feedback can be effectively used to ensure that actual performance is consistent with the intended or agreed-upon standards communicated during the goal-setting encounter. When a deviation occurs, it is in the manager's best interest to act quickly to communicate this fact to the subordinate. Only when subordinates are aware of deviation can they be corrected. Conversely, if subordinates are performing according to agreed-upon standards, or are performing above standards, managers should communicate their satisfaction to the subordinates. Such recognition is likely to ensure continued performance.

2. Development of an Accurate Self-Image. For a subordinate to maximize his or her contribution to departmental success, it is important that he or she has an accurate self-image. One of the most effective mechanisms for obtaining this is interpersonal feedback, especially from one's boss. If a subordinate's self-image is low because of no feedback, or inaccurate feedback, the subordinate may withdraw, reduce personal effort, or fail to take advantage of training opportunities. In other instances, an inaccurate low self-image may motivate the subordinate to take training, or otherwise engage in self-development, in areas where he or she is already competent.

Conversely, if subordinates develop a self-image that is too positive because of inaccurate feedback, they may not engage in necessary training and development activities. Even worse, subordinates who have an inflated self-image may engage in activities they should not attempt. For example, assume that an employee incorrectly believes that he or she is able to diagnose and repair equipment breakdowns. When a breakdown occurs that is beyond his or her ability to fix, the employee may try anyway. The result may be damaged equipment, alienated clients, or personal injury to someone in the department.

3. Fulfillment of Interpersonal Needs. All individuals within the work environment want to fulfill personal needs. If the subordinate wants to belong and have a feeling of self-worth, feedback from his or her boss can satisfy this need. Simply put, managers who are willing to spend the time giving subordinates constructive feedback can help make subordinates feel good about themselves.

4. Improvement in Information Content. Feedback increases the probability that both sides of the manager–subordinate interface will have the needed information to function effectively. By providing feedback to the subordinate, the manager ensures that the subordinate knows what the boss is thinking. Once the subordinate has access to this information, he or she can further enhance the informational content available to the two parties by either agreeing or disagreeing with the feedback received.

5. Facilitation of Mutual Problem Solving. Ultimately, many individuals give and receive feedback because they want to solve an existing problem. For example, in the case of performance evaluation, feedback can be used by a manager to improve the performance of a marginal employee. To the degree that feedback improves informational content, helps correct undesirable behavior, can be used to reinforce desired behavior, and helps improve one's self-concept, it will facilitate the problem-solving process.

Summary

Performance evaluation plays a key role in ensuring that subordinates are performing at acceptable levels and that the manager–subordinate interface is being properly managed. Performance evaluation provides the manager with the required data to make decisions in the areas of motivation, development, and administration. To be effective, however, the process of development must be separated from the motivational and administrative elements. This separation can be accomplished by emphasizing subordinate development on a day-to-day basis and using the PAR data to facilitate semi-formal coaching, counseling, and feedback. Administrative and long-term motivational issues should be emphasized during the formal end-of-period meeting with the subordinate.

To effectively carry out performance evaluation, the manager must develop a set of integrated behaviors necessary to carry out the process. Specifically, the manager must be able to analyze the jobs he or she is responsible for. Once relevant job dimensions and support behaviors have been identified and communicated to subordinates, it is the manager's responsibility to observe, record, classify, and rate subordinate performance. It is the manager's personal assessment of the subordinate's performance that acts as the basis for periodic feedback, coaching, and counseling.

The test of whether the PAR process has been a success is the degree to which subordinates develop over time. This assessment can only be achieved if the PAR process is fully integrated with the goal-setting process. When goal setting and performance evaluation are linked within an ongoing PAR process, the manager has the greatest probability of developing and motivating subordinates.

APPENDIX

KEY LEARNING POINTS FOR CARRYING OUT PERFORMANCE APPRAISAL MEETING

1. Prepare for the meeting.
2. Open the PAR meeting.
3. Where appropriate, review strengths and areas of past performance.
4. Where appropriate, identify and discuss areas of weakness or poor performance.
5. Discuss and set goals with subordinate for the next relevant planning period.
6. Close the meeting.

Process Guidelines:

1. Establish rapport/two-way communication.
2. Control the meeting.
3. Probe/mirror/summarize to ensure meaningful content.

Key Learning Points

1. Effectively Prepare for the Meeting

- Select and establish an appropriate meeting environment—when and where.
- Develop, as best as possible, pre-session understanding of the individual you are meeting with (e.g., strong points, weak points; review behaviorally specific support material).
- Develop your meeting strategy prior to the actual meeting session—especially for initial meetings. Should the meeting center around development, maintenance, or remedial action?
- Complete your own planning/goal-setting activities prior to the meeting.
- Determine job goals for subordinate.
- When appropriate, review subordinate's progress.

2. Effectively Open the PAR Meeting

- Meet the employee at the door, say hello, be sincere, and show enthusiasm.
- Deliver a structured opening statement designed to explain key points to the employee and to explain typical employee questions. For example:
    Inform employee of what will happen during the meeting.
    Indicate the overall/general importance of the PAR meeting.
    Emphasize the importance of development.
    Indicate that the employee should feel free to make any comments or ask any questions that appear relevant.
    Indicate that you will be taking notes, and why.
    Reassure the employee.

An Example: Structured Opening Statement

As you know, we are here to review your performance over the last six months. Since this is your first evaluation, I plan to review your performance on the six job dimensions we discussed when you were first hired. As you recall, these were the general skill dimensions most directly related to success as a personnel director. By jointly discussing your performance on these dimensions, I believe we can best assess how well you have been doing. I will also point out those areas where I believe improvement could be obtained. However, it is important that I get your opinion in these potential areas of improvement. With your help we can jointly set future goals designed to further develop you as a personnel director. I also want to make it clear that you should feel free to make any comments you want and to ask any questions you might want answered. This is your meeting and I want your input. If we work together on these dimensions, I think we can make some real progress. Finally, I should mention that I will be taking notes, which I will keep as part of your general file in my office. They will be for my eyes only. Before we continue, are there any questions or comments that you would like to make?

3. Review Strengths and Areas of Past Performance

- If appropriate, present those areas where you rate the subordinate more highly than he/she rates himself/herself or where improvement has occurred.
- Review attainment steps set during previous session.
- Assess past performance and reinforce where appropriate.

4. Review Weaknesses and Areas of Poor or Unsatisfactory Performance

- If self-appraisals are used carefully and without criticism, present your view on areas where you rate the employee more poorly than he/she has reported.
- Discuss problem areas in an open and receptive manner.
- If required, support your general observations with specific support statements.
- Help individual identify constraints which may have inhibited progress.
- Attempt to identify behaviors which prevented the subordinate's success and those behaviors which facilitated the subordinate's success.
- Allow subordinate adequate opportunity to respond to negative observations.
- When consensus on problem areas has been reached, establish improvement objectives and related attainment steps.

5. Discuss and Set Goals

- Specify (agree upon) the standard or target to be reached.
- Specify (agree upon) how the performance in question will be measured.
- (Jointly) prioritize goals.

- Optional step: specify (agree upon) relevant set of attainment steps.
- Clearly articulate the consequences of successful performance—ensure that consequences are acceptable to the subordinate.
- Specify (agree upon) follow-up procedure.

6. Closing the Meeting

- Indicate your personal appreciation for the subordinate's help, time, and cooperation.
- Repeat agreed-upon goals and objectives as well as relevant attainment steps.
- Repeat the benefits to him or her and the organization.
- Indicate the type of follow-up, if any.
- Ask for any final questions, concerns, and comments.
- If it appears that this employee is a problem employee, it may be necessary to write down the agreed-upon attainment steps.
- Thank the employee again for his or her cooperation and escort him or her to the door.

Process Guidelines

1. Establish Rapport/Two-Way Communications

- Ask open-ended questions rather than those permitting a simple yes/no answer.
- Allow the subordinate to respond fully without cutting him or her off.
- Use good eye contact when listening/talking to the subordinate.
- Nod in agreement where appropriate.
- Respond in full to all the subordinate's questions.
- Encourage the subordinate to express whatever he or she feels.
- Reinforce the subordinate's cooperation.
- Attempt to put to rest any early concerns the subordinate might have.

2. Control the Meeting

- Keep track of time.
- Move from one topic/issue/dimension to the next as each is adequately dealt with.
- Skip topics/issues/dimensions that have already been adequately dealt with.
- Keep the subordinate from getting off on an unrelated (unimportant) tangent.
- Keep the subordinate from rambling on about a point already explained.
- Follow up on earlier topics/issues/dimensions if new information is offered.

3. Probing/Repeating/Summarizing to Ensure Meaningful Content

- Obtain clarification of subordinate's point by further questioning.
- Obtain understanding by repeating or paraphrasing the subordinate's comments.
- Ask for elaboration by using such words as: how, what, when, why, and where.
- Ask for critical incidents of on-the-job events to support statements made.
- During the session, periodically summarize what the subordinate has stated.

Exercises

13.1 Individual Feedback

The relevant question concerning feedback is not "Should we give feedback?" but "How do we give feedback so that it works?" This is especially true when negotiating new role responsibilities within a functioning work group. (The instructor will distribute a list of 17 characteristics of effective feedback.) The degree to which you exhibit these behaviors will greatly determine the success of your feedback efforts. However, knowledge is only part of the answer. You also must be able to carry out these steps effectively in a real-life encounter with another person. Before giving feedback or negotiating new role responsibilities with others, take time to practice your skill. Please carry out the steps outlined below.

Step 1. The class will break up into groups of two. Group members should determine who should be classified A and B.

Step 2. Individually read the Mini Case: Facts about Larry Benton (p. 577). Next, complete the feedback sheet, using the information in the mini case. You can also make additional assumptions about Larry and the situation being described. The only constraint is that assumptions are reasonable for a utility employing about 5,000 workers. The additional assumptions may prove helpful when completing Item 4 of the feedback sheet.

Step 3. Plan a feedback session with Larry. Build into your planned feedback session many of the characteristics of effective feedback on the list provided by the instructor. Individuals should also consider how they might respond to an actual feedback session if they were Larry Benton. (Approximately 20 minutes)

Step 4. Individual A will begin giving meaningful and accurate feedback to individual B. In this case, B will play the role of Larry Benton. Attempt to build in as many as possible of the characteristics of effective feedback. After A has completed the feedback process, reverse roles. At both times, the receiver of the feedback is allowed to ask for clarification and/or offer additional information.

At the end of each feedback exchange, the two group members should assess the degree to which the 17 steps of effective feedback were carried out. They should also assess the degree to which the receiver understood and accepted as accurate, the feedback sent, and proved willing to change or maintain his or her behavior.

Step 5. The class will assemble and group members will share their experiences.

Feedback Sheet

Instructions: *Please take 10 minutes to complete the items below. You should complete each item with Larry Benton as the focus.*

It would be more comfortable and beneficial for me if you would...

1. *Continue doing the following things:*

2. *Do the following things more often:*

3. *Do the following things less often or stop doing them:*

4. *Begin doing these things:*

MINI CASE:
FACTS ABOUT LARRY BENTON

You are a member of a small task force established by the president of EverBright Electrical to address several key issues facing the organization. The president also wants the task force to demonstrate how effective teams can be at EverBright. Given the utility's move to privatization, your task force is considering how to maintain high levels of motivation. For the most part, you are satisfied with the performance of the task force. The sole exception is Larry Benton. Larry appears to be so self-centered that he seems to be unaware of the impact that he has on other members of the task force. His behavior, however, is threatening the team climate the president hopes the task force will develop.

Unfortunately, no one has taken the initiative to deal with Larry's behavior. Task force members lack the skills to handle this problem. Consequently, they have avoided the issue and have directed their attention to the technical issues of motivation and privatization. In order to determine what you should do about changing Larry's behaviors, you review the past several meetings.

- Larry never appears to have free time to attend scheduled meetings. As a result, the task force has on two occasions postponed its meeting.

- Second, when the group discussed the location of future meetings, Larry continually argued that they should be held in his office.

- Larry is always late, even when they are scheduled for his office.

- Larry is rarely prepared to discuss the matter at hand unless he is making the presentation. Considerable time is wasted waiting for Larry to arrive and bringing Larry up-to-date.

- Larry has a bad habit of talking out of turn in a loud voice when someone else has the floor. This may explain why Larry is never on top of the current discussion.

- Larry rambles in discussions. Two meetings ended with Larry talking endlessly about an issue that had already been decided.

- Larry is inflexible and rarely changes his mind once made up. This occurs even when sound and logical arguments by other members show why his position is wrong. This behavior tends to increase the frustration of other task force members more.

- On several occasions, Larry has upset task force members with his personal comments (e.g., he told Hal that his report was a mess—that Larry's five-year-old daughter could have done a better job; he told Bob he would not allow his staff to take part in Bob's attempt to streamline the MIS system; he badgered Janet to the verge of tears).

- On at least three occasions, several members believed that Larry had fabricated information about the operations of his department and how he had motivated his people.

Fortunately, there are several examples of positive behavior in Larry's performance as a task force member.

- Larry takes the initiative in bringing others into the conversation, especially members who have remained quiet for a long period of time.

- Larry makes well-prepared and organized presentations before the task force. He also is a whiz in the use of visuals.

- Whenever the meeting begins to flounder, Larry is the first to step in and take charge.

13.2 The Personnel Manager's Case: Evaluating Performance

The purpose of this exercise is to give students practice evaluating the performance of a subordinate. The case describes a typical day in the life of Alan Foster, the director of personnel for the municipality of Centerville, a small community in the Midwest. Please follow the steps outlined below.

Step 1. Read the case provided, The Administrator Performance Appraisal and Review. As you read, jot down behaviorally specific examples of the dimensions that appear on the Performance Appraisal form. For your convenience, you have been provided with two appraisal forms, that is, Behavior Observation Scales and Behaviorally Anchored Rating Scales (BOS and BARS). Your instructor will inform you which one to use for this exercise. Do not attempt to group or classify the behaviors listed.

Step 2. If you have been instructed to use the BOS appraisal instrument you are to indicate your rating for each of the 29 items listed. Each skill dimension is supported by five or six behavioral statements. In the event that you have been instructed to use the BARS instrument, you should proceed as follows. With your list of observed behaviors in front of you, group or classify each behavior under the appropriate job dimension. Use the five dimensions described on the PAR form. Rate each dimension based on your understanding of the PAR dimensions. (One and one-half hours.)

Also remember that this is a single day in the organizational life of Alan Foster; therefore, assume that behaviors described in the following case occur often.

(*Note:* **Ideally, this exercise could be assigned for nonclass time.**)

BOS Instrument

Key Behavior

A. Decisiveness—The ability to make decisions quickly, take action, make commitments, and not change one's position when challenged.

1. When given sufficient information on an important issue makes decision within allotted time.

   Almost never   1   2   3   4   5   Almost always

2. Able to make up mind and does not change position unless presented with new and contrary information to the position taken.

   Almost never   1   2   3   4   5   Almost always

3. In response to an employee's single request for a preferred vacation schedule (or work schedule) and one that is consistent with company policy and supervisory needs, immediately accepts or rejects.

   Almost never   1   2   3   4   5   Almost always

4. When allocating resources able to quickly make "yes" or "no" decisions.

   Almost never   1   2   3   4   5   Almost always

5. When confronted with multiple pieces of information easily selects the information he or she will use to make decisions.

   Almost never   1   2   3   4   5   Almost always

6. When asked by subordinate for instructions does not hesitate to give him or her directions.

   Almost never   1   2   3   4   5   Almost always

B. Leadership—The ability to take charge; to direct and coordinate the activities of others; to maintain control; to delegate where appropriate and follow up when required on a subordinate's progress.

1. During meetings is able to maintain control, complete the agenda as stated, and keep side conversations from disrupting the meeting's rhythm.

   Almost never   1   2   3   4   5   Almost always

2. When assigning a new, difficult, or important task follows up on employee's performance.

   Almost never   1   2   3   4   5   Almost always

3. Varies his or her level of monitoring of employees' progress in response to their level of experience, past performance, and importance of the task.

   Almost never   1   2   3   4   5   Almost always

(BOS Instrument continued)

4. Before delegating work ensures that subordinate is interested, has the ability, will learn from the experience, has the time, or is next employee scheduled to do the task.

Almost never   1   2   3   4   5   Almost always

5. If the team becomes sidetracked or appears unwilling to perform, steps in to give direction or set group goals.

Almost never   1   2   3   4   5   Almost always

C. Organization and Planning—The ability to establish courses of action for both one's self and others in order to accomplish desired goals; to make proper use of available resources; to be able to establish timely schedules and goals; and to set priorities when and where appropriate.

1. When making presentations comes prepared, follows agenda, and is able to find material as needed.

Almost never   1   2   3   4   5   Almost always

2. Before acting (i.e., attending meetings, making important telephone calls, assigning work to subordinates) collects appropriate support information to ensure its availability if needed.

Almost never   1   2   3   4   5   Almost always

3. Makes information and schedules available to others before asking them to participate in meetings.

Almost never   1   2   3   4   5   Almost always

4. Manages his or her time effectively by establishing schedules and setting aside time both for crises and quiet times.

Almost never   1   2   3   4   5   Almost always

5. Sets aside sufficient amounts of time to carry out planned activities or to account for environmental constraints (e.g., sets realistic timetables).

Almost never   1   2   3   4   5   Almost always

6. Informs relevant others of his or her activities so as to keep them aware of what is happening.

Almost never   1   2   3   4   5   Almost always

D. Dependability—To be willing to accept tasks and responsibilities that are within one's authority and ability zone; to provide the required time and energy to accomplish accepted tasks; to finish the tasks on time; and if unable to complete the tasks as assigned, inform the appropriate other of this fact and explain why.

(BOS Instrument continued)

1. Carries out responsibilities and attends meetings as scheduled or assigned.

   Almost never   1   2   3   4   5   Almost always

2. If work cannot be completed as assigned, informs affected individuals, and explains why as well as what the likely consequences are.

   Almost never   1   2   3   4   5   Almost always

3. Shares all relevant information with others to ensure high levels of performance from all staff.

   Almost never   1   2   3   4   5   Almost always

4. When the individual says something will get done, it gets done.

   Almost never   1   2   3   4   5   Almost always

5. Stands behind his or her staff and effectively represents their interests to top management.

   Almost never   1   2   3   4   5   Almost always

6. Carries out personal work and activities in the time allotted.

   Almost never   1   2   3   4   5   Almost always

E. Interpersonal Sensitivity—The ability to respond to and perceive the needs, emotions, and feelings of others; to deal openly with others regardless of their status, power, or position; to tolerate individual differences; and to develop positive relations with others.

1. Listens and responds to the concerns of others.

   Almost never   1   2   3   4   5   Almost always

2. Before acting or making decisions takes into consideration the interests and schedules of others.

   Almost never   1   2   3   4   5   Almost always

3. Shares information that directly affects the performance of others.

   Almost never   1   2   3   4   5   Almost always

4. Does not attack others, especially in public, for their personal shortcomings or merely because they are different or disliked.

   Almost never   1   2   3   4   5   Almost always

5. Gives recognition and support to employees.

   Almost never   1   2   3   4   5   Almost always

6. When responding to others takes into consideration their needs and values.

   Almost never   1   2   3   4   5   Almost always

BARS Instrument

Decisiveness—The ability to make decisions quickly, take action, make commitments, and not change one's position when challenged.

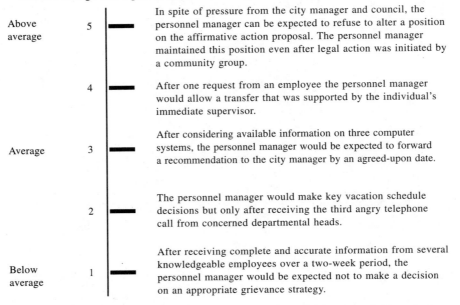

Above average	5	In spite of pressure from the city manager and council, the personnel manager can be expected to refuse to alter a position on the affirmative action proposal. The personnel manager maintained this position even after legal action was initiated by a community group.
	4	After one request from an employee the personnel manager would allow a transfer that was supported by the individual's immediate supervisor.
Average	3	After considering available information on three computer systems, the personnel manager would be expected to forward a recommendation to the city manager by an agreed-upon date.
	2	The personnel manager would make key vacation schedule decisions but only after receiving the third angry telephone call from concerned departmental heads.
Below average	1	After receiving complete and accurate information from several knowledgeable employees over a two-week period, the personnel manager would be expected not to make a decision on an appropriate grievance strategy.

Leadership—The ability to take charge; to direct and coordinate the activities of others; to maintain control; to delegate where appropriate and follow up when required on a subordinate's progress.

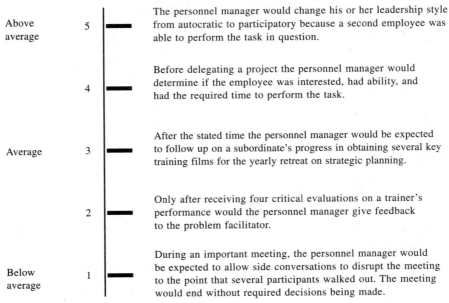

Above average	5	The personnel manager would change his or her leadership style from autocratic to participatory because a second employee was able to perform the task in question.
	4	Before delegating a project the personnel manager would determine if the employee was interested, had ability, and had the required time to perform the task.
Average	3	After the stated time the personnel manager would be expected to follow up on a subordinate's progress in obtaining several key training films for the yearly retreat on strategic planning.
	2	Only after receiving four critical evaluations on a trainer's performance would the personnel manager give feedback to the problem facilitator.
Below average	1	During an important meeting, the personnel manager would be expected to allow side conversations to disrupt the meeting to the point that several participants walked out. The meeting would end without required decisions being made.

Organization and planning—The ability to establish courses of action for both one's self and others in order to accomplish desired goals; to make proper use of available resources; to be able to establish timely schedules and goals; and to set priorities when and where appropriate.

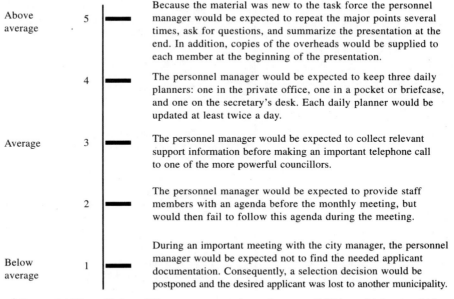

Above average	5	Because the material was new to the task force the personnel manager would be expected to repeat the major points several times, ask for questions, and summarize the presentation at the end. In addition, copies of the overheads would be supplied to each member at the beginning of the presentation.
	4	The personnel manager would be expected to keep three daily planners: one in the private office, one in a pocket or briefcase, and one on the secretary's desk. Each daily planner would be updated at least twice a day.
Average	3	The personnel manager would be expected to collect relevant support information before making an important telephone call to one of the more powerful councillors.
	2	The personnel manager would be expected to provide staff members with an agenda before the monthly meeting, but would then fail to follow this agenda during the meeting.
Below average	1	During an important meeting with the city manager, the personnel manager would be expected not to find the needed applicant documentation. Consequently, a selection decision would be postponed and the desired applicant was lost to another municipality.

Dependability—To be willing to accept tasks and responsibilities which are within a zone of authority and ability; to provide the required time and energy to accomplish accepted tasks; to finish the tasks on time; and if unable to complete the tasks as assigned inform the appropriate manager of this fact and explain why.

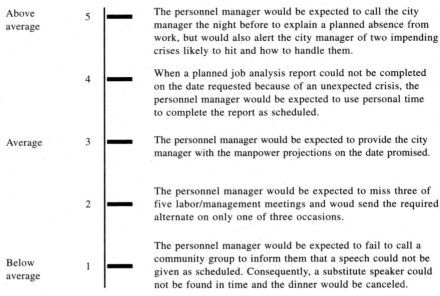

Above average	5	The personnel manager would be expected to call the city manager the night before to explain a planned absence from work, but would also alert the city manager of two impending crises likely to hit and how to handle them.
	4	When a planned job analysis report could not be completed on the date requested because of an unexpected crisis, the personnel manager would be expected to use personal time to complete the report as scheduled.
Average	3	The personnel manager would be expected to provide the city manager with the manpower projections on the date promised.
	2	The personnel manager would be expected to miss three of five labor/management meetings and woud send the required alternate on only one of three occasions.
Below average	1	The personnel manager would be expected to fail to call a community group to inform them that a speech could not be given as scheduled. Consequently, a substitute speaker could not be found in time and the dinner would be canceled.

Interpersonal sensitivity—The ability to respond to and perceive the needs, emotions, and feelings of others; to deal openly with others regardless of their status, power, or position; to tolerate individual differences; and to develop positive relationships with others.

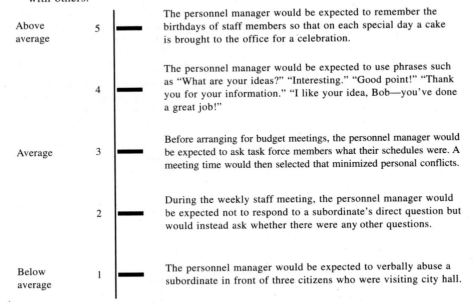

Above average	5	The personnel manager would be expected to remember the birthdays of staff members so that on each special day a cake is brought to the office for a celebration.
	4	The personnel manager would be expected to use phrases such as "What are your ideas?" "Interesting." "Good point!" "Thank you for your information." "I like your idea, Bob—you've done a great job!"
Average	3	Before arranging for budget meetings, the personnel manager would be expected to ask task force members what their schedules were. A meeting time would then selected that minimized personal conflicts.
	2	During the weekly staff meeting, the personnel manager would be expected not to respond to a subordinate's direct question but would instead ask whether there were any other questions.
Below average	1	The personnel manager would be expected to verbally abuse a subordinate in front of three citizens who were visiting city hall.

The Administrator Performance Appraisal and Review

This is the tale of Alan Foster, the director of personnel for a small municipality in the Midwest. Alan is an energetic individual who likes to be in control at all times. Unfortunately for Alan, the volume of activity in Centerville has increased dramatically. Specifically, Centerville has been earmarked as a staging and supply area for the new offshore oil drilling scheduled to begin next year. As a result, Alan has found it increasingly more difficult to stay ahead of the new demands placed on his office. A graph of his blood pressure over the past several months would remind you of a roller-coaster ride at an amusement park.

Let's spend some time with Alan to better assess how he performs as a manager. The organizational chart shows Alan's position in the city government, to whom he reports and who reports to him. Alan has recently been promoted to the director's position. Also, Centerville's city government is undergoing a series of organizational changes and an upgrading of its work environment. These changes in turn are the result of the transition in the area. The city manager has indicated that he expects a great deal from the Personnel Department.

Each morning Alan leaves for work about 7:30 A.M. so that he can pull into the parking lot about 8:00 A.M. He likes to arrive at his office 15 to 20 minutes before starting time so that he can plan his day and collect his thoughts. Today, however, as Alan drives into the parking lot he is confronted with a sign that reads "Lot Full

Today." Alan suddenly remembers the memo that came across his desk that informed staff of several special events that were being held at the Town Hall. As a result, Alan has to start hunting for a parking space downtown.

Unfortunately, few spaces are available after 8:00 A.M. (This is primarily due to the large number of construction projects in the area.) Alan spends about 25 minutes finding a parking space that is a 10-minute walk to City Hall. Instead of having 15 to 20 minutes to plan his day, Alan now is about 10 minutes late. Coming in late is becoming a habit for Alan. As he breezes into his office, he fails to say good morning to Mary, his secretary, and rushes past her.

After getting a cup of coffee, Alan begins to open his mail. Alan believes that opening his own mail is the best way to keep on the pulse of the organization. As a result, this morning is no different from any other morning, and Alan spends the first 30 minutes going through his mail to set his priorities. Today, however, he is starting 45 minutes later than usual. He carefully goes through each piece of mail and determines what should be acted on, what should be filed, what represents reference material or should be forwarded to a different department and what should be thrown out. He pencils in the appropriate response at the top of each sheet. Alan puts all his opened mail in one pile on his desk. At 9:43 A.M. he finishes this task.

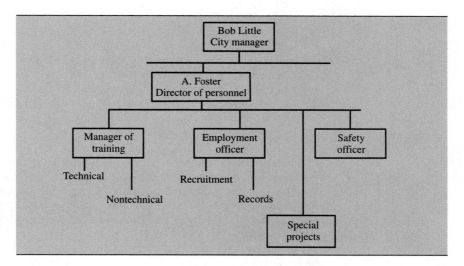

Next, Alan opens his daily planner. To his chagrin, Alan finds that he is supposed to be at a meeting with the city manager and two other department heads at 9:45 A.M. and he has not yet collected the necessary data or reviewed the agenda. Alan mumbles to himself that if they hadn't been paving the wretched parking lot he would have had plenty of time. He grabs what he can and rushes off to the meeting, reading the agenda on the way. He again rushes past Mary and fails to tell her where he is going or for how long he will be gone. Mary reaches out to check her copy of Alan's daily planner, but the only thing listed is the meeting from 9:45 A.M. to 10:45 A.M.

Fortunately, although Alan is 10 minutes late, the city manager has not arrived at the meeting because of a surprise visit from the mayor. John Busybody (Parks and Recreation) and Peter Hestent (Engineering and Safety) are already there. Alan says good morning to the two men but does not wait for their response. Instead, he continues to review the agenda and support material he has brought to the meeting. Alan ignores all comments directed at him. Five minutes later, the city manager's secretary comes in and informs them that Bob will be another 10 minutes late and would like the group to start without him. For the first minute or so the men sit there and review their notes.

Alan is the first to speak and the following conversation takes place:

> *Alan:* We might as well get started. The first thing we should look at is what we want to accomplish this morning
>
> *John:* Well, I think that if we are going to open an indoor skateboard arena for the town kids, I would like to suggest we use Buildall, Inc. I heard that they just lost a major contract and are looking for work.
>
> *Alan:* That might be a fact to keep in mind because it could save us some money, but my reading of the memo I received from Bob is that we have not yet made up our mind to open an arena and that we first want to look at the pros and cons of such a move.
>
> *John:* Believe what you want, but I think Bob has made up his mind. My sister plays bridge with Bob's wife, and their kid is really into this skateboard stuff. She says that the only reason he is pushing it is so that his kid will have a safe place to skate.
>
> *Alan:* That may be true, I have no way of knowing. Therefore, I would like to look at the facts, then list what might be the advantages and disadvantages of such a venture, and finally consider if this year's budget can handle the cost. Peter, this relates to your area. What do you think?
>
> *Peter:* Whatever you guys think we should do....
>
> *Alan:* I appreciate your confidence in us, but the design and safety issues are critical factors. As a result I would really appreciate it if you would spell out your views, especially in the area of liabilities.

At that point Bob enters the room and takes charge. He indicates that the group is only there to consider the pros and cons of an arena and that each member should make his view known. He then asks what the group has discussed. After a moment of silence, Alan describes what happened in Bob's absence. The meeting continues until 11:00 A.M. with all the participants openly discussing the pros and cons of a skateboard arena.

Before Alan has a chance to leave, the city manager asks him if the report on salary differentials between men and women working for the city is finished. Alan says he didn't think Bob wanted the report until next Friday. The following exchange then takes place between Bob and Alan.

> *Bob:* How could you say that? This is the third time I've asked you for the report. You told me both times that you would have it for me today! As a result, I promised Paul (the mayor) that the report would be on his desk tomorrow.
>
> *Alan:* Gee, Bob, how could you make that kind of commitment without letting me know?
>
> *Bob:* That's the whole point. I did let you know and you said I would have the report today! I wish you were a bit more organized. It would sure make my job a lot easier!

> *Alan:* I don't think I'm the one who needs organization around here. Anyway, there is nothing I can do for you today. Right now I have to meet with a local trainer. [*Alan turns and walks away.*]
>
> *Bob:* [*calling after Alan as he walks down the hall*] I'll expect something on my desk by four o'clock!

On the way back to his office Alan stops in the cafeteria for a cup of coffee and to take a break from all the pressures of the job. While there, he runs into Tim Needsit. Tim is working on personnel projections for the city and needs some background material. Alan indicates that he probably has the material somewhere in the office files and tells Tim he will find the material when he returns to his office.

After about 15 minutes Alan returns to his office and as promised begins to search his files for the material Tim needs. Mary notices his rummaging through the file and asks if she could be of assistance. Alan responds by saying, "Thanks for the offer, but it will only take a few moments to find what I want." As it turns out, it takes Alan about 25 minutes to realize that he cannot find the material and has to ask Mary to locate the manpower figures. Mary finds them in about 30 seconds.

It is now about 11:30 A.M. and Harry, the Manager of Training, pops his head in Alan's office and asks if Alan has a minute. Alan looks at his watch and then his daily planner. At that point he looks up at Harry and the following conversation takes place.

> *Alan:* I have to leave in a few moments for an appointment across town—is it something critical or can it wait until after lunch?
>
> *Harry:* It's important, but it can wait until this afternoon. Jim Baker in Works wants to know if he can get funded for some training this summer and we have only a couple of days before the registration deadline.
>
> *Alan:* That's no problem. We have the money; he's a good man, send him.
>
> *Harry:* But if we send him we may get a bunch of other requests from people who need it more then he does.
>
> *Alan:* I can see your point—it will have to wait until I get back. Can you stop back at 2:30 P.M.?
>
> *Harry:* Sure, no problem.
>
> *Alan:* OK, let's meet then—also bring the personnel files of the people who you think will want to go, or are in need of training. That way we can go through each case and see who really needs the training. Also, while I have you here, how is Linda doing? (Linda is one of the new trainers who handles some of the in-house orientation sessions.) Last week you mentioned that she was having some problems maintaining control during the sessions.
>
> *Harry:* Well, she seems to have it under control now. It must have just been that she was nervous the first few times—you know, some of those new drivers can be a little rough.
>
> *Alan:* That's great, I was hoping she would work out. By the way, did you order the new training film we had previewed last week?
>
> *Harry:* No, not yet. I am hoping to do that this afternoon. I have to check with purchasing about a PO number and determine from what budget account it is going to come.
>
> *Alan:* No problem, so long as you order it in the next day or two. We will need to use it in the new safety session at the end of the month.
>
> [*Harry nods his head and leaves.*]

Shortly thereafter Alan leaves his office for a lunch appointment. On the way out, he tells Mary where he is going and asks her to pull the data on pay differentials for males and females working for the city. He continues to explain how he wants her to handle the data and what totals and subtotals he would like. He explains that he has to finish the report by 4:00 P.M. for Bob. He asks Mary if she has any questions. When she says there are none, Alan thanks her for her cooperation, tells her he will be back at 2 o'clock, and leaves.

On the way to his car, Alan remembers belatedly that it is not in the parking lot so now he has to rush if he wants to get to his appointment on time. On the way out the Town Hall's front door, Alan runs into Paul Fixit from maintenance. Paul tells Alan that he was just on the way to see him to discuss a problem about one of his men. The subordinate has a drinking problem that is affecting his work. Paul wants to know how and what he should document. Instead of responding to Paul's problem, Alan states, "I'm on my way out. In the future give me a call before you stop by—that way you will save us a lot of time." Alan does not wait for a response from Paul and rushes off. He mumbles to himself about the poor organization and planning around this place.

We follow Alan to lunch at a local restaurant where members of the Midwest Association of Quality Circles are having a meeting. Bob, the city manager, has asked Alan to meet with the group to see if the city might benefit from quality circles (QCs). Alan is 10 minutes late and finds that the group has already started to eat. They bring him up-to-date on the conversation and then start to explain how QCs could help a municipal organization.

As they talk, Alan pulls out a number of 3-by-5-inch cards he always carries in his pocket and takes notes. After listening and asking several questions, Alan informs the group that he believes the city will gain a lot from joining the Midwest Association of Quality Circles. He will arrange for the membership fee to be sent out that very afternoon. Alan also informs the group that the city will send two employees to take part in the week-long training session the association will hold in August. Alan says, "I know whom I will send without even thinking about it!" (Alan takes out another card and adds the two names to his things-to-do list, which now has 10 items on it requiring immediate action.) The luncheon meeting ends about 2:00 P.M. and the participants shake hands and leave.

While driving back to his office, Alan remembers that he had promised the children that he would pick up some videos for the weekend. He decides to save some time and stops at the video shop to pick them up now rather than on the way home. Unfortunately, Alan considers himself an amateur movie buff—once he gets into one of these shops he loses all track of time. This time is no exception and before Alan realizes it, it is almost 3:00 P.M.

Although Alan had told his secretary that he would be back at 2:00 P.M., he does not return until 3:00 P.M. He enters Mary's office and says, "Mary, bring me in the differential data now." He rushes into his office and slams the door. Mary knows better than to bother him now. Whatever happened over lunch will just have to take its course.

At 3:30 P.M., John Dontno (manager of special projects) enters Mary's office and informs her that he has to see Alan right away. Mary indicates that Alan is busy, but John insists that he must see Alan about a project that Alan has to complete by week's end. Finally, Mary buzzes Alan to see if he will see John. You can hear Alan shout back, "Not John again! What does he want this time? Oh well, you might as well send him in."

John enters Alan's office and the following conversation takes place. (Alan thinks to himself, John must come into this office at least five times a day with some type of problem he can't solve. Yet John has his MBA and takes nearly every course he can to upgrade his skills. There must be a solution to this problem somewhere, but I don't have the time to solve it now.)

Alan: What is it this time, John? [*John lowers his head in response to Alan's tone of voice.*]

John: Well, Alan, it has to do with the performance appraisal form we are setting up for the Police Department. It appears that we are having a hard time developing anchors for the dimensions we selected.

Alan: John, I thought that problem was solved last week when we decided to bring in those guys from the University. Now what seems to be the problem?

John: Well, the consultant has us developing the dimensions in parallel groups and the boys simply haven't been able to get the level of detail required by the consultant.

Alan: I still don't understand why you are coming to me. You are in charge of this project and have the authority to handle these problems. In fact, you are the one who came to me requesting to be put in charge of the project, and I said OK because I thought it might give you a chance to prove yourself. I wish you would start bringing me solutions instead of problems!

John: [*about 15 seconds of silence*] Sure, I'm in charge, but I want your input on what I should do. It's the first time I've worked on anything this large, and its results are likely to have a significant impact on this department....

Alan: Get back to your office and do what you are supposed to do. You will get no help from me! In fact, if you can't do the job, I'll find someone who can.

Without saying another word, John turns around and leaves Alan's office. Alan buzzes Mary and tells her that if John comes in again he is to be told that he (Alan) is not available. It is now nearly 3:45 P.M. and Alan has not finished the report for Bob. Alan assesses what has to be done and decides that he can't finish it now. Bob will have to wait. Alan thinks it's mostly Bob's fault anyway.

Alan again pulls out his daily planner to see what else he has to do before he leaves for the day, usually around 5:00 P.M. He is surprised to see 10 items on his list that require "immediate action" written next to them. Alan grabs a pencil and crosses off those items that can wait. When he is finished, only two items remain that have to be done now. One is Betty's proposal for a new training program on report writing; the other is a vacation schedule for his department. He puts the files for both into his briefcase, figuring that there will be plenty of time to do both items tonight. The other eight items can wait.

It is now 4:00 P.M. Alan pats himself on the back for putting up with all the silliness and incompetence of the people around him. Alan thinks, why not go home early as a reward for surviving the day. Alan grabs his briefcase, telling Mary that he has to leave for the day.

As Alan is walking out he meets Harry, who stops him and says that he is getting quite a bit of heat from his subordinates. They are concerned about the office space in the new wing. They are really excited about the space and want to move in as quickly as possible. "I wonder whether we have any policy on how the space will be allocated." Without hesitation Alan states, "Allocate the space on the basis of seniority. That's the way everything else is decided around here." With that, Alan leaves.

If we were to continue to follow Alan, we would learn that he is about to visit several boat distributors. Alan has been thinking about buying a sailboat for the family. Today is a good day to stop at one or two of the larger ones since he is leaving early.

As Alan gets behind the wheel of his car he wonders how long he can take all this nonsense in the Town Hall. It's not quiet any more.

13.3 Group Discussion: Gaining Consensus on Performance Evaluation

Excercise 13.2 must be completed before you begin this exercise.

Managers should use pre-established standards, based upon job analysis, to rate their subordinates' performances. In our case a BOS and BARS appraisal instrument has been provided. It is also important to base any rating on observable behaviors that have been recorded and classified by the manager. However, ratings should not vary because a different manager has observed an employee's behavior. There must be interobserver reliability for employee evaluation to work. This exercise is designed to give you practice in gaining consensus on ratings given an employee. Please follow the steps outlined below.

Step 1. The class will break up into small groups of five or six students each.

Step 2. The small groups will discuss the various ratings given Alan Foster (see Exercise 13.2). Review each member's rating for the first job dimension: decisiveness. If everyone in the group has selected the same ratings (either for the BOS or the BARS), you should spend 5 to 10 minutes reviewing the behavioral support statements each member used to obtain their ratings. This will allow members to see whether they missed any relevant examples of specific behavior that support the job dimension under consideration.

If the group members disagree on the appropriate rating (for the BOS this is for each item listed under each skill dimension, and for the BARS this is for the job dimension itself), discuss the rationale behind each group member's rating and the behavioral support he or she has used. If agreement does not exist, use group consensus to achieve agreement on an appropriate rating. If the group cannot agree on a single rating and all members are within one rating point of each other, select the majority rating. (15 minutes for skill dimension #1) Allocating your time effectively is especially important if you have been instructed to use the BOS appraisal instrument. Remember you are considering each item listed under the skill dimension being considered.

Step 3. Repeat Step 2 for each of the remaining job dimensions on the evaluation form. (Approximately 50 minutes)

Step 4. The class will assemble to compare and discuss group scores. In addition, group scores will also be compared with the instructor's scores.

13.4 Role Play: The Administrator's Performance Appraisal and Review

The purpose of this role play is to practice carrying out a performance appraisal review (PAR) interview. Assume you are the city manager for a small municipality and will be meeting with Alan Foster, the director of personnel, to assess his performance over the past six months and agree upon appropriate goals for the next evaluation period. Please follow the steps outlined below.

Step 1. The class will break up into small groups of five to six individuals each.

Step 2. Each group will select one of its members to play the role of the city manager in the meeting with Alan Foster. The role of Alan Foster will be played by the instructor.

Step 3. Each group will develop an interview script to be used in the meeting. Time constraints do not allow coverage of all dimensions, so limit the group's preparation to one or two behavioral dimensions. Alan's strengths and weaknesses have been identified; this information should greatly facilitate your task. However, you need to determine what Alan's goals should be for the next evaluation period. Make any additional assumptions you believe appropriate to give life to your script. The only constraint is that your assumptions be consistent with the facts presented in the original case.

If necessary, the instructor will review the steps to follow in carrying out a performance appraisal review with subordinates.

Step 4. Practice the role play within your group. One of the group's members should play the role of Alan Foster and the remaining group members should act as observers.

Step 5. During the next class, one or more groups will be selected to carry out the role play between the city manager and Alan Foster.

End Notes

1. R. P. Delamontagne and J. B. Weitzal, "Performance alignment: The fine art of the perfect fit," *Personnel Journal,* Vol. 59, No. 2, 1980: 115–117.

2. Rand Corporation, 1988, *Annual Report—The Institute for Civil Justice,* Rand, Santa Monica, Calif.

3. W. Holley and H. Field, "Performance appraisal and the law," *Labor Law Journal,* January–February, 1982: 59–64; R. Romberg, "Performance appraisal, 1: Risks and rewards," *Personnel,* August 1986: 20–26; P. S. Eyres, "Legally defensible appraisal systems," *Personnel Journal,* July 1989: 58–62; G. P. Latham, D. Skarlicki, D. Irvine, and J. P. Siegel, "The increasing importance of performance appraisal to employee effectiveness in organizational setting in North America," in *International Review of Industrial and Organizational Psychology,* Vol. 8, ed. C. L. Cooper and I. T. Robertson, New York, John Wiley & Sons, 1993: 87–132.

4. A. H. Locher and K. S. Teel, "Assessment: Appraisal trends," *Personnel Journal,* September 1988: 139–144. Reprinted with the permission of *Personnel Journal,* ACC Communications, Inc., Costa Mesa, Calif., all rights reserved.

5. Ibid.

6. G. P. Latham and K. N.Wexley, *Increasing Productivity through Performance Appraisal,* 2nd ed., Reading Mass., Addison-Wesley Publishing, 1994; Latham, Skarlicki, Irvine, and Siegel, 1993: 88.

7. Latham and Wexley, 1994.

8. A. Gates, "The smartest way to give a performance review," *Working Woman,* May 1991: 65–68.

9. K. Ludeman, "Measuring skills and behavior," *Training and Development Journal,* November, Vol. 45, 1991: 61–66.

10. Latham, Skarlicki, Irvine, and Siegel, 1993.

11. K. E. Apt and D. W. Watkins, "What one laboratory has learned about performance appraisal," *Research Technical Management,* July–August 1989: 22–28.

12. B. R. Nathan, A. H. Mohrman, and J. Milliman, Jr., "Interpersonal relations as a context for the effects of appraisal interviews on performance and satisfaction: A longitudinal study,"

Academy of Management Journal, Vol. 34, 1991: 352–369.

13. L. M. Field, "Performance Appraisal: It's the intent that counts," *Canadian Manager,* Spring 1986: 19–22.

14. Latham and Wexley, 1994; H. H. Meyer, E. A. Kay and J. R. P. French, Jr., "Split role in performance appraisal," *Harvard Business Review,* Vol. 43, 1965: 123–129.

15. J. M. Harackiewicz and J. R. Larson, "Managing motivation: The impact of supervisor feedback on subordinate task interest," *Journal of Personality and Social Psychology,* Vol. 51, 1986: 547–556.

16. Latham and Wexley, 1994.

17. J. B. Prince and E. E. Lawler, "Does salary discussion hurt the development performance appraisal?" *Organizational Behavior and Human Decision Processes,* Vol. 37, 1986: 357–375.

18. P. W. Dorfman, W. G. Stephan, and J. Loveland, "Performance appraisal behavior: Supervisors' perceptions and subordinate reactions," *Personnel Psychology,* Vol. 39, 1986: 579–595.

19. Latham and Wexley, 1994: 206.

20. Latham and Wexley, 1994.

21. H. Levinson, "Appraisal of what performance?" *Harvard Business Review,* July–August 1976: 30–32; G. P. Latham, L. Cummings, and T. R. Mitchell, "Behavioral strategies to improve productivity," *Organizational Dynamics,* Winter 1981: 5–23; M. G. Friedman, "10 steps to objective appraisal," *Personnel Journal,* June 1986: 66–71; M. G. Derven, "The paradox of performance appraisal," *Personnel Journal,* February 1990: 107–111.

22. Levinson, 1976: 30.

23. W. C. Borman, "Format and training effects on rating accuracy and rater errors," *Journal of Applied Psychology,* Vol. 64, 1979: 410–421.

24. J. T. Austin and P. Villanova, "The criterion problem: 1917–1992," *Journal of Applied Psychology,* Vol. 77, 1992: 836–874.

25. Austin and Villanova, 1992.

26. Latham and Wexley, 1994.

27. Latham and Wexley, 1994.

28. P. Smith and L.M. Kendall, "Retranslation of expectations: An approach to the construction of unambiguous anchors for rating scales," *Journal of Applied Psychology,* Vol. 47, 1963: 149–155; Latham and Wexley, 1994.

29. G. P. Latham and K. N. Wexley, "Behavioral observation scales for performance appraisal purposes," *Personnel Psychology,* Vol. 30, 1977: 255–268; G. P. Latham, K. N. Wexley, and T. M. Rand, "The relevance of behavioral criteria developed from the critical incident technique," *Canadian Journal of Behavioral Science,* Vol. 7, 1975: 349–358; Latham and Wexley, 1994.

30. Latham and Wexley, 1994.

31. Latham and Wexley, 1994.

32. Latham and Wexley, 1994: 94.

33. U. Wiersma, P. van de Berg, and G. P. Latham, "Dutch reactions to behavioral observations, behavioral expectations, and trait scales," *Group and Organization Management,* in press.

34. Latham and Wexley, 1994.

35. U. Wiersma and G. P. Latham, "The practicality of behavioral observation scales, behavioral expectations scales, and trait scales," *Personnel Psychology,* Vol. 39, 1986: 619–628; Wiersma, van de Berg, and Latham, in press.

36. A. Tziner and R. Kopelman, "Effects of rating format on goal-setting dimensions: A field experiment," *Journal of Applied Social Psychology,* Vol. 73, 1988: 323–326; A. Tziner and G.P. Latham, "The effects of appraisal instrument, feedback, and goal setting on worker satisfaction and commitment," *Journal of Organizational Behavior,* Vol. 10, 1989: 145–153; A. Tziner, R. Kopelman and N. Livneh, "Effects of performance appraisal format on perceived goal characteristics, appraisal process satisfaction, and changes in rated job performance: A field experiment," paper presented at the Annual Meeting of the Academy of Management, Las Vegas, Nev., 1992.

37. For a detailed description of the specific steps required for developing BOS instruments see Latham and Wexley, 1994: 86–91.

38. Example based upon material presented in Latham and Wexley, 1994: 89.

39. R. J. Benford, "Found: The key to excellent performance," *Personnel,* May–June 1981, 68–77.

40. P. Bobko, "Employee reactions to performance standards: A review and research propositions," *Personnel Psychology,* Vol. 47, No. 1, 1994: 1–29.

41. Latham, Skarlicki, Irvine, and Siegel, 1993.

42. J. Lawrie, "Prepare for a performance appraisal," *Personnel Journal,* April 1990: 132–136.

43. A. P. O'Reilly, "Skill requirements: Supervisor–subordinate conflict," *Personnel Psychology,* Spring 1973: 75–80.

44. M. J. Villareal, "Improving managerial performance," *Personnel Journal,* February 1977: 86–89.

45. H. Bernardin and E. C. Pence, "Effects of rater training: Creating new response sets and decreasing accuracy," *Journal of Applied Psychology,* Vol. 65, No. 1, 1980: 60–66.

46. Latham, Skarlicki, Irvine, and Siegel, 1993.

47. Latham and Wexley, 1994.

48. Latham, Skarlicki, Irvine, and Siegel, 1993.

49. M. Beer, "Performance appraisal: Dilemmas and possibilities," *Organizational Dynamics,* Winter 1981: 24–36.

50. A. Bandura, "Organizational applications of social cognitive theory," *Australian Journal of Management,* Vol. 13, 1988: 275–302.

51. The following discussion is based upon material presented in Latham and Wexley, 1994.

52. Latham and Wexley, 1994; Latham, Skarlicki, Irvine, and Siegel, 1993.

53. The following discussion is based upon material presented in Latham and Wexley, 1994: 111–136.

54. Latham and Wexley, 1994.

55. C. Longnecker, H. Sims, and D. Gioia, "Behind the mask; The politics of employee appraisal," *Academy of Management Executive,* Vol. 1, 1987: 183–193.

56. R. S. Barrett, "The influence of the supervisor's requirements on ratings," *Personnel Psychology,* Vol. 19, 1966: 375–387; Latham and Wexley, 1994.

57. From an organizational perspective, it is possible to use outsiders to appraise an employee's performance. For example, organizations can use assessement centers to evaluate an employee's current skill level, have internal human resource specialists do a field review of employee performance, or seek input from outsiders (such as customers) to assess current performance. For a detailed discussion of these points, see Latham and Wexley, 1994.

58. S. Foc, Z. Ben-Nahum and Y. Yinon, "Perceived similarity and accuracy of peer ratings," *Journal of Applied Psychology,* Vol. 74, 1989: 781–786; J. F. Kremer, "Construct validity of multiple measures in teaching, research and service and reliability of peer ratings," *Journal of Educational Psychology,* Vol. 82, 1990: 213–218; G. M. McEvoy and P. Buller, "User acceptance of peer appraisals in an industrial setting," *Personnel Psychology,* Vol. 40, 1987: 785–797.

59. Latham and Wexley, 1994.

60. L. V. Gordon and F. F. Medland, "The cross-group stability of peer ratings of leadership potential," *Personnel Psychology,* Vol. 18, 1965: 173–177.

61. Latham and Wexley, 1994: 115.

62. Latham and Wexley, 1994.

63. Latham and Wexley, 1994.

64. Latham and Wexley, 1994.

65. H. H. Meyer, "A solution to the performance appraisal enigma," *Academy of Management Executive,* Vol. 5, 1991: 68–75.

66. J. L. Farh and J. D. Werbel, "Effects of purpose of the appraisal and expectation of validation on self-appraisal leniency," *Journal of Applied Psychology,* Vol. 71, 1986: 527–529; S. Fox and Y. Dinur, "Validity of self-assessment: A field evaluation," *Personnel Psychology,* Vol. 41, 1988: 581–592.

67. J. L. Farh and G. H. Dobbins, "Effects of self-esteem on leniency bias in self-reports of performance: A structural equation model analysis," *Personnel Psychology,* Vol. 42, 1989: 835–850.

68. R. W. Eder and D. B. Fedor, "Priming performance self-evaluations: Moderating effects of rating purpose and judgement confidence," *Organizational Behavior and Human Decision Processes,* Vol. 44, No. 3, 1989: 474–493.

69. H. J. Bernardin and R. W. Beatty, "Can subordinate appraisals enhance managerial productivity?" *Sloan Management Review,* Vol. 28, No. 4, 1987: 63–73.

70. Bernardin and Beatty, 1987; G. M. McEvoy, "Evaluating the boss: Should subordinate appraisals of managers be allowed?" *Personnel Administrator,* Vol. 32, No. 9, 1988: 115–120.

71. Bernardin and Beatty, 1987.

72. G. P. Latham, C. Fay, and L. M. Saari, "The development of behavioral observation scales for appraising performance of foremen," *Personnel Psychology,* Vol. 32, 1979: 299–311.

73. Bernardin and L. A. Klatt, "Managerial appraisal systems: Has practice 'caught-up' with the state of the art?" *Personnel Administrator,* Vol. 30, 1985: 79–86; Bernardin and Beatty, 1987.

74. McEvoy, September 1988.

75. McEvoy, September 1988.
76. Information presented in Table 13.2 based upon material presented in McEvoy, September 1988.
77. For a detailed discussion of rater error and supporting research see Latham and Wexley, 1994: 137–167.
78. Latham and Wexley, 1994: 138.
79. R. Klimoski and L. Inks, "Accountability forces in performance appraisal," *Organizational Behavior and Human Decision Processes,* Vol. 45, 1990: 194–208.
80. Latham, Skarlicki, Irvine, and Siegel, 1993.
81. Latham and Wexley, 1994.
82. Latham and Wexley, 1994: 141.
83. B. R. Nathan and R. G. Lord, "Cognitive categorization and dimensional schemata: A process approach to the study of halo in performance ratings," *Journal of Applied Psychology,* Vol. 68. 1983: 102–114.
84. G. P. Latham, "Job performance and appraisal," in *International Review of Industrial and Organizational Psychology,* ed. C. L. Cooper and I. Robertson, Chichester, U. K., Wiley, 1986: 117–155.
85. B. R. Nathan and N. Tippins, "The consequences of halo 'error' in performance ratings: A field study of the moderating effect of halo on test validation results," *Journal of Applied Psychology,* Vol. 75, 1990: 290–296.
86. D. D. Steiner and J. S. Rain, "Immediate and delayed primacy and recency effects in performance evaluation," *Journal of Applied Psychology,* Vol. 74, 1989: 136–142.
87. Latham and Wexley, 1994: 152.
88. W. H. Cooper, "Conceptual similarity as a source of illusory halo in job performance ratings," *Journal of Applied Psychology,* Vol. 66, 1981: 302–307.
89. G. P. Latham, K. N. Wexley, and E. D. Pursell, "Training managers to minimize rating errors in the observation of behavior," *Journal of Applied Psychology,* Vol. 60, No. 5, 1975: 550–555.
90. H. J. Bernardin and M. R. Buckley, "Strategies in rater training," *Academy of Management Review,* Vol. 6, No. 2, 1981: 205–212.
91. Latham and Wexley, 1994.
92. Our definition is based upon the material presented in W. G. Dyer, "Forms of interpersonal feedback,"

Training and Development Journal, Vol. 35, June 1981: 102–109.
93. M. Erez, "Feedback: A necessary condition for the goal-setting performance relationship," *Journal of Applied Psychology,* Vol. 62, 1977: 624–627; D. R. Ilgen, C. D. Fisher, and M. S. Taylor, "Consequences of individual feedback on behavior in organizations," *Journal of Applied Psychology,* Vol. 64, 1979: 349–371; K. N. Wexley, "Performance appraisal and feedback," in S. Kerr (ed), *Organizational Behavior,* Grid Publishing Co., Columbus, Ohio, 1979: 241–259; E .A. Locke, K. N. Shaw, L. M. Saari, and G .P. Latham, "Goal setting and task performance: 1969–1980," *Psychological Bulletin,* Vol. 90, 1981: 125–152; M. S. Taylor, C. D. Fisher, and D. R. Ilgen, "Individuals' reactions to performance feedback in organizations: A control theory perspective," in *Research in Personnel and Human Resources Management,* Vol. 2, ed. K. Rowland and J. Ferris, JAI Press, Greenwich, Conn., 1984: 81–124; P. A. McCarthy, "Effects of feedback on the self confidence of men and women," *Academy of Management Journal,* Vol. 29, 1986: 840–847; M. DeGregorio and C. D. Fisher, "Providing performance feedback: Reactions to alternate methods," *Journal of Management,* Vol. 14, No. 4, 1988: 605–616.
94. J. R. Larson, Jr., "Supervisors' performance feedback to subordinates: The impact of subordinate performance valence and outcome dependence," *Organizational Behavior and Human Decision Processes,* Vol. 37, 1986: 391–408.
95. A. Tesser and S. Rosen, "The reluctance to transmit bad news," in *Advances in Experimental Social Psychology,* Vol. 8, ed. L. Berkowitz, Academic Press, New York, 1975: 193–232; C. D. Fisher, "Transmission of positive and negative feedback to subordinates: A laboratory investigation," *Journal of Applied Psychology,* Vol. 64, 1979: 533–540; D. R. Ilgen and W. A. Knowlton, "Performance attribution effects on feedback from superiors," *Organizational Behavior and Human Performance,* Vol. 25, 1980: 441–456.
96. J. R. Larson, Jr., "The performance feedback process: A preliminary model," *Organizational Behavior and Human Performance,* Vol. 33, 1984: 42–76; Larson, Jr., 1986.

97. G. E. Myers and M. T. Myers, *The Dynamics of Human Communication,* 3rd ed., McGraw-Hill, New York, 1980; our list represents an amalgamation of material presented in W. G. Dyer, 1981: 102–109; P. Diffie-Couch, "How to give feedback," *Supervisory Management,* Vol. 28, August 1983: 27–31; P. C. Earley, "Trust, perceived importance of praise and criticism, and work performance: An examination of feedback in the United States and England," *Journal of Management,* Vol. 12, No. 4, 1986: 457–473; B. Wood and A. Scott, "The gentle art of feedback," *Personnel Management,* Vol. 21, April 1989: 48–51; R. F. Verderber and K. S. Verderber, *Using Interpersonal Communication Skills,* 5th ed., Wadsworth, Belmont, Calif., 1989; S. C. Bushardt, J. M. Jenkins, and P. B. Cumbest, "Less Odious Performance Appraisals," *Training & Development Journal,* March 1990: 29–35; R. E. Levassiur, "People skills: Effective communication—a critical skill for MA/OR professionals," *Interfaces,* Vol. 21, No. 2, 1991: 22–24.

98. Latham, Skarlicki, Irvine, and Siegel, 1993.

COUNSELING TECHNIQUES: A MUST FOR EFFECTIVE MANAGEMENT

14

Objectives:

- Identify the conditions under which counseling is appropriate as a management intervention.
- Describe the steps necessary to effectively prepare for, and carry out, a counseling session.
- Give students an opportunity to practice and fine-tune their skills when engaging in counseling behavior.

Introduction

A situation likely to threaten managerial success is the number of marginal, or problem employees currently reporting to the manager. A problem employee is an individual who is performing at minimal or substandard levels, but present performance does not warrant dismissal.

It is estimated that problem employees cost U.S. companies from $100 to $195 billion each year because of absenteeism, accidents, poor performance, and sick leave.[1] Not only do problem employees directly threaten departmental and organizational success because of their own behavior but there is also likely to be a spillover effect to other employees.[2] Although problem employees only account for 20 percent of total work force, they cause as much as 75 percent of all performance deficiencies across all jobs.[3] Problem employees also use up a scarce resource most managers have too little of, including personal time. Hall and Fletcher estimated that up to 20 percent of the U.S. work force can be classified as problem employees, and that this 20 percent can account for 80 percent of a manager's time attempting to correct or offset performance-related problems.[4]

Recognizing the negative consequences of problem employees, and the expanding role of management, the next decade is likely to be a period in which organizations will increase their efforts to help problem employees.

What Is Counseling?

Two definitions of employee counseling help clarify what will be covered in the following pages. The first definition states that counseling is done to facilitate self-analysis by the subordinate, which in turn combines with the manager's own insights and knowledge to produce: (*a*) self-understanding by the subordinate, (*b*) increased commitment to mutually accepted goals, and (*c*) a plan of action for achieving them.[5] Alternatively, counseling programs can be defined "to include any formal or informal counseling designed to accomplish one of the following objectives: (1) further an employee's career pursuits, (2) aid the employee in adjusting to a major transitional change, and (3) improve an employee's mental, physical, or social health."[6]

Implicit in these two definitions is the belief that employee counseling involves helping the employee solve personal or organizational problems that are negatively affecting job performance.

The primary focus of this chapter is on the goals typically associated with counseling interventions, and how the manager's role as counselor fits within the organization's overall effort to help the problem employee.

Counseling Goals

As a counselor, the manager interacts with employees to help them to understand cause-and-effect relationships that exist between personal behavior and environmental consequences. Once this is understood, the participants can identify behaviors and cognitive changes capable of improving personal interactions with the environment. There are at least *five* goals counseling can seek to achieve. They are: behavior change, positive mental health, personal effectiveness, problem resolution, and improved decision making.

1. Behavior change. Once employees can understand how their behavior impacts on personal consequences or the consequences of others, it is possible for them to alter their dominant behavior style. This is especially true when they identify acceptable alternatives to existing behavior.

2. Positive mental health. The goal of improving the mental health of an employee can be integrated into a proactive management style. Knowing one's subordinates and peers allows the manager to develop baseline data regarding their normal behavior. Alertness to behaviors or communications at variance with these baseline data can signal that a potential problem is developing. The proactive manager can act early to help an employee correct a problem before it becomes significant.[7]

3. Personal effectiveness. Employees must understand and accept the limits that exist within the environment, and how these limits restrict their behavior. This range, as described in Chapter 1, will vary depending upon the group in which the individual functions, the position held within the organization, and the needs and expectations of others. Once the individual's unique range has been identified, it is then necessary to have the employee fully develop his or her personal abilities. The counseling objective is to afford the individual the greatest level of freedom and choice within the functional limits of the situation. When both states of awareness are achieved, individuals are most likely to maximize their effectiveness.

4. Problem resolution. Individuals cannot always solve existing problems themselves. The counseling process described below can be used by managers to help the employee solve such problems as drug and alcohol abuse, career uncertainty, interpersonal conflict, family problems, and low self-esteem. At the very least, the counseling process can be used to help a problem employee identify (*a*) the source of his or her problem and (*b*) others with the skills and resources needed to continue working with the employee. For example, if a substance abuse problem is identified, the employee can be directed to EAP (Employee Assistance Program) personnel within the company or community agencies established to handle such problems.

5. Improved decision making. Improved decision making is a need of many employees. Employees must learn how to make decisions that maximize personal satisfaction and future growth. Effective decision making by the employee involves the following steps: (*a*) employees must identify goals that are important to them; (*b*) once those are identified, employees must then be willing to devote the time and energy to collect and process relevant information that currently exists within the environment; (*c*) as individuals collect and process the available information, an effort is made to identify cause-and-effect relationships that exist and the consequences of them; (*d*) once employees understand how their environment works, and understand their role in cause-and-effect relationships, they can search for alternative courses of action that will enhance their personal well being.

For example, counseling can help a problem locomotive engineer make the following connections and decision about possible courses of action. "My current poor performance (slow response time to signals, irritability, increases in sick days and absences) is related to my drinking problem. If I continue to drink, my performance as a locomotive engineer is likely to decline further. If that happens, and I cause an accident that results in personal injury or property damage, I will be fired. I want to keep my job but I understand the company's rules about drinking on the job or coming in tired or drunk. To prevent losing my job because of my drinking problem, I should seek help before it gets worse. Finally, these are the options available to me, and their consequences."

Having identified the available options, employees then assess the consequences of identified alternatives. In the example above, the counseling process can be used to help the employee to identify the advantages and disadvantages of available alternatives. Such analysis will help employees select a course of action that satisfies their long-term needs. However, to be effective within one's environment, the process does not end with a decision. Instead, the decision is implemented and the actual consequences of that decision are assessed during follow-up sessions. Actual consequences then become the input for further decisions. If the locomotive engineer decides to seek help through an internal EAP program, the success of these sessions will have to be evaluated. Assessment data collected will determine whether the session will continue or other alternatives will be sought.

The Process of Counseling

By undertaking employee counseling, the manager focuses on environmental or personal problems that negatively affect performance. There are, however, four issues often raised by would-be counselors. Managers interested in using counseling as a helping technique often ask, "How does it differ from what I do every day or my end-of-period reviews?" "How much time and energy should I put into the counseling process?" "What is the best style to use during the counseling session?" and "Are there any personal qualities that are better than others when counseling?" Each of these questions represents a legitimate concern that should be addressed before a detailed discussion of the manager's role as counselor or where counseling fits within the organizational context.

As a process, counseling is often confused with other employee encounters. Figure 14.1 attempts to clarify this potential confusion. The major characteristics that distinguish counseling from other similar techniques available to the manager when attempting to manage the problem employee are: (*a*) degree of formalization, (*b*) immediacy of problem objectives, and (*c*) the time frame in which results are to be achieved.

Although not listed in Figure 14.1 it is also desirable to differentiate between counseling and coaching.[8] Coaching is a process primarily designed to improve the job skills and the knowledge of the employee. During coaching encounters, the manager emphasizes the technical content of the job or task being considered. Critical to the coaching process is the manager's ability to observe behavior and discuss a deficiency in an open and constructive manner. As part of this discussion, the manager will use leading (stem) questions designed to involve the employee in the coaching process. Defined in this manner, coaching is closely related to advising as a helping technique. Counseling, on the other hand, attempts to solve problems associated with employee attitudes, motivation, or interpersonal difficulties.

The issue of how long the counseling process should be continued before negative sanctions are applied represents another issue or concern to many managers. The amount of time a manager is willing to devote to a problem

FIGURE 14.1

Three subordinate-oriented helping techniques

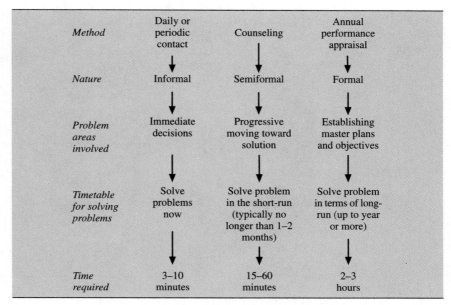

Method	Daily or periodic contact	Counseling	Annual performance appraisal
	↓	↓	↓
Nature	Informal	Semiformal	Formal
	↓	↓	↓
Problem areas involved	Immediate decisions	Progressive moving toward solution	Establishing master plans and objectives
	↓	↓	↓
Timetable for solving problems	Solve problems now	Solve problem in the short-run (typically no longer than 1–2 months)	Solve problem in terms of long-run (up to year or more)
	↓	↓	↓
Time required	3–10 minutes	15–60 minutes	2–3 hours

depends on such issues as importance of consequences, length of service of the problem employee, legal considerations, availability of replacements, the organization's philosophy, the manager's own personality, and availability of resources.

The question of counseling style has received considerable discussion in the literature.[9] This is because differences in counseling style can have a significant effect on the session's outcome. When faced with the need to help problem employees, managers must use the helping style that will best achieve the desired results for themselves, the employees, and the organization.

De Board argued that when attempting to make this decision, the manager should consider two important issues.[10] The first is whether the manager's primary concern is with the problem or with the employee. In other words, is the problem technical or people based? The second issue is the degree of employee involvement that would be appropriate, given the unique characteristics of the situation. Using these two dimensions (technical/employee and employee excluded/included) it is possible to identify *four* styles that can be used to help the subordinate (see Figure 14.2).[11]

1. Telling

In those situations where the manager is concerned primarily with the technical issues associated with a performance problem, a telling style of helping should be used. The technical aspects of a problem become critical when

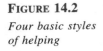

FIGURE 14.2

Four basic styles of helping

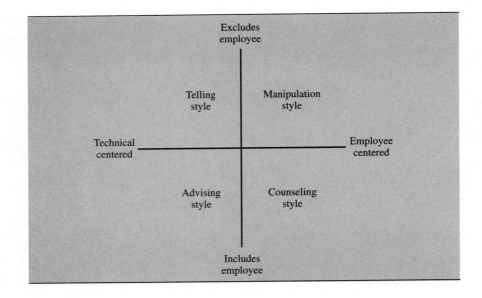

performance deficiencies are produced by technologies that are poorly designed, implemented, or maintained. When the manager is the technical expert, and when subordinates neither understand nor control the process, the manager can increase efficiency and solution accuracy by using a telling style.

Before using a telling helping style, one must decide who truly possesses the expert knowledge to solve the technical problem, and whether others want to participate in finding the solution. A telling style of helping has at least two important consequences. First, by unilaterally making decisions about cause and solutions to performance problems, the manager takes full responsibility for both success and failure. Second, a telling style perpetuates the dependency of subordinates on the manager and can reduce the employee's desire to develop and grow.

2. Advising

The advising style of helping also reflects an emphasis on the technical cause of an existing problem. However, the manager recognizes the long-term benefit of allowing a subordinate to participate in the problem-solving activities associated with solution identification. The willingness to involve others reflects a recognition that the subordinate is interested in participating in the search for a workable solution. As a result, the employee's problem-solving skill is developed. Employees thus learn to solve their own problems rather than to rely on the manager. This frees significant amounts of the manager's time to pursue other initiatives.

3. Manipulating

Under this condition, managers believe that employees play a greater role in the performance deficiency than do the technologies supporting performance. However, managers make the decision that it is best to exclude employees from the problem-solving process. This is due to the perception that employees cannot be trusted, that their goal structure is in conflict with the manager's, or that employees do not want to participate in finding a solution. The consequence of such perceptions is that managers make the decision that they know what is best for the employees and that the most efficient style choice would be manipulation. Managers can manipulate employees by filtering information, linking rewards to preferred subordinate behaviors, selectively using position power, moral persuasion, and by linking personal goals to superordinate goals or senior management preferences.

The use of a manipulative style can have negative consequences for the long-term relationship between managers and subordinates. If employees recognize that they have been manipulated by their superiors, then they may develop negative attitudes toward the would-be helper. Specifically, if subordinates believe that they are being forced to do something that they do not want to do, then they may respond by sabotaging the manager's plans. The likelihood of subordinates acting in this way increases if managers fail to give the reasoning behind their action.

4. Counseling

The underlying assumptions of counseling are that the employees are more important contributors to the problem than the technologies used, and that a solution can best be implemented if they participate in the problem-solving process. There are significant differences between the counseling style of helping and the other three available styles.[12] First, the manager does not have to be a specialist in terms of problem content. Instead, the manager's strength is at the process level. For example, managers must be active listeners; probe, reflect, summarize, and empathize; and use creative problem solving to work with subordinates to jointly identify and solve existing problems. Second, before the counseling exchange the manager does not have to formulate a solution to the problem. It is during the dynamic interaction between managers and employees that solutions to problems are identified. Last, the counseling process is designed to allow the employees to find their own solution, thereby increasing the probability of buy-in and follow-through during implementation of the proposed change.

The manager's choice of counseling styles will be affected by one's interpersonal orientation, that is, the way he or she relates to others. Two interpersonal orientations likely to affect style choice are reflected in the hostility–warmth and assertive–passive dimensions.[13] The hostility–warmth dimension reflects the degree of caring and responsiveness toward the employee.

Included in the manager's responsiveness will be an attempt to interpret and understand the employee's behaviors and feelings. Clearly, the warm individual would rate high on these characteristics, while the hostile person would rate low on these characteristics. The assertive–passive dimension reflects the degree to which the manager takes an active role in controlling and stimulating the tenor of an interactive exchange. The assertive manager takes an active role ensuring that the counseling session remains on task and that the employee is an active participant in the process. This will require the assertive counselor to build into the counseling session the required counseling process elements capable of facilitating cause and solution identification. In other words, the manager will have to include initiating, listening, probing, and controlling behaviors during the counseling session. The passive manager believes that problem employees can solve their own problems with minimum guidance. (The situational nature of this assumption will be considered when we discuss the issue of when to act—see below.)

Managers who are high on assertiveness and warmth are more likely to exhibit a counseling style when interacting with subordinates. Such managers believe that solutions to employee problems can be achieved through mutual input from both the superior and the subordinate. Alternatively, managers who are assertive and hostile are likely to use a telling or forcing style when interacting with employees. Under this condition, managers assume that employees only change if they are told or forced to act.

When discussing these styles during counseling workshops, participants sometimes express skepticism that any manager would use anything but counseling process behaviors reflecting warmth and assertiveness, and still call it counseling. Unfortunately, some organizations and managers still behave in ways consistent with the other three styles and expect results. A local example found in a large organization will demonstrate the point. The organization in question has a policy that problem employees will automatically be counseled by a member of the human resource department after an observed second infraction of company policy. If an individual is late two days in any given month, the immediate boss is required to send him or her immediately to the human resource department for counseling. Once there, the employee is seen by one of the department's staff members and told that if a third infraction occurs punitive sanctions will be taken. The degree of punitive action taken varies with the type of infraction. Although this is what the company calls counseling, it does not fit the authors' definition and clearly reflects a telling or forcing style.

Organizational Options for Employee Counseling

Any attempt to understand the manager's role as a counselor begins with an understanding of the organization's overall strategy for helping problem employees. Managers are not trained as full-time professional counselors, and are therefore limited in the degree to which they can achieve any of the five counseling goals. As a result, the manager's counseling efforts are usually limited to localized attempts to solve problems before they go beyond departmental boundaries. Turning a problem employee into a productive one usually involves a series of phases through which the employee passes. Figure 14.3 shows how an organization may sequence its efforts to help a problem employee.

Counseling often involves four interrelated phases.[14] As is the case with any attempt to solve a problem, it is first necessary to recognize that a problem exists. If the manager remains unaware of a problem employee until someone else acts, others are likely to believe that the manager has allowed the problem to go unattended for too long. The consequence may be significant loss of credibility if the manager allows this to happen often.

The importance of the manager's role in identifying the problem employee is amplified if we consider the probability that appropriate action may not be taken at the other three levels. At the individual level, there is a natural tendency for employees to deny that they are the cause of their own problems. Instead, marginal employees are likely to transfer blame to others, at least until environmental evidence overwhelmingly points to them as the cause of the existing problem. Similarly, unions cannot be expected to act quickly, because such behavior is often in conflict with their perceived mandate to protect the employee. Finally, third parties within the organization are slow to act because they do not want to encroach on the manager's territory. Therefore, failure by the manager to act may result in a delay of efforts to solve the employee's problem. Such delays may result in inappropriate behavior becoming ingrained or being perceived as acceptable because no one has acted to prevent its occurrence. In either case, delay will often mean that greater effort will be required to turn the problem employee around.

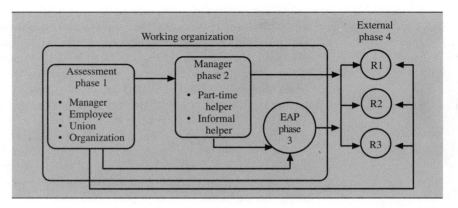

FIGURE 14.3

Strategic phases of the organizational counseling process

R1 to R3 represent *external* resources capable of providing counseling services either on a voluntary or contractual basis.

To facilitate the identification of a problem employee, Bruce recommends that managers monitor their subordinates' or peers' environments for cues that can indicate that an employee is experiencing some type of trouble and that he or she may soon become a problem employee.[15] These 10 cues are presented below:

- Excessive, unexcused, or frequent absences.
- Tardiness and early departures.
- Altercations with fellow employees.
- Causing other employees injuries through negligence.
- Poor judgment and bad decisions.
- Increased spoilage and breakage of equipment.
- Unusual on-the-job accidents.
- Involvement with the law.
- Deteriorating personal appearance.
- Mood shifts.

Once a problem employee has been recognized, there are a number of action alternatives that can be brought on line to correct the situation. Each action alternative may be considered as another phase (Figure 14.3, phases 2–4) of the organization's overall strategy designed to deal with poor performance resulting from problem employees. Although there is no fixed sequence, in the most common scenario initial attempts to help the problem employee are in the form of feedback and coaching sessions—between the employee and his or her immediate boss. As noted in Chapter 13, feedback and coaching are activities associated with an organization's performance evaluation program and are designed either to alter or maintain subordinate behavior. If coaching and feedback interventions do not produce the desired result then counseling is likely to follow.

The type of counseling used will likely vary with the situation and the underlying philosophy, or culture, of the organization. If managers feel comfortable with their counseling skills, and manager-based counseling is supported within the organization, then counseling will likely take place at the manager level (phase 2). If the problem can be solved at the manager level, the counseling process is concluded as the problem employee becomes a productive member of the manager's team. If the problem cannot be solved at this level, the manager can refer the problem employee to an employee assistance program.

When compared to early programs, organizations have broadened the scope of EAPs to include such concerns as substance abuse, mental health, family or domestic problems, health problems, job stress, organizational conflict, financial planning, housing, retirement, and legal problems.[16] At the same time, EAPs appear to be an alternative frequently used by organizations to address employee problems. A recent survey indicated that 84 percent of the organizations questioned used EAPs for alcohol and other drug abuse, 68 percent for psychological problems, 41 percent for marital problems, and 40 percent for financial problems.[17] Similarly, it is estimated that over 10,000 EAP vendors have entered the market in the past 10 years to provide organizations with employee assistance programs.[18]

EAPs allow organizations to meet their responsibility to care for the needs of their employees, reduce exposure to legal risk, and increase the overall productivity of employees. For example, according to Department of Labor regulations, substance abuse may be considered a serious health condition under the guidelines of the Family and Medical Leave Act (FMLA). This means that employers may have to provide recovering alcoholics with up to 12 weeks of unpaid leave. EAPs can be used to help employees and at the same time minimize the organization's exposure to such risks.[19] Research also indicates that EAPs can increase employee productivity by 6.7 days a year, while saving organizations an average of $1,000 per employee.[20] Although EAPs can be expensive to provide in-house, they can be contracted out to qualified vendors. Contracted programs can cost from $1.00 to $3.50 per employee per month.[21] The actual cost will vary, depending upon the services required and the number of employees taking part in the program.

Two assumptions supporting the use of a manager-driven sequence are that managers can be trained in the necessary helping skills designed to facilitate limited counseling interventions (e.g., problem identification; use of probing, reflecting, summarizing, and supportive statements; active listening; creative problem solving), and that such efforts are supported by the organization's culture. Limited counseling by managers is consistent with current trends toward increased employee empowerment and organizational cultures that perceive managers as helpers rather than policemen. In those cases where these assumptions do not hold, the would-be helper can by-pass the manager's phase of the organization's counseling strategy, i.e., go directly to an EAP (phase 3), or an external counseling resource (phase 4).

Understanding the Manager's Role of Counselor

Figure 14.4 describes a process that can be used to help guide the manager in determining when and if counseling can be useful in solving an existing employee problem.[22] This process helps identify the underlying cause of an observed performance deficiency so as to introduce the changes necessary to correct the situation and thereby ensure that appropriate levels of performance are achieved and maintained. Let us walk through the recommended steps and assess their effect on the manager's choice of action alternatives.

Step 1. Before managers take corrective action, they must assess the importance of the perceived behavioral deficiency. Is it worth their time and effort to correct the problem? The subset of questions presented in Figure 14.5 can help the manager assess the relevance of a perceived behavioral deficiency.

Figure 14.4

Role of counseling

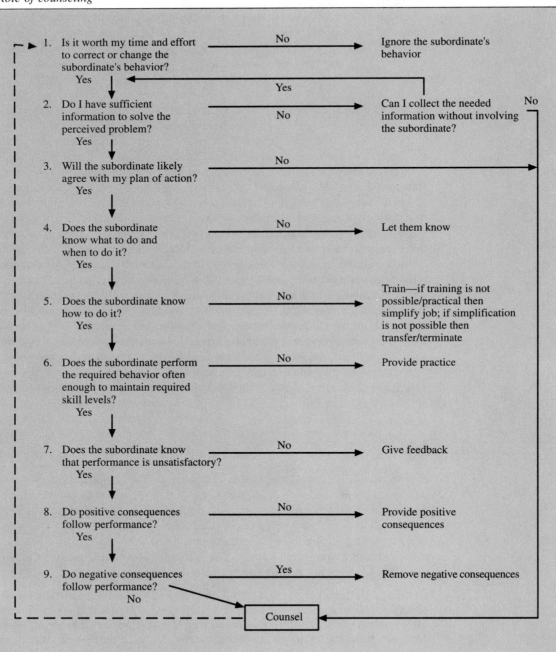

FIGURE 14.5

Assessing the need to act

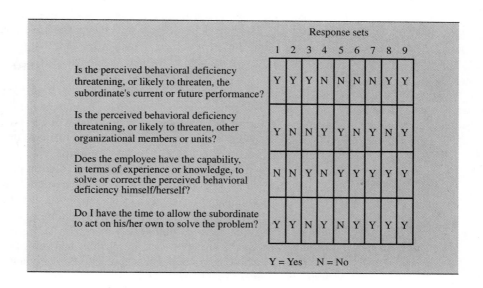

The matrix presented in Figure 14.5 describes the possible response alternatives open to managers. If a manager's response set matches any of the first five columns then it is in the manager's best interest to take steps to correct the perceived problem. For example, in Response Set 1, the behavior not only will prevent subordinates from achieving their goals, but it will also affect other organizational members or units. Unfortunately, the subordinates are not able to correct the deficiency themselves. Under such conditions, the manager must act to solve the problem. If, however, the manager's response set matches any of the conditions indicated in Columns 6 through 9, then the manager would be wasting time attempting to change the employee's behavior. Response Set 9 indicates that although the behavioral deficiency will adversely affect the subordinates and others within the organization, they are able to correct the problem, and the managers have the time to wait for the subordinates to act. In this case, it is in the managers' best interest to allow the subordinates to solve their own problems and at the same time learn from the experience.

Step 2. Once it is determined that action should be taken to correct a behavioral deficiency, managers must assess whether they have sufficient information to identify cause-and-effect relationships existing within the environment, and then implement a correct solution to the problem. If the answer to the first question is no, then managers must collect the needed information. The issue then becomes: can managers collect the needed information without involving the subordinates, or will it be necessary to consult with the employees. If the employees need not be consulted, managers will collect the needed information and introduce changes designed to correct the deficiency. However, where the managers cannot collect such information without the subordinates' help, the managers will want to initiate counseling exchanges with the subordinates.

Steps 3 to 9. These steps represent a set of questions that managers will want to ask themselves to identify and correct the underlying cause producing the behavioral deficiency. (The actual order of internal questioning followed by a manager will reflect the demands and characteristics unique to each situation. Therefore, the order presented in Figure 14.4 is not to be considered the required questioning sequence.) Each question is designed to direct the manager's attention to a potential cause resulting in the behavioral deficiency. The manager's response determines the course of action that will be taken.

The logic behind such a strategy is that behavioral deficiencies occurring within organizations may be the result of multiple causes. When this occurs it may be necessary to introduce a multifaceted solution package.

At the end of Step 9 (Figure 14.4), managers may find that although they initially assumed that sufficient information was available to effectively introduce change, their failure to determine an appropriate course of action demonstrated that the assumption was incorrect. When this occurs, managers should reassess the situation to collect additional information. As part of this information-gathering process, managers will likely initiate a counseling session with the problem employee.

The Manager's Limited Role as Helper

It is important to remind students that most managers will only have a limited role as helper. The typical manager does not have the benefit of professional training designed to develop those behaviors required to perform effectively as a helper or counselor. Mistakes made by the untrained, would-be helper can cause more damage than good or can lead to legal suits by employees who acted unwisely because of the advice or guidance they received when being counseled by an untrained manager.[23] Perry points out some of the more common mistakes that would-be counselors make when attempting to help others.[24] The following are examples of several common mistakes or errors of would-be helpers:

- Get so caught up in the helping process that they begin to behave as if they were a full time social worker or psychologist.
- Prematurely convince helpees that they have a problem when in fact no such problem exists.
- Fail to keep current on the number of counseling resources which exist within the local community, being totally unaware of community services that can be used to help employees when internal resources are not available.
- Remain ignorant of relevant laws within their community, state, or province.

- Divulge confidential information.
- Discuss areas that are not specifically job-related.

Therefore, the manager's efforts to problem solve should be limited to job-related problems that he or she has technical competence to help solve. Once a performance problem is linked to personal problems, the manager's efforts should be limited to initial attempts to get the employee to recognize the link between his or her behavior and poor performance, and the personal consequence of poor performance. If it is determined that poor performance is related to a personal situation, the manager should seek help from the human resource department or direct the employee to an existing EAP. What managers must recognize is that they should leave the counseling of troubled employees to professionals.[25]

The Basic Counseling Model

The model described in Figure 14.6 can be used as a basic guide in the design and implementation of an employee counseling session. The following discussion will draw heavily on the material presented by Carkhoff and Berenson[26] and Nelson-Jones.[27] Their philosophy and recommendations closely parallel the authors' and are consistent with the material already presented in this chapter.

As described, the counseling exchange not only functions on two distinct levels (the counselor or helper level and the helpee or learner level), but it is also time integrating. The counseling exchange is past oriented because what takes place during the actual counseling exchange reflects past encounters between the participants and between the participants and their environment. The counseling session is also future oriented because what is decided in the

FIGURE 14.6

The basic counseling process

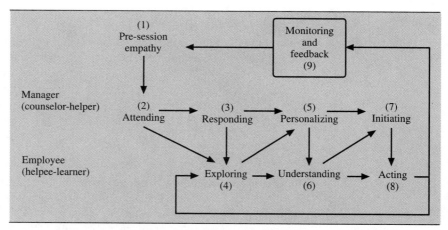

Source: *Beyond Counseling and Therapy*, 2d ed., R. R. Carkhoff and B. G. Berenson, Holt, Rinehart & Winston, New York, 1977, p 23.

session will affect how each participant behaves in the future. Last, what takes place during the counseling exchange plays a critical role in determining the ultimate success of the counseling session.

1. Pre-Session Empathy

Pre-session empathy refers to the manager's ability to develop, through day-to-day interaction, an understanding of who the employee truly is. Specifically, what are the employee's needs, long-term objectives, capabilities, potentials, fears, etc.? The better that managers understand (know) subordinates, the greater the probability that they will conduct successful counseling sessions in the future. In this way, managers demonstrate their ability to enter into the client's internal frame of reference, and thereby see the world through the eyes of the employee. Understanding increases the level of trust, respect, and positive rapport between manager and subordinate. (Trust, respect, and positive rapport, as discussed elsewhere in this text, are also a function of perceived manager fairness, dependability, predictability, and interpersonal sensitivity.) Such a climate increases the probability that managers can maintain open channels of communications between themselves and employees.

The key to the development of pre-session empathy is the desire of the manager to increase the level of contact with others. Observation of, and discussions with, employees expand the information base the manager can draw upon when interacting with others. Such information provides the manager better insight into potential causes of poor performance, the appropriateness of suggested solutions, and can facilitate an assertive counseling style designed to keep the counseling session on track.

Personality and organizational problems may also produce unproductive behavior.[28] The severity of the observed unproductive behavior will affect the likelihood of managers taking action and the appropriateness of counseling interventions. Table 14.1 summarizes a number of these key problems.[29]

Relevant information about others also allows the manager to make effective predictions about how the problem employee may respond to counseling efforts. The manager must consider whether the subordinate is (*a*) susceptible to interpersonal influence, (*b*) likely to agree that a problem exists and that there is a need to change, and (*c*) can cope with the issues to be discussed during the counseling session.[30] If such client-specific characteristics are not in place, there is an increased probability that the counseling effort will fail.

2. Attending Skills

The purpose of attending behaviors is to ensure that both the manager and the subordinate are active participants in the counseling process. There are specifically three types of attending behaviors available to the counselor: *physical attending, observing,* and *listening.* They are described below in some detail.

TABLE 14.1   Personality and Organizational Problems, Level of Severity, and Behavioral Consequences

	Level of Severity and Behavioral Consequences		
	Minor	*Serious*	*Acute/Chronic*
Problems at the Individual Level			
Low self-image/high opinion of others	Shy, uncertain about the future, seeks to please others, and is easily influenced	Fears success, avoids responsibilities, and finds it difficult to make decisions	Withdraws from relationships, refuses to make decisions, but at the same time is envious of others—likely to exhibit signs of depression
Low self-image/low opinion of others	Pities self, blames others for personal mistakes—likely to feel watched by others	Often confused and displays inconsistent action, begins to fall behind on assignments—likely to be defensive and secretive	Individual's actions become irrational, fails to complete assigned work, increasingly isolated and paranoid—personal breakdown near
Inflated assessment of personal abilities	Aggressive, expresses strong views, dominates interpersonal encounters	Not easily influenced by others, seeks control, critical of others, and unwilling to let go of job responsibilities	Totally inflexible, ignores feedback, contemptuous of others, bullies, and finds pleasure in winning at the expense of others
Problems at the Organizational Level			
Technical deficiencies	Begins to experience self-doubt when performing some work, following procedures, or using available technologies	Fears making serious errors in his or her work, or has begun to make such errors	Becomes dysfunctional, can not carry out assignments, frequently argues with technical experts, and begins to miss work

(continued)

TABLE 14.2 *(concluded)*

	Level of Severity and Behavioral Consequences		
	Minor	*Serious*	*Acute/Chronic*
Low work demands	Begins to feel bored	Continually bored, becomes restless, and begins to consider a career move	If the individual does not leave, he or she becomes negative about work, and may withdraw emotionally or physically (e.g., daydreams, comes to work late, or takes unscheduled days off)
Poor interpersonal relationships	Begins to feel personal dissatisfactions with the level of social interaction on the job	Feels isolated and begins to question self-worth, competencies, and interpersonal attractiveness	Withdraws and isolates him or herself, becomes critical of others, and may verbally or physically attack others

Physical attending takes place on several levels. First, managers ensure that employees realize that they are available to fulfill the counseling role. However, to have the desired effect, words must be followed up with acts. Managers can accomplish this by physically making themselves accessible to individuals who request counseling services. Unfortunately, there are instances where relevant others are unaware of an existing problem or are too passive to personally approach others for help. As a result, the manager must first act to tactfully initiate a counseling exchange with the troubled other.

Closely related to the issue of awareness, accessibility, and initiative is the question of where to hold the counseling session. The appropriateness of a setting will likely differ from situation to situation. For example, by calling a lathe operator into a private management office for a closed-door counseling session, the manager could cause the employee to become highly anxious and doom the session to failure. Therefore, in certain situations some managers may find it beneficial to hold a planned counseling session in a location other than a private office. Conversely, a counseling session held in a manager's private office may be completely acceptable to an office worker. The key is to select a neutral area that will not intimidate the subordinate. Moreover, it is necessary to select a location that will (*a*) keep interruptions at a minimum and (*b*) be quiet enough to facilitate effective communication.

Attending behavior also refers to the manner in which the manager physically interacts with the subordinate during the counseling session. Nelson-Jones recommended the following behaviors when physically attending to the relevant other.[31]

1. During a counseling exchange, the subordinate is likely to respond to the nonverbal cues exhibited by the would-be helper. If the manager appears tense, this tension is likely to be transmitted to the subordinate. Therefore, the manager should appear physically relaxed. This can be accomplished by minimizing such behaviors as crossed arms; stiff and erect upper torso when in a sitting position; fidgeting behaviors likely to communicate impatience or tension, such as finger-tapping, leg-bouncing, clock-watching; and standing while the client sits down.

2. To take full advantage of the verbal and nonverbal messages being sent by the relevant other, the manager must ensure open visual access to the individual. Two options assure the manager the desired level of physical openness. One option is for the manager to sit directly in front of the other individual. A second option, for those individuals who find physical mirroring of the subordinate too formal or threatening to the subordinate, is to sit at a slight angle from the subordinate. This second option, while still providing visual openness, offers increased opportunity for visual variety. It is also argued that the counseling setting should be organized to facilitate involvement and motivation by both parties. For example, it is considered undesirable to have a large desk placed between the two individuals. Such a barrier is likely to reduce effective interaction and the free flow of communication.

3. Posture while sitting can also affect the subordinate's behavior during the counseling session. It is suggested that the manager take a sitting position directly in front of, or angled to the side of the subordinate. It is important in terms of distance to position oneself close enough, and with the upper torso leaning slightly toward the subordinate, to demonstrate interest and involvement. However, the manager must not impinge on the subordinate's personal space so as to not be perceived as threatening or dominating. Clearly, the better the manager's pre-session empathy, the better he or she will be able to judge appropriate distancing.

4. To facilitate the development of manager–employee rapport during the counseling session, allow for interpersonal assessment of facial behavior, and at the same time create a positive listening climate, it is recommended that the manager maintain good eye contact with the relevant other. Excessive eye movement, lack of eye contact, and extended periods of note taking, or reading of personal notes, can communicate negative messages to the subordinate. Such behavior can imply nervousness, lack of sincerity, or disinterest by the manager, and subsequently cause the subordinates to withdraw or be less candid than they should be.

5. The manager can stimulate subordinate dialogue by intrinsically rewarding the employee for messages sent and his or her overall responsiveness during the counseling session. Most individuals respond well to facial expressions that are in harmony with their mood and statements. Smiles are appropriate when the subordinate says something that is appropriate or supportive of the problem-solving process or when the general mood of the subordinate is positive. If, on the other hand, the subordinate is upset or expressing a high level

of stress or anxiety, the manager's facial expression and overall demeanor should communicate concern, support, or patience. Other nonverbal behavior designed to intrinsically reward the client's active participation in the counseling session includes positive nods of the head, use of nonwords like "mm, hmm," or the use of such terms as "interesting" or "I see." The only caution here is that the counselor's use of intrinsic reinforcements be sincere and not overdone. Excessive or inappropriate use of these behaviors can have an effect opposite to the one planned.

In addition, the manager can communicate the potential for extrinsic rewards should the counseling session be successful. In other words, during the initial attending sequence, usually in the form of an opening statement, the subordinate can be informed that the manager wishes to work with the subordinate to address concerns about current or past performance. The implication is that if the subordinate and the manager can work together to solve work-related problems, then the subordinate will likely receive extrinsic positive reinforcement due to increased levels of performance, such as job security, good interpersonal relations, and future pay increases.

Observing skills refer to the manager's ability to correctly perceive and understand the relevant other's nonverbal behavior during the counseling session. Therefore, the manager must be alert to all behavioral cues that might indicate the individual's emotional level, intellectual state (alertness and preparedness to evaluate and make decisions), needs, etc. Effective observing also facilitates effective listening—the next required attending skill. Here again, pre-session empathy can be helpful in assessing the current emotional or intellectual state of the employee. Pre-session empathy increases the likelihood of having base-line measures of what can be considered normal behavior for the employee. Any deviations from these base-line measures will alert the manager to what is happening internally to the employee.

As the counseling session unfolds, the manager is constantly monitoring the situation for relevant verbal or nonverbal cues that will signal the need to alter the counseling style. This process is depicted in Figure 14.7. (Topics that have already been adequately discussed elsewhere will not be reviewed at this time; that is, nonverbal behaviors were discussed in Chapter 4.) What is important

FIGURE 14.7

Observation inputs likely to affect counseling behavior

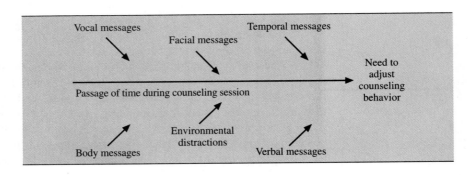

is that counselors tune in to these six input channels and be willing to adjust their counseling behaviors to reflect the specific needs of the clients or external environments. The student examples that follow in this chapter demonstrate the level of attending and response flexibility that is needed.

Listening demonstrated by most individuals is not effective. To overcome this deficiency, counselors should follow a simple rule—"learn to STOP, LOOK, and LISTEN." Managers cannot be listening if they are doing all the talking, or probing using yes or no questions. Second, managers cannot be effective listeners if they do not work at observing the nonverbal behaviors of the employee. When it comes to emotions, feelings, or personal problems, the subordinate's words rarely transmit the entire message. As noted in Chapter 4, good listeners must work to overcome the pitfalls likely to cause them to fail as listeners, and at the same time develop the rapport-building and active-listening styles necessary to tune into the true message being transmitted by the troubled employee.

The Effect of Attending

The attending phase of the counseling model ensures that both parties become aware of the problem or issue that can potentially be resolved by the counseling session. There are two alternative triggering mechanisms that are likely to produce the desired results. First, it is possible that the helpee, or subordinate, will bring the problem to the forefront by making a statement that he or she is unhappy or concerned about some aspect of his or her life. Once this opening statement has been made, the manager can use his or her communication and interpersonal skills to probe more deeply into the problem. If the troubled individual does not verbally take the initiative, it then becomes the responsibility of the would-be helper to respond to nonverbal cues and ask stem-type questions to initiate the desired exchange and begin the counseling process. For example, if the employee looks upset, anxious, or is fidgeting, the would-be helper might state, "I can't help noticing that you appear concerned about something—did something happen that upset you?" In this case, the counselor is using an understanding statement to elicit information or more specifically initiate a counseling encounter. Ideally, the manager would prefer that the troubled individual make the first move to initiate the helping process. However, if this does not occur, the would-be helper must act to motivate the troubled individual to become involved.

A Student Example Model

A description of a counseling exchange with a problem student will be used to breathe life into our discussion. We will describe a portion of this exchange as each of the remaining counseling steps is considered. To give these fictitious individuals an identity we will call the student Pat and the professor Will Helpim. The course in which Pat's problem occurs is entitled Management Skill Development (MSD).

We will assume that Will has already established pre-session empathy with his students. For example, Will has laid the groundwork for student trust and respect by demonstrating fairness in assigning work, testing, and grading. He has also maintained a high level of contact with students by coming to class early, building frequent office hours into his time schedule, and making an effort to attend as many student activities as possible.

Also assume that Pat has failed the midterm in his management skill development class. Pat's professor, to ensure awareness and initiative, announced in class (and inserted a similar written statement of policy into the course syllabus) that any student receiving a D or F grade should make an appointment to come in and discuss the poor grade. The professor also stated that anyone unhappy with the grade given should also set up a meeting to discuss how to improve before the final examination. In response to a desire to improve and the stated course policy, Pat set up a meeting with his professor, Will Helpim. Before meeting with Professor Helpim, Pat asked around to find out what he was like. The following are some of the adjectives used to describe Professor Helpim: sensitive, fair, firm, no-nonsense, willing to listen, not the type of person who would force a solution on anyone and would prefer to jointly work with troubled students so that they could solve their own problems. Given this information, Pat felt comfortable setting up an appointment with Professor Helpim.

Whenever he met with a student in difficulty, Will made every effort to ensure that the meeting time was convenient for both him and the student. Before all student meetings about grades, Will requested that his secretary hold all calls and ensure that no interruptions were allowed. In addition, Will had set up his office so that both he and his student could sit comfortably in two easy chairs in one corner of the office. The chairs themselves were at a slight angle to one another thus allowing for a clear, unobstructed view for both parties.

At the meeting, Pat took the initiative by stating, "I'm really upset that I failed the midterm. I know that if I fail this course I'm in big trouble. If I fail, I think my family will disown me—also I doubt if I will get into the MBA program I'm applying to."

Such a statement is likely to produce a sequence of probes, reflective statements, understanding statements, and summarization. Such behavior allows the helper to move to the responding phase, and the helpee to the exploring phase, of the counseling model.

3. Responding

Theory—Let us leave Will and Pat for a moment to consider the issue of appropriate responding behavior. Responding refers to the manner in which the manager empathizes with the needs, feelings, and emotions of the employee to demonstrate understanding of, or insight into, the individual's reality. Effective responding also demonstrates to the individual seeking help that the manager understands the nonemotional content of the message as well. Response statements are structured so as to reflect and mirror back what the individual has said. By so doing, the manager attempts to cause the employee to explore his or her environment to better understand how it works.

You say _____

You feel _____

You feel _____ because_____

If I hear you correctly, you are saying _____

It should also be realized that correct responding will help ensure increased subordinate involvement throughout the counseling session and at the same time allow the counselor to reach higher functional levels of the counseling process—personalizing and initiating.

Student example—Now that Pat has indicated that there is a problem and that he is unhappy about the situation, Will can respond to feelings, emotions, and the nonemotional content of the message. The following exchange took place between Pat and Will.

> *Pat:* "I'm really upset that I failed the midterm. I can't fail the final."
>
> *Will:* "You're upset about your grade and would like to do something about better preparing for the final?
>
> *Pat:* "Yes, that's right—I know that if I fail this course I'm in big trouble. My family will disown me—and I doubt if I will get into the MBA program I'm applying to."
>
> *Will:* "Would you like to take some time to work together to see what went wrong on the midterm?"

4. *Exploring*

Theory—As managers demonstrate understanding through responding behaviors and statements, they help employees to identify potential solutions to their problem. As discussed earlier, the goal of counseling is also to develop subordinates so that they learn skills necessary to facilitate personal problem solving. In the initial stages of learning, the employees explore their environment. The exploration stage is designed to help employees understand themselves emotionally or psychologically. Through self-exploration, the subordinates better understand who and what they are, and how they fit into the present situation. The employee's ability to explore his or her environment and his or her own self is closely related to the manager's ability to effectively respond (e.g., use of probing questions, reinforcement, correctly summarizing, reflecting, etc.) and attend to the employee. In this way, exploration is a self-diagnostic process by which the subordinate can determine what are important cause-and-effect relationships within the environment. At a minimum, employees will be exploring how the environment works and the experiences they have had in that environment.

Research has demonstrated that when individuals are able to determine the true problem through their own efforts, there is a greater likelihood that they will be willing to undertake appropriate steps to solve it. Through effective exploration, employees are also free to cognitively experience and experiment with their environment. Such activities allow employees to better understand their position or problems. Finally, subordinates' understanding of the problem, as well as their present situation, is critical in any attempt to determine where they want to be, how to get there, and what role they play in the process.

Student example—Before the professor and student can move to higher levels of the helping exchange, the upset student must explore his feelings and the cause-and-effect relationships that exist within the environment. Again, attending and responding behaviors by the professor facilitate this process.

Will: "Let's see if we can figure out what went wrong. Why don't you begin by telling me how you found the test."

Pat: "It was OK, I guess. Just like any other test."

Will: "How did you find the mix between lecture questions and text questions?"

Pat: "Well, I really didn't give it any thought—I just answered the questions the best I could."

Will: "Take a few minutes to review your test and see if you can tell me what percentage came from the lectures and your text."

Pat: "I'd say it's a fifty/fifty split."

Will: "Do you feel that's a reasonable, or fair, split?"

Pat: "Well, I guess so. It's just that I seem to do better on the lecture questions."

Will: "Why don't we try to determine why that happens? For starters, how did you go about studying for this particular test?"

Pat: "Like any other class, I go to lectures, take notes, and review my notes before the examinations. I've always got good grades in the past."

Will: "If you take good notes and know them well before the test you shouldn't have any problem. Do you do well on tests in other classes that deal with lecture material?"

Pat: "Yeah, I always do well on lecture questions—I guess you could say lecture questions are my strong suit."

Will: "OK then, tell me how you approach studying the text."

Pat: "What do you mean?"

Will: "Well, do you read the text and take notes or do you underline with one of those fluorescent markers—and if you take notes or just underline the text, how do you study this material?"

Pat: "I usually read each assignment once through and then the next day I read the assignment again and take notes. When it comes to studying for the test I just review my notes."

Will: "I noticed that you qualified your last statement with the word usually. Did you use that approach to study for your midterm?"

Pat: [*Pat hesitates.*] "No, not really."

Will: "What did you do for this test?"

Pat: "Well, to be honest, professor, I didn't get a chance to study the text."

Will: "Any particular reason?"

Pat: [*Again, Pat hesitates, and then proceeds to blurt out what has been happening in his personal life.*] "Well Prof., my spouse and I have been having some real problems. This program is a lot more demanding than I thought and I'm always studying or working in groups. Well my spouse likes to go out and do things. What makes it worse is that we're not from here. Well it all came to a head last week. I returned from a policy meeting and no one was home. There was just a short note wishing me good luck in the program and the explanation that my spouse had moved back home. Well now I'm all alone, I'm all confused, and I don't know what to do. I can't study and I've missed a lot of classes because I'm not sleeping. Maybe you could tell me how I can get my spouse back?"

Will: "Well Pat I can see that you are really upset, but I'm not in a position to advise you how you should deal with your spouse. But I can work with you to see how this might affect your performance in the program and consider some of the options available here on campus."

As Will and Pat continue to interact, they move into the personalizing and understanding phase of the counseling model.

5. *Personalizing*

Theory—Personalizing is the process by which managers help employees to become increasingly aware of their role in what occurs around, or within, themselves. Specifically, once emotions, feelings, and cause-and-effect relationships in the environment have been discussed, personalization increasingly draws the subordinates closer to a realization of their own personal responsibilities. In this way, managers hope to make the employees personally accountable for what happens to them within the situation being discussed. Personalization can be accomplished through the following type questions:

You feel _____ because *you* _____

You feel _____ because *you* cannot _____

You feel _____ because *you* cannot _____

and *you* want to _____

This happened because *you* _____

This would likely occur if *you* _____

In this way the personalization process increases the subordinates' awareness that they are critically involved in what happens, as well as the realization that any attempt to change that environment will, to a large extent, be a function of the employee's behavior.

Student example—Recall, if you will, that Pat realizes that MSD tests come 50 percent from the text and 50 percent from lectures. Pat also realizes that he wants to get into graduate school and to do so requires good grades. Finally, Pat realizes that if he does poorly on the final he will receive a failure as a term grade. Although not mentioned above, it has also been established that a

65 percent mark is required to pass the MSD course, and that a mere pass is likely to reduce his chances to get into a graduate system. The following dialogue demonstrates how the professor, through attending and responding behavior, can help the troubled student recognize that he plays an important role in determining environmental consequences.

> *Will:* "Tell me, Pat, how are you going to feel if you fail this course?"
> *Pat:* "As I said, I'm going to feel really bad—especially if I don't get into the graduate program I want."
> *Will:* "But you now recognize that if you do poorly this semester you jeopardize those goals?"
> *Pat:* "I understand that I have to be treated like everyone else even though I am a mature student, and that if I don't turn this around I'm in trouble. "
> *Will:* "And you believe that what has been happening is a result of your spouse leaving you last week?"
> *Pat:* "Yes [*a long pause*] I know that because I'm confused and I cannot sleep or concentrate. As a result, I start to miss notes in class and have not been doing the assignments as I should."
> *Will:* "You know what's going to happen if something doesn't change?"
> *Pat:* "Yes ... I'm going to fail."

6. Understanding

Theory—It is at this point that attending, responding, exploring, and personalizing should produce understanding in the mind of the troubled individual. Understanding allows individuals to have insight into their environment and be able to relate behaviors to the consequences of the behaviors. Specifically, helpees should understand (*a*) where they are in relationship to where they want to be, (*b*) how the environment works, and (*c*) consequences of personal behavior (that is, if employees come to work late, they will be docked a certain amount of pay). If the lateness continues, they will be fired. It is this understanding that will allow the two participants to work together to find an acceptable solution and increase the probability of successful behavior in the future.

7. Initiating

Theory—Once the participants in a helping exchange have successfully gone through steps 1 to 6, it is now possible to move into the action, or solution, phase of counseling. At this point, through mutual interaction, both manager and employee are aware of (*a*) the underlying problem, (*b*) personal responsibilities, (*c*) where the employee wants to be, and (*d*) the cause-and-effect relationship between certain behaviors and resulting consequences. However, at this point the appropriate course of action must be operationalized by means of establishing observable and measurable steps necessary to solve the problem or change the situation as desired. Therefore, the objective of initiating activities by the manager is to assist employees to develop an action, or solution, program. It is critical, however, that employees believe that the action program is theirs and that it is not being unilaterally determined by the managers.

This last point is probably the most critical element of the "initiating" step. It is often tempting for managers to dictate a solution. The problem is that employees are more likely to make a personal commitment to the solution if they believe it is theirs. Furthermore, a "know-it-all" position by counselors may threaten the helpees and as a result cause them to become defensive. Initiating statements are typically in the following form.

You would like to achieve ———————————————
The steps you will follow are ———————————————
Your first step would be to ———————————————

As discussed elsewhere in the text, goals, objectives, and attainment steps should be objective, measurable, and temporally based. It is therefore the responsibility of counselors to ensure that clients build these dimensions into any action plan designed to change future behaviors and outcomes.

8. Acting

Theory—At some point the subordinate must decide upon and implement the action program that results from the counseling activities. Therefore, when considering the action learning level it is possible to talk about the identification and decision-making process that takes place and the implementation of the generated action plans. In this way, new behaviors are identified and action plans are willingly implemented by the helpee. The net impact of these behaviors is the increased likelihood that the objectives of the counseling process will be achieved.

This does, however, imply some type of implementation after the session is over. Unfortunately, there is no guarantee that what has been decided upon in the counseling session will in fact be implemented. Therefore, it will be the manager's responsibility to monitor the employee's progress and give meaningful feedback, if appropriate (step 9, Figure 14.6). It may even be necessary to engage in another counseling session if the subordinate's action program becomes disrupted or appears to be failing. This iterative nature of the counseling process is reflected in the external feedback loop in the basic counseling model.

Student example—The joint efforts of the helper and helpee during the initiating and action phases are designed to produce a solution package that both parties find agreeable and will accept. It is this joint acceptance that energizes the process and allows action to be taken by the parties. In the case of Pat and his professor, the following initiating and action-oriented dialogue would produce the desired result. (Assume that steps 1 to 6 resulted in agreement that if Pat's behavior does not change he will fail, current behavior is resulting from the anxiety and confusion caused by his spouse leaving, and that Pat recognizes that he must do something to correct the situation.)

Will: "Then you agree that things cannot continue the way they are going if you want to do well this semester."

Pat: "Well, I know that to get a minimum of a B+ in this course I'm going to have to get at least an A- on the final, and I can't do that if I don't get my life straightened out."

Will: "Do you think that is a realistic goal, given the situation?"

Pat: "I know I can do that well. I've gotten mostly A's in the past, and you've indicated a willingness to take into account improvement if someone has done poorly on the midterm."

Will: "Yes, I'm willing to do that, but what are you going to do to cope with your personal situation?"

Pat: "Well—I don't think I can handle this myself—I've been trying to, but I just can't. That's why I asked if you could help. You've always been willing to listen to student problems."

Will: "I'm more than willing to help, especially if the problem has to do with course work and how to study. In your case, I can help you get back on track but counseling someone on personal problems is something I can't do. But if I hear you right, you think that if you can get some help you may be able to cope with what's happening?"

Pat: "I think so, but I don't know where to start. My wife and I have no friends in town, and we've never had the time to practice our religious faith. I thought about the counseling services group at the student center but I would feel funny just walking in off the street and talking to a total stranger about my wife walking out. I'm not even sure what they do over there."

Will: "I understand how you would feel, it's a very personal issue. However, if you don't mind I could make a suggestion."

Pat: "Not at all, at this point I need somebody to help me."

Will: "Well, my brother has been the director of student counseling for several years and he is a trained clinical psychologist. In fact, they have several good people over there. I also know that they do more than just counsel students on how to study. For example, my brother has been a practicing psychologist for about 20 years. In fact, his staff probably has about 80 years of combined experience dealing with both student and nonstudent problems. If you want, I can talk to my brother and set up an appointment for you."

Pat: "Would I have to meet with him?"

Will: "No, I don't believe so. I'm sure they would let you select the person you would feel most comfortable with. Would you like me to talk to him?"

Pat: [*Pat hesitates.*] "Well ... Ok, I guess I better, as I said, if I don't get someone to help me I'm in big trouble. How soon could you arrange something?"

Will: "I'll give him a call this morning. Give me a call this afternoon, say between 2:00 P.M. and 3:00 P.M. to verify that I've talked to him, and then you can give him a call to set up an appointment."

Pat: "That's great." [*Pat sits quietly but still looks concerned.*]

Will: "You still look a bit concerned, is there anything else?"

Pat: [*Pat hesitates.*] "Yes, there is. I'm still concerned about catching up. I've missed a couple of important lectures and some of the assignments have been pretty confusing. I'd ask some of the other students but they're busy and I'm not sure how much help they would be."

Will: "Can I be of any assistance?"

Pat: "Is there any chance we could meet a couple times to review some of the new material? I know you are busy, but if I review the material again we could just work on those areas I'm having problems with."

Will: "That will be fine, Pat. Why don't we meet once or twice a week to get you back on track. How about Wednesday afternoon?"

We can see from this exchange that there has been an attempt to jointly work together to identify a course of action that will help the student cope with his problem. The first step the student must take is to contact the university's counseling center and set up an appointment. We also see that because the professor's brother is the director of the university's counseling services, and because the student appears hesitant to contact counseling services himself, professor Helpim is willing to make the initial contact for the student. The professor has agreed to meet once a week with Pat. By meeting with Pat, professor Helpim demonstrates support, a desire to help Pat catch up on course material, and at the same time ensures some degree of follow-up. Finally, the professor's response is consistent with our position that managers play a limited role when counseling employees. In our student example, the professor was quite willing to counsel Pat on course-related material or on the students study habits. However, once the session turned in the direction of a personal problem, the professor limited his intervention to helping the student understand (*a*) the link of his performance to behavior, (*b*) the link between behavior and personal problems, and (*c*) the need to seek outside help.

Generally Accepted Do's and Don'ts of Counseling

To help the reader fully understand the counseling process, a list of behaviors considered both desirable and undesirable is presented in Table 14.2. Although there will be some overlap with the above discussion, such a listing

TABLE 14.2   Desirable and Undesirable Counseling Behavior

Desirable	*Undesirable*
Know one's subordinates	Treat subordinates as production resources unworthy of respect or personal interest
Attempt to demonstrate genuine interest and trust in subordinates during day-to-day interactions	Keep on-the-job interaction at a minimum
Keep an open mind and listen	Become argumentative and defensive—take a know-it-all position
Seek mutual agreement	Unilaterally decide on issues
Utilize probing open-ended questions	Ask questions which restrict the subordinate to yes/no answers
Attempt to mirror the subordinate's attitudes and feelings by summarizing	Keep interaction and openness at a minimum
When summarizing attempt to interpret subordinate's statements	
Avoid tendency to come up with hasty solutions	Become impatient and accept the first solution without thinking through consequences
Attempt to obtain verbal commitment with pressure	Set up counseling session in locations convenient to only you
Attempt to make the counseling environment and location as comfortable as possible	

is usually helpful to readers when attempting to organize their thoughts with respect to counseling responsibilities.

Table 14.2 does not necessarily represent a complete listing of desirable or undesirable counseling behaviors. After you have read and fully understood this chapter you should be able to articulate your own do's and don'ts of counseling.

Summary

It should be clear by now that employee counseling is a responsibility every manager will be called upon to perform. Similarly, it should be realized that the counseling process itself is a complex one that requires considerable practice if it is to be performed correctly. More important, research indicates that the manager who develops effective counseling skills will often prevent minor problems from developing into major ones. Therefore, behavioral scientists would argue that although employee counseling is not a hundred percent cure-all, it is a managerial response that should come before issuing a formal punishment or reprimand, and before an employee is discharged or demoted.

The key to managerial success is for the manager to recognize counseling as an available tool in attempting to analyze and solve subordinate problems. The counseling process works well in those areas where the manager does not have complete access to relevant information, and the subordinate does, and where subordinate cooperation is critical to the successful implementation of any change strategy. It is also important to understand the limits to which counseling can be used by the manager. The manager is not a trained psychologist and will in most cases be limited to (*a*) identifying the underlying cause of the behavioral deficiency through counseling, and (*b*) helping the subordinate identify a solution package that the employee will have the responsibility of implementing.

Exercise

14.1 South Shore General Hospital: Counseling the Problem Employee

Your group has the task of developing a script for a meeting about counseling a problem employee. You are L. Murphy, the newly hired head nurse of Unit B at South Shore General Hospital. You were hired to replace the retiring J. Connors, who had been the head nurse for seven years and a staff member for 22 years. Today's date is April 15, 1994. The head nurse is responsible for 12 nurses and nurses' aides on the day shift, 8:00 A.M. to 5:00 P.M. In addition to your direct supervisory responsibilities, you also must attend to first-stage grievances, requests for schedule changes, requests for time off, disciplinary problems, and so forth.

Although you have not had much time to familiarize yourself completely with your new responsibilities or with all the individuals on your nursing staff, you have been asked by the director of nursing, Janet Hill, to handle a problem concerning one of the nurses, Ralph Johnson. Material is presented to acquaint you with the problems surrounding Ralph Johnson prior to your meeting with him. You should draw heavily upon this material in developing the counseling script. The primary purpose of this meeting is to discuss Ralph's recent performance problems in order to (*a*) identify the underlying causes of his behavior and (*b*) agree upon an action program/solution designed to overcome them. Please follow the steps outlined below.

Step 1. The class will be divided into small groups of five or six students each. (Steps 2, 3, and 4 should be completed prior to the next class. Actual role plays will be carried out at that time.)

Step 2. Each group will select one of its members to play the role of L. Murphy, head nurse.

Step 3. Each group will develop an interview script to be used in the meeting with Ralph Johnson. Make whatever additional assumptions you believe appropriate to give life to the script. The only constraint is that your assumptions be consistent with the information provided in this simulation. You should attempt to build into your script many of the learning points relevant to the counseling and feedback process.

Step 4. Practice your script. One of the group's members should play the role of Ralph Johnson and the remaining group members should act as observers.

Step 5. During the next class, one or more groups will be selected to carry out the role play between L. Murphy and Ralph Johnson.

Background

Ralph Johnson has been working in Unit B (see chart) for four years. Until recently, he was considered one of the more conscientious nurses on the floor. Although the average seniority of nurses in your unit is about seven years, Ralph is considered highly knowledgeable of the activities and procedures used by your staff. He is frequently called upon to provide clarification and advice to other nurses and nurses' aides.

However, several incidents involving Ralph have recently occurred that are causing concern among nurses, patients, and individuals outside the department. If something is not done to reverse this trend, it is rumored that the director of nursing will have to take drastic steps. The executive director of the hospital, John Norwood, may even have to be involved. Specifically, Ralph's overall performance has declined, and this has had a negative impact on the performance of the entire work group. Other problems include excessive use of sick days, and returning late from lunch and other breaks. Finally, people have mentioned several instances in which Ralph has antagonized individuals inside and outside the unit. It should also be noted that the nursing staff is nonunionized.

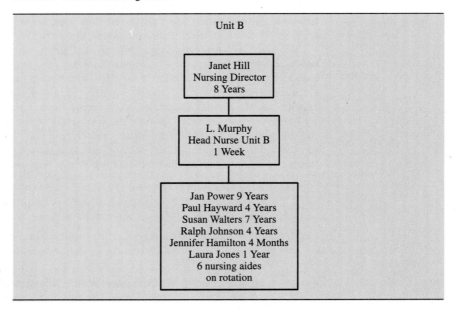

The following items will also help you to develop your counseling/feedback script. Please follow the steps outlined below.

Item 1

To: L. Murphy
From: Janet Hill
Date: April 15, 1994

First, let me again welcome you to South Shore General. I am sure that you will find working here much more relaxing than at Seattle General. Unfortunately, even though you have only been here a week, I must ask you to deal with a problem employee named Ralph Johnson.

Over the past several weeks, I have been reviewing the personnel records of the various nursing units. I have discovered what appears to be a severe problem with one of your staff. In addition, the overall performance of your unit relative to other units has shown signs of deterioration. I have received several complaints from patients and staff alike, and in the past two weeks I have received two requests for transfers out of your unit. I am sensitive to the fact that you have inherited this problem, but because you are now head nurse of Unit B, I believe that any corrective action should be your responsibility. If the problem is not corrected soon, I will be forced to take stronger measures.

In particular, I have noted that Ralph Johnson has become a central figure in many of the problems in your unit. Therefore, I suggest that you start with him in your efforts to bring departmental performance up to acceptable levels. I have attached material from Ralph's personnel file dating back to May 12, 1993. This information will give you a clearer understanding of why I believe that he should be your most immediate concern.

I have complete confidence in your ability to handle this issue. However, if I can be of any help please feel free to contact me. Please give me an update on actions you have taken by week's end.

Item 2

To: Ms. J. Connors, Head Nurse Unit B
From: Laura Jones
Date: May 12, 1993

I am the type of person who likes to give credit where credit is due. Now that I have been with South Shore General for several months, I am finally getting the hang of how things work. Unfortunately, this wasn't the case when I first started working here. If it wasn't for Ralph Johnson, I don't know what I would

(Item 2 concluded)

have done. He was most helpful in showing me the ropes and encouraging me when things got rough. I cannot remember one instance where he complained when I asked him for help.

We should have more people like Ralph around.

Item 3

To: Ms. J. Connors, Head Nurse Unit B
From: Mary Anderson—Nursing Aide
Date: July 18, 1993

Just a short note to thank you for getting Ralph Johnson to help me adjust to the fast pace of activities in our unit. He has been most helpful orienting me in the hands-on activities of patient care typically required of aides. Ralph's assistance was particularly helpful since many RNs are too busy to assist aides.

Thanks again.

Item 4

September 14, 1993

Ms. Janet Hill
Director of Nursing
South Shore General
118 Shore Drive
Westgate, Maine 54321

Dear Ms. Hill:

I usually find it quite hard to write and express myself, but because of the sensitivity and ability of one of your staff I felt that I should write this letter. Our new baby was born prematurely and because of his early birth had respiratory distress syndrome. Being a new mother and not well educated I had no idea what this was. All I knew was that my child was quite ill. One of the nurses on staff at the time, Ralph Johnson (not even one of the regular nurses in the natal unit) was nice enough to sit with me and my husband and explain to us

(Item 4 concluded)

what was wrong with our child. He made it easier to understand than our own doctor. The baby had premature lungs because of an early birth. Mr. Johnson was also nice enough to explain how the new equipment in the unit would help my baby breathe until his own lungs were strong enough and what type of long-term treatment was planned for the next several weeks. Although Mr. Johnson was only in the unit for three days, each time he saw me and Jim he would again spend some time with us to bring us up-to-date. Needless to say, he made those first few days bearable. I was sorry to see Mr. Johnson go back to his own unit.

Happily we have Jim Jr. (our baby) home now and he is doing just fine. When you see Mr. Johnson would you please thank him for all three of us.

Sincerely,

Item 5

To: Janet Hill, Director of Nursing
From: John Norwood, Executive Director
Date: December 15, 1993

This is to inform you that the results of this year's competition for Nurse of the Year are in. The individual receiving the largest number of patient/peer votes (545 votes) was Mary Parker, Unit A. The two runners-up this year were Gail Sherman (514 votes) Unit C, and Ralph Johnson (486 votes) Unit B. All three should be congratulated. The Nurse of the Year award will be presented during the executive committee meeting December 18, 1993. As you know, the winner also receives a 7 percent bonus for the year.

Item 6

To: J. Connors
From: Susan Walters
Date: February 14, 1994

I am writing to formally protest some recent behavior of Ralph Johnson. In the past, he was a real pleasure to work with. However, lately he has been making the rest of us miserable. It is the continual interference that is starting to anger

(Item 6 concluded)

the rest of the nurses. They feel that if I write, you might take some action to correct what we believe is an intolerable situation. Let me give you several examples. The other day I was helping Dr. Penton with a lumbar puncture procedure. We had a seven-year-old girl who needed the procedure to determine if she would test positive for meningitis. Well, I had prepared the patient and was holding her in position for proper back positioning. About then Ralph came by and, in front of the doctor and the patient's parents, started to tell me that I had the patient positioned all wrong. When asked to leave, he refused to leave and continued to make negative comments about the procedure.

This has not been the only occurrence of interference on Ralph's part. Only yesterday I was about to set up an IV with one of my patients and all of a sudden Ralph pulled back the curtain, observed what I was doing, and told me I was using the wrong-size needle. I have been a nurse for 20 years and I don't appreciate this type of interference. If we cannot work as a team, life around here becomes too stressful. We need to be able to support one another.

I would greatly appreciate your help in this matter.

Item 7

To: Paul Simms, Personnel Manager
From: J. Connors, Head Nurse, Unit B
Date: March 25, 1994

I've been having a problem with one of my staff. Oddly enough, he was one of my better nurses in the past. However, in the last few months his attitude has deteriorated significantly. He has been taking excessive sick days and frequently comes in late. I've told him that unless he changes his behavior, I will have to take drastic action. Unfortunately, I've not seen any dramatic change in his behavior. If anything, it's gotten worse.

Since this is your area of expertise—and I will be retiring in the next few days—I thought you might have a chat with Ralph. Please let me know what you plan to do.

Item 8

To: J. Connors, Head Nurse, Unit B
From: Paul Simms, Personnel Manager
Date: April 1, 1994

In response to your memo of March 25, 1994, I will be out of town until April 28. Upon my return, I will meet with you or your replacement to discuss this matter further. However, to be totally honest, I believe that changing Nurse Johnson's behavior should be your responsibility.

Item 9

March 5, 1994
John Norwood, Executive Director
South Shore General
118 Shore Drive
Westgate, Maine
54321

Dear Mr. Norwood:

I am a person who believes that people should receive some feedback on how well they are performing. During the past three weeks, I was a patient in your hospital because of injuries sustained in a sailing accident. For the most part, I have no complaints about your facilities or staff. They compare very favorably with other hospitals with which I am familiar. There was, however, one exception, a nurse by the name of Ralph Johnson, who was supposed to be assisting me in my recovery. Specifically, I found Mr. Johnson rude, uncooperative, and generally disinterested in the well-being of the patients he was assigned to care for. On at least three occasions, I had to inform him that the medication he wanted me to take was not mine. If I had taken this medication I'm not sure what would have happened. I don't believe I ever got my pills on time when Nurse Johnson was dispensing medication. On several of my trips to therapy sessions, I also observed Mr. Johnson sleeping at the nurse's station. Perhaps this is why he responded to patient calls so infrequently.

Again, I am sorry to have to write this letter, but I believe that if such behavior is left unchallenged it will eventually affect others within your hospital.

Respectfully,
Rita Metcalf

Item 10

To: J. Connors
From: Ray Burns, Manager of Pharmacy
Date: March 2, 1994

I thought it would be appropriate to inform you that my staff is having considerable trouble with one of your nurses. As you know, we fill medication requests based on a 10:00 A.M., 4:00 P.M., and 8:00 P.M. distribution schedule. To meet these deadlines, we need to receive requisitions no later than two hours prior to these times. However, whenever Ralph Johnson is responsible for delivery of requests or medication pickups, he is usually one to two hours late. I am already short of staff and as a result find it difficult to keep everybody happy. Therefore, when nurses do not cooperate or fail to perform, my people fall further and further behind. I would appreciate it if you would have a word or two, or three, with Mr. Johnson. So far, my complaints have been ignored.

Item 11

April 1, 1994

Janet Hill, Director of Nursing
South Shore General
118 Shore Drive
Westgate, Maine
54321

Dear Ms. Hill:

I am writing to request a transfer out of Unit B. Although I have worked here for only four months, I believe I have given the unit a fair chance. It appears that the working environment has become quite negative and gives every indication of worsening in the future. Unfortunately, Ms. Connors was unable to cope or change the situation, and I don't believe the new head nurse, Ms. Murphy, will have much luck either. Things have gone too far.

Although there are several factors causing problems in the unit, Ralph Johnson appears to be a major contributing factor. He is insensitive to the needs and feelings of patients and staff alike. When you tell him that something needs to be done, he tells you why it cannot be done or shouldn't be done. In addition, he refuses to listen to any constructive criticism about his performance

(Item 11 concluded)

and has verbally threatened several of the other nurses. He has told me personally on at least five occasions to mind my own business. When Ms. Connors pointed out that he had overextended his coffee and lunch breaks, he denied everything. The bottom line is that Ralph's negative attitude is affecting everyone else and making Unit B an unpleasant place to work. Therefore, could I speak with you personally to discuss my transfer? I should mention that if I cannot transfer, I will seek employment elsewhere.

Respectfully,
Jennifer Hamilton

Item 12

Employee Attendance Summary

Name: Ralph Johnson
Department: Unit B—Nursing
Location: South Shore General, Chester Wing
Period Covered: April 1993–March 1994

	Late Days		Absences	
Month	*Recorded for Employee*	*Average for all Nurses*	*Recorded for Employee*	*Average for all Nurses*
April 1993	0	4	0	1
May 1993	0	4.5	0	1.5
June 1993	0	4	0	.5
July 1993	1	5	0	1
August 1993	0	5	0	2
September 1993	0	5	0	1.5
October 1993	2	5	1	2
November 1993	0	4	0	1.5
December 1993	0	4.5	1	3
January 1994	7	5	3	1
February 1994	6	5.5	7	1.5
March 1994	10	5	6	2

Item 13

Performance Appraisal and Review
Nursing Form 2–12A

Employee: Ralph Johnson
Department: Unit B, Nursing
Location: South Shore General, Chester Wing
Period Covered: January 1, 1993–December 31, 1993

Supervisory ratings of employee are for the period shown. Upon completion, this form will be placed in the subordinate's permanent file.

Scale: 1 = Unacceptable.
2 = Needs some improvement.
3 = Satisfactory.
4 = Good.
5 = Outstanding.

1. Technical understanding of job.   5
2. Work quality.   5
3. Dependability.   5
4. Decision making.   4
5. Interpersonal sensitivity.   5
6. Ability to handle stress.   3

Supervisor's signature _____

Employee's signature _____

Employee's signature signed to
acknowledge PAR meeting only,
subordinate does not accept ratings _____

Date of interview _____

End Notes

1. R. Cooke, "Low-cost help for troubled employees," *Credit Union Management,* Vol. 14, No. 2, 1991: 50–51; J. Hall and B. Fletcher, "EPA potential to save money unknown," *Business Insurance,* Vol. 17, No. 35, 1983: 14.

2. P. Cairo, "Counseling in industry: A selected review of the literature," *Personnel Psychology,* Vol. 36, No. 1: 1–18.

3. D. W. Myers, *Employee Problem Prevention and Counseling,* Quorum Books, Westport, Conn., 1985.

4. J. Hall and B. Fletcher, "Coping with personal problems at work," *Personnel Management,* Vol. 16, No. 2, 1984: 30–33.

5. V. R. Buzzotta, R. E. Lefton, and M. Sherberg, "Coaching and counseling: How you can improve the way it's done," *Training and Development Journal,* Vol. 31, No. 11, 1977: 50.

6. D. W. Myers, 1985: 4.

7. W. M. Bruce, *Problem Employee Management,* Quorum Books, Westport, Conn., 1990.

8. Buzzotta, Lefton, and Sherberg, 1977.

9. M. B. Parloff, I. Waskow, and B. E. Wolfe, "Research on therapist variables in relation to process and outcome," in *Handbook of Psychotherapy and Behavior Change and Clinical Psychology,* ed. S.L. Garfield and A.E. Bergin, John Wiley & Sons, New York, 1978; H. H. Strupp, "The outcome problem in psychotherapy: Contemporary perspectives," in *The Master Lecture Series, Volume 1: Psychotherapy Research and Behavior Change,* ed. J. H. Harvey and M. M. Parks, Washington, D.C.: American Psychological Association, 1982; J. D. Frank, "The present status of outcome studies," *Journal of Consulting and Clinical Psychology,* Vol. 47: 310–316; J. W. Lieberman, I. D. Yalom, and M. B. Miles, *Encounter Groups: First Facts,* Basic Books, New York, 1973.

10. R. De Board, *Counselling People at Work,* Aldershot, Hants, England, Gower Publishing Company Limited, 1983.

11. Figure 14.2 is based on material presented in De Board, 1983.

12. De Board, 1983.

13. Buzzotta, Lefton, and Sherberg, 1977.

14. For a discussion of a number of alternative sequences refer to J. F. Dickman, W. G. Emener, and W. S. Hutchison, *Counseling the Troubled Person in Industry,* Charles C Thomas, Publisher, Springfield, Ill., 1985.

15. Bruce, 1990: 6

16. T. H. Stone and N. M. Meltz, *Human Resource Management in Canada,* Toronto, Dryden, 1993.

17. Anonymous, "EAP programs and productivity," *Supervisory Management,* Vol. 39, No. 1, 1994: 5.

18. S. Rosenzwig and E. P. Kramer, "Getting with the program," *Small Business Reports,* Vol. 17, No. 8, 1992: 20–24.

19. J. A. Segal, "Alchoholic employees and the law," *HR Magazine,* Vol. 38, No. 12, 1993: 87–94.

20. D. Hockley, "Assisting employees at B.C. Tel," *Canadian Business Review,* Vol. 19, No. 2, 1992: 25–28.

21. Rosenzwig and Kramer, August 1992.

22. Similar decision-tree models have been used to identify training needs, C. O. Longenecker and P. R. Liverpool, "An action plan for helping troubled employees," *Management Solutions,* Vol. 33, No. 7, 1988: 22–27.

23. Longenecker and Liverpool, 1988.

24. P. M. Perry, "Problems of counseling troubled staff members," *Law Practice Management,* Vol. 18, No. 4, 1992: 40–44.

25. P. M. Perry, "Dealing with troubled employees," *Legal Assistant,* Vol. 9, No. 5, 1992: 78–85.

26. R. R. Carkhuff and B. G. Berenson, *Beyond Counseling and Therapy,* Holt, Rinehart & Winston, New York, 1977.

27. R. Nelson-Jones, *Practical Counselling and Helping Skills,* Cassell Educational Limited, London, 1989.

28. Bruce, 1990.

29. Table 14.2 is based on material presented in De Board, 1983: 25 and 27.

30. L. Luborsky, "Perennial mystery of poor agreement among criteria for psychotherapy outcome," *Journal of Consulting and Clinical Psychology,* Vol. 37, 1971: 316–319; S. L. Garfield, "Research on client variables in psychotherapy," in S.L. Garfield and A. E. Bergin (eds.), *Handbook of Psychotherapy and Behavior Change,* John Wiley & Sons, New York, 1978: 191–232.

31. Nelson-Jones, 1989.

15

UNDERSTANDING THE ORGANIZATION AND ITS ENVIRONMENT: A MACRO PERSPECTIVE

Learning Objectives:

- To sensitize students to the importance of understanding the system in which they will function as managers.
- To identify major environmental components that, when understood, enhance the manager's ability to maximize the level of subordinate productivity.

Understanding the Organization

Most adults will spend approximately 50 percent of their waking hours within an organizational setting. Therefore, one of the first tasks that should be carried out by employees is to develop an understanding of the system in which they are working. Managers can only effectively manage the manager–subordinate interface if they (a) understand the major environmental components relevant to managerial activity, and (b) effectively use this information when dealing with subordinates and others within the organization.

Figure 15.1 shows those factors that must be understood by all managers if they are to be successful. The model indicates that the success of managers will be affected by their ability to collect and understand critical information existing within the organization's internal and external environments. With the appropriate understanding of this information, the manager will significantly increase the likelihood of making correct decisions in the future. The student should realize that while each topic area is discussed separately, in the real world these areas are highly interactive. For example, what happens within the organization's external environment will likely have an impact on strategic planning, which in turn will alter power relationships, reward systems,

639

FIGURE 15.1

Knowledge critical to effective management

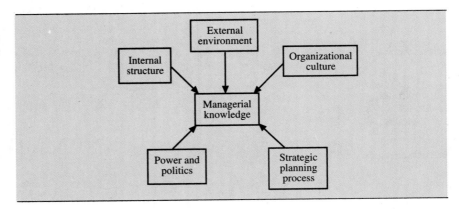

etc. Finally, the selection of the information areas discussed reflects what the authors believe should be understood by managers in their efforts to increase the performance of others. The precise set of variables that will be most relevant to a particular manager will be a function of the organization in which he or she performs.

The Organization's External Environment

Since the early works of Dill,[1] Thompson,[2] Lawrence and Lorsch,[3] and of Duncan,[4] it has generally been shown that the organization's environment plays a crucial role in determining what does, and should, occur within that organization. Specifically, what exists within the organization's external environment is likely to impact upon all subsystems within that organization and specifically on the management subsystem. The easiest way in which to articulate what the manager must be aware of is to list those environmental components that are typically considered to have the greatest effect on the organization and therefore are most relevant to the manager. Here Duncan's original conceptualization serves our purpose quite well. As indicated in Table 15.1, Duncan showed that the organization's external environment is made up of five major components that are particularly important to industrial organizations.[5] (Again, the exact listing may vary depending on the type of organization being considered.)

More recently, other behavioral scientists have suggested that Duncan's dimensions can be reduced. Boulton and his associates have argued that when managers act as planners it is possible for the competitor dimension to be incorporated into the customer and supplier dimensions.[6] Others have suggested that Duncan's five dimensions can be collapsed to two dimensions, that is, unpredictability of the market (e.g., product demand), and technological volatility

TABLE 15.1   Factors and Components Constituting the Organization's External Environment

Customer Component
- Distribution of product or service
- Actual users of product or service

Suppliers Component
- New materials suppliers
- Equipment suppliers
- Product parts suppliers
- Labor supply

Competitor Component
- Competitors for suppliers
- Competitors for customers

SocioPolitical Component
- Government regulatory control over the industry
- Public political attitude toward industry and its particular product
- Relationship with trade unions with jurisdiction in the organization

Technical Component
- Meeting new technological requirements of own industry and related industries in production and service
- Improving and developing new products by implementing new technological advances in the industry

Source: R. B. Duncan, "Characteristics of organizational environments and perceived environmental uncertainty," *Administrative Science Quarterly,* Vol. 17, 1972, p. 315.

(e.g., uncertainties about technological advances).[7] Unfortunately, by reducing the number of dimensions considered, managers may begin to oversimplify the organizational environments they face, and ultimately reduce their environmental scanning efforts.

The model found in Figure 15.2 attempts to reconcile these differences. When dealing directly with customers, suppliers, and competitors, the organization is able to negotiate with and influence their behavior. However, because of market dynamics or volatility, managers are unable to predict with complete certainty what is likely to happen in each sub-environment. Nevertheless, based upon past contacts, and the ability to affect suppliers, customers, and competitors, managers can link statements of probability or risk with future environmental outcomes. In contrast, organizations have only indirect contact with the sociopolitical and technological dimensions of their external environments. As a result, they are less likely to feel capable of predicting what will occur in the future.

FIGURE 15.2

*Sources of
environmental
uncertainty*

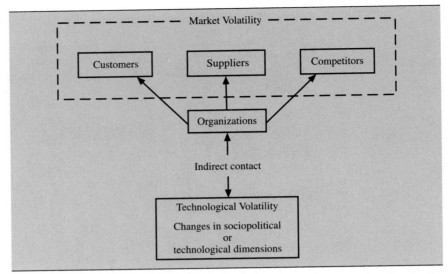

Source: S.J. Hartman, M.C. White, and M.D. Crino, "Environmental volatility, system adaptation, planning requirements, and information-processing strategies: An integrative model," *Decision Sciences*, Vol. 17, Fall 1986: p. 458. The *Decision Sciences* journal is published by the Decision Sciences Institute, located at Georgia State University.

Environmental Uncertainty

In addition to the two categories of environmental dimensions described in Figure 15.2, behavioral scientists have also used the dimensions of complexity and dynamics to define the actual level of environmental uncertainty faced by the organization.[8] However, managers need to be more specific when dealing with the concept of uncertainty. This can be accomplished by differentiating among *three* types.[9]

State Uncertainty

First, there is s*tate uncertainty,* which results from the level of change, complexity, and difference (number of different participants or constituent units) found within each environmental component. Clearly, the slower the rate of change, the more simple the relationships and processes in that environmental component, and the fewer and more homogeneous the participants, the more certain one can be about environmental predictions.

Effect Uncertainty

A second type of uncertainty about the environment deals with the type of cause-and-effect relationships that exist between the environmental component and the organization and its sub-units. Therefore, managers may know what is happening within their environment, but be unable to predict the nature, severity, or timing of the impact on their organization or unit. This second type of uncertainty can be referred to as *effect uncertainty.*

Response Uncertainty

The third type of environmental uncertainty occurs when an organization or manager attempts to assess available response options, or the potential consequence of such response options. In this case we can talk about *response uncertainty,* when the manager is unable to clearly articulate available options, or cannot clearly assess their impact on the organization or its environment.

What is important to realize is that each type of uncertainty will likely require a different behavioral response by the manager. For example, if the major type of uncertainty facing the manager is state uncertainty, then managers would be best advised to expend their energies on scanning and forecasting activities to better understand the environment. Similarly, if state uncertainty is high, then managers may alter the strategic planning process to reflect this uncertainty, that is, attempt to muddle through the process,[10] use the so-called garbage-can approach to decision making,[11] or attempt to buffer and protect internal subsystems from an uncertain external environment.[12] If the uncertainty facing managers is best described as effect uncertainty, then it is likely that they will direct more and more resources to the threats and opportunity phase of the strategic planning process (see block 5, Figure 15.8). The emphasis here is to identify as best as possible the implications of known changes on organizational, or departmental, outcomes. Finally, if the uncertainty faced by the manager is response uncertainty, then the manager is likely to direct increased time, energy, and resources to response analysis. In this case there is likely to be (*a*) an increased effort to network with other organizations to determine what others are doing, (*b*) merely copy other successful managers or organizations, or (*c*) delay one's actual response until more information is collected.

The Manager as Boundary Spanner

By collecting information about the organization's environment, and by inputting this information into the appropriate decision-making process, managers fulfill an important boundary-spanning function. Research has indicated that boundary-spanning activities (e.g., representing the organization, scanning, monitoring, transacting, and coordinating) increase as environmental complexity and dynamics increase.[13] Boundary-spanning activities also increase when the significance, accountability, and irreversibility of decisions made increase.[14]

When collecting and transferring information, boundary spanners must be able to communicate and translate information across boundaries.[15] To facilitate this transfer, boundary spanners must also be linked to internal and external constituencies. Described in this way, the information transfer process becomes a multistepped process as managers interact with different groups, cross organizational boundaries, and engage in multiple activities (e.g., scanning, data collection, translation, mediation, and transfer). Boundary spanners who fill the information-transfer role control an important resource within the organization and as a result are likely to have considerable influence on the organization's decision-making or strategic-planning process.

Organizational Culture

Having considered the organization's external environment, managers should now turn their attention to its internal environment. It is the internal environment that will directly impact on managers as they attempt to perform their day-to-day responsibilities. Managers must realize that organizations are composed of social and technical subsystems that interact to help determine organization and employee behavior. (The combination of social and technical systems within organizations is referred to as the sociotechnical system.) Such behavior will also be affected by past practices and future goals. To function effectively within these systems, managers must understand and master a number of important dimensions that will directly affect their long-term success. One of the most crucial dimensions they must understand is the organizational culture in which they are immersed.

While the study of culture has been important in anthropology and folklore studies, it was not until the 1980s that management scholars became widely interested in the topic.[16] One of the first appearances of the term "organizational culture" occurred in 1979 with Pettigrew's article "On Studying Organizational Cultures."[17] There is no consensus in the management literature on what organizational culture means. Nevertheless, Hofstede and his colleagues have listed six characteristics that are likely to be associated with any attempt to define the concept. Organizational culture is "(*1*) holistic, (*2*) historically determined, (*3*) related to anthropological concepts, (*4*) socially constructed, (*5*) soft, and (*6*) difficult to change."[18]

Recognizing the limited usefulness of defining organizational cultures, we will provide the reader with the following common definitions found in the literature.

> Culture is to the organization what personality is to the individual—a hidden, yet unifying theme that provides meaning, direction and mobilization.[19]
>
> A pattern of basic assumptions—invented, discovered, or developed by a given group as it learns to cope with its problems of external adaptation and internal integration—that has worked well enough to be considered valid and therefore to be taught to new members as the correct way to perceive, think, and feel about those problems.[20]
>
> Organization culture means the patterned ways of thinking, feeling, and reacting, acquired and transmitted mainly by symbols, constituting the distinctive achievements of the organization, including how those are embodied in artifacts, technology, and symbols: the essential core of culture consists of traditional (i.e., historically derived and selected) ideas and especially their attached values.[21]

No two organizational cultures are exactly the same. Such differences result because (*a*) organizations differ in terms of their past successes and failures, (*b*) organizations function in different environmental settings (i.e., markets, competitors, the surrounding societal culture, external regulations, etc.), and (*c*) the characteristics and personalities of key figures—especially early founders or leaders—are rarely, if ever, the same. The result of these differences is to produce a culturally unique environment in each organization. Therefore, a complete understanding of organizational culture cannot be obtained in an abstract manner before entering the organization or by merely studying structural or systems elements. A model of sources and consequences of organizational culture is presented in Figure 15.3. It is important to realize that an understanding of organizational culture helps the manager predict, explain, and control organizational behavior—actions that are crucial to managerial success.

To further explain the complexity and dynamics of organizational culture, Schein articulated a model of organizational culture that clarified the distinction between those theorists who believe that observable events act as the basis of organizational culture and those who believe that what is shared in members' minds acts as the basis for organizational culture.[22] As can be seen (Figure 15.4) Schein argued that to understand organizational culture it must be analyzed from all *three levels*, that is, *artifacts, values,* and *basic assumptions*.

Levels of Organizational Culture

Level 1 is the most concrete, and consequently reflects the view that organizational culture can be described in terms of observable characteristics. It consists of those organizational artifacts and creations that are the observable behavioral patterns and the visible, tangible and/or audible consequences of behavior. Therefore an organizational culture will be reflected in such things as office layout, organizational structures, dress, norms, oral and written communications, jargon, etc. Also included in this first level are such organizational characteristics as behavioral habits, rites and rituals.[23]

FIGURE 15.3

Organizational culture: Sources and consequences

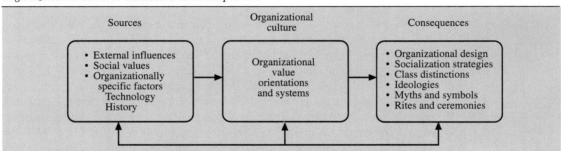

Source: Tosi et al., *Managing Organizational Behavior*, Marshfield, Massachusetts, 1986, p. 66.

FIGURE 15.4

Levels of organizational culture and their interaction

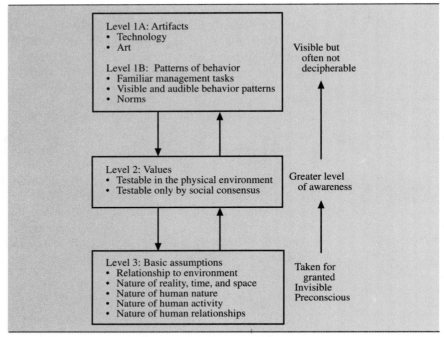

Source: Reprinted from E. H. Schein, "Coming to a new awareness of organization culture," *Sloan Management Review*, Vol. 25, No. 2, pp. 3–16, by permission of publisher. Copyright © 1984: by the Sloan Management Review Association. All rights reserved. Revised in J. S. Ott, *The Organizational Culture Perspective,* 1989.

Even at this level of exactness, it is possible for managers to be uncertain about how to interpret, respond, and use the various aspects of culture. For example, Trice and Beyer have categorized several types of rites.[24] The following represent three examples and their overall relevance to any manager:

Rites of passage—These are used to facilitate entry of the new employee into the organization by communicating organizational norms and values. The level of complexity and formalization of such rites will vary from organization to organization. In the case of the military or a social fraternity they may be very complex and formalized. In other organizations they may represent little more than a policy manual presented to the employee on the first day or a five-minute chat with the boss designed to set the employee straight. Managers should be able to recognize these rites so that they can effectively learn from the experience but at the same time apply them to new employees entering their departments.

Rites of enhancement—These are designed to enhance the status or overall position of an employee who has been performing well within the organization, and often involve the use of symbols or announcements on either a formal or an informal level. They may come in the form of being invited to special functions by a senior executive or being asked to sit on a special task force. Whatever the symbol or announcement, the manager must be able to recognize its existence and act accordingly.

Rites of conflict reduction—Given the complexity, variety, and dynamics of today's organizations, conflict is unavoidable. Rites of conflict reduction represent generally accepted techniques within a particular organization for managing these conflicts. As we saw in Chapter 12, there are numerous alternatives open to the manager for conflict management. Which alternative will be considered appropriate will likely reflect the cultural norms of the organization. Therefore, new managers must educate themselves to what is considered organizationally acceptable. To behave otherwise would likely result in a negative contrast effect and thereby reduce the likelihood of long-term success or acceptance.

Level 2 centers on the set of values and beliefs that define "what ought to be" rather than "what is." In other words, it is the set of values and beliefs that cultural members use to define and explain their behavior or actions. Level 2 includes organizational ethos, philosophies, ideologies, ethical and moral codes, and attitudes.[25] When dealing with Level 2, it is important that the new manager recognizes the difference between "espoused values" and "values in use."[26] The problem here is that Level 2 analysis may produce "espoused values" (that is, what people say), rather than "values in use" (what people do). Such a distortion may prove debilitating to managers as they attempt to learn the ropes of the organization. Having recognized this pitfall, Level 2 information is still important because it allows the manager to better predict the behavior of others within the organization and at the same time better understand how he or she should act within the organizational context to increase the probability of personal success.

Level 3 is by far the most abstract level used to describe the nature of organizational culture. Nevertheless, it may be the most important and powerful in understanding why and how the other two levels exist. Schein defined basic underlying assumptions as a set of fundamental beliefs, values, and perceptions that are taken for granted and exist on an unconscious level, in that they are nonconfrontable or nondebatable.[27] Nevertheless, basic assumptions are passed on as each new organizational member joins the firm. This occurs through the unconscious learning process as individuals interact with others within the organizational setting, or are rewarded or punished for behaving in a certain way.

As managers observe and record occurrences on Levels 1 and 2, they will unconsciously be creating a set of assumptions about basic questions relating to the organization, its environment, and its people. More specifically, as managers are exposed to stories, myths, and modeled patterns of behavior and their consequences, there is a learning process by which they piece together a meaningful set of basic assumptions. Again, we should note that the driving force behind this process is the employees' desire to be successful within their environment.

Two examples should clarify how underlying assumptions act as the driving force behind organizational behavior. One classic example deals with AT&T. Before the company's breakup, and for some time afterward, the basic underlying assumption that appeared to be the driving force behind corporate behavior was the belief that technological superiority was sufficient to ensure success within the marketplace and that all customers should be treated equally.[28] It was soon learned, after AT&T's breakup and the appearance of significant competition, that such assumptions were not valid. To compete in a differentiated market, AT&T had to change its underlying cultural assumptions. Unfortunately, as some experts point out, it can take years to alter an organization's culture sufficiently to match environmental realities with organizational behavior.[29]

A second example describes how a set of basic assumptions can affect an organization's climate and its approach to doing business. The basic assumptions made by Jim Treybig, president of Tandem Computers, have had a significant effect on how the company does business and how it relates to employees.[30] Treybig assumes that all employees are good; you should not differentiate between people, workers, and management, and that every one in the organization can and must understand the business and how it operates. He also believes that organizational success must benefit everyone in the organization and that it is management's responsibility to ensure that the organization's climate reflects these assumptions. Treybig and his staff have made every effort to reflect these assumptions in the way they manage. At Tandem, employees are encouraged to provide the best quality product and service possible to customers, have no time clocks to punch, and attend weekly beer busts to mingle with co-workers, customers, and suppliers. Employees are also required to take sabbaticals every four years to revitalize themselves. Although such a management style is not typical for most organizations, it is likely one of the reasons for Tandem's success.

These two examples indicate that underlying assumptions can have a positive or negative effect on organizational performance. To obtain a positive effect, managers must take steps to ensure that basic assumption fit both the reality and the needs of the situation, that they support productive behavior, and that managers periodically engage in organizational self-analysis to ensure existing assumptions are supporting long-term goals. Similarly, the manager must be aware of basic underlying assumptions not only to ensure appropriate personal behavior but to add his or her voice to the ongoing critical evaluation of these basic assumptions.

Table 15.2 presents a typology of terms and definitions of organizational culture and how one might classify them into Schein's three-level model. Such a classification may help the manager to identify cultural elements and

TABLE 15.2 A Typology of Elements of Organizational Culture

Elements of Organizational Culture	Level Of Culture				
	Artifacts 1A	Patterns of Behavior 1B	Beliefs and Values 2	Assumptions 3	Not Clear
Anecdotes, organizational	x				
Art	x				
Assumptions that people live by				x	
Assumptions, patterns of basic				x	
Assumptions, shared				x	
Attitudes		x	x		
Behavioral regularities		x			
Being		x	x		
Beliefs			x		
Beliefs, patterns of shared			x		
Celebrations		x			
Ceremonies		x			
Climate, organizational					x
Cognitive processes, patterns of			x		
Commitment to excellence			x		
Communications, patterns of	x				
Consensus, level of			x		
Core			x	x	x
Customs		x			
Doing things, way of		x			
Ethic, organizational			x		
Expectations, shared		x			
Feelings			x		
Glue that holds the organization together				x	
Habits		x			
Heroes	x				
Historical vestiges	x				
Identity			x	x	
Ideologies			x		
Interaction, patterns of		x			
Jargon	x				
Justifications of behavior			x		
Knowledge			x		
Language	x				
Links between language, metaphor, and ritual	x	x			
Management practices		x			

(continued)

TABLE 15.2   *(concluded)*

Elements of Organizational Culture	Artifacts 1A	Patterns of Behavior 1B	Beliefs and Values 2	Assumptions 3	Not Clear
Manner		x			
Material objects	x				
Meaning, patterns of			x		
Meanings			x		
Meanings, intersubjective			x		
Mind-set			x	x	
Myths	x				
Norms		x			
Philosophy			x	x	
Physical arrangements	x				
Practical syllogisms			x		
Purpose			x		
Rites		x			
Ritualized practices		x			
Rituals		x			
Roots				x	
Rules, informal system of		x			
Scripts, (organizational— transactional analysis)			x		
Sentiments				x	
Sources of norms, rules, attitudes, customs, and roles			x		
Specialness, quality of perceived					x
Spirit				x	
Stories, organizational	x				
Style			x		
Symbols	x				
Thinking, way of			x		
Traditions	x	x			
Translation of myths into action and relationships	x				
Understanding, tacit			x		
Values			x		
Values, basic core			x		
Values, patterns of shared			x		
Vision			x		
Way			x	x	x
Worldviews			x	x	x

Source: J. S. Ott, *The Organizational Culture Perspective*, 1989.

at the same time to assess their impact on his or her own personal behavior. Ultimately, listed elements may also help to identify avenues through which the manager may successfully attempt to change the organization.

Modifications to Schein's Basic Model

While some behavioral scientists have directly used Schein's model, others have questioned his approach.[31] For example, some management scholars have argued that Schein's model fails to take into account the existence of organizational subcultures, the importance of symbols as a distinct variable, the key role played by individuals, or cultural dynamics inherent in organizational systems. Furthermore, while Schein's model considers underlying assumptions the key element in understanding organizational culture, others would prefer to place emphasis on the relationships existing between elements. By modifying Schein's basic theory, Hatch provided a model that attempts to address many of these criticisms[32] (see Figure 15.5).

Hatch's model reflects a number of fundamental changes in Schein's approach to organizational culture. First, it describes organizational culture as a dynamic process that does not place primary emphasis on underlying assumptions. Second, symbols are described as a separate element. Last, there is a dynamic interplay between each of the elements that allows for cultural change to be initiated at all four levels. In other words, you can introduce a stimulus for cultural change at any level and move either in a clockwise or counterclockwise direction. This dynamic interaction is reflected in the dual arrows surrounding the processes of *manifestation, realization, symbolization,* and *interpretation.*

Proactive/Retroactive Manifestation. Proactive manifestation is defined as the process by which organizational members translate assumptions into perceptions, cognitions, and emotions.[33] Of particular interest to our discussion is how individuals translate assumptions into recognizable values. For example, if managers within the organization assume that all employees were lazy, they are likely to develop perceptions, cognitions, or emotions about unproductive behavior. Managers will in turn develop values toward controlling laziness that activate their underlying assumptions. Such values may be expressed in the statement that employees cannot be given autonomy because they will take advantage of increased levels of freedom.

As mentioned above, the arrows surrounding *manifestation* indicate that it occurs in both directions. Retroactive manifestations occur when new values act to maintain or change underlying assumptions. New values can be imported into the organization as new employees enter the organization, as organizational members interact with other cultural systems, as employees import values from other institutions with which they interact, and when employees produce random variations through successful innovations and experimentation. Once these new values are introduced, they act to maintain or change

FIGURE 15.5

*The cultural
dynamics model*

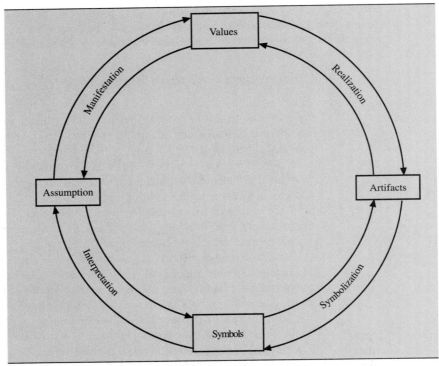

Source: M. J. Hatch, "The dynamics of organizational culture," *Academy of Management Review,* Vol. 18, 1993, p. 660.

underlying assumptions existing within the system. Since employees are uncon-scious of underlying assumptions, they will not initially recognize conflicts between values in use and existing assumptions. However, over time, these new values will act to reinforce or realign existing assumptions.

Proactive/Retroactive Realization.   Proactive realization is the process by which values are translated into organization artifacts (e.g., rituals, rites, stories, and physical objects). Let us continue the example where assumptions about employee laziness have produced a positive value toward controls on employee behaviors. In this case, managers may act to introduce time clocks, produc-tivity reports, and performance reviews to ensure employee compliance to orga-nization policies and high productivity.

Retroactive realizations address the issue of how artifacts affect employee values and their expectations of "how things should be done." New artifacts act to maintain or change the existing value structure found within the organization. As with the case described above, new artifacts can be intro-duced by new employees, interactions with other organizational cultures, and through random innovations and experimentation. Even if the new artifact is not accepted by everyone, it may attract sufficient support to be maintained within the system. Over time, the new artifact will likely gain increased acceptance. When this occurs, the general acceptance of new artifacts are likely to change the value structure of organizational members. For example, in organizations where computers were first resisted, employees now actively seek out the new technology.

Prospective/Retrospective Symbolization. Symbols are defined as "anything that represents a conscious or an unconscious association with some wider, usually more abstract, concept or meaning."[34] In Hatch's model, symbols are given separate status because they incorporate meaning that goes beyond the artifact itself. Training within an organization may merely represent an intervention by the human resource department to remove an existing or future deficiency. As a result, it has little or no symbolic meaning. However, a particular type of training may take on special symbolic meaning because of top management's response to employees who have successfully taken the training, the history of training within a particular department, the individual experiences of past participants, or the behavior of the facilitator providing the training. It is this additional or surplus meaning that we will refer to as prospective symbolization. In other words, when organizational members transform artifacts into symbols, they are considered culturally significant.

Retrospective symbolism occurs when a particular artifact stands out from the rest because of the added meaning provided by employee members. Hatch uses the example of an employee's desk as compared to the desk of other organizational members. If the employee begins to associate memories (positive or negative feelings) with the desk, then it stands out from all other desks because its enhanced symbolic significance. In other words, the symbolic meaning associated with the desk changes its literal meaning for the employee.

Prospective/Retrospective Interpretation. It is at this point that Hatch's model runs full circle by closing the loop between assumptions and symbols. In the case of retrospective interpretation, employees draw upon what is already known (set of assumptions) to define or help interpret new symbols. At the same time, however, new symbols facilitate the process by which cultures absorb newly symbolized knowledge into its basic structure (set of assumptions). This is referred to as prospective interpretation.

Although Hatch's model increases the complexity of the organizational culture model, it nevertheless introduces a holistic and dynamic view of the cultural process within organizations. More specifically, the four relational components of the model described in Figure 15.5 should not be considered "as four separate processes, each with forward and backward modes of operation, but as two wheels of interconnected processes, one moving forward and the other backward with reference to the standard concept of time."[35] Therefore, at least in principle, the manager can affect organizational culture at any point of the model. In other words, revision is inherent throughout the circle.

The Individual's Role within the Organization's Culture

A potential bias in the cultural literature is an emphasis on the unifying role that culture plays within organizations and the importance of individuals adapting to the norms of behavior set forth by the dominant culture.[36] Such a view by management scholars biases our organizational perspective toward one of harmony and cooperation. Also important, however, in any organizational culture is the way individuals act, especially when attempting to introduce change or stimulate creativity. Simply put, employees can become active agents within their environments.

Unfortunately, the ability of individuals to act is relegated to a secondary or peripheral role when discussing organizational cultures. The implication becomes that individuals only act when the organization's culture is weak, when a number of strong subcultures exist, or when cultural norms are ambiguous.[37] By assuming that such conditions are prerequisites for employee action, one minimizes the proactive role members can play within their organizations.

It is also important to recognize that organizational members are members of other cultural institutions and, as part of their role responsibilities, must often interact with other organizational cultures. Both conditions are likely to exert a powerful influence in determining employee behavior within organizations. What must be recognized therefore, is that employees may not only adhere to cultural norms but also depart from them. As a result, organizational members can engage in four strategies of acting when performing within organizations. They are (*1*) unequivocal adherence, (*2*) strained adherence, (*3*) secret nonadherence, and (*4*) overt nonadherence.[38] Only in the case of unequivocal adherence does the reality of employee performance match the requirements of the organization's culture. However, given the need for organizational change and creativity within organizations, such a strategy is not always appropriate.

Cultural Transmission in Formal Organizations

The study of cultural content implies that organizational cultures are relatively stable. An organization with a strong culture is able to maintain employee allegiances and loyalty across time by ensuring transmission of cultural beliefs.[39] In situations where new members enter and leave the culture slowly, it is possible for the mechanisms of cultural transmission to be slow and diffuse. However, if new members enter and leave the culture rapidly, then the mechanisms for transmission must be extensive and dramatic. In relative terms, organizations fit the second scenario while societies fit the first scenario. As a result, managers must become familiar with the process of cultural transmission within their organizations. Managers should also be interested in the process of transmission because they have some control of the very factors that will be used to transmit cultural assumptions, values, artifacts, and symbols from one organizational generation to the next.

Harrison and Carroll identify recruitment, socialization, and turnover as three activities that play a central role in the transmission process.[40] In the area of recruitment, managers can affect selection standards, the selection decision, and the "selling" procedures designed to attract desired candidates to the organization. To effectively maintain a culture, managers must determine desired cultural content and, where possible, build such assumptions, values, and behavior into the recruitment process. The intensity of such activities will reflect the manager's desire to maintain or control cultural content.

Socialization allows managers to transmit desired assumptions, values, and behaviors to lay the groundwork for effective employee performance. Of primary importance for managers are those activities undertaken after the new employee enters the organization and attempts to learn how to behave on the new job. Managers can design orientation programs, training experiences, early assignments, comprehensive reward systems, and provide meaningful feedback to produce the desired adherence to cultural norms. It is also possible for managers to interpret organizational events for new staff with the desire of reinforcing existing cultural norms.

Finally, the turnover process can be used to affect employee adherence to desired cultural norms. Managers can take steps to retain those individuals whose values and behaviors match those of the dominant culture and encourage the turnover of employees who do not adhere to cultural norms. This can be accomplished through performance feedback, promotions, job assignments, and pay for performance schemes. However, managers must recognize that such action must support organizational goals. For example, if the organization's goal is to stimulate creativity, broaden the existing employee experience base, and challenge the status quo, then it may be desirable to retain a proportionally larger number of less socialized employees.

Power and Politics

Power and its use must be considered an important thread in the fabric of internal organizational life.[41] Power affects not only how managers interact with their subordinates, but also affects relationships between departments, and the strategic decisions made by organizations.[42] As a result, managerial success is often a function of the manager's ability to understand the power distribution currently existing within the organization, and to use the positive effects of power to achieve personal and organizational goals.[43]

Two Changing Views of Power

Many researchers and practitioners have traditionally equated power only with competition, or the process by which one organizational member gets others to do what they would not otherwise do.[44] Such a view assumes that social players within the organizational context have conflicting goals and therefore must always compete. As a result, some researchers have recommended minimizing power and politics within organizations. The problem with such a one-dimensional view of power is that it prevents managers from recognizing potential positive benefits of power and its use.

Managers who empower subordinates, engage in principled negotiations, increase organizational interdependencies, and use symbolic or charismatic management facilitate goal achievement by taking advantage of the cooperative benefits of power.[45] For example, Tjosvold and his colleagues found that cooperative and powerful managers were perceived as competent, effective, and supportive by their subordinates.[46] They found that, taken together, power and cooperation accounted for approximately 73 percent of the variance in perceived manager effectiveness. A possible explanation for this finding is that powerful and cooperative managers will use their resources to help others succeed by promoting common objectives. Similarly, Eisenhardt and Bourgeois found that managers who share decision-making power with subordinates reduce the occurrence of organizational politics while facilitating organizational performance.[47]

A second shift in how power is viewed reflects a de-emphasis of exchange theory as an explanation of organizational power, especially when describing departmental interactions.[48] It has been argued that dyadic exchanges occur when organizational members are dependent upon one another for information, physical resources, financial support, or authority to act. If manager A has need for something of value from manager B, but cannot reciprocate in kind, A may find it necessary to give B control over how he or she behaves. In other words, manager B has gained power or influence over manager A. According to this approach, managers can increase their power over others by increasing the dependence of others on them, while reducing their dependence on others.

An alternative view is that power reflects the strategic contingencies that exist within the organization.[49] Instead of power resulting from imbalances in dyadic exchanges, it reflects the position of individuals or departments within the organization's work flow and the existing level of interdependency between organizational sub-units. According to this approach, individuals or departments become critical or strategic to the organization when they are (*a*) able to deal effectively with uncertainty, (*b*) linked to the work flows of other departments (persuasiveness), (*c*) likely to have an immediate and significant impact on the success of the organization, and (*d*) provide skills, activities, or information that are not easily replaced (nonsubstitutability).

Although researchers disagree on how these variables should be combined,[50] it is our view that immediacy and significance must be present. In other words, the other three variables provide individuals and departments with the potential for power, but it is the issue of strategic importance, that is, the degree to which individuals or departments affect the organization's ability to function and achieve its goals, that allows them to gain power or influence. For example, while accounting departments may be staffed with highly trained professionals (nonsubstitutability), are linked with many departments, and provide information that reduces uncertainty, they are often given low power ratings.[51] This occurs because accounting information is not typically critical to the operation or success of the departments receiving the information. However, should their services become strategic to the organization's success (e.g., during a merger or hostile takeover battle), then their organizational power or influence would significantly increase.

Power, Authority, and Politics

To fully understand the concept of power, the reader should also differentiate between power, authority, and politics. As defined above, power is the ability of individuals to both effect and affect organizational outcomes. Organizational members who seek to use power to influence the outcomes and activities of organizations can be defined as influencers.[52] Power cannot, however, be used in isolation. When discussing individuals' ability to influence organizational outcomes and activities, one must consider their power relative to other organizational members. The actual level of power possessed by any one organizational member will reflect the general building blocks of power he or she has control over (that is, resources, technical skills, and knowledge), how important each building block is to the ultimate success of the organization, and the individual's desire to have influence. The distribution of power within organizations is also likely to change over time as organizations and their environments change.[53]

Organizational power can be described as either legitimate or illegitimate.[54] In any social system, participants will over time develop a set of values, attitudes, and beliefs as to what is appropriate in terms of behavior and relationships. When this set of values, attitudes, and beliefs becomes broadly accepted across social groupings, then it becomes legitimized. When power is legitimized within an organization, it is said to be formalized as authority. Such authority is typically associated with a social actor's position within the organization. For example, both a superior and a subordinate can have power over one another. However, only the superior can have authority over the subordinate.

Conversely, politics, according to Mintzberg, is a subset of power that exists on an informal level and, when compared to legitimate authority, is illegitimate in nature.[55] Organizational politics are normally covert behaviors taken by organizational members to increase their power to influence the decision-making process.[56] Such behaviors can take the form of secret meetings, forming coalitions, lobbying, co-optation attempts, manipulating meeting agendas, and the withholding of information from other organizational members. Such behaviors take place outside the boundaries of position power. Consequently, they have not been formalized within the organization.

With these definitions in mind, it is possible to be more specific about why managers, as part of their knowledge base, seek to map out both the formal (authority) and informal (political) power structures within the organization. To begin with, an understanding of power relationships allows the manager to identify those individuals whose support must be obtained to help ensure *success or acceptance* of departmental, as well as personal, goals. Because organizations represent sociotechnical systems, and because most organizations function under conditions of scarce resources, change, and uncertainty, organizations are political, power-based structures.

It is also important for the manager to identify the power and political relationships for a more personal reason. Specifically, the manager's likelihood of success is often facilitated by an ability to link up, or otherwise be identified with, a mentor. A mentor is someone within the organization who is willing to guide, support, and protect the manager during the early stages of organizational entry and establishment. Unfortunately, the use of power and political activity often has its cost. For example, if the manager increases personal power and influence by identifying with a particular mentor, he or she may alienate other power influencers within the organization. Similarly, gaining support and protection from others also produces an obligation to reciprocate in like value some time in the future. Both factors therefore require not only that the manager understand how power is distributed in the organization, but the consequences of its development and use.

Conditions for the Use of Power and Politics

To appreciate the complexity and dynamics of power and politics within organizations, it would be helpful to consider the conditions under which both are likely to be used. With a model of levels acting as a road map for the new manager, the task of functioning within such an environment is greatly facilitated (see Figure 15.6).[57]

Level 1.   The first condition necessary for the use of power and politics is a differentiated internal structure (that is, in terms of department activities, reporting relationships, technologies used, etc.). Although the level of internal differentiation varies among organizations, it will always be present because of two factors. First, internal structures are functionally dependent upon the organization's external environment. Consequently, as the organization's external environment becomes more complex, varied, and turbulent, managers should not be surprised to find the organization's internal structure becoming more differentiated. (More will be said about structure when it is discussed below.) Second, by definition, organizations are built upon the principle of specialization. Once the organization grows it is impossible for any one manager or department to carry out the activities of the organization. As a result, the natural process is to break down these activities and specialize. The consequence of these two forces is an organization that is by definition departmentalized.

FIGURE 15.6

Model: Conditions for the use of power and politics

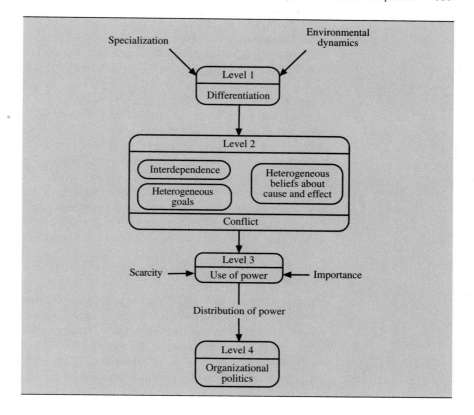

Level 2. This internal variety increases the likelihood of multiple goals associated with different areas of activity, units, or functions. Individuals within each area of activity, unit, or function are likely to have different sets of beliefs about cause-and-effect linkages that help to explain internal and external events. Such differences frequently occur because of differences in background, education, on-the-job experiences, personal needs, etc. Internal differentiation, however, does not typically imply independence. Instead, organizational units share varying levels of interdependence and, as a result, one unit's success depends upon the success of other units within the organization (that is, the success of production is often a function of purchasing, maintenance, training, and the quality control department, etc.). In those organizations where Level 2 conditions have been met, conflict is likely to occur.

Level 3. Although there are a variety of responses open to the manager to reduce the negative effect of conflict (see Chapter 12), the use of power is likely to be a dominant response when the conditions of scarcity and importance are also present. The greater the scarcity of resources and importance of desired outcomes to the individuals involved, the greater the use of power in overcoming the conflict. In the case of scarcity, choices must be made in terms of allocation of those resources which fall short of organizational demand. Importance, on the other hand, is related to the likely impact of a resource shortfall on the manager's, or the department's, success.

Level 4. Finally, the degree to which a manager will engage in organizational politics will be a function of the relative distribution of power among the involved managers. The relevant point here is that the more centralized the distribution of power, the easier it is for one manager to force his or her will on others. Conversely, the more evenly the sources of power are distributed, the more difficult it is for one manager to use power in its raw form to force his or her will on others. In the latter case, it is more likely that the manager will turn to organizational politics as the preferred vehicle for the use of power. For example, the manager faced with evenly dispersed power is likely to use such techniques as bargaining and coalition formation.

Identifying Who Has Power

Merely understanding the conditions under which the process of power and politics will be used is insufficient to guide the manager through the potential pitfalls of organizational life. The manager must attempt to map out the distribution of power within the organization by identifying powerful individuals within the organization. The key here is to know what to look for. The analysis process should begin with an attempt to identify individuals, groups, or departments that can be described as highly visible, permanent, and active entities within the organization context. This step is an initial screening designed to reduce the number of social actors being assessed for power. Once a short list has been developed, a manager should consider a number of factors that give some indication of the presence of power. The following represents a partial list of such clues.

General Sources of Power

One of the first clues to the presence of power is the identification of its sources and who controls or possesses them. It is important for organizational participants to be able to recognize sources of power for two reasons. First, it allows the individual to identify those social actors likely to be power brokers in the organization. Second, since power rests upon some type of dependency among organizational participants, it helps individuals to develop a personal strategy of how to increase their own power.

If an organizational participant has control over a valued resource, object, piece of information, or is able to offer personal support, then he or she will likely have power and influence over interested parties. However, the degree to which dependence will result in actual power for one organizational participant over another will be affected by several factors. First, Pfeffer and Salancik argued that the potential influencer must have discretionary control over the resources in question to have power over the interested parties.[58] Dependence will also be affected by the degree to which the potential influencer can monitor the compliance of the other participant to his or her demands. Last, Pfeffer pointed out that dependence, and ultimately power, will be a function of the ease with which the influencer can be replaced or substituted.[59] In other words, if the potential influencer can be replaced, his or her power base is greatly reduced.

Mintzberg identified five bases of power.[60] An individual may possess power over others because he or she has control over needed resources. Therefore, if one individual (or department) controls the distribution of land, labor, or capital that is needed by others, then that individual will have power. Furthermore, the greater the other's need for such resources, and the more monopolistic the manager's control over such resources, the greater will be his or her potential influence over others. Next, if one social actor has control of, or privileged access to, valued information then he or she again can influence others. A third basis of power reflects an individual's skill level in those areas considered crucial to the success of the organization. Consequently, the internal experts find themselves wielding significant power within the organizational system. Fourth, rights and privileges are given to managers based upon their position within the organization. Such prerogatives in turn provide a legal basis for power (e.g., owners or boards of directors have the right, within legal limits, to hire and fire others within the organization). Finally, power can be obtained merely from the fact that one individual within the organization has access to (and influence over) another individual who has power because of the first four sources of power just described.

Expenditure of Time and Energy

A second clue to who has power is the level of time and energy expended by individuals to achieve their goals. If individuals want to become influencers within the organization they must be willing to expend personal time and energy. The expenditure of time and energy will have several positive consequences for potential influencers. First, it will increase their personal credibility as they are perceived to be willing to personally invest in the issue under consideration. Furthermore, by visibly pursuing a particular issue or point of view they are demonstrating a willingness to place their reputations on the line. The expenditure of time and energy will also increase the probability that potential influencers will become members of the critical mass, or inner circle. Should this group be recognized as one of the organization's internal power groups, the new member will, by definition, have power. The philosophy here is "no investment, no pay back."

The expenditure of time and energy also relates to what takes place after an issue has been decided, or an order has been given. If there is no followup or subsequent consequence for participant behavior, then the individual attempting to exert influence will eventually be perceived as weak. For example, if employees are told not to behave in a certain way and they ignore the order but are not reprimanded in any way, the giver of the order loses power. Conversely, if an employee is requested to perform in a certain way and does so, that employee expects some type of recognition. If such recognition is not forthcoming, then the maker of the request is likely to lose power.

Political Skill

As the third clue to who has power, social actors within the organization must have the political skill to develop and maintain their power base. Because most organizational members are free to leave, have their own personal need structures, and because organizations have multiple power centers (with power equally dispersed) the effort to control or influence the behavior of others may still fail. Consequently, power within organizations is likely to be a function of the level of political skill and sensitivity exhibited by the potential influencer. If the potential influencer does not consider the values, attitudes and beliefs of others, he or she may face significant resistance. Similarly, if the potential influencer is not sensitive to timing, tradition, and the existence of other political forces within the system, personal failure may result. Ultimately, such consequences will lead to a reduced power base in the future. Finally, interpersonal skills in developing and maintaining coalitions and support networks within the organization will affect the ability to wield power within the organization. Put another way, it is not only what you do that counts, but how you do it.

The remaining set of clues to power depends less on the characteristics of the social actors being assessed and more on the observable events in the environment.

Access to the Decision-Making Process.   Few would argue with the position that central to the success of most organizations is their ability to make sound decisions. Consequently, decision making becomes a crucial process in its own right. Therefore, to identify who the power influencers are in the organization, one must merely identify those individuals who play a crucial role in the decision-making process. More specifically, an individual's level of power may be measured by the degree to which he or she affects decision premises (i.e., the constraints that define the decision domain), the number of alternatives considered, and the amount of information known about each alternative. Therefore, a manager's role in influencing the decision-making process greatly affects his or her actual, or perceived, power within the organization.

Working Backward from Outcomes.   In any organizational setting, it is possible to identify major occurrences in the life of an organization. Once identified, it is often, but not always, possible to identify those individuals who play a key role in causing an outcome to occur or who significantly benefit from its occurrence. In both cases, individuals so identified are likely to be power influencers within the organization.

Assessing the Symbols of Power.   Sociologists frequently point out that it is nearly impossible for managers to remove status symbols from organizational environments. If this is true, the manager's ability to identify social actors wielding power is greatly facilitated. Such factors as physical location and size of offices, office furnishings, special eating facilities, washrooms, parking spaces, titles, etc., will give a clear indication of who does or does not have power within an organization. Simply put, locate the symbols and you locate the social actors with power.

Reputations and Stories.   As discussed in the section headed Organizational Culture, much can be learned about an organization and its members by the stories told about past events and perceived reputations of key individuals. To plug into this information the new manager merely has to ask or listen to what is being talked about within the organization. Most individuals on an informal, off-the-record basis, are more than willing to divulge information about the power influencers within the organization. This information adds one more piece to the puzzle of organizational power.

Representational Indicators.   As organizational environments become more dynamic and complex, employee interests, power, and resources remain dispersed; and the organization moves toward a more participative decision-making style, the use of task forces, committees, project teams, and coalitions will continue and grow. Realizing that such groups traditionally are brought together to make decisions, and influence the organization's direction, it follows that such groups have power. Concomitantly, individuals who participate in such groups also have power. The new manager's task, therefore, is to identify such groups and then identify those individuals and departments that are most frequently represented. Such representation will imply power.

Consensus.   The issue of consensus deals primarily with the power of groups when dealing with others within the organization. The relevant point here is that the greater the internal consensus, the greater the perceived external power and influence. Groups that are internally split, loosely organized, or in the process of change are frequently perceived as weak because they are unlikely to maintain effort or keep control over their members, and can be more easily divided and conquered.

It should be realized that although each of these factors can stand alone, they often interact, thereby having a cumulative effect on the level of power possessed by a particular social actor.

Strategic Planning

If an organization does not have a strategy, it is unlikely to move effectively into the future. To be effective, managers must understand the major components, of strategic planning how the process works within their organization, how it is affected by the distribution of managerial power, and how organizational strategies are linked to employee behavior. In its simplest terms, strategy is the organization's overall game plan for achieving desired objectives. At a general level, it specifies the organizational action, market, and customer base.

Defining Strategy

For Mintzberg, strategy is a plan, ploy, pattern, position, and/or perspective.[61] As a *plan,* it is a conscious and intended course of action developed before organizational action is taken. When defined as a *ploy,* strategy is used to maneuver or otherwise outwit an opponent or competitor. There may, however, be no intention to implement the strategy as the manager's purpose is to manipulate others into committing resources or taking action. Next, strategy as a *pattern,* in Mintzberg's words, is a stream of actions or a consistency in behavior irrespective of whether it was planned. Such strategies are emergent rather than deliberate, and become strategies only because they work. The fourth definition of strategy as a *position* locates the organization within an environment (i.e., its choice of a niche or place within the environment where the organization will concentrate its resources). Finally, strategy as a *perspective* appears to be the most general definition of the five. In this case, strategy is defined as "an ingrained way of perceiving the world." As such, it implies that strategy is a concept that cannot be seen or touched, but yet produces a joint perspective (collective mind) for organizational participants. At this level of definition, the organization can be described from a cultural perspective. These five definitions as five different levels of strategy help us to understand the broad range of planning structures found within business. At the same time, they help define the dynamics and complexity of the planning process itself.

Figure 15.7 integrates these five definitions and demonstrates the evolutionary and dynamic nature of the strategic planning process. Not only are the various cells interrelated, but the starting point for any organization is the function of organizational tradition, the situation, and the personalities involved. Consequently, some organizations plan their way to success (or failure), while others evolve (blocks 1, 6 or 7). Second, when something works, those activities, markets, etc., usually continue into the future because principles of inertia, parsimony, and motivation cause organizations to repeat what has worked well in the past (block 2). Such behavior will continue until there is some precipitating event (e.g., the oil embargo of 1973 for the auto industry), a key change in management, or the introduction of a new product by a competitor. The obvious consequence of repetitive successful behavior will likely be an identifiable market position (block 3) and a shared internal perspective of how the organization will behave in the future (block 4). The wavy lines leading to these blocks show that this occurs over time. Furthermore, it takes more time for a shared perspective to develop than an identifiable market niche to be recognized. Finally, the actual characteristics of long-term planning within any organization are affected by the dynamics and uncertainty of the external

FIGURE 15.7

*Strategic planning:
Evolutionary and
dynamic properties*

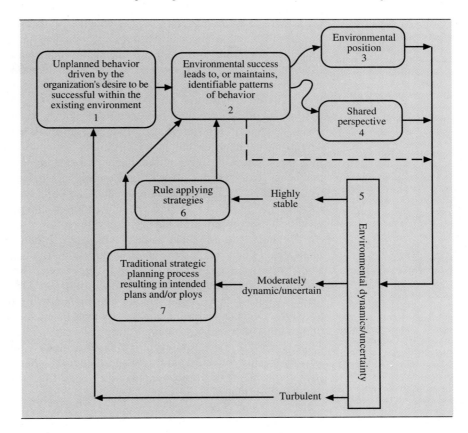

environment (block 5). As a result, firms facing a highly stable and certain environment are likely to be rule-applying organizations with a minimum long-term planning effort (block 6). Moderate levels of uncertainty and dynamics are likely to result in a traditional form of long-term strategic planning (block 7). Such a structure is discussed below. Last, a highly turbulent environment results in unplanned, delegated responsibilities designed to adjust and evolve as the environment adjusts and evolves (block 1).

Why Organizations Need Strategy

The level of success achieved by any strategic planning process depends upon the match between that process and the existing situation. Organizations frequently engage in behaviors that reduce the effectiveness of planning.

Mintzberg, in addition to giving five definitions of strategy, identified four key reasons why organizations should develop strategies and also why they fail.[62] *First*, organizations need strategies to give the organization direction. The problem here is that direction often reduces the motivation by organizations to monitor and keep in touch with their environment. Worse is the possibility that because one is constantly told to plan, the organization plans even when the future is so uncertain or turbulent that planning is of little value. In fact, it may even be counterproductive. *Second*, strategies allow the organization to focus employee effort and the coordination of organizational activity. Although both objectives are desirable, such focusing can produce rigidity and therefore an unwillingness to change when required. *Next*, strategies help define the organization to its members and to others. The problem, here, is that such definitions can be simplistic and as a result fail to indicate the true complexity of the system. *Finally*, clearly defined and accepted strategies afford organizations a required level of consistency to allow for prediction and control. Such an objective is again desirable as long as the premises behind these strategies are occasionally tested to ensure that accepted strategies remain relevant.

By understanding these issues, managers can better deal with the output of strategic planning, have a positive impact on the process itself, and *effectively* integrate existing goals and objectives into present and future behavior. Only when this has been accomplished can managers *effectively* interact with top management, peers, or subordinates, and at the same time *effectively* carry out personal responsibilities. Keeping the above points in mind, let us consider how the traditional strategic planning process works. Steiner describes a conceptual planning model (see Figure 15.8) that *effectively* integrates the strategic and tactical (sometimes referred to as the strategy implementation phase) planning activities typically associated with the strategic planning process.[63]

Phase I of the Strategic Planning Process: Premises

The process itself begins with top management planning to plan (Figure 15.8, box 1). Here management clearly articulates what they want the process to produce, who will be involved, and how it is going to work. Without these decisions, it is unlikely that others will buy into the process and consequently create the critical mass needed to help ensure an effective strategic planning process. Once a critical mass and planning infrastructure has been created, the next step is to collect and assess the relevant information needed to make high-quality decisions about the future. The information traditionally collected during this organizational scanning process (also referred to as a corporate appraisal or situational audit) is outlined in boxes 2 to 5.

The primary purpose of organizational scanning is to provide the relevant information necessary to successfully carry out the strategic planning process. As indicated in boxes 2 to 5, the sources of information available in the scanning process are broad and must consider both internal and external environments. The degree to which internal and external stakeholders are involved in the process will have a significant impact on (*a*) the level of internal support and therefore the level of potential future resistance, and (*b*) the organization's ability to effectively identify and adjust to changes within its external

Figure 15.8

Companywide strategic planning process

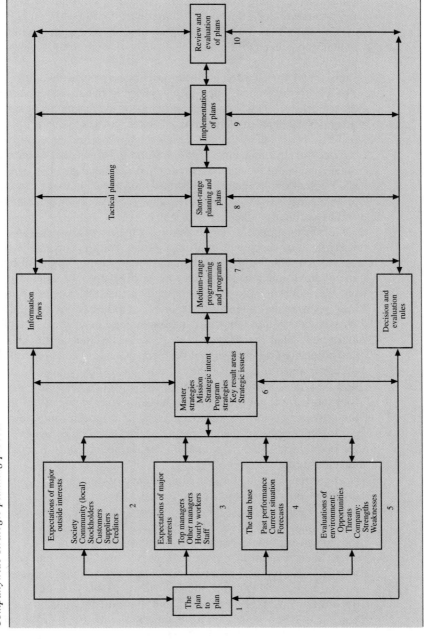

Source: G. A. Steiner, *Strategic Planning: What Every Manager Must Know*, The Free Press, New York, 1979, p. 17.

environment. It should also be realized that an organization's approach to environmental scanning may be informal, formal, or some combination, depending upon the dynamics of the environment faced (see Figure 15.6).

Boxes 1 to 5 represent the planning premises upon which the strategic planning process will be built.

Phase II of the Strategic Planning Process: Formulation

The key to the second, *formulation,* phase of the strategic planning process is the progressive narrowing (fine-tuning) of the strategies being developed. In other words, the formulation phase (boxes 6 to 8) of strategic planning can best be described as a process by which the appropriate decision makers go from the general (mission statement being the most general) to the specific (short-range plan being the most detailed action component of the formulation phase). The ultimate objective of the formulation phase is to develop a set of short-term strategies that can be easily translated into operational tactics, behaviors, and operational budgets.

To fully appreciate the dynamics of the formulation phase, several dimensions must be discussed in greater detail. The first deals with the concept of "strategic intent." Although strategic intent was initially developed to describe an organization's strategy for establishing global leadership, the identical process can apply to any organization that seeks to give direction to its long-term behavior.[64] Strategic intent should exhibit the following characteristics: (*a*) a clear and measurable statement of the level of performance and results that the organization seeks in the long term (i.e., a measurable end point), (*b*) stated levels of performance and results remaining stable over time, (*c*) an expression of the organization's desire to win, and (*d*) articulation of a goal that has meaning to organizational members and will therefore motivate them (e.g., to beat a major competitor rather than to improve the bottom line for stockholders). What is important to realize is that strategic intent establishes the end point but does not fix the means of getting there. Consequently, the process allows for flexibility as the organization moves into the future.

A second dimension is the importance of establishing priorities at several levels in the formulation phase (that is, key result areas, strategic issues, and strategic directions). Once planners have articulated the organization's mission and strategic intent, it is crucial that there is an attempt to identify those key result areas (KRAs) in which results must be achieved and progress made to ensure future movement toward some desired end point. Figure 15.9 identifies KRAs that might be relevant for academic institutions, municipal governments, and private industry. However, because of the complexity and dynamics of most organizations, and the limited quantity of resources available, it is often necessary to establish priorities as to which and/or how many KRAs can be addressed. The underlying issue is the degree to which each KRA is likely to affect future progress toward the organization's perceived mission or strategic intent.

FIGURE 15.9

KRAs for universities, municipal government, and private industry

Universities	Municipal Government	Private Industry
• Academic programming	• Physical plant	• Physical plant
• Student services	• Protection of people and property	• Management development
• Alumni relations	• Economic development	• Corporate growth
• Community involvement	• Social and community development	• Employee/labor relations
• Physical plant		• Government/consumer relations
• Continuing education	• Leisure facilities and services	• Technology
• Support staff relations	• Management and staff relationships	• Financial performance

FIGURE 15.9
KRAs for universities, municipal government, and private industry

Planners should then turn their attention to strategic issues associated with high priority KRAs. A strategic issue represents an internal or external situation (event) that is likely to have, or is having, a significant impact on the future performance of the organization. The ability of the organization to correctly identify strategic issues is a function of the scanning process and an understanding of the organization's mission, strategic intent, and emerging policy. In the case of a university, a strategic issue might be a local competing institution offering a new program, thereby requiring program modification; for a municipality, it might be the loss of a major industry, resulting in the need for economic development; and in the case of a manufacturing firm, it may be new government regulations requiring the development of new pay equity procedures. The key to understanding strategic issues is the realization that they are future oriented, are likely to affect the gap between where the organization is now and where it wants to be in the future, and that strategic issues will directly impact on the development of new initiatives.

However, as with KRAs, planners have to evaluate strategic issues and set priorities relevant to the organization and its desired future state. Each *identified issue* should be evaluated against these following five criteria:[65]

Urgency   • The likely negative consequences in the short run of not acting in response to a particular strategic issue.

Strategic importance • The degree to which the issue relates to strategic intent identified by the organization.

Controllability	• The degree to which the organization can affect the situation/events linked to the strategic issue.
Mandated importance	• The degree to which external bodies impose future action by the organization (e.g., government, or action-oriented groups).
Ease of action	• The degree to which the organization has either free or transferable resources required for taking action in response to the strategic issues.

If an issue rates high on the above criteria, then it will be assigned a high priority.

The next step in the formulation phase is the identification of the strategic direction that the organization will take in response to each strategic issue deemed to have a high priority for action. Direction will articulate the general response and level of resources the organization will commit to the strategic issue. This step leads the strategic planner into the medium-range and short-range planning stages—boxes 7 and 8. When determining *directional priorities*, it is important to consider the following five criteria:[66]

Effectiveness	• The degree to which the strategic direction will contribute to movement toward the organization's agreed-upon strategic intent.
Consistency	• The degree to which the strategic direction complements, or otherwise supports, other strategic initiatives taken or being considered.
Pragmatism	• The degree to which the strategic direction is likely to be implemented, given existing levels of resources and the political realities of the organization.
Flexibility	• The degree to which the strategic direction allows for alteration in response to a changing environment.
Parsimony	• The degree to which the strategic direction represents the simplest and least expensive alternative while at the same time achieves effective movement toward the organization's strategic intent.

If strategic planners are fortunate enough to have agreement on mission, strategic intent, and strategic issues and direction, the remaining work during the formulation phase emphasizes the continual narrowing of strategic plans to the point where planners articulate how objectives will be achieved. The output, therefore, will be action oriented, short-range plans that are ready for implementation.

Phase III of the Strategic Planning Process: Implementation

Implementation of the strategic plan usually requires organizational changes of varying magnitude. Such changes are likely to occur within the organization's structure, systems and processes, management style, and ultimately in the organization's culture. With this reality in mind, it may be necessary to pay particular attention to the possibility of employee resistance to change well before it is likely to occur. Such changes will also require that managers eager to implement strategic plans clearly establish standards against which to measure performance. However, it is equally important that managers clearly communicate such standards to those involved in the change and its implementation. The important question to ask is, what level and what type of standards are we talking about? Typically, we can identify three types of standards that may be used to guide and evaluate the implementation process. First, we can articulate the results desired at each level of the planning process. Such results may act as clear bench marks as to how well implementation is working. One of the most common standards used to assess the overall success of implementation is the budgeting process. As one moves from strategies to tactics (the detail of the strategic planning process) the issue of resource allocation becomes the focal point of consideration. It is this allocation of resources that drives the budgeting process and ultimately acts as a second standard against which to assess implementation. Finally, as the organization establishes action-oriented plans, it is possible to describe specific behaviors or activities that will be assigned or expected from particular employees. Such behaviors themselves can act as standards to assess implementation and its success or failure.

For strategy implementation to work, management must achieve total corporate integration, free flow of communication, and full participation of relevant others throughout the process. When such conditions are met during the premise building and formulation phases of the strategic planning process, the probability increases that line managers will buy into the decisions made and that a much needed critical mass will be created. It is this critical mass that helps ensure implementation. Full integration, communication, and participation also ensure that changes in strategies can be made, if they are needed, during the implementation phase. Without these conditions being met, information gaps and staff rigidity will increase the likelihood of failure.

Finally, implementation requires that support systems be built into the implementation phase to facilitate long-term success. Support activities also reduce the negative consequences of stress likely to be produced by change and uncertainty. Such support should occur on the following levels: (*a*) training, (*b*) structural changes, and (*c*) rewards. First, implementation will likely require new knowledge, skills, and attitudes. If the acquiring of these much needed factors is left to chance, or self-development, the organization increases the likelihood that failure will occur. Second, to ensure total integration and full participation it is often necessary to alter structure to allow for a free flow of information. A specific example of a structural change designed to improve such integration is the introduction of quality circles into the organization's decision-making or leadership structure. Last, employees must perceive that intrinsic and extrinsic rewards are linked to behaviors designed to help strategic implementation.

Assessing the Accuracy of the Rational Model of Strategic Planning

Our description of the strategic planning process has thus far reflected a rational approach to the decision-making process.[67] Provan pointed out that this model reflects the belief that "strategy formulation should be based on a rational consideration by top management of strategically important elements of the organization's external environment coupled with an assessment of the organization's strengths and weaknesses."[68] Although it is important to understand the rational model and its components, it should be recognized that this model may fail to provide an accurate representation of how strategic decisions are made within organizations.[69]

- One reason for this failure is that the rational model ignores the important role managerial perceptions play in interpreting environmental events and uncertainty. In those situations where managers' perceptions do not fit the realities of the organization's environment, their decisions will be less effective or rational. Managers can act to overcome such a mismatch by increasing their environmental scanning and boundary-spanning activities.
- It is also possible that managers do not have the desire, resources, or skill to carry out the sequence of steps described above. When this occurs, rational decision making cannot take place. In other words, decision quality will suffer because of an inadequate data search.
- A third factor that can prevent rational decision making is the use of power. As indicated above, power is likely to be distributed unevenly within organizations. When an existing power imbalance is linked with organizational segmentation and heterogeneous goals and beliefs, managers will often use their power to achieve personal or departmental goals at the expense of others. The effect of organizational power is accentuated when managers form coalitions to obtain desired goals.
- Finally, some behavioral scientists argue that the rational model does not accurately reflect the role that top management decisions play in determining the environment organizations face.[70] As a result, managers should be less concerned with the development of strategy based upon the organization's environment, and begin to consider the opportunities and threats that result from the decisions made by top management.

The points presented here demonstrate that the link between the organization's environment and decisions made during the strategic planning process may be moderated by the actions and perceptions of top management. This is especially true if one considers the important role that implementation plays in determining the ultimate success of any strategic or operational plan. Simply put, strategic plans will not be implemented unless managers accept them as appropriate or desirable.

Organizational Structure

A crucial dimension of any organization is its internal structure. It is within this structure that managers must achieve productivity through their subordinates, and at the same time (*a*) introduce changes supporting personal success and (*b*) implement changes demanded by others within the organization. What is important to realize is that the strongest direction of influence when considering the interface between the organization's structure and the employee is from the structure to the employee. Consequently, new managers must make the effort to clarify the important structural characteristics of the system in which they will be expected to perform. For new managers to fully understand organizational structure, they must consider the factors that determine its form and the structural characteristics most likely to have an impact on performance. It is also important to realize that structural characteristics will interact with the employee's personality. The degree of match, or mismatch, at the structure–personality interface will have an effect on employee satisfaction, turnover, and productivity. Therefore, it is important that managers take steps to understand the structural dimensions they are likely to face. The total systems model outlined in Figure 15.10 will be used to articulate key factors associated with organizational structure.

It should be realized that the type of structure one is likely to find within any given organization will be a function of several key factors:

1. The dynamics, complexity, and degree of uncertainty of the organization's *external environment* are likely to impact on internal structure. This occurs because of the required linkages between internal units and their external environment or subenvironments. Consequently, as internal units attempt to adjust to differences and changes in the external environment, structural variations are likely to occur.

2. The organization's own *size* and degree of geographic dispersion also play a role in determining the desired or appropriate organizational structure.

3. The *technologies* used and the nature of the tasks performed will also influence the type of structure designed for the organization.

FIGURE 15.10

*A total systems model
of the organization's
macro–micro
elements*

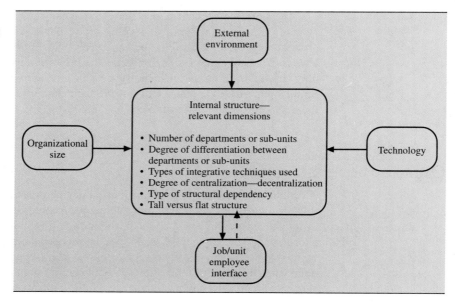

4. The personalities of dominant organizational *participants* are likely
   to shape the manner in which the organization is structured. This is
   especially true when the dominant figures are the original founders,
   or a group of key senior managers. The relevant point here is
   that their dominant style will likely be reflected in a preferred
   organizational structure.

However, as mentioned above, influence strength is greatest when moving from
the structural level to the employee level. Therefore, understanding the current characteristics of organizational structure will be crucial to the knowledge base being developed by the manager. Figure 15.10 identifies six *dimensions*
frequently associated with the discussion of internal structure.

Departmental Structure

At a very basic level, managers should attempt to identify the departmental
structure that exists within the organization. The issue is how departments are
grouped (e.g., by function, product, geographic location, or customer). Such
information allows managers to build a road map of the organization. It will
also facilitate the manager's attempts to identify and clarify power or political relations within the system. However, knowing what is out there is insufficient if the manager cannot articulate the differences and similarities between
organizational units. Crucial to any managerial knowledge base is an understanding of each department's goals, time frame (short versus long), control
and reward system, interpersonal orientation (task versus relationship), and
internal structure.

Interdependence

Because organizations will invariably have a level of differentiation or departmentalization, managers would be wise to assess the manner in which organizational units relate to one another. More specifically, what is the level of interdependence among the various units found within the organization? As discussed in Chapter 12, pooled interdependence implies that organization units are only indirectly related. Their performance affects the organization's overall performance but does not directly affect other units. An example of pooled interdependence is a group of teachers who share a common budget, but do not interact when it comes to teaching their students. A more direct relationship exists when the output of one unit becomes the input of another. This is called sequential interdependence. Sequential fabrication within a manufacturing environment is a case in point. Similarly, the input–output relationship between two organizational units may move in both directions simultaneously, as would be the case in reciprocal interdependence. A classic example of reciprocal interdependence is the relationship between the operational and maintenance units of an airline. Information about interdependence becomes crucial when managers attempt to assess their department's role in the organization and how to prioritize the numerous relationships that must be established within the organization.

Integration

Related to the issue of unit interdependence is organizational integration. The range of techniques used to integrate a segmented organization into a functioning whole is quite broad, and the actual mix is a function of the existing situation. Separate units may be integrated simply through informal day-to-day contacts between unit members, or something as basic as Likert's linking-pin concept. Employees who act as linking pins link, or integrate, two separate organizational units or levels, and by so doing, coordinate their overlapping interests.[71] Conversely, integrating techniques may be complex and highly formalized. Examples of such integrating techniques are permanent or temporary task forces, project or matrix structures, and corporatewide information systems. It is important that new managers identify how integration is accomplished so that they can effectively tap into the system and, if necessary, critically assess the appropriateness of the techniques that are being used.

Centralization/Decentralization

A structural characteristic that has recently attracted significant attention is the issue of whether decision-making and control processes should be centralized or decentralized. As the organization's external environment becomes more turbulent, new technologies increase the ease and accuracy of information flow. Consequently, employees demand an active role in decision making. The pressure for organizational decentralization thus grows. However, the move has risks and roadblocks.

Even though there may be legitimate pressures demanding a decentralized structure, two factors may prevent its implementation. First, the "hero" approach to leadership assumes that a central figure leads the group. In the case of the total organization, such hero figures are likely to be senior managers, such as Lee Iacocca of Chrysler, DeBenedetti of Olivetti, and John Sculley of Apple. Such a philosophy is likely to introduce resistance to the process of decentralization. Similarly, top managers may fail to share information downward because they fear giving the impression that they are not on top of things, or they believe that subordinates cannot handle the problems that need to be solved.

A risk associated with decentralization is that by allowing smaller and smaller areas of decision making, employees find it difficult to identify with the overall objectives and needs of the organization. Furthermore, decentralization may make it difficult to develop and/or identify the core competencies of the organization that are likely to increase the organization's chances of survival or growth.

Tall versus Flat Structures

Two major characteristics are typically associated with the concept of tall versus flat organizational structures. The first is the number of levels between the chief executive and the lowest nonmanagement position. The second is the average span of control at each level. When there are few levels and wide spans, the structure is considered flat. Conversely, when there are many levels with narrow spans the organizational structure is considered tall. Structural characteristics affect performance, control, and psychological behavior of organizational participants as follows.

First, whether a structure is tall or flat appears to affect how decisions are made and how tasks are performed. In a tall structure, the vertical flow of information is frequently interrupted because of the multiple levels that exist and because managers at each level have time to provide close levels of supervision. Conversely, flat organizational structures tend to encourage participants to engage in participative decision making and a looser style of supervision. Next, there appears to be a difference in the sheer magnitude of evaluation. In the case of tall structures, the numerous intermediate levels allow for repeated evaluation of decisions. Clearly, this cannot be the case under a flat structure. Similarly, in tall organizations, managers appear to have more time to engage in a broader range of managerial activities because they are not as burdened with the problem of having many subordinates. Furthermore, tall structures tend to produce more orderly communication and decision processes. A flat structure produces conditions that are opposite to those just described. Finally, tall structures allow for greater identification with one's immediate boss and in this way can have a positive effect on one's security. The point here is that the boss is more accessible if a problem arises. Conversely, a flat structure tends to satisfy the subordinates' need for autonomy, self-actualization, and a sense of making it on one's own. A flat structure fosters the process of self-learning—experimenting and learning from one's mistakes.

Knowing where the department or organization fits in terms of structure allows managers to assess what behaviors they should develop and fine-tune. For example, a client of one of the authors was recently engaged in a companywide reorganization. An organizational audit recommended flattening and widening the existing structure to bring organizational levels closer together, and at the same time remove two levels of middle management. Soon after the restructuring process began, managers quickly recognized the importance of delegation, team building, and group facilitation skills. In response to this perceived need, requests for training in these three areas increased significantly. Structural understanding also increases the probability that managers can critically assess the degree to which decision making, control, and communications procedures fit the requirement of the situation, and whether changes are warranted in the future.

Summary

Managers must understand their organization's internal and external environments if they are to perform effectively. Knowledge about the organization's external environment, its culture, power structure, strategic planning process, and internal structure allows managers to avoid the numerous pitfalls that exist within any sociotechnical system and, at the same time, provides the needed information, allowing managers to influence and alter their environment. Thus, managers are better able to create a departmental climate that fosters performance, enhances personal credibility, and provides for sufficient time to adjust to organizational changes. Finally, environmental knowledge facilitates managers' ability to protect, buffer, and inform subordinates.

Exercises

15.1 Understanding the Macro Organizational Environment

Important to managerial success is the ability of individuals to understand the environment in which they perform. Without this information, it is unlikely that managers will make good decisions or use organizational and personal resources effectively. Poor performance results. Such managers are likely to be classified as marginal performers. They rarely get growth oriented or challenging assignments, or get promoted, and often they are forced to leave the organization. Therefore, it is critical for new managers to analyze their environments and collect the necessary information to perform effectively. This exercise is designed to help students identify the types of questions that should be asked to get the right information. To complete this exercise please follow the steps outlined below.

Step 1. The class will break up into groups of five or six individuals. Each group will develop a set of questions that all managers must answer if they hope to be successful within today's complex organizations. You should assume that you have just been hired from another province or state as the new dean for your school (e.g., School of Business Administration, Commerce Department, or School of Public Administration).

Step 2. Your task is to develop a set of detailed questions you believe are relevant for each general macro area and which must be answered if the new dean is to succeed. The following macro areas should be included: organization culture, external environment, internal structure, power, strategic planning, mission, and staff. The questions developed should be specific enough to give guidance on (*a*) what information is needed and (*b*) where one might obtain this information. It is important to realize that correct information in the hands of an effective decision maker represents power, that is, the power to make correct decisions, to influence others, and to navigate through the pitfalls that exist within any organization. Remember, you are approaching this exercise from the point of view of a newly hired dean. Therefore, all questions should relate to the situation at your present institution.

(Approximately one hour to one hour and 30 minutes. In classes of shorter duration, each group should be assigned a particular macro area. The time allotment can be reduced to 30 minutes or less.)

Step 3. The class will assemble and each group will present its questions. Following the presentations and discussion, the class will construct a master list of questions.

Step 4. Time permitting, groups will assemble and map out a strategy for collecting and presenting the relevant information called for in Step 2, that is, where to obtain this information, what individuals (internal or external to your school) are likely have the information, and which members of the group will have the responsibility for collecting the information. If groups are unable to carry out Step 4 during regular class time, they are responsible for completing it outside class. They should prepare a written report on the collection of information due in one week. (Step 4 is optional.)

15.2 My Commitment to the Future

You have now completed a full semester course on management skills. However, this course has only been of value if you are willing to apply in the real world what you have learned. This exercise is designed to motivate you to think about how you will apply what you have learned. To accomplish this, please select a partner with whom you would like to work. Please follow the steps outlined below.

Step 1. Select a partner.

Step 2. Individually, write out what you plan to do differently as a result of taking this course, when you become a manager. Be as behaviorally specific as possible; general statements do not tend to act as motivators or effective standards by which to measure success.

Step 3. In each group of two, take turns explaining to your partner what you will do differently now that you have taken this course. Articulate why you intend to behave in this way. The other partner should be prepared to comment on the appropriateness of the behavior, its desirability as a management style, and whether the behavior could be improved in some way.

Step 4. Take this information home with you and write a report about what you have discussed. You will be required to hand in your report on or before the final examination. (*Option:* Assign students a specific date by which they must hand in their reports.) It is recommended that each student keep a copy of the report as a reminder of what it means to be an effective manager.

End Notes

1. W. Dill, "Environment as an influence on managerial autonomy," *Administrative Science Quarterly,* Vol. 2, 1958: 409–443.
2. J. D. Thompson, *Organization in Action,* McGraw-Hill, New York, 1967.
3. P. R. Lawrence and J. W. Lorsch, *Organization and Environment,* Harvard University Press, Boston, 1967.
4. R. B. Duncan, "Characteristics of organizational environments and perceived environmental uncertainty," *Administrative Science Quarterly,* Vol. 17, 1972: 313–327.
5. Duncan, 1972.
6. W. R. Boulton, W. M. Lindsay, S. G. Franklin, and L. W. Rue, "Strategic planning: Determining the impact of environmental characteristics and uncertainty," *Academy of Management Journal,* Vol. 25, No. 3, 1982: 500–509.
7. H. Tosi, R. Aldag, and R. Storey, "On the measurement of the environment: An assessment of the Lawrence and Lorsch environmental uncertainty subscale," *Administative Science Quarterly,* Vol.18, 1973: 27–36.
8. M. I. A. At-Twaijri and J. R. Montanari, "The impact of context and choice on the boundary-spanning process: An empirical extension," *Human Relations,* Vol. 40, No. 12, 1987: 783–798.
9. F. J. Milliken, "Three types of perceived uncertainty about the environment: State, effect, and response uncertainty," *Academy of Management Review,* Vol. 12, No. 1, 1987: 133–143.
10. C. E. Lindblom, "The science of muddling through," *Public Administration Review,* Vol. 19, 1959: 79–99.
11. M. D. Cohen, J. G. March, and J. D. Olsen, "A garbage-can model of organizational choice," *Administrative Science Quarterly,* Vol. 17, 1972: 1–25.
12. Thompson, 1967.
13. At-Twaijri and Montanari, 1987.
14. D. W. McAllister, J. R. Mitchell, and L. R. Beach, "The contingency model for the selection of decision strategies: An empirical test of the effects of significance, accountability, and reversibility," *Organizational Behavior and Human Performance,* Vol. 24, 1979: 228–244.
15. M. L. Tushman and T. J. Scanlan, "Boundary spanning individuals: Their role in information transfer and their antecedents," *Academy of Management Journal,* Vol. 24, No. 2, 1981: 289–305.
16. M. J. Hatch, "The dynamics of organizational culture," *Academy of Management Review,* Vol. 18, 1993: 657–693.
17. A. M. Pettigrew, "On studying organizational cultures," *Administrative Science Quarterly,* Vol. 24, 1979: 570–581.
18. G. Hofstede, B. Neuijen, D. D. Ohayv, and G. Sanders, "Measuring organizational cultures: A qualitative and quantitative study across twenty

cases," *Administrative Science Quarterly,* Vol. 35, 1990: 286–316.

19. J. S. Ott, *The Organizational Culture Perspective,* Brooks/Cole Publishing Company, Pacific Grove, Calif., 1989: 1.

20. E. H. Schein, *Organizational Culture and Leadership,* Jossey-Bass, San Francisco, 1985: 5.

21. H. Tosi, J. R. Rizzo, and S. J. Carroll, *Managing Organizational Behavior,* Pitman Publishing, Marshfield, Mass., 1986: 65.

22. E. H. Schein, "Does Japanese management style have a message for American managers?" *Sloan Management Review,* Vol. 23, No. 1, 1984: 55–68; E. H. Schein, "Coming to a new awareness of organizational culture," *Sloan Management Review,* Vol. 25, No. 2, 1984: 3–16; Schein, 1984.

23. Ott, 1989.

24. H. M. Trice and J. M. Beyer, "Studying organizational culture through rites and ceremonials," *Academy of Management Review,* Vol. 9, 1984: 653–669.

25. Ott, 1989: 60.

26. C. Argyris and D. A. Schon, *Organizational Learning: A Theory of Action Perspective,* Addison–Wesley, Reading, Mass., 1978.

27. Schein, 1985.

28. E. F. Huse and T. G. Cummings, *Organization Development and Change,* West Publishing, St. Paul, Minn., 1985.

29. B. Uttal, "The corporate culture vultures," *Fortune,* Vol. 108 Pt 2, October 17, 1983: 66–72.

30. R. L. Daft, *Organization Theory and Design,* West Publishing, St. Paul Minn., 1986; M. Magnet, "Managing by mystique at Tandem Computers," *Fortune,* June 28, 1982: 84–91; "An acid test for Tandem's growth," *Business Week,* February 28, 1983: 63–64; "What makes Tandem run," *Business Week,* July 14, 1980: 73–74.

31. Hatch, 1993.

32. Hatch, 1993.

33. Hatch, 1993.

34. Hatch, 1993: 669.

35. Hatch, 1993: 686.

36. K. A. Golden, "The individual and organizational culture: Strategies for action in highly ordered contexts," *Journal of Management Studies,* Vol. 29, No. 1, January 1992: 1–21.

37. Golden, January 1992.

38. Golden, January 1992.

39. J. R. Harrison and G. R. Carroll, "Keeping the faith: A model of cultural transmission in formal organizations," *Administrative Science Quarterly,* Vol. 36, 1991: 552–582.

40. Harrison and Carroll, 1991.

41. I. Mangham, *Power and Performance in Organizations,* Basil Blackwell, New York, 1988; D. Tjosvold, I. Andrews, and J. T. Struthers, "Power and interdependence in work groups," *Group & Organizational Studies,* Vol. 16, No. 3, 1991: 285–299.

42. Tjosvold, Andrews, and Struthers, 1991; W. G. Astley and E. J. Zajac, "Beyond dyadic exchange: Functional interdependence and sub-unit power," *Organizational Studies,* Vol. 11, No. 4, 1990: 481–501; K. M. Eisenhardt and L. J. Bourgeois III, "Politics of strategic decision making in high-velocity environments: Toward a midrange theory," *Academy of Management Journal,* Vol. 31, No. 4, 1988: 737–770; K. Provan, "Environment, departmental power, and strategic decision making in organizations: A proposed integration," *Journal of Management,* Vol. 15, No. 1, 1989: 21–34.

43. A. M. Pettigrew, *The Politics of Organizational Decision Making,* Tavistock, London, 1973: 240.

44. R. P. Dahl, "The concept of power," *Behavioral Science,* Vol. 2, 1957: 201–218; R. M. Emerson, "Power-dependence relations," *American Sociological Review,* Vol. 27, 1962: 31–41; J. Pfeffer, *Power in Organizations,* Pitman Publishing, Marshfield, Mass., 1981; Tjosvold, Andrews and Struthers, 1991.

45. N.C. Roberts, "Organizational power styles: Collective and competitive power under varying organizational conditions," *The Journal of Applied Behavioral Science,* Vol. 22, No. 4, 1986: 443–458.

46. Tjosvold, Andrews, and Struthers, 1991.

47. Eisenhardt and Bourgeois III, 1988.

48. Astley and Zajac, 1990.

49. C. S. Saunders, "The strategic contingencies theory of power: Multiple perspectives," *Journal of Management Studies,* Vol. 27, No. 1, 1990: 1–18; Provan, 1989; D. J. Hickson, C. R. Hinings, C. A. Less, R. E. Schneck, and J. M. Pennings, "Strategic contingencies theory of intraorganizational power," *Administrative Science Quarterly,* Vol. 16, 1971: 216–29; C. R. Hinings, D. Hickson, J. M. Pennings, and R. E. Schneck, "Structural

conditions on intraorganizational power," *Administrative Science Quarterly,* Vol. 19, 1974: 22–44; H. Mintzberg, *Power In and Around Organizations,* Prentice Hall, Inc., Englewood Cliffs, N.J., 1983.

50. C. S. Saunders, "The strategic contingencies theory of power: Multiple perspectives," *Journal of Management Studies,* Vol. 21, No. 1, 1990: 1–18.
51. C. S. Saunders, 1990.
52. Mintzberg, 1983.
53. Mintzberg, 1983.
54. Pfeffer, 1981.
55. Mintzberg, 1983.
56. Eisenhardt and Bourgeois III, 1988.
57. The model presented in Figure 15.8 and the subsequent discussion is based upon the material presented in J. Pfeffer, 1981.
58. J. Pfeffer, G. R. Salanick, *The External Control of Organizations: A Resource Dependence Perspective,* Harper & Row, New York, 1978.
59. Pfeffer, 1981.
60. Mintzberg, 1983.
61. H. Mintzberg, "Five Ps for Strategy," in H. Mintzberg and J. B. Quinn, *The Strategy Process: Concepts and Contexts,* Prentice Hall, Englewood Cliffs, N.J., 1992; H. Mintzberg, "The strategy concept I: Five Ps for strategy," *California Management Review,* Vol. 30, No. 1, 1987: 11–24.
62. Mintzberg, 1987.
63. G. A. Steiner, *Strategic Planning: What Every Manager Must Know,* The Free Press, New York, 1979.
64. G. A. Hamel and C. K. Prahalad, "Strategic intent," *Harvard Business Review,* Vol. 89, No. 3, 1989, 63–76.
65. Criteria reflect material presented in The Coopers & Lybrand Consulting Group, *Strategic Management: An Introduction for Municipal Managers and Councils,* Queen's Printer for Ontario, Ontario, Canada, 1989.
66. Criteria reflect material presented in The Coopers & Lybrand Consulting Group, 1989.
67. Provan, 1989; M. E. Porter, *Competitive strategy: Techniques for analyzing industries and competitors,* The Free Press, New York, 1980; Steiner, 1979; K. R. Andrews. *The Concept of Corporate Strategy,* Irwin, Homewood, Ill., 1971.
68. Provan, 1989: 21.
69. Provan, 1989.
70. R. L. Daft and K. E. Weick, "Toward a model of organizations as interpretation systems," *Academy of Management Review,* Vol. 9, 1984: 284–295; L. Smircich and C. Stubbart, "Strategic management in an enacted world," *Academy of Management Review,* Vol. 10, 1985: 724–736.

Name Index

Subject Index